BOTTOM LINE'S SuperFoods Rx

How to unlock the power of foods to prevent and even cure disease!

STEVEN PRATT, MD
AND KATHY MATTHEWS

Bottom Line Books
www.BottomLinePublications.com

Bottom Line's SuperFoods Rx

How to unlock the power of foods to prevent and even cure disease!

By Steven Pratt, MD, and Kathy Matthews

Published by arrangement with William Morrow, an imprint of HarperCollins Publishers.

This book is adapted from:

SUPERFOODS RX. Copyright © 2004 by Steven G. Pratt, MD, and Kathy Matthews, Inc.
SUPERFOODS HEALTHSTYLE. Copyright © 2006 by Steven G. Pratt, MD, and Kathy Matthews, Inc.

ISBN 0-88723-670-7

10 9 8 7 6 5 4 3 2 1

This book is written as a source of information about the effects of foods, vitamins and lifestyle choices on the body. It is based on the research and observations of the author. The information contained in this book should by no means by considered a substitute for the advice of the reader's personal physician or other medical professional, who should always be consulted before beginning any diet or other health program.

The information in this book has been carefully researched, and all efforts have been made to ensure accuracy as of the date published. Readers, particularly those with existing health problems and those who take prescription medications, are cautioned to consult with a health professional about specific recommendations for supplements and the appropriate dosages. The author and the publisher expressly disclaim responsibility for any adverse effects arising from the use or application of the information contained in this book.

Bottom Line Books® is a registered trademark of Boardroom Inc.
281 Tresser Blvd., Stamford CT 06901
www.bottomlinepublications.com

Bottom Line Books® publishes the opinions of expert authorities in many fields. The use of this book is not a substitute for health or other professional services. Please consult a competent professional for answers to your specific questions.

Offers, prices, addresses, telephone numbers and Web sites listed in this book are accurate at the time of publication, but they are subject to frequent change.

Bottom Line Books® is an imprint of Boardroom® Inc., publisher of print periodicals, e-letters and books. We are dedicated to bringing you the best information from the most knowledgeable sources in the world. Our goal is to help you gain greater wealth, better health, more wisdom, extra time and increased happiness.

Printed in the United States of America

TABLE OF CONTENTS

About the Authors

Steven Pratt, MD, is a world-renowned authority on the role of nutrition and lifestyle in the prevention of disease and optimizing health, and the author of the bestselling *SuperFoods Rx* and *SuperFoods HealthStyle.* He is a senior staff ophthalmologist at Scripps Memorial Hospital in La Jolla, California, and is board certified by the American Board of Holistic Medicine. He lives in Rancho Sante Fe, California.

Kathy Matthews has coauthored several health and medical best sellers, including *SuperFoods Rx, Medical Makeover* and *Natural Prescriptions.* She lives in Fleetwood, New York.

Foreword

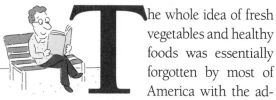

The whole idea of fresh vegetables and healthy foods was essentially forgotten by most of America with the advent of fast-food chains and TV dinners. But little by little we are seeing a resurgence of interest in and commitment to healthy foods, with greenmarkets springing up and organic foods being sold in supermarkets. *Bottom Line's SuperFoods Rx: How to Unlock the Power of Foods to Prevent and Even Cure Disease!* is the next major step forward in the food-health connection, and I am certain that people are ready to appreciate that what we eat can act as good or bad "medicine."

While most of us are well aware that food choices are important to health, very few people realize that foods can actually *promote* health. This is good news to all of us because it means that instead of worrying about what foods we should avoid, it introduces an era when we can, at last, embrace foods—particularly SuperFoods—as allies in our quest to live long, healthy lives.

We are constantly increasing our awareness and knowledge that "we are what we eat." *The Wall Street Journal* has featured articles including "Yes, There Are Some Healthy Snacks That Your Kids Will Actually Eat," "Toward Smarter Snacks," and "Big-Brand Logos Pop Up in Organic Aisle." The very next day in the same publication was a half-page color spread of fruits and vegetables by a major food company welcoming the message, "Diets rich in fruits and vegetables may reduce the risk of some types of cancer and other chronic diseases" (July 10, 2003, U.S. National Cancer Institute, as endorsed by the U.S. Food and Drug Administration).

SuperFoods Rx is an exciting concept based strongly in academic science and peer-reviewed research clinical trials conducted by some of the world's leading clinicians and research scholars. My close friend Steve Pratt, M.D., has devoted many hours to nutrition and its science and implementation, and this book is the exciting culmination of those efforts.

Steve and I have been practicing physicians, colleagues and close friends in southern California for more than twenty years. In addition to being practicing specialists, we are also interested in the entire patient. My original background was in family medicine, where I first became board certified in family practice. Steve is also a physician interested in the entire well-being of his patients. Thus, the inquiry and journey from treatment to prevention to concern for the whole patient has always been an important part of our medical practices. As the former CEO of the world-renowned Scripps Clinic, I can state that physicians in all of our specialties are gaining an increasing awareness of the role that nutrition and foods play in our patients and their disease processes. I think the important underlying concept of SuperFoods Rx—that certain foods can promote and enhance health—will be embraced by all health-care practitioners as well as the general public. It's a book whose time has come.

The SuperFoods Rx Lifestyle Pyramid, on page 8, is of particular interest to those looking for a balanced, healthy lifestyle. It includes more than just food. Steve correctly includes exercise, stress management, faith, friendship, laughter, daydreaming, sleep and other elements necessary for a longstanding, healthy life.

I am pleased to be continuing to work with Dr. Pratt in all aspects of medicine, especially our research efforts. Together we are looking at what foods might function as natural sunscreens in the plant world and how such information can help and protect us in the future. Both the eye and the skin provide a window into the inner aspects of our bodies, so our research is important for a variety of reasons.

Change can be both challenging and difficult for all of us. To think that overnight you and I could fully incorporate the twenty-three SuperFoods into our daily routine may be unrealistic. A gradual plan is a good way to go. Try to add one SuperFood every two weeks. By next year you should be and feel healthier than ever!

Steve remains at the forefront of helping each of us live better, longer and more productive lives with his research, leadership and forward thinking in nutritional medicine. I hope that *Bottom Line's SuperFoods Rx* will help you find a better, healthier future.

—Hubert (Hugh) T. Greenway, M.D.,
CEO emeritus, Scripps Clinic
Chairman, Mohs Dermatologic Surgery

Introduction

Each time you sit down to a meal, you're making life-and-death decisions. Does that sound scary? At first blush it truly is. But here's how I see it: You have an exciting opportunity—one that wasn't available even a few years ago—to make choices that will change the course of your lifespan *and* your health span. You are making decisions right now, at your very next meal, that will affect how you spend the rest of your life, whether you're 22 years old or 62.

See this book as a fork in the road: One way leads to a handicapped space in front of the mega-drugstore. You're 68 years old and you're struggling to navigate to the back of the store where the pharmacist has your meds waiting. He greets you cheerfully; he knows you well. You're taking nine prescription medications and on a good day, you can walk around the block with your grandson. On a bad day, you log a lot of TV time. You fill your basket with your prescriptions and a few over-the-counter medicines. You shake your head sadly when the elderly man behind you in line says, "Old age isn't for the faint of heart, is it?"

There's another choice. You pull up to the farmers' market. You're 68 years old, and you've just finished a tennis game with some pals or an hour of satisfying work in your garden. You grab a basket and fill it with delicious fruits and vegetables. You're thrilled to see that blueberries have come into season and you stock up on spinach and orange bell peppers. There are no ripe tomatoes yet but the broccoli looks perfect. You've got friends coming over for dinner so you'll stop by the fish market for some wild Alaskan salmon. Maybe you'll pick up some almonds; you've been meaning to try that new dessert recipe. You duck out of line for a moment to grab a small red cabbage and smile when the cashier says, "I don't know where you get your energy!"

It's a simple choice, really: the right foods or prescription drugs.

Of course no one can guarantee that one will ensure you'll avoid the other. But there is enough evidence—some published, some just being reported at medical conferences—that the power of certain foods can make a significant difference in your risk of developing a host of diseases. This is extremely exciting because it puts the tools in your hand, and on your plate, to change your future.

The Terrific Twenty-three

Bottom Line's SuperFoods Rx is based on a very simple concept: Some foods are better than others for your health. We could all guess that an apple is better for you than a potato chip. But what about choosing between a couple of pretzels and a few walnuts? Did you know that eating a handful of nuts a few times a week can reduce your risk of getting a heart attack by at least 15 percent and perhaps as much as 51 percent? Even if you smoke, are overweight and never exercise. That's how powerful certain foods are.

This book presents the twenty-three known nutritional powerhouse foods that can help you extend your health span—the extent of time you have to be healthy, vigorous and vital—as well as, perhaps, your lifespan. These are the foods that have been proven to help prevent and, in some cases, reverse the well-known scourges of aging, including cardiovascular disease, type II diabetes, hypertension, certain cancers and even dementia.

Many SuperFoods may already be part of your diet. Most people routinely enjoy **broccoli** and **oranges** and even **spinach,** for example. **Blueberries** could possibly be everyone's favorite SuperFood, but most people eat them only as a treat, when they're in season. When you learn about the awesome power of this berry, and some others, I'm sure that you'll try to eat them every day. Frozen berries in a shake are delicious. Some SuperFoods, like **pumpkin** and **turkey,** make occasional appearances in the average diet. (You'll soon see why they should be eaten far more frequently.) Other SuperFoods may be brand-new to you, like **soy** or perhaps **yogurt,** and I'll show you how to enjoy them even if you think you don't like them.

Walnuts are the surprising SuperFood. Surprising because most people think nuts belong in the "avoid" category because they're fatty. But the power of nuts is almost stunning. I try never to go a day without eating some nuts and seeds. Some SuperFoods are less of a surprise. Perhaps you've read about **wild salmon** recently. Wild salmon has so many health benefits that it seems just foolish not to eat it regularly.

Some SuperFoods are so easy to incorporate into your diet that you'll be able to begin your overall improvement in the time it takes to boil some water for a cup of **tea** to sip while you finish reading this book. Others will take a little more planning. Some SuperFoods, such as pumpkin (or one of its sidekicks, like orange bell pepper), should be eaten a few times a week; others, like yogurt, should be eaten more frequently, even if in small amounts. And when you discover the power of **tomatoes,** even in the form of ketchup or sauce, you'll find yourself choosing pizza over other fast foods.

You may be surprised to learn from SuperFood shopping tips that a dramatic improvement in your nutrition can be a simple matter of learning to read a label. For example, most of us eat bread every day and we serve it to our families. Many of us think we're eating **whole-grain** bread and would be surprised to learn that we're not. Did you know that by checking the nutrition label on a loaf of bread and making sure it has at least 3 grams of fiber, you could turn an ordinary sandwich into a *SuperFoods Rx* sandwich?

Most of us tend to get set in our ways: We eat the same things on a fairly regular basis. To break out of your particular rotation, you need convincing that it's worth it and also that it's easy to do. I know that when you read about the individual SuperFoods you'll be convinced that it's worth eating them. To make it easy, *Bottom Line's SuperFoods Rx* gives you a hand in the kitchen. Each section has lots of tips and suggestions that will help you choose and prepare each SuperFood. I've also included my favorite, simple, everyday family recipes that will get you right on the SuperFood way to health.

In addition, two of the best chefs in the country, Michel Stroot, from the Golden Door spa, and Mark Cleveland, from the Avanti Café, both in California, were given free rein to develop some great-tasting recipes using SuperFoods. Some of these recipes are quick and easy; others are more suitable for a splurge. They're all absolutely delicious and perhaps the most healthy recipes you'll find anywhere.

There are excellent, healthy, prepared foods out there if you just know what to look for. Of course, most of us don't have time to read and compare countless labels in the supermarket. You don't have to—I've done it for you. To make it all super easy, I've created the SuperFoods Rx Shopping Lists (page 211) that will direct you right to the best products our markets have to offer, and you'll be delighted to find another tool to help you improve your everyday diet. My patients love these lists, and I'm sure you will too.

Feeling Super

Remember that *Bottom Line's SuperFoods Rx* is not just about avoiding disease. The fact is, few people are willing to make changes in how they live every day and just hope that they won't develop a disease in a few decades. But it's not just the last quarter or third of your life that's affected by making the wrong food choices; it's every day. Once you're beyond those enviable, vigorous teen years, you hear your "health clock" beginning to tick. Small aches show up. You feel tired in the late afternoon. You don't have much enthusiasm for a bike ride or any vigorous activity, for that matter. Your skin loses some of its glow. In many cases these minor symptoms are the easily dismissed, early-warning signs of what can develop into future chronic ailments.

I often tell my patients, "I wish you could feel like I feel." I'm not boasting. I'm encouraging them to alter their eating patterns because I know that once they begin to feel really good, that will be all the encouragement they'll need to make their changes permanent.

Many people find it hard to believe that they could be developing disease if they feel okay and have reasonably good health habits. Sadly, if this were true, we wouldn't have the host of chronic and disabling diseases that we're observing today.

DO A SELF-TEST

Take this quick test: Get a mirror, preferably a magnifying mirror, and examine your eyes. Look at the white part, particularly the area of the eye just to the left or the right of the iris—the colored part. Do you see some yellow discoloration? Sometimes it can look like yellowish ropey globs. These are called "pinguecula." They're a kind of callus that the thin mucous membrane that covers the eye develops as a result of exposure to pollutants and, in particular, ultraviolet light. Perhaps you also notice a yellow ring around the peripheral part of your cornea (the front, clear part of the eye). This is a warning sign that your cholesterol may be high and you should have a blood test to check your cholesterol levels. If you have one or both of these signs, your body is telling you that your diet and your environment may be taking a toll on your immune system and your eventual health.

Foods—the right foods—can actually change the course of your biochemistry. They can help to stop damage at the cellular levels that can develop into disease. The goal of this book is to help you stop the incremental changes in your body that can lead to disease and/or dysfunction. The delightful side effect to this effort is that you feel better, have more energy, look better and can embrace all that life has to offer you with more optimism.

The Beginnings of SuperFoods

My mom introduced me to the concept of optimum nutrition. I had no choice: I had to eat the crusts on the sandwich (we now know they really are the healthiest parts). I ate salads every day. There was always a jar of wheat germ in our fridge, and I was encouraged to eat the white part of the orange peel. My mom was an early devotee of nutritionists like Adele Davis. While I might have resisted some of her efforts as a kid, when I became a serious athlete and a doctor, I saw that she was right.

As an athlete I was aware that nutrition affected performance. It was clear that what I ate affected my ability to compete. Gradually, I became interested in how foods affected performance on a biochemical level: What was there about certain foods that made them especially beneficial?

As an ophthalmologist and a plastic and reconstructive surgeon, I found myself working in an area of medicine that gave access to the body's first warning signals of age and disease—the eyes and the skin. You can't see your arteries narrowing. But you can experience your eyes losing clarity and developing pinguecula, and you can see your skin developing discolorations and losing elasticity.

Skin health, ocular health and overall health are inextricably linked. For example, if you're diagnosed with cataracts or macular degeneration, you have a significantly increased risk of developing cardiovascular disease. It's the same story with skin cancer. If you develop skin cancer before the age of 60, you may have a 20 to 30 percent increased mortality rate from multiple systemic cancers, including colon cancer, breast cancer, prostate cancer and leukemia.

My practice at the Scripps network of clinics and hospitals in San Diego, California, provides a wealth of clinical material. Most research centers struggle to get patients. Many researchers aren't really clinicians. They don't work with patients, and they don't get to see real results in

HOW I'VE INCORPORATED SUPERFOODS INTO MY LIFE

I've always followed a version of the *SuperFoods Rx* diet, which gets updated regularly as I learn new things and new research reports are published. I thought you'd find it interesting to get a quick snapshot of some of the changes I've made in my own diet as a result of working on this book.

- In my fridge there are separate plastic containers for dry-roasted sunflower seeds, almonds, walnuts, dry-roasted peanuts, pistachios and pumpkin seeds. I have a handful of at least two different nuts and/or seeds every day.
- I drink one Odwalla C Monster juice almost every day. I sip it slowly over hours to keep my vitamin C blood levels high, instead of drinking it all at once.
- I put lots of Knott's Boysenberry Preserves or Trader Joe's Organic Blueberry Fruit Spread on my toast.
- I drink a lot of green and black tea.
- I usually have 5 ounces of Trader Joe's 100% Unfiltered Concord Grape Juice or pomegranate juice with sparkling water with my dinner or lunch at home.
- I eat a cup of berries almost every day.
- I put some ground flaxseed on my cereal.
- The SuperFoods Rx Salad (page 198) is a daily must.
- I always check food labels for sodium content.

real people. I'm a practicing clinician who also does research. I can draw on my clinical practice to study anything. The Scripps health care system is world famous, and we draw an excellent and cooperative patient base. In addition, I'm surrounded at Scripps by researchers who are on the cutting edge of their fields—researchers who are only steps away when I have a question or need clarification on an arcane point of biochemistry or medicine. The combination of top-notch experts and world-class library and research facilities at the University of California at San Diego (UCSD), where I'm a member of the clinical teaching faculty, has been a tremendous advantage to me in my work. It's given me access to the cutting-edge advances in nutritional therapy.

It was serendipitous that these interests—nutrition, ocular and skin health, and preventive medicine—meshed. It quickly became clear to me from clinical research, as well as from my own work with patients, that the connections between food and specific nutrients and health were inevitable.

I also realized that the public, despite a hunger for such information, was finding it increasingly difficult to find simple, safe dietary recommendations. The public thirst for knowledge has, ironically, been part of the problem. People are eager to hear about the latest advances. Nutrition updates hit the front pages. Unfortunately, oftentimes headlines don't translate into sensible, practical recommendations. People become discouraged by conflicting information. They begin to think that there's no point in trying to improve their diet—what they're told to eat today turns out to be a problem tomorrow.

I have taken the best of what's known about the best foods available in order to show you how to develop an "optimum" diet. This book will help you fine-tune your diet to get the most out of the good foods you already eat, while introducing other powerful, health-promoting foods to amplify the overall beneficial effects.

Introducing HealthStyle

HealthStyle is a fresh new way of living. It embraces every aspect of life that promotes health and optimism. HealthStyle is not a diet or an exercise program or a few isolated principles that promise you'll feel better in a few days or weeks.

HealthStyle recognizes that achieving optimal health in the twenty-first century is a synergy of information, motivation, good habits and inspiration. Many people are aware that the current accepted course of much of traditional medicine—end-stage care of chronic, often fatal, ailments with drugs or surgery—may not be the solution for a long, healthy, fulfilling life. Disease and disability take years and years to develop. Once we experience symptoms, our lives are often changed forever, usually for the worse. What if you could stop that microscopic cancer cell that showed up in your kidney when you were twenty-five years old and prevent it from thriving? What if by eating a diet high in phytonutrients and fiber, exercising to regulate your metabolism, sleeping enough to maintain a strong immune system—what if all of these and other aspects of your HealthStyle resulted in that tiny cell being flushed harmlessly from your system? What if instead of getting a diagnosis of kidney cancer at age 55 after a few years of mild nagging back pain, instead you sailed right on to 60 and 70 and 80, still playing tennis, still gardening, still enjoying the spring sun on your face?

This is what HealthStyle does for you. The information that you read here can be your ammunition against disease, frailty and the host of indignities that come with poor health. HealthStyle will help you dodge those potential bullets. With luck, you'll never know how close they came. You'll simply feel good. Energetic. Optimistic. Some sections in this book are expressly designed to help you dodge some of the biggest bullets around. Can the section "How to Avoid Alzheimer's" or "How to Avoid Hypertension" guarantee freedom from these increasingly common chronic ailments? Of course not, but you'll increase your odds. And while the end result is not guaranteed, the process is: If you follow these suggestions, you will feel better both physically and emotionally because you'll be doing the best you can to live well on this earth.

If you're reading this book you probably already make some effort to achieve health. Perhaps you have a pretty good diet. Maybe you exercise regularly. Or maybe you hope that your good diet will make you "immune" from an exercise requirement. Maybe you eat pretty well and exercise but get only about six hours of sleep a night and feel pretty good. But what you don't know is that you're really suffering from a chronic sleep debt that's not only impairing your performance but could also be promoting hypertension and diabetes as well as impairing your immune system and even promoting obesity. Health is a web. Each strand is doing a job; no part can be ignored.

Perhaps the big news of HealthStyle is the role that *certain simple habits* play in keeping us at our best. Sleep, attention to our spiritual side, social contacts—all of these affect health in profound and usually unrecognized ways. I find the research studies on these practices particularly exhilarating because they seem to confirm instinct. Doesn't it make sense that achieving what I call "personal peace" will actually promote health and perhaps even longevity?

How HealthStyle Works

HealthStyle creates a blueprint for optimal health based on the latest peer-reviewed research on the importance of nutrition, exercise, sleep and stress control in your life. "Peer-reviewed" is important. It means that every bit of information in this book has been published in respected journals (all the substantiating data can be found in the back of this book). It's not just my theory or a suggestion that seems reasonable. It's actual, proven data. My own feeling is that research data is often mishandled by the media. There's too much focus on single studies that can have conflicting and sometimes alarming results. Many more headlines are written on the one study that confounds previous ones or even common sense. Sometimes animal studies yield results that may not be transferable to humans yet still make headlines and confuse consumers. Except where noted, I rely on studies conducted on humans.

Information is one thing; implementation is another. The goal of HealthStyle is literally to help you change your life. You've already taken the first step: You're reading this book. You might be mildly curious—perhaps you'd like to lose a few pounds or eat more healthfully—or you might be absolutely determined to improve your health because a condition or illness has made you realize that your HealthStyle is a life-and-death decision. It doesn't matter how you came to read this book; it should be comforting and encouraging to know that just by doing so, you're going in the right direction. Your goal is change. However, change isn't always so easy. Many of us have tried and failed before. This time will be different because, with the help of HealthStyle, you'll have different skills and constant motivation.

Life is change. Tomorrow will be different from today. You will be a different person—on molecular, physical and emotional levels—a year from today. Will you be better or worse off? The choice is yours. HealthStyle will put the tools in your hands to improve; you need only decide, each day, to use them.

The start of the new year is often a time of recommitment and resolution, but you can begin at any point. It's useful to take a look at the process of personal change. If you are aware of all of the elements of effective change, there is no doubt that you'll be more successful in achieving your goals.

In a book published more than a dozen years ago, *Changing for Good,* three psychologists studied thousands of people who were able to alter their lives positively and permanently. The authors learned that change isn't dependent on luck or willpower as many of us believe. It is a *process* that can be successful if certain guidelines are met. As a doctor who actively works to promote health with his patients, I've always known that positive change isn't just a matter of willpower. I've seen too many patients who were determined and committed but who failed to achieve change in the long run for many reasons. Making positive, permanent change is a skill. You can learn how to do it. It's a gradual process of learning to know yourself, learning to set goals, maintaining motivation and learning what tools you need to reach your goals. I find it useful to take a close look at the process of change. It will help us as we go forward trying to improve our overall health and well-being.

LEARNING VITAL SKILLS

Some of the life-changing skills I'll describe may seem obvious to you. But each one needs attention if you want to give yourself the best chance for success. Take a minute now and think about each skill and how you can implement it in the season and year ahead.

• One of the important skills of permanent change is the ability to evaluate yourself realistically. Take a hard look at the year ahead. What are your goals? How do you want your life to improve? What do you think will be better about your life if you adopt the HealthStyle lifestyle? Do you primarily want to look better by losing some weight? Do you want to extend your active, vital lifespan? Do you want to live to enjoy your grandchildren? Do you want to feel the inner peace that comes with living a healthy and directed life? You probably have enough basic information about health improvement to know the weak links in your own HealthStyle. Maybe it's your diet. Maybe you've never exercised. Maybe the stress in your life is so out of control that you're losing sleep and feeling anxious all the time. Or perhaps you have a very specific issue—high cholesterol, a family history of heart disease, being overweight, a recent diagnosis of type II diabetes. Whatever your health issue, look it square in the face. One year from now, one year of HealthStyle, and you are going to be a different person.

• Change doesn't happen by wishing it so. You must make the decision to change. It's not enough to think about how your life *could be better.* You have to determine that *you will make it better.* Too often we daydream about change. We often think about how nice it would be if we were healthier, if we ate better, if we exercised. We have a moment of resolve when stepping on the scale or sitting in the doctor's office. But we never actually *decide to take action.* You'll be surprised at how empowering it is actually to make a decision to veer from your routine. Make a promise to yourself that by this time next year, you're going to be better and maybe even look better. Commit to it by writing it down right here, right now:

____

____

You've got nothing to lose and everything to gain.

• Of course, you have to do more than read this book—you have to take active steps to incorporate suggested changes in your life. HealthStyle doesn't insist that you follow a single blueprint for success. You'll learn how to make decisions based on your lifestyle and tastes and on what changes will work for you. You'll be shown how to substitute good health habits for poor ones. This isn't as hard as it might seem, because there are literally hundreds of ideas in this book that will help you. As you go through a year of HealthStyle, you can pick and choose the tips that work for you. Sometimes you'll have to push yourself a bit to make these changes work. But if you've made the decision to change and you refer back to your written commitment, you will surely keep on track and your HealthStyle year will be a success.

• You must keep motivated. HealthStyle acknowledges: Its core is motivation. Anyone who makes a commitment to change knows that it's important to search for motivation everywhere. You'll find it in the headlines. Former President Bill Clinton's heart surgery was motivating for many people who had been cavalier about their heart health. Many people were shocked that someone who seemed so vigorous, who had lost weight and seemed to be exercising—someone who certainly got good medical care—suddenly found that he needed major heart surgery to avoid a possibly fatal heart attack. Calls to cardiologists spiked in the weeks following Clinton's surgery.

One interesting and exciting aspect of positive change is that motivation grows and strengthens as a result of the positive actions you're taking. Improvement is self-reinforcing. All my patients tell me this and I've found it to be so in my own life. When you eat well, you feel better and want to continue eating well. When you exercise, you have more energy and want to continue exercising and eating well. If there's any magic bullet to health improvement, that's it: *Act better to feel better to get better.*

• You need support from friends and family. You need to make decisions about how to ask for help and who will help you. Perhaps you should tell your children that certain foods the family is eating will ultimately cause health problems, but sometimes it's hard to resist these foods, so you need their help. Maybe they can help prepare salads at dinnertime. Maybe they can help prepare some healthier recipes. If they feel like collaborators rather than victims of change, they're far more likely to be enthusiastic supporters. Don't forget co-workers. Ask their support in avoiding sugary treats on coffee breaks or at office parties. Suggest a quick, healthy lunch followed by a walk with an office mate instead of a fatty, high-calorie midday extravaganza. If you suggest providing fruit instead of doughnuts at the next meeting, others will surely embrace your suggestion.

• You need rewards. Many people think of rewards in this context as a major gift to oneself, like a new coat or theater tickets or even a trip. This is fine if it works for you and your budget, but I prefer to think of rewards in smaller, everyday terms. Rewards are stepping-stones to a goal. They help you cross a river of temptation and conflicting demands. For example, buy that fancy green tea or a soothing CD if you reach your week's exercise goals. Treat yourself to some new exercise clothing or a reflexology session once you go a month without junk food. Call a friend you haven't spoken with in ages as a reward for skipping dessert at a buffet. You know yourself best and you know what your short-term HealthStyle goals are.

Let *Bottom Line's SuperFoods Rx* be your road map to a better, healthier future.

1

SuperFoods Rx: The Basics

The foods that you eat every day, from the fast food you mindlessly consume to the best meals you savor in a top restaurant, are doing much more than making you fat or thin. Their effects on your body are making the difference between the development of chronic disease and a vigorous extended life. They can prevent or greatly reduce your risk of vision problems, stroke, heart disease, diabetes and a host of killers. These are not just vague promises; they are *facts* that are now supported by an impressive and irrefutable body of research.

How Your Diet Is Killing You

Most respectable scientists in the world today agree that *at least* 30 percent of all cancers are directly related to nutrition. Some would argue that the figure is as high as 70 percent.

For example, we know that the people who eat the most fruits and vegetables are *half* as likely to develop cancer as those who eat the least amount of these foods.

It's not just cancer that's nutrition-related—about *half* of all cardiovascular disease and a significant percentage of hypertension cases can be traced to diet as well. In the Nurses' Health Study (an ongoing study of more than 120,000 female nurses, begun in Framingham, Massachusetts, in 1976), the nonsmoking women with a median daily intake of 2.7 servings of whole grains were *half* as likely to suffer a stroke as other women in the study. Given this, it's particularly alarming to learn that fewer than 8 percent of Americans eat this much whole grains.

Indeed, most of us are eating ourselves to death—only about 10 percent of American eat the foods that would enable them to be free of chronic disease and premature death.

Our Western diets are literally killing us. While man evolved on a plant-based diet more than fifty thousand years ago, our modern diet—the one our parents ate and the one we're eating—developed only during the past fifty to eighty years. It is not serving us well. We humans are genetically "wired" for starvation, not an overabundance of food. Our genes are set for hunter-gatherer mode and a diet rich in fruits, vegetables, whole grains, nuts and seeds, and lean, wild game—not for the majority of foods and beverages found in today's supermarkets.

It has been estimated that 300,000 to 800,000 preventable deaths per year in the U.S. are nutrition related. These include deaths from atherosclerotic disease, diabetes and certain cancers.

Here are 11 disastrous developments in nutrition that are ruining your health and the health of most everyone in modern industrialized societies...

1. Increased portion sizes.
2. Decreased energy expenditure; people just don't exercise enough.
3. Unhealthy balance of fats in the diet: an increase in saturated fat, omega-6 fatty acids and trans-fatty acids, along with a huge decrease in omega-3 fatty acids.
4. An increase in consumption of processed cereal grains.
5. An overall decrease in fruit and vegetable intake from historical standards.
6. A decrease in lean meat and fish intake.
7. A decrease in antioxidant intake and calcium intake (especially from whole foods).
8. The unhealthy ratio of omega-6 to omega-3 fats, which is associated with a long list of chronic diseases.
9. A marked increase in refined sugar as an overall percentage of caloric intake.
10. A decrease in whole food consumption, which has led to a marked decrease in phytonutrient intake.
11. A decrease in the overall variety of foods eaten.

Few people, including health professionals, are aware of the significant recent decline in our overall health status. More than 125 million Americans have at least one chronic condition like diabetes, cancer, heart disease or glaucoma. The Centers for Disease Control and Prevention estimates that one-third of Americans who were born in 2000 will develop diabetes in their lifetime. Sixty million Americans have more than one condition. It's getting worse every day. In 1996, estimates were made projecting the rate of chronic disease in the future.

Four years later, in 2000, the number of people with chronic ailments was twenty million *higher* than had been anticipated. By the year 2020, a projected one-quarter of the American population will be living with multiple chronic conditions, and estimated costs for managing these conditions will reach $1.07 trillion.

The most shocking nugget of information in this dismal overview of American health is that the age of the "chronically ill" is declining. About half of chronically-ill Americans are under age 45 and, stunningly, 15 percent of that number are children who are suffering from diabetes, asthma, developmental disabilities, cancer and other disorders.

Recognizing the crisis in pediatric health care, for the first time in the spring of 2003, the American Heart Association has offered guidelines for screening kids.

They include...

- Checking a child's blood pressure at every visit after age 3.
- Talking to kids about not smoking as early as age 9.
- Testing cholesterol levels and blood fats in kids who are overweight or at risk.
- Reviewing family history for signs of early heart disease.

As a doctor, I see the imperfections of the system every day. The general unspoken assumption among many people is that you can eat whatever you feel like eating and count on a pill or a surgery to take care of the fallout down the line. For many of us, the only diet-related concern, if we have one, is weight control.

Two of three U.S. adults are either overweight or obese compared with fewer than one in four in the early 1960s. Obesity accounts for more than 280,000 deaths annually in the U.S.

What's the answer? Clearly, we need to do better if we want to live longer and avoid chronic disease. In simplest terms, we need to work with a system—our bodies—that's geared to thrive in times of starvation and high-energy expenditure and adjust for greatly-reduced activity levels in a world where food is overabundant. In other words, *we need to get as much nutrition as possible from fewer calories.* This is possible only if we select the most nutrient-dense, low-calorie foods and make these foods the backbone of our daily diet. *Bottom Line's SuperFoods Rx* will show you how easy this is to do.

Micronutrients: The Keys to Super Health

Do you know what a "healthy diet" consists of? Fruits? Vegetables? Low fat? Lean protein? This advice is okay as far as it goes, but given what we now know about the relative nutritional values of foods, these vague guidelines are only a part of a larger picture. Many people who believe they are eating a "good" diet would be shocked at how poor their nutritional balance actually is. It's a paradox that nutritional deficiencies are common in the overfed. Many people, even those of us who are eating a "healthy diet," are deficient in many of the nutrients that could be helping us to prevent disease.

SuperFoods Rx is based on the premise that we must develop a more sophisticated appreciation of the familiar building blocks of diet—the macronutrients of fat, carbohydrates and protein—and then move on to an examination of the micronutrients in foods. All foods are not created equal. We're familiar with the idea that some proteins are better than others. Striped bass, for example, is better for you than a fatty pork chop. Many of us know that low-fat or nonfat dairy foods are better for us than full-fat ones. But the idea that one vegetable or fruit might be better than another is entirely new. We've only been able to make these kinds of distinctions because we can now examine the micronutrients in fruits and vegetables and assess which ones have more health-promoting qualities.

Micronutrients include two categories we're all familiar with—vitamins and minerals. The most exciting category of micronutrients and one that you'll hear more and more about in the coming years is phytonutrients. Phytonutrients ("phyto," from the Greek word for plant) are naturally-occurring substances that are powerful promoters of human health. This book provides specific information on phytonutrients and their effect on your health and daily energy.

Introducing Phytonutrients

Phytonutrients are nonvitamin, nonmineral components of foods that have significant health benefits. There are literally thousands of them in our foods, appearing in everything from our cup of morning tea to a handful of popcorn at the movies. Some phytonutrients help facilitate the ability of our cells to communicate with one another. Some have anti-inflammatory abilities. Some help prevent mutations at the cellular level, while others prevent the proliferation of cancer cells. Some have functions that we are only beginning to understand, and many have yet to even be identified.

Here are just three important types of beneficial phytonutrients...

Polyphenols act as antioxidants, have anti-inflammatory properties and are antiallergenic, among other health-promoting abilities. Some foods that contain polyphenols are tea, nuts and berries.

Carotenoids are the pigments found in red and yellow vegetables—think tomatoes, pumpkin, carrots, apricots, mangoes, sweet potatoes. They are an important category of phytonutrients that includes beta-carotene, lutein and lycopene.

These nutrients function as antioxidants; they protect us from cancer and help defy the effects of aging.

Phytoestrogens, literally "plant estrogens," are naturally-occurring chemicals found particularly in soy foods as well as in whole wheat, seeds, grains and some vegetables and fruits. They play a role in hormone-related cancers such as prostate and breast cancers.

How Micronutrients Can Prolong Your Health Span

Your body is a complicated, interrelated system that is remarkably resilient. Nonetheless, over a lifetime, the tiny links in the chain that your health depends upon begin to break down. The micronutrients in whole foods provide the reinforcements that retard this breakdown.

One critically important function of micronutrients in maintaining your health is their activity as powerful antioxidants. Just as a bicycle frame in the back of the garage will eventually begin to rust, so our bodies at the cellular level "rust," or oxidize. This oxidation creates long- and short-term health problems. Antioxidants protect the body from oxidation. The antioxidants that have been the most studied and have received the most attention include vitamin C, vitamin E, beta-carotene and minerals such as selenium. You can see the antioxidant activity of vitamin C in your own kitchen: A slice of apple will begin to turn brown shortly after being cut, but if it's rubbed with lemon juice (high in vitamin C) it will be preserved. The vitamin C slows down the oxidation process. The list of antioxidant nutrients grows almost daily. *Here's a brief synopsis of how antioxidants help preserve our health…*

Our bodies are heat-generating machines that depend on oxygen to carry out basic metabolic functions. One of the by-products of this use of oxygen, or "oxidation," is oxygen molecules that have been transformed into what are known as "free radicals." Free radicals are generated by the body's own metabolic systems. In addition, the environment is teeming with them in the form of cigarette smoke, pollution, certain foods and chemicals. Even your drinking water and the sun that warms your face on an April morning are creating free radicals.

These free radicals, which are constantly proliferating throughout our bodies, are missing an electron. This makes them highly unstable. Driven to restore the missing electron, they seek out replacement molecules from whatever neighboring cells they can attack. Sometimes their targets are DNA, sometimes enzymes, sometimes important proteins in neighboring cells and sometimes they attack the cell membrane itself. It's been estimated that each cell experiences ten thousand free-radical hits each day.

Clearly, no living being could survive for long without some powerful system of defense against free radicals. Antioxidants are the foot soldiers in the battle to disarm free radicals in our bodies. They neutralize free radicals and, in effect, minimize their threat by giving up an electron in an effort to stabilize them. Stabilized, the free radicals are no longer a threat to cellular health.

Our bodies produce many antioxidants on their own, but the antioxidants in foods play a critical role in keeping free radicals in check. Indeed, it's the antioxidants in foods that inspired the once shocking but now commonly-held belief in the medical community that certain foods promote health beyond their ability simply to nourish the body.

Scientists now believe that successfully combating free radicals, and the damage they instigate, is one of the keys to long-term health. In other words, we now know that it's no longer just genetics or medical advances that are responsible for your longevity and your ability to avoid chronic disease: It's your body's ability to handle free radicals. Unchecked free-radical activity has been conclusively linked to heart disease, cancer, diabetes, arthritis, vision problems, Alzheimer's disease and premature aging.

It's this idea—that the body benefits immeasurably from a constant rich infusion of phytonutrients, as well as all macro- and other micronutrients—that is one of the cornerstones of *SuperFoods Rx,* and identifying the richest sources of micronutrients in foods is one of its important features.

The Four Principles of SuperFoods Rx

Bottom Line's SuperFoods Rx presents a very simple idea that rests on a cluster of important principles. Understanding these principles will help you shift the focus of your diet and thereby improve your short- and long-term health.

PRINCIPLE ONE: SuperFoods Rx Is the "Best Diet In the World"

The first question most people have about the *SuperFoods Rx* diet is what makes one food more super than another? How were the foods chosen?

As you might imagine, choosing one food over another is not a simple matter. The guiding principle is which food, within a given category, is at the top of its class in promoting health. Also, I had to consider which foods had the most desirable nutrient density, in other words, the most known beneficial nutrients and the least negative properties like saturated fat and sodium.

Today's sophisticated computers have enabled researchers to determine which human populations are the healthiest and live the longest. These epidemiological studies have also allowed us to discover the particular foods eaten by those healthy populations. Certain foods pop up over and over again when you look at the diets of the healthiest people in the world. For example, the traditional Greek diet prior to 1960, including the traditional diet of Crete, is known to be one of the most healthful diets in the world. This Mediterranean diet is primarily a plant-based diet with a number of protective substances in the most popular foods such as selenium; glutathione; resveratrol; a good balance of essential fatty acids (omega-3s to omega-6s); and high amounts of fiber, folate, antioxidants and vitamins C and E. You've probably heard of the Okinawan diet, also recognized as healthy. (Okinawa reportedly has more centenarians—people 100 and older—as a percentage of the population than any region in the world.) My approach in selecting the SuperFoods was to analyze these diets along with other healthy consumption patterns to discover the critical foods that show up over and over.

Approaching from the other direction, in an effort to see which foods were the best proven health promoters, I also studied many highly-respected databases and sets of recommendations, including those of the American Heart Association, the American Cancer Society, the National Cancer Institute and others. These groups have made very specific recommendations based on literally countless studies on what constitutes a healthy diet. The U.S. Department of Agriculture (USDA) has very useful information. There is something called an ORAC score, in which foods are ranked according to their Oxygen Radical Absorption Capacity, or how well they act as antioxidants. Spinach and kale are the two vegetables with the highest ORAC score. That's important information, but it's not the whole picture. The ORAC score, for example, doesn't count fiber, but it does give you a starting point. Multiple charts exist on the relative amounts of nutrients in foods. I have tried to use the most accurate and up-to-date data in all cases.

I turned to the researchers themselves. I've attended many research meetings where I had the opportunity to discuss the latest findings with those who are in the front lines of nutrition research. It's extremely exciting to hear a paper presented for the first time that outlines a new finding that will affect the way people think about food. The fascinating information that has emerged on fats is something that has been getting a great deal of attention lately and is frequently discussed at these meetings. We are in a dual crisis right now: We're eating too much fat, and much of it is the wrong kind of fat. Good fat is essential to life, as you'll see in the section on wild salmon (page 80).

It would have been impossible to do this work even a few years ago, as much of the information I can now access is brand-new. In one instance, I hired a renowned scientist to do the analyses for me. For example, the polyphenol amounts in selected, readily available brand-name 100 percent fruit juices and jams have never been published before. You'll see in the section on blueberries how impressive certain juices are (and, conversely, how unimpressive others are!). The *SuperFoods Rx* guiding goal is to identify the best, buy the best and eat the best!

WHAT ABOUT ORGANIC FOODS?

There's no question that organic foods are better for the environment and thus for all creatures (including us) in that environment because they reduce the threat of pesticides. But are they better from a nutrient standpoint? This is a developing story. There are preliminary and still very controversial data suggesting that organically grown food—particularly some fruits and vegetables—may have more vitamin C, minerals and polyphenols than conventionally grown varieties. Confirming evidence doesn't yet exist. Until larger studies are done confirming these preliminary data, the only definite benefit to organic foods (and one that I believe is considerable) is to the environment.

PRINCIPLE TWO: SuperFoods Are Whole Foods

This is a *very* important principle. I am not at all opposed to supplements; I take them myself. But if there's one thing you should learn from this book, it's that nutritious whole foods must be at the center of your nutrition plan; you can't rely solely on supplements to do the job.

Whole foods are the answer. What are whole foods? While perhaps there will always be some disagreement on a precise definition of the term, in general, whole foods are those that are unprocessed or are minimally processed and in such a way that none of their nutritional characteristics have been intentionally modified. Canned tomatoes, for example, are processed. In the processing, some of the vitamin C is lost, but the processing actually increases tomatoes' nutritional value by concentrating the remaining nutrients. For the purposes of this book, I consider canned tomatoes a whole food.

Phytonutrient research is an emerging science. Optimal as well as safe intakes of phytonutrients have not yet been established for many of these compounds. So we are left with whole foods to provide them in a safe and much more satisfying way. Once again, it's the synergy that matters. It's not just one particular phytonutrient in a food that makes the difference; it also seems that fiber, vitamins, minerals and other substances in that food also enhance and regulate the actions of the phytochemicals.

Whole foods are complex. They contain as-yet-unidentified compounds that can magnify the effects of identified phytonutrients. A growing body of research from laboratory and

About 25 percent of the population is "salt sensitive," which means that their bodies are particularly sensitive to sodium in their diet, and as a result, they are particularly vulnerable to developing hypertension. Everyone tends to become more salt sensitive as they grow older. I recommend that you try to avoid as much added salt in your diet as possible. Learn to read food labels and avoid products with lots of sodium. Remember: You can always add salt to your taste at home. It's far better for you to control the amount.

human studies suggests that these phytonutrients work best in concert. Moreover, just as the phytonutrients in a particular food team up to combat disease and enhance well-being, so do the phytonutrients from a wide range of foods work together to promote good health.

While many studies have focused on beta-carotene, for example, there is still some uncertainty about whether the benefits associated with that carotenoid are actually due to the action of beta-carotene or to one or more of the other carotenoids found in our food. Most likely, the answers lie in the synergistic effect of multiple carotenoids working together or in some compound that hasn't yet been identified. Until all the answers are in, and that surely won't happen in the near future, the safest and most effective way to benefit from the bounty of nutrients in nature's precisely calibrated form is to eat whole foods.

PRINCIPLE THREE: SuperFoods Rx Equals Synergy

We now know a great deal about the rich array of micronutrients in various foods, but we still only have part of the picture. We do know that food synergy is critical to health. Food synergy refers to the interaction of two or more nutrients and other healthful substances in foods that work together to achieve an effect that each is individually unable to match. For example, the power of nuts to prevent cardiovascular disease is far greater than one would assume by looking at any single nutrient they contain. Nutrients work in a precisely calibrated relationship—the kind of relationship that nature has provided when the nutrients are obtained from food. There are, after all, thousands of chemicals present in food and researchers have only identified a fraction of this number. Surely, with this many chemicals present, interactions are taking place that science doesn't fully understand. You can't shortcut your way to good nutrition; you must rely on whole foods.

We don't have the full picture on foods and how they behave in the body. Remember, too, that some foods have attracted more attention and research interest than others, so we know more about those foods. What we don't know is precisely how all the nutrients in a given food work together to promote health. Sometimes we know the result, e.g., a high level of lutein in the macula of the eye is a predictor of visual health. We may not, however, be certain about what other substances are working along with the lutein to achieve a lifetime of excellent vision.

Spinach is a good example of the synergy of multiple nutrients. Spinach is the single food that most epidemiological studies associate with the lowest levels of cancer, heart disease, cataracts and macular degeneration. It's very clear: The more spinach people eat, the less likely they are to develop any of those diseases. It would make sense that if you could develop a pill containing the significant substances in spinach, you'd have a potent weapon against cancer. In an effort to do just this, researchers have tried to deconstruct spinach to see what makes it so effective. Here's what they have come up with: Spinach contains a stunning collection of micronutrients, including

SuperFoods Rx
LIFESTYLE PYRAMID

- Aerobic exercise most days (30 to 90 minutes)
- For those not currently exercising, begin with walking a minimum of 1 hour per week
- Resistance exercises (weight training) 2 to 3 times per week
- Stress-management practice (15 minutes most days)
- Hydration: Drink 8 or more 8-ounce glasses of water daily (may include tea and/or 100% fruit/vegetable juice)
- Sleep (7 to 8 hours for most people)

FRUITS: 3 to 5 servings daily; include berries (fresh or frozen) most days

VEGETABLES: Unlimited (minimum 5 to 7 servings); include dark, leafy greens most days

WHOLE GRAINS: 5 to 7 servings per day (see SuperFoods Rx List); include whole-grain noodles/pasta, tortillas, breads, and cereals

PROTEIN: *Animal Protein:* 1 to 2 servings daily of skinless poultry breast, fish* (see SuperFoods Rx List); may include 3 oz lean red meat every 10 days (*2 to 4 servings per week) *Vegetarian Protein:* 1 to 3 servings daily of legumes, lentils, soy (i.e., tempeh, tofu), egg whites, eggs (1 per day maximum)

FOR HEALTHY BONES: 1 to 3 servings daily of non- or low-fat dairy, tofu, soy, fortified soy milk, fortified OJ, fish with bones (i.e., sardines, canned salmon), shellfish, dark leafy greens

HEALTHY FATS: 1 to 2 servings daily of nuts, seeds, avocado, extra virgin olive oil, canola oil, soybean oil, peanut oil, flaxseed oil

Up to 100 calories daily dark chocolate, butter, buckwheat honey, sweets, or refined breads and grains

SUPPLEMENTS:
- Multivitamin and mineral supplement daily for most people
- Consider a fish oil supplement (250 to 1,000 mg daily)

SEASONINGS:
Cook frequently with dried or fresh parsley, rosemary, oregano, tumeric, garlic, ginger, citrus zest, chives, red onion and white onion

ALCOHOL:
If you choose to consume alcohol, we recommend: 1 to 3 drinks per week for women; 2 to 8 drinks per week for men

FOOD FOR THOUGHT:
- Daydream
- Enjoy friendships and laughter
- Embrace spiritual values
- Spend some time outdoors each day

SAMPLE SERVINGS:
Fruits = 1 medium piece, 1 cup, ½ cup juice, 2 tablespoons raisins, 3 prunes
Vegetables = ½ cup cooked, 1 cup raw
Grains = ½ cup cooked grains/pasta; 1 slice bread
Meat and Fish = 3 oz lean meat, poultry, or fish
Vegetarian Protein = 1 egg, 2 egg whites, 3 oz tofu or tempeh, ½ cup cooked beans or lentils
Dairy = ½ cup non- or low-fat cottage cheese, 8 oz non- or low-fat yogurt or milk
Fats = 1 oz (24) raw almonds, 14 walnut halves, 1 tablespoon oil, ⅜ avocado

SUPERFOODS RX IS AN SPF DIET

Eating the foods recommended in this book can actually increase the SPF (sun protection factor) of your skin. The key nutrients of lutein/zeaxanthin, beta-carotene, alpha-carotene, lycopene, vitamins C and E, folate, polyphenols, glutathione, isoflavones, omega-3 fatty acids and coenzyme Q_{10} all help protect your skin from sun damage. This is extremely important because as the ozone layer has decreased, the ultraviolet exposure of all living organisms on earth has increased.

lutein, zeaxanthin, beta-carotene, plant-derived omega-3 fatty acids (only a very few vegetables contain these fatty acids), the antioxidants glutathione, alpha lipoic acid (spinach is the best food source of this amazingly potent antioxidant), vitamins C and E, polyphenols, coenzyme Q_{10}, thiamine, riboflavin, vitamin B6, folate, vitamin K, and the minerals calcium, iron, magnesium, manganese and zinc. It also has chlorophyll, which may be a potent anticancer substance.

Wouldn't it make sense for a pharmaceutical company to formulate a capsule version of spinach? Not really. A pill containing all these substances (in the quantity available in whole-food spinach) would be hopelessly large and impossible to swallow, not to mention expensive and unprofitable. Moreover, there's no certainty that we understand the exact proportions of nutrients as they exist in spinach. We know that the synergy of micronutrients is critical, but we don't know yet how to achieve this in a man-made substance. The bottom line is that it's most likely impossible to make a supplement that fully duplicates the synergistic power of food. But there's really no need to: If you want to have all the health-promoting power of spinach, it's available right in your market.

The synergy of *SuperFoods Rx* really extends beyond diet. Not only do all the nutrients in food work together to make something greater than the whole, the organ systems in your body do the same. We now know that disease isn't usually something that strikes out of the blue and hits an isolated organ. For example, did you know that obesity is a risk factor for age-related macular degeneration (AMD)? Who would guess that being overweight would affect your vision?

While the focus of this book is certainly food, if you want to achieve optimum health, you must incorporate other lifestyle changes into your daily life. The SuperFoods Rx Lifestyle Pyramid, on the preceding page, visually summarizes the components of a healthy life. It's critically important to improve your diet, but if you don't exercise, you won't get the most benefit from optimum nutrition. Similarly, if you do nothing to control the stress in your life, even a perfect diet won't work to your best advantage. So, it's diet, exercise, positive social interaction, stress reduction, sufficient sleep and even sufficient fluid intake that work together—that's synergy!—to maximize the benefit of each.

PRINCIPLE FOUR: SuperFoods Rx Are Simple; SuperFoods Rx Are Positive

Food is an emotional subject for many people. For some, it's a great, unmitigated pleasure. For many, it's a source of worry and confusion. There's the nutrition issue, the weight issue, the preparation issue...A healthy diet is the essential core of a healthy lifestyle, along with exercise, routine preventive medical care, adequate sleep and stress reduction. We all live busy complicated lives, and any nutrition recommendations or advice that I or anyone else offer will be ignored if it is too complicated or challenging.

Fortunately, nature agrees, so choosing from a range of whole SuperFoods is simple.

Fresh isn't always best. Some canned or frozen vegetables often have the same nutritional content as fresh. Frozen fruits and vegetables are usually flash-frozen just after being harvested, so their nutrients are locked in. Many are available already chopped, which saves you a prep step. Take the time to become familiar with the products that are easily accessible to you.

The best approach to any health change is one that is positive. I believe that "diets" that forbid foods or make eating satisfying meals a challenge are counterproductive.

Once most people understand the *SuperFoods Rx* principles, they feel liberated.

SuperFoods Rx is about what you should eat, not what you shouldn't eat. It's not about what you shouldn't do.

If you eat a healthy diet of SuperFoods, there's room for a bit of most any kind of food that gives you pleasure, whether it's vanilla ice cream or bacon. The good stuff in the SuperFoods will help to mitigate any damage done by the bad stuff. Of course, you have to be sensible about this.

I attended a medical conference in Spain where I lectured on the dietary prevention of cataracts. The next morning when I went to breakfast with a few colleagues, it became clear that they wanted me to order first because they were afraid I'd disapprove of their choices. I ordered scrambled eggs topped with fresh salsa, a bowl of berries and a glass of delicious fresh squeezed orange juice. They were shocked. I guess they expected me to eat a bit of unsweetened granola and drink some mineral water.

Food is pleasure. When you sit at the table, you're not a patient, you're a person. Eating should be a satisfying part of your life. *SuperFoods Rx* will help make it so.

SuperFoods Rx in Your Kitchen

No eating plan will work if you can't adapt it to your lifestyle. I think *SuperFoods Rx* offers the easiest, healthiest eating plan ever! To make it even easier, I've worked closely with nutritionists and super chefs—who are feeding real people every day—to come up with tips and suggestions on how to integrate SuperFoods into your busy lifestyle.

Here are some very practical considerations and some basic information that will help you get started with *SuperFoods Rx*.

SuperFoods Rx and Portion Control

The amounts of food many of us eat are out of control. When I tell people that they should be eating five to seven servings of vegetables a day, they are shocked, claiming they could never eat that much food. It's quite true that one couldn't eat seven servings of vegetables a day if their serving size duplicated the portions in many restaurants. The Food and Drug Administration (FDA) says that the standard serving of pasta, for example, is 1 cup. In most restaurants, pasta portions typically measure about 3 cups. That's about three servings! We'd be eating vegetables out of buckets if we extrapolated from restaurant-portion sizes. I believe that many people have been discouraged from following good dietary guidelines because they've come to believe that a serving is a super-size amount of food. They believe that if they really ate that much, they'd gain a tremendous amount of weight.

✪ A survey by the American Institute for Cancer Research found that more than 25 percent of Americans polled said that they decided how much food to eat at a single sitting based on how much food they were served.

When it comes to fruits and vegetables, getting the optimum number of servings isn't hard at all when you understand what a serving size really is. For most fruits and vegetables, it's one-half cup.

Here is the *SuperFoods Rx* breakdown of serving sizes in various food categories…

Vegetables

½ cup cooked or raw vegetables
1 cup raw greens
½ cup vegetable juice

Fruits

½ cup chopped fruit
½ cup fruit juice
1 medium piece of fruit
2 tablespoons raisins, 3 prunes

Vegetarian Protein

1 egg or 2 egg whites
3 ounces tofu or tempeh
½ cup cooked beans or lentils

Nuts

2 tablespoons peanut butter or 1 ounce raw nuts and seeds

Fish and Meat

3 ounces cooked lean meat, poultry or fish

Whole Grains

1 slice whole wheat bread
½ cup cooked grain or pasta

High Calcium Foods

½ cup nonfat cottage cheese
8 ounces nonfat yogurt or milk

Fats

1 ounce (24) almonds, 15 walnut halves
1 tablespoon oil
⅜ avocado

Here is a general idea of what you should be eating on a weekly basis…

	Daily Servings
Vegetables	5 to 7; include dark leafy greens most days
Fruits	3 to 5
Soy	1 to 2
Animal protein	0 to 3
Vegetarian protein	3 to 6
Healthy fats	1 to 2
Whole grains	5 to 7
High calcium foods	2 to 3
	Weekly Servings
Nuts and seeds	5
Fish	2 to 4

Here are some tips from the American Dietetic Association on how to recognize appropriate serving sizes…

- A medium potato should be the size of a computer mouse.
- An average bagel should be the size of a hockey puck.
- A cup of fruit is the size of a baseball.
- A cup of lettuce is four leaves.
- Three ounces of meat is the size of a cassette tape.
- Three ounces of grilled fish is the size of your checkbook.
- One ounce of cheese is the size of four dice.
- One teaspoon of peanut butter equals one dice.
- One ounce of snack foods—pretzels, etc. —equals a large handful.

Understanding Each SuperFood

There are 23 SuperFoods. That does not mean that any diet should be limited to these foods! Variety in food choices is absolutely critical to health. The 23 SuperFoods are the "flagship" foods in a given category. They were chosen because of the high concentrations of nutrients or the otherwise hard-to-get nutrients they contain, as well as the fact that many of them are low in calories. You will see that under each SuperFood is a list of the primary nutrients that have elevated them to SuperFood status. This is not meant to be a complete list of every single nutrient that food contains, but rather a list of the high-profile nutrients that have demonstrated definite health benefits and are present in that food in sufficient quantity to make a difference.

Each SuperFood has "Sidekicks." These are foods that are generally in the same category as the flagship SuperFood and offer a similar nutrient profile. For example, almonds, along with sunflower seeds and pecans and a few others, are sidekicks to the SuperFood walnuts. Some foods like soy have few sidekicks, so while soy is available in a variety of food forms, including soymilk, soy nuts and tofu, it's the nutrients in soy and only soy that make it a SuperFood.

At the beginning of each SuperFood section there is a "Try to Eat" recommendation. This is a guideline on how much of that particular SuperFood you should attempt to incorporate into your diet and how often.

At the end of every SuperFood section, you'll find a few quick-and-easy recipes that my family and I enjoy at home on a regular basis.

The SuperFoods Rx Recipes

You'll find enticing recipes specifically created for us by our two wonderful chefs, the Avanti Café's Mark Cleveland and the Golden Door's Michel Stroot, starting on page 157. The recipes highlight the various SuperFoods and a nutritional analysis accompanies each recipe. Chef Stroot has also developed a sample week's worth of delicious recipes, followed by a daily nutritional breakdown, beginning on page 184. You will see how easy it is to incorporate SuperFoods into your life.

Here is an extremely abbreviated outline of the major *SuperFoods Rx* recommendations...

- Eat at least eight servings of fruits and vegetables daily.
- Think healthy fat: Try to increase your intake of seafood, nuts and seeds, avocado, extra virgin olive oil and canola oil.
- Eat one handful of nuts about five days per week.
- Eat fish two to four times a week.
- Substitute soy protein for animal protein a few times a week. Try to have one or two servings of soy daily.
- Buy bread and whole grain cereals that have at least 3 grams of fiber per serving.
- Drink green or black tea, hot or chilled, daily.
- Have some yogurt for breakfast, or in a smoothie, dip or dessert every day.
- Add phytonutrient-rich 100 percent juices and jams to your diet.
- Avoid commercial snacks and baked goods, which contain many unhealthy fats, including saturated fat, trans-fatty acids, an overabundance of omega-6 fatty acids and sodium.
- Eliminate soft drinks, sweetened or "diet," except as an occasional treat.

2

THE TERRIFIC TWENTY-THREE: THE SUPERFOODS

APPLES

An apple a day is the most delicious and effective prescription ever to be given out. Apples have been proven to be potent weapons against cancer, heart disease, asthma and type II diabetes, when compared to other fruits and vegetables, according to a recent major review study. The reasons for apples' powerful health benefits are varied and synergistic.

For one thing, apples are a rich and important source of phytochemicals, including flavonoids and phenols. In the U.S., 22 percent of the phenolics (a class of polyphenols) consumed from fruits are from apples, making them the largest source of phenols in the American diet.

APPLES ARE A SOURCE OF:

- Polyphenols
- Fiber
- Vitamin C
- Potassium

Sidekicks: Pears

Try to eat: An apple a day

Apples also contain two polyphenols—phloridzin and phloretin xyloglucoside—which to date have not been detected in any other fruits. Not only are apples particularly rich in phenols, they also have the highest concentration of "free phenols." These are phenols that seem to be more available for absorption into the bloodstream.

Eat a wide variety of apples. Different apple varieties have different skin colors, meaning the phytonutrient content of the skins varies in concentration and type of polyphenols.

Apples are also filled with superantioxidants. The antioxidant activity of approximately one apple is equivalent to about 1,500 milligrams of vitamin C, even though the amount of vitamin C in one apple is only about 5.7 milligrams. And, by the way, apples with peels have a *far* greater antioxidant capacity than those with the peel removed. In cell culture in the laboratory, apple peel alone inhibits cancer cell proliferation better than whole apples. The apple peel contains more antioxidant compounds, especially polyphenols and vitamin C, than the flesh. A peel provides anywhere from two to six times (depending on the variety) more phenolic compounds than the flesh, and two to three times more flavonoids. The antioxidant activity of apple peels is about two to six times the activity of the apple flesh. So, eat the peel if you want to get the full protective benefits of apples.

In the U.S., Fuji apples have the highest total phenolic and total flavonoid content; Red Delicious apples are also quite high. But don't limit yourself: Variety is the key.

One of the flavonoids found in apples, quercetin, seems to play a protective role against chronic conditions like heart disease and cancer. Quercetin is a plant pigment that has anti-inflammatory and antioxidant properties. It may be helpful in preventing the oxidation of bad cholesterol and in inhibiting cancerous changes to cells. Studies have suggested that people with the highest intakes of quercetin may have a reduced risk for heart disease and lung cancer.

Apples and Your Heart

Regular apple consumption seems to be a delightful way to protect yourself from heart disease. The fiber in apples—both soluble and insoluble—helps to reduce cholesterol levels, thus promoting heart and circulatory health. One large apple supplies almost 30 percent of the minimum amount of the government's DV (daily value) for fiber (5.7 grams), and about 81 percent of the fiber in apples is soluble—the type that helps to reduce cholesterol levels.

Apples, along with pears, are loaded with soluble fiber, which plays an important role in normalizing blood lipids. In fact, adding just one large apple to your daily diet can reduce serum cholesterol levels 8 to 11 percent and eating two large apples daily has lowered cholesterol levels by up to 16 percent in some people.

In one study, ten thousand Americans were studied for nineteen years. In this group, those eating the most fiber—21 grams daily—had 12 percent less coronary heart disease and 12 percent less cardiovascular disease compared with those eating the least fiber—5 grams daily. The folks who ate the most water-soluble dietary fiber did better yet, with a 15 percent reduction in their risk for coronary heart disease and a 10 percent reduced risk for cardiovascular disease.

Apples are also useful in preventing cardiovascular problems. A study of forty thousand women from the Women's Health Study found a 35 percent reduction in the risk for cardiovascular disease in the women with the highest flavonoid consumption, and in this study both apple and broccoli intake were associated with reductions in the risk for cardiovascular disease and events. Women ingesting apples had a 13 to 22 percent decrease in cardiovascular disease risk. Some of the apples' protective effect against cardiovascular disease may come from their potential cholesterol-lowering ability. In a 2003 study, it was found that combined apple pectin and apple phenolics (a class of polyphenols) lowered plasma and liver cholesterol, triglycerides and apparent cholesterol absorption to a much greater extent than either apple pectin or apple phenolics alone. This once again demonstrates that it is the synergy of the whole food that makes the best insurance against disease.

Moreover, in a Finnish study, those who had the highest consumption of apples had a lower risk of thrombotic stroke compared with those who had the lowest consumption. In addition, apple and wine consumption was inversely associated with death from coronary heart disease in postmenopausal women in a study of nearly 35,000 women in Iowa. This would argue for the healthful effects of a wine and apple party.

Apples can help you lose weight. Soluble fruit fiber has been shown to be inversely associated with long-term weight gain, and in one study the daily consumption of either three apples or three pears was associated with weight loss in overweight women.

Apples and Cancer

Apples have proven themselves to be potent cancer fighters. In the Nurses' Health Study and the Health Professionals Follow-up Study, fruit and vegetable intake was associated with a 21 percent reduced risk of lung cancer in women. Subjects who consumed at least one serving per day of apples and pears had a reduced risk of lung cancer (apples were one of the individual fruits associated with a decreased risk).

A study in Hawaii found that apple and onion intake was associated with a reduced risk of lung cancer in men and women. There was a 40 to 50 percent decreased risk of lung cancer in participants with the highest intake of apples and onions compared with those who consumed the lowest amount of these foods.

Apples and Lung Health

In addition to all the ways that apples boost heart health, they're beneficial to lung function. Apple consumption has been inversely linked with asthma and has also been positively associated with general pulmonary health. For example, an Australian study found apple and pear intake to be associated with a decreased risk of asthma, and a United Kingdom study found that apple intake, as well as selenium intake, was associated with less asthma in adults. In the latter study, the clearest effect was in those consuming at least two apples per week.

In a study of more than thirteen thousand adults in the Netherlands, it was found that apple and pear intake was positively associated with pulmonary function and negatively associated with chronic obstructive pulmonary disease.

Another study showed that those who consumed five or more apples a week had a significantly greater forced expiratory volume (a measure of pulmonary function) compared with those who did not consume apples.

Apples and Diabetes

Not only may apples help decrease the risk of heart disease, cancer and asthma, but apple consumption may also be associated with a lower risk for diabetes. In a study of ten thousand Finnish people, a reduced risk of type II diabetes was associated with apple consumption and higher intake of quercetin (a polyphenol), a major component of apple peels, was also associated with a decreased risk of type II diabetes.

Apples in the Kitchen

While they are at their freshest obtained from local sources in the autumn, apples are readily available all year long. When shopping for apples, look for ones that are firm and unblemished. Choose different types of apples depending on how you plan to use them. Sweet apples like Red or Golden Delicious are great eaten out of hand. So are slightly tarter Fuji and Braeburn apples. Granny Smith and Pippins are good choices for cooking, as they are tart and retain their texture. Apples should be kept cold after purchase.

The key to getting the best from apples is to eat the whole fruit, peel and all, and to eat a variety of apples, as each type offers different health-promoting benefits.

Here are some ideas for getting more apples into your life...

• A great snack is a sliced apple smeared with peanut or soy butter.

• For a healthy dessert, wash and core an apple. Put it in an oven-safe dish with a dash of honey, a sprinkle of walnuts, and a dusting of cinnamon (all SuperFoods). Bake in a preheated 350° F oven for about 30 minutes. Serve warm or cold.

• Dice an unpeeled, washed, cored apple and mix it with raisins, cranberries (dried or fresh), and any chopped dried fruit. Bake until soft and use to top yogurt or oatmeal.

• Add thinly sliced apples or pears to a spinach salad and top with walnuts and diced red onions. Dress with raspberry vinaigrette.

• Homemade applesauce, made with cored, unpeeled apples, is always a favorite, served either as a dessert or a side dish. Don't forget the cinnamon.

See our Shopping Lists (pages 211, 212, 216, 218 and 219) for some recommended products.

AVOCADO

How about a buttery green fruit that you can spread on a sandwich, dice into a salad or mash into America's favorite dip? If avocados were only delicious and versatile, they would still be a treat worth serving frequently. Recent research has demonstrated that avocados also offer some surprising and powerful health benefits. One of the most nutrient-dense foods, avocados are high in fiber and, ounce for ounce, top the charts among all fruits for folate, potassium, vitamin E and magnesium. Indeed, the very impressive health benefits of eating avocados regularly have encouraged me to adopt them as a SuperFood.

THE HISTORY OF THE AVOCADO

Avocados have been cultivated for thousands of years. A favorite of the Aztecs, they were native to Central America. There are generally two types of avocados available in U.S. markets—the Hass avocado from California and the West Indian avocado from Florida. The green-black Hass avocado was named for Rudolph Hass, a Wisconsin mailman who retired to Pasadena and obtained a patent for the "Hass" avocado tree in 1935. Hass avocados are nutty and buttery and rich in healthy monounsaturated oil—from 18 to 30 percent oil in each avocado. The light green Florida avocado is larger and juicier than the Hass variety, but it is less buttery and considerably lower in oil. The Florida avocado contains just 3 to 5 percent oil and roughly 25 to 50 percent less fat than the Hass variety.

MANY HEALTH CLAIMS

The delicious healthy monounsaturated fat in the avocado is one of its biggest SuperFood health claims. The only other fruit with a comparable amount of monounsaturated fat is the olive. The monounsaturated fat in avocados is oleic acid, which may help lower cholesterol. One study found that after seven days on a diet that included avocados, there were significant decreases in both total and LDL ("bad") cholesterol as well as an 11 percent increase in the HDL ("good") cholesterol. Half a California avocado has a really excellent overall nutrient profile. At 145 calories it contains approximately 2 grams of protein, 6 grams of fiber, and 13 grams of fat, most of which (8.5 grams) is monounsaturated fat.

AVOCADOS ARE A SOURCE OF:

- Monounsaturated fatty acids
- Fiber
- Magnesium
- Folate
- Vitamin E
- Carotenoids
- Glutathione
- Beta-sitosterol
- Chlorophyll
- Polyphenols
- Lutein

Sidekicks: Asparagus, artichokes, extra virgin olive oil

Try to eat: ⅓ to ½ of an avocado multiple times weekly

Avocados are rich in magnesium. Magnesium is an essential nutrient for healthy bones, the cardiovascular system (particularly in the regulation of blood pressure and cardiac rhythms), prevention of migraines and prevention of type II diabetes. Ounce for ounce, avocados provide more magnesium than the twenty most commonly eaten fruits, with the banana, kiwi and strawberry in second, third, and fourth place, respectively.

Among the twenty most commonly eaten fruits, avocado ranks number one for vitamin E, lutein, glutathione and beta-sitosterol.

Avocados also have plenty of potassium, a critical nutrient that up until now has not gotten deserved attention. Potassium helps regulate blood pressure, and an adequate intake of this mineral can help prevent circulatory diseases, including high blood pressure, stroke and heart disease. For more information on potassium, see page 146.

RICH IN FOLATE

Avocados are a wonderful source of folate. One cup of avocado contains 23 percent of the daily value for folate. Various studies have shown a correlation between diets high in folate and a reduced risk of cardiovascular disease and stroke.

In addition to their other heart-healthy qualities, avocados are rich in beta-sitosterol, a so-called phytosterol. Along with peanut butter, cashews, almonds, peas and kidney beans, avocado is one of the best sources of beta-sitosterol from whole foods. A phytosterol is the plant equivalent of cholesterol in animals. Because beta-sitosterol is so similar to cholesterol, it competes for absorption with cholesterol and wins, thus lowering the amounts of cholesterol in our bloodstream. Beta-sitosterol also appears to inhibit excessive cell division, which may play a role in preventing cancer-cell growth. In both animal and laboratory studies, this phytonutrient helps reduce the risk for cancer.

Perhaps the most interesting research on avocados demonstrates that it is a powerful "nutrient booster": Avocados actually improve the body's ability to absorb nutrients from foods. It's important to remember that it's not just the presence of nutrients in foods that matter, it's also our body's ability to absorb these nutrients. In one study, adding about half an avocado (75 grams) to a carrot/lettuce/spinach salad increased the absorption of the following nutrients in the subjects who ate the salad: alpha-carotene by 8.3 times, beta-carotene by 13.6 times and lutein by 4.3 times compared with the absorption rate of the same salad without avocado. In a second study, adding a medium avocado (150 grams) to a serving of salsa increased the absorption of lycopene 4.4 times and the absorption of beta-carotene 2.6 times, compared with eating the salsa without the avocado. Both studies concluded that the healthy monounsaturated fat in the avocado caused a significant increase in the absorption of the fat-soluble carotenoid phytonutrients in the meal.

Avocado has more soluble fiber—the best fiber for lowering cholesterol—than any other fruit.

Avocado can play a role in a weight-loss diet if eaten in moderate amounts. While high in calories—at 48 calories per ounce, avocados are equivalent to skinless roast chicken breast—avocados help fight obesity because they boost satiety. Satiety is the feeling of fullness that signals us to stop eating and thus helps us control our calorie intake.

Perhaps more interesting, research suggests that exercise burns monounsaturated fat more rapidly than saturated fat. This means that even though an avocado is high in monounsaturated fat, this fat will be burned more quickly than saturated fat. The body prefers to burn this fuel over the saturated fat found in meat and dairy.

Recent research shows that avocado seems to be a potent warrior in the fight against prostate cancer. Avocados contain the highest amount of the carotenoid lutein of all commonly eaten fruits. In addition, they contain related carotenoids, including zeaxanthin, alpha-carotene and beta-carotene, as well as significant amounts of vitamin E. Another study showed that an extract of avocado containing these carotenoids and tocopherols inhibited the growth of prostate cancer cells. Interestingly, when researchers used lutein alone, the cancer cells were unaffected, thus demonstrating once again that it's the synergy of health-promoting nutrients in whole foods that makes the difference.

Research at Tufts University suggests that avocado can play an important role in optimizing brain health and function.

How to Buy and Eat an Avocado

An unripe avocado will have none of the delicious creaminess of a ripe one. When shopping for avocados, select fruit that is unblemished, without cracks or dark sunken spots. A ripe avocado will yield slightly to the touch when pressed, and this slight softness indicates it's ready to eat. It's often difficult to find a ripe avocado in the store, but it will ripen at home in a few days in a paper bag or on the kitchen counter. Plan in advance so you'll have ripe avocados when you need them. Do not refrigerate avocados.

My favorite ways to eat avocados are...

- Guacamole is a favorite use for avocado and I've included a great "guac" recipe on page 165. There are many variations on this basic recipe, the simplest probably being mashing a ripe avocado with a roughly equal amount of prepared salsa.
- Spread on toasted whole-grain bread and topped with salsa
- As a garnish for turkey tacos
- Diced into any green leafy salad

If you're counting calories, that's no reason to exclude avocados from your diet. Just use them judiciously. *For example...*

- Spread a bit of mashed avocado on a sandwich in place of mayo.
- Chop and sprinkle avocado on top of a bean soup.
- Add to tofu and spices and blend to make a delicious, creamy dressing.

See our Shopping Lists (page 217) for some recommended products.

BEANS

I love spreading the good news about beans. They're one of my favorite SuperFoods for many reasons. Of course, most important are their health benefits. One recent study of older people revealed that those who regularly ate beans had a *significantly lower risk of overall mortality* compared with nonlegume eaters. In fact, for every 20 grams of beans consumed daily, they experienced an 8 percent lower risk of mortality. It's not surprising then that bean eaters live longer given the multiple health benefits of the lowly bean.

Many people have relegated beans to the back of the pantry for a few reasons: They assume that beans, while good for vegetarians and "back to the land" types, don't have much to offer the average meat-eating diner. They also figure that beans take way too long to cook. *Oh, yes, and then there's the gas issue...*

The truth is that beans are a virtual wonder food. A delicious source of vitamin-rich, low-fat, inexpensive, versatile protein, beans deserve a place at the table for those reasons alone. But the full power of beans to lower cholesterol; combat heart disease; stabilize blood sugar; reduce obesity; relieve constipation, diverticular disease, hypertension and type II diabetes; and lessen the risk for cancer make this ancient food an extraordinary and important addition to any diet.

If the health benefits weren't enough, the practical reasons for eating beans would push them into the top ranks of desirable foods. Beans are versatile and delicious. Stars in many signature dishes from around the world, they adapt beautifully to myriad seasonings and cooking methods. They're great served hot or cold. They're inexpensive and, fresh or canned, readily available all year round. Just stock up on them when convenient. With a can of beans in the pantry, you have the beginning of a healthy, nutritious, delicious, and almost instant meal.

Legumes include fresh beans like peas, green beans and lima beans as well as lentils, chickpeas, black beans and the whole dried bean family.

BEANS ARE A SOURCE OF:
- Low-fat protein
- Fiber
- B vitamins
- Iron
- Folate
- Potassium
- Magnesium
- Phytonutrients

Sidekicks: All beans are included in this SuperFood category, though we'll discuss the most popular and readily available beans such as pinto, navy, Great Northern, lima, garbanzo (chickpeas), lentils, green beans, sugar snap peas and green peas

Try to eat: At least four ½-cup servings per week

Let's now get any perceived objections about beans out of the way. While it's true that most beans take a while to cook, they don't take up much *active* cooking time. In other words, beans simmer without your having to hover over a pot. An alternative to cooking beans is to use canned beans. This actually is the most practical way to introduce beans to your diet. You can open a can of chickpeas (garbanzo beans), cannellini beans (small white beans) or black beans and just toss them on top of a salad or add them to chili.

There is a negative to relying on canned beans: Many varieties and brands are too high in sodium. Look for low-sodium or no-salt-added beans, which are becoming increasingly available or, alternatively, rinse the beans in cold water, which will remove much of the salt. Keep a variety of canned beans in the pantry for a quick meal. It's helpful to mark the tops of the cans with the date purchased so you can use them in the order of freshness.

In 1992, less than one-third of Americans ate beans during any three-day period. As income levels rise, bean consumption tends to decrease.

As for the complaint that beans can cause gas, it is true that beans can cause flatulence. This is because bacteria attack the indigestible matter that remains in the intestine. *Here are some hints for reducing any discomfort associated with eating beans...*

- Some people find that canned beans as well as mashed beans are less gas producing.
- If you eat beans frequently in small amounts, your body will become accustomed to them and you'll reduce any digestive problems.
- Soak the beans before cooking: Rinse and pick over the beans, then boil them for two or three minutes. Turn off the heat and let them soak for a few hours. Pour off the liquid, add fresh water and continue cooking. This boiling

and soaking releases a large percentage of the indigestible carbohydrate in the beans, making them easier to digest. Even though some vitamins are lost to this method, if it allows you to enjoy beans, it's to your benefit.

• Some people find that pressure-cooking beans reduces their gas-producing qualities. It also considerably speeds the cooking process.

• Try using Beano, an enzyme product that helps reduce the gas associated with foods like beans. Put a few drops of the product on the first bites of the food. It goes to work digesting the carbohydrates that would have fed the gas-producing bacteria.

Bean History

Beans, peas and lentils are ancient foods. Originating primarily in Africa, Asia and the Middle East, they spread over most of the globe, carried by nomadic tribes. They have been cultivated all over the earth for thousands of years. Evidence also suggests that many beans were first grown on the American continent. In North America, most of the dried beans commonly eaten are descendants of beans cultivated in Central and South America seven thousand years ago. Portable, tasty, highly nutritious, nonperishable and adaptable to any cuisine, beans show up in the signature dishes from many lands. Dal from India, hummus from the Middle East and rice and beans from Latin America all make use of the versatile bean.

Beans are also known as legumes or pulses. They're an extensive family of plants distinguished by their seed-bearing pods. Some beans, like string beans, are eaten fresh, pod and all. Other legumes or relatives of beans included here are lentils and peas. (While soybeans are also beans, because of their special nutritional characteristics they have their own section, on page 89. Peanuts are also, strictly speaking, legumes, but because many people think of them as nuts, we've included them in the section on walnuts, on page 125.) Most of the beans that we refer to in this chapter are those that are eaten, when fully mature, in their dried form.

Don't forget that peas, as well as string beans and green beans, are members of the bean family. These fresh beans are readily available, are frequently served in restaurants and make it easy to reach or exceed your weekly quota of bean servings.

Low-fat Protein

Beans are not just for vegetarians. Long regarded as "poor man's meat" because they offer an excellent source of protein, beans lost favor while Americans binged on animal protein. But as the ailments associated with animal protein have skyrocketed—particularly heart disease, some types of cancer and diabetes—savvy consumers are beginning to recognize the value in the humble bean.

Beans are an incredible source of vegetable protein. In an era when high-protein diets have become popular, it's important to understand that there are a variety of protein sources, and there is some evidence that eating more meat and dairy products in place of carbohydrates is linked to greater coronary heart disease mortality. In one study of over 29,000 postmenopausal

Polyphenols occur at relatively high concentrations in legumes. High levels of these important phytonutrients are present in colored beans, e.g., black, yellow, beige, red. The beans with the highest antioxidant concentrations, highest to lowest, are:

- Broad beans/fava beans
- Pinto beans and black beans
- Lentils

Iowa women who were initially free of cancer, coronary heart disease, and diabetes, it was found that the women who ate the most vegetable protein instead of either carbs or animal protein were 30 percent less likely to die from heart disease.

We don't know why different sources of protein have different health effects, but it could be that vegetable protein delivers minerals, vitamins, and phytonutrients that promote health, or perhaps vegetable protein has a more positive effect on our hormones.

Beans offer many healthy components with virtually no fat and very few calories. Loaded with fiber—an often-neglected aspect of a healthy diet—they're also a rich source of antioxidants. Indeed, black beans are as rich in the antioxidant compounds anthocyanins as are grapes and cranberries. In a recent study, researchers found that the darker the bean, the higher the level of antioxidant activity. Black beans were the stars, followed by red, brown, yellow, and then white beans. Interestingly, the overall level of antioxidants found in black beans was ten times that of oranges.

The American Cancer Society's 2006 Dietary Guidelines recommend choosing beans as an alternative to meat. It's a simple recommendation that stands on a huge and impressive body of research associating increased risk for a wide variety of diseases with animal protein, and a decreased risk for those same diseases when plant-derived protein (such as that from beans) is substituted for animal food sources in the diet.

Beans are one of the most healthy and most economical sources of protein available. For example, 1 cup of lentils provides 17 grams of protein with only 0.75 gram of fat. Two ounces of extra-lean trimmed sirloin steak has the same amount of protein but *six times* the fat.

Lysine is the principal amino acid deficient in a large percentage of plant protein, and most beans have a generous concentration of it. As a result, beans are an ideal complementary protein for most other vegetarian protein choices. Lysine is one of the two amino acids essential for carnitine synthesis, and carnitine is essential for efficient energy production in the mitochondria—the cellular energy factory.

THE COMPLETE-PROTEIN ISSUE

The traditional objection to the protein from beans—that it's not a complete protein—is a somewhat old-fashioned idea. It's true that beans (with the exception of soybeans, which are a complete protein) are missing two amino acids and are therefore not complete in the sense that these acids are necessary for the body to make use of the beans' protein.

However, bean protein is completed by other common foods, such as nuts, dairy and grains or even animal protein. In fact, many popular bean dishes—rice and beans, couscous and chickpeas, lentils and barley—capitalize on this combination. Many people used to believe that it was essential to eat beans and the complementary food at the same time. We now know that eating them in the same day is sufficient. For most people who eat a varied diet—certainly those eating a SuperFood diet—the bean protein would be readily available.

Beans and the complete protein issue is an interesting example of how too often we become distracted by relatively insignificant details concerning nutrition. When we eat fast-food burgers and fries at the drop of a hat, eschewing beans because they're not a complete protein, we've lost sight of the forest as we stare at the trees. I do know it's a bit more complicated than that. Many people have grown up believing that meat is an important part of most meals and this cultural influence is difficult to shed.

It does deserve some rethinking, now that studies suggest that substituting bean protein for red meat will help extend our health span and aid us in avoiding a host of chronic diseases. It's not just that you don't get the negatives of saturated fat with beans; you also get the positives of all the fiber, vitamins, minerals and phytonutrients without the fat.

Keep in mind that eating plant protein leads to less calcium loss than animal protein, a benefit to those who are vulnerable to osteoporosis. In general, as you increase your protein intake, you increase the amount of calcium lost from your bones. The acidity that occurs with eating meat increases the calcium loss compared with plant protein. Moreover, plant protein provides phytonutrients plus vitamins and minerals that are bone-friendly.

Another recent study revealed that eating beans—or at least relying on vegetable protein—could reduce the risk for gallbladder surgery. In this study, women who ate the most vegetable protein from sources like beans and nuts were least likely to need gallbladder surgery. While we knew that vegetable protein seemed to inhibit gallstone formation in animals, now there's evidence that it can play a protective role in humans as well.

Beans are a good source of water-soluble vitamins, especially thiamine, riboflavin, niacin and folacin. Canned beans are often lower in these vitamins than are dried ones. Because of the other substantial nutritional benefits, this shouldn't be a reason to avoid canned beans.

Beans and Your Heart

Beans are a superb heart-healthy food. One study involving dietary patterns over a twenty-five-year period examined the risk of death from coronary heart disease in more than sixteen thousand middle-aged men in the United States, Finland, the Netherlands, Italy, the former Yugoslavia, Greece and Japan. Typical food patterns included a higher consumption of dairy products in Northern Europe; higher consumption of meat in the U.S.; higher consumption of vegetables, legumes, fish and wine in Southern Europe; and higher consumption of cereals, soy products and fish in Japan. When researchers analyzed these data in relation to the risk of death from heart disease, they found that legumes were associated with a very impressive reduction in risk.

In another study, conducted over a period of nineteen years, 9,632 men and women were followed. None of the participants had heart disease when the study began. Over the nineteen years, 1,800 cases of coronary heart disease were diagnosed. But the follow-up data revealed that those men and women who ate beans at least four times a week had a 22 percent lower risk of coronary heart disease compared with those who consumed beans less than once a week. Moreover, those who ate beans most frequently also had lower blood pressure and total cholesterol and were much less likely to be diagnosed with diabetes.

Beans Lower Cholesterol

Eating beans frequently is associated with lower cholesterol levels. This isn't simply because bean protein is substituted for animal protein that adds dietary cholesterol to the diet. There's a certain amount of confusion out there regarding cholesterol.

Cholesterol is a fatlike substance manufactured by the body and is also found in foods in conjunction with fats. Cholesterol is found *only* in animal foods. Many people think that if you eat a lot of cholesterol, your blood levels of this substance will be high, but this isn't really the case. There's a wide range of variation in people's responses to dietary cholesterol. Some people are quite sensitive to cholesterol in their food.

However, many of us will have a minimal response to our dietary cholesterol intake. The bottom line? It's the intake of saturated fat and trans fat that really counts. This doesn't mean you should totally disregard cholesterol intake. Since cholesterol is present only in animal fats, if you focus on the amount of saturated fat and partially hydrogenated oils in your diet and try to substitute plant-derived protein like beans, you're well on your way to reducing your blood cholesterol levels and improving your overall health.

That said, it is still a healthy goal to keep your blood cholesterol levels low. How do you achieve this? Increase the amount of beans in your diet by eating ½ cup of beans each day. We all remember hearing about the power of oat bran to lower your blood cholesterol. Beans are just as effective, it turns out, and in lower quantities. In one study, people who ate 1½ cups of cooked dried beans each day experienced similar reductions in blood cholesterol to those who consumed a cup of raw oat bran. Moreover, by combining both beans and oat bran, there was a similarly successful outcome with lower, more realistic amounts of oat bran. The most important result in this study, as far as most readers are concerned, is that even eating only about ½ cup of canned beans per day made a significant difference in both cholesterol and triglyceride blood levels.

Beans are also an excellent source of fiber. (Animal protein, by the way, provides no fiber at all.) This fiber helps to keep LDL ("bad") cholesterol levels down while helping to boost the HDL ("good") levels.

It's not just the cholesterol-lowering ability of beans that's good news for your heart. Beans are also a rich source of the B vitamin folate. Lentils are particularly high in both folate and fiber. Folate plays a critical role in the reduction of homocysteine levels. Without adequate folate, homocysteine levels rise. Since homocysteine is damaging to blood vessel walls, when it accumulates, it poses an increased risk of cardiovascular disease. Elevated homocysteine levels are found in between 20 to 40 percent of patients with coronary artery disease. Just 1 cup of cooked garbanzo beans provides 70.5 percent of the daily requirement for folate.

Along with the folate, beans deliver a healthy dose of potassium, calcium and magnesium, a mineral and electrolyte combination that's associated with a reduced risk of heart disease and hypertension. Magnesium is a kind of natural calcium channel blocker, which relaxes the arteries and veins, thus reducing blood pressure and improving blood flow. A cup of black beans provides over 30 percent of your Daily Value (DV) for magnesium.

BEAN FIBER ALL-STARS

Most of us don't get nearly enough fiber in our diets. In 1909, it was estimated that fiber intake per capita was 40 grams a day; in 1980, it was about 26.7 grams a day. It's now about 15 grams a day. That's too low!

Beans give you a great fiber boost. *Here's the fiber content of a few beans in ½-cup servings...*

Lentils	8 grams
Black beans	7.5 grams
Pinto beans	7.5 grams
Kidney beans	5.5 grams
Kidney beans (canned)	4.5 grams
Chickpeas	4 grams

Beans and Blood Sugar

The plentiful soluble fiber in beans is a boon to your blood sugar. If you have insulin resistance, hypoglycemia or diabetes, beans can help you balance blood sugar levels while providing steady slow-burning energy. The fiber in beans keeps blood-sugar levels from rising too rapidly after a meal. Researchers compared two groups of people with type II diabetes who were fed different amounts of high-fiber foods. One group ate a diet that provided 24 grams of fiber per day. The other group ate a diet containing 50 grams of fiber a day. The higher-fiber diet resulted in lower levels of both blood sugar and insulin. The high-fiber group also reduced their total cholesterol by almost 7 percent, their triglyceride levels by 10.2 percent and their VLDL (very low density level) by 12.5 percent.

Beans and oats are the less expensive way (instead of costly medications) to lower total and LDL cholesterol levels.

Beans and Obesity

Beans play an important role in weight management. The simple fact is that beans fill you up: They provide lots of bulk without a lot of calories. When you add beans to your diet, you're more likely to get full before you can get fat. Beans' high-fiber content controls blood sugar and thus helps to keep hunger at bay while helping to maintain energy levels.

Beans and Cancer

There is promising evidence that beans may help to prevent cancer, particularly pancreatic cancer and cancers of the colon, breast and prostate. In one study, the bean consumption and cancer rate of fifteen countries was compared, and the analysis revealed that higher rates of bean consumption were associated with a decreased risk of colon, breast and prostate cancers. Beans contain phytoestrogens called "lignins" that have been shown to have estrogen-like properties. Researchers speculate that a high consumption of foods that are rich in lignins may reduce the risk of cancers that are related to estrogen levels —particularly breast cancer. The lignins may also have a chemopreventive effect on cancers of the male reproductive system.

There are other compounds in beans called "phytates," which may be able to help prevent certain types of intestinal cancer. Epidemiological studies have shown a lower rate of cancer among people who consume higher quantities of beans, and the thought is that this result is in part because of the phytates in beans.

Shopping for Beans

The most important thing to remember when shopping for dried beans is to find a source with a good turnover. If you have ever boiled a pot of beans for hours and hours only to find them as tough as when you began, you can testify to the importance of using fresh beans. Even though beans are dried, they shouldn't be too old or they'll never become tender when cooked. The problem is that it's hard to tell if they're old: There's no change apparent to the naked eye. Buy beans and use them soon. People get into trouble when they buy beans, put them in the back of the cupboard and, a year later, try to cook them!

If you shop for beans in a store with open bins, be sure that the bins are covered and kept clean. Check bags of beans for powder, which indicates older beans. Be sure that the beans you buy are whole and not broken.

Here are a few popular varieties of beans...

- **Adzuki beans** are small, russet-colored beans. They have a thin white line on the ridge. They're somewhat thick-skinned with a sweet, nutty flavor.
- **Black beans** or turtle beans have a beautiful matte black color. The flesh is cream-colored with a rich, earthy flavor.
- **Cannellini** or white beans are white and kidney-shaped. They have a creamy, smooth texture and are good in soups and salads.

• **Chickpeas** are round, cream-colored legumes. Extremely popular in the Mediterranean, India and the Middle East, they have a nutlike flavor. Very high in fiber and nutrients, they're great when tossed on a salad, mixed with some chopped onion and olive oil, or pureed into hummus.

• **Fava beans** or broad beans are usually available whole in their pods or peeled and split. They're large and light brown with a nutty taste and a slightly grainy texture.

• **Great Northern beans** are large white beans with a creamy texture. Use them in baked-bean dishes.

• **Navy beans** are small white beans and are so called because the U.S. Navy used to keep them aboard ships as a standard provision.

• **Pinto beans** are perhaps the most popular beans in the United States. Pale pink with streaks of brown, once cooked, they turn entirely pink. They have a rich, meaty taste.

Cooking Beans

Before cooking beans, spread them out and pick them over, looking for tiny stones, bugs, or clumps of dirt. Rinse the beans in a strainer under cold running water. Ideally, you'll then soak the beans for an hour or even overnight. In general, the longer you soak them, the shorter the cooking time and the less gas they'll produce. Beans that have been recently harvested generally require shorter soaking and cooking times. Beans respond well to pressure-cooking, which cuts down considerably on cooking time. Most pressure cookers have accompanying cookbooks that describe the best method to use to cook beans in that model pressure cooker.

Beans in the Kitchen

It is so easy to get more beans and other legumes into your diet. You can cook your own, save money and have the luxury of picking from a wide variety of dried beans. Or you can buy canned beans and at a moment's notice have a delicious, healthy meal on the table.

Everyone can find some beans that they like. Most people like green beans, though they often forget that they're part of the legume family. Many home gardeners grow sugar snap peas, which are sweet and delicious. They can be enjoyed raw or cooked, and many children who refuse other vegetables will enjoy raw sugar snap peas.

If you or your family is dried-bean–resistant, start your bean exploration with lentils. They're delicious, extremely nutritious and they're less gas producing than some other beans.

✪ Be sure that lard is not an ingredient listed on canned refried beans. Look for beans that are labeled "vegetarian" on the can.

Lentils are quick to cook—no soaking required—and very versatile. Add a bit of curry powder to give them an Indian flavor or some chopped garlic, celery and olive oil for a more traditional spin. Most lentils take about twenty minutes to cook in boiling water. Cook up a batch and keep them in a plastic container to eat as a side dish or to add to broth with other seasonings for an almost instant, filling, healthy soup.

Here are some other ideas on how to get beans into your life...

• Hummus is quick and easy to make. Puree canned garbanzo beans with chopped garlic and olive oil.

• Bean salads are fast to make. Toss different varieties together for a colorful salad with some fresh herbs and olive oil.

• Baked beans count, too! Buy or make them...but keep an eye on the sugar and salt levels.

• Don't forget about lima beans or green peas. They're available year-round, frozen, in the supermarket. Baby lima beans are delectable.

• Combine beans with pasta. Try pasta e fagioli.

• To make an "instant" black bean soup, add a can of low-sodium black beans to a jar of salsa and thin it with vegetable or chicken stock. Add oregano, chili powder and Tabasco to taste. Mash some of the beans and return them to the pot to thicken the soup.

• Mash garbanzo or black beans with finely chopped garlic and chopped red onions or scallions. Fill a whole wheat wrap or pita with the beans, sprouts or some shredded romaine lettuce, and some chopped tomatoes for a packable lunch.

• For a different kind of salad, combine a half cup of black beans, a few spoonfuls of salsa, some diced red onion and diced avocado.

• Roast green beans by placing them in a single layer in a baking pan, drizzle with olive oil and sprinkle pepper and perhaps some finely diced garlic on top. Roast in a preheated 400° F oven for about twenty minutes, shaking the pan a few times during cooking.

See our Shopping Lists (page 214) for some recommended products.

BLUEBERRIES

Blueberries—now here's a SuperFood you can take to the bank! Everybody loves blueberries and there are few foods more densely packed with healthful benefits. I tell my patients that blueberries are one of the three major SuperFoods, along with spinach and wild salmon. If you learn nothing else from *Bottom Line's SuperFoods Rx,* remember to eat blueberries and spinach most days and wild salmon, or its sidekicks, two to four times a week. These three foods alone will change your life and health.

A small but mighty nutritional force, the blueberry combines more powerful disease-fighting antioxidants than any other fruit or vegetable. As one positive report after another has come out on blueberries, the media have taken to calling them "brain berries" and "youth berries," and they certainly deserve the good press: Just one serving of blueberries provides as many antioxidants as five servings of carrots, apples, broccoli, or squash. In fact, two-thirds of a cup

BLUEBERRIES ARE A SOURCE OF:

- A synergy of multiple nutrients and phytonutrients
- Polyphenols (proanthocyanins, anthocyanins, ellagic acid, quercetin, catechins)
- Salicylic acid
- Carotenoids
- Fiber
- Folate
- Vitamin C
- Vitamin E
- Potassium
- Manganese
- Magnesium
- Iron
- Riboflavin
- Niacin
- Phytoestrogens
- Low calories

Sidekicks: Purple grapes, cranberries, boysenberries, raspberries, strawberries, fresh currants, blackberries, cherries and all other varieties of fresh, frozen or freeze-dried berries

Try to eat: 1 to 2 cups daily

of blueberries gives you the same antioxidant protection as 1,733 international units (IU) of vitamin E and more protection than 1,200 milligrams of vitamin C.

INCREDIBLE HEALTH BENEFITS

The extraordinary health and antiaging benefits of blueberries include their role in lowering your risk for cardiovascular disease. They contain a compound called pterostilbene, which may be able to lower cholesterol as effectively as many drugs. In an experiment conducted on rats, researchers found that the pterostilbene activates a cell receptor that plays a role in lowering cholesterol and other blood fats. This effect is similar to the effect of the cholesterol-lowering drug ciprofibrate. It's not yet known how many blueberries one would have to eat to duplicate this effect, but it is further evidence of the power of this delicious fruit to promote health.

And we can't forget blueberries' help in maintaining healthy skin and reducing the sags and bags brought on by age.

One recent study, published in the *Journal of Clinical Nutrition,* found that people who ate the equivalent of one cup of blueberries daily had an increased level of antioxidants in their blood—an increase which is now being studied as a "physiologic state" that plays an important role in the prevention of cardiovascular disease, atherosclerosis, diabetes, senility, cancer and degenerative eye diseases like macular degeneration and cataracts.

We know that increased blood levels of antioxidants have been shown to favorably modify incidences of breast cancer. (I found this study to be particularly interesting, as it was based on the use of whole foods rather than extracts or supplements.) The berries also contain carotenoids, fiber, folic acid, and vitamin C, each of which makes a major contribution to long-term health. Antioxidant carotenoids work to modulate your immune system, increase the UV protective capacity of your skin, decrease the redness of your skin after sun exposure, decrease the incidence of age-related macular degeneration, inhibit abnormal cell growth, and decrease the mutation rate of cells.

Perhaps the most exciting recent news in connection with blueberries and your health is the discovery that blueberries can help to protect the brain against oxidative stress, which may reduce the effects of age-related conditions such as Alzheimer's disease and dementia. Thus far the results on the power of blueberries have been based primarily on animal studies, but if the human clinical studies that are under way go half as well, it will be one of the most important advances in recent medicine and nutrition.

The All-American Blueberry

Blueberries are native to North America. Long recognized as nutritional powerhouses, blueberries were an important part of the American Indians' diet. Originally called star fruit because of the star shape at the blossom end of each berry, blueberries were used, among other things, as a preservative. Because of their high levels of antioxidants, the berries, when pounded into dried meat, slowed the rate of spoilage of the food. Early settlers learned from the Indians to use blueberries for medicinal purposes: They brewed the berries as well as the entire plant to make medicines to treat diarrhea and to ease the discomfort of childbirth.

I think of the polyphenols in berries as the choir directors. The other nutrients are all members of a huge, effective choir, working together to create something much more powerful than each individual voice.

With that in mind, and remembering that each polyphenol in each berry has something to contribute, mix it up! Don't limit your berry consumption to any particular kind. Eat them all!

Blueberries (called "bilberries" in Europe) work their magic primarily because of their incredibly high levels of antioxidant phytonutrients—particularly one type in the flavonoid family called "anthocyanin." Anthocyanin pigments give blueberries their intense blue-purple color. Indeed, the darker the berry, the higher the anthocyanin content. Blueberries, particularly wild blueberries, have at least five different anthocyanins. The anthocyanins are concentrated in the skin of berries because, as with many other fruits and vegetables, the plant skin protects the fruit from the sun and other environmental assaults by concentrating antioxidants in this key location.

Berries, especially cranberries, are an excellent source of the flavonoid quercetin, which has been shown to possess significant anti-inflammatory properties.

A recent article on the flavonoids (a class of polyphenols in berries and grapes) concluded, "Although there is still much to be learned, there are indications that the scientific approach may reaffirm the basis for many of the remedies known from traditional therapeutic use of grapes and berry products in folk medicine."

Anthocyanins are one of the phytonutrients that give blueberries their powerful antioxidant and anti-inflammatory abilities. As we know, free radicals are the culprits that damage cell membranes and DNA and ultimately cause many of the degenerative diseases that plague us as we age. Anthocyanins are key players in neutralizing free-radical damage to cells and tissues that can lead to a multitude of ailments. The anthocyanins also work synergistically with vitamin C and other key antioxidants. They strengthen the capillary system by promoting the production of quality collagen—the building block of tissues. This important subclass of flavonoids also promotes vasodilation and has an inhibitory effect on platelet aggregation—an aspirinlike effect on blood clot formation.

In an interesting study of nineteen male rowers, it was found that dietary supplementation of anthocyanin-rich chokeberry juice limited the exercise-induced oxidative damage of red blood cells, most likely by enhancing their antioxidant defense system.

The Benefits of Berries

The health benefits of blueberries are truly impressive. For many years, researchers paid little attention to the fruit because they knew that its vitamin C levels were relatively low compared with other fruits and it didn't seem to offer any other impressive benefits. But gradually, as the power of antioxidants and in particular flavonoids—a class of polyphenols—was discovered, blueberries gained more and more attention.

The research that really put blueberries on the health map because it gained so much national attention had to do with the exciting news that the berries seemed to slow and even reverse many of the degenerative diseases associated with an aging brain. As we're now facing a ballooning population of aging adults—by the year 2050 more than 30 percent of Americans will be over age 65—any positive news that relates to preventing degenerative diseases like Alzheimer's or dementia is greeted with tremendous enthusiasm.

This particular berry/brain research was conducted at the USDA Human Nutrition Research Center on Aging, at Tufts University. Dr. James Joseph, director of the study, supplemented the diets of aging rats (comparable to a 65- to 70-year-old human) with the equivalent of one-half to one cup of blueberries, a pint of strawberries or one large spinach salad. The blueberry-supplemented group not only performed better than the others on the various rat brainteasers, they also showed actual *improvements* in coordination and balance.

This was very impressive news indeed, as previously it was thought that degeneration due to aging was virtually irreversible. Dr. Joseph's continuing research has confirmed that blueberries have a functional antioxidant and anti-inflammatory effect on brain and muscle tissue.

THREE DISTINGUISHING FACTORS

How exactly did the blueberries—in an amount that would be the equivalent of a human serving of one cup of blueberries a day—accomplish this dramatic improvement? Three factors seem to distinguish the blueberry-fed rats: Their brain cells seemed to communicate better, their brains seemed to have fewer damaged proteins than would be expected and, finally and most encouraging, their brains actually developed new brain cells. Studies are currently under way to see if these extremely impressive results can be duplicated in humans. Preliminary studies show that people who consumed a cup of blueberries daily have performed 5 to 6 percent better on tests of motor skills than a control group. We also know that there has been a positive effect on people with multiple sclerosis. This isn't surprising because the nutrients in blueberries have an affinity for the areas of the brain that control movement.

> ✪ My kids tease me about the mountains of jam I put on my toast and pancakes. I tell them that jam consumption has been inversely associated with skin wrinkling. So I'm actually doing my face two favors: the smile I have when I eat the jam and the smooth skin I'll have in the future.

Here's a breakdown of some of the polyphenol contents of various juices and jams found in American markets. Some of these analyses are published here for the first time; all the juice and jam data are from independent research. Optimum daily amounts of this class of phytonutrient have not yet been determined.

Juices	*Milligrams of Polyphenols per 8-ounce Serving*
Odwalla C Monster	845
Trader Joe's 100% Unfiltered Concord Grape Juice	670
R.W. Knudsen 100% Pomegranate Juice	639
R.W. Knudsen 100% Cranberry Juice	587
R.W. Knudsen Just Blueberry	425
L & A Black Cherry Juice	345
27% cranberry juice cocktail	137
100% apple juice	61

Jams	*Milligrams of Polyphenols per 20 Grams—a trace over 1 tablespoon*
Trader Joe's Organic Blueberry Fruit Spread	400
Knott's Berry Farm Pure Boysenberry Preserves	300
Trader Joe's Organic Blackberry Fruit Spread	280
Trader Joe's Organic Strawberry Fruit Spread	120
Trader Joe's Organic Morello Cherry Fruit Spread	120
Sorrell Ridge Wild Blueberry Spreadable Fruit	100
Knott's Berry Farm Bing Cherry Pure Preserves	100
Welch's Concord Grape Jam	60

While the brain research is perhaps the newest and most positive news about the power of blueberries, there are other equally impressive data on their health-promoting abilities.

In addition to the brain-boosting anthocyanins, blueberries provide another antioxidant known as ellagic acid. Research suggests this antioxidant blocks the metabolic pathways that can promote cancer. Various studies have demonstrated that people who consume fruits with the most ellagic acid were three times less likely to develop cancer than those who consumed little or no dietary ellagic acid. Ellagic acid is found in black and red raspberries, boysenberries, Marionberries and blackberries. This phytonutrient tends to be concentrated in the seeds (berry seeds are loaded with bioactive components). The aforementioned berries have three to nine times as much ellagic acid as three other good sources—walnuts, strawberries and pecans—and as much as fifteen times the ellagic acid found in other fruits and nuts.

While the polyphenol amounts in certain juices can be quite high, the calorie count can be high, too. Whole fresh fruit will always have the lowest number of calories. Don't become so enthusiastic about polyphenols that you sip juice all day and develop a calorie overload. Get your polyphenol boost by mixing half water or seltzer and half 100 percent juice.

American Indians were right about the blueberry's ability to promote digestive health: Rich in pectin, a soluble fiber, blueberries work to relieve both diarrhea and constipation. Moreover, the tannins in blueberries reduce inflammation in the digestive system, and polyphenols have also been shown to have antibacterial properties.

Like cranberries, blueberries are a plus for urinary-tract health. Components in blueberries reduce the ability of *E. coli*, a bacterium that commonly causes urinary tract infections, to adhere to the mucosal lining of the urethra and bladder.

Commercially produced berry-grape-pomegranate juice can be very rich in anthocyanins. Commercial pomegranate juices, for example, show antioxidant activity three times higher than red wine and green tea. This is because the processing extracts some of the tannins in the rind.

To find the best juices, look for those with sediment at the bottom of the bottle. This indicates bits of skin, which are the prime sources of the beneficial berry-grape-pomegranate antioxidants. Shake before serving.

The French Paradox

You've probably heard of the French Paradox. It refers to the seeming contradiction discovered in regions of France where, despite a high intake of dairy fat, the people had low incidences of cardiovascular disease. At first, it was believed that the alcohol in the wine people drank was the factor that helped reduce their risk. As time went on, it was discovered that the paradox is only partly explained by the ability of alcohol to increase HDL ("good") cholesterol. Recent research has concentrated on the ability of the flavonoids in wine to play an active role in reducing the risk of coronary artery disease.

The extremely high level of polyphenols in red wine, which is about twenty to fifty times higher than white wine, is due to the incorporation of the grape skins in the fermenting process. The polyphenols in grape skins are known to prevent the oxidation of LDL ("bad") cholesterol, a critical event in the process of the development of coronary artery disease. As Tufts University's James Joseph, who did the original blueberry research, says, "What's good for your heart is good for your brain." Researchers also discovered that blueberries deliver 38 percent more free-radical-fighting anthocyanins than red wine. In one study, a 4-ounce drink of white wine contained 0.47 mmol of antioxidants, red wine contained 2.04 mmol, and a drink made from highbush blueberries delivered 2.42 mmol of these powerful antioxidants.

Researchers have also noted a decreased risk of age-related macular degeneration with the consumption of limited amounts of red wine.

Health professionals are always cautious about recommending the consumption of alcohol because of its close association as a risk factor in other diseases. Nonetheless, for men who consume only a glass of red wine with dinner or women who consume a half glass, the health benefits are positive.

I drink juice every single day. I start the day with a sip of high-polyphenol juice, have some green tea in the midmorning and drink juice with dinner.

Have juice—make sure it's 100 percent juice—or wine with dinner because the polyphenols in those beverages help to neutralize the adverse effects of the oxidized oils and fats in foods like the char on grilled foods. Straight fruit juice can be too sweet, so mix a couple of ounces of juice with seltzer or plain water and garnish with a lemon or lime slice.

Juices can be high in calories, so don't forget to figure that into your lifestyle and compensate with more exercise or taking in fewer calories from other sources.

If you want to enjoy most of the benefits of a moderate consumption of red wine without the alcohol, drink purple grape juice, 100 percent dark cherry juice, 100 percent pomegranate juice, 100 percent cranberry juice or 100 percent prune juice with added lutein, or alcohol-free red wine. Both purple grape juice and pomegranate juice have been shown to increase the antioxidants in your system. There's nothing more refreshing than adding a splash of grape juice or pomegranate juice and a slice of lemon in a glass of sparkling water.

Dried SuperFruits

Dried fruit can be a good source of health-promoting nutrients, as their benefits remain and are actually concentrated if you measure them by volume. Indeed, dried fruits have a greater nutrient density, greater fiber content, increased shelf life, and significantly greater polyphenol content compared with fresh fruit (except for vitamin C; there's little of it in dried fruit).

Dried fruit seems to possess significant anti-wrinkle properties.

It's getting easier to find variety in dried fruits beyond raisins, dates and prunes in local markets. Blueberries, cranberries, cherries, currants, apricots and figs are now more readily available. One thing to think about when you buy dried fruit is pesticides. Some fruit is heavily sprayed with chemicals to prevent pests and mold. Of course, when the fruit is dried, the chemicals are concentrated. Blueberries and cranberries are not a heavily treated crop, but strawberries and grapes (and thus raisins) are, and so I buy organic dried fruit when possible. Avoid dried fruit that has been sweetened with high-fructose corn syrup.

Top-ranked dried fruits are apricots and figs, which share the highest nutrient score. Dried plums are second, followed by raisins, dates and dried cranberries. So don't miss out on the fiber, vitamins, minerals, phytonutrients, potassium and complex carbs to be found all year round in dried fruits. Add dried fruits to oatmeal in the last five minutes of cooking, to quick breads, cookies and other baked goods. Don't forget that raisins make great lunchbox snacks. A recent study suggests that, contrary to what most of us used to think, the phytonutrients in raisins actually decrease the risk for cavities.

Two Powerful SuperSidekicks

Don't forget about two blueberry SuperSidekicks: cranberries and purple grapes. Cranberry consumption has been associated with protection against urinary tract infections, kidney stone formation, periodontal disease and also genital herpes, among other benefits.

A recent study reported that drinking one glass of light cranberry juice cocktail daily was associated with a 6.4 percent increase in heart-protective HDL cholesterol. It's not surprising that this cousin of the blueberry is so powerful. Cranberries contain among the highest levels of phenols of commonly consumed fruits.

Another study at Cornell University that compared the phenolic compounds in common fruits found that cranberries were richest in phenolics, followed in descending order by apple, red grape, strawberry, pineapple and banana.

Purple grapes are packed with disease-fighting phytonutrients. They're readily available and can be fresh, in 100 percent juice or in jams. They're delicious out of hand and also good, believe it or not, from the freezer. Frozen grapes make a refreshing snack on a hot day.

Berries in the Kitchen

Berries are available fresh, dried or frozen, so they can be eaten year-round. I love to munch on fresh berries while having my morning hot beverage. My favorite way to eat them is to take a bowl of berries, add a sliced banana, pour over one-half to one cup of soymilk, drizzle the whole thing with one to two teaspoons of buckwheat honey, and mash it all with a fork. Sound weird? Try it; you'll be a convert.

Fortunately, as the health benefits of blueberries have come to the attention of the public, growers and producers have worked to make their fruit more widely available. You can now find frozen wild and cultivated blueberries in most every supermarket. It's not difficult to find organic berries, too. More and more 100 percent fruit juices (blueberry, cherry, pomegranate, cranberry, grape) can be found on store shelves, like Wyman's Wild Blueberry juice.

✪ Keep dried blueberries and cranberries on hand. They are a great addition to oatmeal along with raisins, prunes and other dried fruit. Add them in the last minute or two of cooking.

Fresh blueberries in season may be cultivated or wild. The cultivated blueberries are more widely available; the wild ones only grow in the cool climates of the northern United States and Canada and are usually available at roadside stands or local markets, though you can also find them frozen in many supermarkets.

Cultivated blueberries are plump with a deep blue color and a pale protective "bloom" that protects the berries from spoiling. Shake the container before buying—if they don't all move freely it could be because some are moldy or crushed.

Wild blueberries are smaller with more intense flavor.

By the way, ounce for ounce, you'll usually get more antioxidants in the wild blueberries, as

FRESH VERSUS FROZEN

New data on frozen berries yields some very interesting and encouraging news for those of us—probably most people—who can only get fresh berries for a short period of time. Indications are that frozen berries provide all the benefits of fresh.

A European study compared two groups of healthy older men (age 60) and found that those eating frozen berries daily had a 32 to 51 percent higher blood level of quercetin—a powerful anticancer, antioxidant flavonoid—than those who ate no berries. The results showed that eating even frozen berries can significantly boost your body's level of powerful disease-fighting flavonoids.

their small size means you're getting more skin per ounce and, of course, the skin is where the health-promoting goodies are.

When adding fresh blueberries to batter for baking, dust them first with flour and they'll be less likely to fall to the bottom of the baking pan.

Fresh blueberries are delicate and deserve care. They should be washed briefly but only just before you're going to use them. If you need to store them in the fridge, be sure to pick out and discard any moldy or crushed fruit first. They will store in the fridge for a day or two in a container that allows air to circulate. They'll freeze well, but to prevent them from sticking together, scatter them on a cookie sheet and put them in the freezer. Don't wash them before freezing. Once frozen, they can be put into airtight bags for storage. I put a cup or so of frozen berries in a container in the fridge to defrost overnight so I can sprinkle them on my cereal or yogurt the next morning. (When making a smoothie, I just use frozen berries.) You can toss berries while still frozen into pancake, muffin and quick-bread batter.

MY FAVORITE WAYS TO EAT BLUEBERRIES

I'm lucky enough to be able to pick ripe berries in my organic garden, so I enjoy them in season.

- Sprinkle some berries and wheat germ on yogurt.
- Toss onto cold cereal.
- Whip some into a smoothie with yogurt, banana, ice and soy or nonfat milk.
- Drop some onto whole wheat buttermilk pancakes just before turning them.
- Nibble from a big bowl of fresh blueberries while sitting on the porch.

Frozen blueberries greatly expand the fruit's possibilities, and it's important to know that all the animal studies on blueberries and black raspberries have been done with freeze-dried berries.

Fresh cranberries are harvested in the fall and are usually only available in markets from October through December. I always buy extra bags at this time of year to put into the freezer. When spring comes and my frozen cranberry supply dwindles down, I rely on dried cranberries to toss in oatmeal or yogurt or even on salads.

A warning on cranberries: If you take the blood thinner warfarin, you may need to avoid drinking cranberry juice, as it seems to amplify the effect of the drug. This can lead to serious bleeding issues.

See our Shopping Lists (pages 212, 216, 217, 219 and 220) for some recommended products.

BROCCOLI

It was 1992 and then-president George H. W. Bush made a daring proclamation…"I'm president of the United States, and I'm not going to eat any more broccoli." The horrified gasps of nutritionists could be heard from sea to shining sea. But in the end, broccoli triumphed. Perhaps in part because of the president's statement, the press took up the cause of broccoli, and anyone who had doubted its power as one of our most valuable foods ultimately became a believer.

The timing was right for broccoli: In that same year, a researcher at Johns Hopkins University announced the discovery of a compound found in broccoli that not only prevented the development of tumors by 60 percent in the studied group, but that it also reduced the size of tumors that did develop by 75 percent. Broccoli is now one of the best-selling vegetables in the U.S.

Indeed, broccoli and its cruciferous sidekicks are among the most powerful weapons in our dietary arsenal against cancer. That alone would elevate it to the status of a SuperFood. In addition, broccoli also boosts the immune system, lowers the incidence of cataracts, supports cardiovascular health, builds bones, fights birth defects, promotes the production of the primary intracellular antioxidant, glutathione, and decreases inflammation. Broccoli is one of the most nutrient-dense foods known; it offers an incredibly high level of nutrition for a very low caloric cost. Of the ten most common vegetables eaten in the U.S., broccoli is a clear winner in terms of total polyphenol content. It's got more polyphenols than all other popular choices—only beets and red onions have more polyphenols per serving.

Broccoli is a member of the *Brassica* or cruciferous family of vegetables. "Cruciferous" comes from the Latin root *crucifer,* meaning bearing a cross, which refers to the cross-shaped flowers of vegetables in this family. The name "broccoli" is derived from the Latin word *brachium,* meaning arm or branch, which describes the stalks of broccoli topped by a head of florets.

BROCCOLI IS A SOURCE OF:

- Sulforaphane
- Indoles
- Folate
- Fiber
- Calcium
- Vitamin C
- Beta-carotene
- Lutein/zeaxanthin
- Vitamin K

Sidekicks: Brussels sprouts, red and green cabbage, kale, turnips, cauliflower, collards, bok choy, mustard greens, Swiss chard, rutabaga, kohlrabi, broccoflower, arugula, watercress, daikon root, wasabi, liverwort

Try to eat: ½ to 1 cup most days

Originally found growing wild along the coast of the Mediterranean, broccoli was cultivated by the Romans, enthusiastically adopted by Italians and is now available worldwide. Italian immigrants brought broccoli to America.

✪ Broccoli is an excellent source of vegetarian iron.

Broccoli is prized because of its delightful taste as well as the variety of textures it offers, from its flowery heads to the smooth and fibrous stalks. Most of the broccoli found today in our supermarkets comes from California. The fact that broccoli consumption doubled in the last decade of the twentieth century, following news of its cancer-fighting abilities, is encouraging. And the news on broccoli and its health-promoting abilities has become even more impressive in the intervening years.

Broccoli and Cancer

The development of cancer in the human body is a long-term event that begins at the cellular level with an abnormality that typically only ten to twenty years later is diagnosed as cancer. While research continues at a furious pace to find ways to cure this deadly killer—after heart disease, the greatest killer of Americans—most scientists have come to recognize that cancer might well be more easily prevented than cured.

Diet is the best tool we all have at hand to protect ourselves from developing cancer. We know that a typical Western diet plays a major role in the development of cancers, and we know that at least 30 percent of all cancers are believed to have a dietary component. Population studies first pointed to the role that broccoli and other cruciferous vegetables might play in cancer prevention. One ten-year study, published by the Harvard School of Public Health, of 47,909 men showed an inverse relationship between the consumption of cruciferous vegetables and the development of bladder cancer. Broccoli and cabbage seemed to provide the greatest protection. Countless studies have confirmed these findings. As long ago as 1982, the National Research Council on Diet, Nutrition and Cancer found that "there is sufficient epidemiological evidence to suggest that consumption of cruciferous vegetables is associated with a reduction in cancer."

A recent meta-analysis, which reviewed the results of eighty-seven case-controlled studies, confirmed once again that broccoli and other cruciferous vegetables lower the risk of cancer. As little as 10 grams a day of crucifers (less than one-eighth cup of chopped raw cabbage or chopped raw broccoli) can have a significant effect on your risk for developing cancer. Indeed, eating broccoli or its sidekicks is like getting a natural dose of chemoprevention.

One study showed that eating about two servings a day of crucifers may result in as much as a 50 percent reduction in the risk for certain types of cancers. While all crucifers seem to be effective in fighting cancer, broccoli, cabbage and Brussels sprouts seem to be the most powerful. Just one-half cup of broccoli a day protects from a number of cancers, particularly cancers of the lung, stomach, colon and rectum. No wonder broccoli is number one on the National Cancer Institute's list of nutrition all-stars.

A recent study confirms the power of these vegetables to fight cancer. A seven-year study in Australia followed 609 women who had been diagnosed with ovarian cancer—an aggressive form of cancer. It seems that by including five servings a day of vegetables, particularly cruciferous vegetables, in their diet, the women experienced a beneficial effect on their survival rates. The women who survived the longest after diagnosis ate the most vegetables, especially cruciferous ones.

RAW VS. COOKED

It's important to eat cruciferous vegetables both cooked and raw to gain optimum health benefits. For example, the bioavailability of a phytonutrient called an isothiocyanate from raw broccoli is approximately three times greater than from cooked broccoli.

Best solution: Eat cooked broccoli and Brussels sprouts and raw shredded cabbage—red and green—in salads. Eat raw broccoli sprouts on sandwiches and in salads; eat kale, collards and mustard greens cooked.

Broccoli is the vegetable with the strongest inverse association with colon cancer, especially in those younger than 65 with a history of smoking. If you've ever smoked, eat your broccoli!

The sulfur compounds in cruciferous vegetables are a major reason these foods are such powerful chemopreventive foods. The strong smell that broccoli, cabbage and other cruciferous vegetables share comes from the sulfur compounds that protect the plant as well as you. The strong, sometimes bitter taste and smell of these vegetables protect them from insects and animals.

POWERFUL COMPOUNDS

The particular compounds in broccoli that are so effective against cancer include phytochemicals, sulforaphane and indoles.

Sulforaphane is a remarkably potent compound that fights cancer on various fronts. It increases the enzymes that help rid the body of carcinogens, actually kills abnormal cells and helps the body limit oxidation—the process that initiates many chronic diseases—at the cellular level.

An interesting recent study found that the sulforaphane in broccoli stopped the proliferation of breast cancer cells, even in the later stages of their growth. This is excellent news and also a reminder that it's never too late to improve your health by adopting a healthy diet and trying to include a wide variety of SuperFoods routinely in your meals.

Men, too, can benefit from a diet rich in broccoli as well as other fiber-rich vegetables. In one recent study, it was reported that men whose diets were highest in fiber had an 18 percent lower risk of prostate cancer compared with men in the study who ate the least fiber. It was mainly fiber from vegetables like broccoli, cabbage and peas that made the difference.

The sulforaphane in broccoli has been shown to be effective against *Helicobacter pylori,* a bacterium that is a common cause of most peptic ulcers as well as gastric cancer.

Indoles work to combat cancer through their effect on estrogen. They block estrogen receptors in breast cancer cells, inhibiting the growth of estrogen-sensitive breast cancers. The most important indole in broccoli—indole-3-carbinol, or I_3C—is thought to be an especially effective breast cancer preventive agent.

In a study at the Institute for Hormone Research in New York, sixty women were divided into groups, some eating a high I_3C diet containing 400 milligrams of I_3C daily, another eating a high-fiber diet, and a third control group on a placebo diet. The women consuming the high I_3C diet showed significantly higher levels of a cancer-preventive form of estrogen. The other diets showed no increase in this substance.

I_3C is now available in the form of a supplement. As this supplement hasn't yet been widely tested, I recommend, as always, to rely first on a food source: Eat some broccoli.

SPROUTS = SUPER BROCCOLI

Researchers estimate that broccoli sprouts provide ten to one hundred times the power of mature broccoli to neutralize carcinogens. A sprinkling of broccoli sprouts in your salad or on your sandwich can do more than even a couple of spears of broccoli. This is especially good news for those few people—particularly children—who refuse to eat broccoli. Check *www.broccosprouts.com* to learn more about this nutrition-packed veggie and where you can buy it.

Broccoli also has other components that help make it an all-star anticancer vegetable. We know that vitamin C plays a role in preventing cancer, and broccoli, and many other crucifers, are rich in this particular antioxidant vitamin. One cup of cooked broccoli contains more than 100 percent of the adult male/female RDA (Recommended Daily Allowance) for vitamin C and 27 percent of my recommended daily dietary beta-carotene goal. Broccoli is rich in fiber as well, which plays an important role in reducing cancer risk.

It's All Better with Broccoli

If broccoli did nothing but protect us from cancer, that would be enough, but this mighty vegetable works on other fronts as well.

RICH IN FOLATE

Broccoli and its related crucifers have high levels of folate, the plant form of folic acid, and it is this B vitamin that is essential to preventing birth defects. Neural tube defects like spina bifida have been linked to folic acid deficiency in pregnancy. A single cup of raw, chopped broccoli provides more than 50 milligrams of folate. Folate is also active in helping to remove homocysteine from the circulatory system; high levels of homocysteine are associated with cardiovascular disease. Folate also plays a role in cancer prevention. Interestingly, folic acid deficiency may be the most common vitamin deficiency in the world.

HELP FOR CATARACTS

We all know how common cataracts are in our aging population. Broccoli to the rescue! Broccoli is rich in the powerful carotenoids lutein and zeaxanthin (as well as vitamin C). Both of these carotenoids are concentrated in the lens and retina of the eye. A single cup of raw, chopped broccoli provides 1.5 milligrams of lutein and zeaxanthin—8 percent of the *SuperFoods Rx* goal of 12 milligrams daily. One study found that people who ate broccoli more than twice weekly had a 23 percent lower risk of cataracts when compared to those who ate broccoli less than once a month. Lutein/zeaxanthin and vitamin C also serve to protect the eyes from the free-radical damage done to the eyes by ultraviolet light.

Broccoli Builds Bones

Broccoli and cruciferous vegetables are bone builders. One cup of raw broccoli provides 41 milligrams of calcium along with 79 milligrams of vitamin C, which promotes the absorption of calcium. While this is not a huge amount of calcium, it's at a low cost of calories and with the benefit of the many other nutrients in broccoli. Whole milk and other full-fat dairy products, long touted as the main sources of calcium, contain no vitamin C and are often loaded with saturated fat and many more calories than the 25 in 1 cup of raw, chopped broccoli. Broccoli also supplies a significant portion of vitamin K, which is important for blood clotting, and also contributes to bone health.

Vitamin K is a fat-soluble vitamin known as the clotting vitamin because of its role in promoting blood clotting. If you take a prescribed anticoagulant or blood thinner, you should be careful about your K intake. Don't increase your consumption of K-rich foods like broccoli, cauliflower or cabbage, leafy greens or Brussels sprouts without checking with your health care professional.

A HEART HELPER

Broccoli is a great source of the flavonoids, carotenoids, vitamin C, folate and potassium that help prevent heart disease. It also provides generous amounts of fiber, vitamin E and vitamin B6, which promote cardiovascular health. Broccoli is one of the few vegetables, along with spinach, that are relatively high in coenzyme Q_{10} (CoQ_{10}), a fat-soluble antioxidant that is a major contributor to the production of energy in our bodies. At least in people with diagnosed heart disease, CoQ_{10} may play a cardioprotective role.

The Women's Health Study found both apples and broccoli intake to be associated with reductions in the risk of both cardiovascular disease and cardiovascular events.

About 25 percent of the population inherit an aversion to the bitter taste of cruciferous vegetables. If this describes you, add salt, since that makes them taste sweeter. Use them in a stir-fry with low-sodium soy sauce or add them to casseroles and lasagnas.

Broccoli in the Kitchen

The good news about broccoli is that it's one of our most popular vegetables; the bad news is that we're not eating enough of it. In one study, only 3 percent of Americans surveyed reported eating broccoli in the prior twenty-four-hour period.

What vegetables and fruits are we eating instead? Iceberg lettuce, tomatoes, french fries, bananas, and oranges. This isn't good! While tomatoes and oranges, as well as bananas, are good for you, iceberg lettuce and white potatoes, often in the form of french fries, are the top choices of many Americans when it comes to vegetables. We need to have a seismic shift in our vegetable choices. I'll give you some ideas here on how to get more broccoli and other cruciferous vegetables into your life.

One of the excellent features of broccoli is its ready availability. It's in season October through May, but it's easy to find in supermarkets all year long. While broccoli is probably most nutritious when bought at a roadside stand from an organic farmer, even frozen broccoli packs a valuable nutritional wallop. If buying it fresh, it pays to look for young broccoli: Older broccoli can be tough and can also have a strong odor. Broccoli comes in a variety of green shades, from a rich sage green to deep forest green. You can even find broccoli in shades of purple. In the broccoli family are broccolini—a combination of broccoli and kale—and broccoflower—a combination of broccoli and cauliflower.

Because manufacturers usually remove most of the stalk when preparing broccoli for freezing, the remaining florets dominate the portion. Because the carotenoids, as well as other nutrients, are concentrated in the florets, this means that you can get up to 35 percent more of certain nutrients per portion from frozen broccoli than from fresh broccoli. Broccoli leaves have even more carotenoids than the florets.

When shopping for broccoli, choose tight, deeply colored, and dense florets, or flowers. (The deeper the color, the more phytonutrients!) Usually, the smaller the head, the better the flavor. Yellowing florets are signs that the broccoli is past its prime. If there are still leaves on the stalks, they should be firm and fresh-looking; wilted leaves are also a sign of an aged vegetable.

Broccoli will keep in the fridge in a crisper for five to seven days. Never wash the broccoli before storing, as it can develop mold when damp.

Wash fresh broccoli thoroughly before using, soaking it in cold water if the florets seem to have

Does your child hate broccoli? It could all be in the genes.

A study done in Philadelphia found that a gene called TAS2R38 could be responsible for your child's aversion to certain vegetables. Each of us carries two of these genes, and one version of the gene is more sensitive to bitter tastes than the other. In the study of 143 children, almost 80 percent had two copies of the "bitter gene." The presence of this gene had a big impact on a child's food choices; the same gene in the mother didn't seem to play as big a role in diet.

The solution? Serve vegetables like broccoli with a slightly sweet or salty sauce. And don't give up. It sometimes takes a half dozen tries before a child will develop a taste for new foods.

Here are two broccoli toppers kids are sure to like...

- Mix ¼ cup peanut butter with 2 tablespoons brewed hot black or green tea. Mix until smooth and stir in 1 tablespoon reduced-sodium soy sauce, 1 tablespoon lemon juice and 1 teaspoon brown sugar.
- Mix 2 tablespoons reduced-sodium soy sauce with 2 tablespoons orange juice, 1 tablespoon rice vinegar, 1 tablespoon toasted sesame oil, 2 teaspoons honey and 2 teaspoons minced fresh ginger.

sand or dirt in them. Don't discard the leaves; they're rich in nutrients. Cut off any tough part of the stalk, slicing up a few inches of the remaining stalk to hasten its cooking time, since the florets cook faster. Steaming or microwaving broccoli in very little water is the best way to cook it. Boiled broccoli can lose more than 50 percent of its vitamin C.

Some quick ways to get cruciferous vegetables on the table...

• Keep fresh or frozen broccoli on hand to use in stir-fries, soups and side dishes.

• Puree leftover broccoli with some sautéed onions and mix with low-fat milk or soymilk and add a grind or two of nutmeg for a great, fast soup.

• Toss shredded raw broccoli with red cabbage and red onion, some homemade vinaigrette and maybe some poppy seeds, for a quick homemade slaw.

• I snack on leftover cooked broccoli just as it comes from the fridge; it's also good with some salad dressing and toasted sesame seeds.

• Shred Brussels sprouts and stir-fry them with a bit of minced garlic, olive oil, some coarsely chopped toasted walnuts or pine nuts and a squeeze of fresh lemon juice. Toss with pasta or enjoy as a side dish.

• Stir-fry shredded cabbage with a tablespoon of sesame oil and serve as an accompaniment to an Asian meal.

• Coat cut-up broccoli or cauliflower with a little olive oil and salt. Roast at 425° F for 20 to 30 minutes, until they become browned at the edges. The vegetables become sweet and intense.

• Serve a bowlful of raw broccoli florets with hummus dip.

• I shred red cabbage into most every salad I eat at home. You don't have to put in much; just a bit gives you a great nutritional boost.

• Add chopped broccoli to pasta sauces, lasagnas, and casseroles.

• Top whole wheat pasta with sautéed garlic, olive oil and broccoli (all SuperFoods). Add a dash of red pepper flakes if you like.

This is one class of vegetables where too much of a good thing may have adverse affects. Broccoli contains goitrogens, naturally occurring substances that can interfere with the function of the thyroid gland.

Nonetheless, 2 cups a day of cooked Brussels sprouts or broccoli are completely safe. Consumed in moderation, this class of vegetables confers a remarkable number of health benefits.

See our Shopping Lists (pages 219, 221 and 223) for some recommended products.

DARK CHOCOLATE

Here's the health update of the century: Dark chocolate is a SuperFood! For many of us, this is a dream come true. The interesting thing is that many people have told me that once they think of chocolate as a food that's beneficial to health, even though they still love and enjoy it, because it is no longer "forbidden," they're somehow less tempted to gorge on it.

This news doesn't mean that you should toss out the oatmeal and fill your cabinets with chocolate. *Pause for a moment and let the HealthStyle chocolate watchwords sink in...*

DARK CHOCOLATE IS A SOURCE OF:

• Polyphenols

Try to eat: For those who enjoy it, have about 100 calories daily, adjusting your calorie intake and exercise appropriately

• Keep your daily dark chocolate intake to about 100 calories per day.

• Eat only *dark* chocolate.

First, and most important, is the amount of chocolate: You *cannot* eat as much as you want. It's high in calories and eating too much of it can sabotage your diet. If you eat excessive amounts of chocolate, *you can gain weight.* Depending on your weight and activity level, chocolate should be a small treat, a little healthy indulgence that will have to be accounted for in your overall calorie intake/activity equation.

When you do indulge in chocolate and you're looking for a health benefit, choose *dark* chocolate. Milk chocolate or white chocolate (the latter isn't even real chocolate) won't do. While both contain some of the beneficial polyphenols (though in lower amounts than dark chocolate), preliminary data suggest that the presence of milk in the chocolate somehow mitigates the effectiveness of the polyphenols.

Here, in a nutshell, is the good news: Dark chocolate seems to contribute to lowering blood pressure, increasing blood flow and ultimately contributing to a healthy heart.

POLYPHENOLS: THE SUPERNUTRIENTS

One of the most abundant phytonutrients in the human diet, polyphenols' total daily dietary intake can easily exceed 1 gram per day, which is much higher than that of all other classes of phytonutrients and known dietary antioxidants.

To give it some perspective, this is about ten times higher than the majority of our vitamin C intake and about one hundred times higher than our dietary intake of vitamin E and carotenoids.

Polyphenols act as antioxidants, anti-inflammatories, antimutagens, antimicrobials, antivirals and antifungals. They help protect our DNA and inhibit the growth of unwanted blood vessels.

They also decrease LDL-C oxidation, elevate HDLs, promote blood vessel dilation, decrease blood pressure, have beneficial effects on capillary permeability and fragility, work in synergy with vitamins C and E, lower the risk for cardiovascular disease and lower the risk for some cancers.

In addition, polyphenols seem to play a role in turning on "good" genes and turning off "bad" ones.

What Makes Dark Chocolate A SuperFood?

Yes, there's the taste...the creamy melt-in-your-mouth deliciousness. But when it comes to health, it's none of the above. It's the polyphenols.

Whoever first thought to smash a yellow, hard-shelled cocoa pod, scoop out the cocoa beans meshed in the pulpy inside and turn them into one of nature's most delicious and versatile foods? We can only be grateful. The cocoa beans that yield the chocolate we love come primarily from Africa, Asia or Latin America. It takes approximately four hundred cocoa beans to make one pound of chocolate. The beans are processed into a sticky paste called chocolate liquor, which is then used to make chocolate products. The humble chocolate bar is the product of cocoa butter, chocolate liquor and sometimes powdered cocoa, which is combined with sugar, emulsifiers and sometimes milk. Chocolate is about 30 percent fat, 5 percent protein, 61 percent carbohydrate and 3 percent moisture and minerals. The magic in the mix as far as health benefits are concerned is the polyphenols, specifically the flavonols.

Flavonols are plant compounds with potent antioxidant properties. Cocoa beans, along with red wine, tea, cranberries, and other fruits contain large amounts of flavonols. Research is now suggesting that the flavonols in chocolate are responsible for its health benefits.

Chocolate doesn't just have some flavonols; it has lots. Below is a chart that lists various foods' flavonol content.

Flavonol Content of 100 Grams of Various Foods

red wine	63 mg
black tea, brewed	65 mg
cherry	96 mg
apple	111 mg
dark chocolate	**510 mg**

Chocolate and Blood Pressure

In the early 1990s, a physician and researcher at Brigham & Women's Hospital and Harvard Medical School, Dr. Norman K. Hollenberg, learned that the Kuna Indians, the indigenous residents of the San Blas Islands of Panama, rarely develop high blood pressure even as they aged. Studies indicated that neither their salt intake nor obesity was a factor in this seeming immunity. Moreover, when the islanders moved to the mainland, their incidence for hypertension soared to typical levels, so their protection from hypertension was probably not due to genetics.

Hollenberg noticed one facet of Indian culture that might play a role: The Kuna routinely drank about five cups of locally grown, minimally processed, high-flavonol cocoa each day.

He gave his study subjects cocoa with either high or low amounts of flavonols. Those who drank the high-flavonol cocoa had more nitric oxide activity than those drinking the low-flavonol cocoa. The connection between the ability of the nitric oxide to relax the blood vessels and improve circulation and thus prevent hypertension seemed obvious.

It's a myth that chocolate is loaded with caffeine. While there is some caffeine in chocolate, it's not much. In a typical chocolate bar, the caffeine content ranges from 1 to 11 milligrams. An 8-ounce cup of coffee has about 137 milligrams of caffeine.

Hollenberg is continuing his investigation. He recently completed a pilot study that found that subjects who drank a cup of high-flavonol cocoa had a resulting increased flow of blood to the brain that averaged 33 percent.

Another interesting study looked at the blood flow effects of high-flavonol cocoa compared with low-dose aspirin. The study compared how blood platelets reacted to a flavonol-rich cocoa drink versus a blood-thinning dose of 81-milligram aspirin. It seems that the twenty- to forty-year-olds who participated in this study enjoyed similar blood-thinning results from both the cocoa and the low-dose aspirin. It must be noted that the effects of the flavonol-rich cocoa were more transitory than those of the aspirin.

Chocolate and Atherosclerosis

Research suggests that atherosclerosis begins and progresses as a gradual inflammatory process. It normally involves years of chronic injury to the lining of the blood vessels. As the lining—or endothelial cells—is damaged, atherosclerotic plaques, or fatty deposits, are formed on the walls of the blood vessels. These plaques both impede the flow of blood and can rupture, leading to a blood clot, which could precipitate a heart attack or stroke.

Chocolate to the rescue. The polyphenols in chocolate act to relax the smooth muscle of the blood vessels. In addition, it seems that these polyphenols also inhibit the clotting of the blood. In a 2001 study, volunteer subjects were given a commercial chocolate bar (Dove Dark) containing 148 milligrams of flavonols. The end result

Sip your way to health....In a recent study, researchers at Cornell University found that a mug of hot cocoa has nearly twice the antioxidants of a glass of red wine and up to three times those found in a cup of green tea.

Make your cocoa with 1% low-fat milk, nonfat milk or soymilk and sweeten it with minimal sugar.

Avoid cocoa mixes, as they are high in sugar or artificial sweeteners and some contain trans fats.

Dutch-process cocoa is cocoa powder that has been treated with alkaline compounds to neutralize the natural acids. It's slightly milder than natural cocoa, but it has lower levels of flavonols so, for health purposes, stick with natural cocoa.

was that the volunteers showed reduced levels of inflammation and beneficial delays in blood clotting at two and six hours after ingesting the chocolate.

What About the Fat?

Ordinarily, foods that are high in fat would never make it to SuperFood status. Chocolate is the rare exception for a variety of reasons. While chocolate is approximately 30 percent fat, the fat in it, known as cocoa butter, is approximately 35 percent oleic acid and 35 percent stearic acid.

Oleic acid is a monounsaturated fat that has been shown to have a slight cholesterol-lowering effect. Stearic acid is a saturated fat, but it does not raise blood cholesterol levels. At least two studies have shown that chocolate consumption does not raise blood cholesterol in humans.

Indeed, in one three-week trial, forty-five healthy volunteers were given 75 grams daily of either white chocolate, dark chocolate or dark chocolate enriched with polyphenols. As you might guess, since white chocolate has no chocolate liquor and isn't real chocolate, it had no effect, but the dark chocolate increased HDL ("good") cholesterol by 11 percent and the enriched chocolate increased HDL by 14 percent. As higher HDLs are known to decrease the risk of cardiovascular disease, the argument for including chocolate in your diet is strong.

Chocolate: Some Buyer's Tips

When buying chocolate, select dark chocolate with a high level of cocoa solids. The higher the amount of cocoa solids, the more polyphenols the chocolate will contain. Manufacturers are getting wise to consumer interest, and you'll soon notice more of this type of labeling on chocolate. Look for at least 70 percent cocoa solids. *I had an independent analysis conducted to learn the total polyphenol content of various commercially available chocolates, and here are the results...*

Total Polyphenol Content of a Single 40-Gram Serving of Chocolate

Newman's Own Organics Dark Chocolate	955 mg
Dove Silky Dark Chocolate	811 mg
Endangered Species Chocolate Wolf Bar (with cranberries and almonds)	811 mg
Cadbury Royal Dark Chocolate	765 mg
Hershey's Special Dark Mildly Sweet Chocolate	739 mg
Dina's Organic Chocolate (Infused with Green Tea)	676 mg

Using Chocolate

The best way to get chocolate into your life—for your health—is to eat just a square or two daily.

One hundred calories of one of the chocolate bars I've listed (eaten in divided doses) is a tasty health-promoting strategy.

Don't think that any chocolate dessert is now a health food. Fresh fruit is still the best sweet treat there is. I enjoy eating a square or two of chocolate as an evening treat after dinner. Even just one or two small pieces are satisfying.

See our Shopping Lists (pages 215, 216 and 218) for some recommended products.

GARLIC

Garlic, a small and humble-looking vegetable, plays a huge role in the major cuisines of the world. It's very hard to imagine Italian, French or Asian cooking without garlic. The big news on garlic isn't its ability to flavor a dish, but rather its considerable role as a health promoter. Indeed, recent findings on the power of garlic to fight cancer and cardiovascular disease, as well as its anti-inflammatory and antiviral properties, give garlic the bona fides to elevate it to SuperFood status.

GARLIC IS A SOURCE OF:

- Organosulfur compounds (75 total, with allicin the most active)
- Saponins
- Polyphenols
- Selenium
- Arginine
- Vitamin C
- Potassium

Sidekicks: Scallions, shallots, leeks, onions

Try to eat: Multiple times per week

Garlic, a member of the lily, or *allium,* family, traces its origin to Central Asia. Garlic is a major flavoring agent, particularly in Mediterranean cuisine, but as far back as 2600 B.C., it was used by the Sumerians as medicine. One of the oldest cultivated plants in the world, garlic was recognized by early civilizations as a source of strength and was mentioned in the Bible. Indeed, throughout the history of civilization, the medicinal properties of garlic have been prized, and it's been used to treat ailments, including atherosclerosis, stroke, cancer, immune disorders, cerebral aging, arthritis and cataract formation.

MANY POWERFUL COMPOUNDS

Garlic's power as a heath promoter comes from its rich variety of sulfur-containing compounds. Of the nearly one hundred nutrients in garlic, the most important in terms of health benefits seems to be the sulfur compound allicin —an amino acid. Allicin is not present in fresh garlic, but it is formed instantly when cloves are crushed, chewed or cut. Allicin seems to be responsible for the superbiological activity of garlic as well as its odor.

In addition to allicin, a single clove of garlic offers a stew of compounds with potential health benefits, including saponins, phosphorus, potassium, zinc, selenium, polyphenols and arginine. In addition to these compounds, garlic is a good source of vitamin B6 and also of vitamin C. As with most whole foods, garlic's antioxidant and anti-inflammatory abilities are probably due to the sum of the whole rather than a single agent.

Garlic and Cardiovascular Disease

A number of studies have shown that garlic has an important impact on risk factors for cardiovascular disease. It has been demonstrated that those who make garlic a regular part of their diets enjoy lowered blood pressure and decreased platelet aggregation, as well as decreased triglycerides and LDL ("bad") cholesterol. Garlic may also increase HDL ("good") cholesterol. Consuming one-half to one clove of garlic daily lowers LDL cholesterol levels by approximately 10 percent, partially by decreasing cholesterol absorption.

Garlic extracts have also been shown to decrease blood pressure: In one study, a 5.5 percent decrease in systolic blood pressure and a slight decrease in diastolic pressure were noticed. While these are modest decreases, they could still lead to a significant lessening of the risk for stroke and heart attack.

The end result of all of these benefits is a lowered risk of atherosclerosis and heart disease as well as a reduced risk of heart attack and stroke. Garlic oil has been shown to decrease total and LDL cholesterol and triglyceride levels.

Garlic's primary positive effect on cardiovascular disease comes from its sulfur compounds, but the effects of vitamin C, B6, selenium and manganese can't be ignored. Garlic's vitamin C—the body's primary antioxidant defender—protects LDL cholesterol from oxidation. It's the oxidation of LDL cholesterol that begins the process that damages blood vessel walls. Vitamin B6 lowers levels of homocysteine, a substance that can directly damage blood vessel walls. The selenium in garlic fights heart disease, while it's also working to protect against cancer and heavy metal toxicity. Manganese works on a variety of antioxidant defenses, and studies have found that adults deficient in manganese have lowered their levels of the good HDL cholesterol.

Garlic and Cancer

A number of studies have reported on garlic's ability to fight cancer, although further research is needed to clarify the precise role of garlic in this battle. Several population studies have shown a link between garlic in the diet and a decrease in the risk for colorectal and gastric cancer, and one clove of garlic daily may decrease the risk of developing prostate cancer. Recent reviews of more than thirty-five studies report some protective effect against cancer in about 75 percent of the published articles.

Garlic as Antibiotic

Two recent studies have shown that garlic can be a potent antibiotic. Particularly impressive was that garlic was effective against strains of pathogens that have become resistant to many drugs.

The first study showed that garlic juice showed significant antibacterial activity against a host of pathogens, even including antibiotic-resistant strains such as ciprofloxacin-resistant staphylococci.

The second study, conducted on mice, found that garlic was able to inhibit a type of staph infection that's become increasingly resistant to antibiotics and increasingly common in hospitals. This type of staph infection has become a potential danger for health care workers, as well as for people with weakened immune systems. Sixteen hours after the mice were infected with the pathogen, garlic extract was fed to them. After twenty-four hours, garlic was found to have been protective against the pathogen and to have significantly decreased the infection.

The Best Source of Garlic

Although garlic is available in supplements, I believe that fresh garlic is the far better choice. There is variation among garlic products and some odorless garlic preparations may not contain active compounds.

Here's an interesting example: A dose of 600 milligrams of garlic extract typically produces 3,600 micrograms of allicin. A dose of fresh garlic—about one clove—typically produces approximately 18,300 micrograms of allicin. Obviously, the whole-foods version is more powerful.

Moreover, you're more certain of getting the complete package of health boosters that garlic has to offer.

If you do, however, decide to try garlic powder, a reasonable dose is 300 milligrams of garlic powder, three times a day.

Buying and Using Garlic

Garlic in its fresh form seems to provide the most health benefits. This is good news for cooks and those who love the delicious flavor punch that garlic adds to food. You'll get maximum effect of the phytonutrients by including raw garlic in some of your dishes. The trick here is not to overdo. Just one clove, or even a half clove, of finely minced raw garlic in dressings, dips and guacamole adds great flavor without overpowering the dish.

When shopping for garlic, look for cloves that are plump and without blemishes. Avoid cloves that are soft, shriveled, or moldy or that have begun to sprout. Store your whole garlic heads in a dark, cool place, keeping them away from dampness and sunlight. Once the head of garlic is broken, however, its shelf life is reduced, so keep cloves whole until needed.

It's easy to separate individual cloves of garlic from the head, but some cooks find peeling them a challenge. The most effective way is to place a garlic clove on a cutting board and press down on it with the flat side of a knife. The skin will break and be easy to remove. The green shoot in the center can be bitter, so remove it with the point of a knife.

Garlic in the Kitchen

Here are just a few ideas for incorporating garlic into your diet...

- Add chopped garlic when sautéing greens such as spinach, kale or broccoli rabe.
- Add chopped garlic to soups and stews.
- Roast potatoes and whole cloves of garlic and puree them together with a bit of olive oil for garlic mashed potatoes.
- Add a bit of finely minced garlic to salad dressings.
- Sauté a couple of minced cloves of garlic in a tablespoon or two of extra virgin olive oil, and then add broccoli, carrots or other vegetables and give the pan a shake. Add a few tablespoons of broth or water and allow the vegetables to steam until tender.

See our Shopping Lists (pages 216, 217, 220 and 222) for some recommended products.

Honey

No wonder the word *honey* is a term of endearment. What could be sweeter and more appealing than the rich golden liquid? I've long enjoyed the delights of honey on cereal, toast, yogurt and pancakes, and as a sweetener for green tea, and I'm sure once you know about the nutritional benefits of honey, you'll be eager to use it more frequently.

Honey is much more than just a liquid sweetener. One of the oldest medicines known to man, honey has been used in the treatment of respiratory diseases, skin ulcers, wounds, urinary

HONEY IS A SOURCE OF:

181 different substances including:
- Polyphenols
- Salicylates
- Oligosaccharides

Sidekicks: None

Try to eat: 1 to 2 teaspoons multiple times a week

diseases, gastrointestinal diseases, eczema, psoriasis and dandruff. Today, we know the validity of these timeless treatments, as research has demonstrated that honey can inhibit the growth of bacteria, yeast, fungi and viruses.

The power of honey comes from the wide range of compounds present in the rich amber liquid. Honey contains at least 181 known substances, and its antioxidant activity stems from the phenolics, peptides, organic acids and enzymes. Honey also contains salicylic acid, minerals, alpha-tocopherol and oligosaccharides. Oligosaccharides increase the number of "good" bacteria in the colon, reduce levels of toxic metabolites in the intestine, help prevent constipation and help lower cholesterol and blood pressure.

The key point to remember with honey is that its antioxidant ability can vary widely depending on the floral source of the honey and its processing.

HOW BEES MAKE HONEY

The process begins when bees feast on flowers and collect nectar in their mouths. The bees mix the nectar and enzymes in their saliva to turn it into honey, which is then stored in combs in the hive. The constant movement of the bees' wings promotes moisture evaporation and yield the thick honey we enjoy.

The phenolic content of the honey depends on the pollen that the bees have used as raw material. There's a very simple way to determine the health benefits of any honey: its color. In general, the darker the color of the honey, the higher the level of antioxidants. There can be a twentyfold difference in honey's antioxidant activity, as one test revealed. For example, Illinois buckwheat honey, the darkest honey tested, had twenty times the antioxidant activity of California sage honey, one of the lightest-colored honeys tested. Overall, color predicted more than sixty percent of the variation in honey's antioxidant capacity.

Honey and Your Health

Maintaining optimal blood-sugar levels has a positive effect on overall health, and honey seems to contribute to this goal. Indeed, the ancient Olympic competitors relied on foods such as figs and honey to enhance performance by helping to maintain energy levels and restore muscle recovery.

In one recent study of thirty-nine male and female athletes, the participants ate a protein supplement blended with a sweetener following a workout. Those who ate the supplement sweetened with honey, as opposed to sugar or maltodextrin, enjoyed the best results. They maintained optimal blood-sugar levels for two hours following the workout and enjoyed better muscle recuperation.

✪ There are more than three hundred kinds of honey in the United States, such as clover, buckwheat and orange blossom. Light-colored honeys are generally mildly flavored, while dark honeys are more robust.

Perhaps honey's most important health-promoting benefit is its antioxidant ability. We know that daily consumption of honey raises blood levels of protective antioxidants.

In one study, participants were given about four tablespoons daily of buckwheat honey while eating their regular diets for twenty-nine days. A direct link was found between the subjects' honey consumption and the levels of protective polyphenolic antioxidants in their blood.

In another study, twenty-five healthy men drank plain water or water with buckwheat honey. Those consuming the honey enjoyed a 7 percent increase in their antioxidant capacity.

As the U.S. Department of Agriculture estimates that the average U.S. citizen consumes about 68 kilograms of sweetener annually, substituting honey for at least part of this amount would make an impressive contribution to our overall antioxidant status and would no doubt be a significant health promoter.

HONEY HEALS WOUNDS

Honey, long recognized as a wound healer, has been used for centuries as a topical antiseptic for treating burns, ulcers and wounds. A study in India compared the effectiveness of honey with a conventional wound-healing treatment, silver sulfadiazine, on patients suffering from first-degree burns. Amazingly, in the honey-dressed wounds, early abating of acute inflammatory changes, better control of infection and quicker wound healing were observed. Some researchers attribute this effect to the nutrients in honey that promote skin growth and to the antibacterial substances present in honey. While I'm not recommending that you consider using honey topically, its power in this role is further evidence of its wide range of health benefits.

Never give honey to children younger than a year old. About 10 percent of honey contains dormant *Clostridium botulinum* spores, which can cause botulism in infants.

An additional benefit of honey is found in the oligosaccharides it contains. They increase the numbers of good bacteria in the colon, reduce levels of toxic metabolites in the intestine, help prevent constipation and help reduce cholesterol and blood pressure.

Feeling under the weather? Throat sore and scratchy? Try sipping some hot green tea with a spoonful of honey and a dash of red pepper (cayenne). The potent mix of SuperFoods tea and honey along with red pepper can soothe that inflamed throat.

Researchers think that the red pepper subdues one of the body's pain chemicals, substance P—a neuropeptide that carries pain signals to the brain—so that you can swallow more comfortably.

Honey in the Kitchen

It's not difficult to find uses for honey in your kitchen. It's an obvious substitute for sugar in tea and other hot and cold drinks. You can also bake with honey, but you will have to adjust your recipe, as the honey may cause foods to brown more quickly. Reducing the oven temperature by about 25° F and using one-quarter cup less liquid in your recipe is a good formula. About one-half cup of honey equals a cup of sugar.

Don't keep honey in the fridge, since the cold will cause it to crystallize. If the honey does crystallize, put the container in a bowl of warm water and the crystals will dissolve. Avoid heating honey in the microwave because this can alter the taste.

Here are some suggestions for using honey...

- Add about one tablespoon to smoothies and shakes.
- A super after-school snack is a sliced apple or pear drizzled with honey and sprinkled with cinnamon.
- Some fruit-on-the-bottom yogurts have quite a lot of sugar. Make your own version by adding a bit of honey and some fresh fruit to nonfat or low-fat plain yogurt.
- Make a honey-mustard salad dressing by mixing a few tablespoons each of honey and Dijon mustard, a drizzle of lemon juice and about a quarter-cup of extra virgin olive oil. Delicious served on peppery greens like arugula.
- A great way to start the morning: Steep 2 green tea bags in 3 ounces hot water for 3 minutes. Squeeze the tea bags into the water and add one-half to 1 teaspoon honey plus 4 to 5 ounces Silk vanilla soymilk. Stir and enjoy.

• Toast 1 slice whole-grain bread and spread with natural peanut butter, dark honey and a sprinkle of cinnamon.

See our Shopping Lists (pages 213 and 220) for some recommended products.

KIWI

Kiwis are perhaps the first fruit to be named for a bird—twice. Introduced to New Zealand from China around 1906, the fruit was first known as a Chinese gooseberry (the first bird), probably because, like a green gooseberry, it has pale flesh. As kiwis became more popular, and international demand spread, New Zealanders proudly renamed the fruit after their national bird—the kiwi (the second bird).

Today, California provides 95 percent of the U.S. crop. Kiwis, or kiwifruit, are popular the world over and deservedly so, as their pale green and delicious flesh, reminiscent of strawberries to some and pineapple to others, offers a potent mix of nutrients that elevate it to the status of a SuperFood.

KIWI IS A SOURCE OF:

- Vitamin C
- Folate
- Vitamin E
- Potassium
- Fiber
- Carotenoids (primarily lutein/zeaxanthin)
- Polyphenols
- Chlorophyll
- Glutathione
- Pectin
- Low glycemic index

Sidekicks: Pineapple, guava (any variety)

Try to eat: Multiple times a week

Kiwi the SuperFruit

While many fruits feature one or two nutrients in their profile, kiwis offer an unusual array of health-promoting substances. Extremely rich in vitamin C, kiwis also offer folate, potassium, fiber, carotenoids, polyphenols, chlorophyll, glutathione and pectin. In addition, kiwis are an unusual source of vitamin E, because most sources of this important vitamin, like nuts and oils, are high in both fat and calories. Kiwis, by contrast, offer their rich nutritional bounty for only about 93 calories for two kiwis. In fact, on a calorie-per-nutrient basis, kiwis have only 3.8 calories per nutrient. Of twenty-seven fruits tested, only cantaloupe (2.6), papaya (2.8), strawberry (2.5), and lemon (2.5) had fewer calories per nutrient.

Kiwis are antioxidant all-stars. Offering a rich bounty of vitamin C—more than the equivalent amount in an orange—kiwis can help neutralize the free radicals that damage cells, ultimately leading to inflammation, which, in turn, can lead to cancer and other chronic diseases. Vitamin C plays such an important role in so many bodily functions, including the immune system, and is associated with preventing so many ailments from asthma and atherosclerosis to osteoarthritis and colon cancer, that it's no wonder that high consumption of the foods containing the vitamin is associated with a reduced risk of death *from all causes*, including cancer, heart disease and stroke.

Kiwis and Your Heart

Kiwifruits promote heart health by lowering triglyceride levels and reducing platelet hyperactivity, which in turn seems to play a role in the development and stability of atherosclerotic vascular plaques.

Kiwis can promote heart health by limiting the tendency of blood to form clots. The vitamins C and E in kiwi, combined with the polyphenols and magnesium, potassium, B vitamins and copper, act to protect the cardiovascular system. In one study in Oslo, Norway, people who ate two or three kiwis a day for twenty-eight days reduced their platelet aggregation response—or potential for clot formation—by 18 percent compared with those who ate no kiwis. Moreover, the kiwi eaters enjoyed a triglyceride drop of 15 percent compared with the controls.

Four medium kiwifruit supply about 1.4 milligrams of lutein and zeaxanthin. Therefore, this fruit is a nonleafy green source of these two important nutrients, which have been associated with a decreased risk for cataracts, macular degeneration and the development of atherosclerotic plaques.

Kiwis are reported to have a laxative effect, which can be beneficial to all, but especially to older people who are troubled by constipation.

Kiwis in the Kitchen

Kiwis are generally available in most supermarkets all year round. The most common variety is the Hayward, which has green flesh and is covered with brown fuzz. Gold kiwis have a smooth bronze-colored skin and are pointy at one end. The flesh is mustard-colored and quite flavorful. The gold kiwi is also higher in vitamins C and E, and lutein/zeaxanthin. New hybrids include the baby kiwis, which are green, smooth, about the size of table grapes and eaten much like them.

When you shop for kiwis, choose plump ones that yield slightly to the touch. Avoid those that are shriveled, moldy or have soft spots. You can easily ripen kiwifruit by leaving them at room temperature for a few days, or to speed up the process, put the kiwifruit in a dry paper bag along with an apple or banana.

Most people don't realize that you can eat the kiwi, skin and all, after rubbing off the fuzz. The skin is actually quite nutritious. If you want to omit the skin, simply slice the fruit in half and scoop out the flesh, or you can slice it into rounds and peel the rounds before serving. If you have an egg slicer, use it to slice kiwis into uniform rounds.

Here are a few ways to get more kiwis into your life...

- Toss diced kiwis into a green salad.
- Puree kiwis into smoothies. They're delicious with bananas and/or blueberries and nonfat yogurt.
- Kiwi chunks make a tasty addition to a turkey or tuna salad.
- Serve kiwis with strawberries and add a dollop of low-fat or nonfat yogurt and a dash of honey.
- Blend kiwis with cantaloupe or other melon, and add yogurt for a creamy, chilled

Remember that you should be trying to get "Five a Day" of a wide variety of fruits. It's easier to achieve this goal in the spring, when the cascade of ripening fruits beckons from our markets.

Here's a primer on which fruits will continue to ripen once purchased and which will not...

Never ripen after picking: soft berries, cherries, citrus, grapes, lychees, olives, pineapple, watermelon

Ripen only after picking: avocados

Ripen in color, texture and juiciness but not in sweetness after picking: apricots, blueberries, figs, melons (except watermelon), nectarines, passionfruit, peaches, persimmons

Get sweeter after picking: apples, cherimoyas, kiwis, mangoes, papayas, pears

Ripen in every way after harvest: bananas

soup. Garnish with blueberries and mint for delightful color.

- Make a relish of chopped kiwi, red onion, pineapple, and orange. Serve with grilled meat or fish.

See our Shopping Lists (page 212) for some recommended products.

OATS

The humble oat made nutrition history in 1997 when the Food and Drug Administration (FDA) allowed a label to be placed on oat foods claiming an association between consumption of a diet high in oatmeal, oat bran or oat flour and a reduced risk for coronary heart disease—our nation's number one killer.

The overall conclusion from the FDA review was that oats could lower serum cholesterol levels, especially the "bad" ones, the LDLs. The FDA stated that the main active ingredient that yielded this exciting positive effect is the soluble fiber found in oats called "beta glucan." The press leaped on this news and oats, particularly oat bran, became touted as the magic bullet against cholesterol. Subsequent research showed that the cholesterol-lowering effect of oat bran was less dramatic than originally thought and the oat bran story faded away.

It's time for a renewal of interest in the power of oats. Despite the fact that whole grains form the base of most food pyramids, indicating that they should be a significant part of our diet, many Americans fail to eat even one whole grain serving a day! New discoveries, combined with what's been known about oats for years, have shown that their health-promoting powers are truly impressive. Oats are low in calories, and high in fiber and protein. They're a rich source of magnesium, potassium, zinc, copper, manganese, selenium, thiamine and pantothenic acid. They also contain phytonutrients such as polyphenols, phytoestrogens, lignins, protease inhibitors and vitamin E (they're an excellent source of tocotrienols and multiple tocopherols—important members of the vitamin E family). The synergy of the nutrients in oats makes them an outstanding and formidable SuperFood.

Indeed, the degree of protection against disease offered by oats and other whole grains is greater than that of any of their ingredients taken in isolation. In addition to their power to reduce disease and extend your health span, oats are a flagship SuperFood for practical reasons: They're inexpensive, readily available and incredibly easy to incorporate into your life. Oatmeal is on virtually every menu of every restaurant serving breakfast in America, and if you only remember

OATS ARE A SOURCE OF:

- High fiber
- Beta glucan
- Low calories
- Protein
- Magnesium
- Potassium
- Zinc
- Copper
- Manganese
- Selenium
- Thiamine

SuperSidekicks: Ground flaxseed and wheat germ

Sidekicks: Brown rice, barley, wheat, buckwheat, rye, millet, bulgur wheat, amaranth, quinoa, triticale, kamut, yellow corn, wild rice, spelt, couscous

Try to eat: Whole-grain foods that contain a daily minimum of 10 grams of whole-grain fiber

to eat a bowl of oats regularly, you'll be on your way to better health.

Oats are an excellent source of the complex carbohydrates that your body requires to sustain energy. They have twice as much protein as brown rice. They're also a rich source of thiamine, iron and selenium, and contain phytonutrients that show promise as an aid to reducing heart disease and some forms of cancer.

While oats are the star SuperFood of this section, the entire category of whole grains is an important component of a *SuperFoods Rx* diet.

Oats and Heart Disease

Whole grains benefit the heart, according to an analysis of data from the Iowa Women's Health Study, a nine-year study of more than 34,000 postmenopausal women. When all other factors were considered, it was found that women who ate a serving or more of whole-grain foods each day had a 14 to 19 percent lower overall mortality rate than those who rarely or never ate whole grains. It really is a tragedy that we consume so few whole grains and so much refined grains. If we could shift that balance, we would all be far healthier. We've already seen how oats can lower cholesterol levels and stabilize blood sugar. The complete list of the health-promoting abilities of whole grains is quite long.

In the Nurses' Health Study, women who consumed a median of 2½ whole-grain servings a day experienced more than a 30 percent lowered risk of coronary artery disease.

Other studies also continue to confirm the benefits of including oats in your diet as a way to reduce heart disease risk.

One fourteen-year study at the Harvard School of Public Health of more than 27,000 men ages 40 to 75 found that those with the highest whole-grain intake (about 40 grams per day) cut their heart disease risk by almost 20 percent—but even those eating just 25 grams cut their risk by 15 percent.

Another meta-study, which analyzed data on 91,058 men and 245,186 women who had participated in ten studies in the U.S. and Europe, found that for each 10 grams of fiber consumed daily, there was a 14 percent reduction in heart disease risk and a 25 percent reduction in the risk of dying from heart disease. The bottom line is that the cereal fiber in whole grains appears to make heart disease much less likely—and less serious if it does occur.

But it's the cholesterol-lowering power of oats that draws the most attention to this grain. Study after study has shown that in individuals with high cholesterol (above 220 mg/dL), consuming just 3 grams of soluble oat fiber per day—or roughly the amount in a bowl of oatmeal—can lower total cholesterol by 8 to 23 percent. Given that each 1 percent drop in serum cholesterol translates to a 2 percent decrease in the risk of developing heart disease, this is a significant effect.

One study in the *Journal of the American Medical Association* studied young adults and found those with the highest fiber intake had the lowest diastolic blood pressure readings. Hypertension is consistently the most important risk factor for stroke. Researchers estimated that

TWO TOP TIPS FOR BOOSTING WHOLE-GRAIN INTAKE

- Eat whole-grain cereal for breakfast. While only 5 percent of the grain foods in the U.S. are whole grain, it is the first ingredient listed on the package label in 18 percent of ready-to-eat cereals.
- Choose whole-grain breads. Look for whole wheat as the first ingredient and only buy bread with 3 or more grams of fiber per serving.

a 2-millimeter decrease in diastolic blood pressure would result in a 17 percent decrease in the prevalence of hypertension and a 15 percent reduction in risk for stroke. Whole grains form an important part of the Dietary Approaches to Stop Hypertension (DASH) diet that has repeatedly been found to lower blood pressure (see Web site *www.nhlbi.nih.gov/health/public/heart/hbp/dash.*)

Oats and Stroke

Whole-grain consumption has been linked to a reduction in the risk of strokes. In the Nurses' Health Study, among the group that never smoked, a median intake of 2.7 servings of whole grains a day was associated with a 50 percent reduction in the risk of ischemic stroke. Given that less than 8 percent of adults in the United States consume more than three servings of whole grains a day, it's clear we are missing a major opportunity. When you consider that in the U.S., strokes are a leading cause of morbidity and death, with an estimated 700,000 strokes annually costing roughly 40 billion dollars a year, you can see that convincing Americans to add the SuperFood oats and other whole grains to their diet is well worth the effort.

Oats and Blood Sugar

The beneficial effect of oats on blood-sugar levels was first reported in 1913. In recent years, researchers have discovered some of the mechanisms that make oats so effective. The same soluble fiber that reduces cholesterol—beta glucan—also seems to benefit those who suffer from type II diabetes. People who eat oatmeal or oat bran–rich foods experience lower spikes in their blood-sugar levels than they could get with, say, white rice or white bread. The soluble fibers slow the rate at which food leaves the stomach and delays the absorption of glucose following a meal. As stabilizing blood sugar is the goal of anyone with diabetes, this is an extremely beneficial effect.

One study in the *Journal of the American Medical Association* that was recently published found a low intake of cereal fiber to be inversely associated with a risk for diabetes. The authors conclude: "These findings suggest that grains should be consumed in a minimally refined form to reduce the incidence of diabetes mellitus." This same study also looked at the role of various foods in connection with diabetes. They found a significant inverse association with cold breakfast cereals and yogurt and, not surprisingly, a significant association with colas, white bread, white rice, french fries and cooked potatoes. The more you eat of the latter, the greater your risk for diabetes.

Epidemiological studies continue to consistently show that the risk for type II diabetes is decreased with the consumption of whole grains. We know that people who eat whole grains regularly, especially high-fiber cereals, are less likely

HOW MUCH IS A SERVING?

While eating five to seven servings of whole grains daily sounds like a tremendous amount, the USDA serving size is small, so it's not all that difficult to take in an adequate amount. Look for whole-grain products, which are higher in fiber. Here are some typical serving sizes:

- 1 slice of bread, 1 small roll or 1 muffin
- ½ cup cooked cereal, rice or pasta
- 5 or 6 small crackers
- 1 four-inch pita
- 1 small tortilla
- 3 rice or popcorn cakes
- ½ hamburger roll, bagel or English muffin
- 1 serving of cold cereal (amount depends on type—check box label)

to develop insulin-resistant or type II diabetes and metabolic syndrome.

In one six-year study of 35,988 older Iowa women who were initially free of diabetes, it was found that grains (particularly whole grains), cereal fiber and dietary magnesium played a strong protective role in the development of diabetes.

In another study at Tufts University, researchers found that people who eat three or more servings of whole grains a day, particularly from high-fiber cereals, are less likely to develop insulin resistance and metabolic syndrome, common precursors of both type II diabetes and cardiovascular disease.

Oats and Obesity

It stands to reason that eating a diet high in whole grains would help to prevent obesity. One effect of eating whole grains versus refined grains is that the former fill you up. Whole grains are simply bulkier and thus contribute to satiety, or a feeling of fullness. Research supports the idea that a diet that is rich in whole-grain foods promotes optimum body weight. As part of the Nurses' Health Study, researchers at the Harvard School of Public Health followed more than 74,000 women from 1984 to 1996, and concluded that women who consumed more whole grains consistently weighed less than women who consumed fewer whole grains.

Oats' Powerful Phytochemicals

In addition to the power of oat fiber, researchers have been excited to learn more about the phytonutrients in grains and how they help prevent disease. The germ and bran of oats contain a concentrated amount of phytonutrients, including caffeic acid and ferulic acid. Ferulic acid has been the focus of recent research that shows promising evidence of its ability to prevent colon cancer in

Corn, one of America's favorite vegetables, is actually a grain. Corn is a unique grain, as it is a source of five carotenoids: beta-carotene, alpha-carotene, beta cryptoxanthin, lutein and zeaxanthin.

Only yellow corn has significant amounts of these healthful carotenoids; white corn does not.

animals and other experimental models. Ferulic acid has been found to be a potent antioxidant that is able to scavenge free radicals and protect against oxidative damage. It also seems to be able to inhibit the formation of certain cancer-promoting compounds.

Oats and Cancer

There is substantial and growing evidence to indicate that consumption of oats and other whole grains can play a role in reducing the risk for a variety of cancers. We have known for a number of years that there is a link between whole-grain consumption and the reduction of cancer risk.

One meta-study of forty observational studies found that men and women who ate whole grains had a reduced risk for twenty types of cancers.

More recently, a study at the University of Utah found that high intakes of vegetables, fruits and whole grains reduced the risk for rectal cancer by 28 percent, 27 percent, and 31 percent, respectively. A high-fiber diet (more than 34 grams of fiber per day) reduced rectal cancer by an impressive 66 percent in this study of over two thousand people.

Whole-Grain Confusion

Before I make a case for the truly impressive health-promoting abilities of whole grains, I'd like to clear up some confusion that may have unfortunately encouraged you to avoid whole-grain foods in the past and/or conversely might be encouraging you to buy the wrong "whole grain" foods, which are of little nutritional value.

Few issues in the diet and nutrition wars are more confusing than carbohydrates. Low-carb diets have increased the confusion: They've drawn attention to carbohydrates, but unfortunately have oversimplified the issue of protein versus carbs. Many people have come to believe that carbs equal weight gain and are bad. Foods are now being labeled with banners that claim "no-carb" or "carb-free." Consumers trying to lose weight are being told that eating carbs will destroy any hope of weight loss. What's been lost in this battle, at least for many consumers, is the fact that, like fats and protein, not all carbs are created equal.

Carbohydrates are found in a vast array of foods, from table sugar to vegetables, beans and whole grains. A teaspoon of sugar is a carb. So is a slice of whole-grain bread. You can guess which is better for you, but you may not know precisely why. Not only are carbohydrates—*whole-grain carbohydrates*—good for you, they are also absolutely critical in your quest for lifelong health.

✪ Whole grains contain folate, which helps to lower serum levels of homocysteine—an independent risk factor for stroke and cardiovascular disease.

Whole grains lower your risk of coronary heart disease, stroke, diabetes, obesity, diverticulosis, hypertension, certain cancers and osteoporosis. Despite what you may hear, they do not make you fat (unless you eat way too much of them—which is hard to do!). The reason carbs have the reputation for promoting weight gain is that the vast majority of those eaten by Americans are *refined carbs* like cookies, doughnuts, breads and cakes that are loaded with sugar and fat and often trans fats as well. Yes, they are carbohydrates, but they are a world away from the complex carbohydrates that are whole grains. Many people don't realize what a difference there is between whole and refined grains. While whole grains are actually *health-promoting*, refined grains, such as pasta, white flour, white bread and white rice, have been associated with a variety of negative health effects, such as an increased risk of colorectal, pancreatic and stomach cancers.

If you stick with real whole grains, I promise you, you'll get full before you get fat. (How much brown rice can you eat?) You'll also increase your health span and maybe even your lifespan.

HOW TO READ A BREAD/ CEREAL LABEL

There are two things to look for to ensure a healthy product...

1. The list of ingredients should *begin with the word "whole."* This applies to all baked goods, including bread, crackers, cereals, pretzels, etc.
2. Look at the "Nutrition Facts" part of the label. The fiber content should be *at least 3 grams per serving for bread and cereal.* If it's lower, put the item back.

Will the Real Whole Grains Please Stand Up?

Some of you may avoid all grain products because you've been led to believe that such foods are carbs and will promote weight gain. I hope by the end of this section you'll become whole-grain enthusiasts.

Other people believe they're eating healthy whole-grain foods because food labels have convinced them they're buying wisely. But consider this: Only 5 percent of the grain foods in the American diet are whole grains. What are 95 percent of those refined grains going into? In some cases, products that would have you believe they're healthy and nutritious are not at all. Words like "honey wheat," "multi grain," "hearty wheat," "nutri grain," in fact, do not indicate anything about the healthfulness of the product. Foods that use such words on the labels might be nutritious, but these terms guarantee nothing.

Food producers are beginning to catch on. Scan the bread shelf at your supermarket. You'll probably see a number of new breads that have health claims. They contain higher levels of fiber than you used to find, perhaps with added soy flour, and they're made of whole grains. Major cereal producers are also boosting the amount of whole grains in their cereals, and there is a new "whole grain" stamp that appears on food products that are sources of this important component of a healthy diet. This is all excellent news for consumers, who will now have an easier time identifying the true whole-grain products.

HOW TO GET 15 GRAMS OF WHOLE-GRAIN FIBER A DAY

Uncle Sam Cereal—toasted whole-grain wheat flakes with crispy whole flaxseed (1 cup)	10 grams
½ cup oats	9 grams
Post Shredded Wheat 'N Bran (1¼ cups)	8 grams
2 tablespoons flaxseed	7 grams
¼ cup oat bran (raw—not toasted)	4 grams
1 slice Ezekiel bread	3 grams
2 tablespoons wheat germ (crude—not toasted)	2 grams
½ cup cooked brown rice	2 grams
½ cup cooked yellow corn	2 grams

Vitamin E intake from food, not supplements, has been inversely related to the risk of stroke. Whole grains and nuts are the two major sources of whole food vitamin E.

What Is a Whole Grain?

Whole grains have been part of the human diet for ten thousand years—ever since man adopted agriculture as a method of providing food. Indeed, for the last three thousand to four thousand years, whole grains were a major portion of the human diet.

A whole grain, whether it's oats, barley, wheat, bulgur or a host of others, contains every part of the grain. *The three parts include...*

- **The bran.** A health-promoting, fiber-rich outer layer that contains B vitamins, minerals, protein and other phytochemicals.
- **The endosperm.** The middle layer that contains carbohydrates, proteins and a small amount of B vitamins.
- **The germ.** The nutrient-packed inner layer that contains B vitamins, vitamin E and other phytochemicals.

It's the synergy of these three components that makes whole grains life-sustaining.

Beginning about 1870, a new type of milling allowed for grains to be "refined" so that only a part of the grain was used in food products like white flour and white rice. The bran and the germ were stripped away, leaving only a starchy substance that was missing many, if not all, of the whole grains' natural nutrients, antioxidants, and phytonutrients. Consumption of whole-grain foods plummeted until few people were consuming anywhere near the amount recommended for health.

Does it really matter if your diet is low in whole grains? If you care about reducing your risk for *many* major health concerns, then, yes, it does!

In 1943, some of the nutrients that had been stripped out of white flour in its processing were added back, including some of the B vitamins and iron. In 1998, folic acid was put back in. The lost vitamin E in various forms and the phytonutrients were never returned and, given the complexity of these nutrients, probably could not effectively be added back. Get everything that's missing from refined grains: *Eat whole grains!*

Welcome to the Wide World of Grains

There are many other whole grains besides oats that can help you increase and vary your intake of this valuable food group. Here are a few that you might want to try. Remember, it's the synergy of the various nutrients in a variety of grains that will give you optimum nutrition.

A Host of Grains and Fiber Content	*(¼-cup servings)*
Triticale	8.7 grams
Barley	8 grams
Amaranth	7.4 grams
Wheat bran (raw or untoasted)	6.5 grams
Rye	6.2 grams
Buckwheat	4.3 grams
Wheat germ (raw or untoasted)	3.8 grams
Quinoa	2.5 grams
Wild rice	1.5 grams
Millet	1.5 grams
Brown rice	.9 gram
Enriched white rice	.2 gram

It hasn't always been easy to find whole-grain products. Now the Whole Grains Council, (*www.wholegrainscouncil.org*), a group of more than 170 grain food companies, grain producers, and bakeries have come up with a seal of approval that features shafts of wheat and one of two designations...

- "Whole Grain" for foods offering a half-serving or more of whole grain and containing at least 8 grams of whole-grain ingredients per serving
- "100% Whole Grain" for foods where all grain ingredients are whole grain and containing at least 16 grams of whole grain per serving.

The SuperSidekicks

An unusual feature of oats is that they have two "SuperSidekicks": ground flaxseed and wheat germ. The SuperSidekicks really belong in a very special category because they're so nutrient dense. Both offer super benefits in very small amounts. If you add just 2 tablespoons each of ground flaxseed and wheat germ each day to your cereal, you will be on your way to better health.

FLAXSEEDS

Flaxseeds are a SuperSidekick that deserve special attention because these seeds are the best plant source of omega-3 fatty acids. They're a quick, easy way to get this important nutrient into your diet. (For a more complete discussion of this crucial, and often neglected, component to our diets, see the section on wild salmon.)

Flaxseeds are also a powerful source of fiber, protein, magnesium, iron and potassium: an all-around treasure trove of nutrients. In addition, flaxseeds are the leading source of a class of compounds called "lignins," which are phytoestrogens, or plant estrogens. Lignins influence the balance of estrogens in the body and help protect against breast cancer.

Flaxseeds are slightly larger than sesame seeds, darker in color—they range from dark red to brown—and very shiny. You can buy them in the form of flaxseed meal, or you can buy them in seed form and grind them yourself in a coffee grinder or mini food processor. The seeds must be ground, as the nutrients are difficult to absorb from the whole seed. Since the oil in flaxseeds spoils quickly, ideally it's best to grind them as you go. Some people use a grinder, which they dedicate to flaxseeds, and grind them in small amounts, keeping the ground portion in the fridge in a small glass jar.

I keep flaxmeal—already ground flaxseed, which you can buy in health food stores—in a plastic container in the fridge. I sprinkle 2 tablespoons of ground flaxseed a day on oatmeal, cereal and yogurt, or use it in smoothies, pancakes, muffins and quick breads.

All you need is one to two tablespoons of ground flaxseed a day. This gives you more than the Institute of Medicine's total daily recommendation for alpha linolenic acid (ALA, or plant-derived omega-3 fatty acids). Two tablespoons of ground flaxseed is a safe amount, geared to providing optimal nutrition, and there are no data suggesting that this amount of flaxseed/ALA has any deleterious effect.

WHEAT GERM

Eating wheat germ is one of the easiest ways to increase your intake of whole grains. Wheat is one of the oldest harvested grains and was first cultivated about six thousand years ago. Wheat germ is the embryo of the wheat berry (a wheat kernel that has not been heated, milled or polished), and it's packed with nutrition. Two tablespoons, at only 52 calories, have 4 grams of protein, 2 grams of fiber, 41 micrograms of folate, a third of the Recommended Daily Allowance (RDA) of vitamin E, along with high levels of thiamine, manganese, selenium, vitamin B6 and potassium together with reasonable levels of iron and zinc. Wheat germ, like flaxseed, is also one of the few sources of plant-derived omega-3 fatty acids. Just two tablespoons—the serving size of wheat germ—of Kretschmer toasted wheat germ have 100 milligrams of beneficial omega-3 fatty acids.

Wheat germ contains phytosterols, which play a role in reducing cholesterol absorption. A recent clinical trial reported that slightly less than six tablespoons of wheat germ per day caused a 42.8 percent reduction in cholesterol absorption among the human volunteers in the study.

Sprinkle wheat germ on yogurt, cold cereal, hot oatmeal or smoothies. Add it into pancake and muffin mix and into quick breads. You can even put a dash of it on baked fish or in many casseroles and other dishes. When you think that only two tablespoons of wheat germ can significantly boost your day's nutrition, I don't know why anyone wouldn't keep a jar of it in the refrigerator.

SUPER BREAKFASTS THE WHOLE YEAR

My usual winter breakfast is a bowl of hot oatmeal with raisins or dried cranberries or blueberries, sprinkled with 2 tablespoons each of ground flaxmeal and toasted wheat germ. In the summer, it's flaxmeal, wheat germ and berries on yogurt. You really can't find a better start to your day.

Buying and Cooking Whole Grains

As whole grains become more popular, more markets carry them. If you do buy them from open bins, be sure that the store has a good turnover so the grains are fresh. Make sure that the bins are covered and kept clean.

Store whole grains in airtight containers, in a cool place, preferably the refrigerator. Oats, for example, have more natural oil than many people realize and can become rancid if they're stored in a warm environment.

Soaking whole grains before cooking can reduce the cooking time.

Many grains improve in flavor if they're toasted before cooking. Heat them in a nonstick pan over a low heat until just fragrant and until they become darker, taking care not to burn them.

Once grains are cooked, they will keep in the fridge for two to three days. They freeze well, so it's a good idea to make long-cooking grains in batches that can be frozen in portion sizes. Then they can easily be added to soups, casseroles and salads.

Oats in the Kitchen

Here are some tips for eating more whole grains...

• Make every breakfast an opportunity to eat whole grains. It's the easiest meal of the day in which to include them and it gets your day off to a great nutritional start. Check out the cereals in your pantry and if they don't contain whole grains, get rid of them and shop for some of the new cereals that tout whole grains as a primary ingredient.

• Make steel-cut Irish oatmeal (which takes about a half hour to cook) in a big batch with cranberries, raisins, cut-up apricots and other dried fruit, store it in plastic containers, and heat it in portion sizes in the morning for a quick, delicious breakfast.

• Use whole-grain breads for your sandwiches. Look for whole-grain tortillas and pita breads. There are some excellent whole-grain breads on the market that taste great, have no trans fats, and are good sources of whole-grain nutrition and fiber.

• Try the new whole-grain or partially whole-grain pastas that have recently come onto the market. Some are delicious and will give you more fiber and nutrition than traditional refined-grain pastas.

• Purchase whole-grain crackers. They're just as tasty as the less nutritious refined-wheat crackers.

• Add some oats to fruit crisps, stuffings, turkey meatballs, meatloaf and, of course, oatmeal cookies.

• Try some of the "exotic" grains as side dishes, such as barley or quinoa.

• Look for Japanese soba buckwheat noodles. They're good in soups or cold with a sesame dressing.

See our Shopping Lists (pages 213-218 and 224) for some recommended products.

Extra Virgin Olive Oil

If you were to make one change in your kitchen—one single simple adjustment—to promote health and gain substantial benefits in countless ways, it would be to use extra virgin olive oil in place of other fats. So many studies

OLIVE OIL IS A SOURCE OF:

- Monounsaturated fatty acids
- Vitamin E
- Carotenoids
- Polyphenols
- Phytosterols

Sidekicks: Canola oil

Try to eat: About 1 tablespoon most days

have verified the health-promoting qualities of extra virgin olive oil that the European Union has embraced it as the oil of choice, and is investing more than thirty-five million euros to promote consumption in its member states. In the U.S., the FDA, for only the third time, granted a qualified health claim for conventional foods containing olive oil. These foods are allowed to carry labels saying they may reduce the risk of coronary heart disease due to the monounsaturated fat in the oil.

Olive oil—made from the crushing and pressing of one of the oldest-known foods, olives—has been enjoyed since as early as 3000 B.C. It is a staple of the extraordinarily healthy Mediterranean diet, and it is now believed that the consumption of olive oil is a prime reason for the positive aspects of this particular diet.

It seems that the heart-healthy effects of olive oil are due to a synergy of health-promoting compounds. The monounsaturated fat in olive oil has various impressive health benefits. In addition to healthy fat, olive oil is a good source of vitamin E. One ounce of extra virgin olive oil contains 17.4 percent of the Daily Value (DV) for vitamin E. Interestingly, part of the nutrient synergy of extra virgin olive oil is that the abundant polyphenols not only provide their own health benefits, they also protect and preserve the accompanying vitamin E.

The powerful synergy of all the cooperating compounds in extra virgin olive oil seems to have beneficial effects on health, and a wide range of studies has demonstrated that adding olive oil to your regular diet could reduce your risk for breast and colon cancer, lower your blood pressure and improve your cardiovascular health.

Olive Oil Fights Oxidative Damage

One of the most interesting studies on olive oil suggests what a protective role it can play in preventing cancer and cardiovascular disease. In this study, healthy men consumed 25 milliliters a day of olive oil (a dose similar to what is consumed in the Mediterranean Diet), and after only four days of olive oil intake, beneficial changes were seen in their blood plasma. The ingestion of the olive oil increased the vitamin E and phenolic content of their blood lipids, thus protecting them from oxidative damage that could lead to cardiovascular disease and the development of certain cancers.

Interestingly, this is the first study to show the effect of olive oil on DNA. It's significant that following the consumption of the olive oil, there was less oxidation of the DNA. Oxidation of DNA is linked to the development of diseases such as cancer and even to aging itself.

Olive Oil and Blood Pressure

Perhaps you've heard of the Mediterranean Diet. This name refers to the traditional diet eaten by people in Crete. First studied in the 1950s and 60s, the Mediterranean Diet was recognized as a particularly healthy eating pattern—one that seemed to promote long life expectancies and low rates of heart disease and some cancers. The Mediterranean Diet consists largely of plant-based foods—fruits, vegetables, coarsely ground grains, bread, beans, nuts and seeds—as well as olive oil. Fish, poultry and red meat are rare, special-occasion foods.

Remember that olive oil is a fat. It has 120 calories per tablespoon. If you eat too much of it, you will gain weight. For most people, as a SuperFood it's best used as a substitution for other, less healthy fats, such as butter.

People who ate this Mediterranean Diet seemed to enjoy generally low blood pressure. Of course, the question remained: Was the low pressure a result of other components of the diet?

What particular role did olive oil play? To learn the answer, a team from the University of Athens studied more than 20,000 Greeks who were free of hypertension when the study began. At the end of the study, data confirmed that, overall, the Mediterranean Diet was consistently associated with lower blood pressure. When the effects of olive oil and vegetables were compared, olive oil alone was found to be responsible for the most beneficial effect in lowering blood pressure.

It seems that olive oil has a beneficial effect on the vascular endothelium, the cells lining the blood vessels. A study in Spain found that subjects who used olive oil for four weeks reported both systolic and diastolic blood pressure to drop approximately 8 mm Hg. Another very interesting study found that not only did olive oil lower blood pressure, it also rendered medication less necessary for the participating subjects.

Olive Oil and Cardiovascular Disease

There's no doubt that olive oil is a rich source of antioxidants and other phytochemicals, and it's likely that the lower rates of coronary artery disease in Mediterranean countries are at least partly due to olive oil consumption.

There is ample and impressive research evidence that demonstrates that olive oil can play a role in promoting cardiovascular health over and above its ability to reduce blood pressure.

We know that diets rich in olive oil have been shown to be effective in lowering total cholesterol and LDL ("bad") cholesterol. Certainly, olive oil is one of the significant constituents that contribute to the cardioprotective ability of the Mediterranean Diet. For example, we know that the polyphenols in olive oil are potent antioxidants that help protect LDL from oxidation.

Moreover, the presence of monounsaturated fatty acids help biologic membranes, like those of our cell walls, better resist oxidative damage. We know that the oxidation of LDL plays a fundamental role in the progress of arteriosclerosis. In one study, when olive oil was added to the diet of healthy males, it significantly reduced the vulnerability of their LDL to oxidative damage.

Olive Oil and Cancer

There is reason to believe that extra virgin olive oil could play a significant role in preventing cancer. It's been estimated that up to 25 percent of the incidence of colorectal cancer, 15 percent of the incidence of breast cancer and approximately 10 percent of the incidence of prostate, pancreatic and endometrial cancers could be prevented if the populations of Western countries would consume the traditional Mediterranean Diet. Of course, this would mean an increase in fruit and vegetable intake as well as the substitution of olive oil as a main source of fat in the diet. While we don't know exactly what it is in olive oil that provides this protection against cancer, we do know that once again it seems to be the synergy of the whole food.

There's also evidence that substances in olive oil inhibit the formation of amines—cancer-causing compounds that form during the cooking of meat. This would indicate that a marinade that contains extra virgin olive oil may lessen cancer risk, as it would inhibit these cancer-promoting amines from forming in the first place.

BREAST CANCER PREVENTIVE?

There has been great interest in the role of olive oil in the development and prevention of breast cancer. The role of fat in the diet and its effect on breast cancer is controversial, and a number of studies have been published with conflicting findings.

In case-control studies, consumption of olive oil has been shown to reduce the estimated relative risk of breast cancer in Spain and Greece. Moreover, in animal studies, olive oil seems to have an antitumor effect. Interesting research points to the possible ability of olive oil to reduce breast cancer risk. It seems that oleic acid, the monounsaturated fat found in olive oil, may have the ability to inhibit the growth of certain types of breast cancer cells by inhibiting a gene that stimulates their growth.

MAY HELP COLON CANCER TOO

There is some evidence that olive oil can play a role in the prevention of colon cancer as well. In one large European study, olive oil consumption was associated with a lower incidence of colorectal cancer. Evidence suggests that compounds such as the phenolics in olive oil act directly in the colon to reduce oxidative or free-radical damage of the colon. This reduction of free-radical damage would ultimately have a chemoprotective result.

Olive Oil in the Kitchen

The key to obtaining health benefits from olive oil is to use it as a substitute for corn, safflower and sunflower oils. Remember that the SuperFood recommendation is about one tablespoon a day: That isn't a lot of oil, so use it judiciously.

When shopping for olive oil you should know that there are different grades, depending on the processing method...

Extra virgin olive oil, which because of its higher polyphenol content is considered a SuperFood, is derived from the first pressing of the olives. It has a low acid content. In addition to its considerable health-promoting qualities, it has the most delicate flavor.

Virgin olive oil is from the second pressing of the olives. It has a higher acid content than extra virgin oil.

Fino is made from a blend of extra virgin and virgin oils.

Refined oil is made by using chemicals to extract the oil from the olives. It is often a blend of a variety of oils.

Cold-pressed extra virgin olive oil is the kind to buy, as it will provide the most health benefits as well as the most subtle taste. One study indicates that virgin olive oil (most studies do not differentiate the type of olive oil) provides greater protection against free-radical damage to LDL ("bad") cholesterol—a first step in the development of atherosclerosis—than other oils. I always look for greenish-colored extra virgin olive oil, since the color indicates a high level of polyphenols. Different types of olive oil—from Spain, Greece and even California—have different, interesting tastes.

Extra virgin olive oil is quite perishable. Buy no more than you'll use in two or three months. Decant some oil from the original container into an opaque bottle or tin and keep it from the light; store it in a cool, dark place in your kitchen. Don't keep it near the stove! Store the rest of the oil in the fridge, where it will solidify slightly. Cold olive oil will quickly liquefy when brought to room temperature.

It's easy to use sufficient olive oil in your diet to get its considerable health benefits.

- Make salad dressing with 3 parts extra virgin olive oil and 1 part balsamic vinegar or lemon juice. You'll avoid the high sodium levels in most prepared dressings. Add finely chopped garlic or shallots and fresh herbs plus ground pepper, and use a salt substitute such as Vegit.
- Drizzle vegetables and sautéed greens with a bit of extra virgin olive oil before serving.
- Add extra virgin olive oil and roasted garlic to make delicious mashed potatoes.
- Drizzle asparagus, beets, red and white potatoes, turnips or carrots with extra virgin olive oil. Roast in a 400° F oven until crisp-tender.

See our Shopping Lists (page 222) for some recommended products.

Onions

It's hard to imagine a culinary life without onions. A staple of so many cuisines, onions lend a unique savory and pungent flavor to an endless variety of dishes. Eaten cooked and raw, available all year round, onions are hard to avoid, and once you know about their considerable health benefits, it's difficult to imagine why anyone would want to. While onions' health-promoting abilities have long been recognized, it's only recently that their considerable curative abilities have been conclusively demonstrated; thus, their elevation to SuperFood status.

Cultivated for more than five thousand years, onions are native to Asia and the Middle East. The name "onion" comes from the Latin *unis*, meaning "one" or "single," and it refers to the fact that onions, unlike their close relative garlic, have only one bulb.

Onions are a major source of two phytonutrients that play a significant role in health promotion: flavonoids and the mixture of more than fifty sulfur-containing compounds. The two flavonoid subgroups found in onions are the anthocyanins that impart a red-purple color to some varieties, and the flavonoids, such as quercetin and its derivatives, that are responsible for the yellow flesh and brown skins of many other varieties.

In general, the phytonutrients in onions, and in other fruits and vegetables, are concentrated in the skin and outermost portions of the flesh.

We now know that the health-promoting compounds in onions, like those in garlic, are separated by cell walls. Slicing an onion ruptures these walls and releases the compounds, which then combine to form a powerful new compound: thiopropanal sulfoxide.

In addition to mitigating various diseases, this substance also gives cut onions their pungent aroma and their ability to make us cry.

ONIONS ARE A SOURCE OF:

- Selenium
- Fructans (including inulin)
- Vitamin E
- Vitamin C
- Potassium
- Diallyl sulfide
- Saponins
- Fiber
- Polyphenols

Sidekicks: Garlic, scallions, shallots, leeks, chives

Try to eat: Multiple times a week

To get the most health benefits from onions, let them sit for 5 to 10 minutes after cutting and before cooking. Heat will deactivate the thiopropanal sulfoxide and you want to give it time to develop fully and to become concentrated before heating.

Onions and Your Heart

While chopping onions may make you cry, their considerable cardiovascular benefits should bring a smile through your tears. As with garlic, onion consumption has been shown to lower high cholesterol levels and high blood pressure. Onions, along with tea, apples and broccoli—the richest dietary sources of flavonoids—have been shown to reduce the risk of heart disease by 20 percent in one recent meta-analysis that reviewed the dietary patterns and health of more than 100,000 individuals.

Onions and Cancer

Regular consumption of onions has also been associated with a reduced risk of colon cancer. It is believed that quercetin in onions is the protective factor, since it's been shown to stop the growth of tumors in animals and to protect colon cells from the negative effects of some cancer-promoting substances. There's also evidence that onions may lower the risk of cancers of the brain, esophagus, lung and stomach.

Onions Are Good Anti-Inflammatories

Onions contain several anti-inflammatory compounds that contribute to reducing the symptoms associated with a host of inflammatory conditions like osteoarthritis and rheumatoid arthritis, the allergic inflammatory response of asthma and the respiratory congestion that is a symptom of the common cold. Onions and garlic both contain compounds that inhibit the enzymes that generate inflammatory prostaglandins and thromboxanes. Both vitamin C and quercetin contribute to this beneficial effect. They work synergistically to spell relief from inflammation, making both onions and garlic good choices as ingredients in many dishes during the cold and flu season. Onions also exhibit antimicrobial activity against a range of bacteria and fungi.

Onions in the Kitchen

Onions and their cousins, shallots and green onions or scallions, are widely available all year round. Choose onions that are clean and firm with no soft or moldy spots. Avoid sprouting onions or ones with any dampness. When choosing scallions, look for those having green, fresh-looking tops with a whitish base. Avoid any that look wilted, brown or yellow at the tips.

Onions and potatoes, while delicious combined in foods, are not storage friends. The moisture and ethylene gas from the spuds will cause onions to spoil more quickly. Keep them separate. Onions should be kept in a well-ventilated dark place. Scallions should be stored in a perforated plastic bag in the fridge.

If cutting an onion makes you weep, chill the onion for an hour or so before chopping to slow the enzyme activity. Allow the chopped onion to come to room temperature and rest after cutting to promote the beneficial enzyme activity before cooking.

- Onions are welcome additions to almost any cooked dish, including soups, stews and casseroles.
- Onions are a pungent addition to salads. Use red onions for color and a polyphenol boost.
- Grilled or roasted onions are flavorful and sweet. Brush lightly with olive oil before cooking.

See our Shopping Lists (pages 216 and 220) for some recommended products.

From a health promotion standpoint, the most pungent onions and their sidekicks pack the biggest wallop. In one test of the flavonoid content of onions, shallots had six times the amount found in Vidalia onions, the variety with the lowest phenolic content. Shallots also had the most antioxidant activity. Western yellow onions had the most flavonoids—eleven times the amount found in Western white onions, the type with the lowest flavonoid content. Americans have been opting for the sweeter onions of late. All types of onions are good additions to your diet, but choose the stronger-tasting ones when appropriate to your recipe.

ORANGES

Oranges may well have been America's first "health food." Long recognized as a potent source of vitamin C, oranges are considered by most to be tasty, juicy and perhaps too familiar. No one gets very excited about an orange in a lunchbox—but they should. The discoveries that are being made about the power of oranges to support heart health and prevent cancer, stroke, diabetes and a host of chronic ailments (as well as the common cold) should bring oranges and other citrus fruits back to center stage as crucial components in a healthy diet.

Oranges originated in Asia thousands of years ago and have become one of the most popular fruits the world over. Christopher Columbus brought orange seeds to the Caribbean Islands in the late fifteenth century, and Spanish explorers then brought oranges to Florida in the next century. About two hundred years later, in the eighteenth century, Spanish missionaries brought oranges to California. These two states remain the primary producers of oranges in the United States.

Her Majesty's Life Preserver

The story of how limes and the vitamin C they contained saved Her Majesty's sailors is familiar to many people. It's an interesting tale of the power of food and the importance of getting a wide range of health-promoting nutrients in your diet.

In the fifteenth and sixteenth centuries, sailors were routinely lost on long sea voyages, dying of scurvy. Countless sailors died despite the belief they were getting enough to eat. The Portuguese explorer Vasco de Gama lost nearly half his men to scurvy in the 1490s as he took his first trip around the Cape of Good Hope. It wasn't until the mid-1700s that James Lind, a British naval surgeon, discovered that a daily ration of citrus in lemons, limes or oranges preserved the sailors' health. Thus the life of the British sailor, or "limey," was saved.

This would be quaint old news were it not for the fact that 20 to 30 percent of America's adults have marginal blood levels of vitamin C and 16 percent are reportedly deficient in the vitamin. Humans, along with primates, guinea pigs and a few bird species, can't manufacture vitamin C in their bodies. It's water soluble and not retained in the body, so we need a constant replenishment from dietary sources to maintain adequate cellular and blood levels. Alarmingly, a high percentage of children consume minimal amounts of vitamin C. The Recommended Daily Allowance (RDA) for Americans is 90 milligrams a day for adult males and 75 milligrams a day for adult females. This recommendation, in my opinion, is quite low. I think that the optimal intake of dietary vitamin C is 350 milligrams or more from food. Just one orange supplies nearly a quarter of my daily dietary vitamin C recommendation—along with a host of other significant nutrients. But up to a third of us consume less than 60 milligrams of C daily.

It's fairly shocking that, given today's abundance of food, so many of us are deficient in a

ORANGES ARE A SOURCE OF:

- Vitamin C
- Fiber
- Folate
- Limonene
- Potassium
- Polyphenols
- Pectin

Sidekicks: Lemons, white and pink grapefruit, kumquats, tangerines, limes

Try to eat: 1 serving daily

vitamin that's crucial to good health. While we might not be seeing cases of scurvy, we're certainly seeing epidemics of heart disease, hypertension and cancer. The vitamin C in citrus, along with the other valuable nutrients, can play a major role in reducing these high levels of chronic disease.

Remember, vitamin C is rapidly excreted from the body. Adequate daily intake is critical for optimum health.

The precipitous decline in vitamin C levels has occurred over the past twenty years for largely unknown reasons. One possibility is that many if not most consumers have switched from orange juice in frozen concentrate form to ready-to-drink orange juices and orange drinks. As orange juice is the primary source of vitamin C in our diet, and the frozen form of orange juice is considerably higher in vitamin C than the ready-to-drink juices and drinks, this switch could be having a dramatic effect on our overall health.

We're not getting enough vitamin C from dietary sources, and oranges and orange juice are the prime source of this beneficial nutrient. There are various potent components of whole oranges that make them star performers in the fight against aging and disease. I tell all my patients to eat and drink more citrus. A simple fact: marginal vitamin C status has been linked to an increase in many causes of mortality, especially cancer and cardiovascular disease. A single navel orange, at only 64 calories, provides 23 percent of my daily dietary vitamin C recommendation of 350 milligrams or more. (That same navel orange provides 89 percent of the adult male RDA and 110 percent of the adult female RDA.) Only a limited number of fruits and vegetables are rich in vitamin C. Here are the top common sources of vitamin C. Try to make them a regular part of your daily diet.

Vegetables	**Milligrams of Vitamin C**
1 large yellow bell pepper	341
1 large red bell pepper	312
1 large orange bell pepper	238
1 large green bell pepper	132
1 cup raw chopped broccoli	79

Fruits	**Milligrams of Vitamin C**
1 common guava	165
1 cup fresh sliced strawberries	94
1 cup papaya cubes	87
1 navel orange	80
1 medium kiwi	75
1 cup cubed cantaloupe	68

Juices	**Milligrams of Vitamin C**
1 cup (8 ounces) Odwalla C Monster	350
1 cup fresh orange juice	128
1 cup orange juice from concentrate	97

For all intents and purposes, the only fruit or vegetable with a high level of vitamin C that's consistently consumed in the United States is orange juice. On average, adults with a desirable vitamin C intake consume more than one daily serving of dietary vitamin C.

The Power of Flavonoids

Flavonoids are a class of polyphenols found in fruits, vegetables, legumes, nuts, seeds, grains, tea and wine. There are more than five thousand flavonoids that have been identified and described in scientific literature, and we're learning more about them every day.

Citrus flavonoids, which are found in the fruit's tissue, juice, pulp and skin, are one of the reasons for the health-promoting attributes of citrus fruits and the reason that the whole fruit is so much more healthful than just the juice. Oranges provide more than 170 different phytochemicals and over 60 flavonoids. Two of the flavonoids in citrus—naringin in grapefruit and hesperidin in orange—occur only rarely in other plants and are thus essentially unique to citrus. Hesperidin seems to be the most important flavanone studied thus far, as animal studies have shown that it lowers high blood pressure and cholesterol. What is important to know is that most of this phytonutrient is found in the peel and inner white pulp of the orange, rather than in its liquid orange center, so this beneficial compound is too often removed by the processing of oranges into juice. Other phytonutrients in citrus include anthocyanins, hydroxycinnamic acids and a variety of other polyphenols. These nutrients all work together.

Rutin, a flavonoid found in citrus (and black currants), has an anti-inflammatory effect, possesses antiviral activity and helps protect capillaries from age-related "breakdown."

The power of citrus flavonoids is dazzling. They're antioxidant and antimutagenic. The latter refers to their ability to prevent cells from mutating and initiating one of the first steps in the development of cancer and other chronic diseases. This is accomplished by their apparent ability to absorb ultraviolet light, protect DNA and interact with carcinogens. Citrus flavonoids have been shown to inhibit cancer cell growth, strengthen capillaries and act as anti-inflammatories. They are also antiallergenic, antitumor, antiviral and antimicrobial. Flavonoid intake is inversely associated with the incidence of heart attack and stroke as well as a host of other ailments.

The Curative Power of Citrus

The vitamin C and other phytonutrients in oranges also seem to be of benefit in preventing asthma, osteoarthritis and rheumatoid arthritis—all inflammatory conditions. Free-radical damage to cellular structures and other molecules can result in painful inflammation as the body tries to clear out the damaged parts. Vitamin C, which plays a role in preventing the free-radical damage that triggers the inflammatory cascade, is associated with reduced severity of these three conditions.

In one study, diets high in vitamin C appeared to decrease the risk of an inflammatory joint condition called "inflammatory polyarthritis." Inflammatory polyarthritis is a form of rheumatoid arthritis. It usually involves two or more joints. Compared with people whose diets were highest in vitamin C, subjects in a study whose diets were lowest in vitamin C had three times the risk of inflammatory polyarthritis.

Interesting recent research on animals shows promise that citrus fruits could also play a helpful role in lowering the risk for the development of diabetes. In this study, two of the polyphenols in citrus—hesperidin and naringenin—significantly lowered blood glucose levels. When compared with the control groups, the animals consuming these polyphenols enjoyed a 20 percent reduction (hesperidin) and a 30 percent reduction (naringenin) after five weeks of supplementation. There was also a favorable increase in insulin and leptin levels, and several other studies have shown that people with type II diabetes have significantly lower leptin levels than nondiabetic patients. Remember that lower leptin levels are associated with an increase in obesity.

While further studies in humans are needed, it is always encouraging to be reminded that in the natural whole-foods pharmacy of SuperFoods there are phytochemicals that show great potential to decrease rates of chronic disease, and to prove useful in treating disease.

Perhaps vitamin C is most well known for helping to prevent the common cold. It turns out that the evidence supports this claim. One cup (8 ounces) of orange juice has been shown in studies to help maintain a healthy immune system, which can reduce susceptibility to illness. Studies also report that vitamin C may help shorten the duration or lessen the severity of a cold.

Oranges and Cardiovascular Health

We are certain that an orange a day promotes cardiovascular health. The Framingham Nurses' Health Study found that drinking one daily glass of orange juice reduced the risk of stroke by 25 percent. Countless other studies have confirmed similar benefits from regular consumption of citrus. We're beginning to understand that, as with so many SuperFoods, it's the synergy of multiple foods and the variety of nutrients they contain that combine to amplify and intensify individual benefits.

For example, we know that oranges are rich in vitamin C. They are also rich in flavonoids, such as hesperidin, that work to revive vitamin C after it has quenched a free radical. In other words, the hesperidin strengthens and amplifies the effect of vitamin C in your body. In an interesting human clinical trial, orange juice was shown to elevate HDL ("good") cholesterol while lowering LDL ("bad") cholesterol.

FIBER IS KEY

The fiber in oranges is another major contributor to heart health. Citrus fruit (especially tangerines) are one of the richest sources of high-quality pectin—a type of dietary fiber.

Pectin is a major component of the kind of fiber that is known to lower cholesterol. Pectin is also helpful in stabilizing blood sugar. A single orange provides 3 grams of fiber, and dietary fiber has been associated with a wide range of health benefits. About 35 percent of Americans consume their fruit only in juice form. In most cases, their health would benefit if they would add whole fruit whenever possible.

✪ **The concentration of vitamin C in orange pulp is twice that found in the peel and ten times that found in the juice. Bottom line: Eat the pulp and buy high-pulp juice.**

RICH IN FOLATE

Oranges also help prevent cardiovascular disease by supplying folate, also called "folacin" or "folic acid," when used in supplementary form. Folate is one of the B vitamins. The total folic acid content in the average diet has been found to be below the recommended daily allowances, and mild-to-moderate folate deficiency is common. In fact, folate deficiency is known to be among the most common vitamin deficiencies in the world. This is unfortunate, as we're learning more every day about the importance of this nutrient.

We know that dietary folate can play an important role in the prevention of cardiovascular

Pectin, the dietary fiber that's so effective in helping to reduce cholesterol, is present in large amounts in the white lining of citrus fruit (it's known as albedo). An easy way to increase your pectin intake is to eat the white pith. I always eat the "white stuff" on the inside of orange or tangerine rinds, scooping up a little of the orange color as well in order to boost my limonene intake.

disease; it is essential for the maintenance of normal DNA and also plays a role in the prevention of colon and cervical cancers, and possibly even breast cancer.

Folate plays a very important role in lowering blood concentrations of homocysteine. Homocysteine is an amino acid by-product of protein metabolism, and its role in cardiovascular disease is significant. High levels of homocysteine have been implicated in cardiovascular disease and even vascular disease of the eye.

In one study at Harvard, men with slightly elevated levels of homocysteine were three times more likely to have heart attacks than those with normal levels.

A large U.S. government–sponsored study in 2002 found that there was an inverse risk for heart attack and stroke among people who consumed the most folate: the more folate, the lower the risk. Folate works with the other B vitamins—B12 and B6 and probably betaine (a plant-derived compound that seems to lower homocysteine)—to remove homocysteine from your circulatory system. The homocysteine that is allowed to build up in your body can damage your blood vessels and ultimately precipitate a "cardiovascular event."

Interestingly, there is also evidence that increased folate intake can actually improve heart health in people who have already developed heart disease.

Another study also gave ample evidence that citrus is an important factor in preventing cardiovascular disease, primarily due to the folate in citrus.

Prevents Cholesterol Oxidation

Citrus fruit can also help to mitigate cardiovascular disease because of its ability to prevent the oxidation of cholesterol. Free radicals oxidize cholesterol. Only after being oxidized does cholesterol stick to the artery walls, building up in plaques that may eventually grow large enough to impede or fully block blood flow, or rupture to cause a heart attack or stroke. Since vitamin C can neutralize free radicals, it can help prevent the oxidation of cholesterol.

In one interesting animal study, hamsters with diet-induced high cholesterol were fed a diet that included 1 percent polymethoxylated flavones (PMFs)—a class of compounds found in citrus peels—and it was found that their blood levels of LDL ("bad") cholesterol were reduced by 32 to 40 percent. This result led researchers to speculate that the PMFs in citrus could lower cholesterol more effectively than statin drugs, and without side effects.

PMFs, including nobiletin, are found exclusively in citrus fruit. The Dancy tangerine reportedly has the highest PMF total—about five times the amount found in other sweet orange varieties. Nobiletin and other PMFs also exhibit anti-inflammatory, antimutagenic and anticancer properties.

While more research needs to be done on this, it does argue for the value of consuming well-washed citrus peel in a variety of foods.

POTASSIUM HELPS TOO

The potassium in citrus works to lower blood pressure and this, too, lowers the risk of cardiovascular disease.

A low intake of vitamin C can double the risk of hip fracture.

Citrus and Stroke

Citrus seems to have a protective ability against stroke. In the Men's Health Professionals Follow-Up Study, citrus and citrus juice were major contributors to the stroke-risk reduction from fruits and vegetables. It has been estimated that drinking one glass of orange juice daily may lower the risk of stroke in healthy men by 25 percent while the risk is reduced only 11 percent from other fruits.

It's very interesting that consumption of vitamin C in supplement form does not appear to have the same benefits as the whole fruit when it comes to stroke prevention. This suggests that there must be some other protective substances in citrus juices to account for their power to protect from strokes. The current assumption at this point is that it's the power of the polyphenols that make the difference. Another reason to rely on whole foods for optimal nutrition! On the other hand, more than 350 to 400 milligrams a day of supplemental vitamin C for a period of at least ten years seems to be an effective means of lowering your risk of developing cataracts. (This is one instance where supplements do work.)

In one study, drinking about two glasses of orange juice a day (about 500 milliliters) increased the vitamin C concentrations in the blood by 40 to 64 percent.

Oranges and Cancer

Recent news from researchers has demonstrated that oranges can play a significant role in preventing cancer.

We also know, for example, that the Mediterranean diet, which includes a considerable amount of citrus, is associated with a low incidence of cancers of the breast, lung, pancreas, colon, rectum and cervix. Indeed, citrus fruits have been found to contain numerous known anticancer agents—possibly more than any other food. The National Cancer Institute calls oranges a complete package of every natural anticancer inhibitor known. As you might suspect, the anticancer power of oranges is most effective when the whole fruit is eaten: It seems that the anticancer components of oranges work synergistically to amplify one another's effects.

FIBER HELPS PREVENT CANCER TOO

The soluble fiber, or pectin, which is so effective for heart health, is also an anticancer agent. It contains antagonists of growth factors, which in the future may be shown to have a positive effect decreasing the growth of tumors. We know that in animals pectin has been shown to inhibit the metastasis of prostate and melanoma cancers.

LEARNING ABOUT LIMONENE

One particular phytonutrient has attracted attention lately as a health-promoting agent. Amazingly, we routinely throw out this most potent part of the orange. In the oil of the peel of citrus fruits is a phytonutrient known as limonene. Oranges, mandarins, lemons and limes contain significant amounts of limonene in the peel and smaller quantities in the pulp. Limonene stimulates our antioxidant detoxification enzyme system, thus helping to stop cancer before it can even begin. (It's reassuring to know that a natural chemopreventive phytonutrient can work to prevent the process of carcinogenesis at the earliest stages.) Limonene also reduces the activity of proteins that can trigger abnormal cell growth. Limonene has blocking and suppressing actions that, at least in animals, actually cause regression of tumors.

One study of people in Arizona found that those who used citrus peels in cooking reduced their risk of squamous cell carcinoma by 50 percent. We've long known that Mediterranean people suffer lower rates of certain cancers than

CONSUMER-ACTION ALERT

Ask manufacturers to put lemon peel in lemonade like they do in Europe for an extra boost of health-promoting limonene.

others, and researchers now believe this can partly be ascribed to their regular consumption of citrus peel. Try the Mediterranean lemonade at the end of this chapter for a great limonene boost.

And, by the way, orange juice does contain some limonene but not nearly as much as the peel. Fresh-squeezed juice has the most limonene, along with other nutrients, and orange juice pulp has 8 to 10 percent more limonene than juice with no pulp.

There's lots of nutritional power in the skin of citrus, but if you're going to eat it, be sure to wash it carefully with warm water and a little liquid soap or, better yet, buy organic citrus. Some people occasionally get contact dermatitis from the limonene in citrus peel.

THE IMPORTANCE OF VITAMIN C

Vitamin C, which is abundantly available in oranges, also plays a role in fighting cancer.

Cancer begins in the body long before any sign or symptom indicates the disease is growing and spreading. One instigator of cancer is DNA that is damaged by free radicals. One of the functions of vitamin C is to protect the DNA from free-radical damage and prevent cancer before it even begins.

One study called "The Health Benefits of Citrus Fruits," which was released by an Australian research group, the Commonwealth Scientific and Industrial Research Organisation (CSIRO), reviewed forty-eight studies showing that a diet high in citrus fruits provides impressive protection against some kinds of cancer.

The evidence seems to indicate that citrus can be particularly helpful in preventing the development of DNA damage and possibly cancer in areas of the body where cellular turnover is particularly rapid, such as the digestive system.

Thus citrus shows evidence of lowering the risk for esophageal and oropharyngeal/laryngeal (mouth, larynx and pharynx) cancers as well as stomach cancers. Diets that are rich in citrus fruits can lessen the risk for these cancers by as much as 50 percent.

Vitamin C also protects against nitrosamines, cancer-causing agents found in food that are thought to be responsible for instigating cancers of the mouth, stomach, and colon. One study of Swiss men found that those who died of any type of cancer had vitamin C concentrations about 10 percent lower than those who died from other causes.

There's also evidence that citrus can act to help reduce your risk of developing lung cancer. We know that consuming foods rich in beta-cryptoxanthin—the orange-red carotenoids that are found in high amounts in oranges (as well as in corn, pumpkin, papaya, tangerines and red bell peppers)—may significantly lower lung cancer risk.

In one study, dietary and lifestyle data was collected from 63,257 adults in China over eight years. During this time, 482 cases of lung cancer were diagnosed. However, those eating the most cryptoxanthin-rich foods showed a 27 percent reduction in lung cancer risk. It was also found that even smokers who ate the most cryptoxanthin-rich foods enjoyed a 37 percent reduced risk of lung cancer when compared with smokers who ate the least amount of these foods.

Citrus peel and the white membrane beneath it are a major source of dietary pectin. Dietary pectin plays a role in decreasing LDL ("bad") cholesterol, glucose and insulin levels.

Vitamin C Supplementation

I prefer whole foods for nutrients rather than relying on supplements. However, even adults consuming five servings of fruits and vegetables daily often consume less than 100 milligrams of vitamin C a day, so it's appropriate to take vitamin

C supplements if you desire. Keep in mind that your body can't tell the difference between vitamin C from food and ascorbic acid made in the lab, but vitamin C in foods has polyphenols (bioflavonoids) that amplify its effect. For this reason, it's best to get ascorbic acid with added bioflavonoids, giving yourself a better chance of benefiting from the whole antioxidant network.

Remember that there's a limit to how much vitamin C your body can absorb at a time, so it's best to take, say, a 250-milligram supplement in the morning and a 250-milligram supplement in the afternoon rather than a 500- or 1,000-milligram supplement at one time.

If you do take supplements, be sure to keep your daily supplement intake below the Food and Nutrition Board's tolerable upper limit of 2,000 milligrams a day. In my opinion, 1,000 milligrams of supplemental vitamin C is more than enough to optimize health benefits from this vitamin.

Comparing Grapefruits

Here's an interesting breakdown of two sidekicks, white versus pink grapefruit, from a nutritional standpoint. *It's based on one-half grapefruit...*

	White grapefruit	*Pink grapefruit*
Calories	39	37
Vitamin C	39 mg	47 mg
Potassium	175 mg	159 mg
Lycopene	0	1.8 mg
Beta-carotene	trace	.7 mg
Beta cryptozanthin	0	trace
Lutein/zeaxanthin	0	trace
Alpha-carotene	trace	trace
Flavonoids	present	present

Grapefruit juice increases the bioavailability of certain drugs. It's believed that one of the flavonoids in grapefruit—likely naringin—causes this. Check with your health-care provider if you are on oral medications to see if grapefruit juice will interfere.

Oranges in the Kitchen

Citrus fruit—along with cherries, grapes and ten other fruits—won't ripen after picking. And a bright orange color doesn't necessarily mean ripe: Oranges are routinely gassed and dyed for cosmetic reasons. Splotches of green on an orange are nothing to worry about.

The heavier and smaller the fruit (and, usually, the thinner the skin), the more juice it contains. You'll also get more juice out of a lemon or orange if you let it get to room temperature and roll it on the counter before juicing it.

Whole oranges can be stored either in the fridge or at room temperature. They'll last about two weeks. Don't store them in plastic bags as they can develop mold.

If you have an abundance of oranges, juice them, freeze the juice in ice cube trays and store it in the freezer. Don't forget to zest oranges before juicing and save the zest to use in a variety of recipes.

The amount of vitamin C in 8 ounces of orange juice can vary from about 80 to about 140 milligrams, depending on the oranges and their ripeness, and on how they were processed and shipped. Heat, including pasteurization, reduces the nutrient content of juice. Check the date stamped on the carton of juice before you buy: It will stay fresh for two to four weeks once opened.

Orange juice begins to lose vitamin C (and other nutrients) from the moment it's squeezed, but because the C is so abundant, as long as the juice tastes fresh, it's probably providing you with

Discovered by a Canadian housewife who borrowed one of her husband's woodworking tools and was delighted with the results when she used it to zest a lemon, the Microplane zester makes it very easy to zest any citrus. The zesters are sold in many kitchen stores and online.

You can save the zest you make in plastic bags in the freezer to use in a variety of recipes.

adequate amounts. One trick for revitalizing the C content of orange juice is to squeeze a lemon into the carton.

Be sure to read the labels on juices: Many contain more sugar or corn syrup than juice. Only buy 100 percent fruit juice.

While whole fruits are the best choice, there are times when you can shop for another form of citrus—something to spread on your toast. Citrus marmalade can be good for you: The flavonoids found in citrus fruit, which help strengthen capillaries and enhance the effects of vitamin C, survive the manufacturing process when being made into marmalade, as do many of the antioxidants and liminoids. The pectin, the soluble fiber in citrus fruit that sets marmalade, has cholesterol-lowering abilities. It's a better choice than butter on your muffin or toast!

Get some citrus in your life...

- Eat an orange, tangerine or clementine out of hand daily. Keep a few on hand in the kitchen for quick snacks.
- Add mandarin orange segments to a spinach salad with some chopped red onion. Look for canned mandarin oranges packaged with as little sugar as possible.
- Add orange juice to a fruit smoothie.
- Slice oranges in order to accompany grilled meats.
- Broiled grapefruit halves are delicious. Drizzle each half with a tablespoon of honey and sprinkle with cinnamon, then broil for a few minutes until golden.
- Add thinly sliced oranges on top of fish before broiling or baking.
- Keep some orange and/or lemon zest in your freezer...put it into cakes, cookies, muffins or even drinks for a refreshing boost of nutrition and flavor. Sprinkle it on yogurt, into fruit salads and even chicken salad. Use citrus zest in hot tea. Citrus juice adds a flavor boost to many dishes.
- Bring back orange wedges as a refresher for athletes, young and old. They give a much-needed boost of antioxidants and vitamin C on the playing field or at the gym.

Kumquats are the smallest of the citrus fruits. I'm fortunate enough to have two kumquat bushes outside my front door and when they're in season, I pop one or two a day into my mouth. The thin, sweet rind is jammed with powerful phytonutrients. You can find them in supermarkets, mostly in the winter.

Pinch the fruit between your fingers before eating; you'll release the juice and get a blast of sweet and tart from this little nutrition powerhouse.

See our Shopping Lists (pages 211, 212, 219, 220 and 223) for some recommended products.

POMEGRANATES

Did you know that it may have been a pomegranate—not an apple—that tempted Eve in the Garden of Eden? Ancient and beloved, the pomegranate figures prominently in history and mythology. The art, literature and culinary traditions of Europe, the Middle East, Africa and India all revere this mighty garnet-colored jewel. For the Chinese, pomegranates have traditionally symbolized longevity, immortality and abundance, perhaps because of the roughly eight hundred seeds that each pomegranate contains.

One of the joys of the autumn season, pomegranates are not only beautiful and exotic-looking, but also have health benefits that have long been touted. Pomegranates can range in color from yellow orange to red to deep purple. Rich in potassium, vitamin C, polyphenols and vitamin B6, pomegranates are real phytochemical powerhouses. Pomegranate juice may have two to three times the antioxidant power of equal amounts of green tea or red wine. In one study, pomegranate juice was a potent fighter in the battle against atherosclerosis. As little as one-quarter cup of pomegranate juice daily may improve cardiovascular health by reducing oxidation of LDL ("bad") cholesterol. In addition, animal studies suggest that pomegranates may cause regression of atherosclerotic lesions. So don't avoid pomegranates just because it takes some work to get to the seeds.

Pomegranates possess very potent anti-inflammatory phytochemicals, and consumption of pomegranate juice has been shown to lower blood pressure in hypertensive volunteers. Studies of several fruit juices and wines have reported the highest polyphenol concentration in pomegranate juice followed by red wine and cranberry juice.

POMEGRANATES ARE A SOURCE OF:

- Vitamin B6
- Vitamin C
- Polyphenols
- Potassium

Sidekicks: Plums

Try to eat: 4 to 8 ounces of 100 percent pomegranate juice multiple times a week or any amount of seeds

If you've never tried a pomegranate, autumn is the ideal time. Select a pomegranate by weight: The seeds represent about half the weight of the fruit and so the heavier the fruit the better. The skin should be shiny without any cracks. You can store your pomegranate in a cool place for about a month, but it will keep in the fridge for up to two months.

Pomegranate juice, mixed with seltzer and a slice of lemon or lime, can be enjoyed year-round. This cocktail will give you powerful antioxidants.

What do you do with pomegranates? The best way is to use the juice for sauces, vinaigrettes and marinades. The whole seeds can be added to salads and desserts, or as a garnish for meat or fish dishes. To get to the seeds, cut the top off the fruit and slice the rind vertically (from top to bottom) in about four places. Then put the fruit in a bowl of water. Peel away the sections of the fruit, releasing the seeds from the bitter white membrane. The seeds will sink to the bottom of the water and the remaining part of the fruit will float. Skim off and discard the floating bits and pour the seeds into a colander to rinse. You can then use the seeds in a recipe or put them in a blender or food processor to make juice. If you freeze the seeds first, they'll yield more juice. Each medium fruit yields about a half cup of pomegranate juice.

If you want the benefits of pomegranate without the fuss of preparation, you can buy pomegranate juice such as Pom Wonderful. Avoid brands that contain added sugar. Liven up your recipes with pomegranate molasses, a highly concentrated form of pomegranate juice. It's a traditional ingredient in Middle Eastern dishes and can be found in specialty food markets.

See our Shopping Lists (pages 211, 212 and 219) for some recommended products.

Pumpkin

Most people think of pumpkin as a decorative gourd rather than a highly nutritious and desirable food. We buy a pumpkin to carve at Halloween when it serves as a glorified candleholder that's disposed of once the trick or treaters go home. We only eat it once a year, if at all, in a Thanksgiving pie.

This is unfortunate because the squash known as pumpkin is one of the most nutritionally valuable foods known to man. (By the way, pumpkin is not a vegetable; it's a fruit. Like melons, it's a member of the gourd family.)

Moreover, it's inexpensive, available year round in canned form, incredibly easy to incorporate into recipes, high in fiber and low in calories. All in all, pumpkin is a real nutrition superstar.

Native Americans cherished the pumpkin and used both the flesh and the seeds as a dietary staple—the former as a reliable food, fresh roasted or dried, and the latter as medicine. By the second Thanksgiving, pumpkin had become one of the main attractions of the annual feast. In fact, the early settlers made a version of pumpkin pudding that resembles one of my favorite recipes, my friend Patty's Pumpkin Pudding (page 169), although I doubt it was as delicious. They took a pumpkin, filled it with milk, spices and honey, and baked it in hot ashes.

The Power of Pumpkin

The nutrients in pumpkin are really world class. Pumpkin packs an abundance of disease-fighting nutrients, including potassium, pantothenic acid, folate, magnesium, niacin and vitamins B1, C and E. The key nutrient that boosts pumpkin to the top of the *SuperFoods Rx* list is the synergistic combination of carotenoids. Pumpkin contains one of the richest supplies of bioavailable carotenoids known to man. Indeed, a half-cup serving of pumpkin gives you *more than two times* my recommended daily dietary intake of alpha-carotene and *100 percent* of my recommended daily dietary goal of beta-carotene. When you realize the tremendous benefits of these nutrients, you'll see why pumpkin is such an extraordinary nutrition superstar.

Mix canned pumpkin with low-fat or nonfat yogurt or with applesauce. You can drizzle it with buckwheat honey and a few raisins. Use canned pumpkin in recipes for soups, breads and muffins.

Carotenoids are fat-soluble compounds that occur in a variety of plants and are deep orange, yellow or red in color. They protect the plants from sun damage while they help them attract birds and insects for pollination. So far scientists have identified about six hundred carotenoids, and more than fifty of them commonly occur in our diet.

Not all dietary carotenoids are efficiently absorbed. As a result, only thirty-four carotenoids have currently been found in our blood and

PUMPKIN IS A SOURCE OF:

- Alpha-carotene
- Vitamins C and E
- Beta-carotene
- Potassium
- High fiber
- Magnesium
- Low calories
- Pantothenic acid

Sidekicks: Carrots, butternut squash, sweet potatoes, orange bell peppers

Try to eat: ½ cup 5 to 7 days per week

human breast milk. The six most common carotenoids found in human tissue include beta-carotene, lycopene, lutein, zeaxanthin, alpha-carotene and beta cryptoxanthin.

Both alpha- and beta-carotene and beta cryptoxanthin are what's known as pro–vitamin A carotenoids, which means that the body can convert them to vitamin A. As opposed to animal sources of vitamin A, these plant sources cannot deliver a toxic amount of the vitamin.

DAILY CAROTENOID RECOMMENDATION

The Institute of Medicine's Food and Nutrition Board is charged with setting the recommended daily allowances for various nutrients.

While they have recognized that "higher blood concentrations of beta-carotene and other carotenoids obtained from foods are associated with lower risk of several chronic diseases," as yet they have been unable to arrive at a recommended daily intake of carotenoids.

In the meantime, I've come up with recommendations, based on all the available peer-reviewed literature, that I feel ensures that you are consuming the optimum daily protective amounts of these nutrients.

- Alpha-carotene: 2.4 milligrams or more from food sources
- Beta-carotene: 6 milligrams or more from food sources
- Lucopene: 22 milligrams or more from food sources
- Lutein and zeaxanthin: 12 milligrams or more from food sources
- Beta cryptoxanthin: 1 milligram or more from food sources

Carotenoids are concentrated in a wide variety of tissues, where they help protect us from free radicals, modulate our immune response, enhance cell-to-cell communication and possibly stimulate production of naturally occurring detoxification enzymes. Carotenoids also play a major role in protecting the skin and eyes (from cataracts and macular degeneration) from the damaging effects of ultraviolet light.

The two carotenoids that are richly present in pumpkin—beta- and alpha-carotene—are particularly potent phytonutrients.

Beta-carotene, which began attracting attention in the 1980s, is one of the world's most studied antioxidants. The word *carotenoid*—derived from *carrot*—comes from the yellow-orange color of these nutrients, which at first were linked primarily with carrots. Carrots (and sweet potatoes) also contain rich amounts of beta-carotene. It's abundant in fruits and vegetables, and we've long known that the beta-carotene in foods helps prevent many diseases.

Pumpkin Reduces Cancer Risk

There's ample evidence that consuming carotenoid-rich foods reduces the risk of various types of cancer, including those of the lung, colon, bladder, cervical, breast, prostate and skin.

In one recent study, dietary and lifestyle data collected over eight years from 63,257 adults in Shanghai, China, was reviewed, and it revealed that those who ate the most beta-cryptoxanthin—an orange-red carotenoid—enjoyed a 27 percent lower risk of developing lung cancer. Even the smokers in the analyzed group were found to have a 37 percent lower risk of developing lung cancer when they ate a diet rich in carotenoids compared with those eating the least amount of carotenoids.

Another study, combining data from the Nurses' Health Study and the Health Professional

Follow-up Study, found a significant risk reduction for lung cancer in subjects with a high intake of lycopene and alpha-carotene.

Carotenoids also seem to lessen the risk of breast cancer. At least one study of premenopausal women reported a significant reduction in breast cancer risk in females with an increased dietary intake of alpha- and beta-carotene, lutein and zeaxanthin, and in another study, high lycopene intake was associated with a reduced risk of breast cancer.

Yet another study found an inverse association between increasing levels of carotenoid intake and bladder cancer risk. This same study also suggests that a high carotenoid intake can have special chemopreventive benefits for those people susceptible to DNA damage.

Pumpkin seems to have a dual ability to fight colon cancer. The rich supply of fiber along with the beta-carotene has an ability to prevent cancer-causing chemicals from attacking colon cells. This is one reason why diets that are high in fiber-rich foods as well as beta-carotene have been found to reduce colon cancer risk.

PUMPKIN SEEDS

Pumpkin seeds—often called pepitas, "little seeds" in Spanish—are a nutritional bargain. They're rich in vitamin E, iron, magnesium, potassium and zinc, and are a good plant-based source of omega-6 and omega-3 fatty acids. You can buy them roasted or do it yourself. If you're removing seeds from a fresh pumpkin, remove any pulp or strings from them and rinse them in fresh water. Air-dry them on a cookie sheet overnight. Drizzle with a bit of olive oil and some sea salt and roast at 350° F for 15 to 20 minutes. Sprinkle them with curry or chili powder if you like. Cool completely and store in an airtight container.

However, it was the connection between beta-carotene and lung-cancer prevention that led to some fascinating studies. These groundbreaking studies on beta-carotene were among the first indications that supplements were not the *complete* answer in preventing disease and, indeed, it's this finding that's at the heart of SuperFoods: Whole foods are the answer to disease prevention and health promotion.

Whole Foods Are Better Than Supplements

Scientists reasoned that if the beta-carotene in foods helped to prevent lung cancer, it followed that a beta-carotene supplement would do the same. Unfortunately, and shockingly, two important studies showed that, to the contrary, smokers who took beta-carotene supplements showed an increase in lung cancer.

Perhaps you recall those studies. *They made front-page news around the world...*

In 1996, a Finnish study on 29,000 male smokers, published in the *New England Journal of Medicine,* showed that those who smoked and took beta-carotene supplements were 18 percent more likely to develop lung cancer than those who had not taken supplements.

In the U.S., the Carotene and Retinal Efficacy Trial (CARET) study, which was published in the *Journal of the National Cancer Institute,* was halted almost two years before its expected completion date because of the negative effects of the supplemental beta-carotene and vitamin A on smokers when compared with subjects taking a placebo.

The news of the surprising outcomes was stunning to those who follow health trends. They had become accustomed to regular positive reports that individual micronutrients help to prevent disease. What had gone wrong?

QUICK CAROTENOID BOOSTS

To get your daily dose of carotenoids, enjoy a sliced orange or red bell pepper, peeled baby carrots (which can be quickly steamed, microwaved or eaten raw), a handful of fresh or dried apricots or prunes, a slice of cantaloupe or watermelon, a slice of mango or a persimmon. One other carotenoid boost that everyone loves: Häagen-Dazs mango sorbet.

In simplest terms, the beta-carotene found in foods, working synergistically with the other nutrients present in that food, have a very different effect on the body than a single nutrient isolated from its web of assisting and augmenting synergistic partners. The carotenoids, like many nutrients, work best as a team; break up the team and results can be unpredictable.

DOSAGE IS DIFFERENT

Moreover, the dose of a nutrient in supplement form differs from the dose you'd get from food. For example, we know that 10 milligrams of beta-carotene daily from carrots is good for you and helps prevent disease. But if you give someone 20 milligrams of beta-carotene in a pill, the dose may behave more like a drug than a nutrient, with unintended and possibly adverse health consequences. Why? Because the absorption rate of beta-carotene in uncooked carrots is only about 10 percent. If you cook the carrot, the absorption rate of the beta-carotene in it goes up to about 29 percent. So if you're getting your beta-carotene from carrots, your body is only absorbing a percentage of it. You can't eat enough carrots to get a toxic dose. There is no toxic dose of carotenoids from carrots, pumpkin or other foods. In fact, the only known (harmless) side effect of ingested whole food carotenoids is an orange (beta-carotene) or reddish (lycopene) tinge to the skin.

On the other hand, if you take beta-carotene in supplemental form, your body is absorbing a very high percentage of this micronutrient. Not only is it suddenly a potentially, pharmacological dose of a nutrient, it's a dose that may throw off-balance the synergy of the other nutrients your body depends on to maintain health.

A Potent Heart Disease Fighter

Carotenoids have also shown great promise in their ability to lower rates of heart disease. In one thirteen-year-long study, researchers found a strong correlation between lower carotenoid concentrations in the blood and a higher rate of heart disease. As has frequently been found, the correlation between increased carotenoid consumption and decreased risk of heart disease was higher when all carotenoids, not just beta-carotene, were considered.

The carotenoids so richly present in pumpkin play a significant role in preventing cardiovascular disease. The beta-carotene in pumpkin and its sidekicks has powerful antioxidant and anti-inflammatory abilities.

Beta-carotene is able to prevent the oxidation of cholesterol and, since oxidized cholesterol is the kind that coats the walls of blood vessels and contributes to the risk of heart disease and stroke, a diet rich in beta-carotene would be expected to promote heart health. Indeed, studies have demonstrated this to be true.

A recent laboratory study demonstrates that beta-carotene can downregulate the pro-inflammatory Cox-2 pathway—in other words, suppress the activation of inflammation. This pathway is a major cause of inflammation and the same one that is disabled with non-steroidal anti-inflammatories like Advil and aspirin. Although further work is needed to verify the relevance of these cellular studies, this is the first promising report showing beta-carotene as a natural Cox-2 inhibitor or natural anti-inflammatory. This could help other conditions as well, like asthma, osteoarthritis and rheumatoid arthritis.

Another study examined the reasons for the declining life expectancy in central and eastern Europe. The decline seems to be largely the result of rising rates of cardiovascular disease. Traditional risk factors like smoking, hypertension, obesity, high dietary saturated-fat and cholesterol intake do not appear to explain this decrease in longevity. The researchers ultimately concluded that a diet low in foods containing folate and carotenoids—particularly beta-carotene and lutein/zeaxanthin—appears to be a contributing factor to the increased coronary risk observed in this part of the world.

Good News Concerning Diabetes

Beta-carotene, along with other carotenoids, may also prove to be helpful in preventing the free radical–caused complications of long-term diabetes and the increased risk for cardiovascular disease associated with this common illness.

ANTI-AGING AID

While beta-carotene has long been linked with health promotion, it's the bounty of alpha-carotene in pumpkin that makes it a real nutrition standout. The exciting news about alpha-carotene is that its presence in the body along with other key nutrients is reportedly inversely related to biological aging. In other words, the more alpha-carotene you eat, the slower your body shows signs of age.

FIBER-RICH

Pumpkin is also a terrific source of fiber. Most people aren't aware of the fiber content of canned pumpkin because it seems so creamy. Just one half-cup serving provides 5 grams of fiber—more than you're getting from most supermarket cereals.

A TIP FROM CHEF MARK: HOW TO TAME A WINTER SQUASH

Winter squash are very hard, requiring brute force to penetrate them, even with the sharpest knives. Here's how to tame one: Wash it well and place the whole squash on a parchment-lined baking sheet. Bake in a 325° F preheated oven 15 to 30 minutes, depending upon the size and variety, just until the skin is soft to the touch and the back of a spoon makes a slight indentation. Remove from the oven, and when cool enough to handle, cut in half, scoop out the seeds, then the pulp and proceed with your recipe.

Other Winter Squash

Pumpkin is not the only winter squash that's filled with beneficial carotenes. There are a number of winter squashes that are available in the market for most of the year that come close to pumpkin in their nutritional benefits. Don't make the mistake of thinking that all hard winter squashes taste alike. Not so. Try to experiment with different varieties. Most people are familiar with acorn squash, but it is often tasteless. Try butternut squash (which is highly nutritious and makes a great soup), buttercup squash (it looks like it's wearing a "hat" where the stem is), delicata squash (looks like a fat yellow-orange cucumber with green stripes) or hubbard squash (deep green, more rounded than an acorn squash).

There's a vast difference between an over-the-hill watery acorn squash and a fresh, delicious ripe one. Buy these squashes at farmers' markets where you know they'll be fresh since they come from local producers. *In any case, here are some tips for finding the best-tasting and most nutritious winter squashes…*

• A winter squash should be rock hard. If it's soft, it's either too young or too old. Test the skin—if it nicks easily, it's probably too young.

• Be sure to buy squash that has its stem on. Without the stem, bacteria can get into the squash.

• The skin should be somewhat dull. A shiny squash is either too young or has been treated with wax.

• A deep, rich color usually means a ripe squash. If the squash is dark green, you can still usually see the area that touches the ground and it should be a ripe color, not pale green.

• You'll find the most vivid colors at harvest time—usually late summer to fall. But later in the year, when the squash has been stored, it will be sweeter and more concentrated in flavor.

• Squash that comes from a cooler climate will often have more flavor and sweetness than one that grows in a warmer place. Check your supplier.

Pumpkin Sidekicks

While pumpkin is a flagship SuperFood, there are other terrific choices in this category that provide a bounty of carotenoids as well as other nutritional benefits. Carrots are perhaps the most popular. The nutrients in carrots are more bioavailable when cooked; so, while there's nothing wrong with eating raw carrots, you will get more nutritional benefit from them when they're cooked.

Sweet potatoes are another excellent source of beneficial carotenoids. Pierce them all over with a fork and pop them in the microwave for about five minutes if you don't have time to oven-bake them. If oven-baked, they begin to caramelize as they cook. A baked sweet potato doesn't even need butter—just a bit of salt and pepper. I often brown-bag half a baked sweet potato to eat cold at work. It also tastes great at room temperature if you don't have a microwave in the office to heat it up.

Baby carrots are great little bites that are rich in beta-carotene and alpha-carotene. They're not really "babies"; they are the clever marketing idea of a farmer in California who searched for a way to use up his broken or misshapen regular carrots.

They're easy to use and worth the higher price if they help you serve carrots frequently. Put them out with a healthy dip for an after-school snack. Stick some in lunchboxes. Keep a bowl in the fridge to satisfy snackers.

Pumpkin in the Kitchen

It's all very well that pumpkin is such a nutritional powerhouse, but that doesn't count for much if every time you wanted some pumpkin you had to wrestle one of those big orange gourds into the kitchen.

A winter squash, pumpkin is usually available fresh only in the autumn and early winter and the rest of the year you might have trouble finding one. But one of the best features of pumpkin is that it's readily available all year long in an inexpensive canned form.

Want to boost your carotenoid intake? *Here are some top sources…*

Alpha-carotene	**Milligrams**
Pumpkin (cooked, 1 cup)	13
Carrots (cooked, 1 cup)	6.4
Butternut squash (cooked, 1 cup)	.3
Orange bell pepper (1 cup)	.3
Collards (cooked, 1 cup)	.2

Beta-carotene	**Milligrams**
Sweet potato (cooked, 1 cup)	19
Pumpkin (cooked, 1 cup)	18.8
Carrots (cooked, 1 cup)	12.5
Butternut squash (cooked, 1 cup)	9.4
Spinach (cooked, 1 cup)	9.4

Canned pumpkin is one of those foods that give the lie to the notion that fresh is always best. Not only is it sometimes difficult if not impossible to find fresh pumpkin, canned pumpkin is actually *more* nutritious (except for those pumpkin seeds—see box on page 76). It's also rich in fiber. Canned pumpkin should be a staple in every pantry. It can be called upon at a moment's notice to provide a nourishing soup, casserole or dessert, or even a delicious instant snack when mixed with some yogurt and perhaps nuts and honey. Canned pumpkin puree (don't get it mixed up with "pumpkin pie filling," which has added sugar and spices), has been cooked down to reduce the water content that you'd find in fresh pumpkin. At only 83 calories per cup, it offers more than 400 percent of my recommendation of alpha-carotene and close to 300 percent of my beta-carotene recommendation, as well as almost half of the iron requirement for adult men and postmenopausal women.

Prepare squash by cutting them in half, drizzling on a bit of honey and a sprinkling of black pepper, and baking in a 350° F oven until the flesh is soft.

Sliced orange bell peppers are a good addition to any salad or platter of crudités. I find that kids really love these crunchy treats, and a plate set out in the evening will disappear. Serve them with your favorite healthy yogurt dip.

Sweet potatoes can jazz up a simple meal. Peel and dice them, then toss the cubes in some extra virgin olive oil, dust with cumin, freshly ground pepper and some ground chiles if you like. Roast them on a baking sheet in a 425° F oven for about 20 minutes until they're tender. Drizzle with fresh lime juice before serving.

See our Shopping Lists (pages 212, 214 and 219) for some recommended products.

Wild Salmon

Once upon a time (actually not very long ago), people came to believe that fat was a murderous monster and the ideal diet was completely devoid of any fat whatsoever. It was the era of fat-free. Fat-free salad dressings, nonfat cakes and cookies, no-fat soups and casseroles. Even bottles of fruit juices proudly trumpeted "fat-free food" on their labels. (Was there ever a fatty cranberry juice?) Why this fear of fat?

It all started as a well-intentioned campaign to improve health. The second half of the twentieth century saw an alarming epidemic of heart disease. Countless studies sought reasons for this epidemic. It became clear that smoking, a sedentary lifestyle and a high-fat diet were linked to the rising tide of cardiovascular disease. The lesson was obvious: To reduce your risk of heart disease, a major killer, you should cut as much fat as possible out of your diet. Cholesterol became a household word and Americans became fat-phobic.

Four Types of Fat

It's taken years for the more complicated and interesting truth to emerge. First, research indicating that all fat is not bad began to reach the public. We all needed an education in dietary fat and, bit by bit, we got one. In a nutshell, we learned that we derive four basic types of fat from food: saturated fat, trans fat (partially hydrogenated oils), monounsaturated fat and polyunsaturated fat.

The news on saturated fat hasn't changed: Saturated fat—found primarily in red meat, full-fat dairy products, and some tropical oils—has well-established negative health effects, increasing your risk of diabetes, coronary heart disease, stroke, some cancers and obesity. One researcher, writing in the *Journal of the American Dietetic Association,* concluded that "reducing dietary intake of saturated fatty acids may prevent thousands of cases of coronary heart disease and save billions of dollars in related costs." There's little positive about saturated fat, and it should make up no more than seven percent of your fat calories per day.

Trans fats—listed on food labels as "partially hydrogenated vegetable oil"—are also bad, probably even worse than saturated fat. Trans fats were created by chemists seeking a fat that would store better than animal fats. They were an attempt to lengthen the shelf life of foodstuffs.

The average intake of trans-fatty acids from partially hydrogenated vegetable oils is currently about 3 percent of total calorie intake per day. Currently there is no recommended safe intake of these oils.

The Nurses' Health Study suggests that the incidence of type II diabetes could be reduced by 40 percent or more if these fats were consumed in their original, unhydrogenated form.

Remember, there *are* good fats. The good guys in the fat family are the monounsaturated fats—the kinds found in olive and canola oils. These fats not only protect your cardiovascular system, they also lower the risk of insulin resistance, a physiologic state that can lead to diabetes and possibly cancer.

Finally, we come to polyunsaturated fatty acids. Both omega-6 (linoleic, or LA, fat) and omega-3 (alpha linolenic, or ALA, fat) are so-called essential polyunsaturated fatty acids (EFAs). Our bodies cannot manufacture these two fats and therefore we must rely on dietary intake to avoid a deficiency in these essential (for life) fats. Omega-6 fatty acids are currently overabundant in the typical Western diet. They are present in corn, safflower, cottonseed and sunflower oils. Virtually no one in America is deficient in these ubiquitous fatty acids. If you look at almost any packaged food, you're going to see one of these oils as an ingredient.

Let's look for a minute at the omega-3 class of polyunsaturated fat. Omega-3 fats come in two distinct forms: plant derived (ALA) and largely marine species derived (EPA/DHA). With each passing month, additional studies are being published about the health benefits of omega-3s. Unfortunately, many Americans are currently deficient in the omega-3 class of essential fatty acids. Omega-3 fatty acids—the ones that help make salmon a SuperFood—haven't been included in adequate amounts in our diet, partly because of lack of knowledge on the part of the public and also because they've been "processed out" of our modern diet. This deficiency has long-term and disastrous health consequences for many people. Indeed, William S. Harris, writing in the *American Journal of Clinical Nutrition,* has said: "In terms of its potential impact on health in the Western world, the omega-3 story may someday be viewed as one of the most important in the history of modern nutritional science." Dr. Evan Cameron, from the Linus Pauling Institute, has said: "Our epidemic of heart disease and cancer may be the result of a fish oil deficiency so enormous we fail to recognize it." The bottom

WILD SALMON IS A SOURCE OF:

- Marine-derived omega-3 fatty acids
- B vitamins
- Calcium (when canned with bones)
- Selenium
- Vitamin D
- Potassium
- Protein
- Carotenoids

Sidekicks: Alaskan halibut, canned albacore tuna, sardines, herring, trout, sea bass, oysters, and clams

Try to eat: 3 to 4 ounces 2 to 4 times per week

line—it's not just okay to include omega-3 fatty acids in your diet, it's imperative to do so if you want to restore a critical balance in your body that is most likely out of whack.

Enter salmon. Salmon is one of the richest, tastiest, readily available sources of marine-derived omega-3 fatty acids. By including wild salmon (or its sidekicks) in your diet two to four times a week (see box on tuna, page 84) you should achieve optimal protection against a multitude of diseases that have been associated with low intakes of these critical fats.

The Critical Balance of EFAs

The key to EFAs—as with so many health issues—is balance. Your body can't function optimally without a balanced ratio of EFAs. The optimum balance of essential fatty acids is a balance of omega-6 to omega-3 that is somewhere between 1 to 1 and 4 to 1. Unfortunately, the typical Western diet contains 14 to 25 times more omega-6 than omega-3 fatty acids. This unbalanced ratio that most of us live with determines myriad biochemical events that affect our health. For example, too much omega-6 (the oil that dominates our typical diet) promotes an inflammatory state, which in turn increases your risk for blood clots and narrowing of blood vessels.

We now also know that without sufficient intake of omega-3 fatty acids, the body cannot adequately build an ideal cell membrane. Membranes that are poorly constructed are not capable of optimizing cellular health, which in turn increases your risk for a host of health problems, including stroke, heart attack, cardiac arrhythmias, some forms of cancer, insulin resistance—which can lead to diabetes—asthma, hypertension, age-related macular degeneration, chronic obstructive lung disease (COPE), autoimmune disorders, attention deficit hyperactivity disorder and depression. This list seems to encompass the major ailments of the twentieth century. Some scientists have claimed that the proliferation of these disorders is at least in part due to the lack of omega-3 fatty acids in our diet.

One report estimated that close to 99 percent of Americans do not consume enough omega-3 fatty acids, and 20 percent of us have such low levels of omega-3 fatty acids that they can't even be detected. This EFA deficiency is rarely noticed because the symptoms it produces are so vague. Dry skin, fatigue, brittle nails and hair, constipation, frequent colds, inability to concentrate, depression and joint pain can all result from lack of omega-3 fatty acids in the diet. Many of us live with these conditions, never dreaming that we

TIPS FOR INCREASING YOUR INTAKE OF OMEGA-3 FATTY ACIDS:

- Use omega-3 enriched eggs, such as Eggland's Best, Christopher Eggs or Country Hen eggs.
- Cook with canola oil rather than corn or safflower oil.
- Eat walnuts and soy nuts, pecans and pumpkin seeds.
- Sprinkle wheat germ and/or ground flaxseed meal on cereal and yogurt; add a tablespoon or two when baking.
- Eat wild salmon or its sidekicks two to four times per week.
- Look for salad dressings that contain some soybean or canola oil.
- Use walnut oil when you are preparing homemade salad dressings.
- Add ground flaxseed when baking muffins, breads and pancakes.
- Avoid processed foods, including packaged cakes, cookies and baked goods.

may be suffering from a nutritional deficiency that can ultimately cause serious chronic disease and even death.

Our Deteriorating Diet

The decline of omega-3 fatty acids in our diet is an interesting story. Up until the twentieth century, this group of fatty acids was abundant in our foods. Some scientists even postulate that it was the ingestion of omega-3 EFAs that allowed the brain to evolve to the next stage in human development. Not only found in cold-water fish, omega-3 fatty acids were available in green leafy foods (we eat one-third of the greens eaten by our ancestors) as well as meat from animals that fed on grass (rather than the grain-fed meat we now consume, which is low in omega-3 fatty acids). As foods became more processed, the amounts of omega-3 fatty acids diminished while the amounts of omega-6 fatty acids increased to today's dangerous ratios. In fact, seventy years ago, before solvent-extracted vegetable oils and corn-based animal husbandry, people were not exposed to the high intake of omega-6 fatty acids we experience today. As one researcher said, "We may well be experiencing the 'linoleic acid paradox' in which a supposedly healthy fatty acid (i.e., one that lowers total cholesterol) is associated with increasing rates of cancer, inflammatory and cardiovascular diseases during those same decades. Compounding and confounding this paradox are low intakes of ALA (plant-based omega-3 oils) and other omega-3 fish oils."

People who eat diets with the optimum balance of essential fatty acids manage to avoid many common ailments. Eskimos in Greenland first brought attention to the question of fat in the diet because they had little heart disease despite a diet high in fat (40 percent of their total calorie intake, which included more than 10 grams of EPA/DHA daily).

The Lyon Heart Study compared the effects of a modified Crete diet—one enriched with omega-3 fatty acids—and the American Heart Association diet. This landmark study showed a reduction of risk, 56 percent for total deaths and 61 percent for cancers, in the experimental group (which ate a diet high in ALA) compared to the control group.

The Japanese, who rely on a traditional diet of fish, are likewise protected from heart disease while their neighbors who farm and eat far less fish suffer higher levels of cardiovascular disease.

It's interesting to note that cultures that have high omega-3 consumption in fish have far less depression than those whose diet is dominated by omega-6 fatty acids.

In fact, in one fascinating epidemiological study, fish consumption was the most significant variable in comparing levels of depression and coronary heart disease.

The bottom line: There is a critical and optimal balance of omega-3 and omega-6 essential fatty acids, working with the nutritional cofactors of minerals, vitamins, phytonutrients, fiber, antioxidants and electrolytes, which is important in reducing the incidence of many of the degenerative diseases currently epidemic in Western countries.

WHAT ABOUT COD LIVER OIL?

Patients have asked me if a tablespoon of cod liver oil is the solution to low levels of omega-3 fatty acids. Yes and no. While it's true that cod liver oil contains a good dose of omega-3 fatty acids (which probably protected our grandparents from many ailments), it's also true that, in addition to tasting pretty awful, it may be contaminated by mercury and PCBs.

TUNA GUIDELINES

Canned tuna is a popular source of omega-3 EFAs. *Here are some tips on using canned tuna in your diet...*

- Buy albacore tuna—it's the richest tuna source of omega-3 EFAs.
- Buy tuna packed in spring water so you won't be getting extra fat.
- Low-salt canned tuna is best.
- Adults shouldn't eat more than one can of tuna a week because of the potential mercury content.
- Pregnant or nursing women, women of childbearing age and children should look at the Environmental Protection Agency Web site (*www.epa.gov/mercury/fish.html*) or call 888-SAFEFOOD before consuming tuna.

Benefits of Omega-3 Fatty Acids

Here are some of the benefits you can enjoy from increasing your omega-3 fatty-acid intake by following the SuperFoods recommendation and adding wild salmon and other cold-water fish to your diet...

• Reduce your risk of coronary artery disease. We know that omega-3 fatty acids help to increase your HDL ("good") cholesterol, reduce your blood pressure and stabilize your heartbeat, thus preventing one of the causes of fatal heart attacks: sudden cardiac arrhythmias. Omega-3 EFAs also act as blood thinners, reducing the "stickiness" of platelets that can lead to clots and stroke. In one study, patients who had a heart attack and who were given one gram per day of omega-3s had a 20 percent drop in total mortality, a 30 percent drop in death from cardiovascular disease and a 45 percent drop in sudden death compared with similar patients who were given nothing or vitamin E alone.

• Omega-3s also improve the ratio of good to bad cholesterol and lower triglycerides (another form of fat that may be more dangerous than elevated cholesterol).

• Salmon and its sidekicks also promote heart health by possibly lowering the risk of atrial fibrillation—one of the most common types of heart arrhythmias. In a 12-year study of 4,815 people over age 65, it was found that eating canned tuna or other broiled or baked (not fried) fish one to four times weekly yielded a 28 percent lower risk of atrial fibrillation. Those who ate even more fish—five times weekly—enjoyed a reduced risk of 31 percent.

Finally, in terms of cardiovascular health, a meta-analysis of eight studies found that the risk of ischemic stroke—the type caused by a lack of blood to the brain—drops in inverse relation to fish consumption. Those who ate the most fish enjoyed the most reduced risk; eating fish five times a week yielded a 31 percent reduced risk of ischemic stroke.

• Control hypertension. The bottom line is the more omega-3 fatty acids you eat, the lower your blood pressure. This is because of the beneficial effect of omega-3s on your artery walls' elasticity. A 1993 meta-analysis on the effects of fish oil on blood pressure showed that eating cold-water fish three times a week seems to be as effective as high-dose fish oil supplements in reducing blood pressure in hypertensive patients.

• Prevent cancer. Research is just beginning to demonstrate that omega-3 fatty acids may play a role in preventing both breast and colon cancers.

• Prevents age-related macular degeneration. In the Nurses' Health Study, those who ate fish four or more times a week had a lower risk of age-related macular degeneration than those who ate three or fewer fish meals per month. The most prevalent fatty acid in our retina is DHA, and the primary dietary source of this "good fat" is salmon and other so-called heart-healthy fish. DHA also seems to reduce some of the adverse effects of sunlight on retinal cells.

• Mitigate autoimmune diseases such as lupus, rheumatoid arthritis and Raynaud's disease. Researchers believe that the anti-inflammatory abilities of omega-3 fatty acids are what help reduce the symptoms of autoimmune diseases as well as prolong the survival of those who suffer from them. Multiple studies have substantiated these results.

• Relieve depression and a host of mental-health problems. Perhaps the most interesting research on omega-3 fatty acids involved their relationship to mental health ailments such as depression, attention deficit hyperactivity disorder, dementia, schizophrenia, bipolar disorder and Alzheimer's disease. Our brains are surprisingly fatty—more than 60 percent of the brain is fat. Omega-3 fatty acids promote the brain's ability to regulate mood-related signals. They are a crucial constituent of brain-cell membranes and are needed for normal nervous-system function, mood regulation and attention and memory functions.

Various recent studies have highlighted the role of salmon and its sidekicks in promoting better mental health. One fascinating study found a relationship between the consumption of fish rich in omega-3s and the "hostility score" in 3,581 young urban black and white men. These young adults were enrolled in the Coronary Artery Risk Development in Young Adults (CARDIA) study, which is trying to determine the factors that promote the development of heart disease. As high hostility levels are associated with the development of coronary artery disease, the researchers were interested to find that the young adults with the highest intake of omega-3 fats were 18 percent less likely to exhibit high hostility compared with those who did not eat fish high in omega-3s.

Another interesting recent study found that for people over the age of 65, eating at least one fish meal a week could reduce their risk for developing Alzheimer's disease. The study involved 815 residents of Chicago. Those who ate fish at least once a week had a 60 percent lower risk for developing Alzheimer's compared with those who never or rarely ate fish. Researchers noted that some participants in the study also saw a decreased risk for Alzheimer's after eating vegetables and nuts rich in omega-3 fatty acids.

It's not only young adults and older folks who benefit from salmon and its sidekicks when it comes to mental health and performance. One study found a correlation between salmon and tuna and mental performance in midlife. The five-year study of 1,613 people found that eating fish high in omega-3 fatty acids several times each week reduced the risk of impaired overall cognitive function by almost 20 percent. Those who ate a diet high in cholesterol, by contrast, were found to have a 27 percent greater risk of impaired memory and mental flexibility.

How Much Omega-3 Should You Eat?

There are some overlapping and some individual properties unique to each type of omega-3 fatty acid (ALA and EPA/DHA). Therefore, it's better to have a combination of both in your diet. There are no current published human clinical trials telling us the ideal intake ratio of ALA versus EPA/DHA. Until such studies are available, I recommend a combination of both.

While we often think that if a little of something is good, a lot must be better, be cautious: Too much omega-3 fatty acid can promote a risk of stroke by thinning the blood excessively. Bleeding time is prolonged with an intake of omega-3 fatty acids that exceeds 3 grams a day. (Greenland Eskimos who consume an average 10.5 grams a day of omega-3 fatty acids have an increased risk of hemorrhagic stroke.) Too high a daily dose can also negatively affect your immune system. However, a study published in the *American Journal of Clinical Nutrition* found that an intake of 9.5 grams or less of ALA or 1.7 grams or less of EPA/DHA did not alter the functional activity of three important cells involved in inflammation and immunity. People on blood thinners and/or aspirin should take this into consideration when they alter their fatty acid intake and should consult their health-care professional.

The Institute of Medicine's Food and Nutrition Board recently revised the recommended daily intake of ALA (plant-derived omega-3) to 1.6 grams for adult men and 1.1 grams for adult women. They didn't feel it was possible to set an acceptable range for all omega-3 fatty acids (ALA, EPA, DHA). They therefore recommended that a target amount of EPA or DHA is 160 milligrams a day for men and 110 milligrams a day for women. I personally feel the EPA/DHA recommendation should be higher to achieve optimal health. My goal is about one gram of marine-derived EPA/DHA a day, and I concur with the Food and Nutrition Board's daily recommendation on ALA, which is the amount found in less than one tablespoon of flaxseed.

Wild Salmon to the Rescue

Some of my patients roll their eyes when I begin to talk about the balance of omega-6 EFAs and omega-3 EFAs. They're not very interested in the biochemistry of fat; they just want to know easy ways to improve their health.

When it comes to omega-3 fatty acids, wild salmon is one simple answer. Add it to your diet. Wild salmon is delicious, high in protein, widely available in canned form, easy to prepare, and, more important, high in beneficial omega-3 fatty acids. If you eat wild salmon or other cold-water fish, like sardines or trout, two to four times a week, and incorporate some of the other recommendations in this section about the use of oils, you will "rebalance" the ratio of fatty acids in your body and be on your way to vastly improving your cellular health.

There's ample evidence that including cold-water fish like wild salmon in your diet will have a positive effect on your short- and long-term health. Keep in mind, it can take up to four months to achieve an ideal omega-3 fatty acid concentration in your body. The American Heart Association currently recommends eating two servings of fish a week (preferably fatty fish like wild salmon) for people without a history of coronary heart disease, and more if you do have such a history. I think three to four servings a week gives a broad range of protection against a wide variety of chronic diseases, but eat a variety of these fishes, too.

The "D" Dilemma

Vitamin D deficiency is a major, largely unrecognized epidemic in adult men and women in the United States today. In one survey of healthy people in Boston between the ages of 18 and 29, 36 percent were found to be vitamin D deficient. Another study reported that 42 percent of African-American women ages 15 to 49 and 4.2 percent of white females in the same age group are deficient in vitamin D. This is important because there seems to be an inverse risk of dying from breast, colon, ovarian and prostate cancers with a decreased presence of vitamin D. African Americans, many of whom are chronically vitamin D deficient, have a higher incidence and more aggressive forms of many cancers, including breast and prostate cancers. (It's important to recognize that, while we call it a vitamin,

vitamin D really acts more like a hormone in our bodies.)

Studies indicate that men who are exposed to sunlight can delay the onset of prostate cancer by more than five years, and children receiving vitamin D supplementation beginning at the age of one year had an 80 percent decreased risk of developing type I diabetes. Adequate vitamin D intake is associated with a lower risk of hip fractures due to osteoporosis in postmenopausal women. In one study on this problem, neither milk nor a diet high in calcium seemed to reduce the risk.

The most important source of vitamin D is the skin's synthesis of the vitamin from sunlight exposure. People who live far from the equator (and therefore get less sunlight), who use sunblocks, or who have heavy skin pigmentation (African Americans have high melanin concentrations, which limit vitamin D synthesis), all may be at risk for low levels of vitamin D. Sunblocks can cut vitamin D production by about 95 percent. I am not recommending discontinuing using sunscreen, but this is a good reason why you should increase your dietary sources of vitamin D.

Interestingly, vitamin D deficiency did not become a health problem until after the onset of the industrial revolution, which led to a decrease in exposure to sunlight as more and more people worked indoors. The major food sources of vitamin D include fatty fish like sardines, salmon and tuna, and fortified foods, particularly cereals and some dairy products.

How do you protect yourself from vitamin D deficiency? Add wild salmon, sardines and tuna to your diet. Try to get about 15 minutes of sun exposure to your arms and face at least three times a week, before 10 A.M. and after 3 P.M., when the ultraviolet rays are not as damaging to the skin. Also check the labels of any fortified foods you eat, including cereals, milk and soymilk.

The Food and Nutrition Board has been unable to settle on an RDA for vitamin D. The current recommendations for adequate intakes are: adult males and females ages 19 to 50 should get 200 international units (IU) per day; ages 51 to 70 should get 400 IU a day; over 70 years, 600 IU per day. If you don't get enough vitamin D from all your food sources, you might consider taking a supplement, though you should be careful with vitamin D supplementation, as there is a definite risk of toxicity if you take too much.

A Fish Story

Wild salmon, and all fish for that matter, used to carry a reliable nutritional benefit. The fish, in their natural habitat, love to eat zooplankton (tiny single-celled organisms), which are a rich source of omega-3 fatty acids. People who ate the fish thus delivered this healthy fat to their eagerly awaiting cells. Sadly, as the oceans have become overfished and polluted, the picture has changed. For one thing, U.S. Atlantic salmon are virtually extinct. (Most Atlantic salmon sold in the U.S. is farm raised.) Even worse from a health standpoint, some cold-water fish are contaminated with mercury. These include swordfish, shark, tilefish and king mackerel. Avoid eating these fish.

Approximately eight percent of women in the U.S. between the ages of 16 and 49 have mercury concentrations higher than the U.S. Environmental Protection Agency's recommended reference dose.

In general, haddock, tilapia, salmon, cod, pollock, canned albacore tuna, sole and most shellfish are relatively low in mercury.

Today, farmed fish have come to dominate many sectors of the market. You've no doubt noticed a wide variation in the price of salmon, from very inexpensive farmed salmon to very expensive, fresh Alaskan salmon. Many environmental groups

CONSUMER-ACTION ALERT

Studies have regularly shown that the vitamin D content of fortified milk is highly variable. It is supposed to have 100 IU per eight-ounce serving. Manufacturers should make this addition consistently. Moreover, consumers should ask that yogurt and fermented milk products be fortified with vitamin D.

are opposed to farm-raised salmon, and there is some controversy about their omega-3 content, as they're not always fed the marine diet that produces high amounts of omega-3 fatty acids. In my opinion, the best salmon is U.S. Pacific wild Alaskan salmon, whether it's fresh, frozen or canned. The Marine Stewardship Council certifies Alaskan salmon as a "Best Environmental Choice."

Other heart-healthy, environmentally safe seafood choices include the following: Arctic char, catfish (U.S. farmed), clams (farmed), crab (Dungeness), crayfish, halibut (Alaskan), herring, mahi mahi, mussels (farmed), sablefish, sardines, scallops (farmed), striped bass and tilapia (farmed).

Wild Salmon in the Kitchen

Most Americans don't eat enough seafood—or enough of the right kind of seafood (fried shrimp does not count!). The reason is obvious: It's not always easy to find good, fresh fish locally. Some of us have great local seafood markets; others are miles from any fresh fish outside a pet store. Here are two solutions: canned wild Alaskan salmon or canned albacore tuna and/or frozen fish.

Canned wild Alaskan salmon can sit in your pantry for months. Canned sockeye salmon has 203 milligrams of calcium—17 percent of your daily requirement—as an added bonus if it's canned with the bones; don't worry, the fish has been cooked and the bones are so soft as to be unnoticeable.

Frozen fish can be an excellent alternative to fresh. Many stores—Trader Joe's and Whole Foods—make a point of offering environmentally safe, high-EFA frozen fish. Just be sure to defrost it slowly in the refrigerator, to preserve texture and flavor.

Of course, fresh wild salmon, trout, or sea bass is also terrific. Get to know your fishmonger and don't be shy about asking which is the freshest fish he has available. Don't hesitate to give it a sniff test; if it doesn't smell like the sea, don't buy it. A "fishy" smell is really the sign of seafood that is past its prime.

Here are some other ways to get more fish into your life...

- You can add the salmon to a green salad for a delicious light meal.
- You can make salmon-burgers that are irresistible. Canned tuna is another good choice (although without the calcium boost). Just be sure to buy albacore tuna packed in spring water.

Due to the unresolved issues relating to potential environmental toxins in some farmed salmon and the seemingly real threat some salmon farms are to the environment, we cannot at this time recommend farm-raised salmon (whether canned, frozen or fresh). Environmental issues surrounding shrimp are particularly complicated as well.

To be environmentally responsible in your fish choices, consult the following Web sites for the latest information...

- *www.montereybayaquarium.org/cr/seafoodwatch.aspx*
- *www.edf.org* (800-684-3322)

• Canned sardines are another excellent source of beneficial marine-derived fatty acids, vitamin D and beneficial calcium from the hidden soft bones. Select sardines packed in tomato sauce for the added benefit of lycopene, or soybean oil or olive oil.

If you're a beginner at sardines, try the ones packed in olive oil; they have the best taste in my opinion.

Don't think you can get your family to eat fish two or three times a week? Don't give up. As little as one serving of fish a week resulted in a significantly reduced risk of total cardiovascular deaths after eleven years in a study involving more than twenty thousand male physicians in the U.S.

For Those Who Just Won't Eat Fish...Ever

I have patients who won't or can't eat fish. While I always advocate whole foods as a source of nutrients, I do believe that getting adequate omega-3s is important enough to argue for taking a supplement if you can't get them any other way.

If you must rely on a supplement, take at least one gram of EPA/DHA per day with food. I take a supplement if I'm not having appreciable dietary omega-3s on a given day. In those instances, I take 500 mg of EPA/DHA with two of my meals.

Look for fish oil that lists a small amount of d-alpha tocopherol (vitamin E) or other antioxidant on the label. This helps to keep the fish oil fresh. Be sure to store fish oil in the fridge, as it can deteriorate quickly.

My favorite fish oil supplement is wild Alaskan sockeye salmon oil from *www.vitalchoice.com*, which contains all 32 fatty acids as they are found in this fish and which is also preserved with the astaxanthan found in the salmon flesh.

If you burp up a fishy taste when first trying fish-oil supplements, persevere. Take the soft gel capsules with a meal and in almost all cases the fishy burps will stop within a week.

See our Shopping Lists (pages 213, 218 and 219) for some recommended products.

Soy

One of the recent national morning shows featured a cooking segment about the nutritional benefits of tofu.

"This will be great," said the host of the show. "I'm trying to get more soy into my diet."

SOY IS A SOURCE OF:

- Phytoestrogens
- Plant-derived omega-3 fatty acids
- Vitamin E
- B vitamins (thiamin, riboflavin, B6)
- Iron
- Potassium
- Folate
- Magnesium
- Selenium
- Saponins
- Phytates
- Phytosterols
- Lunasin
- Excellent nonmeat protein alternative

Sidekicks in forms of soy: Tofu, soymilk, soy nuts, soy yogurt, edamame, tempeh, miso

Try to eat: At least 15 grams of soy protein (30 to 50 milligrams of isoflavones daily; not from isoflavone-fortified products) and divide total daily soy intake into two separate meals or snacks

"Well, then, this should work out really well," replied the co-host. "You can have mine!"

This brief humorous interchange typifies the way many of us think about soy, and tofu, in particular. We think we should eat more of it, though we may not be sure why, and some of us are convinced we want no part of it whatsoever.

My goal in the next few pages is to convince you that soy is a valuable addition to your diet and, even if you never dreamed you'd eat it and even if you never, ever want to cook tofu, there are other ways to incorporate soy foods into your daily diet.

Here is the good news in a nutshell: Soy truly is a SuperFood. It offers tremendous health benefits when incorporated into your diet. It's an inexpensive, high-quality, vitamin- and mineral-rich plant protein with lots of soluble fiber, plant-based omega-3 fatty acids, and most important, it offers a wealth of disease-fighting phytonutrients. Indeed, soy is the richest known dietary source of powerful health-promoting phytoestrogens.

Soy has been recognized by many researchers as playing a positive role in preventing cardiovascular disease, cancer and osteoporosis as well as helping to relieve menopausal and menstrual symptoms. Moreover, you don't have to eat tons of it to enjoy its considerable advantages. Once you learn about the proven benefits of soy and the simple ways you can incorporate this unique food into your diet, I think you'll become a convert.

A daily intake of 25 grams of soy protein is ideal. *Here are some rich sources...*

- Four ounces of firm tofu contains 18 to 20 grams of protein.
- One soy "burger" includes 10 to 12 grams of protein.
- An 8-ounce glass of Edensoy Original Formula Soymilk contains approximately 11 grams of protein.
- One soy protein bar delivers 14 grams of protein.
- One-half cup of tempeh provides 16 to 19 grams of protein.
- One-quarter cup of roasted soy nuts contains approximately 15 grams of protein.

THE HISTORY OF SOY

Soybeans have been cultivated in China since the eleventh century B.C. Indeed, the soybean is the most widely grown and utilized legume in the world. The Chinese name for the soybean is "greater bean," and soy is also referred to as "meat without bones." Like other beans, soybeans grow in pods, and while we most commonly think of them as green, they can also be yellow, black or brown.

The soybean was introduced to America in the eighteenth century by that innovative, forward-looking American Ben Franklin, who, impressed with tofu—the Chinese "cheese made from soybeans"—had some beans shipped from Paris to a group of farmers in Pennsylvania. It wasn't until the next century that soybeans were extensively planted by American farmers. In the twentieth century, people began to recognize the health-promoting qualities of the soybean, and today, to many people's surprise, the U.S. is responsible for more than half of the world's soybean production.

Soy, the Blank Canvas

One of the most unusual aspects of soy, at least in comparison with other SuperFoods, is also perhaps its great advantage: You can make it taste however you like. You can use it in a wide variety of preparations, and if you're not wild about tofu, you may well enjoy roasted soy nuts. You can add a scoop of soy protein to shakes or pancakes or bake with soymilk and it's undetectable. My own children had been eating soy for years before they even heard the word. The message is that you're sure to find some version of soy that you can happily live with. Soy foods all come from soybeans, but there are many permutations of the basic bean as I'll detail later.

Soy: The Alternate Protein

Before we even consider soy's health-promoting abilities, let's take a brief look at its other, often overlooked plus: It is an excellent protein alternative. For example, a half-cup of tofu provides 18 to 20 grams of protein, which is 40 percent of the daily requirement for most people. That same amount of tofu also provides 258 milligrams of calcium (more than a quarter of our daily needs) and 13 milligrams of iron (87 percent of a woman's daily need and 130 percent of a man's).

Here's a comparison of the percentage of protein by weight of a few foods: Soy flour is 51 percent protein; whole, dry soybeans are 35 percent protein; fish is only 22 percent protein; hamburger is only 13 percent protein; and whole milk is just 3 percent protein.

Substituting 15 grams of soy protein for 15 grams of animal protein would cause the current U.S. dietary ratio of animal-to-plant protein to fall from two to one to a more desirable one to one, the ratio it was in the early 1900s. At this level of intake, soy protein would still represent less than 20 percent of the average protein intake of U.S. adults.

In addition to the high-quality protein you get when you substitute soy for animal protein, you get a bonus of vitamins, minerals and a good dose of phytonutrients. Soy has a healthy mix of fats and no cholesterol.

In one study, the substitution of soy for animal products reduced coronary artery disease risk in the study subjects because of their subsequent reductions in blood lipids (such as LDL), homocysteine and blood pressure. For those of us eating a typical American diet, what this means is that soy is so good because much of what we eat is so bad for us! Many of our protein sources come with additional less-than-desirable components, particularly saturated fat, as well as hormones, pesticides, antibiotics and other negatives.

Tofu is even low in calories compared with other plant-based protein sources. In fact, tofu has the lowest known ratio of calories to protein in any plant food except mung bean and soybean sprouts.

Soy offers the highest-quality protein of any plant food. Available in organic forms (and therefore free of any pesticides or other additives), it offers all nine essential amino acids and is a good source of plant-derived omega-3 fatty acids. So even if you only relied on soy as a meat substitute a couple of times a week, you'd be ahead of the game.

Soy and Your Health

Soy has long been recognized as a highly nutritious food. Western scientists became particularly interested in soy when they noticed that people eating Asian diets enjoyed lower rates of heart disease as well as less cancer and osteoporosis, and had fewer hormonal problems than those eating a typical Western diet. While much research still has to be done, there is now broad

SOY AND LACTOSE INTOLERANCE

Many people have difficulty digesting lactose—the main type of sugar found in dairy products. People with lactose intolerance experience upset stomachs and diarrhea when they consume dairy foods, particularly milk. Fortunately, soy foods allow people with lactose intolerance to consume the required protein and calcium they need without difficulty.

agreement on various connections between soy and health promotion.

A Heart Helper

Soy's most conclusively demonstrated benefit concerns cardiovascular health. There have been extensive studies on the cholesterol-lowering effect of soy. One frequently cited study, published in the *New England Journal of Medicine* in 1995, describes an analysis of thirty-eight different studies. The authors found that consumption of soy protein resulted in significant reductions in total cholesterol (9.3 percent), LDL ("bad") cholesterol (12.9 percent), and triglycerides (10.5 percent) with a small though not significant increase in HDL ("good") cholesterol.

A more recent study in the *Journal of Nutrition* demonstrated that the intake of soy foods among the premenopausal female subjects was inversely related to their risk for coronary artery disease and stroke as well as other disorders.

A recent study investigated the effects of soy protein and soy isoflavones on blood pressure and cholesterol levels in sixty-one middle-aged Scottish men who were at high risk of developing coronary heart disease. For five weeks, half of the men consumed diets that contained at least 20 grams of soy protein and 80 milligrams of soy isoflavones each day. The control group consumed a diet that was without soy but did contain olive oil. The soy consumers were found to have significant reductions in both diastolic and systolic blood pressure. Moreover, their total cholesterol was significantly lower and their HDL ("good") cholesterol was significantly increased. The control group also enjoyed an increase in their HDL cholesterol levels, but their blood pressure was unaffected and their LDL ("bad") cholesterol levels did not drop. The researchers concluded that eating at least 20 grams of soy protein, including 80 milligrams of soy isoflavones for a minimum of five weeks, would be effective in reducing the risk of cardiovascular disease in high-risk, middle-aged men.

In connection with promoting cardiovascular health, it's significant that soy has been found to lower heart disease risk by increasing the size of LDL cholesterol particles. Small, dense LDL is the most dangerous form of cholesterol. Large LDL, especially when accompanied by adequate supplies of HDL, is considered much less risky.

In a study at Tufts University on subjects with high cholesterol, researchers found that those who ate a diet high in soy protein significantly increased the size of their LDL particles compared with periods when they ate diets high in animal protein. The participants were given four different diets, each for a period of six weeks: soy protein with no isoflavones, soy protein enriched with isoflavones, animal protein with no added isoflavones and animal protein with added isoflavones. The isoflavones had no effect, but soy protein consumption resulted in a decrease in the amount of small, dense LDL and an increase in larger LDL particles compared with animal protein.

INCREASES NITRIC OXIDE

Soy protein also has the ability to increase blood levels of nitric oxide—a molecule that can boost blood vessel dilation and reduce the free-radical damage of cholesterol and the adhesion of white cells to blood vessel walls. Preventing these events lessens the risk for the development of atherosclerotic plaques. One study on mice found that when fed soy-protein diets, the mice had increased levels of nitric oxide metabolites compared with mice that were fed other protein sources.

Soy protein is an excellent food for those who suffer from diabetes, particularly non-insulin-dependent diabetes. The protein and fiber in soy foods can help to stabilize blood-sugar levels.

ISOFLAVONES IN SOY FOODS

The U.S. Department of Agriculture, in collaboration with Iowa State University, has compiled a listing of the isoflavone content of soy foods. The values are expressed in milligrams per single serving of the food. The foods are listed from the most isoflavones to the least. (From *Wellness Foods A to Z.* Rebus.)

	Calories	Fat (g)	Isoflavones
Soybeans, dried, cooked (1 cup)	298	15	95
Soybean sprouts (¼ cup)	171	9.4	57
Soy nuts (¼ cup)	194	9.3	55
Tempeh (4 ounces)	226	8.7	50
Soy flour, full fat (⅓ cup)	121	5.7	49
Tofu, firm (4 ounces)	164	9.9	28
Soymilk (1 cup)	81	4.7	24
Edamame, cooked (4 ounces)	160	7.3	16

There's also evidence that soy protein can help to protect both the hearts and kidneys of diabetic patients from the damage that can be caused by the disease.

In a recent study, diabetic patients who were switched to a diet containing 35 percent soy protein and 30 percent vegetable protein showed significant reductions in total cholesterol, triglyceride and LDL blood cholesterol levels as well as an improvement in kidney function. The researchers concluded that a diet that includes soy protein could reduce the risk for heart disease and also improve kidney function in diabetic patients.

No one is precisely certain how soy lowers cholesterol, but the evidence of its doing so is so incontrovertible that in October 1999 the FDA gave soy its official backing by allowing soy-food manufacturers to make health claims on their packages. They are able to claim that soy protein, when included in a diet low in saturated fat and cholesterol, may reduce the risk of coronary heart disease by lowering blood cholesterol levels.

A Cancer Fighter Too

Soy has also been shown to be a potent cancer-fighting food. Various components of soy have demonstrated anticarcinogenic effects. They include protease inhibitors, phytosterols, saponins, lunacin, phenolic acids, phytic acid and isoflavones.

Two of the isoflavones in soy—genistein and daidzein—are worthy of particular attention because soy foods are their primary dietary source. These two isoflavones act like weak estrogens in the body. While their effects aren't completely understood, we do know that they can compete with stronger naturally occurring estrogens and in this way help prevent hormone-dependent cancers like those of the breast and prostate. The isoflavones bind to sites on cell membranes that would normally be inhabited by hormones that can stimulate the growth of tumors. In addition to blocking the action of potent, naturally produced hormones, genistein can also inhibit the activity of enzymes that encourage the growth of blood clots and tumors.

There is evidence that soy protein, which has a significant fiber content, could play a role in reducing the risk of various cancers, including breast, prostate and colon cancers. Fiber seems to be able to bind to some cancer-causing toxins and escort them from the body, thus decreasing the incidence of cancers, particularly colon cancer. It has been noted that in various parts of the world where soy is eaten regularly, the rates of colon cancer, as well as breast and prostate cancer, tend to be lower than the rates in Western cultures where meat proteins are a more dominant part of the diet. A study in mice showed that a combination of soy protein and black tea synergistically inhibited prostate tumor growth. Once again, this demonstrates the beneficial synergy of whole foods in preventing disease.

While there have been some variations in study results linking soy intake to breast cancer reduction, epidemiological studies show that women in Southeast Asian populations who consume diets high in soy protein (10 to 50 grams a day) have a four to six times reduced risk of breast cancer compared with American women who normally consume minimal amounts of soy.

A study in *Nutrition and Cancer* reports that people who regularly consume as little as one and a half servings of soymilk daily enjoy better cancer protection than those who occasionally consume soy.

Try to use soy daily—put soymilk on your cereal or oatmeal, sprinkle soy protein powder in a fruit smoothie or snack on soy nuts. Studies suggest that two separate soy foods a day, in separate meals, work best.

Can Soy Be Harmful?

However, there is some controversy about the effects of soy in the diet and most of the controversy surrounds soy and breast cancer. There have been continuing studies on the role of soy in the diet of women who have been diagnosed with breast cancer and whether soy will stimulate or reduce tumor growth in such women.

The confusion about the health benefits of soy stems from the fact that many people want to take shortcuts and rely on soy products and supplements. Some research suggests that not only is the cancer-preventive ability of soy foods greatly reduced in these supplements and processed soy foods but, indeed, these foods can stimulate the growth of preexisting estrogen-dependent breast tumors in mice.

On the other hand, abundant research exists that demonstrates that soy in the form of whole foods can be beneficial; indeed, soy is a food that has been shown to reduce the risk of breast cancer.

Another study has shown that consuming the amount of soy phytoestrogens that would be eaten when soy foods are included in the diet (in women, about 129 milligrams a day of isoflavones) does not increase the risk of breast or uterine cancer, and appears to be protective.

Once again, Mother Nature has produced a product that is more effective and much safer than those produced by man. The complex mixture of bioactive compounds that act synergistically in soy to promote health is found only in whole foods, and I recommend sticking with minimally processed, whole soy foods.

I can also report that a very recent, very extensive study in *Nutrition Review* has confirmed the safety of soy dietary isoflavones in the diet.

The question does remain whether soy is safe for breast cancer survivors. The most recent expert recommendations from the American Cancer Society provide the following counseling regarding soy during and after cancer treatment: "Because soy has been associated with estrogenic effects in some studies, the safety of consuming high amounts of soy from supplements or a soy-rich diet remains unclear: Consumption of up to three servings per day of soy foods [soymilk, tofu, et cetera] is considered moderate and has not been associated with specific benefit or harm in breast cancer survivors." I recommend that women who have been diagnosed with breast cancer consult with their health-care provider about the safety of consuming soy-food products in their individual case.

There were reports, eventually disproved, that soy led to an increase in the development of senility. Indeed, most populations at the higher end of soy consumption have lower rates of dementia than populations who do not consume soy.

Estrogen-like Properties

Does soy help with menopausal symptoms? While it's controversial, some evidence says it can. For example, researchers from the University of Bologna, Italy, gave two groups of menopausal women 60 grams of either soy protein or a look-alike placebo of dried milk protein daily for twelve weeks. The women eating soy protein experienced significantly fewer hot flashes and night sweats than the placebo group. Again, soy's estrogen-mimicking isoflavones are responsible. As a woman's natural levels of estrogen fall during menopause, the isoflavones seem to help take up the slack.

There is evidence that, because of its estrogen-like behavior, soy contributes to bone health and thus helps stave off osteoporosis. One study of sixty-six postmenopausal women at the University of Illinois found that soy protein added to the diet significantly increased both bone-mineral content and density in the spine after six months.

Many people are confused about how much isoflavone to consume per day. Estimates of dietary intake in people in Asian countries indicate that intake of isoflavone from soy foods range from 15 to 50 milligrams a day. The average intake is 30 to 32 milligrams (from whole foods, not fortified products).

Soy and Your Thyroid

Many people ask me about soy and thyroid dysfunction. In general, adequate dietary iodine seems to be protective against soy's occasional potential for promoting thyroid hormone abnormalities. In addition, epidemiologic studies show that soy consumption may reduce the risk for thyroid cancer.

The Major Components Of Soy

Here's a quick breakdown of the major components of soy and how they promote health…

Isoflavones

Soybeans are the best-known source of these compounds, which act like antioxidants as well as estrogens. Two of the isoflavones in soy—genistein and daidzein—reduce the risk of coronary heart disease, mitigate hormone-related cancers, and decrease the ability of tumors to grow new blood vessels. Preliminary evidence suggests that genistein decreases the growth of new blood vessels in the retina, which can lead to vision loss from age-related macular degeneration.

Lignins

Bind with carcinogens in the colon, speed up the transit time of these carcinogens, thus reducing their potential negative effects, and scavenge free radicals.

Saponins

Phytonutrients that boost the immune system and fight cancer.

Protease inhibitors

Block the activity of cancer-causing enzymes called "proteases" and thus reduce the risk of cancer. Protease inhibitors have been reported to suppress carcinogens.

Phytic acid

Antioxidant that binds with and eliminates metals that can promote tumors.

Phytosterols

Nondigestible compounds that reduce cholesterol absorption in the bowel and may help prevent colon cancer.

Protein

Only plant-based complete high-quality protein, totally cholesterol free and low in fat.

Oil

Healthy oil that is free of cholesterol and offers a beneficial ratio of fatty acids (low in bad fat; high in good fat). It's a source of plant-derived omega-3 fatty acids as well.

Soy sauce is not a good source of soy! It has little to no nutritional benefit and is very high in sodium.

Sources of Soy

As mentioned, soy is available in a wide variety of foods. Soybeans can be eaten whole—fresh or frozen as in edamame or dried as in soy nuts. They can also be fermented to make tempeh, miso or soy sauce (of which the latter two are used primarily to flavor various sweet and savory foods). They can be soaked, mashed and heated to create soymilk or curdled to make tofu or bean curd. They're processed to make oil, flour and soy noodles. The key thing to remember about soy is that, while all soy foods are derived from the soybean, they are, except for soybeans themselves, essentially processed foods. This isn't bad; but it does mean that you should read labels when you choose soy foods, and you will have to do some experimenting to find the soy foods you like best.

Tofu

Tofu is perhaps the best-known version of soy. It's a white, cheeselike food made from curdled soymilk, which has been shaped into blocks. Tofu is available in a few varieties—firm, extra firm, soft and silken. Firm and extra-firm tofu are good for slicing into stir-fries and soups. They can also be broiled, grilled or baked. It quickly absorbs marinades and flavorings. Silken tofu is wonderful for using in smoothies or in dips, dressings and toppings.

There have been questions about whether calcium from soymilk is as bioavailable as the calcium from cow's milk.

A recent study reported that calcium absorption from calcium carbonate–fortified soymilk was equivalent to calcium absorption from cow's milk. (Less well absorbed is the calcium in the form of tricalcium phosphate found in some fortified soymilks.)

Don't forget to shake the container well before pouring, as the calcium tends to settle on the bottom.

Soymilk

Soymilk is a major source of soy protein. Soymilk is made from soybeans that have been finely ground, cooked and strained. It comes with various additives and in a variety of flavors. It's widely available in aseptic packages, which keep for a long time and don't need to be refrigerated until opened. You can find fresh and even fresh, flavored soymilk. Some people find that the fresh soymilk available in the dairy case tastes the best. As Lorna Sass says in her excellent *The New Soy Cookbook*, "...not all soymilks are created equal. Tastes ranged from light, fresh and pleasantly sweet to musky, chalky, oily and intensely 'beany.' Color ranged from creamy white to dark caramel, with lots of shades in between." You really have to experiment with locally available brands to find a soymilk that pleases you.

It's critical that you read the labels on soymilk. The amounts of protein and calcium, as well as other vitamins, fat and sugar, vary considerably from one brand to another. Most brands have six to 11 grams of protein per 8 ounces (1 cup). My favorite soymilks are Westsoy Unsweetened Vanilla Organic Soymilk and Original Edensoy Extra Organic Soymilk. Keep in mind that soy fat is good fat. I personally like full-fat soymilk. Beware of added calories in the form of sugar.

Soymilk can be substituted for cow's milk in baking. Some people—particularly children who are used to cow's milk—may balk at the color and flavors of some brands of soymilk and therefore won't enjoy it on cereal, but if your family resists drinking it straight, try it in pancakes, cakes, muffins, etc.

Soy nuts

Soy nuts are soybeans that have been soaked in water and baked or roasted until they're lightly browned, toasty and crunchy. High in protein, isoflavones and soluble fiber, they are also high in calories, so you have to limit your consumption to a reasonable amount, say, one-quarter cup a day. (Remember that one-quarter cup soy nuts has 136 calories and 15 grams of protein.) While soy nuts are available in a honey-roasted form as well as various flavored and spiced versions, I recommend that you eat soy nuts with no added ingredients. Be sure to read the label and avoid soy nuts with any added oil, sweetener or salt. Soy nuts make a great portable snack. I toss a few on my granola. One-quarter cup has about 15 grams of protein.

FOUR EASY WAYS TO GET SOY INTO YOUR DAY

1 cup soymilk on cereal

1 ounce soy protein powder in a fruit shake

¼ cup soy nuts as a snack

Dried cereals and breads containing soy

Edamame

Edamame are green soybeans still in their pods. Ideal because they're a whole food, they are available in the frozen food section of natural-food markets and many supermarkets. Boil the pods briefly in lightly salted water and then pop them right from the pods into your mouth (kids especially enjoy this). Edamame taste like slightly sweet lima beans. You can also find shelled soybeans frozen in bags, and these are great to add to soups, pasta sauces, salads and stews. One cup of shelled edamame has about 23 grams of protein.

Soy protein powder

There are two kinds of soy protein powder and, I'll admit, it can be quite confusing when shopping for this popular additive to shakes and baked goods.

Soy protein concentrate comes from defatted soy flakes. It contains about 70 percent protein, while retaining most of the bean's dietary fiber. Depending on how the concentrate is prepared, it may or may not contain a significant amount of isoflavones.

When protein is removed from defatted flakes, the result is soy protein isolates, the most highly refined soy protein. Containing 92 percent protein, soy protein isolates possess the greatest amount of protein of all soy products. They are a highly digestible source of amino acids (building blocks of protein necessary for human growth and maintenance). Soy protein isolates are the

If you're new to soy, it's well worth checking out some sources that I'm sure you'll find informative and inspiring. Look for *Amazing Soy* or *The Joy of Soy* by Dana Jacobi. Both books are filled with inspiring recipes and excellent general information on incorporating soy into your diet. Two other books on cooking with soy include *This Can't Be Tofu* by Deborah Madison and *The New Soy Cookbook* by Lorna Sass. Both will change the way you think of cooking with soy.

Also, take a look at some Web sites for more helpful information on soy...

- *www.soyfoods.com*
- *www.soyfoods.org*
- *www.soyconnection.com*

substance commonly used in many soy–heart disease research studies.

Whichever soy protein powder you choose, be sure that it's not fortified with extra soy isoflavones.

Soy flour

Soy flour is processed from whole ground soybeans. Use it to increase the protein content of breads, cakes and cookies. Soy flour contains no gluten, so it cannot be used to replace white or wheat flour entirely in baking. But you can use it to supplement your other flour—in yeast-raised breads, replace 2 tablespoons of each cup of wheat flour with soy flour; with quick breads, you can replace up to one-quarter of the wheat flour with soy flour. You may notice that breads made with soy flour brown more quickly than those made with just wheat. One-quarter cup of soy flour has 8 to 12 grams of protein.

Tempeh

Tempeh is a soy food made from soybeans that have been cracked and inoculated with a beneficial bacterium. It is fermented and then formed into flat blocks. Sometimes grains like brown rice, barley or millet are added. Tempeh has a meaty taste and is often used as a meat substitute in cooking. It can be marinated and grilled as well as added to stews and pasta sauces. It can also be added to chili, sloppy joes or burritos. High in protein, fiber and isoflavones, it is usually found in the refrigerated dairy section of your natural food store or supermarket. Tempeh can be frozen and, once defrosted, must be refrigerated. It will keep for about ten days. Three ounces of tempeh, or about one-half cup, has approximately 16 ounces of protein.

Miso

Miso, a soy ingredient that is gaining in popularity in North America, adds flavor, depth and incremental amounts of soy isoflavones to foods. It is a staple in Japanese cooking. A fermented soybean paste, miso is made when soybeans and various grains such as rice or barley are cooked and cooled, then inoculated with friendly mold and allowed to culture.

Miso ranges in color from pale yellow to dark rich chestnut brown and in flavor from sweet to salty. The lighter misos are sweeter, fruity and more subtle, while dark misos are hearty, robust and complex. There are three kinds of miso: shiro miso (white), aka miso (red) and awase miso (blended), plus many varieties within those categories. Experiment with the various types of miso; like vinegars, they are adaptable to different cooking uses.

Miso keeps well in the fridge for several months. Always use a clean spoon to remove some from the storage container. When used raw in dressings or cold preparations, miso adds healthy bacteria to the system, just as yogurt does. If mold forms on the surface, just scrape it off. It is perfectly safe to eat. Miso is high in sodium, so use it sparingly as a salt alternative and avoid using additional salt when preparing a dish using miso.

How Much Soy Should You Eat?

It can be difficult to figure out how much soy is beneficial to health because many consumers look for amounts of soy isoflavones on soy food labels. Unfortunately, some foods don't list isoflavones. Some others list isoflavone amounts that are inaccurate. And some foods list isoflavone fortification, and I don't recommend relying on added isoflavones. (There isn't enough evidence to confirm the long-term safety of isoflavone-fortified products.) Here's the key to shopping for soy foods: **Check the protein content on the label.**

In general, the best way to learn the isoflavone content of a food is to rely on the listed protein content. The protein content of the food is closely linked to the isoflavone content. You can get the benefits of soy with as little as 10 grams of soy protein a day. For example, one-quarter cup of soy nuts has 15 grams of soy protein. While soy nuts are high in calories, most people love to eat a scant one-quarter cup while relaxing at the end of the day. That's all it takes to get the benefit of soy.

KITCHEN TOFU TIP

Many people are unaware that tofu, like milk or meat, is perishable. It won't last forever in the fridge. Pay attention to the expiration date on the package when you buy it (look for the latest date as you would on milk), keep it refrigerated at all times and change the water in the package daily.

Moreover, remember that tofu, like meat, can host unfriendly bacteria like salmonella. Make sure you work with it on a clean surface and wash prep surfaces (and your hands) with soap and water before and after handling.

Soy in the Kitchen

Some of my patients love soy foods; others do not. Whether you enjoy a tofu stir-fry or have no interest in cooking with soy foods, you can enjoy the benefits of soy in your diet. Many people aren't aware that there are a variety of ways to enjoy soy.

Here are some quick and easy ways to get soy into your diet...

- Mix a scant tablespoon of miso with a cup of warm water for a simple healthful stock.
- For a vinaigrette or a marinade with a delicately complex flavor, combine 2 tablespoons miso (a mix of two types is nice) with a minced shallot, one-half cup fresh lemon or lime juice with zest, one-quarter cup extra virgin olive oil and black pepper. Allow the miso to steep in the liquid for five minutes to soften, then whisk until smooth.
- Use soymilk in place of cow's milk in baking and on cereals. These are both good ways to get children to eat some soy, as most won't even notice the difference from cow's milk.
- Sprinkle soybean sprouts on salads and tuck into sandwiches.
- Add soybeans to soups and casseroles.
- Keep some soy flour on hand to mix into pancakes, cakes and other baked goods.

See our Shopping Lists (pages 213, 215-219, 223 and 224) for some recommended products.

SPINACH

It's very simple...you must eat your spinach. Along with salmon and blueberries, spinach is right up at the pinnacle of the *SuperFoods Rx* powerhouse choices. Spinach has more demonstrated health benefits than almost any other food. Is this because spinach is really one of the best foods in the world? Yes and no. Yes, because it is an incredibly nutritious food with a stunning roster of benefits. No, only because there may be other foods—particularly other dark green leafy vegetables like kale and collards—that are comparably nutritious. We have much more information on the benefits of spinach than any other potential candidate.

SPINACH IS A SOURCE OF:

- A synergy of multiple nutrients/ phytonutrients
- Low in calories
- Lutein/zeaxanthin
- Beta-carotene
- Plant-derived omega-3 fatty acids
- Glutathione
- Alpha lipoic acid
- Vitamins C and E
- B vitamins (thiamine, riboflavin, B6, folate)
- Minerals (calcium, iron, magnesium, manganese and zinc)
- Polyphenols
- Betaine
- Coenzyme Q_{10}

Sidekicks: Kale, collards, Swiss chard, arugula, mustard greens, turnip greens, bok choy, romaine lettuce, orange bell peppers, seaweed

Try to eat: 1 cup steamed or 2 cups raw most days

SUPERSTAR SIDEKICKS

Most of the SuperFoods have sidekicks, but in the case of spinach, the sidekicks listed on this page are powerful foods. Each of the green leafies offers a tremendous nutrient boost. Vary your green-leafie intake among all the sidekicks and have at least two servings most days. Remember, a serving is 1 cup raw or a one-half cup cooked.

Spinach seems to be able to lessen our risk for many of the most common diseases of the twenty-first century. Overwhelming research has demonstrated an inverse relationship between spinach consumption and cardiovascular disease, including stroke and coronary artery disease; a host of cancers including colon, lung, skin, oral, stomach, ovarian, prostate and breast cancers; age-related macular degeneration (AMD); and cataracts.

In addition, preliminary research suggests that spinach may help prevent or delay age-related cognitive decline.

What is it about spinach and the other green leafies that makes them such powerful health promoters? In the old days, nutritionists would have pointed to one or two of the nutrients that elevated them to the top ranks. With spinach it was iron. Remember Popeye? It was supposed to be the iron that made him such a powerhouse. He wouldn't dare take on Bluto without popping a can. But it's almost as if nutritionists were working with an 8-pack of crayons; today we're looking at the 250-pack. Based on what we know and are learning daily about micronutrients, we understand that it's the *synergy* of the wide range of all the nutrients and phytonutrients in green leafies that make them superstars.

Although I've listed the most significant nutrients in spinach in the beginning of this chapter,

Co-Q_{10}

Dr. Lester Packer, one of the world's foremost antioxidant research scientists, considers coenzyme Q_{10} a member of his antioxidant network. It works in synergy with vitamins C, E and glutathione. It's a key player in our skin's antioxidant defense mechanism against sunlight damage and also a significant player in mitochondrial energy production. (The mitochondria are the cells' energy factories.) Spinach is an important source of this critical antioxidant.

here is a more complete list of everything we know thus far that's found in this SuperFood...

- The carotenoids lutein, zeaxanthin and beta-carotene
- The antioxidants glutathione, alpha lipoic acid and vitamins C and E
- Vitamin K (spinach is a major source of vitamin K)
- Coenzyme Q_{10} (spinach is one of the only two vegetables with significant amounts of it; the other is broccoli)
- The B vitamins (thiamine, riboflavin, B6, and folate)
- Minerals (calcium, iron, magnesium, manganese and zinc)
- Chlorophyll
- Polyphenols
- Betaine
- Plant-derived omega-3 fatty acids

This list, which, as I said, seems to be growing as we learn more about spinach, is truly formidable. With most SuperFoods, there are one or two nutrients in particular that push an individual food to best in category; with spinach, the list is so long and impressive that the wide range of individual nutrients coupled with the unmatched synergy of those nutrients make it a top SuperFood.

Spinach and Your Eyes

Of all the chronic diseases spinach combats, the ones affecting the eye are of particular interest to me as an ophthalmologist. My mother, who was remarkably healthy until she passed away at age 91, suffered from age-related macular degeneration (AMD). At age 75 she was declared legally blind. For the last 16 years of her life, despite her robust health, she was unable to enjoy life fully. She couldn't read, drive, watch TV, sew or see a movie. Watching my mother during the last years of her life had a major influence on the direction of my work. It inspired me to want to learn everything I could about nutrition and chronic disease.

The macula of the eye is responsible for central vision—the type we need for close work like writing and sewing as well as for distinguishing distant objects and color. Sadly, as many as 20 percent of all 65-year-olds show at least some early evidence of age-related macular changes. By age 90, about 60 percent of Caucasians will be affected by AMD, and close to 100 percent of centenarians reportedly have this leading cause of age-related vision loss. Worse yet, there is no effective treatment that restores 20/20 vision. That leaves us with prevention, and one of the best sources of prevention is certain foods—particularly spinach and its powerful sidekicks—which, along with consumption of

The eye's macular pigment responds very quickly to a rich supply of lutein and zeaxanthin. Within four weeks of increasing your intake of spinach and its sidekicks, you can significantly increase your macular pigment and thus help protect your vision.

dietary marine-based omega-3 fatty acids, can offer real hope.

The macular pigment of the eye protects against age-related macular degeneration (AMD). The lower the macular pigment level, the higher the risk of AMD. The best foods to elevate macular pigment are spinach, kale, collards, and turnip or mustard greens, as well as yellow foods, such as corn, egg yolks and orange bell peppers.

While no one is precisely certain what causes macular degeneration, there's ample evidence that free-radical damage from long-term exposure to light and ultraviolet radiation may play a role. We know for sure that cigarette smoking is a proven risk factor for AMD and most likely cataracts as well. Indeed, smoking is the most preventable cause of AMD.

Enter the two powerful carotenoids in spinach—lutein and zeaxanthin. A number of studies have shown an inverse relationship between dietary intake of foods rich in lutein/zeaxanthin and the incidence of AMD. A similar relationship has been found between dietary lutein/zeaxanthin and the prevalence of cataracts. We know for sure that as the lutein and zeaxanthin levels increase in the macula of the eye, there is a significant decrease in the amount of harmful light rays that reach the retinal cells that produce vision. There seems to be little doubt that the lutein/zeaxanthin combination provide protection.

BETAINE

This is a nutrient you will be hearing more about. Betaine is a derivative of choline, an essential fat, and it plays a role in homocysteine metabolism. Betaine supplementation has been shown to lower homocysteine levels in humans—an important step in lessening the risk of cardiovascular disease. The combination of dietary folate and betaine may be the best way to lower homocysteine. Great sources of betaine are spinach, wheat germ, oat bran, wheat bran and whole wheat bread.

The following people are at higher risk for AMD and cataracts...

- Women
- People with blue eyes
- Smokers
- Those with a history of cardiovascular disease and hypertension
- Obese people
- Anyone who spends a great deal of time outside in the sun
- People who have a low intake of fruits and vegetables
- People who are farsighted (AMD risk only)

Most of us involved in AMD research feel that long before we can see clinical evidence of AMD, adverse events are occurring in the retina. Preliminary data from my studies of people at high risk for later development of AMD are highly supportive of this hypothesis. Prevention of this devastating visual disability is most likely a lifelong job. The earlier you start, the better off your retina will be. At the same time, it is never too late to take action.

Lutein and zeaxanthin also help prevent other eye maladies. Cataracts are a common occurrence in older people. Eighteen percent of people age 65 to 74 have cataracts, and 45 percent of people age 75 to 84 have developed them. A cataract forms over the lens of the eye when, over time, damaged cells accumulate and cloud the lens.

In one twelve-year Harvard study, 77,466 nurses over age 45 were found to demonstrate a clear relationship between lutein and zeaxanthin

LUTEIN ALL-STARS	***Milligrams***
1 cup cooked kale	23.7
1 cup cooked spinach	20.4
1 cup cooked collards	14.6
1 cup cooked turnip greens	12.1
1 cup cooked green peas	4.2
1 cup raw spinach	3.7
1 cup cooked broccoli	2.4

ZEAXANTHIN ALL-STARS	
1 medium raw orange bell pepper	6.4
1 cup canned sweet yellow corn	.9
1 raw Japanese persimmon	.8
1 cup degermed cornmeal	.7

levels and the rate of cataract development. Overall, the nurses who ate the most dietary lutein and zeaxanthin had 22 percent fewer cataract surgeries.

Another study of 36,000 male physicians had comparable results. Virtually every study on eye health has come to the same conclusion: the more lutein and zeaxanthin-rich food consumed—particularly spinach, kale, collards and broccoli—the healthier the eye. I think of these powerful carotenoids as natural sunglasses for the eye.

Lutein and zeaxanthin are always found together in varying proportions in foods. There is preliminary evidence that zeaxanthin may exert an independent beneficial role in preventing macular degeneration. My recommended goal is 12 milligrams of lutein daily, which provides a variable amount of zeaxanthin. Optimum amounts of zeaxanthin are not yet known.

People often ask me why orange bell peppers are included as a sidekick to spinach, since it's not a leafy green. Orange bell peppers are extremely high in lutein and zeaxanthin. I tell my patients who hate spinach that they should eat orange bell peppers by cutting one up into a salad or adding it to a stir-fry. Most markets carry orange bell peppers all year round. I often put out a plate of cut-up peppers and baby carrots for the staff at my medical office, and they disappear in no time.

The data I've presented on these peppers (see box) are preliminary and based on the most reliable published information available as well as on personal conversations with the holder of the patent for orange-bell-pepper seeds. The USDA should analyze this food, as it has not as yet included this nutrition powerhouse in its database.

Another source of lutein/zeaxanthin, and one that's the most bioavailable of all, is the humble egg. While there's not a tremendous amount of lutein and zeaxanthin in egg yolks, what's there is so bioavailable that it's taken up into the bloodstream with great efficiency, giving a significant boost to the serum levels of these protective carotenoids. Eggs are quite nutritious. They're a good source of vitamin B12, riboflavin, selenium, vitamin A and vitamin D as well as lutein and zeaxanthin. They have a high quality of protein, due to their good balance of amino acids. An egg a day for most people (at least those who don't suffer from very high cholesterol and/or diabetes) is a fine addition to a healthy diet.

It's important to buy high omega-3 eggs, as they make a considerable contribution to your healthful balance of fatty acids. Be sure to look for "high omega-3" or "vegetarian fed" or "high DHA omega-3" on the carton. Here's a comparison between a typical supermarket egg and an omega-3 enriched egg.

	1 large egg	***Egglands Best egg***
Calories	75	70
Protein	6.3	6
Total fat	5	4
Saturated fat	1.5	1
Cholesterol	213	180
Vitamin E	0.5	3.8

One medium orange bell pepper contains...

- .4 mg beta cryptoxanthin
- 1 mg lutein
- 6.4 mg zeaxanthin
- .3 mg alpha-carotene
- .4 mg beta-carotene
- 223 mg vitamin C
- 4.3 mg vitamin E

Spinach and Vitamin K

Spinach is a rich dietary source of vitamin K—a vitamin that unlike other fat-soluble vitamins is not stored by the body in appreciable amounts and must be replaced on a regular basis. We're discovering more each day about the importance of this vitamin, and it seems the more we learn, the more diverse and critical these functions are. (Here's yet another argument for the *SuperFoods Rx* approach of making sure you get a wide range of nutrient-dense foods.)

What we know so far: Vitamin K is essential for the production of six of the proteins necessary for proper blood coagulation. Blood simply won't clot properly without it. It's been hypothesized that vitamin K plays a role in vascular health. Early work in this area is promising, though more studies must be done.

We do know that low levels of vitamin K have been linked with lower bone density and an increased risk of hip fracture in women and that a serving a day of spinach significantly reduces this risk. Just one cup of fresh spinach leaves a day gives you 190 percent of your daily requirements of vitamin K.

Cardiovascular Disease And Spinach

Spinach is a heart-healthy food. The rich supply of carotenoids and other nutrients helps protect artery walls from damage. The greens highest in carotenoids include spinach, beet and mustard greens, kale, collards, and turnip and dandelion greens. Just a half-cup of cooked spinach supplies 95 percent of my suggested daily intake of beta-carotene and 85 percent of my suggested daily intake of lutein/zeaxanthin. Usually, we think of beta-carotene as associated with the color orange, as in pumpkins or sweet potatoes, but in spinach the orange beta-carotene is masked by the dense green of the chlorophyll in the spinach leaves.

An excellent source of both vitamin C and beta-carotene, which your body may convert to vitamin A, these nutrients in spinach work together to prevent oxidized cholesterol from building up in blood vessel walls. A cup of fresh spinach leaves can provide you with a substantial amount of your daily requirement of vitamin A (via beta-carotene) and 11 percent of the adult female requirement for vitamin C, and 9 percent of the RDA for males.

Spinach is also an excellent source of folate. Folate plays a significant role in preventing cardiovascular disease because it works to escort a dangerous amino acid—homocysteine—from the body. We know that elevated levels of homocysteine are associated with an increased risk of heart attack and stroke.

To enhance your absorption of carotenes, toss cooked greens with a teaspoon of healthy extra virgin olive oil and/or some chopped nuts and avocado, or as a side dish with a piece of salmon.

Folate is also a key nutrient in DNA repair. This important B vitamin thus plays a major role in cancer prevention. The potassium and magnesium in spinach also contribute to cardiovascular

SALAD SENSE

Don't rely on fat-free salad dressings if you want a full nutrient boost from salads. Too many people try to cut calories by using nonfat salad dressings. We now know this can inhibit your body's absorption of nutrients from the greens and other vegetables.

In a recent study, volunteers ate spinach, romaine lettuce, tomatoes and carrots topped with two ounces Italian dressing containing either zero, six or 28 grams of canola oil. Blood tests revealed that the people who ate fat-free dressing absorbed a negligible amount of beta-carotene, a carotenoid that's been linked to protection against cancer and heart disease. The highest-fat dressing offered the greatest absorption of beta-carotene as well as alpha-carotene and lycopene.

My suggestion is to use homemade dressings (to reduce the sodium level). Try a combination of extra virgin olive oil, balsamic vinegar, ground pepper, Vegit or other salt substitute, and herbs and spices of your choosing. Be sure to use the dressing sparingly—don't drench the greens!

health, as they both work to lower blood pressure and reduce the risk of stroke.

Spinach and Cancer

In epidemiological studies, it's been found that the more spinach consumed, the lower the risk of almost every type of cancer. It's not surprising that spinach would be a powerful anticancer food given the high level of nutrients/phytonutrients it contains.

There are a number of different flavonoid compounds in spinach working to prevent different stages of cancer development. Glutathione and alpha lipoic acid are two antioxidants that some researchers believe are the most important in the body. Normally these life-preserving nutrients are manufactured in the body itself, but our ability to produce them seems to diminish as we age. However, spinach contains a ready-made supply of both.

Glutathione is the primary antioxidant in all cells where its critically important job is to protect our DNA. It repairs damaged DNA, promotes healthy cell replication, boosts the immune system, detoxifies pollutants and reduces chronic inflammation.

Alpha lipoic acid not only boosts glutathione levels, it helps stabilize blood sugar. Studies suggest it has an anti-aging role (e.g., a favorable influence on age-related mental decline) and helps prevent cancer, heart attacks and cataracts. Alpha lipoic acid is unusual in that it's both fat and water soluble. It can work in the fatty part of cell membranes and also in the water portions of our cells to reduce oxidative damage.

As a general rule, the darker the greens, the more bioactive phytonutrients they contain and thus the more powerful they are against cancer and other diseases.

Lutein, another powerful antioxidant in spinach, works to enhance the body's immune system, thus warding off many types of cancers.

LEAFY GREENS AND YOUR BLOOD PRESSURE

An easy way to boost your intake of antihypertensive nutrients is to eat leafy greens. They're high in potassium and low in sodium. They provide calcium, magnesium, folate, polyphenols, fiber and at least a trace to measurable amounts of plant-derived omega-3 fatty acids. Your blood vessels will thank you for this combination of nutrients.

PURSLANE

Many people consider purslane, if they consider it at all, a common weed. It's an annual that thrives in dry, sandy soil and can often be found by roadsides and even, perhaps, at the edges of your own garden.

Purslane is actually a SuperFood. Long regarded—indeed, as far back as ancient times—as a remedy for heart problems, sore throats, swollen joints, dry skin and a variety of other ailments, purslane was and is commonly eaten in Greece, Europe, Mexico and Asia.

Purslane is a worthy addition to any diet: It's actually the very best source of plant-derived omega-3 fatty acids, and a good source of vitamin C, beta-carotene and glutathione. Eaten in a salad with some olive oil and a bit of lemon juice, purslane is delicious.

If you're interested in trying purslane, check websites or books for photos to identify it, and see if you can find some growing wild. Be sure not to pick any from land that might have been treated with chemicals.

Look for purslane at farmers' markets, or try growing your own. It's easy to grow, resists drought and self-seeds readily.

A number of seed suppliers offer purslane seeds. Try Seeds of Change (*www.seedsofchange.com*), Eden Seeds (*www.edenseeds.com.au*) or Bountiful Gardens (*www.bountifulgardens.org*).

Greens seem to be particularly effective in preventing stomach cancer. A Japanese study found that a higher intake of yellow-green vegetables could cut the risk of gastric cancer in half.

Former smokers in particular can benefit from the power of spinach. Studies have found that people who eat a serving of spinach or one of its sidekicks daily, even if they're former smokers, have a significantly reduced risk of developing lung cancer. There's little question that people who consume the least carotenoid-rich food like spinach roughly double their risk of developing lung cancer.

We also know that the chlorophyll in spinach is a potential cancer fighter. Preliminary studies suggest it may be helpful in preventing tumor cell growth and exerting a significant antimutagenic effect against a wide range of potentially harmful carcinogens.

The Leafy Difference

Not all green leafies are created equal. Many of us are used to just grabbing a head of iceberg every time we think salad. If you expand your horizons, you'll get far more nutrition from your salads, as well as sandwiches, tacos and all other dishes that call for something green and leafy.

Green Leafy Comparisons *(based on 1 cup raw of each)*	*Spinach*	*Romaine*	*Iceberg*
Calories	7	9	6
Fiber	< 1 g	< 1 g	> 1 g
Calcium	30 mg	18 mg	11 mg
Iron	.8 mg	.6 mg	.2 mg
Magnesium	24 mg	8 mg	4 mg
Potassium	167 mg	140 mg	84 mg
Zinc	.2 mg	.1 mg	.1 mg
Vitamin C	8 mg	13 mg	2 mg
Niacin	.2 mg	.1 mg	.1 mg
Folate	58 mcg	76 mcg	31 mcg
Vitamin E	.6 mg	.1 mg	.2 mg
Lutein/Zeaxanthin	3.7 mg	1.4 mg	.2 mg
Beta-carotene	1.7 mg	2 mg	.1 mg

CALCIUM AND SPINACH

While spinach is relatively rich in calcium, the calcium it contains is bound to oxalates and is not readily bioavailable. However, the oxalates in spinach have a minimal effect on calcium absorption from other foods eaten with spinach. In other words, if you consume yogurt or any other calcium-rich food along with spinach, you'll still benefit.

As you can see, spinach is king of this crowd. It has the most total carotenoids. Romaine has only 38 percent of the lutein found in spinach but does have slightly more beta-carotene. Iceberg has only 5 percent of the lutein and 6 percent of the beta-carotene that spinach has and 17 percent of the magnesium and 53 percent of the folate. If you're used to iceberg-only salads, try mixing romaine and spinach. I often make a salad of one-half spinach to one-half romaine. You'll get the crispy crunch that you do from iceberg lettuce and lots more nutrients.

Spinach in the Kitchen

Spinach and many greens are available in markets all year round. There are different varieties, ranging from the Savoy type with crinkly, curly leaves to the flat- or smooth-leaf type, which has unwrinkled leaves. Spinach is sold both loose and in bags. Except for the bagged baby spinach, I prefer to buy loose spinach because it's easier to examine for freshness. It should always smell sweet and the leaves should be crisp and intact. Bagged greens can deteriorate quickly and should be carefully examined for darkened leaves that might signal they're past their prime. Yellowed leaves are also a sign that the greens are a poor choice. Spinach and most greens will keep only for three to four days after purchase. Don't wash spinach before storing, as that hastens deterioration. Wrap loose spinach in paper towels and store in the crisper.

Before spinach is cooked or served in a salad, it must be washed and washed! The leaves tend to harbor sand. Tear the leaves from the tough center stem—if using baby spinach, there's no need to do this—and put the leaves in a large bowl or sink filled with cool water. Allow the dirt to sink to the bottom, lift out the spinach, drain the water and sand, and repeat until all the grit is out. Don't soak the spinach; any greens will lose valuable vitamins if they're left to soak in water. A dip, swish and rinse is the way to go.

The worst chore connected with spinach is the washing, rinsing, washing, rinsing and so on. If you find great spinach at a roadside stand, it's worth it to go through the process, but at other times you're just in too much of a rush. My ship really came in when I found Ready Pac brand prewashed baby spinach in the supermarket. You can microwave it right in the bag after slitting it to let the steam escape. We go through several bags a week.

Here are some quick ways to get spinach and other greens into your diet…

- Layer cooked spinach or other greens in a lasagna.
- Steam spinach and serve sprinkled with fresh lemon juice and grated Parmesan cheese, or with a drizzle of soy dressing. This keeps for three days in the fridge, so I enjoy it as leftovers or take some to work.

COOKED OR RAW?

Greens are best eaten both raw and cooked. Cooking liberates the carotenoids, especially beta-carotene, and makes it more bioavailable. It also boosts lutein. But heat degrades both vitamin C and folate. The best approach? Enjoy greens in both salads and cooked form.

- Add a handful of spinach leaves to soups and casseroles.
- Dress leftover greens with balsamic vinegar dressing and sprinkle with some toasted sesame seeds or pine nuts.
- Add chopped greens to an omelet along with chives, tomato, bell peppers, and onion.
- Shred various greens along with romaine lettuce in a salad.
- Shred greens onto tacos and burritos.
- Use spinach in place of lettuce on your sandwiches.
- Make some krispy kale. Preheat the oven to 350° F. Trim and cut up a bunch of kale into bite-sized bits and spread on an aluminum foil–lined baking sheet, lightly sprayed with extra virgin olive oil. Bake for 15 to 20 minutes, stirring every five minutes or so. Sprinkle lightly with seasoned salt, garlic powder or any spice you prefer.
- Spinach Pesto. Puree raw spinach with almonds or walnuts, some garlic, olive oil and Parmesan cheese. This is delicious on chickpeas or bow-tie pasta. It can be frozen.

See our Shopping Lists (pages 219 and 220) for some recommended products.

TEA

How about a SuperFood that's cheap, has no calories, is associated with relaxation and pleasure, tastes good, and is available everywhere, from the finest restaurants to the local diner? And how about if that food lowered blood pressure, helped prevent cancer and osteoporosis, lowered your risk for stroke, promoted heart health, played a probable role in preventing sunlight damage to the skin (such as wrinkles and skin cancer), possibly prevented cataracts and contributed to your daily fluid needs? And if that weren't enough, there's also evidence that drinking tea is associated with beneficial changes in regard to obesity, periodontal disease, diabetes, longevity and neural function. And what if, to boot, it were antiviral, anti-inflammatory, anticavity, anti-allergy and prevented cataracts? Tea is all that. If you're not sipping orange pekoe at the office, gulping refreshing brewed iced green tea on the tennis court, or enjoying some Earl Grey after dinner, you're missing an opportunity to improve your health and longevity with tea, the world's most popular SuperFood.

How Tea Came to Be

According to legend, the discovery of tea occurred quite by accident in 2700 B.C. in the reign of the Chinese emperor Shen Nung. As the emperor rested beneath a shade tree, a servant boiled some drinking water nearby. A breeze came up and blew some leaves from a nearby wild tea tree into the pot. The emperor, impatient to drink, sipped the water and was delighted with the taste. Thus was born a drink that is, after water, the most popular drink in the world.

There are more than 3,000 varieties of tea available around the world, and it's a beverage that, because of its complexity and variety, attracts both connoisseurs and ceremony. From the British institution of tea time to formal Japanese tea ceremonies, no other beverage, save perhaps wine, inspires such ritual and debate.

While the savoring of tea's culinary attractions is an ancient pastime, the health-promoting properties of the beverage have recently drawn wide attention. Interest in the medicinal properties

TEA IS A GOOD SOURCE OF:

- Flavonoids
- Fluoride
- No calories

Try to drink: 1 to 4 cups daily or more

of tea has ebbed and flowed over the centuries, but it hasn't been until recently that research has confirmed ancient suspicions: Tea—the simple, common beverage—is a healthy drink.

All true tea comes from a single plant: the evergreen *Camellia sinensis*. (Herbal teas are not considered true teas, but rather are beverages brewed from herbs, roots and other sources. While some have medicinal properties, they are a separate category from authentic tea.) Three types of tea are produced from this single shrub: green, black and oolong. The differences are in the way the leaves are processed after harvesting. Green tea is lightly processed. Favored in Japan, it comprises about 21 percent of the world's tea production. Black tea, favored in Europe and the West, makes up about 77 percent of tea production worldwide. Black tea is made of leaves that have been left to ferment following harvesting. This fermenting darkens the leaves and allows them to develop a stronger flavor. Oolong tea, popular in China and Taiwan, is partially fermented.

While green tea has received the lion's share of the attention regarding health benefits, in fact, all true teas are beneficial. Green tea has been studied more extensively.

FOUR THOUSAND COMPOUNDS

Tea contains more than four thousand chemical compounds. The ones that have drawn the most attention, and which have proven benefits, include the phytonutrient polyphenols called "flavonoids"—the same type that is found in red wine and berries. There are about 268 milligrams of flavonoids in a cup of brewed black tea, and about 316 milligrams of flavonoids in a cup of green tea. One cup of brewed green tea provides more than five times the flavonoids than red onion, another popular flavonoid all-star.

The most potent polyphenol in tea is a substance known as epigallocatechin gallate, or EGCG, which belongs to a group of flavonoid phytochemicals known as catechins. Research has shown that in a test tube the catechins are more effective antioxidants than even the powerful vitamins C and E. In one laboratory test, the EGCG in green tea was found to be twenty times more potent an antioxidant than vitamin C.

Which Tea is Best?

While it used to be thought that green tea was the standout in promoting health, we now know that both green and black tea have similar, distinct and, in some cases, overlapping biochemical, physiological and epidemiological effects. It's possible that there may be an occasional disease where one is more effective than the other, but overall the message is to choose the tea you like best and enjoy it. I drink both black and green tea at different times in the day.

CAFFEINE IS KEY

There is some evidence that the health benefits of tea may be attributable to its caffeine content. Caffeine seems to have antimutagenic properties, which may be associated with an anticancer effect. Epidemiological studies suggest that caffeine may provide protection from the development of Parkinson's disease. So it would seem to be better to drink it in a caffeinated form. If caffeine is a problem for you, limit your tea drinking to early in the day and try green tea, which is generally lower in caffeine content.

There is less caffeine in tea than in an equal amount of coffee—roughly one-third less—and it seems to elicit fewer of caffeine's typical side effects.

Is All the News Good?

Some of the research on the benefits of tea has been contradictory. For example, some of the evidence pointing to tea's effects has only been gathered in the laboratory. Will the positive results be duplicated in humans? We'll have to wait and see.

In some instances, there have been negative associations with tea and health, but in many of these cases there have been other mitigating factors. Studies have shown tea to be both a positive and a negative influence on the development of esophageal cancer, but researchers speculate that the negative results could have been due to the way in which the tea was consumed. In some countries, tea is drunk boiling hot and/or is heavily salted, and either of these two preparations is known to encourage the development of cancers.

I believe the very positive news about tea is convincing. And, like the other SuperFoods, tea should be viewed as a part of a healthy lifestyle: You can't smoke, abuse alcohol, overeat, and never exercise and expect tea to save you. And you can't think that you can rely on the polyphenols in tea and skip the fruits and vegetables. On the other hand, I believe that tea is a wise addition to a healthy lifestyle for its ability to promote health and prevent disease.

Have a cup of green or black tea before you exercise in the morning. The flavonoids begin to appear in your blood within about thirty minutes, giving you an antioxidant boost and thus preparing your body to handle the free radicals generated by exercise.

Tea and Cancer

There is evidence that tea consumption decreases the risk of stomach, prostate, breast, pancreatic, colorectal, esophageal, bladder and lung cancers. Laboratory studies have consistently shown that tea can inhibit the formation and growth of tumors. Researchers have demonstrated that the catechins in tea prevent cell mutation and deactivate various carcinogens. They also decrease the growth of cancer cells and inhibit the growth of the blood vessels that tumors need in order to grow. Tea has also been found to help neutralize the cancer-promoting properities of certain environmental toxins.

In one Japanese study, researchers showed that women who drank the most green tea—in some cases as much as ten cups daily—had a lower risk of developing cancer when compared to women who did not drink tea.

There is also a belief among some researchers that the prostate-cancer incidence in U.S. males is fifteen times higher than the incidence in Asian males, in part because of the considerably greater amounts of tea drunk by Asians.

It also seems that teas may possess a probiotic effect, which enhances gastrointestinal health.

One study showed that the polyphenols in green tea actually boosted the effectiveness of one of the most common cancer drugs—doxorubicin—by causing the cancer cells to retain the drug rather than repel it.

While even one cup of tea seems to provide health benefits, it may take as many as four cups daily to really achieve a major decrease in cancer risk.

Green and black teas' ability to fight cancer has been amply demonstrated in study after study. Indeed, the Chemoprevention Branch of the National Cancer Institute has even developed a project that will test compounds found in tea to study their cancer-prevention abilities in human subjects.

While research on dementia and the consumption of tea has not been completed, we do know that people with the highest intake of flavonoids seem to have the lowest risk for developing dementia.

Tea and Heart Health

There is solid evidence that tea consumption is associated with a lowered risk of heart disease and stroke. The connection was noticed when the arteries of Chinese-American tea drinkers were compared with the arteries of Caucasian coffee drinkers. The tea drinkers had only two-thirds as much coronary artery damage and only one-third as much cerebral artery damage upon autopsy compared with the coffee drinkers. Another study found that in males, deaths from coronary artery disease were reduced by 40 percent among those who drank one or more cups of tea daily, and another study from Harvard showed that there was a 44 percent lower risk of heart attack in people who drank at least one cup of tea daily.

While some studies on tea and coronary artery disease have been inconclusive, in animal studies we know for sure that the catechins lower cholesterol levels, especially the damaging LDL cholesterol. There's also a definite inverse relationship between tea consumption and homocysteine levels, which are of course associated with an elevated risk for heart disease. Tea also seems to play a role in keeping the lining of the blood vessels plaque-free, which in turn lessens the risk of coronary artery disease. It seems that these positive benefits can be enjoyed if you drink between one and three cups daily, with greater protection conferred as the total consumption increases.

Given the epidemic of hypertension today, it's excellent news that tea can play a beneficial role in reducing blood pressure. A study of more than 1,500 men and women who drank tea regularly for at least a year saw a considerable reduction in their risk for high blood pressure. Those who drank one-half to two-and-a-half cups a day saw a 46 percent reduction in risk while those who drank more than two-and-a-half cups saw a 65 percent reduction. This is an impressive result.

Interestingly, one study showed that tea consumption in the year before a heart attack is associated with a lower mortality following the heart attack. In this study, moderate tea drinkers drank less than fourteen cups weekly, compared to those who drank none and those heavy tea drinkers who drank fourteen or more cups weekly. Both the moderate and the heavy tea drinkers had a lower death rate than those who abstained entirely.

Another study from England reported that green tea seems to inhibit heart cell death after a heart attack or stroke, and also that it appears to speed recovery from same.

The heartening implication of multiple studies is that one does not need to consume tremendous amounts of tea to enjoy health benefits. As little as a cup a day can play a positive role in your health.

Preliminary data suggest that tea may actually help you lose weight by increasing energy expenditure.

More Good News

Tea seems to have a positive effect on your dental health. Drinking tea lowers your risk of developing cavities as well as gum disease. One study found that tea may reduce cavity formation by up to 75 percent. This happens for a number of reasons. The fluoride content of the tea inhibits cavities from developing. Tea also seems to inhibit bacteria from adhering to tooth surfaces, while it also inhibits the rate of acid production of oral bacteria.

There may be a positive association between tea consumption and the prevention of kidney stones. Although some publications suggest the reverse, in the Nurses' Health Study it was found that for every cup of tea consumed daily, the risk of developing kidney stones decreased by 8 percent.

Both men and women can improve bone health by drinking tea. Studies that focused on

Caffeine is a natural component of all teas. In general, a cup of tea contains less than half the caffeine of coffee. Decaf tea has about 85 percent of the flavonoids found in regular tea. However, the actual milligrams of caffeine found in different teas are dependent on the specific brew strength and blends of tea leaves.

Canned, iced and powdered teas all have benefits, but the best bang for your tea buck is from freshly brewed and then consumed tea.

the risk of hip fracture found that habitual tea consumption, especially when maintained for more than ten years, has been shown to have a significant benefit to bone-mineral density. This seems to be due to the fact that some of the flavonoids in tea have phytoestrogen activity, which benefits bone health. Moreover, some tea extracts seem to inhibit bone resorption.

One recent study found that oolong tea is successful in treating atopic dermatitis; this is no doubt due in part to the anti-allergic properties of tea. This benefit was noticed after one or two weeks of drinking tea. In this study, a one-third–ounce tea bag that steeped for five minutes in just over four cups of boiling water was consumed in three parts, one with each meal.

Given the alarming rise in the rate of diabetes worldwide, it's encouraging to learn that recent studies have shown that green tea is effective in improving insulin sensitivity. In one study, healthy subjects who consumed green tea were subsequently given glucose tolerance tests. The green tea actually increased the ability of the body to manage blood sugar effectively.

THE BEST FOR LAST

Finally, if there weren't enough good reasons to drink tea, here's a finding that sends most of my patients right to their teakettles. In a recent study, it was found that green tea not only promoted cardiovascular health by reducing damage to LDL cholesterol and thus reducing plaque formation, it also reduced body fat. In the twelve weeks of the study, thirty-eight normal-to-overweight men who drank one bottle of green tea daily had significantly lower body weight, BMI, waist circumference, body-fat mass and amount of subcutaneous fat compared with men who had consumed a bottle of oolong tea daily. It seems that the amount of catechin flavonoids made the difference. The green tea contained 690 milligrams of catechins while the oolong tea had just 22 milligrams of catechins.

Some Tea Tips

Here is some information to keep in mind...

- Brewed tea confers more health benefits than instant tea.
- Tea bags are as potent as loose tea in their health benefits.
- Brew tea for at least three minutes.
- Squeeze the brewed tea bag to almost double the polyphenol content.
- If you're sensitive to caffeine, reduce brewing time to one minute or so.
- Avoid drinking extremely hot tea.
- The flavonoids degrade with time, so it's best to drink freshly brewed tea that's hot or quickly iced.
- Add a wedge of lemon or lime with the rind for a polyphenol boost.

An animal study suggests that eating black pepper at the same time as drinking green tea can significantly increase the amount of the cancer-fighting EGCG absorbed by your body. So, the next time you're drinking tea with a meal, grind some black pepper into your soup, salad or main course.

Tea in the Kitchen

As promising and indeed almost astonishing as some of these findings are, I really don't think anyone should drink tea with the single intention of, say, lowering blood pressure or losing weight. On the other hand, given the incredibly impressive ability of tea, particularly green tea, to promote health, I can't imagine why anyone wouldn't drink it regularly. I sip it often during the course of the day.

When I travel, I tuck some green-tea bags into my pocket for an in-flight beverage or something to sip in a hotel room (many hotel rooms have coffeemakers that will heat water for tea).

Here are some ideas for using tea, particularly green tea...

- Brew green tea with a few slices of fresh peeled ginger and lemon.
- Brew green tea in room-temperature water for a half hour and use in marinades, dressing, soups and sauces. Brewing at room temperature or in cool water will prevent bitterness.
- Mix brewed tea with fruit juice and pour over ice.

See our Shopping Lists (page 223) for some recommended products.

TOMATOES

Many people feel certain that there's going to be bad news along with the good news when they learn that the tomato is a SuperFood. Of course, they like tomatoes, they think, but in many locations tomatoes are only tasty for a couple of months each year. Well, there's good news and more good news about tomatoes. Not only do they pack a nutritional wallop, but you can enjoy their benefits all year long. That's because their power is available in processed tomatoes. The spaghetti sauce and taco sauce that you love, along with that slice of pizza and even, yes, ketchup and barbeque sauce, all have the power of tomatoes. So, no matter where you live, it's easy to get more tomatoes into your diet and begin to enjoy their considerable benefits.

The tomato—a critical ingredient in some of our favorite foods, including pizza and lasagna—has had a checkered past. Once scorned as a sinister and poisonous food (one Latin name, *lycopersicon* or "wolf peach," refers to the belief that tomatoes were like a wolf—dangerous). It wasn't until the late nineteenth century that tomatoes became popular. Originally grown and enjoyed by the Aztecs in Mexico, tomatoes were imported to Europe by Spanish missionaries. Viewed as a dangerous food by all but the Italians and Spanish, it took years for tomatoes to lose their unsavory reputation.

There was some basis for the original skepticism that clung to tomatoes: Their leaves do

TOMATOES ARE A SOURCE OF:

- Lycopene
- Low in calories
- Vitamin C
- Alpha- and beta-carotene
- Lutein/zeaxanthin
- Phytuene and phytofluene
- Potassium
- B vitamins (B6, niacin, folate, thiamine and pantothenic acid)
- Chromium
- Biotin
- Fiber

Sidekicks: Red watermelon, pink grapefruit, Japanese persimmons, red-fleshed papaya, strawberry guava

Try to eat: 1 serving of processed tomatoes or sidekicks per day and multiple servings per week of fresh tomatoes

contain toxic alkaloids. Embraced by Americans by the end of the nineteenth century, tomatoes have gone on to become one of our most popular vegetables and are now recognized as one of our favorite SuperFoods.

It should be noted that tomatoes are not really vegetables. Botanically classified as a fruit, they are the seed-bearing portions of a flowering plant. However, in 1893, a case came before the Supreme Court of the United States relating to shipping tariffs on tomatoes. Should farmers pay fruit or vegetable rates on them? The Court came down on the side of vegetables, and so vegetables they became.

There are two new carotenoids on the scene with promising health benefits—phytoene and phytofluene. They are both found in tomatoes and tomato products. Phytoene has been shown to possess antioxidant capabilities and also anticarcinogenic action. More study needs to be done, but preliminary work indicates that they play a role in tomatoes' ability to combat cancer and other diseases.

LYCOPENE IN FOOD

(22 milligrams of lycopene is the ideal daily amount)

	Milligrams
Tomato puree (½ cup)	27.2
Tomato juice (1 cup)	22
R.W. Knudsen Very Veggie vegetable juice cocktail (1 cup)	22
Tomato sauce (½ cup)	18.5
Watermelon wedge	13
Tomato paste (2 tablespoons)	9.2
Watermelon balls (1 cup)	7
Ketchup (2 tablespoons)	5.8
Stewed tomatoes, canned (½ cup)	5.1
Pizza (3-ounce slice)	4
Tomato (fresh, medium)	3.2
5 cherry tomatoes	2.2
½ Pink grapefruit	1.8

The Power of Red

Lycopene, a member of the carotenoid family and a pigment that contributes to the red color of tomatoes, is a major contributor to their health-promoting power. Lycopene has demonstrated a range of unique and distinct biological properties that have intrigued scientists. Some researchers have come to believe that lycopene could be as powerful an antioxidant as beta-carotene. We do know that lycopene is the most efficient quencher of the free-radical singlet oxygen, a particularly deleterious form of oxygen, and lycopene is also capable of scavenging a large number of free radicals.

Lycopene is a nutrient whose time in the spotlight has come. It's been the subject of great interest lately as more and more researchers have focused on the particular power of this nutrient. The attention began in the 1980s when studies started to reveal that people who ate large amounts of tomatoes were far less likely to die from all forms of cancer compared with those who ate little or no tomatoes. Many other studies echoed the positive findings about the effect of eating tomatoes.

It's not only cancer that the lycopene in tomatoes helps mitigate. Lycopene is an important part of the antioxidant defense network in the skin, and dietary lycopene by itself or in combination with other nutrients can raise the sun protection factor (SPF) of the skin. In other words, by eating tomatoes (in this case, cooked or processed tomatoes) you're enhancing your skin's ability to withstand the assault from the damaging rays of the sun. It acts like an internal sunblock!

Lycopene may also indirectly lower the risk for cataracts and age-related macular degeneration by "sparing" lutein oxidation so that lutein can be transported to the macula in its unoxidized, protective form.

Perhaps you've heard of the nun study in which Dr. David Snowdon of the Sanders-Brown Center on Aging at the University of Kentucky assessed eighty-eight Roman Catholic nuns ranging in age from 77 to 98. The nuns with the highest blood concentrations of lycopene were the most able to care for themselves and complete everyday tasks. Overall, those with the highest levels of lycopene were 3.6 times better able to function in their everyday lives than those with the lowest levels. Most interestingly, no similar relationship between vigor and the presence of other antioxidants (such as vitamin E and beta-carotene) was found.

Lycopene is rare in foods, and tomatoes are one of only a few that are rich in this powerful antioxidant. Indeed, ketchup, tomato juice and pizza sauce account for more than 80 percent of the total lycopene intake of Americans.

TWO LYCOPENE-RICH SUPERSIDEKICKS

Red watermelon is another excellent source of lycopene. Some food sources say that ounce for ounce, watermelon is even richer in lycopene than tomatoes because it has a very concentrated, bioavailable source of the nutrient. Watermelon definitely results in a blood-level boost of lycopene comparable to that of tomatoes.

Pink grapefruit has not been studied as extensively as tomatoes and watermelon, but the lycopene in this food is nonetheless substantial. When watermelon and pink grapefruit are eaten, the efficient absorption of the lycopene depends on the presence of a bit of dietary fat. Tomatoes are often served with olive oil or cheese, while pink grapefruit and watermelon are often served on their own. Just be sure that you eat them in conjunction with some fat; even a couple of nuts will do, or with pink grapefruit, have a slice of whole-grain toast with some cheese or avocado. A salad of cubed watermelon and some feta cheese is refreshing and does the trick. Or enjoy watermelon as a dessert following a meal that has included some healthy fat.

Watermelon, strawberry guava, pink grapefruit, red-fleshed papaya and persimmons are other dietary sources of lycopene. All make excellent additions to the diet.

While lycopene has received a lot of attention recently, tomatoes are rich in a wide variety of nutrients, which seem to work synergistically to promote health and vitality. Low in calories, high in fiber, and high in potassium, tomatoes are not only a rich source of lycopene, they are also a source of beta-carotene, alpha-carotene, lutein/zeaxanthin, phytuene/phytofluene and various polyphenols. They contain small amounts of B vitamins (thiamine, pantothenic acid, vitamin B6 and niacin), as well as folate, vitamin E, magnesium, manganese and zinc.

It's the synergy of this multitude of nutrients, as well as the special power of lycopene, that boosts tomatoes to a spot in the all-star SuperFood pantheon.

Tomatoes and Cancer

Some of the most exciting studies on tomatoes have focused on their ability to protect against cancer, especially prostate cancer.

Dr. Edward Giovannucci of the Harvard Medical School has published two interesting studies that investigated the effects of foods, particularly tomatoes, on cancer risk. In his 1995 study, Dr. Giovannuci found that of the 48,000 men surveyed, those who ate 10 or more servings of tomatoes a week reduced their risk of prostate cancer by 35 percent and their risk of aggressive prostate tumors by almost 50 percent. Indeed, it seemed the higher the tomato intake, the lower the cancer risk. Interestingly, lycopene is the most abundant carotenoid in the prostate gland.

Dr. Giovannucci's subsequent study in 1999 showed that, of all tomato products, tomato-sauce consumption—at just two servings a week—was by far the most reliable indicator of reduced risk for prostate cancer.

Two important points emerge from these studies. The first, which I mentioned earlier, is that processed tomatoes—sauce and paste—are more effective than raw tomatoes at reducing cancer risk. In the raw tomato, the lycopene is bound into the cell walls and fiber. Processing breaks down these cell walls and frees the lycopene to be absorbed by the body. Ounce for ounce, processed tomato products and cooked tomatoes contain two to eight times the available lycopene of raw tomatoes. While processing does diminish the levels of vitamin C in the tomatoes, it elevates the total antioxidant activity, thus ultimately providing an enhanced benefit.

Tomato paste is a super ingredient to use in cooking. It has the power of a fresh tomato, but it is more concentrated!

Eating tomato paste will increase the SPF (sun protection factor) of your skin, protecting you from damaging ultraviolet rays. In one study, ingesting 40 grams daily (less than one-quarter of a small can) of tomato paste, which provides about 16 milligrams of lycopene, resulted in a 40 percent increase in the amount of sun exposure it takes to cause reddening of the skin.

Small amounts of tomato paste can enrich soups, stocks and stews. Tomato paste comes in a can and squeezable tube. No-salt-added varieties are available. At our house we often double the amount of tomato paste called for in a recipe.

The second important point, which Dr. Giovannucci mentions in his article, once again highlights the importance of whole foods. While he notes the association between tomato consumption and reduced cancer risk, particularly lung, stomach and prostate cancers, he makes it clear that "a direct benefit of lycopene has not been proven and other compounds in tomatoes alone or interacting with lycopene may be important." Given the rich array of nutrients in tomatoes it wouldn't be surprising if, once again, the synergy of those nutrients were the reason for the positive effects.

Other studies also confirm emphatically that a diet rich in tomatoes helps prevent prostate cancer. In a meta-study of 21 studies, it was found that men who ate the highest amount of raw tomatoes had a 19 percent reduction in prostate cancer risk. Even one 6-ounce daily serving reduced the risk of this disease by 3 percent.

CONSUMER-ACTION ALERT

Urge manufacturers to offer more varieties of canned tomato products with less sodium.

Prostate cancer isn't the only type of cancer that tomatoes seem to help protect against. Exciting new research shows that high lycopene consumption is inversely related to the risk for pancreatic cancer, a frequently deadly, fast-progressing cancer. In this study, data showed that men consuming the most lycopene had a 31 percent reduction in their risk for pancreatic cancer. Among subjects who had never smoked, those whose diets were rich in beta-carotene or total carotenoids reduced their risk by 43 percent and 42 percent, respectively.

A growing body of evidence also suggests that lycopene provides some degree of protection against cancers of the breast, digestive tract, cervix, bladder and lung.

Lycopene seems to reduce the risk of cancer in several ways. As a particularly powerful antioxidant, it helps block the ongoing destructive effects of the free radicals in the body. It's especially effective in this mission when sufficient vitamin E is present. Lycopene also seems to interfere with the growth factors that stimulate cancer cells to grow and proliferate. And finally, it seems to stimulate the body to mount a more effective immune defense against cancer.

As mentioned, lycopene, which is fat soluble, needs a bit of dietary fat to transport it into the bloodstream. A whole, fresh tomato, eaten out of hand, is not a good source of this nutrient. The top-ranked tomato-based foods that seem to be the most cancer-protective are all prepared with some oil. A salad of tomatoes with some extra virgin olive oil is really a health-promoting food. The green color of olive oil indicates the presence of polyphenols. Those polyphenols combined with the powerful nutrients in tomatoes are a healthy taste treat on spaghetti sauce, as a pizza topping or in tomato-based soups.

TOMATOES ALL THE TIME

Compared to other carotenoids that are efficiently stored in the body, the plasma level of lycopene falls rather quickly when lycopene-rich foods are not included in the diet. Therefore, it seems prudent to get some lycopene from tomatoes in your diet on a daily basis if possible. Fortunately, this isn't difficult—most of us have an opportunity to eat a tomato-based food frequently.

Tomatoes and Your Heart

In addition to being cancer-protective, there's ample evidence that tomatoes also play a role in reducing your risk for cardiovascular disease.

The antioxidant function of lycopene, combined with the other powerful antioxidants in tomatoes such as vitamin C and beta-carotene, work in the body to neutralize free radicals that could otherwise damage cells and cell membranes. This preservation of cells and their membranes reduces the potential for inflammation and thereby the progression and severity of atherosclerosis.

In one study, German scientists compared the lycopene levels in the tissues of men who had suffered heart attacks with those of men who had not. The men who had suffered attacks had lower lycopene levels than those who hadn't. Interestingly, the men with the lowest levels of lycopene were twice as likely to suffer a heart attack as those with the highest levels.

In another large European study that compared carotenoid levels among patients from ten different countries, lycopene was found to be the most protective against heart attack.

A daily glass of tomato juice is a good idea not only for those with diabetes but also for anyone susceptible to blood-clot formation. People who have recently had a surgical procedure, who travel long distances by plane, who smoke or who have high cholesterol might all consider drinking a daily glass of tomato juice. Look for low-sodium tomato juice, and if you find that it is too bland, add a dash of hot sauce, a sprinkle of celery seed, a squeeze of lemon juice or a dash of Vegit All-Purpose Seasoning to improve the taste.

Another study published recently followed 39,876 middle-aged and older women who were free of both cancer and cardiovascular disease at the start of the study. After more than seven years of follow-up, those who consumed seven to 10 servings each week of lycopene-rich foods were found to have a 29 percent lower risk for cardiovascular disease compared with women who ate fewer than 1.5 servings of tomato foods weekly.

Interestingly, tomato juice has been identified as an effective blood thinner in recent research. People in the study had type II diabetes. They drank 8 ounces of tomato juice or a placebo daily. In three weeks, the platelet aggregation (clumping together of blood cells) in the tomato-juice drinkers was significantly reduced. No change was seen in those drinking the placebo. As diabetes can cause blood vessel damage, which encourages platelets to clump and stick to vessel walls and ultimately leads to cardiovascular disease, it's welcome news that a glass of tomato-juice a day has potent health benefits.

Tomatoes are also a good source of potassium, niacin, vitamin B6 and folate—a great heart-healthy combination of nutrients. Potassium-rich foods play a positive role in cardiovascular health, being especially effective in helping to achieve optimal blood pressure. Niacin is commonly used to lower elevated blood cholesterol levels. The combination of vitamin B6 and folate effectively reduces levels of homocysteine in the blood. Elevated levels of homocysteine are associated with a higher risk of heart disease.

The easiest way to increase your daily lycopene intake dramatically is to drink 8 ounces of R.W. Knudsen Low Sodium Very Veggie Vegetable Cocktail. It contains a whopping 22 milligrams of lycopene per 8 ounces.

The Power of Skin

Growing out in the wild, even if it's the wild of your backyard, plants must protect themselves from attack. They're under constant assault from ultraviolet rays, pollution and predators. It's important that they have a first, powerful line of defense. Skin is that defense. Whether it's the skin of an apple, the peel of a grape or the rind on an orange, this part of the fruit has a tremendous antioxidant ability that permits it to withstand the assaults of nature. The outer leaves of spinach and cabbage, for example, have the highest levels of vitamin C, and broccoli florets have more C than the stalks. One hundred grams of fresh apples with the skin contain about 142 milligrams of flavonoids, but the same amount of apples without the skin has only 97 milligrams of flavonoids. Quercetin—a common flavonoid with anti-inflammatory properties—is found only in the skins of apples, not in the flesh of the fruit. The antioxidant activity of 100 grams of apples without the skin is 55 percent of the activity of 100 grams of apples with skin. The skinless apples are about half as powerful. The papery brownish skins on almonds and peanuts are loaded with various bioactive polyphenols.

As a general rule, the greater the proportion of skin to interior fruit, the higher the antioxidant ability. For example, blueberries and cranberries are extraordinarily high in antioxidants. The rule holds true for tomatoes: The smaller the tomato think cherry tomato—the higher its antioxidant ability. You can use that antioxidant power by simply eating the skin!

Try to eat appropriate fruits and vegetables with the skin on. Of course, the skin is where the pesticides and potentially harmful bacteria reside, so a careful washing is mandatory. Don't forget that juices with sediment on the bottom

PIZZA FOR THE PROSTATE

The prostate gland does most of its growing between the ages of 13 and 20. If a boy eats lots of saturated fat during those years (the major "fast food" span for most Americans), it may increase his chances of developing prostrate cancer later in life. This is a strong argument for making pizza (double the sauce, halve the pepperoni and sneak in some veggies) the fast food of choice for your kids, particularly your sons.

I've always recommended ketchup as an excellent source of lycopene. (It's nice to be able to tell kids, in particular, that there's at least one healthy food at fast-food restaurants!) It turns out that you'll boost your lycopene intake considerably if you buy organic ketchup.

In a recent comparison study, it was found that a sample of regular ketchup contained approximately 59 micrograms of lycopene per gram while the sample of organic ketchup contained about three times that amount, or about 183 micrograms per gram.

If you rarely use ketchup, this difference probably won't matter. But if, like many families with children, you use a fair amount of it, it may well be worth getting the extra nutritional benefits of organic ketchup.

are the ones to choose. That sediment contains bits of skin and pulp and is a great source of antioxidants. You'll notice that many organic juices as well as those that are 100 percent juice contain this sediment.

Avoid cooking tomatoes in aluminum cookware. The acidity of the tomatoes may interact with the metal, causing it to migrate into your food, affecting the taste and possibly having negative effects on your health.

Tomatoes in the Kitchen

Shopping for tomatoes that will have the most powerful, reliable effect on your health is surprisingly easy. As I've mentioned, processed tomatoes are actually of more benefit than fresh tomatoes. In fact, you probably already have in your pantry most of the tomato preparations that can help you boost your intake of this powerful food. Now, you simply have to remember to use them regularly!

Patients love it when I tell them that pizza can be a "health food." I always order it with extra sauce to boost my lycopene intake. It tastes great, too. If I'm eating pizza at home, I blot the slice with a paper napkin to soak up the fat.

Here are some quick ideas for getting more tomatoes into your life...

- Sauté a bunch of cherry tomatoes in some olive oil and herbs. Toss over pasta or serve as a side dish.
- Use sun-dried tomatoes (no salt added) in sandwiches.
- Toss a can of diced tomatoes into soups and stews.
- Make homemade pizza with extra sauce and top with your favorite vegetables. Many supermarkets sell pizza dough that needs only to be shaped, topped and baked.
- A delicious quick meal is a turkey or chicken cutlet, pounded thin, quickly sautéed to brown it slightly, topped with a favorite salsa and baked in the oven until done. Sprinkle a bit of grated cheese on top near the end of cooking and shower it with chopped cilantro or parsley before serving if you like.
- Place one pint of cherry tomatoes, covered with one-half cup of extra virgin olive oil in a small roasting dish. Sprinkle with salt and pepper. Bake in the oven (450° F) for 20 minutes. *Optional:* Add fresh basil before serving.
- One of my favorite sandwiches is a toasted slice of whole wheat bread topped with sliced avocado and some chunky salsa.
- To make huevos rancheros, sauté chopped onions in a tablespoon of extra virgin olive oil until golden. Add some canned diced tomatoes and cook until most of the liquid has evaporated. Add some diced jalapeño pepper. Crack some high-omega-3 eggs into the sauce

and cook to your liking. Sprinkle with chopped cilantro before serving.

See our Shopping Lists (pages 211, 214, 216, 220, 222 and 223) for some recommended products.

TURKEY (SKINLESS BREAST)

At last! Turkey receives the recognition it has long deserved. Passed over as the official national bird in favor of the eagle (despite Ben Franklin's enthusiastic support), the turkey is too often relegated to a once-a-year meal. Ignored and virtually invisible eleven months of the year, it's been a quiet few hundred years for the poor bird.

Turkey is a SuperFood. Highly nutritious, low in fat, inexpensive, versatile and always available, the turkey has finally come into its own. When you discover all of turkey's terrific nutritious benefits, it will surely become part of your regular diet.

Skinless turkey breast is one of, if not *the,* leanest meat-protein sources on the planet. This alone could make it a SuperFood, but turkey also offers a rich array of nutrients: niacin, selenium, vitamins B6 and B12, riboflavin, iron and zinc. These nutrients are heart-health valuable in helping to lower the risk for cancer.

Low-fat Protein

Because skinless turkey breast is so low in saturated fat, it closely approximates the lean sources of animal protein present during Paleolithic times. Studies suggest that the Paleolithic diet was a healthy one. There is also a broad consensus that the traditional Mediterranean/Japanese/Okinawan diets are also low in saturated fat and have multiple health-promoting qualities.

In general, there are no scientifically validated healthy dietary patterns that are high in saturated fat. There's no doubt that the leaner the protein source the better, but low-fat, healthy animal protein is very hard to find. Much of the poultry and red meat available in our markets has too much bad fat and little or no good fat. For example, 3 ounces of fresh ham has 5.5 grams of saturated fat. Three ounces of flank steak has 4.5 grams of saturated fat. The same amount of skinless turkey-breast meat has less than .2 gram of saturated fat.

We are well aware these days that saturated fat is linked to a host of health problems, including everything from cardiovascular disease to cancer. Many studies indicate a relationship between increased dietary saturated fat and colon cancer, coronary heart disease, and Alzheimer's disease. Remember that your dietary intake of saturated fat has a much stronger influence on increasing serum cholesterol than does your dietary intake of cholesterol. Saturated fat raises LDL cholesterol, which in turn promotes cardiovascular disease. This means that turkey can make a valuable contribution to your diet.

TURKEY IS A SOURCE OF:

- Low-fat protein
- Riboflavin
- Niacin
- Vitamin B6
- Vitamin B12
- Iron
- Selenium
- Zinc

Sidekicks: Skinless chicken breast

Try to eat: 3 to 4 servings per week of 3 to 4 ounces (maximum, 4 ounces per serving)

Meat (3 ounces)	Calories	Protein	Cholesterol*	Saturated Fat
Turkey (skinless, white meat)	115	26 grams	71 mg	.2 gram
Chicken (skinless, white meat)	140	26 grams	72 mg	.85 gram
95% Lean ground beef	145	22 grams	65 mg	2.4 grams

*Saturated-fat content is more important than the amount of cholesterol. You are "allowed" 300 milligrams of cholesterol per day, and the amount of cholesterol in these meats is not high; by comparison, one egg yolk has about 213 milligrams of cholesterol.

This is especially welcome news to those who are eager to improve the quality of their everyday diets but are not willing to rely exclusively on vegetarian sources of protein.

What about chicken? Many people think of chicken and turkey as virtually interchangeable. They're surprised when white-meat chicken breast isn't listed along with white-meat turkey breast as a SuperFood. But skinless roasted white meat of chicken is higher in calories and saturated fat than roasted white meat of turkey.

Protein in Our Diets

Protein has become a loaded word these days. High protein, low carb...they're concepts that have dominated nutrition discussions in recent years. What's the truth?

First, let's have a very brief chemistry lesson. Much of our body, including muscles, organs, skin, hair and enzymes, is made primarily of protein. Protein is in every cell and is necessary for life. Protein, in turn, is composed of amino acids. Some amino acids are manufactured by the body. Nine others called essential amino acids must come from the foods we eat. Some foods, including all animal proteins like eggs, meat and fish, contain all of the essential amino acids, and they're known as "complete" proteins. Other foods, particularly plant foods, are incomplete proteins; they must be made complete by getting their missing amino acids from other sources. That's why vegetarians must rely on certain combinations of foods, e.g., brown rice and beans, peanut butter and whole-grain bread, and whole-grain macaroni and cheese, in order to get complete protein. The only plant exception to this is soybeans and/or soy foods like tofu: They are complete proteins.

Don't worry too much about your total protein intake. Instead, think about healthy sources of protein and how to increase them in your diet. Remember that vegetarian sources of protein like soy foods, nuts and grains are good choices, as is seafood like salmon, oysters, clams and sardines, and low-fat or nonfat dairy products.

Our bodies need a constant supply of protein. We don't store it as we do fats. However, getting enough protein isn't a problem for the vast majority of people. Most of us, in fact, get too much protein in our diets, or at least more than we need. The average woman eats 65 grams of protein daily; the average man eats 90 grams a day. Some high-protein diets recommend double or even triple that amount.

In 2002, the National Academy of Sciences published a new Dietary Reference Intake on everything from fiber to fatty acids. They recommend that, in order to reduce the risk of developing chronic degenerative diseases, an optimal range of protein intake is 10 to 35 percent of calories. (On a 2,000-calorie-a-day diet, this would be 50 to 175 grams of protein.) This recommendation is based on extensive scientific review and in my opinion is an excellent guideline.

What does this translate to in everyday terms? Well, adult women need at least 46 grams of protein; adult men, 56 grams (very active and elderly people may well need more). It's very easy to achieve this protein recommendation. A woman can reach her daily goal with 3 ounces of tuna (20 grams of protein) plus 3 ounces of turkey breast (26 grams of protein). A slice of whole wheat bread has about 3 grams of protein and an ounce of almonds, 6 grams. Since many foods contain protein (a cup of lentil soup has about 7.8 grams; an egg, 6 grams; and a baked potato, 3 grams), you can see how quickly most people would reach their protein goal on a daily basis.

What About High-Protein Diets?

Many people mistakenly believe that there's some special "fat burning" paradise that you enter when you severely restrict your carbohydrate intake and simultaneously boost your protein intake. There is nothing magical about a high-protein diet, despite our eagerness to believe so. The simple, irrefutable fact is that if you eat more calories than you burn, you'll gain weight; if you burn more than you eat, you'll lose. Most people who follow a high-protein diet and lose weight do so simply because their food choices are such that they automatically cut down on calories. When you restrict or severely limit one group of foods (carbohydrates), a group that ordinarily comprises over half your calorie intake, you can't help but lose weight. And once you go off the diet, all or most of the weight usually comes back.

✪ Try to substitute nut and soy protein for some of your red-meat consumption. This will definitely lower your risk for cardiovascular disease and possibly lower your risk for cancer.

There are a few proven dangers in an exceptionally high protein intake. For one thing, the more protein you take in, the more calcium you excrete in your urine, thus raising your risk for osteoporosis. In the Nurses' Health Study, women consuming more than 95 grams of protein a day (an extra-lean 6-ounce hamburger has 48.6 grams of protein) had an increased risk of fractures. While there is ongoing debate on this subject, it seems that vegetable protein causes less bone loss than animal protein.

A high-protein diet is also associated with some risk for kidney damage among susceptible people. If you have below-normal renal function, you should talk to your health-care professional prior to trying a high-protein diet.

Another danger of excessive protein in the diet has to do with insulin levels. One of the arguments for a high-protein diet is a claim that too many carbs raise the blood insulin level, which in turn causes weight gain by forcing the calories into fat cells rather than allowing these same calories to be burned as energy. A recent Michigan State University study seems to disprove this argument. In reality, higher insulin levels are a risk factor for developing diabetes and perhaps cancer.

VEGETARIAN PROTEIN

It's relatively easy to consume sufficient protein if you're a vegetarian. *If you select from two or more of these three groups in a given day, you're set...*

- Whole grains
- Legumes
- Nuts and seeds

Unfortunately, for most people in the United States, a high-protein diet means an increase in their consumption of red meat. It's this type of protein—with its associated saturated fat—along with the increased and disproportionate amount of it, that has the greatest negative impact on long-term health.

There is wide consensus that it is prudent to keep one's intake of saturated fat to less than 7 percent of fat calories. Two significant sources of saturated fat in the typical American diet are red meat and full-fat dairy products. Numerous studies suggest there is a relationship between increased dietary saturated fat and colon cancer, coronary heart disease and Alzheimer's disease.

In addition, a number of studies have shown a link between red-meat consumption and prostate cancer. It is also important to remember that saturated-fat intake has a much stronger influence on increasing serum cholesterol than does dietary-cholesterol intake. Substituting skinless turkey breast for higher-saturated-fat protein choices is an easy strategy to help lengthen your health span.

One complete protein source a day is enough. Scientists once believed that some complete protein was needed at each meal. We now know that the amino acids from protein remain in our bodies for at least four hours and for as long as 48. So, don't worry about trying to eat complete protein at each meal. Think in terms of your daily intake.

Where's the Beef?

There's nothing intrinsically wrong with red meat. Red meat from American buffalo, for example, is high in protein and low in saturated fat. The problem with most of the commonly available red meat in the United States is that it supplies too much of the fat we don't need—saturated fat and omega-6 fatty acids—and too little of the fat we do need—omega-3 fatty acids.

In theory, free-range and free-roam cattle should offer a better alternative to meat raised in feedlots. Cattle are ruminants, which means their digestive systems are primed for grass, not grain, but it's faster and easier to fatten them up on corn. A corn diet is rich in omega-6 fatty acids (which we get too much of), and so the meat of corn-fed cattle becomes high in this fatty acid, too. Corn-fed cattle will also tend to have higher residues of hormones and antibiotics.

Antibiotics are often used as growth promoters in farm animals. It is estimated that farmers administer approximately more than 26 million pounds of antibiotics to animals each year, with only about 2 million pounds used for treatment of infections. Remember, antibiotic-resistant strains of bacteria have been found in commercial meat products and in consumers' intestines! Let's lobby to lower the antibiotic use in animals that we use for food.

Grass-fed beef is leaner and has a healthier balance of omega-6 to omega-3 fatty acids. Grass-fed beef contains the plant-derived omega-3 fats and vitamin E found in green leafy vegetables, and it is lower in saturated fat compared with meat from corn-fed cattle. Of course, grass-fed, free-range beef is harder to find and more expensive than corn-fed supermarket beef. That's why leaner sources of protein—like turkey breast—make a better choice.

If you do choose beef of any type, trim all visible fat. On those occasions when my wife and I have ground beef, we rinse the browned beef in a strainer under hot water to get most of the fat out before adding spices and completing the recipe.

In the Mediterranean diet, red meat and meat products are consumed four to five times a month. Less is better, but this is a reasonable beginning goal for the majority of Americans. Ideally, you should have no more than 3 ounces of lean beef about every 10 days.

Turkey for Your Heart

Turkey is a good source of niacin, vitamin B6 and vitamin B12. All three of these B vitamins are important for energy production and DNA health. Niacin seems to be associated with lowering the risk for heart attack and heart attack deaths. Low levels of vitamin B12, as well as of B6 and folate, are associated with high levels of homocysteine—an amino acid–like substance that may be an independent risk factor for heart disease.

Turkey for Your Immune System

Turkey is rich in zinc, a remarkable nutrient that is present in all tissues of the body. Suboptimal zinc intake is common, and frequent consumption of turkey could play a role in improving overall zinc levels in the population. The zinc that is in turkey is far more bioavailable than the zinc in nonmeat sources of this important mineral. Zinc is critical for a healthy immune system. It helps promote wound healing and also normal cell division. A four-ounce serving of turkey breast provides about 20 percent of the daily value for zinc.

Super Source of Selenium

Turkey is a good source of the trace mineral selenium. Selenium is of critical importance to human health. It is involved in a number of bodily functions, including thyroid hormone metabolism, antioxidant defense systems and immune function. Evidence seems to suggest that there is a strong inverse relationship between selenium intake and the risk for cancer. While research is ongoing, there are a variety of explanations for selenium's role in preventing cancer. Proposed anticancer mechanisms associated with selenium include improved immune system function, inhibition of cancer cell growth, enhanced detoxification of carcinogens and improved antioxidant status. Other good sources of selenium include Brazil nuts, crabmeat, wild Alaskan salmon, halibut and whole grains. Finally, there is epidemiological evidence that selenium intake may be related to a reduced risk of coronary artery disease. In areas of the country with a high level of selenium in the soil, there seems to be a lower incidence of this disease.

Turkey in the Kitchen

For the weeks leading up to Thanksgiving, food writers discuss turkey at a feverish pitch: frozen or fresh? How long to defrost? To brine or not to brine? And then turkey is forgotten until the next year. But things are changing, as turkey is beginning to increase in popularity. You do see recipes popping up that make use of this SuperFood. Years ago, turkeys were available primarily whole, but today you can buy turkey as whole or half breasts, cutlets, ground turkey, drumsticks, thighs, wings and even tenderloins. All these parts cook quickly and make it easy to enjoy turkey frequently.

Fresh-ground turkey can be an excellent food, but read the label carefully. It should be ground from breast meat with no added skin. Sometimes it's ground including the skin, fat and dark meat. Look for ground turkey that's 99 percent fat-free. If the fat content is higher, it probably contains dark meat and/or skin.

Some of our favorite ways to use turkey...

- A turkey dinner made with a roasted whole fresh turkey breast. We remove the skin after cooking. It cooks quickly and goes with all the traditional trimmings.
- A turkey sandwich on toasted whole-grain bread with spinach leaves and romaine lettuce, sliced onion and avocado, and a smear of mayo and/or mustard.
- Turkey tacos or burritos using cooked, shredded turkey, stir-fried in olive oil with some onions and peppers.

• Turkey slices with a bit of barbeque sauce (love that lycopene!). I take this to work in a container with some cranberry sauce.

When buying sliced turkey at a deli, ask for fresh roasted turkey meat. Avoid "turkey breast," which contains fillers as well as high amounts of fat and sodium. Buy fresh, roasted white meat to get all the SuperFood benefits.

• Turkey soup with plenty of vegetables.

• Lean, ground turkey breast meat in spaghetti sauce.

• Make a quick turkey chili by lightly browning chopped onions and garlic, then adding ground turkey and cooking it until the meat is browned. Add two cans rinsed and drained red or white beans, a can of diced tomatoes and a chopped jalapeño, if you like. Then sprinkle on your favorite chili spices, including cumin, oregano, fresh-ground black pepper, paprika and cayenne.

Buy only whole turkey without added fats or oils. Self-basting birds may contain partially hydrogenated soy or corn oil or butter. Check the label carefully.

• Make turkey Sloppy Joes by sautéing onion, garlic, green bell pepper and fresh-ground turkey in a bit of extra virgin olive oil. Add a can of diced tomatoes, a drizzle of honey and 2 tablespoons tomato paste, and simmer until the flavors blend. Serve on toasted whole wheat buns.

See our Shopping Lists (page 218) for some recommended products.

WALNUTS

People have a predictable response when I tell them nuts are a SuperFood. Most say, "I can't eat nuts—they're too fattening." Some of my patients have said, "I can't even have nuts in the house. If they are around, I eat them." These responses are understandable; nuts are just plain delicious.

My brother-in-law scarfed down as many nuts as possible after I told him about their considerable health benefits, and gained five pounds in one month. He tuned out when I told him the other part of the nut equation: Moderation! Certainly nuts are high in calories, but they have extraordinary health benefits and are an important addition to your diet. And I'll give you some tips on how to enjoy them judiciously so you won't get fat.

First a simple fact: If you are overweight, smoke, never get off your sofa and eat five fast-food meals a week, there's one thing you could do to improve your health and reduce your risk of cardiovascular disease without even taking your right hand off the remote—eat a handful of nuts about five times a week. This simple act would

WALNUTS ARE A SOURCE OF:

- Plant-derived omega-3 fatty acids
- Vitamin E
- Magnesium
- Polyphenols
- Protein
- Fiber
- Potassium
- Plant sterols
- Vitamin B6
- Arginine
- Resveratrol
- Melatonin

Sidekicks: Almonds, pistachios, sesame seeds, peanuts, pumpkin and sunflower seeds, macadamia nuts, pecans, hazelnuts, cashews

Try to eat: 1 ounce, five times a week

reduce your chances of getting a heart attack by at least 15 percent and possibly as much as 51 percent. That's how powerful nuts are.

Nuts have attracted a great deal of attention lately. As a new nutritional era emerges that moves well beyond macronutrients like fat and protein and into the exciting world of phytonutrients, nutritionists are rediscovering these little nutrition powerhouses. I can safely say that nuts will play an important role in maximizing the human health span during this century.

It's a simple but astounding fact that people who eat nuts regularly can enjoy a significant reduction in their risk of developing coronary heart disease. They'll also reduce their risk of diabetes, cancer, Alzheimer's disease and a host of other chronic ailments. There's also evidence that nuts could play a role in reducing inflammatory diseases like asthma and rheumatoid arthritis as well as eczema and psoriasis.

Indeed, the evidence supporting walnuts' important contributions to health is so convincing that the U.S. Food and Drug Administration in March 2004 allowed walnuts to be the first whole food that can be labeled with a qualified health claim: "Eating 1.5 ounces per day of walnuts as part of a diet low in saturated fat and cholesterol may reduce the risk of heart disease." Shortly after that date, the FDA allowed two walnut sidekicks, peanuts and almonds, to be so labeled as well. One study that looked at all causes of death across various racial, gender and age groups found an inverse ratio between nut consumption and all causes of mortality. If I could develop and patent a drug that could safely deliver the benefits of a daily handful of nuts, I'd be a billionaire!

Which Nuts?

You'll notice that walnuts are the flagship nuts in this *SuperFoods Rx* category. I want to stress, however, that all nuts and seeds are significant contributors to your good health. It makes sense that nuts and seeds are rich sources of a wide variety of nutrients. They are, after all, nature's nurseries. A nut or seed is basically a storage device that contains all the highly concentrated proteins, calories and nutrients that a plant embryo will require to flourish.

My other two top choices include almonds and pistachios. My top-choice seeds are pumpkin and sunflower seeds.

WALNUTS

Walnuts are the headliner for a number of reasons. They are one of the few rich sources of plant-derived omega-3 fatty acids (called alpha linolenic acid, or ALA) along with canola oil, ground flaxseed and flaxseed oil, soybeans and soybean oil, wheat germ, spinach and purslane. They are rich in plant sterols—plant sterols can play a significant role in lowering serum cholesterol levels—a good source of fiber and protein, and they also provide magnesium, copper, folate and vitamin E. Finally, they're the nut with the highest overall antioxidant activity.

PEANUTS

Peanuts are American's favorite nuts, even though they're not really nuts at all, but legumes closely related to beans. We consider them nuts here because they share a similar nutritional profile. Peanuts comprise two-thirds of our total nut consumption and rank third in snack-food sales in the United States. One ounce—about 48 peanuts—provides 15 percent of your daily vitamin E requirement, 2.5 grams of fiber plus calcium, copper, iron, magnesium, niacin, folate and zinc, along with 7 grams of protein.

ALMONDS

Almonds are the best nut source of vitamin E, and a powerful plant source of protein. In fact, at 20 percent protein, one-quarter cup of almonds contains 7.6 grams of protein—more than a large egg, which contains 6 grams. Almonds also contain riboflavin, iron, potassium and magnesium, and they're a good source of fiber. Almonds are also an excellent source of biotin, a B vitamin essential to the metabolism of both sugar and fat. One-quarter cup of almonds provides 75 percent of your body's daily requirement of this nutrient, which promotes skin health as well as energy levels. Almonds are also rich in arginine; only peanuts contain more. Due to its ability to promote the production of a specific chemical, arginine is a natural vasodilator, which promotes increased blood flow by relaxing the blood vessel wall. Also the skin of almonds has a number of polyphenols, many of which have significant free-radical scavenging properties.

Finally, almonds and peanuts also contain sphingolipids. At the moment, there's no known nutritional requirement for these lipids, but they seem to play an important role in cell membrane structure and function. Cancer involves numerous defects in cell regulation, and sphingolipids have been found to affect almost every aspect of defective-cell regulation in cancer. We need more information on this, but for now I believe it is safe to assume that sphingolipids play a role in optimizing our health and represent another component of whole foods that works in synergy with other nutrients and phytonutrients.

PISTACHIOS

Pistachios are one of the oldest edible nuts on earth. In China, they are known as the "happy nut" because of their characteristic half-opened shell. A one-ounce serving of pistachios equals 47 nuts—more nuts per serving than any other except peanuts at 48 per serving. Pistachios are loaded with fiber: You get more dietary fiber from a serving of pistachios than from a half-cup of broccoli or spinach. Pistachios are also rich in potassium, thiamine and vitamin B6. It's interesting to note that the B6 in a one-ounce serving of pistachios is equal to the B6 in a typical three-ounce serving of chicken or pork. Like all nuts, pistachios are particularly rich in the phytonutrients that are associated with reducing cholesterol and with protecting you from a variety of cancers.

NUTS IN A NUTSHELL

A serving of shelled nuts is one ounce. One ounce of nuts is 10 to 48 nuts, depending on their size. A single serving of nuts provides between 150 and 200 calories.

Seeds

While walnuts are the flagship food in this category, as we know by now, it's the synergy of multiple nutrients that provides the most benefits. Though seeds don't, as yet, have the research backing for their health benefits that nuts do, we can assume given their nutrient profiles that they also offer multiple health benefits. Even though we eat seeds in small quantities, they are a good source of protein, especially for vegetarians.

It's really a misnomer to separate nuts from seeds. In fact, just about any seed or fruit that contains an edible kernel inside a brittle covering is called a nut. So nuts and seeds include everything from almonds to walnuts as well as sunflower seeds, sesame seeds, pumpkin seeds and pine nuts. For the purposes of *SuperFoods Rx,* my top picks include sunflower seeds and pumpkin

POWERFUL PUMPKIN SEEDS

One ounce contains...

- Over 50 percent of the RDA for iron
- Over 30 percent of the RDA for magnesium
- Over 20 percent of the RDA for vitamin E
- About 20 percent of the RDA for zinc
- A generous amount of potassium

seeds. I encourage people to include seeds in this food category and use them regularly as snacks, and also in salads, cereals and casseroles. I eat a handful of nuts and/or seeds every morning. I also prefer jams with seeds, and I even eat watermelon seeds.

Don't Nuts Make You Fat?

My brother-in-law will be the first to tell you that nuts do make you fat. Any food that you *add* to your current diet can make you fat. And it's true that nuts are high in calories. But the key concept with nuts is *substitution*. Add a few nuts to your daily diet, substituting them for other foods. You won't gain an ounce if you add one ounce of nuts at least five times a week and subtract a food of comparable calories, preferably one containing saturated fat like cheese or butter or, better yet, add the equivalent amount of calorie-burning exercise.

The truth is, those who eat nuts in a balanced diet tend to be thinner than those who don't, because nuts are so filling. Because of this, nuts help people stick to a diet of foods that are high in carbohydrates but low in fiber. In one Harvard study, people who ate 35 percent of their calories from healthy fats (the common recommendation is 25 to 30 percent of calories from fat) were three times more likely to maintain their weight loss than dieters who restricted their fat intake to 20 percent. While it's true that 79 percent of the energy of nuts comes from fat, it's also true that nuts are low in saturated fat and high in unsaturated fatty acids. Interestingly, saturated fat raises blood cholesterol levels about twice as much as polyunsaturated fats lower them.

Here's a breakdown of how many calories there are in common nuts followed by a few activities you can incorporate into your life to help you keep your nut intake in perspective. I have two recommendations on how to eat nuts and stay thin: substitute exercise for equivalent nut calories consumed or eliminate equivalent "bad" calories, say from saturated fat, from your diet.

Nut Calories ***(All, except where noted, are for one ounce)***	***Calories***
Almonds (24 nuts, raw)	164
Almonds (22 nuts, dry-roasted)	169
English walnuts (14 halves)	185
Hazelnuts (20 nuts, raw)	178
Peanuts (48, dry-roasted, no added salt)	166
Peanut butter (2 tablespoons)	190
Pecans (20 halves, raw)	195
Pistachios (dry-roasted, no added salt, 47 kernels)	162
Pistachios (raw, no added salt, 7 kernels)	158

Calories Burned per Activity ***(Each activity would burn off approximately 150 calories, or one serving of nuts)***	***Minutes***
Walking briskly (4 mph)	32
Walking slowly	43
Running (6 mph)	13
Swimming (general)	21
Swimming (vigorous laps)	13
Cycling (vigorous, 14–16 mph)	13
Cycling (leisurely, 10–12 mph)	21
Stationary cycling (low setting)	26
Tennis, singles	16
Golf with cart	37
Golf, no cart, carrying clubs	16
Basketball	16
General gardening	26
Raking leaves	32

How Nuts Help Your Heart

A powerful body of evidence now conclusively demonstrates that nut consumption correlates with reduced coronary artery disease. To date, at least five large epidemiological studies have demonstrated that frequent consumption of nuts decreases the risk of coronary artery disease. In each of these studies, the more nuts consumed (about five servings a week), the lower the risk. Even when adjusted for other factors, such as age, sex, race and lifestyle variables, the results held. Overall, people who eat nuts five or more times a week had a 15 to 51 percent reduction in coronary heart disease. And amazingly, even people who ate nuts just once a month had some reduction.

The fat in nuts is the healthy monounsaturated fat that is known to have a favorable effect on high cholesterol levels and other cardiovascular risk factors. Walnuts contain alpha-linolenic acid (ALA), a precursor to the omega-3 fatty acids found in fish oils. The ALA that is abundant in walnuts makes a major contribution to heart health.

THE INCREDIBLE OMEGA-3s

One of the main contributors to heart health in nuts, particularly in walnuts, is the omega-3 fatty acids. We know that this particular component of fat works in various ways to help guarantee a healthy heart and circulatory system. They help prevent erratic heart rhythms. And like aspirin, omega-3s "thin" the blood, helping it to flow freely and preventing clots from forming and adhering to the vessel walls. Omega-3s also act as an anti-inflammatory, preventing the blood vessels from becoming inflamed—a condition that reduces blood flow.

Omega-3s are essential for the optimal development and function of every cell in our bodies. Unfortunately, evidence of mercury in certain types of fish—a rich source of omega 3s—has led to warnings about safe levels of fish consumption for pregnant and postpartum women.

If you are trying to consume essential omega-3 fatty acids, and are concerned about the mercury content in some fish, plant-food sources of omega-3s, such as walnuts, are an alternative choice. While the type of omega-3s found in walnuts, its sidekicks and other plant sources, such as flaxseeds and dark leafy field greens, are different from the type of omega-3s found in fish, they still have many similar benefits.

In one study of 67 patients with borderline-high total cholesterol, it was found that adding 64 grams (a little over two ounces) a day of walnuts to a low-fat, low-cholesterol diet caused a significant reduction of total cholesterol and "bad" low-density lipoprotein cholesterol (LDL) and a slight increase in "good" high-density lipoprotein cholesterol (HDL).

Another study followed 21 men and women with high cholesterol who ate either a typical low-calorie Mediterranean Diet or, alternatively, one in which walnuts were substituted for about one-third of the calories supplied by other sources of monounsaturated fats like olive oil. After four weeks, the subjects switched diets for an additional four weeks. Walnuts made an impressive contribution to the heart health of those consuming them: The walnut diet reduced total cholesterol and LDL "bad" cholesterol and, in addition and most impressively, walnuts increased the elasticity of the arteries by 64 percent.

Lowered blood pressure is another benefit of the omega-3s and, of course, reducing hypertension (or high blood pressure) is an excellent way to decrease your risk of cardiovascular disease and even macular degeneration.

CONSUMER-ACTION ALERT

Petition the large peanut producers to market raw or dry-roasted peanuts *with the skins on* so we can get the considerable benefits of all those polyphenols.

Walnuts are also rich in arginine, which is an essential amino acid. Arginine helps to keep the inside of the blood vessels smooth while it also promotes the flexibility of the vessels, thus increasing blood flow, reducing blood pressure and thereby alleviating hypertension.

The top nut and seed sources of arginine in descending order include: watermelon seeds, pumpkin seeds, peanuts, almonds, sunflower seeds, walnuts, hazelnuts and pistachios.

The extraordinary antioxidant ability of walnuts helps in other ways as well. In one recent study, researchers identified various polyphenols in walnuts that, along with the polyphenols ellagic and gallic acid, demonstrate "remarkable" antioxidant abilities.

These polyphenols seem to play an important role in reducing free-radical damage to cholesterol, thus promoting cardiovascular health.

The hormone melatonin has also recently been identified in walnuts, and when walnuts were introduced in animal studies the blood levels of this substance increased to values that could be protective against cardiovascular damage and cancer.

It's interesting to note that while the beneficial fatty acid composition of nuts would account for some of their positive effects on blood lipids, and thus their benefits to heart health, that doesn't explain the whole picture. In other words, in addition to the known health-promoting factors in nuts, including the omega-3s, the B vitamins, magnesium, polyphenols, potassium and vitamin E, there are other elements, which we've yet to identify, that work to lower cholesterol levels and promote heart health.

SUPER SUNFLOWER SEEDS

One ounce contains...

- 95 percent of the RDA for vitamin E
- Over 50 percent of the RDA for thiamine
- Close to 30 percent of the RDA for selenium
- 25 percent of the RDA for magnesium
- 16 percent of the RDA for folate

Sunflower seeds are...

- Very high in polyunsaturated fatty acids
- A fairly rich source of potassium

A study of U.S. male physicians found an inverse association between nut consumption and sudden cardiac death. Doctors who consumed nuts were less likely to die from the sudden arrhythmias that often accompany a heart attack.

Nuts and Diabetes

Given the impending epidemic of type II diabetes, it's encouraging to learn that just a handful of nuts can prove beneficial to those diagnosed with this disease. In one study, men and women with diabetes were assigned to follow one of three diets in which 30 percent of calories were from fat: a low-fat diet, a modified low-fat diet and a modified low-fat diet that included an ounce of walnuts daily. After six months, the subjects who had been on the walnut diet enjoyed a significantly greater improvement in their "good" HDL-to-total-cholesterol ratio than the other groups. Moreover, the walnut folks had a 10 percent reduction in their "bad" LDL cholesterol. Another study that included more than 83,000 nurses found that women who ate nuts at least five times a week had a 30 percent lower risk of diabetes than women who almost never ate nuts. Even women who ate nuts one to four times a week or ate peanut butter at least five times a week enjoyed a 20 percent lower risk. As people with type II diabetes are at increased risk for heart disease, it's encouraging to know that a simple handful of nuts can help them to reduce that risk.

Just one ounce of walnuts—a handful—contains 2.5 grams of omega-3s, which more than satisfies the recommendation by the Food Nutrition Board of the National Academies' Institute of Medicine that women consume 1.1 grams per day of alpha-linolenic acid (an omega-3 fatty acid) and that men consume 1.6 grams per day.

Think Nuts

Walnuts have had a reputation as brain food, probably because their wrinkled shape actually resembles a human brain. However, there's more than appearance to link walnuts and the brain: As our brains are more than 60 percent fat, they rely on a steady supply of good fats—like the type found in walnuts—to promote the varied activities of the brain.

PEANUT BUTTER

Peanut butter, eaten in moderation, has good health benefits (a serving size is two tablespoons, just enough to cover a slice of whole wheat bread). Buy peanut butter from a manufacturer with good quality control; sometimes those grind-it-yourself arrangements that you may see in health-food stores or farmers' markets, for example, are not as rigorously maintained in terms of cleanliness as they should be.

Look for peanut butter with no trans fat, no added sugar, no salt, if possible, and, most important, with no partially hydrogenated oils. I like Laura Scudder's All-Natural Old-Fashioned Peanut Butter, with no added salt. I store it upside down in the pantry for a few days before I open it so the oil is dispersed throughout and I don't have to stir it quite so much.

Other healthy nut butters include almond, cashew and soy.

Interestingly, there have been studies that have proposed a connection between increased rates of depression and our decreased consumption of omega-3 fats. Some of the research has suggested that there may be a connection between low omega-3 fat intake and ADHD (attention deficit hyperactivity disorder) in children. One recent study from Purdue University showed that children with a low consumption of omega-3 fats are significantly more likely to be hyperactive, have learning disorders and exhibit behavioral problems.

There also may be a link between dietary intake of certain antioxidants—particularly vitamins C and E—and the development of Alzheimer's disease. Various studies have pointed to this connection. In one study, more than 5,000 participants were followed for six years, beginning at age 55. Of that group, 146 developed Alzheimer's. When adjustments were made for age, sex, cognitive ability, alcohol intake, education, smoking habits and other variables, a high dietary intake of vitamin C and vitamin E was definitely associated with a lower risk of Alzheimer's disease. Since nuts are one of the richest dietary sources of vitamin E, this is yet another argument for making them a part of your diet.

Interesting recent research shows that a rich supply of dietary vitamin E may help to protect against Parkinson's disease, the chronic neurological condition that impairs motor function. Almonds, as well as other nuts, are good sources of vitamin E.

Nuts for Your Eyes

A 2003 study reported that a high intake of nuts reduced the risk for the progression of age-related macular degeneration. Elevated C-reactive protein has been shown to be an independent risk factor for both cardiovascular disease and age-related macular degeneration, and results from another study showed that eating walnuts and walnut oil can significantly reduce C-reactive protein and other markers of inflammation.

Nuts to the Rescue

While the evidence supporting nuts' contribution to heart health and diabetes prevention is impressive, we must remember that nuts, like every other SuperFood, don't target just a few isolated systems in our bodies. Indeed, they're categorized as SuperFoods because of their amazingly powerful effect on our overall health. Nuts are an extraordinary SuperFood because the range of their known health-promoting abilities is so wide. And surely there's even more to discover about the synergistic power of nuts.

FIBER

Nuts are a rich source of dietary fiber. In one study, a 10-gram-a-day increase in dietary fiber resulted in a 19 percent decrease in coronary heart disease risk. One ounce of peanuts or mixed nuts provides about two-and-a-half grams of fiber—a good contribution to overall daily fiber consumption.

VITAMIN E

Most of us don't get nearly enough vitamin E in our daily diets, and nuts and seeds are a rich source of this nutrient. One of the components of vitamin E—gamma tocopherol—has powerful anti-inflammatory properties. It's my guess that this is one reason why nuts contribute so significantly to heart health, although studies still need to prove this.

Different nuts provide different ratios of the components of vitamin E, which is a good reason to vary your nut consumption. Almonds, for example, are a rich source of alpha tocopherol. Pistachios, on the other hand, are low in alpha tocopherols but very high in gamma tocopherol and also contain gamma tocotrienols. Most vitamin E supplements, by the way, contain only d-alpha tocopherol and thus provide only a fraction of the benefit of vitamin E from whole food.

FOLIC ACID

This nutrient has gotten some attention lately because of its ability to prevent birth defects, particularly neural tube defects such as spina bifida. Nuts are rich in folic acid, whose benefits go beyond its critical role in birth-defect prevention. Folic acid also lowers homocysteine (an independent risk factor for cardiovascular disease) and helps prevent cancer and various causes of aging.

COPPER

The copper in nuts is helpful in maintaining healthy levels of cholesterol. It also contributes to healthy blood pressure and helps prevent abnormal glucose metabolism.

MAGNESIUM

This important nutrient shows up in impressive amounts in nuts. Thus it's no surprise that low intakes of magnesium have been associated with increased risk of heart attack. Magnesium decreases heart arrhythmias and helps prevent hypertension. It's also critical for normal muscle relaxation, nerve impulse transmission, carbohydrate metabolism and maintaining healthy tooth enamel. Low magnesium

NUTS GO TO YOUR HEAD

In 2002, the *Journal of the American Medical Association* published a report that found that a high dietary (not from supplements) intake of vitamins C and E may lower risk of Alzheimer's disease.

In another study, vitamin E consumption was linked to a 70 percent reduction in the risk of developing Alzheimer's over a four-year period.

Nuts are known to be one of the richest dietary sources of vitamin E.

NUTS TO WINE

A handful of walnuts has significantly more polyphenols than a glass of apple juice or even a glass of red wine. In one study, a serving of shelled walnuts (14 halves) had the polyphenol content of 2.2 servings of red wine.

intake is also a risk factor for migraine headaches. It's interesting to note that almost half of patients who suffer from migraines have magnesium levels that are below normal.

RESVERATROL

This flavonoid, which is found abundantly in grapeskins as well as peanut skins, has anticancer properties. It is also an anti-inflammatory and has been associated with helping to maintain healthy cholesterol levels.

ELLAGIC ACID

This polyphenol is found in high concentrations in nuts, particularly walnuts. Animal research studies have demonstrated that ellagic acid is beneficial in the prevention of cancer by affecting both the activation and detoxification of potential carcinogens.

Nuts in the Kitchen

Because of their high concentration of fats, nuts have a tendency to go rancid. Heat, humidity and light all hasten their spoilage. Be sure you shop for nuts in a store with a high turnover, especially if you buy from bulk bins. All nuts should smell sweet or "nutty." A sharp or bitter smell indicates that the nuts may be rancid. In general, whole nuts keep better than pieces, unprocessed nuts keep better than processed ones and nuts in the shell keep better than shelled. Keep nuts in a cool place in a sealed container for up to four months. They'll keep in the fridge for about six months and in the freezer for up to a year.

Dry-roasted nuts are always a good choice. Avoid nuts with added oil. As always, check the labels—sometimes you'll find added preservatives, corn syrup or other sweeteners plus salt. No-salt nuts are ideal, but if you can't eat nuts without salt, it's safe to enjoy them that way; just cut down on other sources of salt in your diet.

You can roast nuts yourself, but do so carefully: High temperatures destroy the omega-3s in the nuts. Spread the nuts on a cookie sheet and place in a 160° F to 170° F oven for 15 to 20 minutes, or until they turn dark.

Many of my patients have found that the freezer is the key to healthy nut consumption, especially if you're a nut nut who can't sleep if you think there's an open jar of mixed nuts in the house. (I use this trick with my daughter's oatmeal-raisin cookies; if they're out, they're eaten. If they're frozen, I have to give it a little thought before I eat one.) Try keeping a variety of nuts and seeds in heavy-duty freezer bags in the freezer. Then you can take out only small amounts at a time so that you'll have what you need—no more! If you prefer to keep them in the fridge, they should keep for about six months.

Most nuts taste better roasted or toasted. I often toss a handful of crushed walnuts or pine nuts or sliced almonds into a nonstick pan on medium heat while I'm assembling a salad. I shake the pan every few minutes until the nuts are lightly toasted, then toss them into the salad.

Here are some easy ways to make your life a little nuttier…

- Use nuts to top frozen yogurt.
- Stir peanut butter into stews and curries to enrich and add flavor.
- Use finely chopped nuts to coat fish or poultry cutlets.
- Gently sauté chopped nuts in olive oil along with bread crumbs and chopped garlic and toss with freshly cooked pasta.

• Don't forget that American classic—a peanut butter–and-jelly sandwich. Make it on whole wheat bread; it's nutritious.

• Toss two tablespoons roasted sunflower seeds on your cereal.

• Sprinkle chopped, toasted nuts on a salad. Walnuts are delicious on a spinach salad with a raspberry vinegar dressing and red-onion rings. Pine nuts, toasted briefly in a nonstick skillet, add flavor and crunch to any mixed-green salad.

• Whole wheat toast with 2 tablespoons peanut butter is a healthy snack.

• Top steamed spinach or kale with toasted pine nuts, walnuts or any chopped nuts instead of cheese.

• Sprinkle nuts on top of oatmeal or yogurt in the morning to add fiber and protein to your breakfast.

• Nut oils also have health benefits and make good choices for salad dressings. Try almond, walnut and hazelnut oils.

• Nuts make a tasty "instant" snack. Take some with you in a small container when you travel or to keep at your desk. Add raisins or other dried fruit and a handful of oatmeal to nuts for a supernutritious snack.

See our Shopping Lists (pages 215, 216 218, 220, 221 and 224) for some recommended products.

Low-fat or Nonfat Yogurt

Remember the ads that featured those elderly people from the Caucasus mountain region of the Soviet Union who ascribed their extreme longevity to yogurt? Some had lied about their age to avoid conscription in the Soviet army. Many others simply realized that the older they claimed they were, the more excited their visitors became. Before you knew it, everyone in the neighborhood was nearly 120 years old, thanks to yogurt.

Those ads were created at a time when yogurt had to be "sold." It was assumed that no one would eat it if it didn't promise something remarkable. Times have changed. Today, we eat yogurt simply because we like it. But many of us have forgotten about the health benefits of yogurt, which were undiscovered or at least unproven in the days of those ads. And, because yogurt now comes in so many varieties and types—from frozen dessert bars to squeeze tubes of flavored yogurt—there are some facts that we need to know to reap the benefits of this extraordinary SuperFood.

The Synergy of Pre- and Probiotics

One of the most important aspects of yogurt as a source of health benefits is the synergy of two health-promoting substances it provides: prebiotics and probiotics.

YOGURT IS A SOURCE OF:

- Live active cultures
- Complete protein
- Calcium
- Vitamin B2 (riboflavin)
- Vitamin B12
- Potassium
- Magnesium
- Zinc
- Potassium
- Conjugate linoleic acid

Sidekicks: Kefir, soy yogurt

Try to eat: 1 to 2 cups daily

PREBIOTICS

Prebiotics are nondigestible food ingredients that beneficially affect the gut by selectively stimulating the growth and/or activity of one or more beneficial bacteria in the colon, thus improving host health. Fructooligosaccharides (FOS) are one of the many classes of prebiotics, and they're found in legumes, vegetables and cereals as well as yogurt. These nonabsorbed fibers inhibit potentially pathogenic organisms as well as increase the absorption of minerals such as calcium, magnesium, iron and zinc.

PROBIOTICS

Probiotics are defined as live microorganisms that, when taken in adequate amounts, can be of benefit to our health. The evidence for the role of prebiotics and probiotics in promoting health and fighting disease is increasing on a monthly basis and is now supported by many double-blind, placebo-controlled human trials. What used to be folklore has become scientific fact. This mounting body of very recent news simply confirms ancient wisdom. In 76 B.C., the Roman historian Plinius recommended fermented milk products (yogurt) for treatment of gastroenteritis. And a Persian version of the Old Testament (Genesis 18:8) states: "Abraham owed his longevity to the consumption of sour milk."

THE GERM THEORY OF DISEASE

Flash forward to about a hundred years ago when Louis Pasteur developed the germ theory of disease. He was one of the first to postulate that our health is intertwined with the living beneficial microorganisms residing on our skin and in our bodies. Yogurt is the most commonly eaten probiotic food that contributes to the balance of microorganisms in our system. With contemporary, cutting-edge research, folklore has become scientific fact: Yogurt is indeed a SuperFood.

Like all of the SuperFoods, yogurt works synergistically to promote health and fight disease: It provides a range of health benefits that include live active cultures, protein, calcium and B vitamins, which work together in such a way that the sum is greater than the parts. Yogurt's primary benefit—as a probiotic—is something that at first blush runs counter to the trend of most modern medicine. With the success of antibiotics beginning shortly after World War II, doctors and the public have come to view microorganisms as evil disease-promoters, which must be relentlessly eradicated. In fact, however, the key to health is *balance:* The goal is not to eradicate all microorganisms but rather to promote the health of the beneficial ones. Yogurt plays a primary role in this promotion by encouraging the growth of "good" bacteria and limiting the proliferation of "bad" ones.

Yogurt has multiple immune-stimulating activities both inside and outside the gastrointestinal (GI) tract. An interesting study has shown that if you eat yogurt with live active cultures, you decrease the amount of a common pathogenic bacterium—Staphylococcus aureus—in the nasal passages. This is a clear sign that the yogurt is stimulating the immune system, and there is a beneficial communication between the immune system lining the GI tract and the immune system lining the upper airway passages.

Our gastrointestinal tracts are home to over 500 species of bacteria—some helpful and some harmful to our health. We rely on these beneficial microbial "partners" for a number of important functions, including carbohydrate metabolism, amino acid synthesis, vitamin K synthesis and the processing of various nutrients. Yogurt is a source of beneficial bacteria, and the positive results that are ascribed to introducing this bacteria to our system are not relegated to the digestive tract. While a host of beneficial health effects are linked to yogurt, those that have attracted the most attention include its anticancer properties, its ability to lower cholesterol and its ability to inhibit unfriendly bacteria.

One of the great benefits of the probiotics in yogurt is its ability to strengthen the immune system and thereby help the body prevent infection. In an era of antibiotic-resistant pathogens and seemingly new infectious threats like SARS and West Nile virus, the value of boosting one's immune system becomes immeasurable.

Inulin, a dietary fiber, is an additive used in Stonyfield Farm yogurt. It's been shown to increase calcium absorption. For example, an intake of eight grams of inulin a day increased calcium absorption among teenage girls by an average of 20 percent.

Live Active Cultures

Before we explore yogurt's extraordinary abilities, it's important to understand that in order to be effectively health-promoting, the yogurt you buy *must contain live active cultures.* Yogurt is, quite simply, milk that has been curdled. To make yogurt, pasteurized, homogenized milk is inoculated with bacteria cultures and kept warm in an incubator where the lactose or milk sugar turns into lactic acid. This thickens the yogurt and gives it its characteristic tart, tangy flavor. The process is very similar to that used when making beer, wine or cheese, in that beneficial organisms ferment and transform the basic food.

This is the standard process for producing yogurt, but there's a wide range of techniques adopted by manufacturers of differing brands. For example, some manufacturers pasteurize the yogurt after culturing it. In this case, the label will indicate "heat treated after culturing." This process kills all the friendly bacteria and, while it may taste good, its health benefits will not extend to those provided by live active cultures. You might be surprised to learn that some frozen yogurts have live active cultures. Check the labels; with live active cultures, frozen yogurt offers a low-fat advantage over ice cream.

CONSUMER-ACTION ALERT

Ask yogurt manufacturers to add vitamin D, a key player in calcium metabolism, to their yogurts.

When you shop for yogurt, look for...

- Low-fat or nonfat varieties
- No artificial colors
- The expiration date on the carton (make sure it's very fresh)
- Whey protein listed on the label (increases the viability of probiotic bacteria—as does the inulin in Stonyfield Farm yogurt)
- Rich in live active cultures (check for specific cultures—the more, the better)

The National Yogurt Association has created a "live active cultures" (LAC) seal that guarantees that yogurt so labeled contain at least 100 million organisms per gram at the time of manufacture. Many yogurt-covered candies and pretzels, and yogurt-flavored salad dressing, do not contain live active cultures. "LAC" yogurt must be refrigerated and date-stamped to indicate its relatively short shelf life. After the expiration date on the yogurt, the bacteria numbers go down. Since the seal program is voluntary, some yogurt products may have live cultures but not carry the seal.

There are three basic types of yogurt, depending on the milk used to make it—regular yogurt, low-fat yogurt and nonfat yogurt. Yogurt made from whole milk has at least 3.25 percent milk fat. Low-fat yogurt is made from low-fat milk or part-skim milk and has between 0.5 and 2 percent milk fat. Nonfat yogurt is made from skim milk and contains less than 0.5 percent milk fat. I favor nonfat yogurt.

Yogurt is most commonly made from cow's milk, but it can also be made from goat, sheep or buffalo milk.

One of the most common yogurts is the FOB, or "fruit on the bottom" product. Some FOB yogurts have live active cultures, but they also have a lot of added sugar. Some fruit-flavored yogurts have up to 7 teaspoons of sugar per cup! I leave the fruit on the bottom of the carton, but the yogurt still has some of the nice fruit taste. Ideally, the best yogurt to buy is plain nonfat or low-fat yogurt that is clearly labeled as containing "live active cultures." The label should also specify which cultures are in the product. The most popular yogurts use only two live cultures—*L. acidophilus* and *S. thermophilus*. Natural yogurts also include other beneficial bacteria, including *L. bulgaricus, B. bifidus, L. casei* and *L. reuteri*. Be sure to check the label on your yogurt carefully—in general, the more beneficial cultures listed, the better. If you like fruit in your yogurt (and who doesn't?), add your own fresh or dried fruits to taste. I usually sprinkle mine with wheat germ, ground flaxseed and berries for added taste and nutrition.

A small study in Japan found that yogurt could be helpful in fighting bad breath (halitosis). The participants ate yogurt twice a day for six weeks. Eighty percent of those who had had halitosis showed lowered levels of the sulfide compounds that contribute to bad breath compared with samples taken during a time when no yogurt was consumed.

The folks who had eaten yogurt also had less plaque and gingivitis, indicating that yogurt can make a real contribution to oral health when eaten regularly.

The Benefits of Probiotics

Ultimately, it's yogurt's activity in the gastrointestinal tract that argues most conclusively for its inclusion as a SuperFood. The bottom line is that a healthy digestive system is critical to good health. Our ability to absorb nutrients from our food depends on our GI health. Even if we eat the most nutrient-dense foods in the world, if our digestive ability is impaired, we won't be able to benefit from those foods. As we age, our digestive ability is often diminished. All the more reason to rely on yogurt as a food that will promote and help preserve intestinal health.

Probiotics as Disease Fighters

The list of the health-promoting abilities of probiotics is quite long. Some benefits have been proven absolutely conclusively while others require more study. *Here is a summary of the conditions where yogurt has efficacy…*

CANCER

Probiotics absorb mutagens that cause cancer, particularly colon cancer, though there's also evidence that they're effective in fighting breast cancer. They stimulate the immune system, partly by promoting immunoglobulin production, and help lower the risk for cancer by decreasing inflammation and inhibiting the growth of cancer-causing intestinal microflora.

In one French study, people who ate the most yogurt had half as many precancerous colon polyps as those who ate no yogurt.

ALLERGIES

Probiotics are helpful in alleviating atopic eczema and milk allergy. In relation to eczema, it's important to remember that probiotics are working on promoting healthy skin as well as a healthy digestive tract. Indeed, probiotics affect all surfaces of the body that have interaction with the external world, including skin, nasal passages, gastrointestinal tract and so forth. There is some evidence that babies who are exposed to probiotics (after the age of three months) will have a better chance of avoiding some allergies later in life.

LACTOSE INTOLERANCE

Some people cannot tolerate milk because they lack the enzyme to break down milk sugar (lactose). In fact, only about a quarter of the world's adults can digest milk. This condition eliminates an important source of highly bioavailable calcium from the diet. Probiotics in yogurt digest the lactose for you, thus helping to relieve this condition. As significant numbers of the lactase (the enzyme that "digests" lactose)-producing bacteria survive for less than an hour after ingestion, it is important to consume probiotics frequently if you suffer from this malady. Yogurt is also a calcium- and vitamin-rich food that is readily digestible by those who suffer from lactose intolerance and is therefore an excellent addition to their diets.

INFLAMMATORY BOWEL DISEASE (IBD)

Probiotics help regulate the body's inflammatory response, which relieves the symptoms of this condition. The probiotics in yogurt have been accepted as a form of therapy that can actually help maintain remission in people suffering from IBD. A review of human studies on probiotics, for example, concluded that "the use of probiotics in IBD clearly will not provide a panacea, but it does offer hope as an adjunct form of therapy, specifically in maintaining a state of remission."

Older people, in particular, can benefit from yogurt. One research study tracked a population of 162 very elderly people for five years. Those who ate yogurt and milk more than three times per week were 38 percent less likely to die compared to those who ate those foods less than once a week.

Yogurt helps people absorb nutrients, fight infection and inflammation, and get sufficient protein—all special challenges as we age.

CONSUMER-ACTION ALERT: WE ALL NEED MORE CULTURE!

Many yogurts claim to have live active cultures. Mainstream yogurts must contain *L. acidophilus* and *S. thermophilus* in order to be so labeled. Some yogurts add more, including *L. bulgaricus, B. bifidus, L. casei,* and *L. reuteri.* Look for yogurts that contain the most variety of live active cultures. Since certain species of probiotic cultures have health benefits, let's urge manufacturers to put them in commonly available yogurts.

HYPERTENSION

Probiotics stimulate the production of drug-like substances that act in the body like pharmacological blood-pressure-lowering medicines.

CHOLESTEROL REDUCTION

More than 30 years ago, scientists were intrigued to find that the Masai tribesmen of Africa had low serum levels of cholesterol as well as low levels of coronary heart disease, despite a diet that was extremely high in meat. The distinguishing characteristic of their diets, aside from high meat consumption, was an extremely high intake of fermented milk (or yogurt)—up to 5 liters daily. Research has now confirmed that yogurt is beneficial to those trying to reduce cholesterol. The probiotics in yogurt reduce the bile acids, which in turn decrease the absorption of cholesterol from the gastrointestinal tract. This effect seems to be seen most reliably in people who already have elevated cholesterol.

ULCERS

Probiotics help to eliminate the pathogen *Helicobacter pylori,* a bacterium that is one of the main causes of ulcers, chronic gastritis and may also be a cause of gastric cancer.

DIARRHEA

Yogurt has potential benefit in relieving what in many countries around the world is a serious threat to the health of millions. It fights diarrhea by stimulating the immune system, crowding out negative microflora in the intestines and stimulating the growth of beneficial bacteria. Probiotics in yogurt are also helpful in treating diarrhea associated with antibiotic use, and some doctors are amazed that yogurt is not routinely recommended to all patients who are being treated with antibiotics.

WEIGHT CONTROL

The evidence has been mounting that yogurt can play a role in a weight-reduction diet. A recent study showed that obese people on a low-calorie diet who included three 6-ounce servings of nonfat yogurt daily for twelve weeks lost 22 percent more weight than dieters who ate little or no dairy foods. Perhaps more important, they lost 60 percent more body fat and maintained more lean muscle mass. It does seem that calcium-rich foods are helpful in reducing or controlling weight. Nonfat yogurt is a low-calorie, high-protein, high-calcium food that may make a significant contribution to your efforts at weight control.

VAGINAL INFECTIONS AND URINARY-TRACT INFECTIONS

Once again, the probiotics in yogurt fight pathogens while crowding out the "bad" microflora and stimulating the growth of beneficial bacteria. One study concluded that eating eight ounces of yogurt containing *L. acidophilus* on a daily basis decreases candidal yeast colonization and infection threefold when compared with control groups.

Yogurt: Best in Dairy Class

Most people are surprised to learn that in the U.S., *nine out of ten women and seven out of ten men don't meet their daily requirement for calcium.* Worse and even more troubling news is that nearly 90 percent of teenage girls and 70 percent of teenage boys don't meet their daily calcium requirement. For many, soda has replaced the old "milk at every meal" custom. This portends disastrous future health consequences for large numbers of people. A single one-cup serving of nonfat plain yogurt supplies 414 milligrams of calcium—an amazing 40 percent of your daily calcium needs and at a cost of only 100 calories. This compares favorably with nonfat milk, which has only 300 milligrams of calcium. The rich amount of potassium in yogurt combined with the calcium also plays a role in normalizing your blood pressure.

Yogurt is also a better source of B vitamins (including folate), phosphorus and potassium than milk. Of course, the calcium in yogurt is of great benefit to pre- and postmenopausal women and to men in their struggle against osteoporosis. A rich source of calcium to begin with, the milk sugar in yogurt actually aids in calcium absorption. Moreover, dairy foods are a source of IGF-1, a growth factor that promotes bone formation, which benefits women over and above the bone-preserving contribution of calcium.

BEST QUICK ALL-STAR SUPERFOODS RX BREAKFAST

One of my breakfast favorites couldn't be easier to fix. I take a bowl of nonfat yogurt and top it with a handful of blueberries (and/or raspberries, cherries or whatever fruit is in season) and some sliced banana. I toss in a small handful of chopped walnuts and about a tablespoon of wheat germ or ground flaxseed. It's delicious and nutritious.

Yogurt: A Great Source of Digestible Protein

Yogurt is a great source of readily digestible protein. In fact, yogurt supplies double the protein of

MAKE YOGURT CHEESE

Line a sieve with a coffee filter and drain the yogurt for a few hours in the fridge—the longer it drains, the thicker it becomes. Use the resulting liquid or whey in pancakes or muffins as a milk substitute. Mix the yogurt cheese half and half with mayo in tuna or other salads to reduce fat and boost protein. Use yogurt cheese in dips, spooned onto a bowl of chili or as a fruit topping.

milk because it's usually thickened with nonfat milk solids, increasing its protein content. Some people, particularly the elderly, just don't consume enough protein or calcium. Studies have shown there's a positive association between protein intake and bone-mineral density of older women and men when they're supplemented with calcium. The lesson: Optimum bone health and prevention of osteoporosis depend not just on calcium supplementation but on sufficient protein intake as well. Yogurt, with its easily digestible protein and calcium, is the answer.

The typical adult human body harbors about 100 trillion bacteria from at least 500 species—ten times the number of human cells. Most of these "friendly" bacteria perform biological functions that are important for survival. It's the proper balance of good bacteria versus bad bacteria that helps to maintain optimum health.

Yogurt in the Kitchen

Here are a few ideas to get yogurt into your daily diet...

- Use yogurt to make healthy dips to keep in the fridge to enjoy with baby carrots, celery stalks and pepper strips. Mix yogurt with fresh herbs, freshly ground pepper, some chopped garlic or some chopped jalapeño. Process the yogurt and spices in a blender or food processor for a few seconds and store in the fridge. Put the dip out for an after-school snack, while watching TV or before dinner when everyone is "starving."
- Add yogurt to smoothies. A half-cup or so of yogurt added to some frozen banana slices, frozen pineapple chunks, blueberries and a splash of orange juice is an excellent start to your day.

Hats off to Dannon for their probiotic product called DanActive—a cultured dairy drink with three types of beneficial bacteria. Peer-reviewed scientific studies have demonstrated that the probiotics in this drink—each bottle has over ten billion bacteria—survive the acidity of the stomach and go to work in the intestine establishing a healthy balance of bacteria.

- Yogurt makes a great salad dressing. Use yogurt cheese or yogurt right from the container. Blend it with fresh herbs and spices or make a sweet dressing to use on fruit. For the latter, blend yogurt with honey, orange or lemon zest and perhaps a dash of ground coriander.
- A cooling salad of diced cucumber and yogurt is a refreshing summer side dish. Add diced red or green onion and fresh chopped herbs like dill or cilantro.
- Use fat-free yogurt as a healthy substitute for sour cream. When adding it to hot mixtures, stir it in at the very end of cooking and warm it only briefly so it won't separate and curdle.

See our Shopping Lists (pages 219 and 224) for some recommended products.

3

Nutritional Information You Need to Know

If you analyze all of the most health-promoting, disease preventing, antiaging, risk-factor-limiting diets in the world, 14 nutrients consistently turn up. They are associated with reducing a wide range of chronic ailments. Countless studies demonstrate that the higher your level of these nutrients, the slower you age and the less chronic disease you suffer.

The 14 Super Nutrients

Here is a list of the top 14 Super Nutrients, along with the foods that offer the richest sources of the "super 14."

If you have a bleeding or clotting problem, or are taking anticoagulants, consult your health-care professional before adopting any of the recommendations listed in this chapter.

1. Vitamin C

Aim for at least 350 milligrams (mg) per day from a combination of the following foods...

1 large yellow bell pepper = 341 mg
1 large red bell pepper = 312 mg
1 common guava = 165 mg
1 large green bell pepper = 132 mg
1 cup fresh orange juice = 124 mg (97 mg/cup from frozen concentrate)
1 cup fresh sliced strawberries = 97 mg
1 cup fresh broccoli, chopped = 79 mg

2. Folic Acid

Aim for 400 micrograms (mcg) per day from a combination of the following foods...

1 cup cooked spinach = 263 mcg folic acid (in food, folic acid is called folate)
1 cup boiled kidney beans = 230 mcg
1 cup boiled green soybeans = 200 mcg
½ cup soy nuts = 177 mcg
1 cup orange juice from frozen concentrate = 110 mcg
4 cooked asparagus spears with ½-inch base = 89 mcg
1 cup (frozen) chopped cooked broccoli = 103 mcg

3. Selenium

Aim for 70 to 100 micrograms per day from a combination of the following foods...

3 ounces cooked Pacific oysters = 131 mcg
1 cup whole grain wheat flour = 85 mcg
1 dried Brazil nut = 68 to 91 mcg
½ can of Pacific sardines = 75 mcg
3 ounces of canned white tuna = 56 mcg

3 ounces cooked clams = 54 mcg
6 farmed oysters = 54 mcg
3 ounces roasted skinless turkey breast = 27 mcg

4. Vitamin E

Aim for at least 16 milligrams per day from a combination of the following foods...

2 tablespoons wheat germ oil = 41 mg (total tocopherals)
2 tablespoons soybean oil = 2.6 mg
2 tablespoons canola oil = 13.6 mg
2 tablespoons peanut oil = 9.2 mg
2 tablespoons flaxseed oil = 4.8 mg
2 tablespoons olive oil = 4 mg
1 ounce raw almonds (23–24 whole kernels) = 7.7 mg
¼ cup hulled dry-roasted sunflower seeds = 6.8 mg
2 tablespoons raw, untoasted, wheat germ = 5 mg
1 medium orange bell pepper = 4.3 mg
1 ounce hazelnuts (20–21 kernels) = 4.3 mg
2 tablespoons peanut butter = 3.2 mg
1 cup blueberries = 2.8 mg

5. Lycopene

Aim for 22 milligrams per day of this carotenoid from a combination of the following foods...

1 cup canned tomato sauce = 37 mg
1 cup R.W. Knudsen Very Veggie vegetable cocktail from concentrate = 22 mg
1 cup tomato juice = 22 mg
1 watermelon wedge (1⁄16 of a melon 15 inches long, 7½ inches diameter) = 13 mg
1 cup canned stewed tomatoes = 10.3 mg
1 tablespoon tomato paste = 4.6 mg
1 tablespoon ketchup = 2.9 mg
½ pink grapefruit = 1.8 mg

Keep in mind that tomato sources of lycopene are far more bioavailable from cooked vs. raw (unprocessed) tomato products.

The lycopene found in watermelon is very bioavailable. (To date we are not aware of any studies evaluating the absorption characteristics of other fruit sources of lycopene; presumably they are similar to watermelon.)

6. Lutein/Zeaxanthin

Aim for 12 milligrams per day of this carotenoid from a combination of the following foods...

1 cup cooked kale, chopped = 23.7 mg
1 cup cooked spinach = 20.4 mg
1 cup cooked collard greens, chopped = 14.6 mg
1 cup cooked turnip greens = 12.1 mg
1 large sweet orange bell pepper = 9.2 mg
1 cup cooked green peas = 4.2 mg
1 cup cooked broccoli = 2.4 mg

7. Alpha-carotene

Aim for 2.4 milligrams per day of this carotenoid from a combination of the following foods...

1 cup canned pumpkin = 11.7 mg
1 cup cooked carrots (slices) = 6.6 mg
10 raw medium baby carrots = 3.8 mg
1 cup cooked butternut squash (cubes) = 2.3 mg
1 large sweet orange bell pepper = .3 mg
1 cup cooked collard greens (chopped) = .2 mg

8. Beta-carotene

Aim for 6 milligrams per day of this carotenoid from a combination of the following foods...

1 cup cooked sweet potato = 23 mg
1 cup canned pumpkin = 17 mg
1 cup cooked carrots (slices) = 13 mg
1 cup cooked spinach = 11.3 mg

1 cup cooked chopped kale = 10.6 mg
1 cup cooked butternut squash (cubes) = 9.4 mg
1 cup cooked collard greens (chopped) = 9.2 mg

9. Beta Cryptoxanthin

Aim for at least 1 milligram per day of this carotenoid from a combination of the following foods…

1 cup cooked butternut squash (cubes) = 6.4 mg
1 cup cooked red bell pepper (strips) = 2.8 mg
1 Japanese persimmon (2½ inches diameter) = 2.4 mg
1 cup mashed papaya = 1.8 mg
1 large sweet red bell pepper (raw) = .8 mg
1 cup fresh tangerine juice = .5 mg
1 medium tangerine = .3 mg

10. Glutathione

Optimum daily recommendation amounts are not yet known. *Foods high in glutathione include…*

asparagus
watermelon
avocado
walnuts
grapefruit
peanut butter
oatmeal
broccoli
oranges
spinach

11. Resveratrol

Optimum daily recommendation amounts are not yet known. Data suggests that this phytonutrient plays a role in preventing inflammation and cancer. It seems to have cardioprotective activity. *Foods high in resveratrol include…*

peanuts
purple grape skins
red wine
purple grape juice
cranberries/cranberry juice

12. Fiber

The Institute of Medicine's Food and Nutrition Board released dietary reference intakes for fiber. *They are…*

Females 19 to 50 years old: 25 grams
Females 51 to 70 years old: 21 grams
Males 19 to 50 years old: 38 grams
Males 51 to 70 years old: 30 grams

I feel these should be minimum goals, and if one's fiber intake is higher through the consumption of whole food and whole food products, so much the better.

Whole foods:
1 cup cooked black beans = 15 grams fiber
¼ cup dry pinto beans = 14 grams
1 cup cooked garbanzo beans = 13 grams
¼ cup dry lentils = 9 grams
1 cup fresh raspberries = 8 grams

13. Omega-3 Fatty Acids

The Institute of Medicine's Food and Nutrition Board set an adequate target intake of 1.6 grams per day of plant-derived omega-3s (alpha linolenic acid, ALA) for adult men and 1.1 grams per day for adult women. They set a target amount of marine-derived omega-3s (EPA/DHA) of 160 milligrams per day for adult males and 110 milligrams per day for adult females.

I agree with the Food and Nutrition Board's daily ALA recommendations (they are great minimums; if you reach higher daily intake levels eating the *SuperFoods Rx* way, that is OK). My personal daily recommendations for marine-derived omega-3s are 1 gram per day of EPA/DHA for adult males and .7 gram (700 milligrams) for adult females.

Aim for the above goals through a combination of the following foods...

Alpha linolenic acid (ALA) = plant-derived omega-3 food sources

Oils

1 tablespoon canola oil = 1.3 grams
1 tablespoon soybean oil = .7 gram
1 tablespoon walnut oil = 1.4 grams
1 tablespoon flaxseed oil = 7.3 grams

Green leafies

1 cup cooked spinach = .2 gram
1 cup cooked collard greens = .2 gram

Other foods

½ cup dry-roasted soy nuts = 1.2 grams
1 tablespoon flaxseed = 2.2 grams
½ cup wheat germ = .5 gram
1 ounce (14 halves) English walnuts = 2.6 grams
1 omega-3 "vegetarian" hen egg = amounts vary; check the carton

EPA/DHA = primarily marine-derived omega-3 food sources

3 ounces cooked Alaskan king salmon = 1.5 grams
3 ounces sockeye salmon = 1 gram
3 ounces farmed rainbow trout = 1 gram
1 can sardines = .9 gram
3 ounces canned white tuna in water = .7 gram

Consider using an EPA/DHA supplement on days when you do not eat marine sources of omega-3 fats.

14. Polyphenols

Optimum daily recommended amounts for this class of phytonutrients has not yet been determined. *The following foods and beverages have significant amounts of polyphenols...*

Whole foods

berries
dates and figs
prunes
kale, spinach
parsley, dried parsley
apples with skin
citrus
grapes

The top three jams we tested for total polyphenol content...

Jams

Organic blueberry fruit spread
Knott's Pure Boysenberry Preserves
Organic blackberry fruit spread

Beverages

green, black or oolong tea
soymilk
100 percent fruit juices (berry, Concord grape, pomegranate, cherry, apple, citrus, prune)

The top three 100 percent fruit juices we tested for total polyphenol content were Odwalla C Monster, Trader Joe's 100 percent Unfiltered Concord Grape Juice and R.W. Knudsen 100 percent Pomegranate Juice.

Are You Getting Enough Vitamin D?

A recent national survey found that many adults, particularly those over age 50, do not reach their recommended daily intake of vitamin D. Many of us are vaguely aware that vitamin D helps preserve bone, but we are now learning that this essential nutrient is also important in protecting us from diseases, including cancer of the prostate, breast and colon as well as non-Hodgkin's lymphoma, rheumatoid arthritis, type I diabetes, macular degeneration, multiple sclerosis, fibromyalgia, gingivitis and muscle aches and pains in elderly people.

Vitamin D is vital in various bodily processes. It maintains normal blood levels of calcium and phosphorus and, by promoting calcium absorption, it helps to form and maintain strong bones. It also works with other nutrients and hormones to promote bone mineralization, which in turn prevents osteoporosis. Vitamin D also seems to play an important role in protecting our immune systems, regulating cell growth and differentiation, and exerting an anti-inflammatory effect.

The Sunshine Vitamin

Vitamin D has a unique feature among essential nutrients: While it's available from food sources, it's also manufactured by the skin and requires ultraviolet light for this process. Women ages 19 to 50, as well as men over age 51, eat the least amount of vitamin D–rich food. And, of course, in the winter, everyone's exposure to sunlight is limited. It's a good time of year to check your vitamin D consumption, as your levels of this important nutrient may be at their lowest.

How Much Vitamin D Do You Need?

The National Academy of Science set the latest daily vitamin D intake on an age-related scale...

19 to 50 years.....200 IU (international units)
51 to 70 years....400 IU
71 and above.....600 IU

My own recommended HealthStyle goal is to try to get 800 to 1,000 IU daily from food and/or supplements.

To put this in perspective, an 8-ounce glass of milk has about 100 IU of vitamin D. Many of us get most of our vitamin D from fortified foods. In the 1930s, when rickets were a major public health problem in the U.S., dairy producers began to fortify milk with vitamin D. Today, about 98 to 99 percent of the milk supply in the U.S. is fortified. A cup of vitamin D–fortified milk supplies one-half of the recommended daily intake for adults between ages 19 and 50, one-quarter of the Reference Daily Intake (RDI) for adults between ages 51 and 70, and about 15 percent of the RDI for those over 71.

Here are some excellent fish sources of vitamin D.

Vitamin D per 100 grams (3.53-ounce serving)*

Alaskan sockeye salmon	687 IU
Alaskan albacore tuna	544 IU
Alaskan silver salmon	439 IU
Alaskan king salmon	236 IU
Alaskan sardines (canned in olive oil)	222 IU
Alaskan sablefish	169 IU
Alaskan halibut	162 IU

Ready-to-eat vitamin D–fortified cereals are also an excellent source. Depending on the brand, they supply approximately 40 IU of vitamin D per serving. As you can see, other than fortified milk, fortified cereals and fish, few foods provide a rich supply of this vital nutrient.

Who's at Special Risk?

There are some folks who are at special risk for vitamin D deficiency...

- Older adults. As people age, their skin is less efficient at synthesizing vitamin D and their kidneys are less able to utilize the vitamin. It's been estimated that as many as 30 to 40 percent

*This analysis was conducted for Vital Choices Seafood Inc. by Covance Laboratories, Inc., Madison, Wisconsin.

of older people with hip fractures are deficient in vitamin D.

• People with limited sun exposure. In the winter, this includes many of us. For example, sunlight exposure from November through February in Boston won't produce significant vitamin D synthesis in the skin. Complete cloud cover halves the energy of UV rays, and shade reduces it by 60 percent. Industrial pollution, which increases shade, also decreases sun exposure. As more of us use sunscreens that prevent skin exposure to UV rays and/or limit our outdoor time to prevent skin cancers, we can become vulnerable to vitamin D deficiencies.

• People with greater melanin in their skin. Melanin is the pigment that gives skin its color. Darker skin is the result of more pigment. Darker skin is less able to produce vitamin D from sunlight, so African-Americans and other dark-skinned people should consume foods containing adequate amounts of vitamin D.

• People with malabsorption disorders. People who suffer from Crohn's disease, pancreatic enzyme deficiency, cystic fibrosis, sprue or liver disease, or who have undergone the surgical removal of part or all of their stomach or intestines can also suffer from vitamin D deficiency.

What's the Solution?

Try to get adequate vitamin D from your diet. Eat fortified low- or nonfat dairy products as well as vitamin D–fortified cereals. Eat the fish listed in the chart on page 145. Spend some (limited) unprotected time in the sun. While it's important to use sunscreen most of the time, a sun exposure of 10 to 15 minutes without sunscreen allows sufficient time for vitamin D synthesis and should be followed by the application of a sunscreen with an SPF of at least 15. When you see the sun shining in the winter, take a brisk 15-minute walk.

Potassium Power

You probably know that if you've been diagnosed with hypertension (high blood pressure), you should cut down on the sodium in your diet (see page 280). Limiting sodium is an important step that everyone should take to preserve health. There's another simple but important dietary modification that you should consider, which, unfortunately, few people know about—increase your potassium intake. Potassium is a mineral—an electrolyte—that helps to balance the acidity/alkalinity of the body's fluids as it also helps control blood pressure. Too much fluid increases blood pressure and potassium plays a crucial role in maintaining optimum fluid levels.

Before the emergence of agriculture, humans consumed a diet that was high in potassium and low in sodium. Lately, with the increase in the popularity of processed foods along with a reduction in the consumption of fruits and vegetables, most of us have decreased our potassium intake as we've increased our sodium intake. While deficiencies of potassium are rare because potassium is widely available in a variety of foods, it's my strong belief that a large percentage of those eating a Westernized diet suffer from a discrete, but important, deficiency of potassium. In the developing world, where diets are rich in potassium and low in sodium, high blood pressure is virtually nonexistent.

Highly refined wheat flour contains less than half the potassium level of whole-grain flour.

Why is a rich supply of potassium important? Research has now established that a high intake of potassium plays a protective role against hypertension, stroke, cardiac dysfunction, (including arrhythmias), as well as kidney damage and osteoporosis. The Dietary Approaches to Stop Hypertension (DASH) diet recommends a rich intake of potassium-rich foods and has shown a marked ability to lower blood pressure.

✪ In an epidemiologic study of 84,360 American women over a period of six years, a high intake of potassium was associated with a lowered risk of developing diabetes mellitus.

We should be getting *three to five times* the amount of potassium as sodium in our diets; unfortunately most of us get about half that amount of potassium. Some of us even get less potassium than sodium. U.S. government guidelines recommend that you consume at least 4,700 milligrams of potassium daily; my own recommendation is that you aim for 8,000 milligrams daily. It's not difficult to reach that goal when you appreciate that green, leafy vegetables, citrus fruits and beans are rich in potassium. Other good choices include dairy products, fish and nuts.

Good Sources of Potassium

(listed in descending order of milligrams [mg])

- Sweet potato, 1 cup cooked, 950 mg, 180 calories
- Potato, 1 medium baked, 926 mg, 161 calories
- Clams, 6 cooked, 705 mg, 166 calories
- Odwalla Chocolate Protein Shake, 12 ounces (oz), 680 mg, 100 calories
- Evolution Incredible Vegetable, 8 oz, 620 mg, 70 calories
- Butternut squash, 1 cup cooked, 582 mg, 82 calories
- Lakewood 100% Fruit Juice Pure Black Cherry, 8 oz, 580 mg, 140 calories
- Figs (dried), 4 large, 541 mg, 194 calories
- R.W. Knudsen Very Veggie Vegetable Cocktail (Low Sodium), 1 cup, 520 mg, 50 calories
- Libby's Canned Pumpkin, 1 cup, 505 mg, 83 calories
- Salsa with mesquite kettle chips, 1 oz, 495 mg, 140 calories
- Cantaloupe, 1 cup, 494 mg, 60 calories
- Lima beans, ½ cup cooked, 478 mg, 108 calories
- Lentils, ½ cup cooked, 475 mg, 115 calories
- Orange juice, 8 oz, 473 mg, 118 calories
- R.W. Knudsen Just Pomegranate, 8 oz, 460 mg, 150 calories
- Naked Juice Strawberry Banana Smoothie, 8 oz, 460 mg, 130 calories
- Oysters, 6 medium, 453 mg, 245 calories
- EdenSoy Extra, Organic Soy Milk, 1 cup, 440 mg, 130 calories
- Avocado, ½ Hass avocado, 439 mg, 145 calories
- POM Wonderful 100% Pomegranate Juice, 8 oz, 430 mg, 140 calories
- Sunsweet Prune Juice, 1 cup, 430 mg, 180 calories
- Banana, 1 medium, 422 mg, 105 calories
- Spinach (cooked), ½ cup, 419 mg, 21 calories
- POM Wonderful 100% Pomegranate Cherry Juice, 8 oz, 390 mg, 140 calories
- Naked Juice OJ, 8 oz, 370 mg, 110 calories
- Salmon (wild coho), 3 oz, 369 mg, 118 calories
- Dried plums (prunes), 6 uncooked, 366 mg, 120 calories
- Naked Juice Power-C, 8 oz, 360 mg, 120 calories
- Trader Joe's Unfiltered Concord Grape Juice, 8 oz, 350 mg, 160 calories
- Oats, ½ cup, 335 mg, 302 calories
- Spinach, 2 cups raw, 334 mg, 14 calories

- Tomato paste, 2 tablespoons, 324 mg, 26 calories
- Dates (Deglet Noor), 6 dates, 324 mg, 138 calories
- Wild salmon (canned), 3 oz, 320 mg, 130 calories
- Raisins, ¼ cup, 309 mg, 123 calories
- Vanilla Silk soymilk, 1 cup, 300 mg, 100 calories
- Pinto beans, ½ cup canned, 292 mg, 103 calories
- Blackberries, 1 cup, 282 mg, 75 calories
- Strawberries, 1 cup, 252 mg, 46 calories
- Turkey (skinless breast), 3 oz, 248 mg, 115 calories
- Apricots (dried), 6 halves, 246 mg, 48 calories
- Orange, 1 medium, 237 mg, 64 calories
- Broccoli (cooked), ½ cup, 228 mg, 44 calories
- Tofu, ½ cup, 221 mg, 183 calories
- Chickpeas (garbanzo), ½ cup, 207 mg, 143 calories
- Tomatoes (raw), ½ cup, 200 mg, .04 calories
- Almonds, 1 oz, 198 mg, 164 calories
- Peanuts, 1 oz, 191 mg, 90 calories
- Applesauce (unsweetened), ½ cup, 183 mg, 50 calories
- Flaxseed, 2 tablespoons, 164 mg, 118 calories
- Figs, 1 large (½-inch diameter), 148 mg, 47 calories
- Wheat germ, 2 tablespoons, 134 mg, 52 calories
- Walnuts, 1 oz, 124 mg, 183 calories
- Nestlé Carnation Evaporated Fat Free Milk, 2 tablespoons, 110 mg, 25 calories

Fiber

HealthStyle is about habits—the everyday behaviors that can boost your health profile and result in vigorous optimum good health. No *single* habit is likely to turn the tide from illness to optimum health, but a *pattern* of good habits can help ensure a vigorous and vital future. My goal is to persuade you to adopt as many HealthStyle habits as you can over the course of a year so that one year from now, you'll feel better than ever, and 10 or 20 years from now, you'll be better yet.

One of the HealthStyle habits I want you to adopt is the fiber habit. Adequate fiber intake is critical for optimum health. Back in the Paleolithic era, the typical Stone-Ager ate about 47 grams of fiber daily. Today, in Western cultures, the average fiber intake is just 17 grams a day. This simply isn't enough. In my opinion, even the guidelines that the Institute of Medicine's Food and Nutrition Board set—38 grams a day for adult men and 25 grams a day for adult women—is low. (Their goal for folks over age 51 is 30 grams a day for men and 21 grams a day for women—lower because of the typical reduced calorie intake at that age.) My own HealthStyle recommendations may be ambitious, but I believe the health payoffs are well worth it.

Here are the HealthStyle Fiber Challenge Goals...

- 45 grams daily for adult men
- 32 grams daily for adult women

If you're like many Americans, this will be more than double the amount of fiber you're eating today, but it's not a difficult goal to achieve once you learn how to choose high-fiber, healthy foods. Meeting this HealthStyle fiber challenge will have a dramatic synergistic effect on your overall health and it could be the most important single change you can make in your diet.

Fiber has traditionally been the Rodney Dangerfield of dietary subjects. Other than a nod to bowel health, the role of fiber just doesn't get much respect. In part, this is because we used to believe that since fiber contained no protein, fat, carbohydrates, vitamins or minerals, its role was pretty much to sweep through the digestive system and add bulk. Not much romance there. We thought that fiber was just cellulose and lignan—the woody part of plants—and that its role was to absorb water and keep things moving along. We now know that fiber is not a single substance, but a powerful variety of compounds that have important and broad-ranging effects on various bodily systems.

WHAT IS FIBER?

It is the general name given to all indigestible carbohydrates. All fiber comes from plant foods, including fruits, vegetables, grains and legumes; meat contains no fiber. In the old days, fiber was divided into two categories—soluble and insoluble. While these simple categories have morphed into more sophisticated ones, they still provide a basic understanding of the role of fiber.

Soluble fiber is fiber that dissolves in water. It plays a vital role in lowering cholesterol levels and promoting cardiovascular health. Soluble fiber also helps regulate blood sugar levels, thus playing an important role in the management of diabetes. And finally, it contributes to maintaining optimum body weight, because high-fiber foods tend to fill you up while being generally low in calories.

Insoluble fiber is fiber that does not dissolve in water. It adds bulk to the stool while it stimulates peristalsis, the intestinal contractions that move food through the digestive system.

Now that we know that both types of fiber are present in many foods, experts prefer to define fiber in relation to its physiological benefits, for example, intestinal transit time (to mitigate constipation and cancer), viscosity (to escort cholesterol from the system) and fermentability (for intestinal health).

If you learn only a few lessons from HealthStyle, one of them should be a new respect for fiber and making an active effort to eat more of it. Fiber is an essential nutrient which is vital to our health.

Here's the simple truth: High-fiber foods are highly nutritious and are associated with health promotion; Low-fiber foods are generally less nutritious and are associated with a greater risk of disease.

Another way to look at it is that people who consume the most fiber-rich foods are the healthiest from the standpoint of a whole host of markers. In one study, it was found that the amount of fiber that people consume may better predict weight gain, insulin levels and other cardiovascular risk factors than does the amount of total fat consumed.

✪ My fiber recommendation is based on fiber that is present in whole foods, not in fiber supplements. Fiber supplements may not contain the health-promoting anticancer and cardiovascular-healthy nutrients that are present in whole, high-fiber foods.

What Fiber Can Do for You

A high-fiber diet has a whole host of health benefits, first and simplest being that these foods tend also to be packed with disease-fighting phytonutrients. This would be reason enough to eat them. But there's more: High-fiber foods have been proven to provide very specific health benefits that promote cardiovascular health, digestive health and improved glucose tolerance, as well as cancer prevention.

LOWERS HEART DISEASE RISK

Research has shown that a high-fiber diet may lower the risk of coronary heart disease. When soluble fiber mixes with water in the digestive tract, it forms a gel that acts to mop up cholesterol and escort it from the system. In one study, women who consumed the most cereal fiber were approximately 35 percent less likely to develop heart disease compared with those who ate the least fiber.

In another study of 42,850 men, the Health Professional Follow-Up Study found that during a fourteen-year period there was an 18 percent decrease in the risk for coronary heart disease in men with the highest daily intake of whole grains and, when adjusted additionally for bran intake, those with the highest bran intake had a 30 percent reduced risk for coronary heart disease.

A recent body of research has pointed to the association of C-reactive protein (CRP) with inflammation and resulting heart disease. Another recent study found that high-fiber intake is inversely associated with CRP levels. In this study, those with the highest fiber intake had almost a 40 percent reduced risk of having a high CRP compared with the participants in the lowest quintile of fiber intake.

HELPS PREVENT AND MANAGE DIABETES

A high-fiber diet can play an important role in both preventing diabetes and managing it. We know that by slowing digestion, fiber helps reduce the rapid rise in blood sugar that occurs after eating foods that contain carbohydrates. One small study had impressive results for the participants. The study group included thirteen patients with type II diabetes. By the end of the study, those who ate 50 total grams of fiber daily had seen a total cholesterol reduction of 6.7 percent, an LDL ("bad") cholesterol reduction of 6.3 percent, a triglyceride reduction of 10.2 percent, a very-low-density lipoprotein cholesterol reduction of 12.5 percent, a blood glucose level reduction of 10 percent and a blood insulin level reduction of 12 percent. These patients achieved these results by consuming unfortified foods, particularly those high in cholesterol-lowering soluble fiber. While it's true that this is more fiber than many people are accustomed to eating, the health benefits were considerable. For example, the decrease in blood glucose levels was similar to that achieved by taking an oral hypoglycemic drug.

A CANCER-FIGHTER TOO

High-fiber foods play a role, in some instances controversial, in fighting cancer. For example, while the relationship between high-fiber foods and colon cancer remains uncertain, at least two observational studies from Europe and the U.S. have found an inverse relationship between total dietary fiber and the incidence of colon polyps or cancer.

It's also been demonstrated that a high dietary fiber intake reduces the risk for rectal, breast, prostate, laryngeal and ovarian cancers. We do know that fiber can play an important role in preventing a recurrence of breast cancer, and now that, thanks to better care, more and more women are living with a history of breast cancer, it's very important to adopt any and all strategies that could prevent recurrences.

Epidemiologic evidence overwhelmingly suggests that a diet low in unhealthy fat and rich in fruits and vegetables is associated with a reduced risk for many primary cancers, including breast cancer. This type of diet also reduces the circulating estrogen levels in breast cancer survivors and could potentially stave off recurrence.

In one study of breast cancer survivors, the intervention group had a significant increase in fiber—from 22 to 29 grams a day—and a significantly lower intake of fat. These women found that their levels of estrogen decreased significantly, and analysis of the data showed that this change was independently associated with the increased fiber intake, but not the decrease in fat intake. As the author of the study said: "...dietary strategies that reduce estrogen stimulation...may help reduce risk of recurrence and improve the likelihood of survival in women with a history of breast cancer."

FIBER FIGHTS WEIGHT GAIN

There's finally good news for those of us who are trying to maintain an optimum weight—a high-fiber diet has been conclusively associated with healthy weight maintenance. It's generally thought that fiber may decrease calorie intake and promote weight loss by inducing satiety—the feeling of fullness—as well as reducing blood glucose concentrations following a meal. We know that soluble fiber intake has been shown to be inversely associated with long-term weight gain. In a recent study, the daily consumption of either three apples or three pears (both fruits are high in soluble fiber) was associated with weight loss in overweight women.

And finally, the old news is still good news: A high-fiber diet promotes normal bowel function and helps prevent constipation, hemorrhoids and diverticulitis.

The 30-Day Fiber Challenge

Here's a way to get you on the fiber bandwagon. It's very simple. It will change your life and get you healthy.

It takes about 30 days for your gastrointestinal system to adjust to an optimum fiber intake. If you go too quickly, you'll experience diarrhea, gas and bloating. In order to meet my HealthStyle Fiber Challenge Goals, you should begin by assessing your current fiber intake. Analyze your fiber intake for a typical day. Write down everything you eat—and the amounts—including all meals and snacks. (This is a great exercise, as it will help you focus on various aspects of your diet.) Once you have your day's food intake charted, find a reference on fiber amounts in foods. The Food and Nutrition Information Center has a Web site that is quite complete: *http://fnic.nal.usda.gov*. Another helpful resource is *Your Personal Nutritionist: Fiber & Fat Counter* by Ed Blonz (Signet).

Once you know what your typical daily fiber intake is, it's time to increase it. Try to increase your fiber intake by 4 to 8 grams per week until you reach the goal of 45 grams daily for adult men and 32 grams daily for adult women. Choose one high-fiber food from each class in the list beginning on page 152. Some foods may cause digestive problems, others will not. At the end of four weeks, you should have reached your fiber goal. You'll probably notice that you get full more quickly and that your normal regularity is enhanced.

- Pay attention to food labels. The labels of almost all foods will tell you the amount of dietary fiber in each serving.
- Choose whole-grain cereals for breakfast that have at least 3 grams of fiber per serving. Top with wheat germ, ground flaxseed meal, bananas, berries or raisins to increase fiber.
- Eat whole fruits instead of drinking fruit juices. Avoid peeling fruits or vegetables when possible.
- Replace white rice, bread and pasta with brown rice and whole-grain products. Snack on raw vegetables instead of chips, crackers or chocolate bars.

It's important to understand exactly what a serving of whole grains is. The following are all considered one serving each: 1 small bran muffin, 1 slice of whole-grain bread, 1 oatmeal cookie, 5 whole wheat crackers, 1 cup of popcorn, 1 cup cooked brown rice, 1 cup cooked oatmeal.

- Substitute beans for meat two to three times per week in chili and soups, and add beans to soups, stews and salads.
- Experiment with international dishes that use whole grains and legumes as part of a meal, as in Indian dals...or in salads, such as Middle Eastern tabbouleh.
- Read the following list of brand-name and whole foods that are top choices for high fiber.

Top HealthStyle Fiber Choices

BREAD

• Manna from Heaven (Julian Bakery), one slice, 8 grams fiber, 110 calories

• HealthSeed Spelt (Yeast-Free, with Soy, Flax and Pumpkin and Sunflower Seeds), one slice, 6 grams fiber, 88 calories

• The Original Bran for Life Bread, one slice, 5 grams fiber, 80 calories

• Vogel's Soy & Linseed Bread, one slice, 3 grams fiber, 80 calories

• Sprouted Grain Bread Ezekiel 4:9, one slice, 3 grams fiber, 80 calories

CEREALS

• Barbara's Bakery Organic Grain Shop High Fiber Cereal, ¾ cup (55 grams), 14 grams fiber, 180 calories

• Bob's Red Mill Organic High Fiber Hot Cereal, ⅓ cup, 10 grams fiber, 150 calories

• Bob's Red Mill Wheat Bran, ¼ cup, 6 grams fiber, 30 calories

• Bob's Red Mill Whole Ground Flaxseed Meal, 2 tablespoons, 4 grams fiber, 60 calories

• General Mills Fiber One Bran Cereal, ½ cup, 14 grams fiber, 60 calories

• Kashi GoLean High Protein/High Fiber Cereal, 1 cup, 10 grams fiber, 140 calories

• Kellogg's All-Bran BranBuds, ⅓ cup, 13 grams fiber, 70 calories

• Kellogg's All-Bran Extra Fiber, ½ cup, 13 grams fiber, 50 calories

• Kellogg's All-Bran Original, ½ cup, 10 grams fiber, 80 calories

• Kellogg's All-Bran Complete Wheat Flakes, ¾ cup, 5 grams fiber, 90 calories

• Mother's Toasted Wheat Germ, 2 tablespoons, 2 grams fiber, 50 calories

• Nature's Path Flax Plus Multibran Cereal, ¾ cup, 7 grams fiber, 100 calories

• Nature's Path Flax Plus Raisin Bran, ¾ cup, 8 grams fiber, 180 calories

• Nature's Path Optimum Cranberry Ginger, ¾ cup, 8 grams fiber, 200 calories

• Post 100% Bran, ⅓ cup, 9 grams fiber, 80 calories

• Post Shredded Wheat, 2 biscuits, 6 grams fiber, 160 calories

• Post Shredded Wheat 'N Bran, ½ cup, 8 grams fiber, 200 calories

• Quaker Oat Bran Hot Cereal, ½ cup, 6 grams fiber, 150 calories

• Simply Fiber, 1 cup, 14 grams fiber, 100 calories

• Uncle Sam Cereal (Whole-Wheat Flakes and Flaxseed), 1 cup, 10 grams fiber, 190 calories

CRACKERS and CRISPBREAD

• Ak-Mak 100% Whole Wheat Stone Ground Sesame Crackers, 5 crackers, 3.5 grams fiber, 16 calories

• Health Valley Amaranth Bran Graham Crackers, 6 crackers, 3 grams fiber, 120 calories

• Health Valley Oat Bran Graham Crackers, 6 crackers, 3 grams fiber, 120 calories

• Health Valley Rice Bran Crackers, 6 crackers, 3 grams fiber, 110 calories

• Ryvita Dark Rye whole-grain crispbread, one slice, 2 grams fiber, 35 calories

• Wasa Fiber Crispbread, one slice, 2.5 grams fiber, 32 calories

FRUITS

• Mott's Organic Unsweetened Applesauce, ½ cup, 1 gram fiber, 50 calories

• TreeTop Applesauce, ½ cup, 2 grams fiber, 80 calories

• Apple, 1 large with peel, 5.7 grams fiber, 125 calories

• Avocado, ½ cup, 4.2 grams fiber, 153 calories

- Blackberries, 1 cup, 7.6 grams fiber, 75 calories
- Blueberries, 1 cup, 3.9 grams fiber, 81 calories
- Dates, 5 to 6 pitted Deglet Noor dates, 3 grams fiber, 120 calories
- Figs, 2 medium, 3.3 grams fiber, 74 calories
- Kiwifruit, 2 medium, 5 grams fiber, 93 calories
- Orange, 1 medium, 3.4 grams fiber, 64 calories
- Papaya, 1 cup cubes, 2.5 grams fiber, 55 calories
- Pears, 1 medium Bartlett, 4 grams fiber, 98 calories
- Persimmons, 1 large, 6.1 grams fiber, 118 calories
- Sunsweet Bite-Size Pitted Dried Plums, 7, 3 grams fiber, 100 calories
- Pavich Organic Raisins, ¼ cup, 2 grams fiber, 120 calories
- Sunmaid Raisins, ¼ cup, 2 grams fiber, 130 calories
- Raspberries, 1 cup, 8.4 grams fiber, 60 calories
- Strawberries, 1 cup, 3.5 grams fiber, 46 calories
- Sweet potato, 1 medium (4 oz), 3.7 grams fiber, 143 calories

JUICES

- Naked Apple Raisin Oat Fruit Juice and Oat Smoothie, 9.5 ounces, 5 grams fiber, 350 calories
- Naked Red Machine, 8 ounces, 4 grams fiber (from fruit and flax), 160 calories
- Sunsweet Prune Juice +, 8 ounces, 3 grams fiber, 170 calories

LEGUMES

- Health Valley Organic Soup—Lentil (no salt added), 1 cup, 8 grams fiber, 110 calories
- Health Valley Organic Soup—Black Bean (no salt added), 1 cup, 5 grams fiber, 140 calories
- Edensoy Extra Organic Soymilk, 8 ounces, 1 gram fiber, 130 calories
- Chickpeas, ½ cup cooked, 6.2 grams fiber, 135 calories
- Green peas, 1 cup cooked, 8.8 grams fiber, 134 calories
- Trader Joe's Dry Roasted Edamame (lightly salted), ¼ cup, 4 grams fiber, 140 calories
- Pinto beans, ½ cup cooked, 7.4 grams fiber, 117 calories

NUTS (all listed per 1 ounce)

- Maranatha Almond Butter, 4 grams fiber per 2 tablespoons (32 grams), 195 calories
- Almonds (24), 3 grams fiber, 160 calories
- Hazelnuts (20), 3 grams fiber, 180 calories
- Pecans (20 halves), 3 grams fiber, 200 calories
- Pistachios (49), 3 grams fiber, 160 calories
- Walnuts (14 halves), 2 grams fiber, 190 calories
- Peanuts (28), 2 grams fiber, 170 calories

PASTA

- Darielle Pasta (penne or elbows), ¾ cup, 8 grams fiber, 160 calories
- DeBoles Organic Whole Wheat Spaghetti Style Pasta, 2 ounces (oz.), 5 grams fiber, 210 calories
- Eden Organic Pasta Company Kamut Spirals, ½ cup, 6 grams fiber, 210 calories

- Eden Organic Twisted Pair Gemelli, 100% Whole-Grain Kamut & Quinoa, ½ cup, 5 grams fiber, 210 calories
- Westbrae Natural Vegetarian Organic Spinach Spaghetti, 2 oz., 8 grams fiber, 180 calories

PIZZA

- A.C. LaRocco Pizza Company, multiple varieties, 3 to 8 grams fiber per serving

VEGETABLES

- Health Valley Organic Soup—Vegetable (no salt added), 1 cup, 4 grams fiber, 90 calories
- Asparagus, 1 cup cooked, 2.9 grams fiber, 43 calories
- Broccoli, 1 cup cooked, 4.7 grams fiber, 44 calories
- Butternut squash, ½ cup baked, 3.5 grams fiber, 49 calories
- Cauliflower, 1 cup cooked, 3.3 grams fiber, 29 calories
- Collards, 1 cup cooked, 5.3 grams fiber, 49 calories
- Corn, 1 cup cooked kernels, 4.6 grams fiber, 177 calories
- Libby's 100% canned pumpkin, ½ cup, 5 grams fiber, 40 calories
- Swiss chard, 1 cup cooked, 3.7 grams fiber, 35 calories
- Tomato, 1 medium, 2.5 grams fiber, 48 calories

SuperSpices

Most of us think of spices as incidental to our diets, but perhaps it's time to update our appreciation of these flavorful, and powerfully health-promoting, seasonings.

Spices are defined as any "aromatic vegetable substance." The key word is *vegetable*. Derived from "vegetables" in the form of tree bark (cinnamon), seed (nutmeg), or fruit (peppercorns), spices have potent anticancer, anti-inflammatory and other health-promoting effects that are daily being confirmed by researchers. Indeed, the following spices have been identified by the National Cancer Institute as having cancer-preventive properties: sage, oregano, thyme, rosemary, fennel, turmeric, caraway, anise, coriander, cumin and tarragon. Indeed, in one comparison of antioxidant power from the Agricultural Research Center, the compounds in oregano rank higher than vitamin E.

Spices also make major contributions to our health by allowing us to reduce the amounts of salt, sugar and fat in our foods.

We've chosen cinnamon as a SuperSpice because of its general popularity and usefulness, but we've also included a few other spices in this section that make major contributions to a healthy diet as well.

Cinnamon

Cinnamon is welcome all year round, but its special scent is a particular treat in the winter months. What could be more welcome and delicious than a warm mug of apple cider sprinkled with cinnamon or a cinnamony baked apple with crushed nuts on a cold snowy day? It's exciting to learn that cinnamon has actual health benefits.

Cinnamon, that delightful spice eliciting memories of Grandma's kitchen and the comforts of home, is actually more than a delicious addition to foods. One of the oldest spices known and long used in traditional medicine, cinnamon is currently being studied for its beneficial effects on a variety of ailments. Indeed, recent findings on the power of cinnamon to promote health, in particular its benefits for people with type II diabetes, have elevated it to the special status of a SuperSpice.

Cinnamon comes from the interior bark of evergreen trees that are native to Asia. The type we most commonly see in the supermarket is cassia cinnamon (*Cinnamomum cassia*). Known as Chinese cinnamon, it has the sweetly spiced flavor we're familiar with. Varieties of Chinese cinnamon come from China and northern Vietnam. There's also Ceylon, or "true," cinnamon (*Cinnamomum zeylanicum*), which is sweeter with a more complex, citrusy flavor. Both types of cinnamon are available in sticks ("quills") or ground.

You can find high-quality cinnamon from China as well as from Ceylon, Indonesia and even Vietnam, at Penzeys Spices. They have a few retail stores and an excellent catalog: 800-741-7787 or *www.penzeys.com.*

Cinnamon and Your Health

Today, we're in the process of learning about the power of cinnamon to affect health, and once you appreciate the special qualities of this mighty spice, I'm sure you'll be eager to use it more frequently.

Perhaps the most exciting recent discovery concerning cinnamon is its effect on blood glucose levels as well as on triglyceride and cholesterol levels, all of which could benefit people suffering from type II diabetes.

In one study of 60 patients with type II diabetes, it was found that after only 40 days of taking about one-half teaspoon of cinnamon daily, fasting serum glucose levels were lowered by 18 to 29 percent, triglycerides by 23 to 30 percent, low-density lipoproteins (LDL) by 7 to 27 percent and total cholesterol by 12 to 26 percent. It's not yet clear whether less than one-half teaspoon a day would be effective. It's particularly interesting that the effects of the cinnamon lasted for 20 days following the end of the study, leading to speculation that one wouldn't have to eat cinnamon every day to enjoy its benefits. This is great news for HealthStylers and points out once again the benefit of a varied diet of whole foods and spices. The cinnamon—and perhaps other spices and certainly many foods—that you're eating today are affecting your health into the future.

Cinnamon, by its insulin-enhancing properties, is not the only spice to show a positive effect on blood glucose levels. Cloves, bay leaves and turmeric also show beneficial effects.

In addition to being a glucose moderator, cinnamon is recognized as being an antibacterial. The essential oils in cinnamon are able to stop the growth of bacteria as well as fungi, including the common yeast *Candida*. In one interesting study, a few drops of cinnamon essential oil in about 3 ounces of carrot broth inhibited the growth of bacteria for at least 60 days. By contrast, bacteria flourished in the broth with no cinnamon oil. Cinnamon has also been shown to be effective in fighting the *E. coli* bacterium.

Try to buy organically grown cinnamon, as it is less likely to have been irradiated. We know that irradiating cinnamon may lead to a decrease in its vitamin C and carotenoid content.

A recent fascinating study found that just smelling cinnamon increased the subjects' cognitive ability and actually functioned as a kind of "brain boost." Future testing will reveal whether this power of cinnamon can be harnessed to prevent cognitive decline or sharpen cognitive performance.

Cinnamon in Your Life

What does this exciting news on cinnamon mean to you? While it may not be practical to eat cinnamon on a daily basis, try to incorporate it into dishes when appropriate. If you have been diagnosed with diabetes, make a special effort to increase your cinnamon consumption.

Almost everyone is a fan of cinnamon, but we may need a little inspiration to get cinnamon into our diets more frequently. A dash of cinnamon in applesauce, pumpkin smoothies and pumpkin pudding, and other foods, is a delightful treat.

- For a healthy dessert, sprinkle cinnamon, a few raisins and walnuts, and a bit of honey, if desired, on a cored apple and bake at 350° F for about 45 minutes until soft.
- Make cinnamon toast. Drizzle some honey and sprinkle some cinnamon on toasted whole wheat bread.
- Simmer, don't boil, milk with a teaspoon of vanilla and a cinnamon stick for a few minutes. Drink the warm milk with a bit of added honey or pour over hot oatmeal.
- Combine one teaspoon cinnamon with two tablespoons honey and one cup yogurt. Serve as a dip for sliced fruit or as a dressing for fruit salad. Spoon a dollop on top of hot oatmeal, whole-grain pancakes, waffles or granola.
- Combine equal parts of cinnamon and cocoa. Sprinkle on yogurt and fruit slices.
- Combine one tablespoon or more ground cinnamon with one-half cup sesame seeds, one-quarter cup golden flaxseeds and one-quarter cup ground flaxseed meal. Use as a topping on cereal, oatmeal, yogurt, grapefruit halves or cantaloupe. Whole flaxseeds add crunch and fiber, though you get more of the nutritional value from ground flaxseeds.

Cumin

Cumin, a nutty, peppery seed, is popular in Indian, Middle Eastern and Mexican cuisines. In addition to being rich in iron, cumin seed has been found in animal studies to have anticancer properties.

Oregano

Oregano, the spice commonly associated with Mediterranean and Mexican cuisines, is a warm, aromatic herb with a variety of health-promoting abilities. The volatile oils in oregano have potent antibacterial properties. In addition, the various phytonutrients in oregano have powerful antioxidant properties. In fact, research has indicated that oregano has demonstrated 42 times more antioxidant activity than apples and 30 times more than potatoes.

Thyme

Thyme is a delicate herb with a delightful fragrance. The primary volatile oil in thyme—thymol—has been found to significantly increase the healthy fats found in the brains of aging rats. Thyme has long been associated with healing abilities in connection with chest and respiratory problems. A rich source of flavonoids, thyme is now recognized as a powerful antioxidant food.

Turmeric

Turmeric, sometimes known as the "Indian saffron" because of its rich yellow-orange color, has been used throughout history as a spice, healing food and textile dye. Numerous studies have shown that the yellow or orange pigment in turmeric—known as curcumin—has anti-inflammatory effects comparable to the potent drug hydrocortisone and other anti-inflammatory drugs. Turmeric has also been associated in preliminary research with providing relief for rheumatoid arthritis and cystic fibrosis, promoting liver function and cardiovascular health, as well as possibly providing protection against Alzheimer's disease.

4

The Amazing SuperFoods Recipes

If you've ever visited Rancho La Puerta or the Golden Door, you know what a remarkable experience they provide. It's not just the utter tranquility and beauty of the locations—it's the combination of attention to the body with exercise and spa treatments, attention to the spirit with an overall atmosphere of mindful serenity, and delicious, healthful food, which refreshes one entirely. It's hard to imagine how a single week can echo for months and months, but it does. My recent week at Rancho La Puerta is such a strong memory that I can close my eyes in the most stressful moment and be transported back to the total peace of that week. I hope that every reader of this book will someday have the opportunity to enjoy a comparable experience.

Introducing... The Incredible Chefs

When the idea for *SuperFoods Rx* first took shape, I realized that I would need more than just nutritional statistics to convince people to adopt the *SuperFoods Rx* lifestyle. Dr. Hugh Greenway, my friend and colleague, suggested that the world-renowned chef, Michel Stroot, of the Golden Door in Escondido, California, and his colleagues at Rancho La Puerta in Tecate, Mexico, would be ideal candidates to create recipes for *SuperFoods Rx* that would be delicious and easy to prepare. Both spas are world famous for their delicious and healthful meals.

Dr. Greenway has had a long relationship with Rancho La Puerta and Golden Door because he treated Alex Szekely, son of the founders of both spas, when he was first diagnosed with cancer. Alex sadly lost his battle with melanoma, but his legacy lives on—he brought his parents' vision of a spa retreat to another level when he shifted the emphasis from weight loss and general pampering to retreats that advocate the ideal of a mind-body-spirit balance.

We are equally as fortunate to have the immensely talented Chef Mark Cleveland also help us turn SuperFoods into super meals.

Mark learned to cook as a child from his wise Italian grandma, mastered the concepts of healthy California vegetarian cuisine while in college, and expanded his repertoire of ingredients, techniques and flavors while living and working in Japan. Once back in California, Mark founded BIAN Personal Chef, a service that specialized in naturally nutritious meals with an international flair. Mark is now busy with his Avanti Café in Costa Mesa, California. Mark's extensive experience teaching cooking techniques is obvious in the care he's taken in developing these recipes.

These amazing chefs immediately grasped the theory of *SuperFoods Rx*—that if you shifted the emphasis of your diet to health-promoting foods, you would feel better, avoid many causes of illness and death, and would even look better as a delightful bonus.

The recipes included here are the best of their creations, working within the guidelines of the *SuperFoods Rx* program. I've also included a handful of much-loved recipes from family and friends. I'm thrilled that my vision has come to life and hope that you and your families will enjoy these recipes.

For more information about Golden Door, call 760-744-5777 or visit *www.goldendoor.com*. For more information on Rancho La Puerta, call 800-443-7565 or visit *www.rancholapuerta.com*. For more information on the Avanti Café, call 949-548-2224 or visit *www.avantinatural.com*.

CHEF MICHEL STROOT

Apple-Oat Crisp

8 large Granny Smith cooking apples, cored and sliced (do not peel)
1½ cups rolled oats
½ cup brown sugar
¾ cup chopped walnuts
1 teaspoon sugar
2 tablespoons Smart Balance buttery spread
3 tablespoons soymilk

Arrange the apple slices in a 13 × 8-inch baking dish. You may need more or less to fill the dish. In a separate bowl, mix all dry ingredients with a fork or pastry blender and cut the buttery spread into the mixture. Drizzle the soymilk over the top; mix. The mixture should be crumbly. Put the mixture over the apple slices. Cover with aluminum foil and bake in a 350° F oven for 45 minutes. Remove the foil and bake until the apples appear bubbly at the bottom of the dish. Top with fresh or frozen yogurt if you like.

Serves eight.

Nutritional analysis per serving...

Calories: 331
Protein: 6.5 g
Carbohydrates: 59 g
Cholesterol: 0
Total fat: 10 g
Saturated fat: 1 g
Monounsaturated fat: 2.7 g
Polyunsaturated fat: 4.8 g
Omega-6: 4 g
Omega-3: .24 g
Sodium: 34 mg
Potassium: 420 mg
Fiber: 8 g

CHEF MARK CLEVELAND

Avocado Goddess Crunch Salad

This salad can be a stand-alone meal or an accompaniment to poached, grilled or roasted wild salmon. If you don't like the anise flavor of tarragon, substitute basil, cilantro, dill or marjoram. Substitute white or champagne vinegar for the tarragon vinegar if you like.

Dressing

2 tablespoons flaxseed oil
2 large ripe avocados
1 cup nonfat yogurt
1 medium shallot
2 tablespoons flat-leaf parsley
1 tablespoon chopped fresh tarragon, optional
3 tablespoons tarragon vinegar, or more
Salt and pepper
1 tablespoon Worcestershire sauce, optional

Salad

1 medium red onion

1 medium green bell pepper
1 medium orange bell pepper
1 medium red bell pepper
2 medium Belgian endive
1 large hothouse cucumber
1 medium jicama
1 medium yellow squash or zucchini
⅓ cup sunflower seeds, roasted

Combine all the dressing ingredients in a food processor or blender and mix until smooth. Add more vinegar if necessary to thin. Cut the onion into quarters and thinly slice. Soak the slices in ice-cold water for about 10 minutes. Drain and place in a salad bowl. Cut the bell peppers into ¼-inch strips. Slice the Belgian endive into ¼-inch slices on the diagonal, to get longer slices. Cut the remaining vegetables into julienne strips, about ¼ inch by 2 inches—similar in size to the pepper strips. Toss the vegetables in the salad bowl with just enough dressing to coat. Garnish with a small dollop more of dressing and top with sunflower seeds.

Serves six.

Nutritional analysis per serving...

Calories: 250
Protein: 7 g
Carbohydrates: 19.4 g
Cholesterol: less than 1 g
Total fat: 18 g
Saturated fat: 2.4 g
Monounsaturated fat: 8 g
Polyunsaturated fat: 6.5 g
Omega-6: 3.5 g
Omega-3: .1 g
Sodium: 72 mg
Potassium: 940 mg
Fiber: 6.6 g

Bean Salad

A simple salad to mix up in the morning and serve as lunch or as a side dish to a dinner entrée. Add some chopped parsley or cilantro, as desired.

1 15-ounce can low-sodium black beans, rinsed and drained
1 15-ounce can low-sodium navy beans, rinsed and drained
2 tablespoons red wine vinegar
2 celery stalks, finely diced
1 small red onion, finely diced
1 fresh tomato or ½ cup canned tomatoes, chopped, liquid discarded
2 to 3 tablespoons extra virgin olive oil
Salt and pepper to taste

Mix all the ingredients together in a bowl and refrigerate for an hour or two before serving.

Serves eight.

Nutritional analysis per serving...

Calories: 122
Protein: 5.3 g
Carbohydrates: 17 g
Cholesterol: 0
Total fat: 5 g
Saturated fat: .6 g
Monounsaturated fat: 3.4 g
Polyunsaturated fat: .4 g
Omega-6: .4 g
Omega-3: .03 g
Sodium: 125 mg
Potassium: 350 mg
Fiber: 6 g

Bean Salad with Orange, Dijon and Balsamic Dressing

This makes a great filling for lettuce or flatbread wraps. Use hothouse cucumbers, sometimes called English cucumbers, since they are not waxed or oiled, have edible seeds and are easy to digest. Kirby, Persian or Japanese cucumbers are delicious alternatives.

1 large orange, zest and juice
2 tablespoons Dijon mustard
2 tablespoons extra virgin olive oil

3 tablespoons balsamic vinegar
Salt and pepper
1 medium red onion
1 medium hothouse cucumber
15 ounces roasted bell peppers
1 garlic clove
⅓ cup flat-leaf parsley
15 ounces garbanzo beans, cooked
15 ounces black beans, cooked
1 15-ounce can pinto beans
1 pound frozen green peas, thawed

Whisk together the orange zest and juice, mustard, oil, vinegar and salt and pepper in a large bowl. Dice the onion, cucumber and roasted bell peppers, and add to the bowl. Mince the garlic, rough chop the parsley and add to the salad. Drain and rinse the beans and add along with the peas. Stir and serve chilled.

Serves eight.

Nutritional analysis per serving...

Calories: 351
Protein: 18 g
Carbohydrates: 60.2 g
Cholesterol: less than 1 g
Total fat: 6 g
Saturated fat: .8 g
Monounsaturated fat: 3.4 g
Polyunsaturated fat: 1.3 g
Omega-6: .7 g
Omega-3: .2 g
Sodium: 256 mg
Potassium: 815 mg
Fiber: 6 g

Black Bean Soup

Homemade beans can be cooked ahead and frozen, allowing you to put this hearty, delicious soup together in 30 minutes. This soup is also good served chilled, garnished with plain yogurt, chopped cucumber and green onions. Be sure to pull out the bay leaves before serving.

2 tablespoons extra virgin olive oil
3 garlic cloves, sliced
Black pepper
1 teaspoon cumin seeds
1 large onion, diced
3 celery stalks, sliced
Kosher salt
½ teaspoon dried oregano, optional
1 tablespoon red pepper flakes
2 bay leaves
1 quart low-sodium organic vegetable or chicken broth
1 15-ounce can black beans, with their liquid
½ cup pumpkin seeds, toasted

In a 4-quart soup pot, heat the oil over medium-high heat. Add the garlic and black pepper, and sauté until the garlic is golden. Add the cumin seeds and toss until the aroma is released. Add the onion and sauté until it starts to brown. Add the celery, salt to taste, oregano (if using) and red pepper flakes, and sauté for a minute longer. Add the bay leaves, broth and beans, raise the heat to high, cover the pot and bring to a boil. Taste and adjust the seasonings, adding more broth if necessary. Serve garnished with pumpkin seeds.

Serves four.

Nutritional analysis per serving...

Calories: 411
Protein: 24 g
Carbohydrates: 39 g
Cholesterol: 0
Total fat: 20.5 g
Saturated fat: 3.6 g
Monounsaturated fat: 9.6 g
Polyunsaturated fat: 6.6 g
Omega-6: 5.8 g
Omega-3: .3 g
Sodium: 742 mg
Potassium: 1,202 mg
Fiber 8 g

Blueberry- and Cranberry-Laced Brown and Wild Rice

Use your favorite method of cooking rice. This works well in a rice cooker or a good heavy pot with a tight-fitting lid. For an al dente crunch, bring the rice to a boil, covered, reduce the heat, simmer, then remove from the heat and let it stand, covered. For a creamier texture, experiment by adding ¼ to ⅓ cup water until you achieve the texture your family most enjoys.

1⅓ cups brown rice
¾ cup wild rice
1 tablespoon white miso
¾ cup dried cranberries
1 cup fresh or frozen blueberries
2 tablespoons maple syrup

Cook the brown and wild rices, along with the miso and cranberries, in about 4 cups water until the rice is tender, about 25 minutes. Remove from the heat and let stand for about 20 minutes, covered. Gently stir in the blueberries and syrup. Serve warm or cool.

Serves eight.

Nutritional analysis per serving...

Calories: 238
Protein: 5 g
Carbohydrates: 52.7 g
Cholesterol: 0
Total fat: 1.2 g
Saturated fat: less than 1 g
Monounsaturated fat: less than 1 g
Polyunsaturated fat: less than 1 g
Omega-6: .4 g
Omega-3: .1 g
Sodium: 66 mg
Potassium: 195 mg
Fiber: 3.9 g

Penne with Broccoli and Nuts

This is a superfast one-dish meal that everyone will enjoy. You can use red or yellow peppers as you wish.

2 heads broccoli
2 medium orange bell peppers, diced
1 pound whole wheat pasta
2 tablespoons grapeseed oil
1 garlic clove or more, minced or sliced
Black pepper
¼ cup orange juice
2 tablespoons soy sauce
5 medium scallions
⅔ cup roasted mixed nuts

Bring a large pot of salted water to a boil. Cut the broccoli into florets. Peel the stems and dice them. Dice the bell peppers. While the pasta is cooking, heat the oil over medium heat in a large skillet. Add the minced or sliced garlic and the black pepper, and toss until just fragrant. Add the broccoli, bell peppers, orange juice and soy sauce, and cook until the broccoli begins to brighten in color and is almost tender. If it gets too dry or sticks, add some of the pasta cooking water. Add the scallions and nuts and heat through. Drain the pasta and toss with the broccoli.

Serves six.

Nutritional analysis per serving...

Calories: 219
Protein: 6 g
Carbohydrates: 21.4 g
Cholesterol: 0 g
Total fat: 13.6 g
Saturated fat: 2 g
Monounsaturated fat: 7.3 g
Polyunsaturated fat: 3.7 g
Omega-6: 3.2 g
Omega-3: .1 g

Sodium: 15 mg
Potassium: 415 mg
Fiber: 3.3 g

Maple Cashew Butter

Use this cashew butter to top pancakes or desserts. Whisk in the yogurt to create a thinner sauce.

1½ cups raw cashews
⅓ cup maple syrup
1 cup brewed green tea
1 cup low-fat yogurt, optional

Soak the cashews in clear water to cover for eight hours or overnight. Drain well, and place cashews and maple syrup in a food processor or blender. Add about ¼ cup of the tea and blend until smooth, adding more tea as necessary to create a thick, creamy texture.

To make a more liquid sauce, whisk in the yogurt, if using.

Serves 10.

Nutritional analysis per serving...

Maple Cashew Butter (Without Yogurt)

Calories: 146
Protein: 3.2 g
Carbohydrates: 14 g
Cholesterol: 0
Total fat: 9.6 g
Saturated fat: 1.9 g
Monounsaturated fat: 5.6 g
Polyunsaturated fat: 1.6 g
Omega-6: 1.6 g
Omega-3: less than .04 g
Sodium: 5 mg
Potassium: 146 mg
Fiber: less than 1 g

Nutritional analysis per serving...

Maple Cashew Butter (With Yogurt)

Calories: 161
Protein: 4.4 g
Carbohydrates: 15.6 g
Cholesterol: 1.5 mg
Total fat: 9.9 g
Saturated fat: 2.1 g
Monounsaturated fat: 5.7 g
Polyunsaturated fat: 1.6 g
Omega-6: 1.6 g
Omega-3: less than .04 g
Sodium: 22 mg
Potassium: 204 mg
Fiber: less than 1 g

Carrot-Chickpea Soup

Here's a great way to get some carrots as well as those fiber-rich chickpeas into your diet. For another layer of flavor, add some baby spinach during the last few minutes of cooking.

2 pounds carrots, peeled and cut into small chunks
1 large onion, diced
1 vegetable stock cube
1 can chickpeas, drained and rinsed
¼ teaspoon cinnamon
Dash of mild curry powder
Dash of ground coriander
Salt and pepper

In a large pot, boil the carrots, onion and stock cube in 10 cups water until the carrots are soft. Turn off the heat and, using an immersion blender, blend the soup until smooth. Add the chickpeas and blend into the soup. Add the remaining ingredients and stir well. Add more spices if needed.

If you prefer a chunkier soup, remove a cup or two of the soup and puree it in a blender or food processor, and return the pureed soup to the original pot.

Serves eight.

Nutritional analysis per serving...

Calories: 104
Protein: 4 g
Carbohydrates: 21 g
Cholesterol: .08 mg
Total fat: 1 g
Saturated fat: .05 g
Monounsaturated fat: .03 g
Polyunsaturated fat: .11 g
Omega-6: .10 g
Omega-3: .01 g
Sodium: 403 mg
Potassium: 399 mg
Fiber: 6 g

Cilantro Dressing

2 cups cilantro leaves
1 teaspoon minced fresh garlic
⅛ cup water
1 10.5-ounce package silken tofu
1 tablespoon lemon juice
1 tablespoon reduced-sodium soy sauce

Put the cilantro, garlic and water in a food processor and process until blended. Add the tofu, lemon juice and soy sauce and process until smooth. Pour into a bowl, cover and chill at least 2 hours before serving.

Serves eight.

Nutritional analysis per serving...

Calories: 24
Protein: 2 g
Carbohydrates: 1.6 g
Cholesterol: 0
Total fat: 1 g
Saturated fat: .13 g
Monounsaturated fat: .2 g
Polyunsaturated fat: .58 g
Omega-6: 0 g
Omega-3: 0 g
Sodium: 53 mg
Potassium: 97 mg
Fiber: .16 g

Cinnamon Maple Macadamias

These slightly gooey nuts make a great topping for oatmeal or yogurt.

1½ cups macadamia nuts, coarsely chopped
1 teaspoon cinnamon
¼ cup maple syrup

Preheat the oven to 300° F. Toss the macadamias with the cinnamon. Spread on a foil-lined sheet pan. Bake until lightly golden and fragrant, about 20 to 25 minutes. Pour the syrup over the nuts and stir to combine. Bake for five minutes more, then cool on the sheet pan.

Serves 10.

Nutritional analysis per serving...

Calories: 166
Protein: 1.6 g
Carbohydrates: 8.3 g
Cholesterol: 0
Total fat: 15 g
Saturated fat: 2.4 g
Monounsaturated fat: 12 g
Polyunsaturated fat: .3 g
Omega-6: .3 g
Omega-3: .04 g
Sodium: 2 mg
Potassium: 90 mg
Fiber: 1.7 g

Cinnamon-Apricot Oatmeal Cookies

If you can't find barley flour, use whole wheat flour for a more crumbly cookie. Date syrup can be found in gourmet and Mediterranean markets. Grapeseed oil is a healthy neutral-flavored oil, but canola or even olive oil works well here.

¼ cup grapeseed or canola oil
¼ cup 100% apple juice
1¼ cups maple syrup or date syrup
¼ cup packed dark brown sugar
1 teaspoon vanilla
2 tablespoons apricot jam
½ teaspoon baking soda
1 teaspoon cinnamon
Pinch of salt
1½ cups barley flour or whole wheat flour
3 cups rolled oats

Preheat the oven to 350° F. Combine the oil, apple juice, syrup, brown sugar, vanilla and jam in a mixing bowl and stir well. Stir in the baking soda, cinnamon and salt, then add the barley flour and oats. Stir to combine. Drop the dough by teaspoonfuls onto parchment-lined baking sheets. Bake 15 minutes, or until cookies just start to brown. Allow to cool for five minutes, then transfer to a wire rack.

Makes 24.

Nutritional analysis per cookie...

Calories: 150
Protein: 2.3 g
Carbohydrates: 28.6 g
Cholesterol: 0
Total fat: 3.2 g
Saturated fat: .4 g
Monounsaturated fat: 1.6 g
Polyunsaturated fat: 1.1 g
Omega-6: .7 g
Omega-3: .2 g
Sodium: 30 mg
Potassium: 128 mg
Fiber: 1.6 g

Granola–Super Fruity Mix

Experiment with these ingredients to create many tasty granola variations. If you don't have millet or quinoa, use all oats. Use either rolled oats or a rolled whole-grain blend. Apple juice is suggested here, but try other 100% juice blends such as cranberry, mango, peach, pear or pineapple. Dried fruits that work well include raisins, cranberries, cherries, blueberries, banana chips, mangoes, papayas, prunes, peaches and nectarines.

½ cup millet
½ cup quinoa
4 cups rolled oats
1½ teaspoons cinnamon
1½ teaspoons pumpkin pie spice
¼ cup sesame seeds
¼ cup flaxseed meal
½ cup sliced almonds or chopped walnuts
1⅔ cups 100% apple juice
⅓ cup honey or maple syrup
¾ cup chopped dried fruit

Preheat the oven to 300° F. Rinse the millet and quinoa well, and combine with the remaining dry ingredients, except the dried fruit, in a large bowl. Stir in the wet ingredients. Toss well, then spread on a foil-lined sheet pan and bake until browned, stirring occasionally, about 30 minutes. Stir in your favorite dried fruits. Store in airtight containers.

Serves 12.

Nutritional analysis per serving...

Calories: 325
Protein: 9.3 g
Carbohydrates: 55 g
Cholesterol: 0
Total fat: 8.7 g

Saturated fat: 1 g
Monounsaturated fat: 3.5 g
Polyunsaturated fat: 3.4 g
Omega-6: 2.6 g
Omega-3: .8 g
Sodium: 7 mg
Potassium: 403 mg
Fiber: 7.6 g

Guacamole

My friend Barbara Swanson shared her recipe with me and said, "I think the reason most people like my guacamole is that I do not overpower it with either too much or too large chunks of onion. That's why it is important to *finely* mince the onion. All ingredients are approximate—start with less and add more to taste. The size of avocados varies, so adjust amounts accordingly. Also, if you are serving this with very salty chips, cut down on the salt."

6 Hass avocados
½ teaspoon extra virgin olive oil
1½ teaspoons lime juice
½ teaspoon (8 to 10 dashes) Tabasco
2½ tablespoons finely minced onion
¼ to ½ cup chopped cilantro
½ teaspoon seasoned salt, such as Lawry's
3 plum tomatoes, diced

Scoop the avocados into a bowl and add the ingredients in the order given. Mix with a fork after each addition (do not overmix) so that the guacamole remains chunky. Cover with plastic wrap until serving time.

Serves 12 (6 cups).

Nutritional analysis per serving...

Calories: 160
Protein: 2 g
Carbohydrates: 7.1 g
Cholesterol: 0
Total fat: 15 g
Saturated fat: 2.3 g
Monounsaturated fat: 9.85 g
Polyunsaturated fat: 1.8 g
Omega-6: .03 g
Omega-3: 0 g
Sodium: 44 mg
Potassium: 672 mg
Fiber: 4.6 g

Balsamic Roasted Onions

8 medium onions, cut into 6 wedges each
¼ cup aged balsamic vinegar
1 tablespoon honey
Freshly ground black pepper
1 tablespoon extra virgin olive oil

Put the onion wedges in a bowl of ice water and soak for about two hours. Drain in a colander for 10 minutes.

Preheat the oven to 400° F. Arrange the onions on an oiled baking dish.

Whisk the vinegar and honey together, and season with pepper. Pour over the onions, tossing gently to coat. Drizzle the onions with the olive oil.

Cover with foil and bake for 25 minutes. Uncover and bake an additional 45 minutes, or until tender.

Serves 12.

Nutritional analysis per serving...

Calories: 51
Protein: 1 g
Carbohydrates: 9.5 g
Cholesterol: 0
Total fat: 1.3 g
Saturated fat: .2 g
Monounsaturated fat: 1 g

Polyunsaturated fat: .15 g

Omega-6: .1 g

Omega-3: .01 g

Sodium: 3.25 mg

Potassium: 120 mg

Fiber: 1.3 g

Cranberry-Orange Relish

Steer clear of the canned cranberry sauce and make your own when serving turkey or chicken. This is the recipe that appears on the bags of Ocean Spray fresh cranberries, which are abundant in the supermarket in the fall. (Buy a couple of extra bags and throw them in the freezer; they keep for a long time. Use them in muffins, pumpkin bread and pancakes, or toss them into oatmeal.)

1 12-ounce package Ocean Spray fresh or frozen cranberries, rinsed and drained

1 unpeeled orange, cut into eighths and seeded

¾ cup sugar

Place half the cranberries and half the orange pieces in a food processor and process until the mixture is evenly chopped. Transfer to a bowl. Repeat with the remaining cranberries and orange slices. Stir in the sugar. Store in the refrigerator or freezer until ready to serve.

Makes about three cups.

Nutritional analysis per serving...

Calories: 101

Protein: .3 g

Carbohydrates: 26 g

Cholesterol: 0

Total fat: .1 g

Saturated fat: .01 g

Monounsaturated fat: .02 g

Polyunsaturated fat: .05 g

Omega-6: .03 g

Omega-3: .02 g

Sodium: .6 mg

Potassium: 58 mg

Fiber: 2 g

Orange-Poppyseed Dressing

A delightful dressing to use on spinach salad or fruit salad all year.

½ cup extra virgin olive oil

Zest of ½ orange

Juice of 1 orange

Juice of 1 lemon

2 tablespoons honey

1 tablespoon poppyseeds or toasted sesame seeds

Put all the ingredients in a lidded jar and shake until blended. Refrigerate for two hours or overnight to let flavors develop.

Serves 12.

Nutritional analysis per serving...

Calories: 106

Protein: .3 g

Carbohydrates: 5 g

Cholesterol: 0

Total fat: 9.7 g

Saturated fat: 1.35 g

Monounsaturated fat: 7.2 g

Polyunsaturated fat: 1 g

Omega-6: 1 g

Omega-3: .07 g

Sodium: .3 mg

Potassium: 35 mg

Fiber: .5 g

French Toast à l'Orange

This is a healthy, low-fat breakfast with a delicious orange flavor. Top with yogurt and honey if desired.

3 egg whites or 2 eggs with Omega-3 content, as noted on label
½ cup soy or nonfat milk
½ cup orange juice
Zest of 1 orange
½ teaspoon cinnamon
4 slices whole wheat bread, stale

Whisk the eggs until blended, then whisk in all the ingredients except the bread. Soak the bread briefly in the egg mixture. Fry the bread slices in a medium sauté pan just until brown. Serve with yogurt topping if desired.

Serves four.

Nutritional analysis per serving...

Calories: 108
Protein: 6.4 g
Carbohydrates: 18.5 g
Cholesterol: .6 mg
Total fat: 1.25 g
Saturated fat: .30 g
Monounsaturated fat: .5 g
Polyunsaturated fat: .3 g
Omega-6: .3 g
Omega-3: .01 g
Sodium: 205 mg
Potassium: 159 mg
Fiber: 2 g

Orange Lemonade

2½ cups water
1 cup sugar (or less)
2 tablespoons orange zest
2 tablespoons lemon zest
1½ cups fresh orange juice, about 5 oranges
1½ cups lemon juice, about 8 lemons
Citrus slices, optional

In a medium saucepan, combine 2½ cups water and sugar. Cook over medium heat until the sugar dissolves, stirring occasionally. Remove from the heat and cool. Add the orange and lemon zests and juices to the sugar mixture. Cover and let stand at room temperature for one hour. Cover and refrigerate until serving time.

To serve, fill glasses with equal parts fruit mixture and water. Add ice and serve. If you like, garnish the lemonade with citrus slices.

Serves 12.

Nutritional analysis per serving...

Calories: 86
Protein: .3 g
Carbohydrates: 22.5 g
Cholesterol: 0
Total fat: .06 g
Saturated fat: .01 g
Monounsaturated fat: .01 g
Polyunsaturated fat: .01 g
Omega-6: .01 g
Omega-3: 0 g
Sodium: 2.3 mg
Potassium: 100 mg
Fiber: .2

Orange Bran Flax Muffins

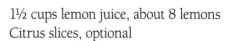

1½ cups oat bran
1 cup all-purpose flour
1 cup ground flaxseed
1 cup natural bran
1 tablespoon baking powder
½ teaspoon salt
2 oranges, washed, quartered and seeded
¾ cup brown sugar
1 cup buttermilk
½ cup canola oil

2 eggs
1 teaspoon baking soda
1½ cups raisins

In a large bowl, combine the oat bran, flour, flaxseed, bran, baking powder and salt. Set aside. In a blender or food processor, combine the oranges, brown sugar, buttermilk, oil, eggs and baking soda. Blend well. Pour the orange mixture into the dry ingredients. Mix until well blended. Stir in the raisins (white chocolate chips can be substituted for the raisins). Fill paper-lined muffin tins almost to the top. Bake in a 375° F oven for 18 to 20 minutes, or until a wooden pick inserted in the center of the muffin comes out clean. Cool in the tins for five minutes before removing to a cooling rack.

Makes 24 muffins.

Nutritional analysis per serving...

Calories: 201
Protein: 5.2 g
Carbohydrates: 28.3 g
Cholesterol: 16.2 mg
Total fat: 9 g
Saturated fat: .6 g
Monounsaturated fat: 3.7 g
Polyunsaturated fat: 3.6 g
Omega-6: 1.75 g
Omega-3: 1.8 g
Sodium: 170 mg
Potassium: 656 mg
Fiber: 5.5 g

Pasta e Fagioli

A thick winter soup of pasta and beans can serve as a hearty lunch or dinner when accompanied by a salad and some rustic whole wheat bread. Use shells, orecchiette, whole wheat penne or farfalle in this soup. Also, use fresh herbs when possible. You can substitute marjoram for the oregano. Any combination of white beans (Great Northern, cannellini, large limas, small white beans, etc.) will work. And, of course, you can use one 15-ounce can of low-sodium canned beans if you prefer.

1 pound dried white beans, such as cannellini or navy beans
4 quarts low-sodium organic vegetable or chicken broth
2 bay leaves
2 tablespoons extra virgin olive oil
1 large onion, minced
3 garlic cloves, minced
1 28-ounce can crushed tomatoes
4 celery ribs, with leaves, sliced
1 tablespoon dried oregano
¼ cup basil, coarsely chopped
1 pound whole wheat farfalle or penne, cooked according to package directions
Salt and pepper

Soak the beans in cold water to cover for six hours or overnight. Discard the water. Cook the beans in the broth in a large pot with the bay leaves until tender, about 45 minutes, skimming off any foam as it forms. In a small skillet, heat the olive oil and sauté the onion and garlic until fragrant and golden. Add to the beans along with the crushed tomatoes and celery with leaves, and simmer for five minutes. Skim foam as necessary. Stir in the oregano, basil, and salt and pepper to taste. Divide the pasta among the bowls and ladle in the soup.

Serves eight.

Nutritional analysis per serving...

Calories: 382
Protein: 22.6 g
Carbohydrates: 63 g
Cholesterol: 19 mg
Total fat: 5.3 g
Saturated fat: .9 g

Monounsaturated fat: 3.2 g
Polyunsaturated fat: .8 g
Omega-6: .3 g
Omega-3: .1 g
Sodium: 1,159 mg
Potassium: 1,437 mg
Fiber: 16 g

Pumpkin Pudding

This is one of my favorite desserts...created by my friend Patty.

¼ to ½ cup sugar
2 to 4 teaspoon cinnamon
¼ teaspoon ground ginger, optional
¼ teaspoon ground cloves, optional
2 large eggs (use eggs with omega-3 content, as noted on label)
1 15-ounce can Libby's 100 percent pure pumpkin
1 12-ounce can Carnation evaporated nonfat milk (or evaporated 2 percent milk)

Mix all the ingredients together and pour into an 8 x 8-inch casserole and bake in a preheated 350° F oven for about 30 minutes. Don't overbake; the center should be slightly wiggly. Cool and enjoy or refrigerate for later use.

Serves eight.

Nutritional analysis per serving...

Calories: 119
Protein: 5 g
Carbohydrates: 23 g
Cholesterol: 46.75 mg
Total fat: 1.4 g
Saturated fat: .35 g
Monounsaturated fat: .4 g
Polyunsaturated fat: .16 g
Omega-6: .15 g
Omega-3: .01 g
Sodium: 70 mg
Potassium: 165.5 mg
Fiber: 3 g

Pumpkin Seed Dip

This is a healthy dip for parties or for snacking. Use a quality, light mayonnaise made with heart-healthy fats such as grapeseed, canola or soy oil. Serve with a platter of cut-up vegetables.

1 small shallot
1 garlic clove
1 small jalapeño pepper
⅓ cup flaxseeds
1 cup roasted and salted pumpkin seeds
½ bunch cilantro
¼ cup light mayonnaise
1 teaspoon ground cumin
½ teaspoon ground coriander
Freshly ground black pepper
2 medium oranges, zest and juice
1 small lemon, zest and juice
Paprika
Extra virgin olive oil

Process the shallot, garlic and jalapeño to a fine mince in a food processor. Add the flaxseeds and pumpkin seeds and process again. Cut the cilantro with scissors into the food processor. Add the mayonnaise, spices, orange and lemon zests and juices, and process to a fine spreading consistency. Add more orange juice if necessary to create a creamier texture. Place in a bowl and garnish with paprika and a drizzle of olive oil.

Serves seven.

Nutritional analysis per serving...

Calories: 234
Protein: 12 g
Carbohydrates: 11.7 g
Cholesterol: 2.9 mg
Total fat: 17.3 g
Saturated fat: 3.2 g

Monounsaturated fat: 4.5 g
Polyunsaturated fat: 6.3 g
Omega-6: 6.2 g
Omega-3: .06 g
Sodium: 112.7 mg
Potassium: 335.5 mg
Fiber: 2.8 g

Emerald Salad

A refreshing salad that is a study in green with lettuces, edamame, cucumbers and apple.

Dressing

1 medium shallot, minced
1 tablespoon any type of miso
1 tablespoon Dijon mustard
¼ cup red wine vinegar
2 tablespoons extra virgin olive oil
Black pepper

Salad

1 medium cucumber, sliced
1 medium Granny Smith apple, cored and sliced
1 pound green soybeans (edamame), cooked according to package directions
1 head romaine lettuce, torn into bite-sized pieces
2 heads Boston lettuce, torn into bite-sized pieces

Whisk together the dressing ingredients and set aside. In a large bowl, toss the cucumber, apple and green soybeans with just enough of the dressing to coat. Add the lettuce and more dressing to coat. Divide among eight salad plates.

Serves eight.

Nutritional analysis per serving...

Calories: 148
Protein: 8.9 g
Carbohydrates: 12.9 g
Cholesterol: less than 1 g
Total fat: 7.8 g
Saturated fat: 1 g
Monounsaturated fat: 3.6 g
Polyunsaturated fat: 2.2 g
Omega-6: 1.7 g
Omega-3: .3 g
Sodium: 83 mg
Potassium: 620 mg
Fiber: 4 g

Cedar Plank Wild Salmon with Garlic Orange Glaze

Slow cooking on a cedar plank results in deliciously moist salmon with a slightly smoky flavor. You can buy individual cedar planks at kitchenware shops, or get untreated cedar planks at a lumber store. If there is only one control for the grill, set it to low. If using a charcoal grill, let the coals die down to pinkish gray, then push them to the outside and cook over indirect heat.

Olive oil spray
¾ cup orange preserves, 100% fruit
2 garlic cloves, minced
1 medium serrano pepper, minced, optional
⅓ cup brewed green tea
1⅓ pounds wild salmon
1 tablespoon sesame seeds
Freshly ground black pepper

Soak the cedar planks in water for at least three hours, and up to 24. If grill has two burners, set one side to medium-high. Spray the top of the planks with oil. Place the planks on the cool side of the grill (indirect heat). In a small saucepan, warm the preserves, garlic, serrano pepper (if using) and green tea just to melt the preserves. Place the salmon on the planks and brush with the sauce. Sprinkle sesame seeds and black pepper on top. Grill for 12 to 25 minutes, checking every 10 minutes. Salmon is done when just firm, but some like it more well done. When grilling a large fillet, the tail end will be more well done, while the thicker end is nicely tender, providing something for everyone.

Serves four.

Nutritional analysis per serving...

Calories: 329
Protein: 34 g
Carbohydrates: 23.6 g
Cholesterol: 68 mg
Total fat: 10.4 g
  Saturated fat: 2 g
  Monounsaturated fat: 3.7 g
  Polyunsaturated fat: 3.6 g
    Omega-6: .8 g
    Omega-3: .3 g
Sodium: 306 mg
Potassium: 724 mg
Fiber: 1.5 g

Garlic and Black Pepper 10-Minute Marinated Wild Salmon

Serve hot or chilled for sandwiches and salads. If there are any leftovers, stuff cold salmon into pita bread with plenty of lightly dressed lettuce and sliced cucumber.

3 garlic cloves, minced
½ cup nonfat plain yogurt
½ teaspoon black pepper
1 tablespoon paprika
2 tablespoons Dijon mustard
¼ teaspoon cayenne, optional
4 5- to 6-ounce pieces wild salmon

Whisk together the garlic, yogurt, black pepper, paprika, mustard, and cayenne, if using. Arrange the salmon in a pan, coat each piece with the sauce, and allow to marinate for 10 minutes. Shake off any excess sauce and broil or grill. Depending upon the thickness of the fish, it will take anywhere from five to eight minutes to cook through.

Serves four.

Nutritional analysis per serving...

Calories: 208
Protein: 32.7 g
Carbohydrates: 4.6 g
Cholesterol: 79 mg
Total fat: 6 g
  Saturated fat: .9 g
  Monounsaturated fat: 1.5 g
  Polyunsaturated fat: 2.2 g
    Omega-6: .2 g
    Omega-3: .1 g
Sodium: 228 mg
Potassium: 625 mg
Fiber: less than 1 g

Poached Wild Salmon Poke

In the Hawaiian language, the word *poke* (pronounced po-*kay*) meant to cut crosswise into pieces. Over time, the word has been used to describe a variety of chopped seafood salads seasoned typically with soy sauce and scallions.

Ponzu is available at many markets or online grocers. If you can't find ponzu, combine 2 tablespoons low-sodium soy sauce mixed with 1 tablespoon orange juice and 2 tablespoons water instead.

Salmon poke looks inviting when served in half an avocado or papaya. Or omit the cherry tomatoes and serve the salad on sliced heirloom tomatoes.

1 lemongrass stalk, optional
2 medium bay leaves
5 green tea bags
2 pounds wild salmon

Poke

1 tablespoon fresh ginger, minced

1 garlic clove, minced
⅔ cup scallions, sliced
1½ cups cherry tomatoes, quartered
¼ cup ponzu
1 tablespoon extra virgin olive oil
2 tablespoons minced cilantro, optional
Black pepper

Garnish

¼ cup macadamia nuts, ground and toasted
1 medium mango
1 medium lime wedge
Lettuce

In a wide, covered pot, bring two quarts water to a boil with the lemongrass (if using) and the bay leaves. When the water boils, reduce the heat to a simmer and add the green tea bags. When the broth gets nicely green after a minute or two, add the salmon and cover. Leave the heat on for two minutes, then turn off the heat and allow the salmon to poach for five to seven minutes. Check for doneness with the point of a knife.

Using a slotted spoon, remove the salmon to a platter and chill. Don't worry if it breaks up a bit when you're taking it out of the water. Meanwhile, combine all the poke ingredients and chill. Crush the macadamias, spread on a small baking sheet, and toast in a preheated 300° F oven until just golden, 10 to 15 minutes. Peel the mango, slice it and squeeze a little lime on it. When the salmon is chilled, break it into large chunks and add to the poke; toss gently to coat. Serve on a bed of lettuce with mango slices on the side, and top with the ground macadamias.

Serves six.

Nutritional analysis per serving...

Calories: 328
Protein: 35 g
Carbohydrates: 12.3 g
Cholesterol: 68 mg
Total fat: 16 g
  Saturated fat: 3 g
  Monounsaturated fat: 8.5 g
  Polyunsaturated fat: 3.4 g
    Omega-6: .4 g
    Omega-3: .3 g
Sodium: 285 mg
Potassium: 981 mg
Fiber: 2.3 g

Wild Alaskan Salmon Burgers

1 14¾-ounce can wild Alaska salmon
2 tablespoons lemon juice
1½ tablespoons Dijon mustard
¾ cup bread crumbs, dried
½ cup green onions, sliced
2 omega-3-enriched eggs

Drain and flake the salmon. Combine the lemon juice and mustard. Blend the flaked salmon with the bread crumbs, green onions and lemon juice–mustard mixture. Mix in the eggs until well blended. Form the mixture into four patties (chilling in the fridge for an hour will help them hold their shape) and cook on a lightly oiled grill or sauté in a skillet until golden brown on both sides. Serve each burger on a whole wheat bun with lettuce, tomato slices and condiments as desired.

Serves four.

Nutritional analysis (burger only)...

Calories: 314
Protein: 28 g
Carbohydrates: 16 g
Cholesterol: 173 mg
Total fat: 15 g
  Saturated fat: 3.3 g
  Monounsaturated fat: 1 g
  Polyunsaturated fat: .4 g

Omega-6: .3 g
Omega-3: .2 g
Sodium: 774.5 mg
Potassium: 85.5 mg
Fiber: 1.1 g

Braised Spinach with Roasted Cherry Tomatoes

CHEF LORNA WYCKOFF

This recipe is from a southern SuperFood fan, Lorna Wyckoff, who mentions that, as a transplanted northerner, she's learned to love her greens. Try this with mustard greens, kale, collards or Swiss chard.

8 ounces organic cherry tomatoes
2 cloves garlic, minced
Extra virgin olive oil
Salt and pepper
1 large shallot, diced
1 bag organic baby spinach leaves
Pinch of red pepper flakes, optional

Preheat the broiler. Arrange eight ounces of organic cherry tomatoes and two cloves minced garlic on a foil-lined baking sheet. Drizzle with olive oil and salt and pepper. Broil, turning with a spatula every couple of minutes until the tomatoes are browned but not burned.

Heat 1 teaspoon extra virgin olive oil in a large skillet over medium heat. Add a diced large shallot and sauté. Add a bag of organic baby spinach leaves, rinsed but not dried, and a pinch of red pepper flakes (optional). When the spinach is just about wilted, add the roasted tomatoes and garlic and cook for another minute.

Serves four.

Nutritional analysis per serving...

Calories: 90
Protein: 4.4 g
Carbohydrates: 9 g
Cholesterol: 0
Total fat: 5.3 g
Saturated fat: .8 g
Monounsaturated fat: 3.6 g
Polyunsaturated fat: .5 g
Omega-6: .45 g
Omega-3: .04 g
Sodium: 122 mg
Potassium: 537 mg
Fiber: 4.4 g

Sesame Noodles with Spinach and Zucchini Sauté

CHEF MARK CLEVELAND

Use buckwheat soba, udon, Chinese noodles, fettuccine or linguine in this dish. Toasted sesame oil, a rich dark brown in color, is used as a flavoring.

1 pound noodles
1 tablespoon extra virgin olive oil
3 garlic cloves, minced
1 medium leek, halved and sliced, white and green parts
1 1-inch piece fresh ginger, peeled and minced, optional
3 small zucchini, halved lengthwise and cut into ½-inch-thick slices
2 tablespoons low-sodium soy sauce
⅔ cup brewed green tea
1 cup fresh or frozen green soybeans, shelled, or green peas
4 cups fresh baby spinach
1 medium lemon, zest and juice
2 teaspoons toasted sesame oil
2 tablespoons sesame seeds

Bring a large pot of water to a boil for the noodles. Note that Asian noodles usually have a higher salt content than Italian pasta, so salt the water accordingly; they also cook much faster than pasta. While the noodles are cooking, heat the olive oil in a large skillet, add the garlic and sauté for a minute, then add the leek and sauté until softened and bright green, about a minute. Add the ginger, if using, and the zucchini; sauté until the zucchini is almost tender, about three minutes. Add the soy sauce, brewed tea and soybeans, and bring to a low boil. Add the spinach, lemon zest and juice, toasted sesame oil and sesame seeds, and stir once. Serve over drained hot noodles.

Serves four.

Nutritional analysis per serving...

Calories: 538
Protein: 23 g
Carbohydrates: 103
Cholesterol: 0
Total fat: 9.4 g
  Saturated fat: 1.4 g
  Monounsaturated fat: 4.7 g
  Polyunsaturated fat: 2.6 g
    Omega-6: 2.2 g
    Omega-3: .1 g
Sodium: 1,251 mg
Potassium: 1,018 mg
Fiber: 13.7 g

Acorn Squash with Pineapple

CHEF MARK CLEVELAND

Pineapple and allspice bring out the inherent sweetness in squash.

2 medium acorn, butternut or delicata squash
⅓ cup pineapple juice
1 tablespoon extra virgin olive oil
¼ teaspoon allspice
Salt and pepper

Preheat the oven to 350° F. Place the whole squash on a baking sheet lined with parchment or foil and roast for 40 to 45 minutes, or until tender. Remove from the oven, allow to cool for 10 minutes and then cut in half horizontally. Scoop out the seeds; reserve them to roast if you would like. Divide the juice, oil, allspice, salt and pepper among the four halves and use a fork to fluff and incorporate. Serve in their shells with a spoon.

Serves four.

Nutritional analysis per serving...

Calories: 128
Protein: 1.8 g
Carbohydrates: 25 g
Cholesterol: 0 mg
Total fat: 3.7 g
  Saturated fat: .6 g
  Monounsaturated fat: 2.8 g
  Polyunsaturated fat: .4 g
    Omega-6: less than .1 g
    Omega-3: .1 g
Sodium: 7 mg
Potassium: 777 mg
Fiber: 3.9 g

Roasted Butternut Squash with Buckwheat Honey Glaze

CHEF MICHEL STROOT

This is great with a turkey or salmon dinner.

Canola oil
1 medium butternut squash, cut in half lengthwise, strings and seeds scooped out and discarded
1 tablespoon butter
2 tablespoons buckwheat honey
Salt and freshly ground black pepper

Preheat the oven to 400° F. Lightly grease a baking sheet with canola oil. Put the squash halves, cut side down to help them caramelize, on the sheet. Bake for 45 to 55 minutes, or until a skewer easily pierces the squash. In the meantime, melt the butter and add the honey with some pepper and salt to taste. When the squash is cooked, remove it from the oven and turn the halves cut side up. Brush them with the honey-butter mixture and return them to the oven for about five minutes. Cut the squash into serving pieces and serve.

Serves two.

Nutritional analysis per serving...

Calories: 270
Protein: 2.25 g
Carbohydrates: 42 g
Cholesterol: 15 mg
Total fat: 12.7 g
Saturated fat: 4 g
Monounsaturated fat: 4 g
Polyunsaturated fat: 2 g
Omega-6: 1.5 g
Omega-3: .7 g
Sodium: 9 mg
Potassium: 750 mg
Fiber: 7 g

Curried Squash Corn Soup

Make this soup with unpeeled organic Yukon gold or purple Peruvian potatoes, but you can use red or white potatoes if you prefer.

1 medium butternut squash
1 medium acorn squash
1 medium potato
1 large red onion, diced
1 tablespoon garlic, minced
2 tablespoons extra virgin olive oil
Black pepper
1 small leek, diced
2 tablespoons curry powder, or more to taste
2 bay leaves
2 quarts soymilk or vegetable stock
¼ cup dark sherry
1½ cups corn kernels
¼ cup pumpkin seeds, roasted

Preheat the oven to 300° F. Wash and roast the squash and the potato for 30 to 45 minutes, or until tender when pierced with a knife. Cool. Cut squash in half and scoop out the seeds. Use a spoon to scoop out the pulp. Sauté the onion and garlic in the oil. Add a few grinds of black pepper, the leek, curry powder, and bay leaves. When fragrant and soft, add the milk and sherry. Add the squash and potato. When the vegetables are tender, add the corn. Divide among warmed bowls and garnish with pumpkin seeds.

Serves eight.

Nutritional analysis per serving...

Calories: 264
Protein: 11.3 g
Carbohydrates: 32.3 g
Cholesterol: 0 mg
Total fat: 12 g
Saturated fat: 1.6 g
Monounsaturated fat: 4.5 g
Polyunsaturated fat: 3.6 g
Omega-6: 1.8 g
Omega-3: .3 g
Sodium: 157 mg
Potassium: 983 mg
Fiber: 6.5 g

Strawberry, Kiwi and Banana Compote

The mixture of honey and orange creates a delicious sauce. You can toast the walnuts in a 300° F oven for about 10 minutes, or until fragrant and golden before stirring them into the other ingredients. I like this fruit compote on oatmeal in the winter and on pancakes year round.

2 pints strawberries, organic
3 medium bananas, ripe
5 medium kiwifruit, ripe
2 medium oranges, zest and juice

2 tablespoons honey
¼ cup walnuts, crushed

Quarter the strawberries, slice the bananas and peel, core and dice the kiwis. Gently toss with the orange zest, juice and honey. Stir in the crushed walnuts. Allow to macerate at room temperature or in the fridge for at least 30 minutes. Serve over soy ice cream, frozen yogurt or breakfast foods such as oatmeal, whole grain pancakes or waffles.

Serves six.

Nutritional analysis per serving...

Calories: 202
Protein: 3.2 g
Carbohydrates: 41 g
Cholesterol: 0
Total fat: 4.4 g
Saturated fat: .5 g
Monounsaturated fat: .6 g
Polyunsaturated fat: 2.8 g
Omega-6: 2.1 g
Omega-3: .6 g
Sodium: 3 mg
Potassium: 707 mg
Fiber: 7.2 g

CHEF MARK CLEVELAND

Sweet Potato, Tofu and Kale Frittata

This is delicious served hot, warm or cool. Frittatas make excellent sandwiches with crusty bread, lettuce and a little mustard. You can use any type of tofu for this frittata. Soft tofu is similar to a creamy cheese, and firm tofu is like a harder cheese. It's good both ways. Most cookware, even those with plastic handles, can go into an oven preheated to 350° F. Check the instructions that came with your pan.

⅔ cup sweet potato, peeled and diced
3 whole kale leaves, finely diced
4 large omega-3 eggs
3 large egg whites
½ cup diced soft or firm tofu
1 garlic clove, minced
1 ½-inch piece fresh ginger, peeled and minced
2 tablespoons chives, minced
⅛ teaspoon sea salt
Olive oil spray

Preheat the oven to 350° F. Steam the sweet potato and kale with a little water in a covered skillet to soften slightly, five to seven minutes (or place in a bowl with a little water, cover and microwave on medium for about three minutes). Whisk the eggs and egg whites. Stir in the tofu, garlic, ginger, chives and sea salt. Pour into a nine- or 10-inch nonstick skillet sprayed with olive oil spray. Cook in the oven for 30 minutes, or until the center is set. Serve. There is no need to turn the frittata over or broil the top unless you would like to do so.

Serves five.

Nutritional analysis per serving...

Calories: 114
Protein: 10 g
Carbohydrates: 7 g
Cholesterol: 148 mg
Total fat: 5.3 g
Saturated fat: 1.2 g
Monounsaturated fat: 1.5 g
Polyunsaturated fat: 1.7 g
Omega-6: 1.1 mg
Omega-3: .1 g
Sodium: 150 mg
Potassium: 209 mg
Fiber: 7.6 mg

RANCHO LA PUERTA

Hibiscus Tea

The hibiscus plant is an annual herb whose flowers have been used to make hot and cold beverages in many of the world's tropical and subtropical countries. Hibiscus flowers contain large amounts of polyphenols with antioxidant, anti-inflammatory and antitumor activity. One study has shown that hibiscus tea can lower blood pressure in patients with hypertension.

Here's a recipe for Hibiscus Tea from the Rancho La Puerta spa in Mexico. Hibiscus (Jamaica) flowers can be found in any market that caters to Hispanics or in the ethnic section of any large supermarket or even in health-food stores.

1 quart water
½ cup dried Jamaica flowers (hibiscus)
1 cinnamon stick
½ cup honey, or agave nectar

Simmer the hibiscus and cinnamon stick in the water for 20 minutes. Let cool slightly before adding honey to taste.

Store in the refrigerator for up to a week. This can also be made as a concentrate and diluted when ready to serve.

Serves four.

Nutritional analysis per serving...

Calories: 122
Protein: less than 1 g
Carbohydrates: 32 g
Cholesterol: 0
Total fat: less than 1 g
Saturated fat: 0
Monounsaturated fat: 0
Polyunsaturated fat: 0
Omega-6: 0
Omega-3: 0
Sodium: 7 g
Potassium: 5 g
Fiber: .14 g

Honey Green Tea Sparkler

This is a refreshing and healthful alternative to soda. If using green tea bags, use 12 or more. Use any type of green tea you like, and family-friendly juices, such as cranberry, all-natural lemonade, peach, orange, grapefruit, pineapple and blueberry. Try black tea with cherry juice for a tasty quencher. Make some into ice cubes to use when chilling the tea. San Pellegrino mineral water is a natural source of calcium.

¼ cup honey
½ cup jasmine green tea leaves
1 quart ice cubes
1 cup white grape juice
Sparkling water

Heat one quart water to boiling. Remove from the heat and stir in the honey, then the green tea leaves. Allow to steep for three to five minutes, then strain into a large pitcher. Add the ice cubes and stir to melt. Add the grape juice. Pour over ice into glasses three-quarters full. Top off with sparkling water, stir once and serve.

Serves 10.

Nutritional analysis per serving...

Calories: 14
Protein: less than 1 g
Carbohydrates: 3.4 g
Cholesterol: 0
Total fat: less than 1 g
Saturated fat: 0
Monounsaturated fat: 0
Polyunsaturated fat: 0
Omega-6: 0
Omega-3: 0
Sodium: 3 mg
Potassium: 76 mg
Fiber: less than 1 g

Sichuan Green Tea, Cauliflower and Tofu Stir-fry

Fermented black beans are available in the Asian aisle of most grocery stores. Keeping the chile peppers whole makes it easy to remove them once the dish is cooked. If you prefer not to use sherry, add two more tablespoons of tea. Grapeseed oil is neutral in flavor and has a high smoking point, but canola oil works just as well.

2 tablespoons grapeseed or canola oil
2 garlic cloves, minced
2 medium shallots, minced
1 1-inch piece fresh ginger, peeled and minced
1 package firm tofu, cut into 1-inch squares and dried
1¼ cups whole almonds
6 small whole chili peppers
1 tablespoon fermented black beans, optional
1 head cauliflower, broken up into florets
2 tablespoons Chinese sherry or dark sherry
2 tablespoons low-sodium soy sauce
½ cup brewed oolong or green tea

Heat the oil in a skillet set over medium-high heat. When hot, add the minced garlic, shallots and ginger. Sauté until fragrant, about a minute. Add the tofu and sauté until lightly golden, about seven minutes. Add the almonds and whole chiles and sauté for several minutes more. Add the black beans (if using) and the cauliflower, and toss. Add the sherry, soy and tea and sauté until the cauliflower is crisp-tender. Divide among six plates and serve.

Serves six.

Nutritional analysis per serving...

Calories: 326
Protein: 17 g
Carbohydrates: 18 g
Cholesterol: 0
Total fat: 23.7 g
Saturated fat: 2 g
Monounsaturated fat: 12.6 g
Polyunsaturated fat: 6.5 g
Omega-6: 0
Omega-3: 0
Sodium: 288 mg
Potassium: 938 mg
Fiber: 8 g

Tofu Dressing

Here's a good mayonnaise substitute for sandwiches. It will keep in the fridge for about a week.

1 10.5-ounce package silken tofu
1 tablespoon balsamic vinegar
1 tablespoon honey
1 teaspoon prepared horseradish
½ teaspoon fresh garlic, finely minced
Dash of dried mustard
Freshly ground black pepper

Combine all the ingredients in a blender or food processor and process until smooth. Adjust the thickness of the dressing to your taste by adding a teaspoon or more of water. Pour into a bowl, cover and chill at least two hours before using.

Serves eight.

Nutritional analysis per serving...

Calories: 30
Protein: 1.8 g
Carbohydrates: 3.6 g
Cholesterol: 0
Total fat: 1 g
Saturated fat: .1 g
Monounsaturated fat: .2 g
Polyunsaturated fat: .6 g
Omega-6: 0
Omega-3: 0
Sodium: 4.4 mg
Potassium: 72 mg
Fiber: .06 g

Roasted Tofu

Even if you're a tofu novice, this tastes good. Roasted tofu is a versatile addition to a green salad, served over brown rice or in place of cheese in a sandwich. Try it with avocado, tomato and lettuce on wheat bread for a taste treat. Dice it up with some peas and corn and have it in a lettuce wrap.

3 garlic cloves
1- to 1½-inch piece fresh ginger, peeled
2 medium shallots, thinly sliced
1 tablespoon chili powder
2 tablespoons any type of miso
2 tablespoons extra virgin olive oil
Freshly ground black pepper
1 cup low-sodium organic vegetable or chicken broth
1 large orange, zest and juice
1 pound firm tofu

Preheat the oven to 425° F. Finely mince the garlic and ginger in a food processor, or slice or mince with a knife, and add them to the shallots, chili powder, miso, oil, pepper, broth, orange zest and juice in small bowl. Rinse the tofu, cut it into ½-inch-thick slices, and pat dry. Lay the tofu in a rectangular baking dish. Pour the marinade over the tofu and bake immediately. (Alternatively, allow to marinate for an hour, or even overnight, in the fridge before baking.) When most of the liquid is evaporated and "saucy," the tofu is ready, 30 to 40 minutes.

Serves six.

Nutritional analysis per serving...

Calories: 133
Protein: 7.4 g
Carbohydrates: 9.1 g
Cholesterol: 0
Total fat: 8.5 g
Saturated fat: 1.2 g
Monounsaturated fat: .8 g
Polyunsaturated fat: 2 g
Omega-6: 1.8 g
Omega-3: .2 g
Sodium: 240 mg
Potassium: 255 mg
Fiber: 1.6 g

Pine Nut–Stuffed Basil Tomatoes

When you can find organic heirloom tomatoes, this recipe is a showstopper!

1 cup pine nuts, toasted
1¾ cups fresh basil, chopped
¼ cup extra virgin olive oil
3 cups cooked brown rice
10 medium tomatoes
Salt and pepper

In a preheated 325° F oven, toast the pine nuts on a baking sheet or in a cast-iron pan until just golden. Toss the pine nuts, basil and olive oil with the brown rice. Cut off and discard the tops of the tomatoes. Remove the pulp and seeds. Fill each tomato with the rice mixture. Serve warm or chilled.

Serves 10.

Nutritional analysis per serving...

Calories: 233
Protein: 6 g
Carbohydrates: 24.5 g
Cholesterol: 0 mg
Total fat: 13.6 g
Saturated fat: 2 g
Monounsaturated fat: 7 g
Polyunsaturated fat: 3.9 g
Omega-6: 3.7 g
Omega-3: .02 g
Sodium: 206 mg
Potassium: 566 mg
Fiber: 4 g

Tomato-Bean Soup

If tarragon is hard to find, use chervil, basil or parsley.

2 tablespoons extra virgin olive oil
3 garlic cloves, minced
1 large red onion, diced
Salt and pepper
1 quart low-sodium organic vegetable or chicken broth
1 28-ounce can crushed tomatoes
1 15-ounce can white beans, rinsed and drained
1 tablespoon fresh tarragon, chopped

Heat the oil over medium-high heat in a soup pot. Add the garlic and stir until fragrant. Add the onion, salt and pepper, and sauté until the onion is tender and translucent. Add the broth, tomatoes and beans. Allow to simmer for about 20 minutes, then stir in the tarragon and remove the soup from the heat. Cool for 15 minutes, then puree with an immersion blender, adding a little more broth or water to thin as necessary. Reheat the soup and ladle into bowls.

Serves six.

Nutritional analysis per serving...

Calories: 213
Protein: 11 g
Carbohydrates: 29 g
Cholesterol: 0
Total fat: 5.1 g
Saturated fat: .8 g
Monounsaturated fat: 3.8 g
Polyunsaturated fat: .5 g
Omega-6: .06 g
Omega-3: .05 g
Sodium: 681 mg
Potassium: 573 mg
Fiber: 7.6 g

Lime Pecan-Crusted Turkey Breast

Roasting a turkey breast means you'll have this SuperFood on hand for sandwiches. Buy organic turkey—it does make a difference.

1¾ pounds cooked turkey breast
2 medium limes, zest and juice
1 tablespoon Dijon mustard
⅔ cup pecans, coarsely chopped
Freshly ground black pepper

Preheat the oven to 375° F. Place the turkey breast in a roasting pan. Whisk together the lime zest and juice, mustard, pecans and black pepper. Pack the mixture on the top of the breast to create a crust, and roast until the turkey is heated through and the pecans are lightly browned. Check after 20 minutes. If the nuts don't brown well, put the breast under a low broiler for a few minutes more.

Serves five.

Nutritional analysis per serving...

Calories: 262
Protein: 35 g
Carbohydrates: 5.1 g
Cholesterol: 84 mg
Total fat: 11.5 g
Saturated fat: 1.2 g
Monounsaturated fat: 6.2 g
Polyunsaturated fat: 3.4 g
Omega-6: 3.1 g
Omega-3: .2 g
Sodium: 84 mg
Potassium: 490 mg
Fiber: 2.2 g

Roasted Turkey Breast

This makes a fine dinner and you can serve the leftovers in sandwiches, tacos, salads and many other dishes. A four-pound turkey breast with bone should yield two-and-one-half to three pounds of meat. Always purchase organic turkey.

4 pounds turkey breast, bone in
1 tablespoon extra virgin olive oil
Salt and pepper
2 medium onions, coarsely diced
4 medium carrots, coarsely diced
3 celery stalks, coarsely diced

Preheat the oven to 325° F. Wash the turkey breast and pat dry. Place the turkey in a roasting pan and rub it all over with oil. Sprinkle with salt and pepper. Roast until the internal temperature is 165° F on an instant-read thermometer. Tent with foil if the breast browns too quickly. Add the diced vegetables to the roasting pan about 45 to 60 minutes before the bird is ready.

Serves eight.

Nutritional analysis per serving...

Calories: 169
Protein: 29 g
Carbohydrates: 6 g
Cholesterol: 6 g
Total fat: 2.6 g
  Saturated fat: .5 g
  Monounsaturated fat: 1.5 g
  Polyunsaturated fat: .4 g
    Omega-6: .2 g
    Omega-3: less than .1 g
    Sodium: 80 mg
Potassium: 517 mg
Fiber: 1.7 g

Tarragon Turkey-Walnut Salad

CHEF MARK CLEVELAND

A good way to use up those turkey leftovers.

¼ cup nonfat yogurt
2 tablespoons light mayonnaise
Salt and pepper
2 cups cooked turkey, cubed
1 large shallot, chopped
2 celery stalks, sliced
¼ cup dried cranberries
2 tablespoons walnuts, chopped
1 tablespoon tarragon or dill, chopped
Lettuce
Whole wheat bread
Sweet pickle slices, low sodium

In a medium bowl, whisk the yogurt and mayonnaise together with the salt and pepper. Add the turkey, shallot, celery, cranberries, walnuts and tarragon. Serve on lettuce leaves or on whole wheat bread with sweet pickle slices.

Serves four.

Nutritional analysis per serving...

Calories: 295
Protein: 22 g
Carbohydrates: 36 g
Cholesterol: 51 g
Total fat: 8.8 g
  Saturated fat: 1.1 g
  Monounsaturated: 2.2 g
  Polyunsaturated: 4.5 g
    Omega-6: 4 g
    Omega-3: .8 g
Sodium: 186 mg
Potassium: 370 mg
Fiber: 6.5 g

Yogurt and Blueberry Shake

CHEF MICHEL STROOT

1 cup nonfat plain yogurt
¼ cup orange juice, freshly squeezed
½ cup fresh or frozen blueberries
½ very ripe banana

Combine all ingredients in a blender. Blend on medium speed until smooth and frothy. Pour into glasses and serve.

Serves two.

Nutritional analysis per serving...

Calories: 115
Protein: 5.7 g
Carbohydrates: 25.4 g
Cholesterol: 2.5 mg
Total fat: .5 g
  Saturated fat: .09 g
  Monounsaturated fat: .06 g
  Polyunsaturated fat: .15 g
    Omega-6: .09 g
    Omega-3: .06 g
Sodium: 68.5 mg
Potassium: 217.5 mg
Fiber: 2 g

Lemon Yogurt Cornbread

Yes, there is such a thing as white whole wheat flour. Go on-line and check out *www.kingarthurflour.com*. Brush the top of the bread, hot from the oven, with a little honey for a sweet glaze.

1 cup whole wheat flour or white whole wheat flour
1 cup white or yellow cornmeal
1 tablespoon brown sugar
2 teaspoons baking powder
1 teaspoon baking soda
Pinch of salt
¾ cup low-fat lemon yogurt
⅔ cup skim milk or soymilk
2 large omega-3 eggs
1 medium lemon, zest and juice
1 tablespoon canola oil
Olive oil spray for the baking tins

Heat the oven to 400° F. Whisk to combine the dry ingredients in a large bowl. In a smaller bowl, whisk together the wet ingredients. Fold the wet ingredients into the dry. Pour the mixture into sprayed muffin tins, loaf pan or preheated 10-inch cast-iron skillet. Place the tins, pan or skillet in the upper portion of the oven. Reduce the heat to 350° F. Cook for 30 to 40 minutes or until a tester comes out clean.

Serves eight.

Nutritional analysis per serving...

Calories: 174
Protein: 6.5 g
Carbohydrates: 29.2 g
Cholesterol: 48 mg
Total fat: 4.5 g
  Saturated fat: less than 1 g
  Monounsaturated fat: 1.7 g
  Polyunsaturated fat: 1.3 g
    Omega-6: 1 g
    Omega-3: .2 g
Sodium: 262 mg
Potassium: 221 mg
Fiber: 3.8 g

Mango Yogurt Cream Sauce

Use this fruity light sauce on desserts such as fruit salad or sponge cake. When mangoes are unavailable, make it with ripe peaches, plums, apricots and/or fresh raspberries or blackberries.

1 medium mango, ripe
1 cup nonfat yogurt
1 tablespoon honey
1 medium lime, zest and juice

Peel the mango and cut the flesh off the pit. Squeeze the pit to release the juice. Place all the ingredients in a food processor or blender and blend until smooth. Refrigerate until serving time.

Serves 10.

Nutritional analysis per serving...

Calories: 36
Protein: 1.6 g
Carbohydrates: 8 g
Cholesterol: less than 1 g

Total fat: .1 g
Saturated fat: less than 1 g
Monounsaturated fat: less than 1 g
Polyunsaturated fat: less than 1 g
Omega-6: less than 1 g
Omega-3: less than 1 g
Sodium: 19 mg
Potassium: 103 mg
Fiber: .6 g

Yogurt and Blueberry Frozen Pops

For kids of all ages.

12 paper or foil baking cups, 2½-inch size
1 small lemon, zest and juices
2 cups plain nonfat yogurt
¼ to ½ cup sugar
1 pint blueberries
12 Popsicle sticks

Line 12 two-and-one-half-inch muffin pan cups with fluted paper baking cups. In a bowl, blend the lemon zest, lemon juice, yogurt and sugar until smooth. Stir in the blueberries. Divide the mixture among the paper-lined muffin-pan cups. Freeze for one-and-one-half hours, or until almost firm; insert a Popsicle stick in the middle of each pop. Freeze until firm, about two hours. For longer storage in the freezer, cover with plastic wrap. To serve, peel off the paper liners from the pops; let stand at room temperature four to six minutes to soften slightly for easier eating.

Makes 12 pops.

Nutritional analysis per serving...

Calories: 64
Protein: 1.9 g
Carbohydrates: 15.4 g
Cholesterol: .8 mg
Total fat: .1 g
Saturated fat: .01 g
Monounsaturated fat: .01 g
Polyunsaturated fat: .04 g
Omega-6: .03 g
Omega-3: .02 g
Sodium: 24 mg
Potassium: 28.4 mg
Fiber: .8 g

Yogurt Cilantro Topping

This is great on a baked sweet potato, grilled turkey breasts or turkey tacos.

1 cup nonfat or low-fat plain yogurt
¼ cup fresh cilantro leaves, minced
2 tablespoons scallions or red onion, minced
2 teaspoons fresh lime juice

Whisk all the ingredients together in a small bowl. Refrigerate, covered, for a couple of hours to let the flavors develop. If you make this with yogurt cheese, it will be thicker.

Serves four.

Nutritional analysis per serving...

Calories: 27
Protein: 2.6 g
Carbohydrates: 5.3 g
Cholesterol: 1.25 mg
Total fat: .02
Saturated fat: 0
Monounsaturated fat: .01 g
Polyunsaturated fat: 0
Omega-6: 0
Omega-3: 0
Sodium: 35 mg
Potassium: 22 mg
Fiber: .15 g

5

HEALTHY MENUS THE GOURMET WAY

Twenty-first-century living is all about time. Most of us have far too little of it. We now know that not only does constant stress wreak havoc with our health, we also realize that taking steps to reduce this stress and enhance family and social ties can actually make us healthier. That fast-food meal, grabbed on the run, not only takes a nutritional toll, but it keeps you and your children from the proven benefits of family mealtime. Food eaten at leisure in a peaceful setting with loved ones is not a luxury; it is actually an activity crucial to your health and the health of your family.

The simple fact is that families who eat together are more healthy in many ways. A survey conducted by the University of Minnesota found that frequent family meals are related to better nutritional intake and a decreased risk for unhealthy weight-control practices and substance abuse. Another study, conducted at Harvard, found that families that ate together every day, or almost every day, generally consumed higher amounts of important nutrients, such as calcium, fiber, iron, vitamins B6, B12, C and E, and consumed less overall fat compared with families who "never" or "only sometimes" ate meals together.

Here are some tips on how you can achieve satisfying family meals...

- Make family meals a priority. Mark them on the calendar. Arrange other activities around family meals whenever possible.
- It's most common to enjoy your family meal right in your own home, but sometimes a family meal can take place in a restaurant, at a sporting event or in the park—anywhere you can be together as a family, eat healthy foods and enjoy conversation with one another.
- Enlist help from the family. You don't have to go it alone—part of the pleasure of family meals can be the prep time that is spent together, engaged in conversation. If your children are small, assign them manageable tasks so that they can be part of the process. Learning to set the table is a valuable lesson for a small child and makes him/her feel competent.
- Eliminate distractions. Don't answer the phone or the door while eating if at all possible. The time your family spends together is precious and shouldn't be interrupted.
- Make mealtimes a pleasure for all. Avoid arguments and emotionally draining conversations. Save lectures for another time. Share news of the day, discuss current events and plan future activities.

The most important thing to remember is to enjoy a wide variety of SuperFoods at meals. Dishes don't have to be fancy or take hours of preparation to be healthy and tasty. Develop a repertoire of quick, wholesome meals like the ones you'll find here, and your health will improve dramatically.

Learn From a Pro

Chef Michel Stroot is the world-famous chef at one of the best-known spas in the world—the Golden Door in Escondido, California. He knows how challenging it can be to satisfy and delight demanding patrons who are used to dining in the finest five-star restaurants. Michel has done an extraordinary job in creating for this book seven days of dazzling menus that rely on the health-promoting benefits of SuperFoods.

All of the *SuperFoods Rx* daily meal plans have been analyzed by a registered nutritionist and measured utilizing the latest nutritional computer software and nutrient databases.

You don't need to be a chef to reproduce these dishes in your own kitchen. Simple and healthful, they make use of supermarket-friendly ingredients with enough of a twist to make you want to rush to the kitchen.

Day 1

Menu

Breakfast: *Oatmeal, fruit, nuts and soymilk*

Morning snack: *1 cup papaya chunks*

Lunch: *Baked Acorn Squash with Quinoa, Tofu, Dried Apricots and Walnuts; Tomato and Cucumber Salad*

Afternoon snack: *½ ounce dry-roasted or raw almonds; 8 ounces Knudsen Very Veggie Cocktail; 1 small carrot*

Dinner: *Grilled Filet Mignon with Cremini Mushrooms on Wilted Greens; Scalloped Sweet Potatoes; SuperFoods Rx Salad (page 198); Watermelon-Banana Sorbet*

Breakfast

Cook ½ cup oatmeal as directed on the side of the box. Add 1 tablespoon ground flaxseed meal, 2 tablespoons toasted pecans, a handful of raspberries and ½ cup soymilk.

Drink 1 cup of unsweetened grape juice.

Lunch

Baked Acorn Squash with Quinoa, Tofu, Dried Apricots and Walnuts

Apricot sauce

¼ cup dried apricots, cut in half
1 cup water
1 tablespoon frozen orange juice concentrate

Baked acorn squash

2 medium acorn squash
1 teaspoon onion powder
2 cups plus 2 tablespoons vegetable stock or water
1 teaspoon sea salt
1 cup quinoa, rinsed and drained
½ cup fresh flat-leaf parsley, minced
½ cup walnuts, coarsely chopped
½ pound firm tofu
1 teaspoon low-sodium soy sauce
½ teaspoon dried oregano
1 teaspoon olive oil
½ cup dried apricots, quartered

1. To make the sauce, simmer the apricots and water over medium heat for 10 to 12 minutes, or until the liquid is reduced by half. Set aside to cool.
2. Transfer the cooled mixture to a blender, add the orange juice concentrate and blend until smooth. Set aside until ready to use. Reheat gently, if necessary.
3. Preheat the oven to 375° F.
4. To prepare the squash, cut them in half horizontally and scoop out the seeds. Trim the

bottoms of the squash halves so that they sit level. Put in a baking dish and sprinkle with onion powder. Pour cold water in the dish to a depth of ½ inch. Cover with foil and bake for about 50 minutes, or until tender. Add more water if necessary during baking. Remove from the dish.

5. Meanwhile, in a saucepan, bring 2 cups of the vegetable stock and the salt to a boil over medium-high heat. Add the quinoa, cover and simmer for about 20 minutes. Remove the pan from the heat and let stand, still covered, for about 10 minutes. Toss with the parsley and walnuts and fluff with a fork. Cover and set aside to keep warm.
6. Cut the tofu into ½-inch dice, put into a bowl, add the soy sauce and oregano and toss gently.
7. In a nonstick sauté pan, heat the olive oil over medium-high heat. Add the tofu and any liquid from the bowl and sauté for about four minutes. Add the dried apricots and the remaining 2 tablespoons of stock to the pan. Stir to scrape up any browned bits on the bottom of the pan.
8. Gently toss the tofu and apricots with the quinoa. Spoon into acorn squash and drizzle with the apricot sauce.

Serves four.

Tomato and Cucumber Salad

Balsamic vinaigrette

2 tablespoons balsamic vinegar
1 tablespoon olive oil
1½ tablespoons Dijon mustard
1½ tablespoons water
½ teaspoon dried basil
¼ teaspoon freshly ground black pepper

Salad

4 ripe medium tomatoes
3 medium cucumbers

1. In a small bowl, whisk the vinegar and oil. Add the mustard and water and whisk until blended. Whisk in the basil and pepper. Whisk again before using.
2. Core the tomatoes and cut into wedges. Cut each wedge in half. Peel the cucumbers and slice into ½-inch-thick rounds. Quarter the rounds.
3. Toss the tomatoes and cucumbers in a large bowl. Pour the dressing over them, stir gently to mix and then set aside at room temperature to marinate for at least 10 minutes or up to one hour.

Serves four.

Dinner

Grilled Filet Mignon with Cremini Mushrooms on Wilted Greens

1 cup cremini mushrooms, stemmed and quartered
2 tablespoons shallots, minced
½ cup red wine, such as Merlot
½ cup Beef Brown Sauce (page 187), or low-sodium canned beef gravy
2 tablespoons olive oil
½ cup yellow onion, finely chopped
2 teaspoons garlic, minced
4 cups turnip greens, torn
1 pound beef tenderloin or filet, sliced into four 4-ounce pieces about 1 inch thick, or bison filets
2 tablespoons fresh flat-leaf parsley, chopped

1. Spray a nonstick sauté pan with canola oil spray, set over medium heat and sauté the mushrooms and shallots for about five minutes, or until lightly browned. Add the wine and cook for about 10 minutes, or until reduced by half. Add the brown sauce, bring to a simmer and cook for two to three minutes, or until the flavors blend.

2. In another large sauté pan, heat the oil over medium-high heat and cook the onion and garlic, stirring, for two to three minutes, or until the onions become translucent. Add the turnip greens and cook, stirring, for a few minutes until the greens wilt. Remove from the heat and keep warm.
3. Prepare a charcoal or gas grill. The coals should be medium-hot to hot. Lightly spray the grill rack with vegetable oil spray.
4. Grill the filets for about five minutes on each side until they reach the desired degree of doneness. Insert an instant-read thermometer in a filet. After about five minutes, the temperature will be 145° F for medium-rare; after six to seven minutes, the temperature will be 160° F for medium. Remove from the grill.
5. To serve, fork the wilted greens onto a plate and top with the grilled steak. Spoon the mushroom sauce over the meat. Garnish with chopped parsley.

Beef Brown Sauce

- 2½ pounds top round, including trimmings, or bison, cut into 1-inch pieces
- 1 small onion, coarsely chopped
- 1 medium carrot, coarsely chopped
- 1 celery rib, coarsely chopped
- 1 tablespoon tomato paste
- 2 teaspoons black peppercorns, crushed
- 2 teaspoons dried tarragon
- 2 sprigs fresh thyme or 1 teaspoon dried thyme
- 2 whole bay leaves
- 2 tablespoons unbleached all-purpose flour
- 2 quarts vegetable broth or water
- 1 tablespoon arrowroot or cornstarch, dissolved in 2 tablespoons water

1. Spray a large skillet with canola oil, set it on medium-high heat and sauté the beef trimmings for 10 to 15 minutes, or until browned on all sides. Add the onion, carrot and celery and sauté for five to 10 minutes longer, or until well browned.
2. Stir in the tomato paste, peppercorns, tarragon, thyme and bay leaves and sprinkle with the flour. Transfer to a large pot.
3. Pour 2 cups of the vegetable broth into the skillet and scrape off any caramelized pieces of meat or vegetables. Pour into the pot with the vegetables. Add the remaining vegetable broth and simmer for about two hours, skimming the foam that rises to the top. Simmer until reduced by about two-thirds. Strain through a fine-mesh sieve into another pot.
4. Return to the stove, bring to a simmer and cook for about 30 to 40 minutes, or until reduced to 1½ cups. Stir in the arrowroot or cornstarch mixture and simmer for another one to two minutes until thickened.

Makes about 1½ cups.

Scalloped Sweet Potatoes

- 2 medium sweet potatoes (about 1 pound)
- ¼ cup fresh orange juice
- ¼ cup vegetable stock or water
- 1 teaspoon ground allspice

1. In a medium saucepan, combine the unpeeled sweet potatoes and enough cold water to cover and bring to a boil over high heat. Reduce the heat and simmer for 15 to 20 minutes, or until the potatoes just begin to soften but are still relatively firm. Drain and set aside until cool enough to handle.
2. Peel the sweet potatoes and cut into ½-inch-thick rounds. You will have about 16 slices.

Place four sweet potato slices in a medium sauté pan, arranging them in a circle and overlapping the edges slightly. Repeat the pattern with the remaining slices. Drizzle the orange juice and stock over the potatoes and sprinkle with allspice. Cover and set aside until ready to serve. Reheat in the oven if necessary.

Serves four.

Watermelon-Banana Sorbet

2 large ripe bananas, peeled and thinly sliced
1 cup watermelon cubes
½ cup freshly squeezed orange juice
⅓ cup fresh lime juice

1. Spread the bananas and watermelon in a shallow metal dish. Pour the orange juice and lime juice over the fruit and freeze for at least four hours, or until frozen solid.
2. Let the fruit thaw on the countertop for about 10 minutes. Break into small pieces and transfer to a food processor fitted with a metal blade and process until smooth and creamy.
3. Spoon into small cups and serve immediately or return to the freezer for no more than an hour. If you freeze the sorbet for longer than an hour, process it again in the food processor before serving.

Serves four.

Day 1 Nutritional Analysis...

Calories: 2448
Protein: 92 g
Carbohydrates: 332 g
Cholesterol: 88 g
Total Fat: 91 g
Saturated fat: 20 g
Monounsaturated fat: 38 g
Polyunsaturated fat: 21 g
Omega-6: 13.6 g
Omega-3: 3.7 g
Sodium: 2315 mg
Potassium: 7318 mg
Fiber: 53 g

Percentage of Calories
Protein 15%
Carbohydrates 53%
Fat 32%

Day 2

Menu

Breakfast: *"Fortified" cereal with soy milk, 8 ounces pink grapefruit juice*

Morning snack: *1 cup fresh papaya chunks*

Lunch: *Spinach Pasta with Turkey-Tomato Sauce; SuperFoods Rx Salad (page 198) with Raspberry Vinaigrette*

Afternoon snack: *½ yellow bell pepper, cut into strips*

Dinner: *Asian-Style Wild Salmon on Sesame Spinach; Millet and Steamed Asparagus Tips; Berry Crisp with Nuts and Oatmeal Topping*

Breakfast

¾ cup Kashi Good Friends cereal
1 tablespoon toasted wheat germ
2 tablespoons toasted slivered almonds
2 tablespoons wheat bran
½ tablespoon ground flaxseed meal

1. Mix together. Enjoy a 4-ounce glass of unsweetened pink grapefruit juice while combining your morning mélange.
2. Pour 8 ounces vanilla soymilk over the cereal.

Serves one.

Lunch

Spinach Pasta with Turkey-Tomato Sauce

9 medium ripe tomatoes (about 3 pounds), halved or quartered, or two 16-ounce cans whole tomatoes with juice, plus two 8-ounce cans tomato sauce
½ cup water
1 8-ounce can tomato paste
2 tablespoons olive oil
1 cup onion, chopped
2 to 3 garlic cloves, minced
1 pound lean ground turkey
1 small fennel bulb, chopped (about 1 cup), or 1 cup celery, chopped, plus ½ teaspoon crushed fennel seed
2 tablespoons fresh flat-leaf parsley, finely chopped, or 2 teaspoons dried parsley
2 tablespoons fresh basil, chopped, or 2 teaspoons dried basil
1 tablespoon fresh oregano, chopped, or 1 teaspoon dried oregano
¼ teaspoon freshly ground black pepper
¼ to ½ teaspoon coarse sea salt
Pinch of cayenne
1 pound spinach pasta, freshly cooked

1. In a large nonstick pot, cook the tomatoes and water over low heat for 30 to 40 minutes, or until tender. Transfer to a blender or food processor fitted with a metal blade, add the tomato paste and process until smooth. (If using canned tomatoes, pour them and the canned tomato sauce and paste directly into the blender or food processor.) Work in batches if necessary.
2. In a large sauté pan, heat the olive oil over medium-high heat. Add the onion and garlic and cook, stirring, for about five minutes, or until softened but not browned. Add the turkey and cook for about 10 minutes, breaking up the turkey with a spoon into small pieces. Add the fennel and cook for one to two minutes longer, or until the fennel softens. Pour contents of pan into strainer and allow fat to drain.
3. Return meat to pan (or heavy pot), add the tomato puree, parsley, basil, oregano, black pepper, salt and cayenne. Cover and cook for about 45 minutes or until flavors are nicely melded.
4. Serve over spinach pasta.

Serves six.

Raspberry Vinaigrette

½ cup raspberries
3 tablespoons balsamic vinegar
1 tablespoon unsweetened apple juice
1 teaspoon canola oil
1 teaspoon honey

Whisk the ingredients together in a small bowl. Toss the dressing with the salad.

Serves two.

Dinner

Asian-Style Wild Salmon on Sesame Spinach

Marinade
½ cup rice wine vinegar
½ cup water
6 tablespoons low-sodium soy sauce
2 teaspoons toasted sesame oil
Juice of 2 small limes
1 knob fresh ginger, about 1½ to 2 inches long, peeled and minced
6 four-ounce wild salmon fillets

Sauce
1 tablespoon shallots, chopped
1 teaspoon garlic, minced
1 teaspoon ginger, minced
¼ cup fresh cilantro leaves, minced

Nests

½ teaspoon sunflower or safflower oil
1 tablespoon shallots, chopped
1 garlic clove, minced
2 bunches spinach (10 to 12 ounces each), washed, stemmed and chopped
1 tablespoon sesame seeds

Garnishes

¼ cup chives, finely sliced
¼ cup red bell pepper, finely minced

1. To make the marinade, combine the vinegar, water, soy sauce, sesame oil and lime juice in a blender. Add the ginger and blend on high speed for two minutes, or until smooth.
2. Lay the salmon fillets in a shallow glass or ceramic dish and pour half the marinade over them. Cover and refrigerate for 30 minutes. Reserve the remaining marinade.
3. Preheat the oven to 350° F.
4. Lift the salmon from the marinade and discard the marinade. Lay the fillets in a shallow baking dish and bake for 15 to 20 minutes, or until the fillets just begin to flake when pierced with a fork and an instant-read thermometer registers 140° F.
5. Meanwhile, put the reserved marinade in a saucepan, add the shallots, garlic and ginger and bring to a simmer over medium heat. Cook for about five minutes, or until the shallots and garlic are tender. Stir in the cilantro, cook for a minute or so and remove from the heat.
6. To make the nests, in a large sauté pan, heat the oil over medium heat and cook the shallots and garlic until softened. Add the spinach and cook just until wilted. Sprinkle with sesame seeds.
7. Divide the spinach among six plates and top each mound of spinach with a salmon fillet. Spoon the sauce over the fish and garnish with a sprinkling of chives and minced red peppers.

Serves six.

Millet and Steamed Asparagus Tips

1 cup millet
2 cups vegetable stock or water
1 teaspoon kosher salt
18 two-inch-long asparagus tips

1. Rinse the millet in a fine-mesh sieve under cool running water. Drain.
2. In a saucepan, bring the stock and salt to a boil over medium-high heat. Add the millet, stir, reduce the heat to a simmer, cover and cook for about 20 minutes, or until the grain is tender. Remove from the heat and fluff with a fork.
3. Meanwhile, put the asparagus tips in a steaming basket and set over boiling water. Steam for two to three minutes, or until crisp-tender.
4. Serve the millet with the asparagus tips on the side or on top.

Serves six.

Berry Crisp with Nuts and Oatmeal Topping

Crisp

⅓ cup almonds, chopped
⅓ cup pecans, chopped
⅓ cup walnuts, chopped
1 cup quick-cooking or regular rolled oats
3 to 4 tablespoons pure maple syrup
2 tablespoons wheat germ
2 tablespoons whole wheat pastry flour or unbleached all-purpose flour
1 teaspoon cinnamon
½ teaspoon nutmeg
½ teaspoon pure vanilla extract

Filling

4 cups blackberries or blueberries or strawberries or raspberries or a mixture of any of these
2 tablespoons pure maple syrup
1 teaspoon ground cinnamon
1 teaspoon lemon or lime zest, finely grated

Topping

16 ounces nonfat regular or frozen vanilla yogurt

1. Preheat the oven to 325° F.
2. To prepare the crisp, spread the nuts on a baking sheet and toast for five to eight minutes, or until golden brown. Stir once or twice during toasting. Transfer the nuts to a mixing bowl.
3. Add the oats, syrup, wheat germ, flour, cinnamon, nutmeg and vanilla. Mix well.
4. For the filling, slice any of the berries that need it. Toss with the syrup, cinnamon and zest. Spread the fruit in an 8- or 9-inch square baking pan or pie plate. Top with the crisp and bake for 15 to 20 minutes, or until the fruit is tender, bubbling around the edges and the crisp is lightly browned.
5. Top each serving with a 2-ounce dollop of yogurt.

Serves eight.

Day 2 Nutritional Analysis...

Calories: 2186
Protein: 99 g
Carbohydrates: 293 g
Cholesterol: 191 mg
Total Fat: 80 g
Saturated fat: 13 g
Monounsaturated fat: 37 g
Polyunsaturated fat: 22 g
Omega-6: 13.8 g
Omega-3: 2.8 g
Sodium: 1916 mg
Potassium: 7259 mg
Fiber: 63 g

Percentage of Calories

Protein 17%
Carbohydrates 51%
Fat 31%

DAY 3

Menu

Breakfast: *Tropical Fruit Yogurt Parfait; 4 ounces orange juice; Whole Grain Toast with Almond Butter*

Lunch: *Poached Wild Salmon Salad with Cucumber Dill Sauce; Sweet Potato Oven Fries*

Afternoon snack: *½ orange bell pepper, cut into strips; ½ ounce unsalted, dry-roasted soy nuts; 1 small carrot*

Dinner: *Stir-Fried Tofu with Soba Noodles; Super-Foods Rx Salad (page 198); Golden Door Blueberry Bread*

Breakfast

Tropical Fruit Yogurt Parfait

½ medium papaya, seeded, cut into ½-inch cubes (about 1 cup)
3 cups nonfat vanilla yogurt (or plain nonfat yogurt mixed with 2 tablespoons pure maple syrup)
4 tablespoons ground flaxseed
½ cup almonds, sliced
1 cup blueberries
1 mango, cut into ½-inch cubes (about 1 cup)

1. Spoon about 2 tablespoons of the papaya cubes into each of four (12-ounce) parfait cups or tall, wide-mouth glasses. Top each with about 2 tablespoons yogurt, 1 teaspoon ground flaxseed and 1 teaspoon almonds.

2. Spoon 2 tablespoons blueberries into each parfait cup and top each with about 2 tablespoons yogurt, 1 teaspoon ground flaxseed and 1 teaspoon almonds. Spoon about 2 tablespoons mango cubes into each parfait cup and top each with about 2 tablespoons yogurt, 1 teaspoon ground flaxseed and 1 teaspoon almonds. Repeat with remaining ingredients to make three more layers of fruit and yogurt.
3. Refrigerate or serve immediately with Whole Grain Toast with Almond Butter (below) and ½ cup fresh, full-pulp orange juice.

Serves four.

Whole Grain Toast with Almond Butter

4 slices whole grain bread
1 tablespoon almond or cashew butter

Toast the bread slices. Spread each with almond butter, cut in half diagonally, and serve.

NOTE: Cashew or hazelnut butter or other tree nut butter may be substituted.

Lunch

Poached Wild Salmon Salad with Cucumber Dill Sauce

Sauce
1 cup nonfat yogurt
½ cup low-fat cottage cheese, ricotta or nonfat yogurt cheese (see page 199)
¼ cup fresh flat-leaf parsley, chopped
2 tablespoons fresh dill, chopped, or 1 tablespoon dried dill
2 medium cucumbers, peeled, seeded and shredded
¼ cup shallots or onion, minced
Pinch of cayenne
¼ teaspoon sea salt
¼ teaspoon freshly ground black pepper

Salmon
1 cup white wine
½ cup vegetable stock or water
Juice of 1 lemon
1 shallot or small onion, minced
1½ teaspoons dried thyme
¼ teaspoon cracked black pepper
6 four-ounce wild salmon fillets

Assembly
6 cups spinach leaves, washed and drained
2 teaspoons olive oil
2 teaspoons balsamic vinegar or fresh lemon juice
1 small unpeeled cucumber or zucchini, thinly cut into rounds
6 large cherry tomatoes, for garnish

1. To prepare the sauce, combine the yogurt and cottage cheese in a blender or food processor fitted with a metal blade and process until smooth. Scrape into a bowl and stir in the parsley, dill, cucumber, shallots, cayenne, salt and pepper. Taste and adjust the seasoning. Cover and refrigerate for at least two hours.
2. To prepare the salmon, combine the wine, stock, lemon juice, shallot, thyme and black pepper in a large sauté pan and bring to a boil over medium-high heat. Reduce the heat to low and simmer the poaching liquid for two to three minutes. Add the salmon and poach for 13 to 15 minutes, or until the fish flakes easily when pierced with a fork and an instant-read thermometer reads 140° F. Using a slotted spoon or spatula, transfer the salmon to a platter, cover and refrigerate for one to two hours, or until chilled.

3. To serve, toss the spinach with the oil and vinegar. Arrange the spinach on each of six plates. Set a fillet on top of the greens and spoon the cucumber-dill sauce over the top. Garnish each plate with 2 or 3 rounds of cucumber or zucchini and a cherry tomato. Serve with whole grain bread or crackers, if desired.

Serves six.

Sweet Potato Oven Fries

Enough sprigs of fresh rosemary to cover a baking sheet
1 teaspoon chili powder
1 teaspoon ground cumin
1 teaspoon paprika
1 teaspoon kosher salt
1 teaspoon freshly ground black pepper
2 medium sweet potatoes (about 1 pound), scrubbed and blotted dry
Olive oil spray

1. Preheat the oven to 400° F. Spray a large baking sheet with olive oil spray, or line it with parchment paper, or use an ungreased, unlined nonstick baking sheet.
2. Spread the rosemary sprigs on the baking sheet in a single layer, making sure that the entire surface is covered.
3. In a small bowl, mix together the chili powder, cumin, paprika, salt and pepper.
4. Square off the potatoes by slicing off the sides lengthwise about ½ inch in from the edge. Cut crosswise into ½-inch strips the size of steak fries, leaving the skin on. Slice the remaining rectangles into ½-inch strips, also the size of steak fries.
5. Lay the potato strips on the rosemary sprigs in a single layer and sprinkle generously with the seasoning mixture. Spray generously with olive oil spray.
6. Bake for 20 minutes, remove from the oven and spray again with olive oil spray.
7. Return to the oven for about 25 minutes, or until the fries are golden and puffed. Brush off the rosemary sprigs and serve warm.

Serves four.

Dinner

Stir-Fried Tofu with Soba Noodles

Tofu

2 teaspoons extra virgin olive oil
1 to 3 garlic cloves, minced
1 tablespoon fresh ginger, minced or grated
2 large red bell peppers, cut into pieces about 2 inches long and ¼ inch wide (about 1 cup)
¼ teaspoon freshly ground black pepper
Pinch of red pepper flakes
1 tablespoon fresh basil, finely chopped, or 1 teaspoon dried basil
2 tablespoons low-sodium soy sauce
1 pound extra-firm tofu, cut into ½-inch cubes

Noodles

6 ounces soba (buckwheat) noodles
1 tablespoon olive oil
2 to 3 garlic cloves, minced
3 tablespoons sesame seeds
1 to 2 tablespoons fresh cilantro, minced
¼ teaspoon freshly ground black pepper

1. To prepare the tofu, in a nonstick skillet, heat the olive oil over medium-high heat and cook the garlic, ginger and red bell peppers, stirring, for about five minutes or until the peppers begin to soften. Add the black pepper, pepper flakes, basil, soy sauce and tofu and stir to coat the tofu. Cook for 10 to 12 minutes, or until heated through.

2. To prepare the noodles, cook the soba noodles in boiling water for five to seven minutes, or until tender. Drain and rinse well under cool running water. Set aside.
3. In a large nonstick skillet, heat the oil over medium-high heat. Add the garlic and cook, stirring, for about 30 seconds, or until tender. Add the sesame seeds and cook for about 30 seconds until fragrant, stirring constantly to prevent burning. Stir in the cilantro and pepper.
4. Add the noodles to the skillet and toss well. Spoon equal portions of noodles into six bowls, divide the tofu mixture among them and serve.

Serves six.

Golden Door Blueberry Bread

1 cup unbleached, all-purpose flour
1 teaspoon baking powder
½ teaspoon baking soda
2 teaspoons ground cinnamon
½ teaspoon ground allspice
1¼ cups whole wheat flour
¼ cup stone-ground yellow cornmeal
½ teaspoon kosher salt
2 ripe medium bananas, mashed (about 1 cup)
½ cup light brown sugar
1 large omega-3 egg
1 large omega-3 egg white
2 tablespoons canola oil
1½ cups low-fat buttermilk
2 tablespoons orange zest, grated
1 cup walnuts, chopped
1 cup blueberries, soaked in warm water for about 15 minutes, and drained
Nonfat vanilla frozen yogurt, optional

1. Preheat the oven to 350° F. Spray a 9 × 5-inch or 8½ × 4-inch loaf pan with vegetable oil spray.
2. In a large mixing bowl, sift together the all-purpose flour, baking powder, baking soda, cinnamon and allspice. Stir in the whole wheat flour, cornmeal and salt.
3. In a blender or food processor fitted with a metal blade, combine the bananas, brown sugar, egg, egg white, canola oil and buttermilk and process until smooth. Add the orange zest and pulse until just combined.
4. Make a well in the flour mixture. Pour the banana mixture into it and mix until almost incorporated. Add the walnuts and drained blueberries and gently mix into the batter. Do not overmix.
5. Pour the batter into the prepared pan and bake for about 55 minutes, or until a toothpick inserted into the center comes out clean, the top is golden brown and the bread begins to pull away from the sides of the pan. Remove from the oven, invert on a wire rack and cool briefly before slicing.
6. Slice into ½- to ¾-inch-thick slices. Serve each slice topped with ½ cup scoop of nonfat vanilla frozen yogurt, if desired.

Makes one loaf.

Day 3 Nutritional Analysis...

Calories: 2040
Protein: 93 g
Carbohydrates: 265 g
Cholesterol: 96 mg
Total Fat: 74 g
- *Saturated fat: 11 g*
- *Monounsaturated fat: 35 g*
- *Polyunsaturated fat: 18 g*
  - *Omega-6: 11.3 g*
  - *Omega-3: 3.7 g*

Sodium: 2192 mg

Potassium: 5131 mg
Fiber: 42 g

Percentage of Calories
Protein 18%
Carbohydrates 51%
Fat 31%

Day 4

Menu

Breakfast: *Sweet Potato Pie*

Morning snack: *8 ounces 100% pomegranate juice (mixed with sparkling water if desired)*

Lunch: *Tuna Salad with Mesclun, Basil and Sprouts*

Afternoon snack: *1 cup of papaya chunks; 8 ounces Knudsen Very Veggie Cocktail; 1 ounce unsalted dry-roasted or raw almonds*

Dinner: *Asian Stir-Fry with Turkey Cutlets, Basmati Rice, Wilted Greens and Peanut-Ginger Sauce; SuperFoods Rx Salad (page 198); No-Bake Pumpkin-Yogurt Cheese Pie*

Breakfast

Sweet Potato Pie

Pie for breakfast? You bet. Make this the night before. Refrigerate once it has cooled.

Crust

1½ cups whole wheat, low-fat gingersnap cookies, crushed, (see Note on page 196)
3 tablespoons ground flaxseed or wheat germ
1 tablespoon dark brown sugar
1 large egg

Filling

2 garnet yams, (see Note on page 196)
1 navel orange
1 ripe banana
½ cup fat-free ricotta cheese or light silken tofu
2 large omega-3 eggs
2 teaspoons pure vanilla extract
1 teaspoon ground cinnamon
¼ teaspoon ground nutmeg or mace
¼ teaspoon ground cloves
⅓ to ½ cup pure maple syrup, or to taste

Garnish

Vanilla yogurt cheese, optional (see page 199)
8 raspberries or strawberries
Mint sprigs

1. Preheat the oven to 350° F.
2. To make the crust, put the gingersnap crumbs, flaxseed and brown sugar in a food processor fitted with a metal blade or in a blender and process to a powder. Add the egg and blend until moist.
3. Press the crumb mixture into a lightly oiled 9-inch pie plate, gently pushing it across the bottom and up the sides. Bake for about 20 minutes, or until the crust is golden brown. Cool the crust completely on a wire rack. Do not turn off the oven.
4. Meanwhile, pierce the yams in a few places with the tines of a fork or a sharp knife. Bake for about one hour and 15 minutes, or until tender when pierced with a knife. Set aside to cool. Do not turn off the oven.
5. When cool enough to handle, peel the yams and mash the flesh. Measure 2 cups of mashed yams.
6. Slice the top and bottom off the orange but do not peel it. Cut the orange into quarters and put it in a food processor fitted with a metal blade or in a large blender. Add the mashed yams, banana, ricotta, eggs, vanilla, cinnamon, nutmeg and cloves. Blend until smooth. Add ⅓ cup of the syrup, blend and taste. Add more syrup if necessary.
7. Scrape the filling into the cooled crust and bake on the center rack of the oven for 40 to 50 minutes, or until set in the center. If

the crust darkens during baking, shield the edges with strips of foil.

8. Cool the pie on a wire rack. Cut into wedges and serve with dollops of yogurt cheese, berries and mint sprigs.

Serves eight.

NOTE: For the crust, you may substitute graham cracker crumbs mixed with 1 teaspoon of ground ginger for the gingersnap crumbs. Eight graham cracker squares yield 1 cup of crumbs.

We recommend garnet or red yams, which are sweeter and creamier than jewel yams. All tubers labeled "yams" in our American markets are actually sweet potatoes.

Lunch

Tuna Salad with Mesclun, Basil and Sprouts

Two 13-ounce cans water-packed albacore tuna, drained
2 ribs celery, cut into ¼-inch dice
½ cup red onion, diced
¾ cup nonfat plain yogurt
2 tablespoons Dijon mustard
2 teaspoons rice vinegar
2 teaspoons dried dill
8 cups mixed mesclun greens, spinach or romaine, washed and torn into bite-sized pieces
½ cup fresh basil leaves, torn
¼ cup alfalfa sprouts
¼ cup radish sprouts
¼ cup Raspberry Vinaigrette (page 189)
⅛ avocado, sliced
1 large hard-cooked omega-3 egg, sliced
½ yellow bell pepper, sliced
4 ripe medium tomatoes, cut into wedges
Freshly ground black pepper
¼ cup edible flowers, such as nasturtiums, geraniums or petunias (optional)

1. Flake the tuna into a small bowl. Add the celery, onion, yogurt, mustard, vinegar and dill and mix well.
2. In a large bowl, toss the greens, basil and sprouts with the vinaigrette.
3. To compose the salad, arrange the tossed greens on four large plates. Add equal portions of avocado, egg, bell pepper and tomatoes to each serving. Using an ice cream scoop, portion the tuna salad in the center of the greens. Garnish with fresh pepper and edible flowers, if desired.

Serves four.

Dinner

Asian Stir-Fry with Turkey Cutlets, Basmati Rice, Wilted Greens and Peanut-Ginger Sauce

Turkey and marinade

1 teaspoon fresh ginger, minced
½ teaspoon toasted sesame oil
2 teaspoons low-sodium tamari or soy sauce
1 tablespoon fresh lime juice
1 teaspoon Szechuan peppercorns, cracked, or chile paste
1 pound skinless, boneless turkey cutlets or breast

Basmati rice

¾ cup brown basmati rice
1¾ cups vegetable stock or water

Peanut-ginger sauce

2 tablespoons fresh ginger, finely chopped
2 to 3 tablespoons low-sodium tamari
2 tablespoons rice vinegar
1 tablespoon red wine vinegar
2 tablespoons honey
1½ teaspoons dried basil
2 tablespoons crunchy peanut butter
2 tablespoons water

Vegetable stir-fry

¼ teaspoon canola oil

1 medium carrot, thinly sliced on the diagonal

1 celery rib, thinly sliced on the diagonal

8 shiitake mushrooms, thinly sliced

¼ cup vegetable stock or water

Wilted greens

¼ teaspoon canola oil

1 teaspoon garlic, minced

1 teaspoon fresh ginger, minced

¼ teaspoon fennel seeds, crushed

1½ small fennel bulbs, thinly sliced (about 1½ cups)

2 to 3 tablespoons vegetable or defatted chicken stock or water

1 cup Swiss chard, torn

1 cup fresh spinach leaves

2 cups bok choy leaves, torn

2 teaspoons low-sodium soy sauce

½ teaspoon toasted sesame oil

1. To marinate the turkey, in a shallow glass or ceramic dish, whisk together the ginger, sesame oil, tamari, lime juice and cracked peppercorns. Add the turkey, turn to coat, cover and refrigerate for at least one hour and up to eight hours.
2. To make the basmati rice, combine the rice and stock in a medium saucepan. Bring to a boil over high heat, reduce the heat, cover and simmer for about 30 minutes or until the liquid is absorbed. Remove from the heat and let stand for five minutes. Remove the cover and fluff the rice with a fork. Cover and keep warm.
3. To make the peanut sauce, put the ginger, tamari, rice vinegar, red wine vinegar, honey, basil, peanut butter and water into a blender and process until smooth. Set aside.
4. Preheat the oven to 350° F. Spray an ovenproof, nonstick skillet pan with vegetable oil spray.
5. Remove the turkey from the marinade and discard the marinade. Heat the oiled pan over medium-high heat, add the turkey cutlets and sear for about one minute, or until golden. Using tongs or a spatula, turn and sear the other side for about one minute. Partially cover the pan and bake for 10 to 15 minutes, or until the turkey is no longer pink in the center but still juicy. An instant-read thermometer inserted into the thickest part of the turkey should register 170° F. Transfer to a warmed platter.
6. To stir-fry the vegetables, heat the oil in a wok or large nonstick sauté pan over medium-high heat. Add the carrot and celery and stir-fry for two to three minutes, or until they begin to soften. Add the mushrooms and cook for one minute longer. Add the stock or water to deglaze the pan, loosening any browned bits from the bottom with a wooden spoon. Transfer the vegetables to a bowl and keep warm.
7. To sauté the greens, in the same wok or sauté pan, heat the oil over medium-high heat. Add the garlic, ginger, fennel seeds and fennel and sauté for one minute. If the vegetables begin to stick, deglaze the pan with a drizzle of vegetable stock, defatted chicken stock or water. Add the Swiss chard, spinach and bok choy and continue cooking just until the greens wilt. Remove from the heat and toss in the soy sauce and sesame oil.
8. Layer equal portions of basmati rice, wilted greens and vegetables on each of four plates. Top each with turkey and drizzle with peanut sauce.

Serves four.

SuperFoods Rx Salad

I eat this salad almost every day—sometimes twice a day. Feel free to vary the ingredients using the *SuperFoods Rx* sidekicks. Add a handful of your favorite chopped fresh herbs, 1 tablespoon grated Parmigiano-Reggiano or 2 tablespoons roasted nuts or seeds. The quantity is for one person, but you can easily multiply the ingredients to serve more.

1 cup spinach, torn into bite-sized pieces
1 cup romaine, chopped
¼ cup red cabbage, shredded
½ cup red bell pepper, sliced
½ tomato, chopped
¼ cup chickpeas; if canned, rinse well
½ cup carrot, grated
¼ avocado, cubed
2 tablespoons extra virgin olive oil
1 teaspoon balsamic vinegar

Combine the spinach, romaine, cabbage, red pepper, tomato, chickpeas, carrot and avocado in a bowl. In a separate bowl, whisk together the olive oil and vinegar. Toss the dressing with the salad just before serving.

Serves one.

No-Bake Pumpkin-Yogurt Cheese Pie

Crumb crust

1 cup whole wheat graham cracker crumbs (from 8 graham cracker squares)
½ cup whole wheat pastry flour
2 tablespoons canola or sunflower oil
2 tablespoons dark brown sugar
2 tablespoons ground flaxseed
2 tablespoons wheat germ or ground pumpkin seeds
2 teaspoons orange zest, finely grated
½ teaspoon ground ginger
1 large omega-3 egg, lightly beaten

Filling

24 ounces canned plain pumpkin puree or 2⅔ cups cooked sugar pumpkin or butternut squash (about 4 pounds uncooked)
1 cup nonfat plain yogurt cheese (see Note on page 199) or 1 cup fat-free ricotta
¾ to 1 cup pure maple syrup
2 ¼-ounce packets gelatin
1 teaspoon ground cinnamon
¼ teaspoon ground ginger
¼ teaspoon ground cloves
¼ teaspoon ground allspice
Mint sprigs, for garnish
Fresh berries, for garnish, optional

1. Preheat the oven to 350° F.
2. To make the crust, mix together the graham cracker crumbs, flour, oil, brown sugar, flaxseed, wheat germ, zest and ginger. Toss the mix. Add the egg and stir until the mixture is moistened.
3. Press the crumb mixture into a lightly oiled 9-inch pie plate, gently pushing it over the bottom and up the sides. Bake for about 20 minutes, or until the crust is golden brown. Cool the crust completely on a wire rack.
4. To make the filling, put the pumpkin puree and yogurt cheese in a food processor fitted with a metal blade or in a blender and puree until smooth.
5. In a small saucepan, heat the syrup over medium heat until simmering. Remove from heat, add the gelatin, cinnamon, ginger, cloves and allspice and stir until dissolved. Pour most of the syrup into the pumpkin mixture and puree until it is incorporated. Taste and add the remainder of the syrup, if needed.
6. Carefully pour into the crust. Cover with plastic wrap and chill for at least two hours or until set.

7. To serve, cut into eight wedges. Garnish each slice with a sprig of mint and a berry or two, if desired.

Serves eight.

NOTE: To make nonfat yogurt cheese, put 1 quart of nonfat plain yogurt in a stainless steel or plastic mesh strainer lined with a large unbleached coffee filter and set over a bowl. Put the bowl in the refrigerator and let the yogurt drain for six to eight hours. You will have 2 cups of yogurt cheese. Reserve the drained whey to use when baking muffins or making pancakes.

Day 4 Nutritional Analysis...

Calories: 2260
Protein: 128 g
Carbohydrates: 304 g
Cholesterol: 474 mg
Total Fat: 64 g
Saturated fat: 12 g
Monounsaturated fat: 30 g
Polyunsaturated fat: 13 g
Omega-6: 7.2 g
Omega-3: 1.2 g
Sodium: 3407 mg
Potassium: 6173 mg
Fiber: 38 g

Percentage of Calories
Protein 22%
Carbohydrates 53%
Fat 25%

DAY 5

Menu

Breakfast: *Breakfast Broccoli Frittata, 4 ounces pink grapefruit juice*

Morning snack: *¼ cup canned pumpkin mixed with ½ cup unsweetened applesauce*

Lunch: *Turkey Burger with the Works; Vegetable Stir-Fry; 8 ounces low-sodium tomato juice*

Afternoon snack: *¼ medium cantaloupe, cubed, mixed with 1 cup nonfat yogurt, 1 tablespoon flaxmeal and 2 tablespoons wheat germ*

Dinner: *White Bean Soup with Greens and Rosemary; Tomato and White Wine–Braised Halibut; Dried Apricot and Cranberry Compote with Apples*

Breakfast

Breakfast Broccoli Frittata

2 medium potatoes, sliced into ⅛-inch-thick rounds
1½ cups broccoli florets
½ medium onion, diced
½ red bell pepper, seeded, ribs removed, and chopped
½ yellow bell pepper, seeded, ribs removed, and chopped
4 large omega-3 eggs
1 cup 1% cottage cheese or fat-free ricotta
½ tablespoon fresh dill or ¾ teaspoon dried dill
3 tablespoons Asiago or Parmesan cheese, grated
4 slices whole grain bread, optional
Tomato slices, for garnish, optional
Melon slices, for garnish, optional

1. Preheat the oven to 350° F. Spray a pie plate with olive oil spray.
2. Lay the potato slices in a single layer in the bottom of the pie plate. Cut the remaining slices in half and arrange them around the sides of the pie plate. Bake for 12 to 15 minutes, or until lightly browned.
3. In a large sauté pan sprayed with olive oil spray, sauté the broccoli, onion and bell peppers for three to four minutes, or until tender. Add a tablespoon of water or vegetable stock if needed to prevent sticking.
4. In a mixing bowl, beat together the eggs and cottage cheese. Stir in the vegetables,

dill and half of the grated cheese. Add the egg mixture to the pie plate and bake for 20 to 25 minutes, or until the egg is set. Sprinkle with the remaining grated cheese and return the frittata to the oven for a minute or two to allow the cheese to melt. Cut into wedges. Serve each wedge with a slice of bread, tomato or melon, if desired.

Serves four.

Lunch

Turkey Burgers with the Works

Burgers

¾ pound lean, ground, skinless turkey breast and thigh meat, (see Note on this page)
1½ teaspoons canola or safflower oil
1½ tablespoons shallots, minced
1 tablespoon ground flaxseed
1 tablespoon whole wheat flour
1 tablespoon fresh flat-leaf parsley, minced
2 large egg whites
Freshly ground black pepper

The works

4 whole grain buns
Dijon mustard
8 large romaine or red lettuce leaves
2 ripe tomatoes, cut into ¼-inch-thick slices
½ medium red onion, cut into ⅛-inch-thick slices
½ medium avocado, sliced in wedges
Ketchup or chunky salsa

1. To make the burgers, in a bowl and using your hands or a large spoon, mix together the turkey, oil, shallots, flaxseed, flour, parsley, egg whites and pepper. Gently form the mixture into four patties. Do not pack the meat tightly. Transfer to a tray, cover and refrigerate until ready to grill.
2. Prepare a charcoal or gas grill so that the coals are medium-hot to hot. Spray the grilling rack with vegetable oil spray and return the rack to the grill.
3. Grill the burgers for five minutes on one side, turn and grill for eight to 10 minutes longer, or until the burgers are cooked through and an instant-read thermometer inserted in the thickest part of the burger registers 170° F and the juices run clear.
4. Meanwhile, toast the buns, cut side down, on the edge of the grill just until lightly browned. Spread the bottom half of each bun with mustard.
5. Divide the lettuce leaves, tomato and onion slices and avocado wedges among the buns. Top each with a burger and spread ketchup or salsa on the burgers. Serve immediately.

Serves four.

NOTE: The best way to ensure that you get quality ground turkey if you buy it in the market is to buy ground turkey *breast* so you know exactly what you are getting.

Turkey is leaner than beef, so it needs the oil and egg whites to keep it moist and the flour for binding.

Vegetable Stir-Fry

1 teaspoon canola oil
2 teaspoons garlic, minced
½ teaspoon fresh ginger, minced
12 asparagus stalks, trimmed and sliced diagonally into 2-inch pieces
1 medium carrot, sliced diagonally into ⅛-inch pieces
1 five-ounce can water chestnuts, drained and sliced into ⅛-inch rounds
6 scallions, including tops, sliced diagonally into ½-inch pieces

4 teaspoons low-sodium tamari
4 tablespoons vegetable stock or water
2 teaspoons cornstarch dissolved in
2 tablespoons water
2 teaspoons sesame seeds

1. In a nonstick saucepan or wok, heat the oil over medium-high heat. Add the garlic and ginger and cook for about one minute, stirring, or until softened.
2. In quick succession, add the asparagus, carrot, and water chestnuts and stir-fry for two to three minutes, or until the vegetables begin to soften. Add the scallions and cook for one minute longer.
3. Sprinkle the tamari in and toss gently with a wooden spoon to distribute the liquid among the vegetables. Add the stock and toss again. Add the dissolved cornstarch and toss once more. Cook for two to three minutes, or until the liquid comes to a simmer and starts to thicken. Sprinkle with sesame seeds and serve.

Serves four.

Dinner

White Bean Soup with Greens and Rosemary

1 cup dried white beans
4 cups vegetable stock or water
1 bay leaf
1 tablespoon olive oil
2 medium carrots, cubed
1 medium onion, cubed
2 garlic cloves, minced
2½ tablespoons low-sodium soy sauce
1 tablespoon fresh rosemary leaves, chopped
1 teaspoon fresh thyme, chopped
¼ teaspoon freshly ground black pepper
Pinch of cayenne
1 bunch spinach, kale or chard (10 to 12 ounces), rinsed and stemmed
3 tablespoons grated Parmesan cheese, optional

1. To prepare the beans, put them in a large bowl and add enough cold water to cover by one or two inches. Set aside to soak for at least six hours and up to 12 hours. Change the water two to three times during soaking. Drain the beans.
2. In a stockpot, combine the drained beans, stock and bay leaf and bring to a boil over high heat. Reduce the heat, cover and simmer gently for about one hour and 30 minutes, or until the beans are tender but not mushy.
3. Meanwhile, in a large sauté pan, heat the oil over medium heat and sauté the carrots and onion for about one minute. Add the garlic and cook for about five minutes, or until softened. Transfer to the pot with the beans.
4. Cook the soup for about 15 minutes over medium-low heat. Add the soy sauce, rosemary, thyme, pepper and cayenne and cook for about 15 minutes longer, or until the flavors meld. Add the spinach and cook for about five minutes, or just until wilted. (If using kale, allow 10 minutes for it to wilt.)
5. Ladle the soup into bowls and sprinkle with cheese, if desired, before serving.

Serves six.

Tomato and White Wine–Braised Halibut

2 tablespoons olive oil
½ medium onion, finely diced
¾ cup celery, finely diced
¾ cup carrot, finely diced
2 garlic cloves, minced
1 cup white wine
1 tablespoon tomato paste

4 cups chicken or vegetable stock
1 cup crushed tomatoes
¼ cup fresh flat-leaf parsley, finely chopped
2 tablespoons fresh thyme, finely chopped
1 teaspoon lemon zest, grated
1 teaspoon orange zest, grated
4 four- or five-ounce halibut, mahi mahi or sea bass fillets
½ teaspoon kosher salt
1 teaspoon freshly ground black pepper

1. Preheat the oven to 375° F.
2. In a large saucepan, heat the olive oil over medium-high heat and cook the onion, celery, carrot and garlic for three to four minutes, or until golden brown. Stir in the wine and tomato paste, bring to a simmer and cook for 10 to 12 minutes, or until the sauce is reduced by half.
3. Add the stock and crushed tomatoes and simmer the sauce for 30 to 35 minutes, or until reduced to about 3 or 4 cups. Transfer to a glass or ceramic dish, cover to keep warm and set aside.
4. In a small bowl, mix together the parsley, thyme, lemon zest and orange zest. Refrigerate until ready to use.
5. Season the halibut fillets with salt and pepper. Arrange the fillets on top of the tomato sauce, cover and bake for 20 to 25 minutes, or until the center of the fish is white but not transparent. Serve the fish with some sauce and a sprinkling of the parsley mixture.

Serves four.

Dried Apricot and Cranberry Compote with Apples

1½ cups dried apricots
¾ cup dried cranberries, dried cherries, currants or raisins
2 medium apples, peeled, cored and cut into large pieces
¼ cup unsweetened apple juice
¾ cup light brown sugar
½ cinnamon stick
2 tablespoons orange or lemon zest, julienned
Nonfat plain or vanilla yogurt or nonfat frozen vanilla yogurt (optional)

1. In a small bowl, combine the dried apricots and cranberries and add enough warm water to cover. Soak for 30 minutes. Drain and discard the soaking liquid.
2. Transfer the apricots and cranberries to a medium-sized saucepan. Add the apples, apple juice, brown sugar and cinnamon stick and bring to a simmer over medium heat. Cover and simmer for 10 to 15 minutes, or until the fruit begins to break down. Uncover the pan and simmer for a few minutes longer, breaking up the fruit with a wooden spoon, until slightly thickened and chunky. Remove the cinnamon stick and set the fruit aside to cool.
3. Meanwhile, in a small saucepan, bring 1 or 2 inches of water to a boil over medium-high heat. Add the orange or lemon zest and blanch for about 45 seconds. Drain and set aside to cool.
4. Spoon the cooled, thickened fruit into small bowls. Garnish with the cooled zest. Serve with a dollop of yogurt, if desired.

Serves eight.

Day 5 Nutritional Analysis...

Calories: 1820
Protein: 127 g
Carbohydrates: 245 g
Cholesterol: 340 mg
Total Fat: 41 g
Saturated fat: 7.8 g
Monounsaturated fat: 17.5 g
Polyunsaturated fat: 8.8 g

Omega-6: 4.4 g
Omega-3: 2.8 g
Sodium: 3094 mg
Potassium: 6184 mg
Fiber: 48 g

Percentage of Calories
Protein 27%
Carbohydrates 53%
Fat 20%

DAY 6

Menu

Breakfast: *Rancho La Puerta Breakfast Crisp; 1 cup papaya chunks; 8 ounces soymilk*

Morning snack: *2 cups watermelon cubes*

Lunch: *Braised Tofu-Stuffed Whole Wheat Pita Sandwich; Pumpkin Soup*

Afternoon snack: *½ medium orange bell pepper, cut into strips; 8 ounces low-sodium tomato juice*

Dinner: *Baked Turkey with Curried Currant Sauce and Wilted Spinach; Ricotta Torte with Blueberries*

Breakfast

Rancho La Puerta Breakfast Crisp

Sip a 4-ounce glass of unsweetened grape juice with this.

Crisp
⅓ cup almonds, chopped
⅓ cup pecans, chopped
⅓ cup walnuts, chopped
1 cup quick-cooking or regular rolled oats
3 to 4 tablespoons pure maple syrup
2 tablespoons wheat germ
2 tablespoons whole wheat pastry flour or unbleached all-purpose flour
½ teaspoon pure vanilla extract
½ teaspoon ground cinnamon
¼ teaspoon ground mace or nutmeg

Filling
3 to 4 pears, apples, peaches or nectarines, peeled, pitted or cored and sliced
½ cup dried berries, cherries, currants or raisins
½ teaspoon ground cinnamon
¼ teaspoon ground mace or nutmeg
2 teaspoons pure maple syrup

Topping
16 ounces nonfat vanilla yogurt

1. To prepare the crisp, preheat the oven to 325° F.
2. Spread the almonds, pecans and walnuts on a baking sheet and roast for five to seven minutes, or until golden brown and fragrant. Remove from the oven and slide onto a plate to halt the cooking.
3. In a mixing bowl, combine the nuts, oats, syrup, wheat germ, flour, vanilla, cinnamon and mace and toss to mix evenly.
4. For the filling, cut the fruit slices into small pieces. Transfer to a mixing bowl and add the dried berries, cinnamon and mace. Put in the syrup and toss until evenly mixed. Spread the fruit in a square 8-inch baking pan or pie plate. Top the fruit with the crisp topping.
5. Bake for 15 to 20 minutes, or until the fruit is tender and the top lightly browned. Serve warm, topped with dollops of yogurt.

Serves eight.

Lunch

Braised Tofu–Stuffed Whole Wheat Pita Sandwich

Roasted Red Pepper Hummus (page 204)
2 medium tomatoes, sliced
Braised Tofu (page 204)
½ cup bean sprouts
½ cup mixed salad greens

½ cup carrots, shredded
½ avocado, sliced into wedges
4 eight-inch whole wheat pitas, halved

Spread 1½ tablespoons of hummus on one half of a pita. Top with tomato slices, two slices of tofu, sprouts, salad greens, carrots and avocado slices. Press closed and serve. Repeat to make three more sandwiches.

Serves four.

Roasted Red Pepper Hummus

1 cup dried garbanzo beans
6 cups vegetable stock or water
2 bay leaves
1 teaspoon cumin seed or ½ teaspoon ground cumin
1 medium red bell pepper
½ cup nonfat plain yogurt or ¼ cup soft silken tofu
¼ cup fresh lemon juice
¼ cup orange juice
2 tablespoons tahini
1 tablespoon olive oil
3 to 5 garlic cloves, minced
½ teaspoon sea salt, or to taste

Garnish

2 to 3 scallions, white and green parts, thinly sliced
¼ cup fresh flat-leaf parsley, minced
1 tablespoon orange zest, finely chopped, optional
Sliced red or yellow bell peppers, carrots, zucchini and broccoli, for dipping
Whole wheat pita bread, cut into triangles

1. To prepare the beans, put them in a large bowl and add enough cold water to cover by one or two inches. Set aside to soak for at least six hours and up to 12 hours. Change the water two to three times during soaking. Drain the beans.
2. In a stockpot, combine the drained beans, stock, bay leaves and cumin and bring to a boil over high heat. Reduce the heat, cover and simmer gently for about one hour and 30 minutes to two hours, or until the beans are tender but not mushy. Drain.
3. Preheat the oven to 350° F.
4. Cut the red bell pepper in half, remove the stem, scrape out the seeds and lay, cut side down, on a baking sheet. Bake until the pepper is tender and the skin begins to wrinkle and color. Using the dull side of a paring knife, peel off the skin and cut the pepper halves into chunks.
5. Put the beans, bell peppers, yogurt, lemon and orange juices, tahini, oil and garlic in the bowl of a food processor fitted with a metal blade. Process until smooth. Add the salt, pulse to mix, then taste and adjust the seasoning.
6. Spoon into a serving bowl and garnish with scallions, parsley and zest, if desired. Serve with sliced raw vegetables and pita triangles. Makes about 5 cups.

Serves eight.

Braised Tofu

1 pound fresh firm tofu, frozen and then defrosted (see Note on next page)
1 teaspoon extra virgin olive oil
8 garlic cloves, coarsely chopped
1 tablespoon low-sodium soy sauce
1 tablespoon fresh lemon juice, balsamic vinegar or Worcestershire sauce

1. Cut the defrosted tofu into ½-inch cubes.
2. In a skillet, heat the olive oil over medium heat and cook the garlic for about one minute. Add the soy sauce, lemon juice and tofu, reduce the heat to low and cook, turning occasionally, for 20 to 30 minutes, or until the tofu is browned.

Makes about 2 cups.

NOTE: Freezing changes the texture of tofu, giving it a meaty "mouthfeel." Drain fresh firm tofu and cut into eight slices. Double wrap the slices in plastic wrap. Freeze for at least eight hours and up to several weeks. Defrost the tofu slowly in the refrigerator, or to hasten the process, submerge the still-wrapped tofu in a pot filled with boiling water. Remove the pot from the heat and let the tofu sit in the hot water for 10 to 15 minutes. Lift the tofu from the water, unwrap and proceed with the recipe.

To give the tofu an Asian tang, substitute sesame oil for the olive oil and add 2 tablespoons of grated fresh ginger with the garlic.

Pumpkin Soup

2 teaspoons olive oil
2 cups leeks, white parts only, washed well and cut into 1-inch slices
½ medium yellow onion, coarsely chopped
2 medium carrots, cut into 1-inch slices
1 medium green apple, peeled, cored and cut into 1-inch chunks
2 sixteen-ounce cans unseasoned pumpkin puree
1 sprig fresh thyme or ½ teaspoon dried thyme
1 bay leaf
2 teaspoons salt
1 teaspoon freshly ground black pepper, or to taste
1 teaspoon ground allspice
1 teaspoon ground cinnamon
7 cups vegetable stock or water
Salt and pepper, to taste
¼ cup frozen orange juice concentrate, thawed
3 tablespoons nonfat yogurt, for garnish
1 medium green apple, peeled, cored and thinly sliced, for garnish

1. In a large soup pot, heat the oil over medium heat. Add the leeks, onion, carrots, apple, pumpkin, thyme, bay leaf, salt, pepper, allspice and cinnamon. Cover and cook for about 10 minutes, stirring once or twice and adjusting the heat if necessary, until vegetables begin to soften.
2. Stir in the stock, bring to a boil, reduce the heat to medium-low and simmer, uncovered, for about 45 minutes, or until the vegetables are tender. Let cool for about 15 minutes. Discard the thyme sprig and bay leaf.
3. Working in batches, transfer to a blender or food processor fitted with a metal blade and process until smooth.
4. Pour the soup back into the pot, and cook over medium heat until hot and the flavors blend. Season with salt and pepper, if necessary, and stir in the orange juice concentrate. Add more vegetable stock if necessary to obtain the desired consistency.
5. Ladle the hot soup into bowls and garnish with dollops of yogurt and sliced apples.

Serves eight.

Dinner

Baked Turkey with Curried Currant Sauce and Wilted Spinach

Turkey and sauce

3 pounds boneless, skinless turkey breasts
1 pound carrots
1 white onion, cut in half
2 sprigs fresh thyme
1 bay leaf
2 teaspoons freshly ground black pepper
1 cup vegetable stock or water, or more as needed
1 teaspoon cornstarch
1 tablespoon curry powder
¾ cup currants, plumped in warm water and drained

Wilted spinach

1 teaspoon canola oil
2 teaspoons garlic, minced

4 cups fresh spinach leaves
⅔ cup long-grain brown rice, cooked
2 tablespoons flaxmeal
Fresh flat-leaf parsley, minced, for garnish

1. To prepare the turkey, preheat the oven to 350° F.
2. Put the turkey in a deep roasting pan that is just large enough to contain it. Scatter the carrots, onion, thyme and bay leaf around the turkey. Season with pepper. Cover with foil to seal it. Bake for about one hour and 45 minutes, until the juices run clear and an instant-read thermometer registers 170° F when inserted in the thickest part of the breast.
3. Remove from the oven and let rest for 15 minutes. Remove the breast from the pan and slice thinly. Reserve the pan's contents.
4. Discard the bay leaf and thyme sprigs from the pan. Using a slotted spoon, transfer the carrots and onion to a blender.
5. Skim as much fat as possible from the pan juices or blot them with paper towels to remove the fat. Pour the defatted juices into a measuring cup, add enough vegetable stock to measure 2 cups and pour into the blender. Add the cornstarch and curry powder, and blend at high speed until smooth.
6. Transfer to a saucepan, add the drained currants and cook over low heat until heated through and the currants begin to pop. Season with black pepper to taste, if necessary. Keep warm until ready to serve.
7. To prepare the spinach, in a large sauté pan, heat the oil over medium-high heat and cook the garlic, stirring, for one minute, or until softened but not browned. Add the spinach and continue cooking just until the greens wilt. Remove from heat and keep warm.
8. Toss the brown rice with the flaxmeal and divide among four warmed plates. Spoon 1 cup wilted spinach and fan several slices of turkey on each plate. Ladle 3 tablespoons warm sauce over the turkey. Sprinkle with minced parsley and serve.

Serves four.

Ricotta Torte with Blueberries

Crust

3 tablespoons flaxseed
3 tablespoons almonds, toasted
2 large whole wheat graham crackers
2 tablespoons light brown sugar
¼ teaspoon almond extract

Filling

4 large omega-3 eggs
1 pound nonfat ricotta cheese (about 2 cups)
3 tablespoons whole wheat pastry flour or unbleached flour
⅓ cup granulated sugar
1 teaspoon pure vanilla extract
1 tablespoon lemon zest, finely grated
3 cups fresh or frozen blueberries (thawed, if frozen)
Confectioners' sugar

1. Preheat the oven to 325° F. Butter or oil a 1-quart soufflé pan.
2. In a food processor fitted with a metal blade, process the flaxseed and almonds until finely ground. Add the graham crackers, brown sugar and almond extract, and process again until ground to fine crumbs and well mixed. Press the mixture into the prepared soufflé pan, gently pushing it over the bottom and up the sides.
3. Wipe out the food processor and add the eggs, ricotta, flour, granulated sugar and vanilla and process until smooth. Or whisk

by hand in a medium bowl. Stir in the lemon zest and carefully pour the batter into the soufflé pan.

4. Bake for about 50 minutes, or until the torte is set and a toothpick inserted into the center comes out clean. Cool on a wire rack for about 20 minutes.
5. To serve, run a knife blade around the edge of the pan. Slice into wedges, serve with berries and garnish with confectioners' sugar.

Serves eight.

Day 6 Nutritional Analysis...

Calories: 1997
Protein: 103 g
Carbohydrates: 288 g
Cholesterol: 221 mg
Total Fat: 57 g
Saturated fat: 9.6 g
Monounsaturated fat: 20 g
Polyunsaturated fat: 21.8 g
Omega-6: 12.7 g
Omega-3: 6.2 g
Sodium: 1803 mg
Potassium: 4635 mg
Fiber: 48 g

Percentage of Calories
Protein 20%
Carbohydrates 55%
Fat 25%

DAY 7

Menu

Breakfast: *Sweet Potato Scones; Grape Cooler*

Morning snack: *1 ounce walnuts; 8 ounces Knudsen Very Veggie Cocktail*

Lunch: *Crab-Stuffed Papaya; Spinach, Mushroom and Egg Chopped Salad*

Afternoon snack: *1 medium carrot, 1 ounce unsalted soy nuts*

Dinner: *Orange-Ginger Chicken with Apricot-Almond Couscous; Sesame Stir-Braised Kale; ½ cup vanilla frozen yogurt*

Breakfast

Sweet Potato Scones

1 cup plus 2 tablespoons whole wheat pastry flour
¼ cup oat or wheat bran
2 tablespoons ground flaxseed
2 tablespoons wheat germ
2 teaspoons baking powder
½ teaspoon baking soda
¼ teaspoon ground cinnamon
⅛ teaspoon ground mace or nutmeg
2 tablespoons dark brown sugar
⅓ cup dried blueberries, currants or chopped raisins
1 cup sweet potato or winter squash, such as butternut, acorn or Hubbard, shredded
⅓ cup nonfat yogurt or buttermilk
1 large omega-3 egg
1½ tablespoons canola or safflower oil
2 teaspoons orange zest, finely grated
Nut butter for serving, optional
Jam or marmalade for serving, optional

1. Preheat the oven to 425° F. Oil a baking sheet.
2. In a large bowl, combine the flour, bran, flaxseed, wheat germ, baking powder, baking soda, cinnamon, mace, brown sugar, dried fruit and sweet potato. Stir in the yogurt, egg, oil and orange zest and mix just until combined.
3. With lightly floured hands, knead the dough in the bowl for several minutes. When smooth, turn the dough onto a lightly floured work surface and pat to a thickness of

¼ inch. Using a cookie cutter or a glass, cut into 2½-inch rounds. Gather the scraps, gently pat into a ball, flatten again and cut out more scones.

4. Place the scones on the prepared baking sheet about 1 inch apart. Bake for eight to 10 minutes, or until golden brown. Serve warm with or without nut butter and jam or marmalade.

Makes about 18 scones.

Grape Cooler

Combine equal parts of chilled unsweetened concord grape juice and club soda and serve with a squeeze of lime.

Lunch

Crab-Stuffed Papaya

Couscous

½ cup whole wheat couscous
½ teaspoon canola or safflower oil
⅛ cup fresh flat-leaf parsley, chopped
1 teaspoon fresh lemon juice

Stuffed papayas

¾ cup celery, diced
2 medium papayas (about ½ pound each), halved lengthwise and seeded
12 ounces cooked crabmeat, diced
2 teaspoons fresh lemon juice
2 teaspoons curry powder
2 tablespoons chives, finely sliced
2 tablespoons sunflower seeds, toasted, (see Note on this page)
Salt and freshly ground black pepper to taste

Garnishes

8 large leaves red leaf lettuce
12 snowpeas, blanched
4 orange wedges

1. To prepare the couscous, pour it into a medium-sized bowl and pour ½ cup boiling water over it. Cover and let stand for five minutes, or until tender. Fluff with a fork. Add the oil, parsley and lemon juice and toss gently. Set aside.
2. To blanch the vegetables for the stuffed papayas: In a medium saucepan, bring 3 to 4 cups water to a boil. Place the diced celery into a heatproof, waterproof strainer and immerse the celery in the boiling water for one minute. Lift the strainer and celery out of the water and cool under cold running water for 30 seconds. Drain well, transfer the celery to a small container and set aside. Place the snowpeas into the strainer and repeat.
3. For the salad, use a small melon baller to make papaya balls, leaving just enough papaya in the shells so that the shells retain their shape. Set the shells aside and place the papaya balls into a medium mixing bowl. Add the crabmeat, blanched celery, lemon juice, curry powder, chives, sunflower seeds and salt and pepper and toss to blend. Add the couscous and mix gently. Spoon equal portions of the mixture into the four papaya shells.
4. Place two red leaf lettuce leaves on each of four salad plates. Place a stuffed papaya half on each plate. Garnish with three snowpeas and an orange wedge and serve.

Serves four.

NOTE: To toast sunflower seeds, spread them in a small dry skillet and heat over medium-high heat for 30 to 45 seconds, shaking the pan until the seeds are fragrant and lightly browned. Immediately slide them from the pan to a plate to halt cooking.

Spinach, Mushroom and Egg Chopped Salad

3 hard-cooked omega-3 eggs, chilled
2 cups fresh baby spinach leaves, chopped
¾ cup white mushrooms, diced
Raspberry Vinaigrette (page 189)

1. To make the salad, discard two of the egg yolks or reserve for another use. Chop one egg yolk and all three egg whites and toss to mix.
2. In a large glass bowl, combine the baby spinach, mushrooms and chopped eggs. Toss with ⅓ cup of the vinaigrette and serve immediately.

Serves two.

Dinner

Orange-Ginger Chicken with Apricot-Almond Couscous

¾ cup fresh orange juice
3 tablespoons low-sodium soy sauce
3 teaspoons fresh ginger, minced
4 boneless, skinless chicken breasts (4–5 ounces each)
2 tablespoons olive oil
20 green beans
8 baby carrots
1 medium red bell pepper, julienned
Apricot-Almond Couscous (see next recipe)
4 sprigs fresh flat-leaf parsley, for garnish

1. To prepare the marinade, in a shallow glass or ceramic bowl, mix together the orange juice, soy sauce and ginger. Pour about half of the marinade into a storage container, cover and refrigerate until needed. Leave enough marinade in the bowl to cover the chicken. Add the chicken breasts, turn several times to coat, cover and refrigerate for at least one hour and up to six hours, turning several times.
2. In a nonstick sauté pan, heat the olive oil over medium heat. Lift the chicken breasts from the marinade and let the marinade drip back into the bowl and discard. Sauté the breasts for two to three minutes on each side or until golden brown. Spoon the reserved, unused marinade over the breasts. Cover, reduce the heat and simmer for five to eight minutes, or until the juices run clear when the meat is pierced with a fork or small sharp knife.
3. Meanwhile, in a steaming basket set over boiling water, steam the beans, carrots and red pepper for three to four minutes or until fork tender.
4. Spoon the couscous onto plates and put a chicken breast on top of the couscous. Coat the chicken with pan juices and spoon the green beans, carrots and peppers on the plate. Garnish with a sprig of parsley. Repeat to make three more servings.

Serves four.

Apricot-Almond Couscous

½ cup dried apricots, diced
¼ cup orange juice
1¼ cups vegetable broth or water
1 cup whole wheat couscous
Pinch of cayenne pepper
⅓ cup toasted sliced almonds
1 tablespoon orange zest

1. In a small bowl, combine the apricots and orange juice and set aside for about 15 minutes to give the apricots time to plump.
2. In a saucepan, bring the vegetable broth to a boil over high heat.
3. In a heatproof mixing bowl, combine the couscous and cayenne pepper. Pour the boiling broth over the couscous and let it stand for five minutes. Fluff with a fork. Stir

in apricots, any orange juice, the almonds and zest. Serve immediately.

Enjoy with ½ cup non-fat frozen yogurt for dessert. Makes about two cups.

Serves four.

Sesame Stir-Braised Kale

1 teaspoon sesame oil
4 garlic cloves, minced
1 tablespoon fresh ginger, minced
2 to 3 tablespoons vegetable stock or water
2 bunches kale (about 1 pound), stemmed and chopped
1 teaspoon low-sodium soy sauce
1 tablespoon sesame seeds

1. In a large nonstick skillet, heat the oil over medium-high heat. Add the garlic and ginger and cook, stirring often, for about one minute, or until softened.
2. Add the stock and kale. Reduce the heat to low, cover and cook for two to three minutes, or until the kale is wilted and tender. Drain excess liquid, if necessary. Add the soy sauce and toss gently. Cover and let stand for at least 20 minutes and up to one hour to allow the flavors to meld.
3. To serve, transfer the kale to a serving platter and sprinkle with sesame seeds. Toss and serve.

Serves eight.

Day 7 Nutritional Analysis...

Calories: 1909
Protein: 110 g
Carbohydrates: 254 g
Cholesterol: 226 mg
Total Fat: 59 g
Saturated fat: 7.9 g
Monounsaturated fat: 17.9 g
Polyunsaturated fat: 21.6 g
Omega-6: 16.3 g
Omega-3: 3.9 g
Sodium: 2047 mg
Potassium: 4123 mg
Fiber: 36 g

Percentage of Calories
Protein 22%
Carbohydrates 51%
Fat 27%

6

SuperFoods Rx Shopping Lists

Everybody knows that many of the foods we eat are not healthy for us. There are fast foods, processed foods and widely available packaged foods that have too much fat and trans fat, sodium, sugar and other nutrition negatives. It can be discouraging to shop. But there is some good news: There are many foods available in local markets that are good for you and are also delicious. I checked thousands of foods in supermarkets and other popular chain stores across the country. Many foods didn't make the cut. The ones that did, I've listed here in a SuperFoods Rx Shopping List. (This isn't meant to be a definitive list and there are other healthy foods out there that are not listed here.) These foods meet my own SuperFood criteria: they're all fairly close to whole foods—they're minimally, or "healthfully," processed...they're low or at least relatively low in sodium and fat (no trans fats)... and they're high in fiber and nutrients. They're health-promoting choices that you'll be happy to have in your fridge or pantry.

A few of these foods are available by mail order; a few are not widely available. In those cases, I've listed the phone number, street address and/or Web site of the companies or stores so that you can contact them if you choose.

Here are some tips which will help you shop for healthier foods...

- Always check the label for partially hydrogenated oils. If they are listed, don't buy the item. There is no safe amount of so-called trans fat.
- Go to the market with the mindset of a hunter-gatherer. First stop is the produce section, and then on to various whole grain products, legumes, nuts and seeds, low-fat/nonfat dairy and so forth.
- On some food labels, both sodium and potassium are listed. A potassium to sodium ratio of 4:1 or more is ideal.
- If you would like information on organic products, check California Certified Organic Farmers at *www.ccof.org.*

I was pleased to find that some chain markets—Trader Joe's and Costco, for example—carry some excellent food choices, and I list some here. I hope as we consumers demand more healthful foods, we'll be able to find these foods and more like them available everywhere.

Applesauce

- Mott's Applesauce Natural Unsweetened

Bottled Fruit/Vegetable Juices

- Ceres 100% fruit juices—multiple flavors
  www.ceresjuices.com

- Evolution Fresh juices—multiple flavors
  www.evolutionfresh.com
- Hain Pure Foods Veggie Juice
- Hain Pure Foods Carrot Juice
- Kedem Concord Grape Juice—100% Pure Juice
- L & A All Cherry, Cranberry, Pomegranate, Prune Juices
- Lakewood 100% Fruit Juices—Pure Apple
- Lakewood 100% Fruit Juices—Pure Prune
- Lakewood 100% Fruit Juices—Pure Concord Grape
- Lakewood 100% Fruit Juices—Pure Blueberry
- Lakewood 100% Fruit Juices—Pure Black Cherry (includes fiber from the fruit, fresh pressed)
  www.lakewoodjuices.com
- Campbell Low Sodium V8 100% Vegetable Juice
  www.v8juice.com
- Martinelli's Certified Organic Apple Juice
- Martinelli's Certified Organic Apple Juice—Unfiltered
  www.martinellis.com
- Minute Maid 100% Pure Apple Juice
- Minute Maid 100% Pure Squeezed Orange Juice
- Minute Maid Home Squeezed Style Calcium + D—100% Pure Orange Juice
  www.minutemaid.com
- Mountain Sun Pure Cranberry (unsweetened)
  www.mountainsun.com
  All 100% pure unsweetened cranberry juice is tart, so mix it with another, sweeter 100% pure fruit juice.
- Naked Juice (multiple flavors). My favorite is Naked Superfood 100% Juice Smoothies.
  www.nakedjuice.com
- Nantucket Nectars Premium Orange Juice
  www.juiceguys.com
- Ocean Spray 100% Juice (no sugar added, multiple flavors)
  www.oceanspray.com
- Odwalla Fruit Juices (multiple flavors). My favorite is Citrus C Monster
  www.odwalla.com
- Organic Sir Real State of the Art Fruit Juices
  www.sirreal.com
- R.W. Knudsen Family Cherry Cider
- R.W. Knudsen Family Just Blueberry
- R.W. Knudsen Family Just Pomegranate
- R.W. Knudsen Family Just Concord Grape
- R.W. Knudsen Family Organic Apple
- R.W. Knudsen Family Organic Cranberry Blueberry Juice
- R.W. Knudsen Family Organic Cranberry Pomegranate Juice
- R.W. Knudsen Family Organic Prune Juice
- R.W. Knudsen Family Organic Tomato Juice
- R.W. Knudsen Family Peach Nectar
- R.W. Knudsen Family Pineapple Nectar
- R.W. Knudsen Family Vita Pomegranate Juice
- R.W. Knudsen Family Very Veggie—Original (22 mg. of lycopene per serving)
  www.knudsenjuices.com
- Sunsweet Not From Concentrate Prune Juice with Pulp
- Sunsweet Prune Juice (100% juice with lutein, potassium and iron)
- Tropicana 100% Pure Premium Orange Juice
- Tropicana Ruby Red 100% Grapefruit Juice
- Walnut Acres Certified Organic Concord Grape Juice
- Walnut Acres Certified Organic Cherry Juice
- Walnut Acres Certified Organic Cranberry Juice
  www.walnutacres.com

- Welch's 100% Grape Juice
  Many markets private-label their fruit juice —look for 100% juice, no added sugar, preservatives, or artificial flavors/colors.

Bottled Sweet Peppers

- Mancini Sweet Roasted Peppers
  www.mancinifoods.com

Bread

- Arnold's 100% Whole Wheat Bread
  www.arnoldbread.com
- The Baker 9-Grain Whole Wheat
- The Baker Cinnamon Raisin
- The Baker Seeded Whole Wheat
- The Baker Whole Grain Rye
- The Baker 7-Grain Whole Wheat
  www.the-baker.com
- Milton's Healthy Multi-Grain Bread
  www.miltonsbaking.com
- Food for Life Sprouted Wheat Burger Buns
- The Original 100% Flourless Sprouted Grain Bread—Ezekiel 4:9 Low Sodium (organic grains)
- The Original Bran for Life Bread (organic grains)
  800-797-5090, *www.foodforlife.com*
- Pepperidge Farms Natural Whole Grain 9 Grain
- Premium Sara Lee 100% Whole Wheat Sliced Bread
  www.saralee.com
- Roman Meal California 100% Whole Wheat Bread
- Rudi's Organic Bakery Honey Sweet Whole Wheat Bread
  www.rudisbakery.com
- Vogel's Soy & Linseed Bread
- Vogel's Original Mixed Grain Bread (third party organic certified flour)
  www.vogels.co.nz

Canned Albacore Tuna

- Bumble Bee Solid White Albacore Tuna (in water)
  www.bumblebee.com
- Chicken of the Sea Low Sodium Chunk White Albacore Tuna
- Chicken of the Sea Chunk Light Tuna (in canola oil)
  www.chickenofthesea.com
- StarKist Solid White Albacore Tuna (in water)

Both Bumble Bee and Chicken of the Sea have "Very Low Sodium" choices.

Canned Clams

- Sea Watch Chopped Sea Clams
  Sea Watch International
  8978 Glebe Park Dr.
  Easton, MD 21601
  410-822-7500
  www.seawatch.com

Canned Salmon

- Bumble Bee Alaska Pink Salmon
- Bumble Bee Alaska Sockeye Red Salmon
  www.bumblebee.com
- Chicken of the Sea Pink Salmon (traditional).
  Includes the skin and bones—the healthiest way to eat salmon, as the content of omega-3 fats and calcium is higher than in the skin-and-bone-removed canned salmon.

  Almost all canned salmon is Alaskan wild salmon. We recommend that you avoid Atlantic Salmon, as it is farm-raised and has a higher mercury content.

Canned Trout

- Appel Fillets of Smoked Trout
  www.appel-feinkost.de

Canned Beans

- Eden Organic Black Beans
- Eden Organic Black-Eyed Peas

- Eden Organic Cannellini Beans
- Eden Organic Garbanzo Beans
- Eden Organic Kidney Beans
- Eden Organic Lentils
- Eden Organic Pinto Beans
- Eden Organic Small Red Beans
  www.edenfoods.com
- Westbrae Garbanzo Beans
- Westbrae Great Northern Beans
- Westbrae Kidney Beans
- Westbrae Natural Vegetarian Organic Black Beans
- Westbrae Organic Lentils
  800-434-4246, *www.westbrae.com*

Canned Chili

- Eden Organic Chili
- Health Valley 99% Fat-Free Vegetarian Chili—Spicy Black Bean
- Health Valley Mild Black Bean
  800-434-4246, *www.healthvalley.com*

Canned Evaporated Milk

- Nestlé Carnation Evaporated Fat Free Milk (vitamins A and D added)

Canned Fruit

- Dole Pineapple Chunks (in own juice)

Canned Olives

- Lindsay Large Pitted Olives

Canned Pumpkin

- Libby's 100% Pure Pumpkin

Canned and Bottled Tomato Products

- Classico Spicy Red Pepper Pasta Sauce
- Classico Tomato & Basil Pasta Sauce
  888-337-2420, *www.classico.com*
- Colavita Marinara 100% Natural
  www.colavita.com
- Emeril's Roasted Red Pepper Pasta Sauce
  www.emerils.com
- Hunt's Tomato Sauce (no salt added)
- Hunt's Tomato Paste
- Hunt's Tomato Paste (no salt added)
  www.hunts.com
- Muir Glen Organic Chunky Tomato Sauce
- Muir Glen Organic Crushed Tomato with Basil
- Muir Glen Organic Chunky Tomato and Herb Pasta Sauce
- Muir Glen Organic Fire Roasted Crushed Tomatoes
- Muir Glen Organic Fire-Roasted Whole Tomatoes
- Muir Glen Organic Ground Peeled Tomatoes
- Muir Glen Organic Tomato Paste
- Muir Glen Organic Tomato Puree
- Muir Glen Organic Whole Peeled Tomatoes
  www.muirglen.com
- S & W Petite-Cut Diced Tomatoes in Rich, Thick Juice
  www.swfinefoods.com
- Walnut Acres Organic Zesty Basil Pasta Sauce
  www.walnutacres.com

Cereal

- Alpen Swiss Style Cereal—Original Alpen Naturally Delicious Swiss Style Cereal (low fat)
- Alpen Swiss Style Cereal—No Added Sugar or Salt Alpen Naturally Delicious Swiss Style Cereal (low fat)
  www.barbarasbakery.com
- Arrowhead Mills Spelt Flakes—Organic
  www.arrowheadmills.com
- Back to Nature Classic Granola
  www.backtonaturefoods.com

- Barbara's High Fiber Original Cereal
- Barbara's Bite Size Shredded Oats Original Cereal
  www.barbarasbakery.com
- Bob's Red Mill Natural Raw Wheat Germ
- Bob's Red Mill Whole Ground Flaxseed Meal
  www.bobsredmill.com
- Breadshop's Granola Crunchy Oatbran with Almonds & Raisins
- Breadshop's Triple Berry Crunch Granola
  www.arrowheadmills.com
- Chappaqua Crunch Simply Granola with Raspberries (additional flavors)
  800-488-4602
  www.chappaquacrunchgranola.com
- Cheerios
  www.cheerios.com
- Familia No Added Sugar Swiss Muesli
- Familia Low Fat Granola
- Familia Original Recipe Muesli
  www.internaturalfoods.com
- Health Valley Organic Oat Bran Flakes
- Health Valley Organic Amaranth Flakes
- Health Valley Organic Golden Flax Cereal
- Health Valley Organic Fiber 7 Multigrain Flakes
  www.healthvalley.com
- Kashi GoLean Protein/High Fiber Cereal & Snack Bars
- Kashi GoLean Seven Whole Grains & Sesame
- Kashi GoLean Good Friends
  www.kashi.com
- Kellogg's All-Bran Complete Wheat Flakes
  www2.kelloggs.com
- Nature's Path Whole O's
- Nature's Path Organic Flax Plus Multigrain Cereal
- Nature's Path Organic Heritage Flakes
- Nature's Path Organic Multigrain Oatbran Flakes
- Nature's Path Organic Optimum Blueberry Cinnamon
- Nature's Path Organic Optimum Cranberry Ginger
  www.naturespath.com
- Organic Weetabix Whole Grain Wheat Cereal
- Post Grape-Nuts-Flakes
- Post—The Original Shredded Wheat 'N Bran
- Post—The Original Shredded Wheat
- Post—The Original Spoon Size Shredded Wheat
  www.postcereals.com
- Stone-Buhr Untoasted Wheat Germ
  www.s-bcereals.com
- Kretschmer Toasted Wheat Germ
  www.kretschmer.com
- Trader Joe's Organic Golden Flax Cereal
- Uncle Sam Original—Toasted Whole-Wheat Flakes & Flaxseed
  www.attunefoods.com

Chocolate

- Newman's Own Organics Dark
- Dove Silky Dark
- Endangered Species Organic Smooth Dark Chocolate
  www.chocolatebar.com
  (see also pages 216 and 218 for cookies and energy bars)

Cooked Cereal

- Hodgson Mill Oat Bran All Natural Hot Cereal
  www.hodgsonmill.com
- McCann's Steel Cut Irish Oatmeal
- McCann's Irish Oatmeal, Quick Cooking
- McCann's Instant Irish Oatmeal (regular)
  www.mccanns.ie
- Mother's 100% Natural Rolled Oats
- Mother's 100% Natural Quick-Cooking Barley
  www.mothersnatural.com

- Quick 1-Minute Quaker Oats
- Quaker Instant Oatmeal (regular flavor)
- Old Fashioned Quaker Oats 100% Whole Grain
  www.quakeroats.com
- The Silver Palate Thick & Rough Oatmeal
  www.silverpalate.com
- Stone-Buhr Cracked Wheat Cereal
- Stone-Buhr 4 Grain Cereal Mate
  www.s-bcereals.com
- Wheatena Toasted Wheat Cereal
  www.homestatfarm.com

Chips and Snack Food

- Abuelita Stone Ground White Corn Tortilla Chips
  S & K Industries, Inc.
  www.abuelita.com
- Certified Organic Chips by Good Health (multiple flavors)
- "Dirty" All Natural Potato Chips (multiple flavors).
  www.dirtys.com
- Eat Smart All Natural Snacks—Snyder's of Hanover Veggie Crisps
  www.eatsmartnaturals.com
- Garden of Eatin All Natural Tortilla Chips/ Sesame Blues
  866-595-8917, *www.gardenofeatin.com*
- GeniSoy Soy Crisps—Apple Cinnamon Crunch
- GeniSoy Soy Crisps—Roasted Garlic and Onion
  www.genisoy.com
- Glenny's Low Fat Soy Crisps (Barbeque, Onion & Garlic, Lightly Salted, and Salt & Pepper are recommended)
  www.glennys.com
- Guiltless Gourmet Baked Mucho Nacho Tortilla Chips (from organic yellow corn)
- Guiltless Gourmet Baked Blue Corn Tortilla Chips (from organic blue corn)
  www.guiltlessgourmet.com
- Just Veggies All Natural Snack Food
- Just Cherries
- Just Raspberries
- Just Blueberries
- Just Pineapple
- Just Carrots
- Just Corn
  www.justtomatoes.com
  The above foods are dehydrated.
- Lay's Simply Natural Sea Salt Thick Cut Potato Chips
- Ruffles Simply Natural Sea Salted Reduced Fat Potato Chips
- Tostitos Simply Natural Yellow Corn (made with organic corn)
  www.fritolay.com
- Organic Just Soy Nuts
  www.justtomatoes.com
- Pennysticks Brand Salted Oat Bran Pretzel Nuggets with Soy Protein
  www.benzels.com
- Terra Exotic Vegetable Chips
  www.terrachips.com

Cookies

- Health Valley Low Fat Mini Chocolate Chip Cookies
- Health Valley Oatmeal Raisin Cookies
  800-434-4246, *www.healthvalley.com*
  You can order from their online store.

Crackers

- Ak-mak 100% Whole Wheat Stone Ground Sesame Cracker
  www.akmakbakeries.com

- Health Valley Original Oat Bran Graham Crackers
- Health Valley Original Amaranth Bran Graham Crackers
- Health Valley Original Rice Bran Graham Crackers
- Health Valley Organic Whole Wheat Crackers
- Health Valley Organic Bruschetta Vegetable Crackers
- Health Valley Organic Garden Herb Crackers
- Health Valley Cracked Pepper Crackers
- Health Valley Sesame Crackers
- Health Valley Stoned Wheat Crackers
  www.healthvalley.com
- Kavli All Natural Whole Grain Crispbread (multiple additional flavors)
  www.kavli.com, purchase on *amazon.com*
- Kashi TLC Tasty Little Crackers
  www.kashi.com
- Wasa Fibre Crispbread
- Wasa Delikatess Crispbread
  www.wasa.com

Dips

- Athenos Mediterranean Spreads Hummus—Roasted Red Pepper
- Athenos Mediterranean Spreads Hummus—Roasted Garlic
  www.athenos.com
- Small Planet Organic Spicy Tofu Dip & Spread
  www.smallplanettofu.com
- Tribe Hummus/Classic
- Tribe Hummus/40 Spices
- Tribe Hummus/Roasted Garlic
  800-8-HUMMUS, *www.tribehummus.com*

Dried Fruit

- Hadley Pitted Deglet Dates (grown in California)
  www.hadleys.com
- Melissa's organic produce:
  - Dried Mango Slices (just mango—from Mexico)
  - Dried Thompson Seedless Grapes (just raisins—from U.S.A.)
  - Dried Papaya (just papaya—from Sri Lanka)
  - Dried Bing Cherries (plus organic cane sugar—from U.S.A.)
  - Dried Blueberries (plus organic cane sugar —from U.S.A.)
  - Dried Cranberries (plus organic cane sugar/canola oil—from U.S.A.)
  - Dried Peaches (just peaches—from U.S.A.)
  - Dried Red Tomatoes (just tomato—from Chile)
  - Pine Nuts (just pine nuts)
  - Roasted Soy Nuts (no salt—from U.S.A.)
    800-588-0151, *www.melissas.com*
- Ocean Spray Craisins Original Sweetened Dried Cranberries
  www.oceanspray.com
- Pavich Organic Raisins
- Sun-Maid Raisins
  www.sunmaid.com
- Sunsweet Gold Label Prunes—no preservatives
- Sunsweet California Pitted Dates
  www.sunsweet.com
- Sunview Certified Organically Grown Raisins
- Sunview Green Seedless Raisins
- Sunview Red Seedless Raisins
  www.sunviewmarketing.com

Eggs

- Giving Nature Organic Cage Free Hens Eggs
  www.givingnaturefoods.com
- Deb-El Just Whites All Natural 100% Dried Egg Whites
  800-421-EGGS, *www.debelfoods.com*

- Egg Beaters 99% Real Eggs
  www.eggbeaters.com
- Egg-Land's Best Grade A Eggs—Large All Natural Vegetarian Fed
  www.egglandsbest.com
- Gold Circle Farms All Natural, Vegetarian Feed Extra Nutritious Eggs (2 eggs provide 300 mg DHA omega-3)
  888-599-4DHA, *www.goldcirclefarms.com*
- Horizon Organic Extra Large Brown Eggs "Cage Free"
  www.horizonorganiceggs.com
- Chino Valley Ranchers Organic Omega-3 Eggs
  www.chinovalleyranchers.com

Enchilada Sauce

- Hatch Select Enchilada Sauce
  www.hatchmexicanfood.com

Energy Bars

- Clif Bars (Cranberry Apple Cherry and Carrot Cake are recommended)
  www.clifbar.com
- Health Valley Fat Free Blueberry Granola Bars
- Health Valley Moist and Chewy Granola Bars
- Kashi GoLean Malted Chocolate Crisp Bar
- Kashi GoLean Oatmeal Raisin Cookie Bar
  www.kashi.com
- PowerBar (Chocolate Toffee Nut and Caramel Triple Threat Peanut Fusion are recommended)
  www.powerbar.com

Frozen Buffalo

- Great Range Brand Ground Buffalo
  Rocky Mountain Natural Meats, Inc.
  2351 E 70th Ave.
  Denver, CO 80229
  www.greatrangebison.com

Frozen Burgers

Veggie "Beef"

- Boca Meatless Burgers (original vegan)
  www.bocaburger.com
- Lightlife Smart Ground Taco/Burrito (veggie ground "beef")
  800-769-3279, *www.lightlife.com*
- Yves Meatless Beef Burger
  800-434-4246, *www.yvesveggie.com*

Veggie "Chicken"

- Yves Veggie Cuisine Meatless Chicken Burger
  800-434-4246, *www.yvesveggie.com*

Veggie

- Dr. Praeger's Meatless All American Burgers
  www.drpraegers.com
- Gardenburger Veggie Medley
  www.gardenburger.com

Frozen Desserts

- Certified Organic Natural Choice Organic Sorbet (blueberry, strawberry-kiwi)
  www.ncf-inc.com
- Dreyer's Whole Fruit Sorbet, sold as Edy's Whole Fruit Sorbet east of the Rockies
  www.dreyers.com,
  www.edys.com
- Häagen-Dazs Fruit Sorbets (multiple flavors). My favorites are Mango and Raspberry.
- Häagen-Dazs Frozen Yogurt (multiple flavors)
- Stonyfield Farm Non-Fat Frozen Yogurt (multiple flavors)

Frozen Fish

- Sea Cuisine Atlantic Cod Loins
  www.seacuisine.com
- Wild Alaskan Salmon
  www.oceanbeauty.com

Frozen Fruit Bars

- Dreyer's Whole Fruit Bars, sold as Edy's Fruit Bars east of the Rockies. (strawberry, lemonade, lime, wild berry)
  www.dreyers.com
  www.edys.com

Frozen Fruit/Vegetables

- Cascadian Farms Organic Blackberries
- Cascadian Farms Organic Chinese-Style Stir Fry Blend
- Cascadian Farms Organic Gardener's Blend Premium Vegetables
- Cascadian Farms Organic Harvest Berries
- Cascadian Farms Organic Red Raspberries
- Cascadian Farms Premium Organic Edamame
- Cascadian Farms Organic Strawberries
- Cascadian Farms Organic Sweet Cherries
  800-624-4123, *www.cascadianfarm.com*
- Flav-R-Pac Oregon Berry Mix (blueberries/Marionberries/raspberries)
  www.norpac.com
- Nutri Verde No Salt Added Vegetables (broccoli & cauliflower florets with slices of carrots, zucchini & yellow squash)
  800-491-2665, *www.nutriverde.com*

Frozen Juices

- Any brand that is 100% frozen concentrated juice with no added sugar and artificial colors

Frozen Waffles

- Kashi GoLean Original 7-Grain All Natural Frozen Waffles
  www.kashi.com
- Nature's Path Made with Organic Grains Flax-Plus Waffles
- Nature's Path Gluten-Free Buckwheat Wildberry Waffles
- Nature's Path Gluten-Free Homestyle Waffles
- Nature's Path Gluten-Free Mesa Sunrise (cornmeal, amaranth and quinoa)
  www.naturespath.com
- Van's All Natural Wheat Free and Gourmet Multi-Grain Waffles
  www.vansfoods.com

Herbs/Spices/Flavor Enhancers

- It's Delish Garlic Granulated
- It's Delish Basil
- It's Delish Parsley Flakes
- It's Delish Oregano
  877-433-5474, *www.itsdelish.com*
- McCormick Granulated Onion

Honey

- Gourmet Honey Store YS/Organic Buckwheat Honey
  www.ysorganic.com
- Rita Miller's Select Honey Premium Gourmet Quality—Buckwheat Blossom
  www.millershoney.com

Jams

- Dickinson's Boysenberry Spreadable Fruit
- Dickinson's Black Sweet Cherry Spreadable Fruit
  www.dickinsonsfamily.com
- Sorrell Ridge Premium 100% Fruit—Wild Blueberry Spreadable Fruit

Ketchup

- Heinz Organic Tomato Ketchup
- Muir Glen Organic Tomato Ketchup

Margarine

- Smart Balance No-Trans Fatty Acids Buttery Spreads
  www.smartbalance.com

Nuts and Seeds

- David's Roasted & Salted Sunflower Seeds
  ConAgra Foods
  800-799-2800, *www.conagrafoods.com*
- Hoody's Classic Roast Peanuts (Original Nut House Brand). The only ingredient is roasted-in-the-shell peanuts. This means the brown skin of the peanut is present, and this is where the polyphenols and resveratrol are concentrated.
  www.hoodysnuts.com
- Kirkland Walnuts—preservative free shelled (Costco)
- Hampton Farms Plain Roasted Peanuts (no salt or oil).
  These are in the shell, which means the brown skin of the peanut is present and this is where the polyphenols and resveratrol are concentrated.
  www.hamptonfarms.com
- Planters Salted Peanuts
  www.planters.com
- Trader Joe's California Premium Walnut Halves
- Trader Joe's Fancy Raw Mixed Nuts

Packaged Fresh Berries

- California Giant Blueberries
  www.calgiant.com
- Surfside Organic Raspberries
- Surfside Organic Strawberries
  www.beachstreet.com

Packaged Greens/Vegetables

- Cut'n Clean Greens—Country Mix (collards/mustard/turnip)
  888-3GREENS, *www.cutncleangreens.com*
- Dole Salad Mix (multiple blends)
  www.dole.com
- Fresh Express Tender Lettuce Mixes (multiple blends)
  800-242-5472, *www.freshexpress.com*
- Green Giant Fresh
  www.greengiantfresh.com
- Grimmway Farms Shredded Carrots
- Grimmway Farms Carrot Chips
  800-301-3101, *www.grimmway.com*
- Mann's Sunny Shores Broccoli & Carrots
- Mann's Broccoli Cole Slaw (broccoli, carrots, red cabbage)
- Mann's Broccoli and Cauliflower
- Mann's Broccoli—Wokly Broccoli Florettes
- Mann's Vegetable Medley (broccoli, cauliflower, baby carrots)
- Mann's Cauliettes (cauliflower florets)
- Mann's Stringless Sugar Snap Peas
  800-285-1002, *www.veggiesmadeeasy.com*
- Organic Earthbound Farm Baby Spinach Salad (multiple blends)
  www.ebfarm.com
- Packaged Greens
  Tanimura & Antle, Inc.
  800-772-4542, *www.taproduce.com*
- Ready Pac (multiple blends)
  800-800-7822, *www.readypac.com*

Pancake and Waffle Mix

- Arrowhead Mills Buckwheat Pancake and Waffle Mix
- Arrowhead Mills Multigrain Pancakes and Waffle Mix
  www.arrowheadmills.com

Pasta

- Al Dente Spinach Fettuccine Noodles
  800-536-7278, *www.aldentepasta.com*
- American Beauty Healthy Harvest Pasta
- American Beauty Whole Wheat Blend Pasta (thin spaghetti style)
- American Beauty Whole Wheat Blend Pasta (spaghetti style)
  800-730-5957, *www.americanbeauty.com*
- Annie's Homegrown Organic Whole Wheat Spaghetti
  www.annies.com
- Bean Cuisine Soups (cooks in 15 minutes)
- Bean Cuisine Florentine Beans with Bow Ties (includes pasta, beans, herbs, and spices)
  Reily Foods Co.
  640 Magazine St.
  New Orleans, LA 70130
  504-524-6131
- DeBoles Organic Whole Wheat Spaghetti Style Pasta
  www.deboles.com
- Organica Di Sicilia Spaghetti
- Organica Di Sicilia Fettuccine
- Organica Di Sicilia Whole Wheat Fettuccine
- Organica Di Sicilia Whole Wheat Spirali
  www.gohunza.com
- Pasta Del Verde Spaghetti 141 Durum Whole Wheat Pasta—Enriched Macaroni Product
  www.delverde.it

Peanut Butter

- Arrowhead Mills 100% Organic Valencia Peanut Butter (no added salt, sugar, preservatives)
- Arrowhead Mills Organic Crunchy Valencia Peanut Butter
- Arrowhead Mills Organic Sesame Tahini
  www.arrowheadmills.com
- Maranatha Almond Butter (crunchy, no salt)
  www.maranathafoods.com
- Adams and Laura Scudder's Old Fashioned Organic Peanut Butters (smooth or chunky, unsalted)
  www.onlinestore.smucker.com

Popcorn

- Great Western Products' Premium America Popcorn
  30290 US Hwy 72
  Hollywood, AL 35752
- Newman's Own Organics Pop's Corn (light butter or butter flavor popcorn)
  www.newmansownorganics.com
  The above popcorn choices have no partially hydrogenated shortening and no trans-fatty acids.

Salad Dressings

- Annie's Naturals Balsamic Vinaigrette
  www.anniesnaturals.com
- Oak Hill Farms Vidalia Onion Vinaigrette
  www.vitafoodproducts.com
- Newman's Own (Recommended: Balsamic Vinaigrette, Olive Oil and Vinegar, Caesar, Ranch, Family Recipe Italian, Lite Italian Dressing, Lite Balsamic Vinaigrette, Parmesan & Roasted Garlic)
  www.newmansown.com
- My favorite salad dressing is extra virgin olive oil (any brand) plus balsamic vinegar.

Salsa—Bottled

- La Victoria Red Taco Sauce
- Santa Barbara Olive Co.—Roasted Garlic Salsa
  800-624-4896, *www.sbolive.com*
- Tostitos Simply Natural Restaurant Style Salsa
- Tostitos All Natural Chunky Salsa
  www.tostitos.com

Salsa—Fresh, Refrigerated

- Santa Barbara Mango & Peach Salsa
  www.sbsalsa.com

Sardines

- Beach Cliff Sardines in Soybean Oil
  www.beachcliff.info
- Crown Prince One Layer Brisling Sardines (oil/no salt added, packed in soybean oil) Product of Scotland.
- Crown Prince Skinless & Boneless Sardines in Olive Oil. Product of Morocco.
  Imported by: Crown Prince, Inc.
  www.crownprince.com
- King Oscar Extra Small Sardines in Purest Virgin Olive Oil
- King Oscar Finest Norwegian Sardines in Olive Oil
  www.kingoscar.com
- Yankee Clipper Lightly Smoked Sardines in Lemon Sauce
- Yankee Clipper Lightly Smoked Sardines in Soybean Oil
- Yankee Clipper Lightly Smoked Sardines in Tomato Sauce
  Purchase at:
  www.walmart.com

Soups

- Health Valley Fat Free Italian Minestrone Soup
- Health Valley Fat Free Corn and Vegetable Soup
- Health Valley Garden Organic Vegetable—Fat Free Soup
- Health Valley Low Fat Chicken Broth
- Health Valley No Salt Added Beef Flavored Broth
- Health Valley Organic Tomato Soup (no salt added)
- Health Valley Organic Split Pea Soup (no salt added)
- Health Valley Fat Free 5 Bean Vegetable Soup
  800-434-4246, *www.healthvalley.com*
- Imagine Natural Organic Creamy Broccoli Soup
- Imagine Natural Organic Creamy Butternut Squash Soup
- Imagine Natural Organic Creamy Potato Leek Soup
  www.imaginefoods.com

Soymilk

- Silk Organic Soymilk
- Silk Organic Vanilla Soymilk
  www.silksoymilk.com
- Edensoy Extra Original Organic Soymilk Fortified with Beta Carotene, Vitamins B12, E and D, and Calcium
- Edensoy Original Organic Soymilk
- Edensoy Extra Vanilla Organic Soymilk Fortified with Beta Carotene, Vitamins B12, E and D, and Calcium
  www.edenfoods.com
- Pacific Organic Ultra Vanilla Soymilk
  www.pacificfoods.com
- Westsoy Organic Unsweetened Soymilk
- Westsoy Plus Soymilk Vanilla
  www.westsoy.biz

Sun-Dried Tomatoes

- Valley Sun Premium California Sun Dried Tomatoes Julienne
  www.valleysun.com

Tea

- Bigelow "Constant Comment" Green Tea (flavored with orange and spice)

- Bigelow Green Tea
  888-BIGELOW, *www.bigelowtea.com*
- Celestial Seasonings Decaffeinated Green Tea
- Celestial Seasonings Wellness Teas
- Celestial Seasonings Green Tea—Organic
  800-434-4246, *www.celestialseasonings.com*
- Traditional Medicinals Organic Golden Green Tea
  www.traditionalmedicinals.com
- Lipton Green Tea
- Lipton Unsweetened Iced Tea
  888-LIPTONT, *www.lipton.com*
- Salada 100% Green Tea
  www.greentea.com
- Twinings of London Lady Grey Tea
- Twinings of London Earl Grey Tea
- Twinings of London China Oolong Tea
- Twinings of London Jasmine Green Tea
  800-803-6695, *www.twinings.com*

Tortillas

- Ezekiel 4:9 Sprouted Grain Tortillas (certified organic)
  www.foodforlife.com
- La Tortilla Factory Whole Wheat Low-Fat, Low-Carb Tortillas
  800-446-1516
  www.latortillafactory.com
- Tumaro's Gourmet Tortillas Honey Wheat (uses organic flour)
  www.tumaros.com

Veggie Hot Dogs

- The Good Dog
  800-434-4246, *www.yvesveggie.com*
- Lightlife Smart Dogs
  800-769-3279, *www.lightlife.com*

Whole Grain Granola

- Bear Naked All Natural Granola (assorted flavors)
  www.bearnaked.com
- Back to Nature Granola
  www.organicmilling.com
- Health Valley Low Fat Granola—Oat Bran Almond Crunch
- Health Valley Low Fat Granola—Date Almond Flavor
- Health Valley Low Fat Granola—Raisin Cinnamon
  www.healthvalley.com
- Kashi GoLean Crunch!
  www.kashi.com

Whole Grains

- Bob's Red Mill Whole Hull-Less Barley
- Bob's Red Mill Organic Medium-Grain Brown Rice
- Bob's Red Mill Organic Quinoa Grain
  www.bobsredmill.com
- Fantastic Foods Organic Whole Wheat Couscous
  www.fantasticfoods.com
- Lundberg Family Farms Organic Long Grain Brown Rice
- Lundberg Family Farms Organic Short Grain Brown Rice
- Lundberg Family Farms Organic Wild Rice Blend
  www.lundberg.com
- Texmati Long Grain American Basmati Brown Rice
  800-232-RICE, *www.riceselect.com*

Yogurt

- Alta Dena Low Fat/Non Fat Yogurt (multiple flavors)
  www.altadenadairy.com

- Cascade Fresh Low Fat/Fat Free Yogurt (multiple flavors)
  800-511-0057, *www.cascadefresh.com*
- Colombo Low Fat/Non Fat Yogurt (multiple flavors)
  www.colomboyogurt.com
- Horizon Organic Low Fat/Fat Free Yogurt (multiple flavors)
  www.horizonorganic.com
- Stonyfield Farm Organic Low Fat Yogurt (multiple flavors)
- Stonyfield Farm Fat Free Yogurt (multiple flavors)
  www.stonyfield.com

Yogurt Smoothies

- Stonyfield Farm Organic Smoothie (multiple flavors)
  www.stonyfield.com

7

LOSE WEIGHT BY EATING WELL

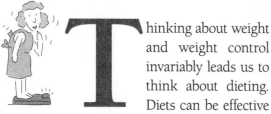

Thinking about weight and weight control invariably leads us to think about dieting. Diets can be effective and healthy. I prefer to take a more positive approach: Instead of limiting what you can eat, I suggest that you focus on making SuperFoods the largest part of your daily food intake and, instead of limiting food types, limit portion sizes. It's the "nondiet diet" that can work for a lifetime.

Portion Control = Weight Control

Recently when I was having breakfast in a hotel dining room, I ordered oatmeal with a side order of fresh fruit, as I often do. When my order arrived, I almost laughed out loud. The waiter put before me what could best be described as a boatload of oatmeal. The bowl was so large that I could almost have bathed in it. A serving of oatmeal should be about one cup—this bowl contained at least three.

Yes, oatmeal is a healthy breakfast. However, eating enough for three people would not make me three times healthier. I'm sure the hotel dining staff felt that they were being lavish in presenting such a grand bowl of food, but in fact these giant-sized portions only make it difficult for those who hate to "waste" food and/or those who simply eat what's put in front of them as they're being distracted by the table conversation.

It's no secret that many of us eat too much and we pay for our overeating with soaring rates of obesity, diabetes and other weight-related ailments. It's not that we have voracious appetites, but that we've become accustomed to eating huge amounts of food at every meal and have lost our sensitivity to what a portion size should be.

When I started working on this book, I knew that I would have to tackle the topic of weight control. Obesity rates among children as well as adults are on the rise and many people are struggling to lose weight. For many of us, weight control is a significant part of our efforts to achieve optimum health. Diet books are always popular and anything that promises to "take off pounds" is a sure bet with the public.

On the other hand, many people, particularly those who read books like this one, recognize that fad diets and weight-loss supplements won't yield results. I hope that reading this book helps you to understand that extreme modifications or limitations in your diet can have negative long-term effects if your body is being robbed of the nutrients it needs to fight disease and achieve vibrant health.

Eat Better, Lose Weight

How can people cope with obesity and/or reduce weight in a healthy but truly effective way? Many people who follow the recommendations in this book will be thrilled to see they are losing weight. This isn't surprising when you consider that the foods we recommend—whole, low-fat foods, plenty of fruits and vegetables, lean sources of protein and healthy fats—are bound to crowd out less desirable and more fattening foods. So, shifting to a higher-quality diet will surely show positive results in terms of weight control.

I also know that approaching food with a positive point of view makes an enormous difference. SuperFoods isn't about what you can't eat —it's about what you should eat. This simple fact is tremendously encouraging to people. They don't feel deprived. All of their energy is spent on finding tasty, whole foods, not on avoiding "forbidden" foods.

There was one piece in the weight-loss puzzle missing, however, and it was the one thing that many—even those knowledgeable about nutrition—forgot about. This was the key that would help people finally achieve weight control with an optimum healthy nutrition plan they could live with forever.

Portion control is the most commonly ignored element of weight control among many people. Even those of us who are eating the right foods are often hampered in our weight-loss efforts due to this single misunderstanding.

Portion Distortion

It's not surprising that we don't pay attention to portion sizes. For one thing, it seems complicated. How the heck do you judge a "portion" of salad? Or a portion of baked potato, when potatoes can be anywhere from marble size to baseball size? And food labels can be deceptive. A quick glance at a label might indicate that the food is relatively low in calories. Only closer inspection will reveal that, say, a small bag of cookies that resembles a single portion is actually designed to feed two and a half people!

Another problem is that most of us suffer from "portion distortion." This became apparent when another new food pyramid was unveiled—it recommended five to nine servings of vegetables a day. Many people were shocked. Who could possibly eat nine servings of vegetables daily? Many patients asked me about this and complained that the goal was unrealistic. They no doubt imagined servings like my hotel oatmeal bowl and figured they'd have to eat bushels of vegetables a day to comply with the new pyramid recommendations. That's when I knew what the missing link in weight control is for people who are already doing their best to follow a SuperFoods diet. The fact is that many people routinely eat two to three servings of vegetables at one sitting. Getting to nine servings isn't that formidable a challenge. But most people don't really know how big a serving size should be.

Over the years we've grown accustomed to the bigger-is-better notion that affects everything from our cars to our houses to those mounds of mashed potatoes on our dinner plates. We regularly eat in restaurants that serve us the equivalent of two dinners. One recent study found that the portion sizes of many popular restaurants and packaged foods have increased substantially over the past 20 years. Some portions exceed standard recommended sizes by as much as eight times.

Many foods and beverages nowadays are two to five times larger than when the items first became commercially available. Chocolate bars, for example, have increased in size more than 10 times since they were first introduced. It's gotten to the point where we'd probably feel cheated if the portions we were served were of normal size.

The Price of Plenty

I'm a big believer in personal choice and self-determination. But the truth is that living the supersized life of steadily increasing portions has made it very difficult for many of us to maintain an optimum weight. Over the years the effect of all those gigantic meals—even the healthy ones—begins to show. Indeed, the average American gains nearly two pounds a year—every year! If you ate just a hundred extra calories a day—for example, the difference between a large and a small potato—you could gain 10 pounds a year.

Here's the common scenario: You are served a supersized soft drink—a mega-42-ounce cup. You drink some of it and are really satisfied after enjoying about 12 ounces—a 150-calorie addition to your daily count. But that giant drink sits there and you absentmindedly sip it until by the time you're ready to toss out the cup you've consumed nearly the entire drink. Now you've sipped away about 410 calories—a whopping dent in your total daily calorie allowance. You didn't really want that much soda—or meat or oatmeal or even vegetables—you didn't even really enjoy it, but it was there and so you ate or drank it.

If you've experienced a gradual weight gain over the years, you're not alone. The average American weighs about 24 pounds more today than he did in 1960. Why? We move less, thanks partly to all those labor-saving devices, and we eat more foods—fast foods, processed foods—that are high in calories and low in nutritional value.

A large order of French fries weighs 6 ounces today...in 1960, the only size available weighed in at 2.5 ounces.

However, perhaps the single most important factor is that we're eating larger portions. According to statistics from the Centers for Disease Control and Prevention, the average number of calories Americans eat each day has risen from 1,996 to 2,247 over the last 20 years. That significant increase—251 calories per day—theoretically works out to an extra 26 pounds every year.

Many of us don't make the connection between amount of food consumed and weight gain, even though it should be apparent. The typical American thinks it's more important to cut out fat than to reduce the amounts of food he eats. When the American Institute for Cancer Research asked more than 1,000 Americans, "Which do you think is more important in maintaining or losing weight, the amount of food you eat or what kind of food you eat?" a remarkable 78 percent answered, "The kind of food you eat," and only 18 percent replied that it was "the amount of food." This is a serious misunderstanding.

Here's another very concrete way to look at the problem of portion creep and how misunderstanding portion sizes—and the calories involved—can sabotage weight control. *A single large bagel with three tablespoons of cream cheese—a typical breakfast for many people—is close to the caloric equivalent of the following...*

One large bagel with 3 tablespoons cream cheese	3 medium bananas (280 calories) Two slices light bread (80 calories) English muffin with 1 tablespoon low-sugar jam (150 calories) A cup of oatmeal (100 calories) A cup of Cheerios (100 calories)
Total calories: 700	710

By this measure, the single large bagel is the caloric equivalent of about three and a half breakfasts.

Once upon a time, a bagel weighed 1.5 ounces and was 116 calories. Today's bagels weigh 4.5 ounces and are 350 to 400 calories.

Huge portion sizes are making our lives difficult. It's not that we're stupid—it's just that we don't pay attention. When it comes to eating, most of us are driven by what we see, not by how hungry we feel. Most people eating the giant bagel described above would be full after finishing about a quarter to a third of it, but few people would stop there.

Large portions encourage you to eat more, and study after study proves it. In one study, adults given a large serving ate 30 percent more calories than when given a small one. Kids are not immune: In another study, children served large portions ate 25 percent more calories.

A particularly fascinating study was conducted by Brian Wansink of the University of Illinois. It was called "At the Movies: How External and Perceived Taste Impact Consumption Volume." Subjects at a movie theater in Chicago were given containers of stale popcorn that tasted pretty terrible. Those who got big buckets ate about 61 percent more than the people who got smaller buckets. When asked to estimate how many calories they'd consumed, both groups figured they'd eaten about the same amount.

What do we learn from this? One lesson is that it's very difficult to judge how much you're eating if the container is oversized. And perhaps the more pertinent lesson is whatever the size of the portion, *and even if it doesn't taste very good,* our impulse is to finish it.

It's time to get control of *how much you're eating* as well as what you're eating.

FAST FOOD RULES

In 2002, fast food restaurants accounted for 74 percent of the average 206 meals purchased by Americans at commercial establishments to be eaten out or taken home. We now have one fast food outlet for each 1,000 Americans, up from one in 1,400 in 1990 and one in 2,000 in 1980.

Get Your Bearings

Do you need to lose weight or maintain the weight you currently enjoy? (So few people need to gain weight that I won't address this challenge here.) Most people have a pretty good idea of where they fall in terms of their optimum weight. If you're uncertain, figure out your BMI (body mass index). Your BMI is a number that relates your height and weight to show approximately how much fat you carry. If your BMI is 25 or more, you're overweight and possibly at risk for adverse health effects. If your BMI is over 30, you're obese and your risk for diabetes and high blood pressure is significant. *To figure out your BMI, here's a simple formula…*

$$\text{BMI} = \left(\frac{\textbf{weight in pounds}}{\textbf{height in inches} \times \textbf{height in inches}}\right) (\times\ 703)$$

You can also go to this Web site, which will calculate your BMI instantly: *http://nhlbisupport.com/bmi/bmicalc.htm.*

A moderate weight loss of 5 percent of body weight can produce significant health benefits and is a reasonable goal for most people.

Once you know roughly how much weight you need to lose to reach your optimum weight, you have to accept a simple reality that's sometimes difficult to face: You cannot lose weight quickly and expect it to stay off. If, like the typical American, you've been gaining a few pounds a year, it may well have taken you 10 years to put on the extra weight. If that's the case, you can't reasonably expect to lose it in a few weeks.

My recommendation is to not set a timetable. Rather, focus on a more positive goal: eating SuperFoods in proper portions. The weight loss will take care of itself. If you follow the HealthStyle recommendations, you'll be exercising, getting a healthy amount of sleep and practicing stress control. These efforts will help you in your quest to lose weight. Health takes time, and weight loss takes time. Give yourself the HealthStyle gift of one *year* of effort. I know that if your goal is to lose weight, you will.

Once upon a time a chair 18 inches wide was standard. Today, auditoriums, stadiums and even subway cars are installing new seats that are several inches wider to carry the new, bigger Americans.

You Really Can Do It

Losing weight and maintaining an ideal weight are important goals for most of us. If you are overweight, this single issue can come to dominate your life, affecting countless daily decisions and ultimately becoming the primary lens through which you see yourself.

Most overweight people have tried and failed to lose weight. Most of us know that diets don't really work for the vast majority of people—certainly not in the long term. I'm also very concerned about the long-term health effects of many diets. Once you appreciate how an optimum varied diet of whole foods predicts short- and long-term health, it's hard to imagine how you can feel comfortable eating a diet that is extreme in any kind of way.

Here is how you can safely, permanently, healthfully lose weight…

SuperFoods + Exercise + Portion Control

The SuperFood information you need is here in this book. You have the exercise information too (see page 236). If you make time to set and reach goals, you'll look back on the year as a turning point. Give yourself the gift of time—the time you need to be healthy. The final part of the equation—portion control—will take just a bit of focus, but it will be a powerful ally in your efforts.

Portion control really works. In one recent study, controlling portion size was the most effective strategy for losing weight and keeping it off. The study of more than 300 people found that those who included portion control as part of their overall weight-loss strategy—in addition to exercise and healthy food choices—were able to lose more weight and keep it off compared with those who simply exercised and ate healthier foods. Another study found significant differences in weight-loss (and cholesterol and fasting insulin) reduction in women who ate portion-controlled entrées versus those who ate the same proportions of fats, carbs and protein but without portion controls. Both groups met weekly and the non-portion-control group was advised on the recommended number of servings of foods. The study concluded, "Accurate portion control is an important factor in weight loss success."

Smaller Is Better

You've got to do a little bit of work if you want to make portion control work for you. But the time you put into it in the beginning will pay off sooner than you think. Just remember, you're fighting an entire supersized culture and you won't succeed without a little preparation.

First, you need to learn what a portion size is. Try this: Take out a bowl and pour dry cereal into it. Pour in what you might have for breakfast. Then pour that cereal into a measuring cup. Most people pour out about a cup of cereal. But a portion of cereal is only one-half to three-quarters of a cup for most cereals.

Pasta is almost always a portion pitfall. Next time you're serving pasta, try the exercise again: Put a portion of pasta in a bowl. Then pour it into a measuring cup. Many restaurants serve about two cups of pasta in a serving. A portion of pasta should be about a half cup!

With packaged foods it's easier to figure out how much you'll be eating because the serving size will be listed on the package. Unfortunately, most of us don't bother to check this information. Right now, pull out some of the packaged foods that you frequently eat and check the serving sizes. Do they correspond to how much you usually eat at a sitting? Following is a list of tips that will help you determine various aspects of portion control, but it's very important that you imprint on your mind what an appropriate portion size actually looks like. Take a few minutes to study this chart below.

Check out the pictures and actual sizes of servings on the new food pyramid. Go to the government pyramid Web site (*www.mypyramid.gov/pyramid/index.html*) and in the "Inside the Pyramid" section, click on the food that interests you. You'll find useful information on actual sizes as well as photos.

Food	**Serving**	**Looks Like**
Chopped vegetables	½ cup	½ baseball or rounded handful for an average adult
Raw leafy veggies	1 cup	1 baseball or fist for average adult
Fresh fruit	1 medium piece	1 baseball
	½ cup chopped	½ baseball or rounded handful for average adult
Dried fruit	¼ cup	1 golf ball or scant handful for average adult
Pasta, rice, cooked cereal	½ cup	½ baseball or rounded handful for average adult
Ready-to-eat cereal	1 ounce, which varies from ¼ cup to 1¼ cups (check label)	
Meat, poultry, seafood	3 ounces (boneless cooked weight from 4 ounces raw)	deck of cards
Dried beans	½ cup cooked	½ baseball or rounded handful for average adult
Nuts	⅓ cup	level handful for average adult
Cheese	1½ ounces (2 ounces if processed cheese)	1 ounce looks like 4 dice

Source: U.S. Department of Agriculture

Here are some practical tips on how to make portion control work for you...

- Practice measuring. Fill a measuring cup with the proper size portion of vegetables, rice, etc. Empty it onto a plate so you can see what these serving sizes look like. Take note of how much of the plate is covered. This will help you in the future, even if you only do it once.

- Downsize your dishes—you eat with your eyes as well as your fork. If you're putting a half cup of cereal in a giant bowl, you will feel deprived. Use smaller plates and bowls at home. You can even buy Mesu "portion control" bowls that could be a great diet aid. One set of six pretty nesting bowls that's available on-line has bowls marked in portion sizes that make serving easy (see *marketplace.hgtv.com*). Of course, you can simply create your own portion-control serving dishes by using measuring cups to determine how much to serve.

- Adjust the balance of food on your plate. A SuperFoods plate is mainly vegetables and healthy whole grains with meat (or fish or a vegetarian substitute) as a side dish. The American Institute of Cancer Research has introduced "The New American Plate," which offers guidelines about portion size and the balance of foods on your plate. A wealth of material can be found on its Web site, *www.aicr.org*.

- Don't serve meals "family style" with platters on the table. It's too easy to continue eating even if you're full when the food is in front of you. Rather, serve food on plates with the appropriate amounts on them. Remember, it takes about 20 minutes to feel satiated. Give yourself some time and you might not be interested in seconds after all.

- Store leftovers in separate, portion-controlled amounts. Consider freezing portions that you won't eat for a while.

- Never eat out of a bag or carton. If you're tempted to eat ice cream from the carton, only buy frozen treats in individual servings.

- If you're eating in a restaurant, consider sharing portions or ask for smaller portions. If the portions are large, make a point of setting some of the food aside and ask the waiter to wrap it for you "to go." My wife and I often each order a salad with dressing on the side and then share one entrée. If you simply can't resist dessert, share it with others at the table.

Be restaurant savvy! Some cuisines are notorious for being served in huge portions. Pasta, for example, is often served in amounts that would be sufficient for three or four meals. Chinese restaurants serve abundant portions as well. Some studies have found that Chinese food servings can be up to a pound and a half each, which would be enough to feed four people.

Keep this in mind when you order in or eat out. Share portions. Don't be shy about asking for a doggie bag so you can finish the meal at another time. Order steamed vegetables and brown rice, and use both to mix with any other entrées to reduce the calorie, fat and sodium content of an individual portion.

- Consider ordering a "child's meal" in a restaurant. The portion will be smaller and you'll save money. Some restaurants won't allow this if you're an adult but few will restrict you if you're getting the meal to go.

- Check the serving sizes of tiny crackers or cookies and count out the proper amount. We often eat more of them than we think we are.

- Check the label before you assume that a tiny package is just one serving. A pitfall of "single portion"–sized packaged foods is that sometimes they're not single portions at all. Some small-portion packages are actually meant to be one and a half servings or more.

- Consider repackaging food into serving-sized packages at home. You probably wouldn't want to bother doing this with cereal, but it could be helpful with cookies or dried fruits, nuts and seeds, popcorn or pretzels. If you measure the appropriate amounts into portion controlled bags or small plastic containers, you'll be less tempted to overindulge.

• Check calorie counts and pay attention to portion sizes of fat-free and sugar-free foods. They still have calories—sometimes as many as their full-fat versions—and those calories count just as much. The same is true for sugar-free foods. Many people think the word "free" means you can eat all you want. Not so.

Regular exercise is critical to any weight-loss program. You must move if you want to lose. Check out the ERA exercise plan. You'll find it simple to work into your daily life.

The Satiety Factor

Controlling weight isn't always about eating less, it's about eating smarter. The simple unchanging fact is that weight loss is a result of taking in fewer calories. Adding exercise speeds the process.

Calories come in all different sizes. If you're eating SuperFoods and watching portion intake, you don't need to be too worried about calories, but there is a trick that will help speed you on your weight-loss way. Satiety is a term that refers to the feeling of fullness after eating. It's the feeling that, if we listen, tells us we've had enough and it's time to stop. If you can promote feelings of satiety, it will be easier to keep portion sizes appropriate and calorie intake low.

There is a simple way to increase satiety: Increase your water intake. Foods that contain a lot of water, in general, are low-calorie-density foods—low in calories and high in volume. Think soups and salads. They fill you up, not out. Barbara Rolls has researched and written extensively on this successful dieting strategy. In her books *Volumetrics* and *The Volumetrics Eating Plan,* she outlines how adding water to foods increases the volume you can consume and the resulting satiety without increasing calories.

Others have confirmed this approach. In one study, researchers found that adding a large, low-calorie salad before the entrée actually reduced overall calorie intake. Study participants were served three cups of salad at 100 calories before their pasta lunch. All study subjects were allowed to eat as much pasta as they liked. Those eating the salad ate 12 percent fewer calories overall compared with those who skipped the salad. Over a year's time, this kind of calorie reduction could lead to about a 10-pound weight loss.

If your diet is primarily made up of SuperFoods, you are already getting a satiety boost. Whole-grain foods, vegetables and fruits are all choices that make you feel full. It can still help, however, to focus on servings of soups and salads before meals that will help to satisfy you and keep you from overeating.

Here is a general idea of what you should be eating...

	Daily Servings
Vegetables	5–7 servings (include dark leafy greens most days)
Fruits	3–5
Soy	1 or more
Animal protein	0–2
Vegetarian protein	3–6
Healthy fats	1–2
Whole grains	5–7
High-calcium foods	2–3
Nuts and seeds	5 (weekly)
Fish	2–4 (weekly)

Note to postmenopausal women who are on diets: A recent study found that postmenopausal women who were dieting absorbed less calcium from food than nondieting women. As women over 50 are supposed to consume 1,200 to 1,500 mg of calcium a day, it appears that women trying to lose weight should shoot for roughly 1,800 mg a day.

A Note on Overweight Kids

It's no secret that too many kids today are overweight. A recent study revealed an interesting, sobering fact: For the first time since the early 1800s, life-expectancy gains could be reversed for our children, who may well live shorter, less healthy lives than their parents. Why? Primarily because of the soaring rates of childhood obesity. Childhood obesity is a large and complex topic. Suffice it to say here that parents should not ignore childhood obesity as "baby fat." An overweight child needs adult help and support.

A Kaiser Family Foundation report recently reviewed more than 40 studies on the role of media in the nation's dramatic increase in the rates of childhood obesity. The report concluded that the majority of scientific research indicates that children who spend the most amount of time with media are more likely to be overweight. However, contrary to common assumptions, most of the research reviewed for this report didn't find that children's media use displaces physical activities. It seems that children's exposure to billions of dollars' worth of food ads and marketing may be a key mechanism whereby media promotes childhood obesity. The report cites studies showing that the typical child sees approximately 40,000 ads a year on TV, and the majority of ads targeted to kids are for candy, cereal, soda and fast food. Many of the ads enlist kids' favorite TV and movie characters to sell these foods.

If you have an overweight child, it can be a challenge to tactfully help him (or her) to get back in shape, but it's critically important for the sake of your child's future health to do so. You are your child's best ally in this effort. There are many excellent books available today that will give you guidance on how to cope with the physical and emotional issues of youthful obesity.

Thirteen Ways to Avoid Childhood Obesity

- Strive for a BMI of less than 25 before becoming pregnant.
- Avoid excessive weight gain during pregnancy.
- Try to breast-feed for 12 months.
- Introduce children to SuperFoods as soon as they begin solid foods.
- Make at least 30 minutes of fun physical activity a daily priority.
- Eliminate foods containing high-fructose corn syrup and/or partially hydrogenated oils.
- Make breakfast mandatory.
- Whenever possible, send your child to school with a homemade lunch and/or snack (e.g., carrots, apples, dried apricots, dried plums, figs, celery with peanut butter, raisins and dates, whole-grain muffins/cookies).
- Have a house rule of no more than one hour daily of TV or computer play time.
- Help your child develop good sleep habits and remember that most teens need eight and a half to nine hours of sleep each night.
- Make family dinners a priority.
- Make fast-food meals an occasional treat, not a habit.
- Encourage three servings daily of low-fat/nonfat dairy foods.

How to Pack a "Grade A" Lunchbox

Now here's a challenge worthy of any survivor-type show: Pack five healthy, nutritious lunches that a third-grader will actually eat. Children can be so finicky in their food tastes and so sensitive to lunchroom food fashions that getting them to eat what you pack is a daunting task. Don't give up: If you're willing to experiment and are open to hearing the truth from your child ("Did you really eat those baby carrots?"), then you can come up with some lunch ideas that are not only nutritious but also popular with your child. *Here are some suggestions and tips for packing a lunch that's both healthy and delicious...*

The first thing parents often forget when packing a lunchbox is the preferences of their child. Many of us pack a lunch for a fantasy child who will eat the foods we believe are nourishing.

Use soda as a special treat, and when possible, choose diet soda. Sugar-sweetened soft drinks contribute 7.1 percent of the total energy intake and represent the largest single food source of calories in the U.S. diet. In general, soft-drink consumption tends to be a marker for a poor overall diet and an unhealthy lifestyle. One can of soda a day can lead to a 15-pound weight gain in one year if the calories aren't subtracted elsewhere in the diet, but studies support the finding that when people increase their soft-drink consumption, they don't reduce their solid-food consumption to balance things out.

So cut out the soda for a quick, easy way to improve your diet and lose weight. Substitute seltzer or club soda with a splash of fruit juice or squeeze of lemon or lime.

Many of us don't know that this lunch lands in the garbage can in the school cafeteria.

So, the first rule in successful lunch packing is to keep your child's tastes in mind. If she never eats a turkey sandwich at home, there's not much chance she's going to eat one at school. This may mean bending the rules a bit. If you know he'll happily eat cereal for lunch, give it to him! If she'd rather have some fresh carrot sticks and onion dip, with perhaps a slice of whole wheat bread smeared with honey, that's fine too.

Parents sometimes lose touch with what their child's daily nutrition needs are. According to the U.S. Department of Agriculture, children between six and 11 years old need about 1,200 to 2,200 calories a day, depending on activity level. This translates roughly to two cups of low-fat milk; two servings of meat or a protein alternative; six servings of whole grains, such as pastas, cereals and breads; and at least five servings of fruits and vegetables.

Of course, these calorie needs will vary widely with your child's activity level. A very active child who plays sports daily will need more calories than one who is more sedentary.

Two important food categories to keep in mind when preparing school lunches are protein and complex carbohydrates. Children's growing bodies need high-protein foods during periods of growth and complex carbs to break down slowly for sustained energy.

Make up a list of foods in both these categories that your child likes. You can even create a "lunchbox menu" so your child can pick which foods he'd like on which day. Often, the more involved a child feels in the process of selecting and preparing foods, the better the chances that she'll actually eat them.

Here are some ideas...

- Use whole wheat flour tortillas to make healthy wraps. Fill them with tuna, turkey or lean ham, and add lettuce, some shredded low-fat cheese, some shredded carrot and a light smear of mayo.

• Most kids love rice cakes. Pack peanut butter or another nut butter separately for the child to spread onto the cake.

• There's nothing wrong with cold pizza if your child likes it. Go light on the cheese and add sliced vegetables if your child will eat them.

• Kids love mini-muffins. Find a recipe for healthy ones without much sugar—a carrot muffin or a raisin bran muffin—and bake them in the small tins.

• Yogurt is a great lunch choice. Send along a separate container of fresh (or no-sugar-added canned) fruit to be mixed in.

• Mix up a personalized trail mix of your child's favorite cereal, adding raisins, unsalted nuts, other chopped dried fruits and mini-pretzels.

• Send along graham crackers spread with cream cheese and dotted with raisins.

• Baked tortilla chips with a small container of bean dip or salsa make a great accompaniment to fresh fruit and perhaps string cheese.

• Use a whole wheat pita pocket instead of bread for favorite sandwich fillings. Stuff with tuna and vegetables, hummus and shredded lettuce, or any other preferred filling.

• Peanut butter and banana bread or even plain old peanut butter and jelly on whole wheat makes a fine lunch.

• Air-popped popcorn is always a welcome treat. Salt it lightly.

• Fruit, of course, makes a great dessert. Just don't send fruit that's too messy or difficult to peel or eat easily. Cut-up fruit is an alternative to whole. Be sure that it's not a fruit that will discolor once exposed to air.

• Look for healthy chips for snacks. Two good choices are salsa with mesquite kettle chips and Trader Joe's Soy and Flaxseed tortilla chips. ❦

8

EXERCISE YOUR WAY TO HEALTH

It's time to look at the most important elements in your HealthStyle. We're tackling that most challenging habit—exercise—because it is perhaps the single critical change you can make in daily life—along with eating SuperFoods—that will improve your health, your spirits and your future.

You must exercise. It's that simple. You cannot fully realize the benefits of HealthStyle if exercise is not a part of your life. If you're thinking right now that this is where you tune out because you've never been able to exercise, let me tell you something that should be encouraging: I have a whole new approach to exercise that works even for confirmed couch potatoes. First I want you to understand how important exercise is to your future health. Once you understand how exercise amplifies all the good things you're doing for your health and how powerful a tool simple movement is in preventing disease, I'm sure you'll resolve to get active.

Here's a way to think about exercise that will motivate you: You are dangling by a line—a lifeline—over the abyss. That line is keeping you alive, keeping you a full participant in life, keeping you hanging on. You want this line to be as strong and reliable as possible. It's made up of four strands woven together. On your "healthline" the four strands are nutrition, exercise, adequate sleep and personal peace. Together, they make up a powerful, reliable health insurance. The synergy of their separate powers can keep you alert, flexible, energetic and optimistic for a long, long time—maybe, with a little luck, to near age 100.

> *Eating alone will not keep a man well; he must also take exercise. For food and exercise, while possessing opposite qualities, yet work together to produce health.*
>
> —Hippocrates, fifth century

Neglect one of these strands and you're in jeopardy. Every fast-food binge, every sedentary month, every frantic year of uncontrolled stress, sleepless nights and spiritual voids fray a few strands in the healthline. Of course, you may be lucky—you may never break a sweat in your life or you may eat fast food daily for a half century and never suffer any consequences. This scenario is highly unlikely but not impossible. Do you want to take the chance of hanging by a frayed rope? Do you want to trust to luck that either one or both of the other two strands will hold?

If you are reading this book you're probably looking to improve your health and if so, exercise must become part of your daily routine.

Yes, I'm repeating myself, but exercise is that important. Now here's the good news: It's time to simplify our approach to exercise. Too many of my patients have been turned off by recommendations that are confusing or don't suit their lifestyles. I have a solution: The HealthStyle ERA Exercise Program, which will be described in detail later once I've demonstrated how important exercise is. It's a simple program and I've yet to meet someone who can't do it.

Perhaps you already exercise regularly. If so, that's great: Keep it up. Most people find that once they begin an exercise program, they see results and stick with it. So bear with me while I convince those who don't exercise, or who've tried and failed, to make physical activity part of their daily lives.

A Nation and a World at Rest

First, a little background...We were born to move. That's literally true. We are here today because many generations ago our ancestors were running around procuring food. The equation was simple: Move or die. In fact, it's been estimated that Paleolithic man burned approximately 1,000 calories a day and consumed about 3,000 calories a day. Today, in affluent Western nations, we consume approximately 2,100 calories a day and burn *only about 300 calories in daily activity.* A little quick math will tell you that we burn less than a third as much as our ancestors did in daily calories.

As recently as a century ago, 30 percent of all the energy used in the American workplace came from human muscle power. Today, the workplace is operating on brain power: Only a tiny percentage of us use our muscles for anything more demanding than moving a computer mouse. It's not only that we don't expend energy at work, we hardly spend energy at all. With our TV remotes and vacuum cleaners that push themselves, our power mowers and snowblowers, and our reliance on cars to get anywhere, we have come to a near total standstill as far as energy expenditure is concerned.

Sedentary individuals may lose 23 to 35 percent of muscle mass over the course of their adult lives. This loss causes a loss of strength and balance, and an overall physical decline.

Statistics highlight the facts: Nearly 30 percent of American adults are entirely sedentary and another 46 percent don't get enough exercise. That means only about a quarter of Americans get sufficient exercise.

Do you think that while you might not be Olympic athlete material you certainly get lots of daily activity? Think again. When researchers from the Centers for Disease Control and Prevention (CDC) evaluated more than 1,500 people who claimed to be walkers, they found that only 5 percent of the surveyed group actually walked enough to realize any benefits.

Where does this leave us? With a genetic makeup that thrives on lots of daily activity and a relatively low caloric intake, we are living in a world that encourages the exact opposite. In other words, we now are watching a lethal mix of a genetic makeup suffering from the toxic circumstances of *increased* daily calorie intake and *decreased* daily activity. It's no wonder that chronic diseases are rampant in our culture.

Obviously we cannot change our genetic heritage. But we can change our behavior: Lower calories...increase exercise!

One in three Americans over age 50 is *completely* sedentary.

Benefits of Exercise

The benefits of exercise are truly extraordinary. Indeed, if some clever salesman could sell exercise as, let's say, "The E Technique," and convince people of all the benefits they'd gain from using this technique, he would be a billionaire! *Here's how exercise can help you live better today and as the years go by...*

- Exercise can make your heart stronger.
- Exercise burns calories and helps you maintain a healthy weight. Exercise is essential for keeping off lost weight.
- Exercise decreases inflammatory markers (e.g., C-reactive protein).
- Exercise helps to control your blood sugar and thus helps to manage or prevent diabetes.
- Exercise can improve circulation, which has myriad beneficial health effects.
- Exercise can decrease blood pressure.
- Exercise increases your cognitive ability, including your ability to concentrate and remain alert.
- Exercise before or after a meal diminishes the postprandial rise in potentially harmful triglycerides (a type of fat).
- Exercise decreases your risk for metabolic syndrome.
- Exercise can decrease the levels of low-density lipoprotein LDL ("bad") cholesterol, and increase the levels of high-density HDL ("good") cholesterol.
- Exercise boosts the immune system.
- Exercise can reduce back pain.
- Exercise lowers your risk for upper respiratory infections.
- Exercise helps relieve arthritis.
- Exercise lowers your overall risk of dying prematurely.
- Exercise can make you stronger and more flexible.
- Exercise, particularly weight-bearing exercise, can make your bones stronger.
- Exercise increases your level of endorphins—brain chemicals that increase your sense of well-being. Thus exercise can improve mood and could even fight depression.
- Exercise reduces the frailty of old age.
- Exercise is an essential activity to prevent cataracts and age-related macular degeneration.

In one study conducted in northern California, approximately 20 percent of the subjects reported that they had had *no vigorous activity for the past 20 years!* In this study, 13 percent of the colon cancer cases could be attributed to physical inactivity.

There's no question that the positive benefits of physical activity are extraordinary. *Here is a list of the diseases and conditions that exercise can help prevent and/or improve...*

- Coronary artery disease
- Heart disease
- Stroke
- Colon cancer
- Endometrial cancer
- Breast cancer
- Prostate cancer
- Osteoporosis
- Obesity
- Type II diabetes
- Depression
- Dementia
- Cataracts and macular degeneration
- Chronic lung disease
- Arthritis
- Disability

This is an impressive list. Keep in mind that many of the physiological benefits will occur *immediately*. While preventing dementia or osteoporosis or coronary artery disease would probably rank as a top long-term goal, you don't have to wait till old age for the benefits of exercise to kick in. Exercise will give you an immediate boost in mood, mental acuity and overall energy levels.

This isn't surprising when you appreciate the dramatic effect that physical activity has on the human body. Yes, you're sweating a bit, probably breathing heavily, and perhaps you feel your muscles aching. However, here's what's happening on a cellular level when you're active: You're increasing the activity of free-radical scavenging enzymes, improving immune function, increasing circulating T- and B-lymphocytes, reducing body fat, increasing gastrointestinal motility, altering hormone levels, improving insulin resistance, reducing triglyceride levels and providing beneficial effects on the inflammatory response. Appreciating the intensely synergistic effects of physical activity makes it easier to see why its health benefits are so extraordinary.

EXERCISE KEEPS YOU YOUNG

Guess what? Much of the overall physical and mental decline we experience between the ages of 30 and 70 has *more to do with a sedentary lifestyle* than with the aging process. Exercise slows the deterioration of a host of bodily systems. It helps reverse impairments in sleep, sexual and cognitive functions as well as loss of muscle mass and bone strength.

Exercise and the Brain

Most of us know that exercise affects our bodies. That's pretty obvious. We become stronger, sometimes slimmer and more flexible. I've found that many people are amazed to learn that exercise has a dramatic effect on the brain. Even those of us who think we can live with some extra body fat or less flexibility or even a higher disease risk will be motivated to exercise when we realize that doing so helps preserve our brains! I'm going to go into detail on this aspect of exercise because it affects everyone (with particular benefits for women, for men, for older folks and for parents) and because it's a powerful incentive to get moving.

It's dismaying to learn that the human brain begins to lose tissue early in the third decade of life. *The average lifetime losses are estimated at roughly 15 percent of the cerebral cortex and 25 percent of the cerebral white matter.* This loss of tissue is closely related to declines in cognitive performance during the same time period.

Exercise to the rescue. In a meta-analysis of eighteen controlled studies conducted over the past 40 years it was found that aerobic exercise improves cognitive ability in people over 55. Interestingly, the people who showed the most dramatic improvement were previously sedentary. Moreover, relatively brief programs (one to three months long) provided as much benefit as moderate programs (four to six months long), though, as you might guess, the longer time a subject exercised, the greater the overall improvements.

There are now other studies that show similar results. *Better cardiovascular fitness will produce a brain that is more plastic and adaptive to change.*

A study published in 2003 demonstrates that physical exercise actually stimulates physiological changes in the brain. In this study, researchers scanned the brains of 55 people ages 55 to 79 and tested their aerobic fitness. Then, using MRIs, researchers found that physically fit subjects had less age-related brain-tissue shrinkage than subjects who were less fit.

One study of normal people 55 years old and older showed that the areas of the brain most gravely affected by aging also showed the greatest benefits from aerobic fitness.

We now have confirmation that the role of cardiovascular fitness as a protector and enhancer of cognitive function in older adults has a solid biological basis. In a nutshell, the simplest and most inexpensive way to delay the effects of senescence on human brain tissue is to get up out of your chair and start moving.

Personally, I find the brain-boosting benefits of exercise powerfully motivating. Many of my patients, especially older folks, agree. It's frightening to think that you could face a future with diminished mental ability. Most of us could imagine a happy life despite many disabilities, but cognitive decline is not one of them.

One study found that physical inactivity was an even greater risk to health than tobacco smoking. In this study, conducted on a Chinese population, one-fifth of deaths of those over age 35 in Hong Kong in 1998 were due to physical inactivity.

Especially for Women

Women have special challenges when it comes to physical activity, but also particular benefits to gain when they are active. Women begin with a disadvantage in the fitness wars: Their reserves of muscle mass are considerably lower than those of men. They are generally weaker than men, with more body fat and less muscle tissue. As they age, their loss of musculoskeletal capacity affects them sooner and more pervasively than men. They begin to feel the impact of reduced fitness at least 10 years before men.

Sadly, the statistics tell us that women are even less active than men: More than 70 percent of adult women do not engage in any regular activity. And women stand to gain a great deal from better fitness—maybe even more than men. One study of 5,721 women found that fitness was twice as strong a factor in preventing death than in men. In another study, previously sedentary women who became active halved their mortality rates from all causes.

Most unfortunately, women who are sedentary often suffer from the results of decline *before they're even aware it's happening.* Half the women in the United States die of cardiovascular disease, and nearly two-thirds of women who die suddenly from cardiovascular disease had no previous symptoms. Also, elderly women can begin to suffer frailty, loss of mobility, balance and so forth, which might never had occurred had they been physically active.

Studies have shown that women in their sixties and seventies, compared with those in their twenties, have lost 30 to 39 percent of their former strength. Again, women often find they're beginning to suffer the damaging results of a sedentary lifestyle before they even realize the extent of their decline.

There is very good news for women, however, on what they stand to gain from regular physical activity. For one thing, adding exercise to your life can lower your risk of cardiovascular disease—the number one killer of U.S. women. Additionally, there's evidence that improved fitness, regardless of any changes in weight, blood pressure or lipid levels, improves your overall health picture. This is extremely good news for women because it puts the focus back on basics: Work on overall fitness with exercise and diet and you'll make giant strides in improving your overall health status. Once you get moving, pay attention to your optimum weight, blood pressure and cholesterol levels.

Exercise has been proven to reduce a woman's risk for coronary artery disease, stroke, type II diabetes, breast and colon cancer, as well as osteoporosis.

I've already mentioned that exercise can reduce a woman's risk for cardiovascular disease. An important meta-analysis concluded that physically active women had half the heart disease of those who were sedentary. Even more exciting for some women: *Vigorous* activity is not necessary for lowering your risk of cardiovascular disease. Women who walk one hour a week had half the coronary artery disease as those who were sedentary.

As little as one hour a week of walking yields a lower risk for heart disease, and the walking need not be fast-paced to prove beneficial. The time spent walking was more important than the walking pace.

Here's the little bonus I share with my women patients who are totally sedentary: One recent study of more than 80,000 women showed that the greatest decrease in disease risk is a result of boosting activity from less than one hour a week to between roughly one and two hours a week. This is not at all difficult to achieve! In this study, walking conveyed approximately the same benefit as more vigorous activities among the middle-aged and older women.

Check out the fitness planner at *MealsMatter.org*. You can find it at *www.mealsmatter.org/eatingforhealth/tools/MFP*.

In addition to a reduction in cardiovascular risk, women derive other important benefits from exercise. Women, particularly early postmenopausal women, must work to fight the bone loss that occurs as they transition to a postmenopausal state. Exercise—especially weight training—plays an important role in fighting bone loss and resulting osteoporosis.

There's also evidence that regular workouts help reduce the hot flashes and night sweats associated with menopause. A Swedish study followed 142 menopausal women who did not use hormones. Regular exercisers in this group reported half the number of moderate and severe hot flashes compared with those who did no regular exercise.

Eight years after this initial study, additional research showed that only 5 percent of very active women experienced several hot flashes compared with 14 to 16 percent of women who were sedentary. In this study, weight, smoking or hormone therapy could not explain the difference in results.

Young women who exercise just a few hours a week in their teenage years can lower their likelihood of developing breast cancer by 30 to 35 percent. The operating theory is that exercise, even in relatively small doses, promotes a kind of biological shield against cancer.

Especially for Men

Many men have an all-or-nothing approach to exercise. The "no pain/no gain" concept really appeals to them (even though it's now generally recognized as *ineffective*). They're either weekend warriors, sweating it out for two hours on the squash court every Saturday, or total couch potatoes, enjoying their golf and tennis on the big screen.

For those of you who go crazy on the weekends and are stiff, sore and immobile for the rest of the week, it's time to educate, moderate and recalibrate your exercise habits with the new HealthStyle ERA Program (see page 247). For those of you who haven't moved since your last phys ed class in high school, hear that sound in the distance? It's the whistle of your new HealthStyle PE instructor getting you back in action.

The health benefits of physical activity are just too powerful to ignore. If you skipped earlier sections in this chapter outlining the specific benefits of exercise, go back and read them now. You need to believe that the effort of physical activity is worth it.

Men have some advantages over women when it comes to health. Yes, women do live longer but the gap is closing. In general, men are larger and tend to have more lean muscle mass. This means that their bodies burn calories more readily than women's bodies. Indeed, preserving and increasing that lean muscle mass is one of the goals of exercise.

While men have the potential for dramatic health gains when they adopt an exercise program, they are often stymied by simple bad habits and the belief that they'll never get back to the "fighting form" they enjoyed in their teens and twenties.

I often see a certain look in a patient's eyes when I recommend exercise. It says, "Don't waste your breath, Doc. I'll listen, if you insist, but there's no way I'm giving up the remote control. I'm not an athlete and I'm not joining a gym."

Here's my favorite response to that look. One study tells the heartening story of middle-aged men who had had a 30-year layoff from exercise. The study showed that in six months, the effects of those sedentary 30 years were actually *reversed* with a program of exercise training. These guys had really declined in 30 years, too. Their weight had increased by 25 percent, their body fat had doubled and their aerobic capacity had decreased by 11 percent.

Despite all that, in six months the men in the study were able to achieve the same degree of cardiovascular fitness they'd enjoyed as *20-year-olds.* The moral of the story is that when it comes to fitness, it's never too late. I've found that many male patients are inspired by this story.

It's a very sad fact of life that most people who are not engaged in athletic or workout activity lose a very large proportion of their physical strength and physical work capacity *before they even notice that something is wrong.*

Tragically, some people cross the threshold of disability and find themselves unable to participate actively in life, an end result that could have been very different with an easily achievable amount of physical activity earlier on.

Remember that big gains in fitness can be achieved without fanatical and intense activity. One study at the University of Colorado found that after a three-month exercise period that consisted primarily of walking, a study of groups of sedentary men with an average age of 53 had improved their endothelial function—a key contributor to vascular health—to a state comparable to that of men who had exercised for years.

It's well known that exercise has impressive beneficial effects on the heart and circulation. It's not surprising that anything that improves circulation could improve erectile function, and indeed it's true. One Harvard study that included some 31,000 men between the ages of 55 and 90 found that men who exercise only 30 minutes a day are 40 percent less likely to develop erectile dysfunction than sedentary men. Given that about 20 percent of men in their sixties and 30 percent of men in their seventies have erectile problems, a little exercise could go a long way to improving the lives of many men and their partners.

Especially for Older Adults

Old age isn't what it used to be. Today we see senior citizens on the tennis court, in marathons and on the bike trail as well as on cruise ships and shuffleboard courts. We're lucky to live in a time when a vigorous old age seems not only desirable but possible.

It's inspiring to see older folks who are as active and engaged in life as any twenty-something. And given that the over-85 segment of the population is the largest-growing segment of all, we can hope to see more and more of them and maybe eventually join them ourselves.

If you're over 65 and sedentary, *exercise may be the single most important habit you can adopt to improve your overall health and well-being.* The evidence is overwhelming. One study revealed a 23 to 55 percent lower mortality rate in highly active men and women over age 65.

If you think that there's not much point in exercising if you're older because you're not really interested in being physically active, you're ignoring the fact that as we age, the benefits we get from exercise—and our own goals—change. Younger folks usually worry more about fitness, appearance and weight. Older folks get those benefits from exercise and more: As balance, mental health and maintaining sexual activity become higher priorities, exercise becomes the best tool for achieving them.

ARTHRITIS AND EXERCISE

If you have arthritis, you may be reluctant to begin an exercise program. More than 32 million Americans and more than half of people over age 65 have some degree of this painful, disabling condition. It's estimated that by the year 2020, 60 million, or 18 percent of the population, will have to deal with the day-to-day impact of arthritis.

While it's often difficult for arthritis sufferers to think about exercise, the fact is that research has shown that exercise can give symptomatic relief. Arthritis sufferers should keep the following in mind: Exercise must be pursued on a regular basis, because once discontinued, muscle strength and symptom relief are quickly lost.

- Exercise programs should have an aerobic component that brings you to 50 or 60 percent of your maximum heart rate for 20 to 30 minutes, three to four times a week (see page 254).
- Make resistance training—lifting weights—a part of your program. Beginners should start with four to six repetitions to avoid muscle fatigue, and two to three sessions a week is sufficient.
- Tai chi (see page 245) is also an excellent exercise for arthritis patients because it achieves strength, stretching and aerobics all in one.

Exciting news for older people is that they stand to gain the most from exercise. For example, a number of studies have demonstrated that older women and men show similar or greater strength gains compared with young individuals as a result of resistance training. In one study, older men responded to a 12-week progressive resistance-training program by more than doubling knee extensor strength and more than tripling knee flexor strength. This refers to keeping the major strength and function muscles of your legs strong. In another study with elderly men working on their quadriceps with resistance training, the average increase in strength after eight weeks of resistance training was a very impressive 174 percent.

One of the great threats of old age is a condition known as sarcopenia. Sarcopenia refers to the loss of muscle mass and decline in muscle quality observed with increasing age. Sarcopenia is also linked to functional decline, osteoporosis, impaired thermoregulation (the ability to control body temperature) and glucose intolerance. Sadly, the effects of sarcopenia can compound: As their physical capacity declines, many older folks avoid physically stressful work and thus

EXERCISE IS FOR EVERYBODY, ALWAYS

While traditional medicine rarely addresses this issue, exercise has been shown to alter the expression and consequences of a disease that is already present.

What this means is even if you already have an ailment or chronic disease, or mobility restriction such as confinement to a wheelchair, exercise can probably help you. Get guidance from a medical professional, but don't miss out on the benefits of physical activity.

become increasingly sedentary and increasingly vulnerable to overall decline.

The best way to fight the ravages of sarcopenia is to exercise. Ample evidence demonstrates that decreasing physical activity levels are related to the development of disability in older adults.

An essential key to improvement in fitness in elderly people is resistance training. Only the loading of muscle and resistance training—weightlifting exercises—have been shown to avert loss of muscle mass and strength in older folks. Studies have shown that even very fit older people—those who run or play tennis for example—do not have the muscle mass and strength of older people who engage in weight training.

Weight training can build muscle and strength. In one study, a weight-training program of three to six months was able to increase muscle strength by an average of 40 to 150 percent. The National Institute on Aging says that even frail, inactive people in their nineties can more than double their strength in a short period with simple exercises.

There's another advantage to resistance training. Elderly people who have been sedentary may have impaired balance and weakened muscles: Aerobic activity could risk a fall. But once a regular program of simple resistance exercises has begun, both weakness and impaired balance will improve.

Resistance training also maintains joint health and function because a joint, particularly knees, elbows and shoulders, is only as strong as the muscles around it. The National Institute on Aging offers exercise videos for seniors. One shows how to use household items such as chairs and towels to tone and strengthen muscles. It costs only $7 and comes with a book of instructional information. Go to *www.nia.nih.gov.* Click on "Publications," and then "Healthy Aging."

Good news for older folks: Even if you have periods of inactivity, you'll still benefit from the effort you put into strength training. In one study, people ages 65 to 81 trained over a two-year period. They exercised twice a week for one hour, performing two to three sets of both upper and lower body exercises at up to 80 percent of the heaviest weights they could once lift.

They were still able to lift up to 24 percent above their baseline three years after discontinuing strength training. Control subjects who performed no strength training over the five years saw declines in strength across the board.

HealthStyle Exercise ERA for Older People

If you're a senior—age 65 and older—shift the order of the HealthStyle ERA Program (see page 247). Begin with **R** for Resistance Training. Go slowly and keep at it. Depending on your age and physical condition, you can incorporate the first part of the program—Exercise Opportunities—when you feel able.

Here are some tips for older folks who are ready to add exercise to their lives...

- If you have a family history of heart disease or are under care for a medical condition, check with your health-care professional before you begin to exercise. You might want to get a complete physical and perhaps take a stress test if your health-care provider advises.
- Wear comfortable clothing and footwear that is appropriate for the activity.
- Seniors generally need to take more care with warm-ups and cool-downs: Don't neglect these exercises. Your muscles need to prepare for activity to avoid injury. If walking is your activity of choice, walk slowly for five or 10 minutes before you up your pace, or slowly jog in place for five minutes before your workout to gradually increase your heart rate and core temperature. The idea is to get your muscles and tendons prepared for activity. Cool down after exercising

Tai chi is an excellent form of exercise for middle-aged people and seniors. Consisting of a series of gentle postures combined in slow, continuous movements, tai chi emphasizes deep, diaphragmatic breathing and relaxation. It's a low-intensity exercise that claims to develop balance and coordination, and helps maintain strength and emotional health.

Tai chi promotes good health, memory, concentration, balance and flexibility, and is also said to improve psychological conditions such as anxiety, depression and the negative health developments normally associated with aging and a sedentary lifestyle.

Tai chi has also been shown to improve balance and reduce falls in elderly people. It definitely conveys the benefits of an aerobic activity in a very appealing format. In one interesting study, folks who practiced tai chi for 12 weeks even enjoyed an impressive drop in blood pressure.

One of the big pluses of tai chi is that it has a high adherence rate—few people drop out once they experience the pleasure and health benefits of this graceful exercise program. Check to see if there's a tai chi class at your local Y or adult education center; Boys and Girls Clubs; health facility; college or university; city recreation department; or local martial-arts school.

with five minutes of slower-paced movement and some stretching. This prevents an abrupt drop in blood pressure and helps alleviate potential muscle stiffness.

- If you walk, choose a place that is safe, well-lit and free of traffic, and make sure the walking surface is smooth and regular. Shopping malls can be great places to walk and some offer walking programs in the morning before they open for business.

- Take it easy. Start slowly and increase your activity intensity slowly. The most common cause of injury and exercise dropouts is going too fast. In general, don't increase your training load—the length or frequency of workouts, the intensity or the distance—by more than 10 percent a week.

- If you're exercising for more than a half hour and/or you're exercising in warm, humid conditions, be sure to drink 4 to 8 ounces of water every 15 minutes. Your body can lose more than a quart of water in an hour. Seniors often find that their sense of thirst is not a reliable guide, and adequate hydration is important.

- A good primer on weight-bearing exercises is *Growing Stronger: Strength Training for Older Adults.* Look for the interactive Growing Stronger Program as well as the booklet itself at *http://growingstronger.nutrition.tufts.edu.* You can download the booklet for free or purchase a copy at the site. Two other useful resources include the American College of Sports Medicine at *www.acsm.org* or 317-637-9200 and the American Council on Exercise at *www.acefitness.org.*

Back pain keeping you from exercising? Cross that excuse off your list. Many people, including doctors, are fearful that exercise will cause excessive wear on spinal structures and thus encourage back pain. In fact, research has shown that exercise has no effect on the development of back pain and that trunk muscles in lower-back-pain patients are frequently weaker than in healthy individuals.

Indeed, exercise can reverse back impairments and result in a more functional, pain-free back. If you suffer from back pain, ask your health care professional about stretching and strengthening exercises. Researchers at Harvard Medical School report the average reduction in back pain with this type of strengthening treatment is 35 percent. They note improvements in 80 percent of patients.

Start slowly and keep at it...as muscles strengthen, your pain will likely decrease.

It's especially encouraging for older people to know that even if they have periods of inactivity, they'll still benefit from any effort they put into strength training. (See "Resistance Training," page 252, for more information on this.)

Especially for Parents

Mom and Dad, you are probably aware of the sad truth: Our kids are tater tots. Many of them have become still lifes. What most parents are unaware of is the fact that their kids are facing future health problems of major proportions if their sedentary lifestyles are not abandoned. As parents, we must make every effort to ensure that our children incorporate plenty of physical activity in their daily lives. The best way to do this is to set a good example. Be active yourself and encourage your kids to be active with you. Turn off the TV and go for a bike ride or a walk or a hike.

In 1999, 14 percent of American adolescents ages 12 to 19 were overweight. This is three times the number of overweight adolescents we saw two decades ago. The Centers for Disease Control and Prevention, the Atlanta-based arm of the federal government charged with the nation's public health, has published research showing that 60 percent of overweight five- to 10-year-old children already have at least one risk factor for chronic disease: elevated fats in the bloodstream, elevated blood pressure or high insulin levels.

Type II diabetes, formerly known as adult-onset diabetes, is now affecting children and adolescents. This is an absolute disaster, as the complications of this serious disease include cardiovascular disease, organ damage, vision problems and amputations. As people develop diabetes at younger and younger ages, the complications will ultimately take a toll on younger and younger people.

Of course, an obvious problem with inactive children is obesity. An obese child may not be concerned about future health issues, but will certainly be concerned with the social issues that arise from being overweight. Social discrimination can cause low self-esteem and depression at a particularly critical time in a child's life.

The tough truth for parents today is that electronic media are more popular than time spent playing outdoors. There is some positive news: There are video games that promote movement.

The EyeToy series by Sony has a motion-tracking camera and players move their bodies to make screen characters do the same. Similarly, players of the Spider-Man 2 Web Action Video Gaming System must move their bodies to move characters on-screen.

Dance Dance Revolution is a floor pad with lighted arrows to show where to step to music. I know some adults who exercise to this. There are TV shows that seem to get the message, too: Nick Jr.'s *Lazy Town* and PBS's *Boohbah* both encourage kids to move.

Encouraging exercise, along with healthy eating habits, is a crucial step that all parents should take to preserve their children's future health. *Here are some simple steps you can take to become a family on the move...*

- Keep in mind that kids should be physically active about 60 minutes each day.
- Encourage your kids to participate in sports for fun. Eliminate the pressure; emphasize the joy.
- Be active yourself. Be a role model.
- Plan active family outings. Hiking, bike riding and ball playing are great ways to spend time together.
- Limit TV and video/computer-game time. These two nonactivities are the biggest drains on kids' time and the biggest encouragements to a sedentary lifestyle. Forty-three percent of teens watch more than two hours of TV daily. Encourage alternative activities.

• Provide a safe environment for your children and their friends to play actively. Provide healthy snacks and drinks, sports equipment and encouragement.

• Don't drive them everywhere. Whenever possible, safe and practical, encourage your kids to walk or ride their bikes to friends' houses and/or school.

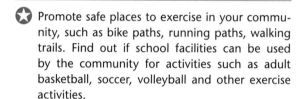

Promote safe places to exercise in your community, such as bike paths, running paths, walking trails. Find out if school facilities can be used by the community for activities such as adult basketball, soccer, volleyball and other exercise activities.

Use Your Head

I hope you're convinced that you need to exercise. Before you move a muscle, however, I want you to use your brain. It's your best asset when it comes to exercise, because success in changing your habits is all about motivation.

You've probably heard that roughly 50 percent of people who begin an exercise program drop out in the first six months. This usually is not because their bodies stopped working (due to injury, for example), but rather because their motivation dried up. Don't let that happen to you.

In one study, the single most important factor that kept people on track with their exercise was that they made it a priority. Interestingly, the people in this study did not focus on their physical appearance nearly as much as on their desire to be fit. I have found this to be true with my patients. The people who are most interested in achieving their best HealthStyle seem to be the ones who manage to stick with their resolutions; those who are focused largely on their appearance often get discouraged when and if they don't see immediate results, and they quit.

Your New HealthStyle ERA

I wish I could tell you exactly what to do in terms of exercise. If there were one, single, ideal exercise program, believe me, I'd tell you. But people and lifestyles are too varied. Actually, that's the fun of it. You have to find activities that suit you—ones you actually enjoy. Pleasure is a great motivator. You have to exercise at a time of day that works for you. With a friend? Alone? With your dog? Doesn't matter. All that matters is that you do it.

You don't even have to stick to a single program. Change with the seasons if you like. Who knows, maybe it was seasonal change that first inspired cross training! Don't feel that exercise is a grind. Sometimes it is, but most of the time it shouldn't be. Are you warmed up now? *It's time to get down to it…*

At the beginning of this exercise discussion I told you that I had a new, simple, flexible approach to getting active. Here it is—the HealthStyle ERA. *Extensive recent research has demonstrated that there are three important aspects to an optimal exercise program, and the HealthStyle ERA incorporates them all…*

Exercise Opportunities
Resistance Training
Aerobics

The HealthStyle ERA Program will make it easy for you to think about exercise because, after all, it begins in your brain. Many of us are

BEFORE YOU BEGIN

Consider your overall health. Do you have any particular health problems? Do you have heart disease, severe arthritis or other chronic health conditions? If so, talk to your health care professional before you begin to exercise. Maybe this is the perfect time to schedule a complete physical.

confused into immobility. The ERA Program will set you free.

The Three-Pronged Exercise Attack

If you're going to do the best for your body in terms of exercise, you've got to fulfill three goals: Increase your overall everyday movement (Exercise Opportunities), do weight training (Resistance Training) and adopt some level of aerobic activity (Aerobics). If just reading about this makes you want to nap, be reassured: Start with just the first goal, Exercise Opportunities. I've never met anyone who was unable to take this first step. *And very few fail to move on to the next one…*

Think Outside the Block

I've found that the most common single excuse that people use to avoid exercise is lack of time. Do you put off exercising because you don't have a "block" of time? Why bother to walk around the block if you only have 10 minutes, right?

Many people believe that exercise has to be done in one relatively long stretch of time. This misunderstanding is keeping too many of us stuck to the sofa. A guiding principle of Exercise Opportunities is that big blocks of time are not essential to achieve physical fitness.

While 60 to 90 minutes of physical activity is optimal, 30 minutes a day is sufficient and beneficial. Best of all, 30 minutes of physical activity can be a 15-minute walk in the morning, 10 minutes of vigorous housework, and five minutes of jogging in place while you watch the news. So don't let limited time stop you from gaining the powerful benefits of regular exercise.

Think you can't get real benefits from this kind of "scattershot" activity? In one report, the Cooper Institute recruited 235 relatively sedentary men and women for a study called "Project Active." Half of the group worked out in a gym three to five times a week. The others were in the "lifestyle" group: They incorporated physical activities such as walking and stair climbing into their everyday lives. After two years, by almost every measure, men and women in the lifestyle group enjoyed the same benefits as those in the gym group. People in the lifestyle group were even burning the same number of extra calories from activity as the hard-core gym folk and they achieved the same improvements in fitness.

> *Those who think they have not time for bodily exercise will sooner or later have to find time for illness.*
>
> —Edward Stanley,
> the Earl of Derby, 1873

How Much Is Enough?

Sixty minutes of exercise daily? Thirty minutes of high-intensity activity daily? Twenty minutes of weight training and a half hour of aerobics? Most people quite reasonably ask, "How much exercise?" But frequently their real question is: "How little exercise can I get away with?" Many patients wonder if they can exercise a little but eat a lot better. Or maybe lose some weight and then stop exercising. Or maybe skip exercise entirely and improve their diet radically. Many people who do their best to exercise are completely discouraged when they learn that what they thought was a good exercise program doesn't come near to a newly announced "goal."

How much is enough? This is the simple question that has kept too many people from enjoying the benefits of physical exercise. The "experts" don't help because, human nature being what it is, if there's any level of confusion on what one should do, it's too easy just to shrug your shoulders and settle onto the sofa with the remote.

There has been some confusion about the recommendations for the optimum amount of physical activity. We've heard recent updates in these recommendations from the new Dietary Guidelines, the American Heart Association and the American College of Sports Medicine as well as the National Academy of Sciences' Institute of Medicine. Many people have found conflicting recommendations to be confusing and discouraging.

Here's the answer: Aim for 30 minutes of at least moderate physical activity on most days. That's a baseline goal. Everyone can achieve that. Once that becomes a regular habit, push the bar a little higher. Sixty to 90 minutes of activity on most days is optimum.

For every pound of muscle you build, your body burns an extra 35 to 50 calories a day.

Exercise Opportunities means seizing every single chance you get to move your body in the course of the day. It's a state of mind.

You probably know people who are exercise opportunists. They walk to the store or take a bike ride on a sunny morning. Many people think of exercise as something that they must add to their day in a big block of time—the gym before work or the exercise class in the evening or the 40 minutes on the treadmill at some odd hour of the day. All of these approaches are good—*if you can achieve them.* But there are many, many people who have never been able to work exercise into their day because they don't have time, they can't afford a gym or they simply don't like to "exercise." If this describes you, Exercise Opportunities is the answer.

Exercise Opportunities is a mind-set that works physical activity into every bit of your day—much like our ancestors did. You don't consciously "exercise"—rather, you make a concerted effort to move whenever possible. You'll be surprised how quickly the perpetual motion of Exercise Opportunities can add up to real gains in terms of all the benefits associated with physical activity. It burns calories so you can maintain a healthy weight (or simply lose weight) and it builds muscles.

There is no "someday" on your calendar. Schedule exercise on a real day! How about today?

There are countless ways to create Exercise Opportunities (EO) in your day. If you consider how modern technology has eliminated virtually all movement from your life, there are countless ways to work it back in. Consider the can opener. Do you have an electric can opener? Think of it as a symbol of physical decline! Every appliance that keeps you from moving your muscles is also keeping you from being healthy. Well, I know that's a bit exaggerated. But if you started using your muscles instead of electricity for more of your daily chores, you might well be healthier and stronger. Once you begin to adopt an EO mind-set, you'll see activity around every corner.

The first and most obvious activity is walking. Walk whenever you can. Walk to work if possible. Walk to the supermarket, to the post office or walk the kids to school. Take a walk with a friend, a spouse, a child or a dog. Take every opportunity to get up and stretch your legs.

Many of my patients have told me that this simple bit of advice has changed their lives. Instead of jumping into the car or onto public transportation without a thought, they now consider if they can turn their journey into a walk. Remember that life is not always about speed—the errand that takes you an extra half hour may be the errand that's saving your life!

Thinking about biking to work? In one study, those who did so experienced a 39 percent lower mortality rate than those who did not—even after adjustment for other factors.

Here are several Exercise Opportunities suggestions. Some I use myself; others have been suggested by patients who delight in finding new ways to spend energy.

At Home

• Use the stairs. Some businesses are even posting signs near the elevators suggesting that workers use the stairs when possible. I always climb the stairs in my building and, in fact, in addition to jogging up three flights to get to my office regularly, I sometimes just run up and down a couple of times just to get my blood flowing.

• Do things standing up! If you're talking on the phone, folding laundry or even writing out a grocery list, stand up. If there's a step nearby, do calf raises: Hold on to a banister to steady yourself, put the ball of your foot on the edge of the step and press your heel downward, and then lift yourself up. Repeat a few times for each leg.

Exercise improves Fido, too! A very interesting recent study showed that older dogs were able to learn new tricks—with the help of improved diet and exercise. The 48 beagles in the study were divided into four groups that got either standard care; a diet supplemented with food-derived antioxidants and supplements; standard care plus exercise; or a special supplemented diet plus the extra play and exercise routine.

The older dogs clearly benefited most from the supplemental diet and exercise program. All 12 of the older beagles who got the SuperDog diet and the SuperDog exercise routine could solve a difficult problem compared with eight to 10 dogs that got only the enriched diet and two of eight dogs who got no special treatment.

• When you walk, walk faster. Pick up the pace and even a short walk can give you a bit of a workout.

• Do housework yourself, with gusto. Vacuum to music. Dust those high shelves.

• Walk the dog. Often. Take him out two or three times a day. Once he's used to this routine, he'll nudge you to keep to it.

• Turn everyday chores into brief exercise sessions: Waiting for the water to boil? The oven to heat up? Do side stretches and leg lifts. I do push-ups against the kitchen counter or steps.

• Don't just watch TV. Use an exercise bike or do sit-ups or use weights while you watch. Keep a set of hand weights right next to the remote control.

• An hour of evening TV has about 15 minutes of commercials. If you do some sit-ups or weight-training exercises during these ads, you'll be *halfway* to your basic goal of a half hour of daily exercise.

• Carry packages to the car instead of putting them in a shopping cart when possible and practical. Try lifting them (as much as you comfortably can) with your arms extended as you walk home or to the car.

• Park the car farther from the store than you'd like! This is an old one but it works.

• Do your own yard work. Shovel snow. Garden. Rake fallen leaves.

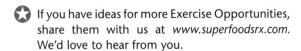

If you have ideas for more Exercise Opportunities, share them with us at *www.superfoodsrx.com.* We'd love to hear from you.

At Work

Most of the time you're probably sitting at a desk, but EOs abound if you pay attention.

• Get off the bus or train early and walk the remaining distance.

KEEPING ACTIVE INDOORS

Sure, it's cold and perhaps snowing where you live, but that's no excuse to become a blob. Keep up with your exercise program no matter the weather. *Here are some tips...*

- If you're doing housework—vacuuming, dusting, making beds—try to do it to music. Dance music with a good beat will keep you moving and will turn a light activity into a moderate one.
- Double shop. When visiting the mall take a brisk walk around the interior of the indoor mall before you even begin to shop. Unless you're at an enormous mall, this tactic will add 10 or 15 minutes to your visit and, if you walk briskly, you could be one-third or even halfway through with your daily activity goal by the time you head home.
- Take a dance class. Many of us are in the habit of going out to dinner as a relaxing activity, but dance classes are fun and can be something to look forward to on a dark winter evening.
- If you sit at a desk all day, you especially need an active break. Set a timer and every hour or so get up and do something. Walk to another office to deliver paperwork or confer with a colleague, get a cup of tea, use the water cooler on another floor or just go up and down a flight of stairs a few times.
- Borrow an exercise tape or two from the library and use them! Ask the librarian which ones are especially popular. Ask a friend or spouse or child to do one with you a couple of times a week in the evening.
- Go ahead and watch your favorite TV show. But do it actively. Jump rope during the commercials. (This can be a real challenge: A commercial break can seem quite long if you're jumping!) Lift weights as you watch. Do a few sit-ups and some push-ups. Get the family to join you.
- Ask a friend or family member to commit to a walk/run event for charity. For information on walking events, check out *www.thewalkingsite.com* and *www.walkingconnection.com.*
- Get a large inflated exercise ball with an instructional video. There are endless exercises—sit-ups, push-ups, leg work—you can do with these.
- Another good option for exercise for women is the many Curves centers. Check out their Web site for more information at *www.curves.com.*

• Instead of meeting a friend or colleague to have lunch or coffee, meet to take a walk.

• While sitting at your desk, put your arms straight out in front of you and grab your elbows with opposite hands. Stretch slowly to the right, then to the left.

• Do seated leg lifts. Sit at the edge of your seat and do five straight leg lifts and five bent leg lifts with each leg.

Don't let traffic slow you down. See it as an exercise opportunity. Pull in your tummy at a red light and hold it till the light turns green. Stretch your neck by dropping your head from one side to the other.

On the Road

Travel can be a special challenge, but it offers its own opportunities for exercise.

HEAD GAMES

Don't feel like exercising today? Take a minute and think about how you'll feel at 9:30 tonight. Pretty disappointed in yourself, no doubt. Turns out that anticipated regret can be a great motivator. In a recent study, folks who took the time to think about how bad they'd feel if they skipped their workout were more likely to do it.

Take time each morning to think about how you'll feel at the end of the day if you don't follow through on your exercise plans.

- Stay in a hotel with a fitness center. They're very easy to find these days. Make sure that the center is open at convenient hours.
- Travel with a jump rope and use it in your hotel room. This is especially useful if your hotel doesn't have a fitness center.
- Walk, walk, walk as you explore new places. You'll see much more than you would in a car or on a bus.

Resistance Training

Resistance training, or weight training, is your best friend when it comes to fitness and longevity. It preserves lean body mass. Remember sarcopenia—that loss of muscle that causes countless health problems as you age? Resistance training is going to help prevent it. If you're in your late thirties or early forties, you're probably already losing muscle mass at a rate of about a quarter pound a year. You need to hang on to that muscle or lean body mass. Lean body mass is metabolically active—it burns more calories than that other body mass, fat—and thus it helps you keep your weight down. Resistance training will also boost your bone density and balance—both particularly important as the years go by.

There's another bonus to resistance training. Do you still fit into those five-year-old jeans? If not, like many people you're experiencing a gradual piling on of pounds that seems part and parcel of the aging process. There are many popular theories to account for this phenomenon, most of which imply that there's no escape from middle-aged spread.

Well, those supertight clothes are not inevitable. Your resting metabolic heart rate (RMR) accounts for about 60 percent of your daily metabolism or calorie burn. Starting at about age 35 or 40, muscle mass begins to decline and with this decline comes a decline in RMR. A lower RMR burns fewer calories. The end result is that what you ate at age 25 to maintain a healthy weight can, at age 45, make you fat.

Fortunately, there's a simple solution to this: Lift weights! You're not looking to build giant muscles—all you're interested in is preserving the muscle mass of your youth, maintaining a higher RMR and thus burning more calories. Who knows, you might just be able to zip up those turn-of-the-century jeans!

There's plenty of excellent information out there on weight-training programs. If you're a beginner, check out a few of the sources I'm listing here. If you're experienced, good for you. You probably already know the benefits of weight training. If you're unsure how to proceed, invest in a couple of sessions with a personal trainer or join a group class to get you started.

- An excellent resource that introduces a complete program of resistance training is the Center for Disease Control and Prevention Web site, Growing Stronger: Strength Training for Older Adults. Although it's geared for older people, it's useful for anyone. *www.cdc.gov/nccdphp/dnpa/physical/growing_stronger.*
- At the American College of Sports Medicine you can download a brochure, "Selecting and Effectively Using Free Weights" or get a free copy

by sending a self-addressed, stamped, business-sized envelope to: ACSM National Center, P.O. Box 1440, Indianapolis, IN 46206.

Here's a simple, basic program that can be very helpful for beginners…

• If you're healthy, you can probably begin weight training today. If you're frail, arthritic or on medications for chronic ailments such as osteoporosis or diabetes, check with a health care professional or exercise therapist before you begin.

• Get some weights.

• Find a comfortable place to use them. You'll need a chair, some steps or a sturdy stool.

• Wear loose-fitting, comfortable clothes.

• Get started!

How often do you have to do these weight-training exercises? The American College of Sports Medicine would like to see you weight-train two or three times a week. If you can do three, great; if not, make twice weekly your regular goal. It's only going to take you a half hour to 45 minutes —enough time to watch your favorite show and pause for a drink of water. Schedule one session for Sunday morning and you can talk back to the political shows while you train. Do it again one evening and you're all set.

Aerobic Exercise

This is the last part of the HealthStyle ERA Program. If you've managed to work on the other two parts, you know you're ready for aerobic exercise.

What is aerobic exercise? It's activity that involves the repetitive use of large muscles to temporarily increase your heart rate and your respiration rate. Aerobic exercise improves your cardiorespiratory endurance, working your heart and lungs to promote cardiovascular fitness. That's the key to aerobic exercise—cardiovascular fitness. It's the reason you do it and the reason it keeps you young and vigorous and energetic.

Deciding to exercise is a Big Decision. It's easier for many of us to make Small Daily Decisions. Decide to exercise today!

Cardiovascular fitness is seen by many as the single best measure of changes that occur in the body with aging. Your cardiovascular fitness normally declines by 8 to 10 percent per decade for both men and women after age 25. That means if you're 50 years old, you could already be 25 percent less fit than you were at 25. That's the bad news. The good news is that it's not that difficult to regain youthful fitness if you're willing to devote a minimum 30 minutes most days of the week to this end. Indeed, while you may never be as fit as you were at 20, studies have shown that even people in their eighties have not lost the ability to improve their aerobic fitness level.

Brisk walking, running, swimming, cycling, aerobic classes, stair climbing, aerobic exercise videos, cross-country skiing, hiking, soccer, rowing, jumping rope, singles tennis and basketball are all examples of aerobic exercise.

HOW MUCH WEIGHT?

In order for resistance training to be effective you have to keep increasing the weight as you go along. If you've been lifting two-pound weights for a year, it's not bad but it's not effective weight training. To determine how much weight to lift, start with a low amount. The ideal training regimen is four sets of eight to 10 repetitions. If you find on the fourth set that it is easy to complete the repetitions, then you need to start adding weight. So if you can easily do four sets of eight reps using three-pound free weights, it's time for you to move up to five-pound weights.

Age	Target Heart Rate Beats per Minute Rate (50–75%)	Avg. Maximum Heart Rate (100%)
20 years	100–150	200
25 years	98–146	195
30 years	95–142	190
35 years	93–138	185
40 years	90–135	180
45 years	88–131	175
50 years	85–127	170
55 years	83–123	165
60 years	80–120	160
65 years	78–116	155
70 years	75–113	150

If you already participate in one of these activities—excellent! You're looking to a healthier future. If, on the other hand, you're one of the millions of Americans who don't get enough exercise, it's time to change your ways.

And, yes, I know you don't have time. Few of us have time to exercise if we don't make it a priority. We all have too much to do. That's why you have to be both clever and determined when it comes to aerobic exercise. You have to find one activity you can count on—something you can do easily and frequently and that you enjoy. For many of my patients, that's walking. Almost everyone can walk—outside in good weather, at a mall in bad weather, with a friend or with music or a book on tape. (For more information on walking, see page 255.)

Thirty minutes a day most days of the week is the ideal beginning goal for exercisers, but many sedentary people think even that sounds like a lot. If that describes you, here's what I suggest: 10 minutes. Decide that you're going to do some aerobic activity for 10 minutes most days this week. Maybe a brisk walk around the block. Maybe it's 10 minutes of bike riding or a short spell on a rowing machine, stationary bike or stair climber. Just do it. Look at your watch and go. If you want to continue for longer, great. If 10 minutes is all you're ready for, great. Just do it almost every day this week and for the next couple of weeks.

Before too long you'll find that you're ready for more than 10 minutes. But don't rush: It's better to get those 10 brisk minutes in each day, building up a good physical and psychological foundation, than to do an hour one day and then give up because you're sore or you can't find that much time the next day. Slow but steady. That's what will get you to an active, healthy old age.

What's Aerobic?

How do you know you're exercising "aerobically"? Patients sometimes get confused about what level of activity is considered to be "aerobic." The best way to measure this is to check your heart rate, which I'll describe shortly. It's not essential to know your heart rate, and if that's going to discourage you or slow you down, forget about it and just focus on this: You're exercising aerobically if you're breathing rapidly but can still carry on a conversation, and you begin to perspire about five to 15 minutes after beginning the activity, depending on the air temperature.

Here's how to gauge your activity level: Your heart responds to changes in your activity levels. When you work harder, it beats faster. Your target heart rate for aerobic exercise is 60 to 80 percent of your maximum heart rate. Most of the time when you begin working out your heart rate should be at 60 to 70 percent of your maximum, occasionally going up to 75 or 80 percent. *Here's the standard formula for estimating your maximum heart rate...*

Maximum Heart Rate: 220 minus your age in years.

Target Heart Rate: 60 to 80 percent of maximum.

Remember, aerobic exercise is going to amplify all the good things you do to keep yourself healthy. It will help keep your weight down, it will make you feel optimistic and in control of your life, it will make you strong and flexible and better able to participate in life and it will reduce your chances of developing many chronic diseases. *If you walk briskly just three hours a week—that's a half hour on six days or even four half-hour sessions and four 15-minute sessions—you will…*

- Reduce your risk of stroke by 30 percent.
- Reduce your risk of type II diabetes by 30 percent.
- Reduce your risk of heart disease by 40 percent.
- Reduce your risk of osteoporosis.
- Reduce your risk of some types of cancer.
- Boost your immune system.

Walking

The weather is improving. The days are a little longer. You're feeling a burst of energy and it's time to take advantage of it all: Start walking! The benefits of exercise are legion. If you're in doubt, read "Exercise." Regular exercise is a must for people who want to reap the most benefits from their new, improved HealthStyle. But perhaps you dread the gym or you're tired of being indoors or maybe you'd just like to try something different. There's one form of exercise that everyone can benefit from and enjoy: walking.

Walking is a form of exercise that I encourage all my patients to participate in. All it takes is comfortable clothing and a good pair of shoes. You could put this book down and head out the door. It's that simple. On the other hand, if you learn a bit about walking and plan ahead, you will have more satisfactory results, both in terms of health promotion and in making walking a staple of your exercise routine.

> *Exercise and Temperance will preserve something of our youthful vigor even into old age.*
> —Cicero

WALK OF LIFE

The HealthStyle goal of a half hour a day of exercise is easy to meet when you walk. Indeed, if you walk with a friend, you may find yourself achieving the optimum goal of one to one and a half hours of exercise daily. Walking is also a good supplement to any other fitness program. Walking is a good choice for people who are just beginning a fitness program or for elderly people who are uneasy about more vigorous exercise.

Many people think that walking for exercise doesn't yield much in the way of results. The fact is that walking briskly for one mile (brisk walking usually means 3.5 to 4 miles per hour) burns nearly as many calories as running a mile at a moderate pace. Even slow walking (about two miles per hour) confers some benefits. There's no question that walking at a moderate pace for 30 to 60 minutes burns stored fat and can build muscle and thus speed up your metabolism.

Walking an hour a day is also associated with cutting the risk of heart disease, breast cancer, colon cancer, diabetes, osteoporosis and stroke. In a Harvard study of more than 72,000 female nurses, it was found that walking as little as an hour a week, at any pace, reduces the risk of coronary artery disease.

As you might imagine, longer and more vigorous walks—three or more hours a week—yielded a greater risk reduction. The authors of this study concluded, "Our results suggest that such a regimen (e.g., brisk walking for three or more hours a week) could reduce the risk of coronary events in women by 30 to 40 percent."

The authors also claim that one-third of heart attacks among women in the United States can be ascribed to physical inactivity.

Walking can help prevent disease, and evidence also exists that it may actually promote a lower mortality rate. A study from the Honolulu Heart Program looked at 707 retired men ages 61 to 81. Those who walked more than one mile a day had a reduction in death during the 12-year follow-up of about one-third; walking more than two miles a day provided only a small additional benefit.

Even after taking into account other activities and other risk factors, the beneficial effects of walking at least one mile a day was evident. The authors of this study concluded, "Our findings indicate that regular walking is associated with a lower mortality rate. Encouraging elderly people to walk may benefit their health."

Shape Up America (*www.shapeup.org*) has useful information on keeping in shape, including tools to help you assess your flexibility, aerobic level, fitness level, etc.

Getting Started

As with any exercise, a little preparation can yield optimum results. Before you begin your walking program, it's very important to think of it as an actual "program." If you just take a walk now and again, you'll derive some benefit, but the effects will be limited and you're not likely to stick with it.

The most important aspect of walking as an exercise is making it a habit and part of your regular routine. If you get used to walking at the same time every day, you don't even have to think about it—just lace up your shoes and go. Find a time of day that will work for you every day. For many people, it's first thing in the morning, but you may find that just after work or after dinner works best.

TOP EXERCISE VIDEOS

There are so many great workout videos and DVDs available. It's easy to find one that you're going to enjoy when bad weather keeps you inside. To find something you'll stick with, borrow tapes or DVDs from the library and use them a few times before you commit to buy one. Here are a few that most people find effective and fun:

- Leslie Sansone—*Walk Away the Pounds*
- Kathy Smith—*Timesaver: Lift Weights to Lose Weight*
- Jamie Brenkus—*:08min. Workouts*
- Petra Kolber—*Trainer's Edge Cardio Interval Training* (You need some weights for this one.)
- Kari Anderson—*Angles, Lines & Curves II*

Here are some other tips that will help to make your walking routine a success…

Set a goal. Walk briskly for at least half an hour every day, or one hour four to six times a week. If it's impossible for you to schedule a full half hour at a time, try to work in that much in smaller stretches—say, three brisk 10-minute walks. Almost everyone can manage that amount, although if you break up your walking, it's more difficult to create a program for yourself and it may be more challenging to reach your goal.

Choose comfortable, appropriate clothes. It's easy these days to find exercise clothing appropriate to any weather condition. Athletic stores carry a wide range of comfortable, attractive clothes that will make your walking workout pleasurable.

Supportive, comfortable shoes are critical. If you have a pair of comfortable sneakers, they're probably fine, but if you're uncertain whether your shoes are appropriate or if you're walking on variable terrain, it's worth a trip to a good athletic supply store to find a pair that will give you support and will be comfortable. Many types of walking shoes are available that have flexible soles and stiff heel counters to prevent side-to-side motion.

Warm-weather clothing is easy: shorts and a T-shirt. For cooler weather, you'll want to dress in layers, so investigate fleece for outer layers and fabrics that wick perspiration from the skin as the best choice for a base layer of clothing.

If walking is your primary physical activity, add some simple weight-training exercises a few times a week to your program (see page 252). Weight training will help you work muscles that don't get used in walking, increase the strength of your musculoskeletal system and help you to amplify all the health benefits you get from walking.

Make sure that your walking site is safe and well lit. Particularly at night or at dusk, you should make sure your walking site is populated and/or well lit, and that you wear reflective clothing. Walking with a friend is the best choice at night no matter where you walk. Avoid uneven terrain that could cause falls, particularly if you are elderly or if you walk alone.

Walk with a buddy. For some people, walking with a buddy keeps them honest: They won't skip their workout so as not to disappoint their friend. This is a very effective technique not only for sticking with your program but also for enjoying it more. Chatting with a friend can make the time fly by, and you may find that you're covering even more distance than you'd planned. The buddy can have four legs too. Dogs generally insist on a daily walk and will be delighted with any extra walks they're offered. Many of my patients tell me that their dogs force them outside regularly, and they are grateful for this.

Listen to books on tape or your favorite music while you walk. Either of these two techniques can make your walking time speed by and be twice as pleasurable.

Vary your terrain. Walking up and down hills varies the muscles used for your workout. Walking on grass or gravel burns more calories than walking on a track, and walking on sand increases caloric expenditure by almost half. Walking on a track is easiest on your joints and also makes it easy to judge distance.

Pay attention to speed and stride. If brisk walking usually means 3.5 to 4 miles per hour and your goal is a half hour of brisk walking, aim for covering about two miles in a half hour. Figure this amount by using a track or, if you don't use a track, drive the distance using your car's odometer to figure out a two-mile distance. Remember that covering more than two miles in that time period or walking more than a half hour may convey more health benefits and will surely burn more calories. Also, if you want to walk faster, instead of taking longer steps, take faster steps. Lengthening your stride can increase the strain on your feet and legs.

Use walks to reconnect with friends and loved ones. Walking is a great way to share time with your spouse, kids, parents or significant others at the end of the day or at any convenient time. A walk can be an effective way to enjoy nature, discuss problems and plan the future. One patient told me that her daily walk with her husband helped to keep their 50-year marriage alive.

Try walking sticks or poles. A walking stick can be helpful for balance, especially for older people or those walking on varied terrain. Enhance your upper-body workout by using lightweight, rubber-tipped poles, available in many sporting-goods stores. Walking with the poles is like cross-country skiing without the skis. Test the poles for the right size in the store: You should be able to grip the pole and keep your forearm about level as you walk. Many poles are now adjustable. Nordic Walker, Exerstrider sticks or Leki poles are three brands that are commonly available.

Keep a log. Many people find that keeping a log helps them stick to their goals. Recording the date, distance and time of your walks in a little notebook will help to keep you motivated.

Train for an event. An excellent way to get motivated is to train for a particular event. Don't think of yourself as a "marathon man"? You don't have to be. Many events today have categories for people who are walking the course. You'll often find participants who range in age from nine to 90. You don't have to cover a tremendous distance either; some events, like 5K walks, are well within the range of someone with a few months of preparation, depending on age and physical condition. Check out the American Volkssport Association (*www.ava.org/index.htm*) or Walkertown USA (*www.walkertownusa.com*) for information on events in your area and other valuable information for walkers.

Take a walking vacation. A number of agencies specialize in setting up walking vacations in various areas of the world. These vacations give you an opportunity to slow down, exercise and see the world while meeting like-minded people or even to arrange your own group to make the trip together. Planning such a trip can give you a training goal as well as a reward. One agency that I recommend is Mountain Travel Sobek, *www.mtsobek.com* or 888-687-6235.

Ped Power

America on the Move (*www.americaonthemove.org*) is a national program developed to encourage people to be more active. The program sets a simple goal, encouraging people to count their daily steps by using a pedometer. A pedometer is a motion-sensitive device that resembles a tiny beeper and clips onto your waistband. The recommended goal is 10,000 steps a day. On average, people walk about 5,310 steps in a day, according to a Harris Interactive online poll conducted for the group. That simply isn't enough to maintain optimum health.

Walking Burns Calories!

See how many calories you will burn every mile by checking your weight against how fast you walk.

	If you weigh...						
	100 lbs.	*120 lbs.*	*140 lbs.*	*160 lbs.*	*180 lbs.*	*200 lbs.*	*220 lbs.*
And walk at...	*You'll burn this many calories...*						
2 mph	65	80	93	105	120	133	145
2.5 mph	62	74	88	100	112	124	138
3 mph	60	72	83	95	108	120	132
3.5 mph	59	71	83	93	107	119	130
4 mph	59	70	81	94	105	118	129
4.5 mph	69	82	97	110	122	138	151
5 mph	77	92	108	123	138	154	169
6 mph	86	99	114	130	147	167	190
7 mph	96	111	128	146	165	187	212

HEALTHSTYLE HOLIDAY GIFTS

Want to give some "healthy" gifts this holiday season? *Here are some suggestions...*

- A gym membership.
- A session or two with a personal trainer.
- A subscription to a healthy cooking magazine like *Cooking Light* or *Eating Well.*
- An exercise video or DVD.
- An "exercise basket" with a set of dumbbells, an exercise ball, a tape or DVD, etc.
- A pedometer and a book on walking, or books on tape or music to listen to while you walk.
- A healthy cookbook.

Many people find that using a pedometer is a great help in reaching exercise goals and particularly walking goals. Pedometers are inexpensive and, while there are variations in accuracy, most people find that just paying attention to how much they move is an eye-opener. I suggest wearing a pedometer for a few days and noting how many steps you're taking. For many people, it's as little as 3,000 or 4,000 steps a day. Try to add to your baseline total week by week. You may find that adding just 50 steps a day for a few weeks will get you to your 10,000-step goal.

Walking 10,000 steps is the approximate equivalent of walking four to five miles. The distance covered depends on the length of your stride.

Many have told me that knowing they needed just a few hundred more steps to reach their daily goal would be enough to get them to take the dog for a walk or to walk to mail a letter instead of driving. Wearing a pedometer can be just the encouragement you need to take the stairs instead of the elevator, to park a few blocks from your destination and to take a walk at lunch instead of sitting at your desk. Of course, all those steps add up to calories burned, muscles built and a host of health benefits.

The About.com Walking Web site has a wealth of excellent information on everything to do with walking, including logs to measure your progress, suggestions on pedometer brands and walking events to keep you motivated. Check out *http://walking.about.com.*

Tips for Long-term Exercise Success

The HealthStyle ERA Program is the answer for busy people who need to get exercise into their lives. Many of my patients have adopted it. Trying an exercise program is easy; sticking with it is the challenge. I've kept ERA open-ended and flexible for that reason, because a rigid program, even if it's quickly adopted, may be quickly abandoned. ERA is more an Exercise HealthStyle: You live it day by day. It's like eating—you do it every single day. Some days you do it better than others, but you never stop. *Here are some tips to help keep you on track on your new ERA...*

- If you've been sedentary for a long time, are overweight or have chronic health problems, see your health care professional before you begin any exercise program.
- Make it fun. Whatever exercise you choose to do, make it a pleasure. Find an exercise buddy or work out while watching your favorite movies or while listening to books on tape.
- Wear comfortable clothes. It was recently discovered that people burned more calories on "casual" days at work. This is probably because they feel more comfortable in their clothes and are more eager to move about. Wear walking shoes when you can and you might well walk more.

9

BETTER SLEEP: IMPROVE YOUR LIFE

You do it every night but probably not enough. Or at least not enough for your health. Many people don't realize how important sleep is to their overall health. With life's ever-increasing demands claiming every second of our day, it's easy to feel overwhelmed. The temptation is to burn the candle at both ends—stay up late to finish a project and get up a bit earlier to pack yet one more thing into the day. It's a good time to take a look at the dramatic effects of sleep loss on our health.

Believe it or not, there's impressive evidence supporting the argument that the amount of time you sleep—even more than whether you smoke, exercise or have high blood pressure or cholesterol levels—could be *the most important predictor of how long you'll live.*

Sleep. It's the most overlooked factor in achieving optimum health in the twenty-first century. We all know we should eat well and exercise. For many of my patients, even those committed to a healthy lifestyle, sleep is seen as a kind of luxury. Indeed, many people who follow sound diets and who routinely exercise are unwittingly sabotaging their efforts by depriving themselves of a pleasurable, satisfying, easy and inexpensive way to insure optimum health—sleep!

Feel yourself nodding off? You're not alone. A 2000 poll by the National Sleep Foundation found that sleep debt is a problem for more than 50 percent of American workers. Data suggests that in the last century we've reduced the average amount of time we sleep by 20 percent.

It's easy to put sleep at the bottom of your to-do list. For one thing, our culture encourages it. We live in a 24/7 world where night and day dissolve into one long stretch of work and family obligations. Get up early to beat traffic and get a few phone calls in, stay up late after squeezing in some family time, so you can send a batch of e-mails and do some paperwork. Awake in the middle of the night? Look at it as a bonus to catch up on a little reading. And if you are up at 3 a.m. scanning magazines, you're likely to read about successful executives who boast about getting by on four or five hours of sleep a night. The implicit message is that sleep is for the weak and undisciplined.

The alarming truth is that sleep deprivation is taking a serious toll on our overall health. Chronic lack of sleep affects daily performance, overall productivity, and now, most significantly to HealthStyle, long- and short-term health.

Sound far-fetched? Well, you may be surprised to learn that the sleep debt of only three to four hours that many of us routinely rack up in the course of a busy week can provoke metabolic changes that mimic a prediabetic state and hormonal changes that compare with those experienced by someone suffering from depression.

In a nutshell the amount of sleep you get has a direct bearing on the following...

- Obesity
- Coronary heart disease
- Hypertension
- Diabetes
- Immune function
- Cognitive performance
- Longevity

Sleep and Your Health

There's no question that sleep and health are intimately intertwined. Up until relatively recently, however, even though it was known that sleep affects performance in humans and sleep deprivation in rodents results in actual death, little attention was paid to the effect of sleep deprivation on human health. We now know that while the main function of sleep seems to be the refreshing of our brains, sleep and its lack affect many bodily systems, including our metabolism, our hormones and our immune function.

The important news, and one of the major messages of HealthStyle, is that chronic sleep deprivation is doing more than just making us tired and reducing our ability to perform at optimum levels. The big news on sleep is twofold: Many of us who think we're getting enough sleep really aren't, and our performance is affected even though we're unaware of our diminished abilities. Moreover, and most significantly, the lack of sleep that many of us endure routinely has now been conclusively linked with diabetes, metabolic syndrome and obesity—all increasingly common conditions that are taking a serious toll on our overall health.

Total sleep deprivation suppresses the immune system and even partial sleep deprivation has an effect on this important protective system.

The summer is a time of no teachers, no books and, for many children, no schedule. It's fun and flexible and allows for travel and visitors and catching fireflies. However, suddenly facing the first day of school without sufficient sleep can make the adjustment to a new teacher and a new classroom all the more difficult.

Sleep deprivation in children affects mood, cognitive ability, memory, decision making, creativity—everything a child needs for good academic performance. Don't wait until the night before school starts to get the children back into a school sleep schedule. You should start at least a week in advance with earlier bedtimes and earlier risings.

A six- to 12-year-old will need between 10½ and 11½ hours of sleep a night. Get them into a good bedtime routine—say, dinner, bath, reading, bed—which they can follow for the full school year. A regular bedtime is critical. Our internal clocks are powerful and we sleep best if we fall asleep and wake up at the same times daily.

If children have a week or two of restful sleep in advance of the start of school, they'll be better able to handle any night-before-the-first-day jitters and catch up on needed sleep quickly.

Even smaller amounts of partial sleep deprivation reduce natural killer cell activity and diminish the effectiveness of communication between our pituitary gland and our adrenal glands. This results in altered stress hormones, which in turn play a role in memory and glucose tolerance.

One fascinating area of research is discovering causative links between lack of sleep and diabetes and obesity. In one study, curtailing sleep to four hours per night for six nights impaired glucose tolerance and lowered insulin secretion in healthy well-rested young men. This condition was entirely reversed when these men made up their sleep debt with adequate rest.

EVEN A LITTLE IS A LOT

The important message for all of us is that you don't have to lose huge amounts of sleep before it takes a toll. Partial sleep deprivation has a substantial effect on sleepiness, as you might guess, but also on motor and cognitive performance and mood.

From a very general standpoint, one study found that sleeping less than four hours per night was associated with a 2.8 times higher rate of mortality for men and a 1.5 times higher rate for women. The author of this study also found that length of sleep time was a better predictor of mortality than smoking, cardiac disease or hypertension. One other study found that people who slept six hours or less a night had a 70 percent higher mortality rate over a nine-year period than those who slept seven to eight hours a night.

It's not only long-term health that's affected by lack of sleep. Did your grandma ever tell you that you'll get sick if you don't get enough sleep? She was right. Studies have shown that people who suffer from acute and chronic sleep deprivation also experience immune changes, including a decreased number of protective natural killer cells and reduced activity of those cells. This reduced ability of our bodies to fight invaders on a cellular level will inevitably make us more vulnerable to colds and infections.

You're not only in danger of getting a cold if you don't get enough sleep, but you're also at greater risk for developing chronic health problems including diabetes, metabolic syndrome and even obesity. While the links between these ailments and sleep deprivation are only emerging, we know for certain that loss of sleep affects hormone function as well as glucose tolerance and insulin resistance.

ATTENTION ATHLETES

There is research evidence that most of the improvement of a motor skill depends on sleep. Improvement of a perceptual or motor skill continues after training has ended, and sleep is very important to maximize this improvement. The sleeping brain does a reprocessing of recent memory patterns involving motor skills. In addition, numerous studies support the idea that sleep is essential for brain memory function.

Sleep and Performance

You might have guessed that sleep deprivation takes a toll on performance. This is certainly true. One study showed that sleep restriction of six hours or less per night produced cognitive performance deficits that mimic the loss of two full nights without sleep. This is actually a relatively moderate sleep debt—many people experience it regularly—never imagining that it could seriously impair their waking neurological functioning.

This same study, which involved 48 healthy adults ages 21 to 38, also reported (and this is critical information) that the study subjects were *largely unaware of their increasing cognitive disability*. Other reports corroborate this finding: We're tired, we're not performing well and we're oblivious to the fact. Most people believe that they function normally despite being sleep deprived. No doubt this helps to explain why sleep deprivation has become a common condition.

We not only perform less well when sleep deprived, we try less. One study of college students who were sleep deprived found that on the day following their sleep loss they not only, as you might guess, were sleepy, fatigued and had longer reaction times, but they also selected less difficult tasks than the control group. The selection of the least demanding option in a complex situation has obvious implications for the safety, reliability and effectiveness of workers.

TIRED=LESS EFFECTIVE

Nearly 25 percent of the population, including night-shift workers and medical residents and interns, are particularly sensitive to sleep loss. A recent study of medical interns showed a clear relationship between the hours slept per day and the number of "attentional failures" during night-shift work. Most significant, this study examined the work performance of a highly motivated, intelligent segment of the population, and clearly their sleep restriction had a significant effect on their ability to perform work.

Another study of medical interns reported that those following a traditional schedule (little sleep and long hours) made 35.9 percent more medical errors than a group following a so-called intervention schedule (more sleep and reduced work hours).

Another interesting study compared performance after being awake 30 minutes to five hours longer than the subjects' normal sleep time versus measured amounts of alcohol intake in the same subjects. The authors concluded that the magnitude of the behavior impairment observed when the subjects were performing tasks just a few hours after their normal time of sleep onset exceeded that observed following a legally intoxicating dose of alcohol in these same subjects.

The fatigue of sleep deprivation is an important factor that is very likely to compromise performance accuracy and speed. In some ways, sleep deprivation is like being drunk without any alcohol in your system. If you believe you can perform well in any endeavor without a good night's sleep, you're wrong!

HEALTHSTYLE BASKET CASE

Every now and again I encounter a patient who is in desperate need of a complete HealthStyle makeover. This patient typically has a poor diet, is highly stressed and is physically inactive.

Here are my instructions: Go home and go to bed. You can't live healthfully if you don't sleep, and chronic sleep debt makes other healthful activities difficult to achieve. You won't exercise if you're exhausted. You won't make good food choices if your appetite control system is out of whack—as it will be if you're sleep deprived. And you sure can't control stress when you're struggling to stay awake and function at a high level.

I prescribe a full week of adequate sleep before you begin to think about setting other healthy goals. When you've achieved that, you're ready to take on all the HealthStyle challenges.

Close Your Eyes: Avoid Diabetes

Data from the Nurses' Health Study showed that healthy women who reported getting less than five hours or more than nine hours of sleep were more apt to develop diabetes in the next 10 years than women who initially averaged seven to eight hours of sleep. A sleep debt of three to four hours a night over a few days can result in metabolic changes that mimic a prediabetic state.

Close Your Eyes: Lose Weight

Perhaps one of the most interesting recent findings about sleep is the effect that it has on obesity. It's interesting to note that as Americans' nighttime sleep duration lessened by one to two hours over the second half of the twentieth century, the incidence of obesity *doubled over roughly the same time period*. While sleep deprivation alone doesn't explain the rise in obesity and diabetes, it surely plays a contributing role.

Trying to lose weight while suffering from sleep deprivation is like walking up a down escalator. You may find yourself trying very hard and getting nowhere.

One study showed that the less you sleep the more likely you are to become obese. This study, conducted at Columbia University, demonstrated a clear link between the risk of being obese and the number of hours of sleep each night even after controlling for depression, physical activity, alcohol consumption, ethnicity, level of education, age and gender.

The study subjects—ages 32 to 59—who slept four hours or less per night were 73 percent more likely to be obese than those who slept seven to nine hours per night. Those who got only five hours each night had a 50 percent higher risk than those who got a full night's sleep, and those who got six hours of sleep were still 23 percent more likely to be substantially overweight.

In another study, adolescents with greater sleep disruption or generally poor quality of nighttime sleep also demonstrated lower daytime activity, and for each hour of sleep lost, the odds of obesity increased by 80 percent.

One of the reasons that sleep seems to have such a dramatic effect on weight is the intimate relationship between sleep and hormones. When you experience sleep deprivation, your blood levels of leptin, a hormone that acts as an appetite suppressant, appear to decrease. Leptin is a hormone that's produced by fat cells. It helps to regulate your appetite and metabolism. High levels of leptin help you to eat less while low levels increase your appetite and cause you to eat more. In a study on sleep and leptin, it was found that subjects who slept less than five hours a night had a significant decrease in leptin and additionally a significant increase in gherlin, a hormone that triggers hunger.

Another factor when considering the relationship between sleep deprivation and obesity is perhaps more obvious: When we're tired we're less likely to make good choices about health-related activities. It's difficult to keep up with exercise routines or to cook a healthy dinner if you're just totally exhausted. So getting sufficient sleep not only contributes to your long-term health and your overall performance, it also helps reduce your chances of becoming obese.

How Much Do You Need?

While we know that adequate sleep is crucial to optimum health, we don't know the precise amount of sleep to recommend for everyone. We do know that as we age over a lifespan, our need for sleep seems to change and diminish.

In the first days of life, our total sleep time is roughly 16 hours, falling to about 14 hours by the end of the first month. At six months of age, we're sleeping about 12 hours, and this amount declines about 30 minutes per year through age five. By adolescence we're sleeping from nine to 10 hours, and as adults, seven to eight hours.

While 50 percent of drivers report driving while sleepy, nearly 25 percent report falling asleep at the wheel, though not crashing. Approximately 5 percent of people have crashed while being drowsy. If you drive while sleep deprived, you're facing a risk comparable to that of someone who drives with an illegal blood alcohol level.

There are, of course, individual differences in needs for sleep and abilities to sleep. We know that women have a greater need for sleep than men, and on average, though they retire earlier than men and fall asleep faster, they report more time spent awake during the night and generally poorer sleep quality.

While not getting enough sleep is clearly associated with increased health risks, so is getting too much sleep. In the Nurses' Health Study, 82,969 women responding to the questionnaire revealed that those who slept five hours or less a night had a 15 percent greater mortality risk compared with those sleeping seven hours. But those who slept nine hours had a 42 percent increase in risk. Other studies have reported similar patterns.

Health care professionals should ask patients in detail about their sleep habits and should stress the importance of adequate sleep for all.

I recommend seven to eight hours of sleep each night. While some people may claim that they do well on less, even six hours of sleep a night does not prevent cumulative performance deficits.

Sleep-Disordered Breathing

Sleep-disordered breathing, or sleep apnea, is a condition that is estimated to affect 2 to 4 percent of middle-aged adults and an even higher percentage of older people. Approximately 30 percent of those who snore regularly may have sleep-disordered breathing. This condition is most often diagnosed in overweight men with a large neck circumference.

Even mild sleep-disordered breathing is related to an increased risk for hypertension, cardiovascular disease, diabetes and mortality. Obesity is a worldwide problem and is probably a cause of sleep-disordered breathing, thus weight loss and prevention of weight gain offer the best hope of reducing the incidence of this disorder. If snoring is an issue for you, an evaluation to rule out sleep-disordered breathing at a sleep clinic near you is a good step to take.

Insomnia

Insomnia is a special problem in the dark world of sleep deprivation. It's a condition affecting 9 to 19 percent of adults in the United States and Europe. The incidence of insomnia seems to increase with age and to be more common in women than men. A 1991 Gallup survey found that insomnia had a direct impact on the daily lives of one-third of American adults.

Insomnia is generally described as the perception or complaint of inadequate or poor quality of sleep due to difficulty falling asleep, waking up frequently during the night with difficulty going back to sleep, waking up early in the morning or, finally and generally, unrefreshing sleep.

Insomnia takes a toll similar to that of sleep debt: Sufferers feel tired, lack energy, have trouble concentrating and are irritable. Insomnia, among 37 other variables, is the most predictive factor for absenteeism at work.

Only one in 20 patients sees a physician specifically about chronic insomnia, even though chronic sleep disturbance is associated with substantial health consequences, including hypertension, chronic lung disease, arthritis, chronic pain or headaches, and diabetes. Untreated insomnia is a major risk factor for the development of psychiatric disorders, especially major depression but also anxiety and substance abuse disorders.

Many people think that insomnia is a function of aging. While it's true that some need less sleep as they age, it's also true that insomnia in the aged is often a function of increased rates of illness, medication usage, other sleep disorders and the isolation and inactivity that is often seen in older folks.

As with sleep debt, the long-term toll that insomnia takes on health can be serious. Chronic insomnia is associated with an increased risk for alcohol and drug abuse, anxiety, neurosis, personality disorders, as well as dependence on sedatives, depression, diminished quality of life and, in the case of older adults with cognitive disorders, placement in long-term-care facilities.

If you suffer from chronic or even occasional insomnia, read "How to Get a Good Night's Sleep" (see page 267) and follow the recommendations. In addition, consult your doctor to be sure that medical problems such as angina, chronic pain, congestive heart failure, chronic lung disorders, endocrine disorders or prescription or over-the-counter medications are not contributing to your difficulty in sleeping.

A Note to Parents

Many of our kids are desperately in need of some sleep. Too often they're stressed both at school and at home with lots of demands on their time and little downtime. Help your kids get a good night's sleep. Learning good sleep habits early on will pay off. One study found that just one hour of additional sleep restriction or extension on boys and girls in the fourth or sixth grade had a considerable effect on neurobehavioral functioning.

Extension of sleep leads to improved memory function and alertness. The study concluded that most children can extend their sleep with demonstrable benefits. This has obvious implications for learning and school success. In another study on children and sleep habits, boys who had trouble sleeping as toddlers were more likely to become early users of alcohol and marijuana. Don't let this strike fear into your heart if your child is a poor sleeper—other factors could well have been at work in this study.

It's worth knowing that healthy sleep hygiene can promote a host of beneficial effects in children, and that children suffer health consequences just as adults do when they suffer regular sleep deprivation. It's also significant to know that REM (rapid eye movement) sleep is important for learning; children who are lacking sufficient REM sleep will be at a disadvantage in the classroom.

Tips for Sleepy Kids and Parents

• Look at the tips for adults on the next page ("How to Get a Good Night's Sleep"). Many of them are good for babies and children as well.

Even our babies are not getting enough sleep. According to a poll of more than 1,400 parents and others who care for children by the National Sleep Foundation, infants average almost 90 minutes less sleep a day than the 14-hour minimum that doctors recommend. The poll also reported that toddlers get on average at least two hours a week less and preschoolers more than four hours less than the minimum sleep they need to function at their best.

• It's particularly important to establish a bedtime routine for your child. Many parents find that a postdinner bath, followed by reading and quiet time, is a good prelude to a restful night's sleep.

• Many soft drinks contain caffeine, which can have a disastrous effect on children's ability to sleep. Eliminate caffeinated beverages from your child's diet, at least in the afternoon hours.

• Sleepless babies are the bane of parents. We now know that good sleep habits are learned and you may have to "teach" your baby to sleep. There are a number of books that give good guidelines on this. *Solve Your Child's Sleep Problems* by Richard Ferber, MD, is especially useful.

High schools should consider later starting times —about one hour later than usual—to accommodate teenagers' biological clocks. Some universities, such as Duke, have already done this by eliminating 8 A.M. classes. Experts are beginning to recognize the close connection that stress, substance abuse and lack of sleep have with the increasing prevalence of depression in college students.

For Older Folks

The amount of sleep we need does not decrease with age, but the ability to sleep well does. Many older people face particular sleep challenges. For one thing, many seniors don't realize that their body rhythms shift as they age—as we get older we feel an urge to retire sooner and wake earlier. Unfortunately, many people fight this urge. They stay up late as they always did, but they wake earlier. This creates a state of chronic sleep deprivation that takes its toll on health.

In addition, many older folks don't sleep as deeply as they once did, waking more often during the night. This, too, can make seniors feel less rested and refreshed.

In addition, the following conditions can affect sleep: hot flashes during menopause, frequent urination from an enlarged prostate, carpal tunnel syndrome or restless leg syndrome, and chronic pain. Keep in mind that untreated depression as well as high blood pressure and heart disease can all encourage insomnia. Consult with your doctor if you think you could be suffering from any of these conditions.

Putting aside time in the early afternoon to nap appears to help older adults compensate for the sleeping problems that tend to occur with age, new research shows. U.S. investigators found that people between the ages of 55 and 85 who had the opportunity to nap between 2 P.M. and 4 P.M. performed better on tests of mental ability, and had little trouble falling asleep at night. Older adults who took naps got an average of one hour more of sleep each day they napped, giving them more than seven hours—close to the average for young adults.

How to Get a Good Night's Sleep

Here are some tips to help you get a long, *restful*, night's sleep…

- Try to go to bed and arise at the same time each day.
- Sleep in a dark, cool room. You sleep more soundly when your body temperature is cool. Indeed, lowering your body temperature is a signal to your body to sleep. If you and your partner cannot agree on a room temperature, use separate blankets or sew a thin twin-sized blanket to a thicker one to create a full-sized two-zone blanket.
- Take a warm bath an hour before bedtime. The resulting boost in body temperature will trigger a corresponding drop in body temperature a short while later, which helps induce sleep. If the bath is too hot, it may cause more difficulty in falling asleep.
- If you exercise in the late afternoon, it should not be less than four hours prior to your regular bedtime. Like a bath, exercise will raise your body temperature and trigger a rise in temperature, but could keep it elevated near bedtime, making sleep elusive.
- Minimize alcohol consumption. Alcohol may help you fall asleep, but it will not be a deep, restorative sleep. You'll also be more likely to wake in the middle of the night. The more alcohol you drink, and the closer it is to bedtime, the greater this effect. You may also find yourself going to the bathroom more often during the night due to alcohol's diuretic effect.
- Avoid caffeine eight to 12 hours before bedtime. Caffeine can stay in your system about 12 hours. Even decaffeinated coffee can cause sleeplessness in some people. So, if you have difficulty sleeping, avoid any caffeinated beverages, including soft drinks, after lunchtime.
- Don't eat dinner too close to bedtime. A late-evening meal can affect your ability to sleep.
- Complex carbohydrates can boost serotonin levels in your brain, which in turn relax you and help induce sleepiness. If you do have an evening snack, make it a complex carb like a slice of toasted whole wheat bread with some peanut butter.

• Be careful about the supplements you use to promote sleep. While the herbal supplement valerian is touted to make you sleepy, studies have been inconclusive. Also avoid the herb kava kava, as there have been several reports of liver damage with this herb.

Studies of Okinawan and Japanese elderly highlight the synergy between lifestyle and sleep health. These studies suggest that exercise, walking, short naps and a healthy diet were important factors in good sleep habits. A 20-minute nap during the day can be beneficial.

• Try melatonin. Melatonin, a hormone produced by the body to promote sleepiness, can help reset your internal clock and thus help you overcome jet lag or temporary difficulty in sleeping. A dose of 0.1 to 0.5 milligrams a day should be enough. I recommend taking it for no more than two to three weeks at a time. There's no long-term safety data on the daily use of melatonin supplements. If you are on any antidepressants, check with your health care professional before taking any oral sleep medication.

• Check any medications you may be taking to be sure that they don't interfere with sleep. Calcium channel blockers like Cardizem and Procardia, as well as steroids, decongestants and some pain relievers, can interfere with a restful night's sleep.

For more information on sleep and sleep-related disorders, here are some resources...

American Sleep Association
www.sleepassociation.org

American Sleep Apnea Association, 202-293-3650, *www.sleepapnea.org*

National Sleep Foundation, 202-347-3471, *www.sleepfoundation.org*

Restless Legs Syndrome Foundation, 507-287-6465, *www.rls.org*

• Some people find that an open window and/or a fan in the room helps them sleep. Circulating air and the steady drone of a fan can be sleep inducing.

• Do you love your pillow? A great pillow is a great encouragement to a good night's sleep. Invest in a new one if you're spending your nights punching and rearranging the one you have now.

• Drink some warm milk before bedtime. Milk and dairy products contain tryptophan, a natural sleep enhancer.

• Throw out the cigarettes. When smokers go to bed they may experience nicotine withdrawal, which has been linked to difficulty falling asleep.

• Let the sun shine in. As sunlight is an essential element in helping us to synchronize our body clocks, leave your sunglasses off until after 8 A.M. ❦

10

The Keys to Avoiding Disease

It's become increasingly common for people to live longer and healthier lives. More and more of us are taking the initiative to actively seek out better ways to live and eat, which ultimately helps to prevent disease. With the right information and motivation, you can take control of your own health care and avoid serious illness. These basics can help you do this.

How to Avoid Diabetes

Diabetes and a prediabetes are both worldwide time bombs that we will soon see detonate. Few families will remain unaffected.

If you're over age 60, you have a one in five chance of already having diabetes. If you're a young person reading this and you think you don't have to worry about diabetes until you're older or maybe not at all, you may well be wrong. One in five Americans has a condition known as prediabetes and many are completely unaware of their precarious state in terms of future health.

Too many of us have been lulled into thinking that chronic health conditions like diabetes are easily managed these days with sophisticated drugs. While chronic ailments are managed better than ever before, it's important to recognize the potential severe consequences of living with a condition like diabetes. The complications of this disease can include cardiovascular disease, cognitive decline, stroke, kidney failure, nerve damage, vision loss and even amputation.

As the risk for diabetes increases among young people and the possibility of living with the disease for many years becomes a reality for many, the long-term physical, emotional and financial devastation of people's lives becomes a huge burden. To live for 10 years with diabetes is one thing...to live for 50 years with it is another thing altogether, both in terms of personal cost and in actual health care dollars. And of course, many people are not so lucky as to live for 50 years with diabetes: It's a significant cause of premature death.

Here's perhaps the most important thing you need to know about diabetes: You can dramatically lower your risk of developing the disease and you can help control it if you already have it, by making informed choices and adopting HealthStyle as your way of life.

Diabetes is a condition that is characterized by a high level of sugar in the blood (hyperglycemia). That's probably the most distinguishing fact about diabetes, but what is most important for you to know is that it affects virtually every cell and organ in the body. The old saw is that a physician who treats diabetes knows the most about how the human body works because this disease affects every part of it.

There are two types of diabetes: type I (juvenile diabetes or insulin-dependent diabetes) and type II (adult-onset or non-insulin-dependent diabetes). With insulin-dependent, or type I, diabetes, the pancreas does not make insulin and thus blood sugar levels rise uncontrolled in the body. In non-insulin-dependent, or type II, diabetes, the tissues resist insulin's efforts to control blood sugar, resulting in uncontrolled glucose levels in the body.

A study recently revealed that drinking a glass of tomato juice daily could help reduce the blood-platelet clumping and resulting heart attacks and strokes in people with type II diabetes. As 65 percent of people with diabetes die from complications of cardiovascular disease, such as heart attacks and stroke, tomato juice could be a simple step to take to reduce your risk. Look for low-sodium tomato juice.

For the purposes of HealthStyle, we're going to concentrate on type II, or non-insulin-dependent, diabetes, because that is the type that is becoming an epidemic. In 2000, approximately 151 million adults worldwide had type II diabetes...it's projected that by 2025, that figure will double to 300 million.

It's no surprise that the overall rise in obesity parallels the rise in diabetes, as the two are interdependent: Obesity is an important risk factor for diabetes and lack of exercise is a major risk factor for both conditions. Worldwide, the estimated number of people who are obese is in excess of one billion.

CHILDREN AT RISK

The shocking news about type II diabetes is that it is a rising plague among children. Type II diabetes used to be called adult-onset diabetes, but today we are seeing a stunning rise in prediabetes among our children. Six million American children—or 25 percent—are obese and one in four of these obese children have impaired glucose tolerance. In 1990, 4 percent of American children were diagnosed with diabetes. By 2001—only 11 years later—the rate skyrocketed to between 8 and 45 percent of children in ethnically diverse populations, of whom fully 85 percent were obese at the time they were diagnosed. (Indeed, the prevalence of child obesity in America has doubled in the past two decades.) This is a sobering figure, since these children could be facing a lifetime impaired by chronic disease.

HealthStyle is your best defense against developing diabetes, as well as your best strategy for controlling it if you've already been diagnosed. Of course, genetics play a role in your risk for diabetes, but for most people the single greatest risk factor is obesity combined with a lack of exercise.

One study suggests that up to 75 percent of the risk for type II diabetes is attributable to obesity. The worldwide obesity incidence is the primary precursor of the type II diabetes epidemic.

Lifestyle changes really work when it comes to fighting this disease. In one study, 3,234 people at risk for developing diabetes were divided into three groups: Group one received medication (glucophage) to lower blood sugar and were encouraged to eat a healthy diet...group two got a placebo and the same lifestyle recommendations as group one...group three received no medications and no placebo, but had "intensive lifestyle interventions" involving diet and exercise. By the end of the study, group three, the lifestyle group, had a 58 percent decrease in the risk for developing diabetes compared with group two. Group one had a 31 percent reduced risk.

This and many other studies have come to the same conclusion: Lifestyle—HealthStyle—is the best preventive and treatment for diabetes. Yes, making a commitment to eat well and exercise regularly is more difficult than taking a pill, but these behavioral changes work better, they are cheaper in the long run and the only side effects are positive ones.

Here's a diabetes preventive that you probably already have in the pantry: A study of women showed that those who consumed 1 ounce of nuts or peanut butter five times a week or more had a 20 percent decreased risk for developing diabetes.

Here's an outline of the steps you can take to help avoid diabetes or control it if you already have it…

- Maintain a healthy weight for yourself. You do not need to reach an "optimum" weight. For many people, a weight loss of 10 to 14 pounds is sufficient.
- Exercise. Countless studies have demonstrated that exercise improves insulin sensitivity. If you're sedentary, our exercise goal of 30 minutes most days is a good start. You don't have to do it all at once. Ten minutes in the morning, 10 at lunch and 10 in the evening are fine. Find time to walk (see page 255). It's the easiest beginning exercise.
- If you're over 45 years old, get your blood glucose tested and ask your health-care professional how often you should repeat this measurement.
- Reduce your fat intake and pay attention to the types of fat in your diet. In general, a high total fat intake and a high intake of saturated animal fats and trans fats, which are found in many processed foods, are associated with a decrease in the ability of insulin to do its job. Polyunsaturated and monounsaturated fats such as extra virgin olive oil have much less tendency to have an adverse effect on insulin sensitivity.
- Increase your fiber intake. In one study of 42,759 men followed for six years, cereal fiber was inversely associated with a risk for type II diabetes. Another study found that people who ate more white bread than whole-grain breads tended to have the highest risk of type II diabetes. Follow a SuperFoods diet and try to get on a daily basis 45 grams of fiber for adult men and 32 grams of fiber for adult women. As whole-grain fiber is so good at lowering insulin resistance, aim for at least 10 grams of whole-grain fiber as part of your total daily fiber intake (see "Fiber," page 148).
- Increase your intake of fruits and vegetables, especially the carotenoid-rich ones like pumpkins, sweet potatoes, spinach, tomatoes, mangoes, apricots and cantaloupes. This will increase your fiber intake as well as your intake of micronutrients that help promote the efficient use of insulin.
- Eat 1 ounce of unsalted nuts daily.
- Get sufficient sleep. Mounting evidence suggests that sleep deprivation can be a causative factor in diabetes. Curtailing sleep to four hours per night for six nights impairs glucose tolerance and lowers insulin secretion in otherwise healthy, well-rested young men. This prediabetic condition was entirely reversed when these men paid back their sleep debt (see "Sleep," page 260).
- Don't smoke.
- If you drink wine, beer or spirits, drink moderately. Published studies suggest a beneficial effect of a moderate (two drinks a day for men, one drink for women) alcohol intake. Don't start drinking alcohol to prevent diabetes. My personal recommendation is a maximum of eight drinks per week for men and three drinks per week for women.
- There are several nutrients that you should pay special attention to…

Magnesium has been associated with diabetes. One study of women showed a strong inverse relationship between dietary magnesium intake and the incidence of diabetes. Magnesium is found in whole-grain bread and cereal as well as unprocessed foods such as fruits, vegetables, beans and nuts. You should consume the recommended 400 milligrams daily intake of magnesium. One ounce of dry roasted almonds has 86 milligrams, one-half cup cooked spinach has 78 milligrams and one cup of plain low-fat yogurt has 43 milligrams.

Studies have also shown there is an inverse relationship between calcium intake (specifically) and dairy intake (in general) called the insulin resistance syndrome. Of course, low-fat or nonfat dairy foods are excellent sources of bioavailable calcium.

Additional nutrients such as dietary vitamin E, chromium, zinc, potassium and omega-3 fatty acids have been mentioned as possibly playing a role in the prevention of diabetes.

Your risk for developing diabetes is higher than normal if you...

- Are age 45 or over.
- Are overweight.
- Are African-American, Hispanic/Latino American, Asian-American, Pacific Islander or American Indian.
- Have high blood pressure.
- Have a blood relative—parent or sibling—with diabetes.
- Have low HDL ("good") cholesterol—under 40 for men...under 50 for women.
- Have high triglycerides—over 250.
- Have had gestational diabetes while pregnant or gave birth to a large baby.
- Are active less than three times weekly.
- Have been diagnosed as having metabolic syndrome (see page 278).
- Consume a high-fat diet, especially one high in saturated fat and trans fats.

How to Avoid Osteoporosis

We think of our bones as the scaffolding to our bodies. From certain standpoints, this is correct. Our bones are the rigid framework that supports our muscles and soft tissue. *But there is a dramatic difference between our bones and a steel scaffold...*

Our bones are living tissue in a constant state of flux. Bones constantly break down and build up. Indeed, as far as your bones are concerned, you're not the person you were 10 years ago—the adult skeleton is replaced about every decade. Bones are also porous. They actually consist of a flexible porous framework of a protein substance known as collagen, plus a lot of calcium phosphate that serves as a mineral filler.

Here are the two most important things to know about your bones: First, because they're in a constant state of rebuilding, today's diet and exercise are creating tomorrow's bones. Second, we are facing a health care crisis because, as many of us tend to live longer, our bones, abused by poor diet and lack of exercise, aren't up to the task of supporting us into old age. *The results:* The estimated risk of lifetime fracture exceeds 40 percent for women and 13 percent for men. In fact, approximately 10 million Americans are currently diagnosed with osteoporosis and, perhaps more alarming, 18 million are at risk because of low bone mass.

The Looming Danger

Osteoporosis or porous bone, is aptly named. If you could see an X-ray of osteoporotic bone it would look like Swiss cheese. As you might imagine, when bones become porous they lose strength. The great danger here is fracture. A young person with strong resilient bones who experiences a simple broken or fractured bone will heal fairly quickly. An older person who experiences a hip fracture—a common occurrence among seniors with osteoporosis—can find that he has crossed the threshold into disability and worse.

For too many older people, a hip fracture can be the cause of nursing home confinement and subsequent immobility and decline. Indeed, in the elderly, hip fractures are associated with mortality in over 20 percent of cases. When you realize that 350,000 hip fractures are reported annually and this number is likely to rise as the number of people over age 65 increases, you can see that osteoporosis is a significant health issue.

While genetics plays a role in the development of osteoporosis, there's a lot you can do now to improve your chances of having a strong, flexible skeleton into old age.

- Boost your calcium and vitamin D intake. Calcium is a mineral used in a wide variety of bodily functions. If you're not getting sufficient calcium from your diet, your body will begin to break down the calcium in your bones to use it elsewhere. Vitamin D helps your body both absorb calcium and deposit it in the bones.

Many studies have demonstrated that adequate amounts of both calcium and vitamin D will improve bone mineral density. In 1997, for example, researchers found that men and women who were given calcium and vitamin D rather than a placebo enjoyed higher bone density and fewer fractures.

Most of us don't get enough calcium in our diets. The typical woman consumes 800 milligrams of calcium daily from food and supplements, but the recommended level is 1,000 milligrams daily to 1,200 milligrams daily for women over 50 years of age. This is of particular concern when you realize that a negative balance of only 50 to 100 milligrams a day over a period of time is enough to result in osteoporosis.

The best sources of calcium are low-fat and nonfat dairy products like yogurt, as well as fortified soymilk and soy foods, cereals, sardines and canned wild Alaskan salmon (with bones), broccoli, collards, kale and calcium-fortified orange juice.

- Adequate vitamin D intake is important to preserve bone strength. Our skin actually makes vitamin D when exposed to ultraviolet rays of the sun. Unfortunately, many of us do not get sufficient vitamin D from either sunlight or dietary sources, so it may be important to consider adding a supplement to your diet. (See "Are You Getting Enough Vitamin D?," page 144.) I recommend 800 to 1,000 IU of supplemental vitamin D3 daily. (All supplemental vitamin D from fish sources is vitamin D3.)

- Resistance exercise plays an important role in preserving bone strength. Resistance training and weight-bearing exercise like walking stimulate new bone formation. Include this type of exercise in your routine two to three times weekly. (See "Resistance Training," page 252.) Remember that balance and flexibility to prevent falls are important also, especially as you age. Exercise in general, particularly tai chi, enhances flexibility.

- Vitamin K is being recognized as an important player in the promotion of bone strength. One recent study in the Netherlands emphasized the importance of vitamin K when subjects who took vitamin K supplements, along with calcium, vitamin D, zinc and magnesium, had significantly less bone loss after three years compared with subjects who took either a placebo or the same supplements minus the vitamin K.

Many people think that osteoporosis is a woman's disease. While it's true that women can be at high risk because of bone loss during and immediately after menopause, men also are commonly afflicted. In fact, one in every eight men over 50 will suffer a hip fracture due to osteoporosis. Men should discuss their risk for osteoporosis with their health care providers and should have bone density tests as indicated.

The current recommended dose of vitamin K is 90 micrograms a day for women and 120 micrograms a day for men, but many researchers believe that this amount is too low. Trials are under way to come up with a more beneficial recommendation, but in the meantime, if you follow a SuperFoods diet, you'll easily get the vitamin K you need. Vitamin K is particularly abundant in spinach and its sidekicks, especially kale and collards.

- Potassium is a real bone booster. Research has shown that people who get a good supply of potassium experience less bone loss than others who do not. Once again, as potassium is readily available in fruits and vegetables, you should have no trouble reaching your HealthStyle potassium goal of 8,000 milligrams a day if you follow a SuperFoods diet. A single potato has 940 milligrams of potassium and a banana, 490 milligrams. (See "Potassium Power," page 146.)

- Soy can promote healthy bones because its phytoestrogens—literally plant estrogens—seem to boost bone mineral density. I recommend 10 to 15 grams of soy protein a day, which supplies about 50 milligrams of soy isoflavones. If you have a history of breast cancer in your family, check with your health care practitioner before eating soy.

- Limit alcohol consumption to a maximum of three to seven drinks per week for women and six to fourteen drinks per week for men. Alcohol consumption at these levels may enhance bone mineral density. However, in larger amounts, alcohol decreases the activity of bone-rebuilding cells. The risk for breast cancer in women begins to climb with four drinks per week. My own HealthStyle recommendations on alcohol are one to three drinks per week for women and two to eight drinks per week for men.

- Limit caffeine consumption. Excessive amounts of caffeine can affect bone strength, as it increases the amount of calcium excreted in the urine. Limit your coffee consumption to two cups a day and don't forget that many brands of soda contain caffeine as well as phosphates, which tend to pull calcium from the bones. (Noncola soft drinks, by the way, do not contain phosphates.) Consider adding nonfat milk, 1% low-fat milk or calcium-fortified soymilk to tea and/or coffee, as this helps to counteract any adverse effects of the caffeine.

- Limit your sodium intake. Excessive sodium intake may trigger calcium excretion. Aim for no more than 2,400 milligrams of sodium per day. Hide the salt shaker, look for low-sodium labels in the supermarket, avoid most processed foods and cured meats and check the labels on canned goods for sodium content. Try Vegit or another salt substitute.

- Watch your intake of vitamin A (in the form of retinol or so-called preformed vitamin A), as it's a nutrient that in excess will increase your risk for bone fractures. While vitamin A is essential for bone growth, too much of it in the form of retinol can be damaging. Limit retinol intake to a maximum of 3,000 IU daily. There is, by the way, no increased risk for fracture from carotenoid sources of vitamin A.

- Don't smoke. Many people don't realize that smoking, along with so many other health negatives, plays a role in promoting osteoporosis. Although the reasons for this are unclear, there's no doubt that smoking has a negative effect on bone strength, which seems to translate into an increased risk of hip fracture. Indeed, the negative effects of smoking on bone health last up to 10 years after quitting.

Eat Your Greens!

One of the great delights of the spring season is the appearance in supermarkets and farmers' markets of the first greens of the season. After months of eating the vegetables of winter—cabbage, rutabaga, carrots (not without their charms, of course...)—we finally begin to see the rich greens of the new season, offering a change and a nutritional jump start from the doldrums of winter. Greens are so rich in crucial nutrients that they have indeed earned their reputation as tonics. They abound in carotenoids and vitamin C as well as folate, iron, calcium and fiber. They're truly essential to a healthy diet and a vibrant HealthStyle.

Chard, kale and spinach are more commonly found, but many markets feature unusual and tempting varieties, such as dandelion, pea shoots, watercress, mustard, purple broccoli, baby bok choy and a host of others. Most can be added to a salad or lightly sautéed with extra virgin olive oil and a minced garlic clove.

Here are some tips...

- Look for fresh-looking, fresh-smelling greens. Avoid any that are yellowed or browned. Avoid any slimy or wilting greens.
- Refrigerate greens and keep them moist but not wet. Roll greens lightly in damp paper towels and store the bundle in a plastic bag (with holes punched in it so humidity doesn't promote spoilage) in the fridge.
- Don't wash greens until just before using.

Some greens are bitter, others are strongly flavored and some are a surprising change from the usual bland winter lettuces. Some folks, especially children, like their greens with a little added flavor. Here are three quick preparations that will make greens even more appealing:

- Blend 2 tablespoons reduced-sodium soy sauce, 1 tablespoon rice vinegar, 1 tablespoon toasted sesame oil, 1 teaspoon honey (buckwheat honey, if you have it), 2 teaspoons minced fresh ginger, 1 small clove minced garlic and 1 teaspoon grated orange or lemon rind. Toss these ingredients with cooked greens such as kale, spinach, Swiss chard or even broccoli.
- Blend ¼ cup peanut butter, soy butter or almond butter with 2 tablespoons hot green tea. To this add 1 tablespoon reduced-sodium soy sauce, 1 teaspoon honey (buckwheat honey, if you have it), 1 tablespoon lime juice, 1 small clove minced garlic and a dash of crushed red pepper flakes, if desired. Use as a dressing for any cooked greens.
- Blend ¼ cup balsamic vinegar with 1 tablespoon chopped shallots. Heat in a small saucepan over medium heat until syrupy. Remove from the heat and add 2 tablespoons raisins or dried cranberries and 1 tablespoon extra virgin olive oil. Toss with cooked Swiss chard, kale or spinach.

How to Avoid Alzheimer's Disease

There are few diseases that are more feared than Alzheimer's, no doubt because any mental disorder is frightening. Moreover, this affliction has become so common that many people find their lives touched by it. Of course, one of the tragedies of Alzheimer's disease is that entire families are affected, as they must bear responsibility for helping loved ones with this disease.

There are currently about 5 million Americans with Alzheimer's and the number is expected to rise to 16 million by the year 2050. Women seem to be most at risk, although the precise reason for the development of Alzheimer's is still somewhat of a mystery. The lifetime risk for Alzheimer's disease is reported to be 12 to 19 percent for women over age 65 and 6 to 10 percent for men of the same age.

We do know that some cases are linked to genetic susceptibility, while others may be due to damage from tiny strokes and resulting decreased blood flow to the brain. It's also clear that cardiovascular risk factors, including obesity, high blood pressure and high cholesterol, are associated with the cognitive decline we recognize as Alzheimer's.

Alzheimer's disease is a form of dementia. Dementia affects about 10 percent of the adult population over age 65 and about 45 percent of those over age 85. Alzheimer's disease is the most common form of dementia and it's generally defined as an irreversible progressive decline in memory, language skills orientation in time and space and ability to perform routine tasks.

Since it now stands that one out of two of us who are reading this are slated to develop Alzheimer's or some form of dementia, if we live long enough, efforts at prevention are certainly well advised.

Fortunately, there are steps we can all take to reduce our risk of developing Alzheimer's. Like all HealthStyle recommendations, the positive changes you adopt to avoid Alzheimer's disease will also help you avoid a host of other chronic disabling conditions. Like most diseases, Alzheimer's begins decades before the onset of clinical symptoms—the brain changes very slowly—so you do have time to take steps now. Indeed, one study of 13,000 women from the Nurses' Health Study found that women who ate the most SuperFood vegetables, like spinach, broccoli and Brussels sprouts, in their fifties and sixties showed less cognitive decline in their seventies compared with women who ate less of these vegetables.

In general, a HealthStyle of abundant SuperFoods, adequate exercise and stress control is the best defense against this disease. Overall, since the brain relies on optimum blood flow, adequate nutrients and the right balance of fats, those are the three areas that need special attention if we want to preserve optimum cognitive ability long into our senior years. We know for sure that a healthy cardiovascular system is the foundation for a healthy brain and so that is the bedrock of an effective Alzheimer's defense.

Here are some guidelines for avoiding Alzheimer's...

- Eat fish, particularly fatty varieties like wild Alaskan salmon, regularly. I recommend 3 ounces four times a week. Since omega-3 fatty acids—particularly DHA, one of the fats found in fish—is a primary component of brain cell membranes and is known to directly promote brain health, an adequate intake of fish—the best food source—is the cornerstone of any Alzheimer's avoidance program.

In one study, people who ate one or more fish meals a week had 60 percent less risk of Alzheimer's than people who ate fish rarely or never. In this study, total intake of DHA fatty acids was inversely associated with risk: People in the top fifth of intake had a 70 percent reduction in risk compared with those in the lowest fifth. Remember, fish is not only for dinner—think salmon salad sandwiches or a salad of fresh greens topped with chunks of leftover grilled salmon. Don't forget high omega-3 eggs. You can put a chopped, hard-boiled egg on top of a salad for a great nonfish source of DHA. A recent study demonstrates that six DHA-enriched eggs a week supply a measurable bioavailable source of this important fat.

- Keep your blood pressure low—ideally below 120/80 or lower. We know that hypertension is a risk factor for developing Alzheimer's.
- Keep your weight at optimum levels. Obesity is another risk factor for Alzheimer's disease.

One exciting recent study showed that both green and black tea hinder the activity of two enzymes in the brain that have been associated with the development of Alzheimer's disease. The effects of green tea were longer lasting—a week—while the effects of black tea lasted only a day. Make both green and black tea part of your regular daily diet (see "Tea," page 108).

- Feed your brain with SuperFoods. A constant supply of glucose is required, so look to complex carbohydrates—whole grains, fruits and vegetables—to provide a steady, healthy source of fuel. In one study, 28 healthy elderly people who took 3.5 tablespoons of sugar enhanced recall and verbal fluency compared with a control group who took saccharin. Yet another study of Alzheimer's patients found that increasing blood glucose levels improved memory by 100 percent in some of the subjects. The point is not to increase your sugar intake, but rather to try to give your brain the steady supply of glucose that it needs from complex carbs. These studies also point to the biological plausibility that long-term low-carb diets might have a negative effect on the brain.

• Check your homocysteine levels. One study found that the presence of elevated homocysteine could nearly double the risk of developing Alzheimer's disease. If your levels are high, be sure to take a multivitamin with the RDA for all the B vitamins, especially folate, B6 and B12.

• Have a complete blood count (CBC) to be sure you're not anemic, as low-iron stores are implicated in neurological deficits. Do not, however, take an iron supplement without consulting with your health care provider.

• Aim for a total cholesterol below 200 milligrams/d and an LDL-C of 70 milligrams. High cholesterol promotes atherosclerosis or hardening of the arteries and may also contribute to the brain plaques that are typical of Alzheimer's.

• Aim for a fasting glucose of less than 100 during your annual physical.

• Be wise about your alcohol intake. A study of older adults found that those who drank one to six alcoholic drinks per week were least likely to have dementia. (In the same study, those who had 14 or more drinks per week were *more* likely to develop dementia than those who never drank.) Red wine contains polyphenols (antioxidants), which may have additional benefits to those of alcohol. Of course, you shouldn't start to drink to stave off Alzheimer's disease, but if you already do, keep within the range of one to six drinks per week. For abstainers, I suggest 4 to 8 ounces of purple grape juice daily.

• Exercise! Exercise increases blood flow to the brain and reduces the production of stress hormones, such as cortisol, that can have an adverse effect on the brain. Follow the HealthStyle ERA suggestions (see page 247) and try to get at least 30 minutes of physical activity daily.

• Socialize. Relationships with others seem to play a role in brain health. Seek out regular social interaction, especially as you age and might have less routine contact with others in work situations.

• Lower your risk for diabetes, as this disease is a risk factor in developing Alzheimer's (see page 269).

• Eat blueberries—one cup fresh or frozen—or its sidekicks daily. Blueberries are "brain berries"—they seem to have powerful effects on the preservation of cognitive ability.

• Eat avocado. Preliminary research suggests that this fruit works in a similar fashion to blueberries in promoting brain health.

• Avoid trans fats.

• Concentrate on a high dietary intake of vitamins C and E. Also consider taking a daily supplement of vitamins C and E. These vitamins may help lower your risk for Alzheimer's. If you take E supplements, be sure they contain all eight forms of vitamin E (four tocopherols and four tocotrienols). Take 100 to 200 IU of natural vitamin E and 200 to 500 milligrams of vitamin C daily.

• As there may be a relationship between low intake of dietary beta-carotene and cognitive decline, boost your intake of this important nutrient with the SuperFood pumpkin. Try pumpkin smoothies, pumpkin soups and pumpkin puddings. Spinach is also a good source of beta-carotene and animal studies suggest that spinach prolongs normal cognition in older animals.

• Consider taking ginkgo biloba extract. Although the data is not clear, the *Cochrane Reviews* stated in 2002: "Overall there is promising evidence of improvement in cognition and function associated with ginkgo." There is no established amount, but a typical dose is 120 to

240 milligrams per day, divided into two or three doses. Consult with your health care professional before using and don't take ginkgo biloba in conjunction with other blood thinners such as aspirin, as there is an additive effect.

• Consider taking acetyl-L-carnitine. This substance mimics the action of acetylcholine—a major neurotransmitter—in the brain. It may have efficacy in retarding the aging of cellular mitochondria, the energy factory in the cells and many feel that this is a key to increasing longevity. To date, acetyl-L-carnitine has been shown to slow the progression of Alzheimer's in at least two studies, though there hasn't been a published report on the effectiveness of this substance to prevent Alzheimer's. Take 500 milligrams twice a day.

• Spice it up. Preliminary data suggests that turmeric may play a role in preventing and/or treating Alzheimer's.

• Calorie restriction may prevent Alzheimer's disease and other aging disorders.

• Increase your niacin intake. A recent study of 6,158 men and women age 65 and older reported an inverse association between Alzheimer's disease and age-related cognitive decline and dietary intakes of total niacin from food and supplements, and also niacin from foods only. Excellent sources of niacin include turkey or chicken breast, tuna, wild salmon, sardines, Alaskan halibut, peanut butter and vitamin-enriched cold cereals.

Syndrome X or Metabolic Syndrome

At least 64 million Americans—nearly a third of adults age 20 and older—suffer from a condition known as metabolic syndrome, called by its discoverer, Dr. Gerald Reaven, "Syndrome X." The rate of those who probably meet the federal government's criteria for the syndrome approaches 50 percent among the elderly. Mexican Americans and African-American women appear to be especially prone. It also turns up in people who are not obese but have recently put on a lot of weight around their middles and, alarmingly, in an increasing number of overweight children.

Researchers speculate that metabolic syndrome is caused by a fundamental malfunctioning of the body's system for storing and burning energy. Contributing to the syndrome are genetics, a sedentary lifestyle, a Western diet high in refined carbohydrates (low in fiber and high in saturated fat), smoking and progressive weight gain.

Metabolic syndrome is a cluster of risk factors that, taken individually, have negative health consequences but, when appearing together, exponentially increase the risk of various health problems, notably heart disease, diabetes and possibly certain types of cancer. It's the synergy of the multiple factors that increases the risk of disease and death. Like the synergy of good factors that we've been exploring in the nutrients in whole foods, the synergy of negative factors present in metabolic syndrome can create a danger much greater than one risk factor alone.

Do you suffer from Syndrome X? If you have three or more of the following risk factors you do have it and you must begin right now to reverse your risk with diet and exercise. It's important to remember that you don't need to be obese to suffer from Syndrome X: Many people who have three or more of the risk factors ignore them because they think that obesity is a crucial factor in the syndrome. This is not the case and it's dangerous to go for a long period of time without any treatment for the syndrome as your risk of developing a serious, if not fatal, ailment increases.

• Waist: More than 40 inches for males, 35 inches for females.

• Serum triglycerides: Greater than 150 milligrams/dl.

• HDLs: Less than 40 milligrams for males and less than 50 milligrams for females.

• Blood pressure: Greater than 130/85.

• High fasting glucose or blood sugar, of at least 110 milligrams/dl of blood.

If you do have three or more of these risk factors, discuss Syndrome X with your health care provider to see if you should pursue a course of medication in addition to the HealthStyle recommendations concerning diet, exercise and stress control.

In general the following steps should be taken if you have metabolic syndrome...

• Lose excess weight.

• Increase physical activity.

• Eat a SuperFoods diet of whole foods with plenty of vegetables and fruits.

• Avoid a very low-fat diet. Any diet that has less than 20 percent of calories from fat could exacerbate metabolic syndrome. Usually, eating very little fat means an increase in carbohydrate consumption and too many carbs can cause both triglycerides and blood glucose to rise, worsening metabolic syndrome.

• Pay attention to your cholesterol levels. Consult with your health care professional and if diet and exercise don't get your blood lipid levels into line, consider taking medications.

• Pay attention to your blood pressure (see the following section, "How to Avoid Hypertension"). Have it checked regularly and take steps to reduce it if it is high.

• Practice stress control. See how to do this in "How to Achieve Whole Mind/Whole Body Health," page 286.

There may be an association between HDL ("good") cholesterol typical of metabolic syndrome and breast cancer. A study of older, overweight women with metabolic syndrome revealed that those who had the lowest levels of HDL had the highest risk for breast cancer. Future studies will reveal the complex nature of the connection between metabolic syndrome and chronic diseases such as cancer.

How to Avoid Hypertension

People are often surprised that I pay attention to the sodium content of foods. Why, they wonder, does a healthy guy bother to look for, say, low-sodium canned tuna or no-salt-added salsa? Excess sodium intake is contributing to a looming crisis in national and international health. I'm talking about hypertension and the disastrous consequences of this syndrome.

Of course, sodium and excess salt intake aren't the sole causes of hypertension. For some people, salt intake seems to have no effect on their health whatsoever. Paying attention to sodium intake is a simple signal and reminder that you should work every day to ensure that your blood pressure is in the optimal HealthStyle zone.

Under Pressure

Blood pressure refers to the resistance created each time the heart beats in an effort to send blood rushing through the arteries. Between beats, when the heart relaxes, blood pressure drops. Blood pressure is routinely expressed in two figures: the systolic (SBP) or peak pressure, created when the heart contracts. This figure is normally written over the diastolic (DBP) or reduced pressure, present between beats. A typical adult blood pressure reading is 120 (systolic) over 80 (diastolic).

Recently, the acceptable levels of blood pressure were reduced. The guidelines recognize that the risk of death from heart disease and stroke begins to increase even at blood pressures as low as 115/75 mm Hg and that it doubles for each 20/10 mm Hg increase beyond that mark. Previously, the normal or optimal mark was 120/80 mm Hg. While this was considered optimal, it is now considered borderline. *High blood pressure is now divided into the following different levels...*

• Prehypertension SBP 120–139 or DBP 80–89

• Stage I hypertension SBP 140–159 or DBP 90–99

• Stage II hypertension SBP 160 or higher or DBP 100 or higher

• Residual hypertension is an SBP of 140 mm Hg or more even after treatment

• HealthStyle goal is an SBP less than 120 and a DBP less than 80

Have your blood pressure checked every time you see a health care professional for whatever reason. If you're over age 60, have your pressure checked at least once a year.

Hypertension is the term that describes a state of chronic elevated blood pressure. More than 60 million people in the U.S. and approximately one billion people worldwide suffer from hypertension. More than half of all Americans aged 65 to 74 and almost three quarters of African-Americans in the same age group also suffer from elevated blood pressure. (The hypertension epidemic is especially dangerous for African-Americans, whose rate of stroke deaths is 40 percent higher than that of the general population.).

Data from the Framingham Heart Study suggests that about 90 percent of Americans will eventually develop hypertension. Ironically and really tragically, many of these people don't even know they're suffering because hypertension generally is painless and has no symptoms.

Here's the truly frightening aspect of hypertension—it isn't an isolated ailment. Hypertension affects many bodily systems. *If you have hypertension, you are also subject to...*

• Increased risk of dying from a heart attack

• Increased risk of congestive heart failure

• Increased risk of dying from a stroke

• Increased risk of developing dementia and Alzheimer's disease

• Increased risk of kidney damage

• Increased risk of atherosclerosis and arteriosclerosis

• Increased risk for developing macular degeneration

If you have hypertension, you are pushing your heart and circulatory system to their limit every single day.

The good news about hypertension is that most people are in the borderline-to-moderate range and most of them can bring their pressure down by making lifestyle and diet changes—in other words, by adopting the general recommendations of HealthStyle.

Don't expect to notice any symptoms from hypertension. It's typically picked up at a routine medical screening. A crisis resulting from hypertension could include the following symptoms:

- **Headache, drowsiness or confusion**
- **Numb or tingling hands and feet**
- **Nosebleeds**
- **Severe shortness of breath**
- **A vague but intense feeling of discomfort**

The Scourge of Salt

There are many reasons why hypertension rates around the world are soaring. For one thing, obesity is on the rise and obesity contributes to hypertension. We also know that the population is aging and as we age, the likelihood of developing hypertension also increases. Indeed, since most adults develop blood pressure readings that put them at risk for negative health consequences, paying attention to your blood pressure and taking steps to control it, whatever your age, is a wise move.

COLD-WEATHER CHOLESTEROL

Did you know that blood contains less water in winter, slightly concentrating cholesterol? This means your total cholesterol reading could be a bit higher in winter than in summer.

One study has found that cholesterol levels naturally fluctuate throughout the year. Researchers at the University of Massachusetts Medical Center in Worcester tracked 517 healthy people for a year and found that their cholesterol levels tended to rise in the winter and fall in the summer.

The biggest changes occurred in those with elevated cholesterol and in women. Their levels fluctuated by as much as 18 points. The seasonal variation put 22 percent more patients over the official high-cholesterol mark of 240 milligrams/dL in winter than in summer.

Cold-season readings could lead to a misdiagnosis of high cholesterol for up to three million Americans, the researchers estimate. *Best bet:* Get several checks and make sure that at least one is in the spring or fall, when levels are at a midpoint.

Myth: Sea salt is a healthier product than table salt. In fact, there are no documented health advantages to sea salt and the sodium content of the two is similar. Sea salt, however, tastes better because it has no additives to make it free flowing.

Salt is a major hidden health menace to us and to our children. If you eat out, eat prepared foods and/or eat fast foods, you're probably eating too much salt. We do need sodium to live. It helps us maintain fluid balance, regulates blood pressure and transmits nerve impulses as well as helping in maintaining the body's acid-alkaline balance and playing a role in muscle movement.

The average adult body contains about 250 grams of salt—enough to fill three small saltshakers. This salt is constantly lost through sweat and urine and replaced through the diet. The problem is that most of us are consuming far more salt than is required for healthy functioning.

While the amount of salt the body needs daily, depending on circumstances like exercise and climate, is usually less than 500 milligrams a day, the typical American diet consists of 4,000 to 7,000 milligrams a day. We know that a diet containing more than 2,400 milligrams of salt a day is associated with higher blood pressure readings and in fact there's some evidence that difficulties begin at consumption of more than 1,500 milligrams of sodium daily. It's generally agreed by researchers that much of the rise in blood pressure that seems inevitable as we age is actually a result of a lifetime of overconsumption of salt.

Attention Parents: A low-sodium diet during the first six months of life not only lowers infant blood pressure, but these "low-sodium babies" become adolescents whose SBP (systolic blood pressure) is lower than that of "normal sodium babies."

There is some disagreement among experts about an acceptable level of salt intake. For example, the Institute of Medicine in 2004 said that for people under 50 years of age, 1,500 milligrams of sodium daily was acceptable, while the 2005 Dietary Guidelines Advisory Committee said that for "young adults" no more than 2,300 milligrams daily was acceptable. If even these two important U.S. groups studying sodium can't agree on an appropriate intake, it's no wonder that the public might be somewhat confused.

I think that we can take our cue from the past: Since our Stone Age ancestors ingested about

813 milligrams of sodium daily and our genetic makeup hasn't changed much since then, it seems obvious that when it comes to sodium, the less the better. Unless you are training for or running a marathon or are physically active in hot, humid environments, the need for sodium above that which you would consume in a whole-foods, low-sodium SuperFoods HealthStyle diet will rarely occur.

Does salt affect us all equally? No. It's true that some people who overuse salt will not elevate their blood pressure. On the other hand, it's difficult to determine who is and is not salt sensitive. We know for sure that where salt has not been added to the diet, there is virtually no hypertension. We also know that only in industrialized countries does blood pressure rise with age.

You say you don't use that much salt and you figure your blood pressure is okay. That's the delusion too many of us labor under until it's too late and we're either on medication or suffering serious health consequences. The truth is that most of us are eating far more salt than necessary and that, combined with obesity and lack of physical activity, is putting our health at risk.

The terms "salt" and "sodium" are used interchangeably, but they're not the same thing. Sodium is an element that joins with chlorine to form sodium chloride or table salt. Sodium occurs naturally in most foods and salt is the more common source of sodium in the diet.

The best way to reduce salt in your diet is to read labels for salt content and avoid fast foods. Many fast foods are loaded with salt and for that reason, as well as the fat in those foods, they should be avoided. People are often surprised to discover how much salt there actually is in prepared foods.

Here's an exercise: Take that bottle of salad dressing in the fridge and a box of any processed food in the pantry—macaroni and cheese or taco seasoning or even salad croutons. Check the sodium content on the labels of these foods. Remember that you're aiming for less than 1,500 milligrams of sodium daily from all sources. Chances are that the labels will reveal that one serving of both the salad dressing and the prepared food will put you over the limit. Two tablespoons of Wishbone Italian Dressing, for example, has 490 milligrams of sodium and Stouffer's Macaroni & Cheese has 1,100 milligrams in a 9-ounce serving. Add to those numbers the salt from all the other sources in your daily diet and it's easy to see that you could be going well over the healthy limit every single day.

Here are some tips on getting the salt out of your diet...

About 10 to 20 percent of the American population is "salt sensitive." The percentages are greater among African-Americans and also in the elderly and those who have diabetes.

- Reeducate your taste buds. If you crave salt, it's because your taste buds have become used to very salty foods. By gradually cutting back on salt, after a few weeks you'll find that heavily salted foods will lose their appeal.
- Avoid bottled salad dressings or look for ones that are low in sodium. Make your own dressing with extra virgin olive oil and balsamic vinegar and fresh herbs. If you use dressing in a restaurant, request that it be served on the side and use it sparingly.
- Remove the saltshaker from the table. Try salt substitutes like Mrs. Dash and Vegit.
- Avoid salt when cooking or reduce the amount called for. You can use less salt in most recipes without anyone noticing.
- Avoid processed meats and deli foods, as they are high in sodium.
- Check all canned foods and processed foods as well as frozen dinners for salt content.

Other reasons to shake the salt habit:

- Sodium increases urinary calcium loss and although the literature is mixed, there is data to suggest that high salt intake may be related to loss of bone mass and to osteoporosis.
- High salt intake may have an adverse effect on lung function and asthma symptoms.
- Salt may promote the formation of kidney stones.
- High dietary salt may lead to a higher infection rate of *Helicobacter pylori*, the bacterium that causes stomach ulcers.
- High salt intake seems to increase your risk for stomach cancer.
- High salt intake has been associated with insomnia and preeclampsia of pregnancy.

• Look for low-sodium canned tuna and salmon.

• Home water softeners can add considerable amounts of sodium to your drinking water. Consider using bottled water for drinking and cooking if your household water has a high level of sodium.

Other Causes of Hypertension

While critically important, salt is not the only cause of hypertension. There are a number of steps you can take to ensure that your blood pressure remains at healthy levels throughout your lifetime.

• Stop smoking.

• Maintain an optimum weight. Obesity is a significant contributor to hypertension. Sometimes losing just a few pounds can make a significant difference to your blood pressure. If you're overweight, your systolic blood pressure drops about one point for every two pounds you lose.

• Exercise. It's important to be physically active. See "Exercise" (page 236) for some suggestions on how to work physical activity into your daily life. Exercise not only can lower your blood pressure, it can also help you lose weight and make major overall positive contributions to your health.

✪ Only two out of three people who have hypertension know they do and only one in three has the condition under control.

• Reduce your saturated fat intake. A high intake of saturated fat has been conclusively linked to high cholesterol levels and atherosclerosis, which in turn contributes to hypertension.

• Increase your potassium, magnesium and calcium intakes by eating a diet that is rich in foods containing these nutrients. Most Americans have a sodium-to-potassium ratio greater than 2:1, which means that we eat twice the amount of sodium as potassium. Researchers suggest that a sodium-to-potassium ratio of 1:5 is optimum (see "Potassium Power," page 146). Many of us also do not consume enough magnesium and calcium, the lack of which contributes to hypertension. A diet rich in fruits and vegetables can help you restore the optimal balance of these nutrients.

• Investigate the Dietary Approaches to Stop Hypertension (DASH) diet. This diet, which

- *Foods rich in magnesium:* Swiss chard, spinach, whole grains, pumpkin/sunflower seeds, soybeans, beans, Alaskan halibut, nuts, avocado.
- *Foods rich in calcium:* Low-fat/nonfat dairy, sardines, canned Alaskan salmon with bones, almonds, kale, collards, tofu, calcium-fortified orange juice or soymilk.

is rich in fruits, vegetables and low-fat dairy products, has been shown to lower blood pressure. Check the DASH homepage at *www.nhlbi.nih.gov/health/public/heart/hbp/dash/introduction.html*.

• Limit alcohol to a maximum of three to seven drinks per week for women and six to fourteen drinks per week for men. My own HealthStyle recommendations on alcohol are one to three drinks per week for women and two to eight drinks per week for men.

• Control stress. A number of studies suggest that relaxation techniques such as meditation can play a role in lowering blood pressure (see page 286).

A recent study reported that drinking alcohol outside of meals increased the risk of hypertension no matter what type of alcohol was consumed. The lesson: It's probably best to drink with your meals or immediately following them.

• Increase your fiber intake. Some studies show an inverse association between the consumption of dietary fiber and both high blood pressure and risk of hypertension (see "Fiber," page 148).

11

HOW TO ACHIEVE WHOLE MIND/WHOLE BODY HEALTH

You are more than the sum of your parts. You are an intensely complicated mechanism of bodily systems, mental states, whims and enthusiasms that react to the weather, the traffic, the noise and a loved one's caress in unique and profound ways. You have good days and bad. Sometimes you turn the key and your engine purrs...other days you get nothing but a backfire.

What am I getting at here? I'm introducing one of the oldest concepts in human health that's become one of the hottest topics in medicine and research: the mind/body connection. Wise men have long known that there is an intimate connection between your inner self and your physical state. They really can't be separated. It's time to look at what, for many people, is a new frontier in medicine.

BODY, MIND, SPIRIT

HealthStyle is about whole body/whole mind health. One of my goals is to have you appreciate that achieving your best healthy self involves more than good nutrition, exercise and other activities that focus on you as a physical machine. True health involves the whole you—body, mind, spirit.

There is a new field of medicine that explores this relationship. It's called psychoneuroimmunoendocrinology (or PNIE). This describes the study of the unity of mental, neurological, hormonal and immunological functions—in effect, the combination of mind, body and spirit.

Here are some intriguing examples to illustrate this field of research...

A study of people who had suffered a heart attack found that those suffering from depression had a threefold risk of dying in the year after the event.

A four-year study of nearly 1,000 folks from Finland found that the group identified as "high-hopelessness" experienced a 19 percent greater thickening of atherosclerotic plaque compared with the "moderate or low-hopelessness" group. This indicates that intensely felt negative emotions can actually promote the development of cardiovascular disease.

A study of nearly 13,000 men and women found that anger was a significant risk factor for death from coronary artery disease, independent of other biological risk factors exhibited by these subjects. Indeed, several studies suggest that risks are greater for emotional distress—depression, anger, grief, hostility, anxiety, frustration, resentment—as well as social isolation, than for conventional medical risks.

One study found a significantly increased risk for suffering a heart attack following the death of a loved one. The elevated risk in the first 24 hours after the loss is fourteenfold higher than if the subject were in a normal state without the loss of a loved one. In the second 24 hours following a loss, the risk is eightfold. Over the ensuing month, the risk is two- to four-fold higher.

Another study reported that among more than 1,000 adults with coronary artery disease, the patients who were depressed felt a greater burden from their symptoms, greater physical limitations, worse quality of life and worse overall health. It's not a simple matter of attitude influencing symptoms—intensely felt negative emotions, including anxiety and fear, anger and rage, and grief and sadness, are all associated with increased incidence of premature cardiovascular death in adulthood as well as greatly increased complications after heart attack.

Don't you find this information powerful but also rather intuitive? In your heart, you've probably always known that your mental state affects your health. HealthStyle's important message is that you can and must do something about this connection *over and above recognizing it.* You can't separate your physical health from your emotional/mental/spiritual health. If you truly want to achieve optimum HealthStyle, you must recognize the power of the mind/body connection and take whatever steps you can to improve on this often neglected aspect of robust health.

How We Got Here

Modern medicine is in constant transition. New findings topple old...time-honored practices are discarded as new ones prove more effective. If you are reading this book, you've no doubt seen dramatic changes in health care. A more recent change has involved my particular specialty—the role of nutrition in disease. It wasn't so long ago that nutrition was virtually ignored by traditional medicine as a factor in precipitating disease. For a period of time, vitamins, sometimes in megadoses, were seen as a solution to health. Today, we know that whole foods are the backbone of a healthy lifestyle and that appropriate supplementation is important but is never a substitute for a healthy diet.

One exciting frontier in nutrition and health involves the precise and delicate interaction of the nutrients in foods and our genes. One day we may be able to prescribe a diet based on your genetic makeup—one that will use foods to enhance protective genes and suppress ones that make you susceptible to certain diseases. Of course, at present we know that a SuperFood diet is your best chance of promoting health, whatever your genotype. We also know that adequate exercise is absolutely fundamental to a healthy lifestyle—not just to lose weight and not just to get strong, but to amplify every single aspect of good nutrition.

We're ready as health care consumers to move into the new frontier of stress reduction and "mindfulness" as a health-promoting activity. To that end I'd like to introduce my HealthStyle version of achieving stress relief and promoting lifelong health: Personal Peace. But before I can explain the goals and practice of Personal Peace, you have to understand the role of stress in your everyday life and its effects upon your long- and short-term health.

Stress

If there's an opposite of Personal Peace, it's stress. Stress is as much a part of living as breathing, but it's something that we ignore at our peril. We all have a general idea of what it is, but it was first studied by Hans Selye, who defined stress as both a psychological and physiological event. It was recognized that there are both good and bad stressors. A positive stress is a challenge; a negative one is overload. Words that define our reactions to a negative stress could include fear, anxiety, frustration, anger, depression and helplessness. Many of us find our days laced with these emotions. Many of us are unaware that these "feelings" are affecting both our short- and long-term health.

Laugh out loud. It's good for your heart. Studies have shown that laughter may reduce the risk of coronary heart disease. In one study, researchers measured 300 subjects' propensity to laugh in a variety of everyday situations.

It was found that, compared with the control group, people who suffer from coronary heart disease were significantly less likely to experience laughter during daily activities, surprise situations or social interactions, leading researchers to propose that the inclination to laughter may be cardioprotective.

SYMPTOMS OF STRESS

- You eat more or less than normal.
- You feel tired constantly.
- You drink more alcohol, smoke more or use drugs more frequently.
- Your sleep habits change.
- You have aches and pains that are not the result of exercise.
- You feel more anxious, nervous or angry than usual.
- You have to use the bathroom more or less often than normal.
- You are more forgetful.
- You notice other changes in the way you behave.

FIGHT OR FLIGHT

When we feel a stress—an unreasonable boss, a sick child, too many bills, sleep deprivation, a rude salesclerk—our body shifts into overdrive. Levels of the stress hormones adrenaline and cortisol elevate and the body shifts into fight-or-flight response with increased metabolism, heart rate, respiration, blood pressure and muscle tension.

In a twenty-first-century world, usually there's no actual physical fight or flight involved as a result of stress. Rather, usually the result is a slow burn with a metabolism in high gear and no physical response that allows us to let off steam.

Too many of us spend too much time all stressed up with no place to go. The end result is more than simple frustration. It's an actual physical disease. An estimated 75 to 90 percent of all adult visits to primary-care physicians are prompted by stress-related complaints.

We now know that unresolved chronic stress can damage the immune and other systems. It is linked to the development of insulin resistance (a risk factor for diabetes) as well as hypertension, coronary heart disease, osteoporosis and other disorders. There's some evidence that it might even promote cancer. There's also evidence that chronic, unrelieved stress causes a variety of physical reactions that may not go away. Eventually, enough stress over a long period of time renders us unable to calm down physiologically. It's as if our engines are locked in overdrive.

Personal Peace

Personal Peace is your weapon against unrelieved stress. Personal Peace allows the ratcheting down of the fight-or-flight response into a state of serenity that actually has positive physiological and psychological benefits. Just as a constant stream of multiple antioxidants fights the unending onslaughts of free-radical damage on a cellular level, so the regular achievement of Personal Peace enables your body to recover from the inevitable daily onslaughts of stress. To achieve optimum health, you need Personal Peace as much as you need the nutrients provided by whole foods. Personal Peace will restore you to your whole mind, body and spirit.

Personal Peace isn't something that you achieve once and for all. Rather, it's a process, a mind-set, a habit of regularly retreating to a place of inner calm. This retreat has actual physiological benefits that can pay off in reducing risk for a host of chronic diseases.

The notion of Personal Peace is not a new idea. It has always existed in the context of religious teachings. In Eastern cultures, it is an essential part of daily existence. The news about Personal Peace or mindfulness or spirituality is that it has measurable definable physiologic effects that can benefit us all.

As I mentioned, *Personal* is a key aspect to this concept. There's no simple prescription for achieving this. It's not comparable to the basic recommendation of eating a cup of spinach daily or getting 30 minutes of exercise. *Personal* Peace is about you and your world. So many factors come into play that will affect how the mind and spirit can best achieve Personal Peace. There are vast cultural, religious and even geographic and gender differences that affect us. There are more elusive, almost inexplicable preferences that guide us in our choices and our achievement of pleasure and serenity.

You must determine your best route to Personal Peace. All I can do is urge you to take active steps to achieve this goal as the evidence is truly overwhelming that it's a route to a healthier and happier life.

How do you achieve Personal Peace? My general recommendation is to select one or more stress-reducing practices from the list below and incorporate them into your daily life. I use a host of these practices, from the relaxation response to prayer to exercise to nature, at various times every single day to achieve my own Personal Peace.

Consciously working on this aspect of coping with stress has changed my life, and I know you'll reap similar rewards when you achieve your own Personal Peace.

Here are some common, proven approaches to Personal Peace that have demonstrated physiological benefits...

The Relaxation Response

When I left home for college, my mother told me that it was important to learn to relax, that it wasn't always something that just "happened," and that learning to relax could help me fall asleep and help me cope with the stresses of school. She told me to lie down and let each part of my body relax until it felt heavy. What my mother was teaching me was progressive muscle relaxation, or the relaxation response.

Herbert Benson, a doctor at Harvard, wrote about the progressive muscle relaxation in his book *The Relaxation Response. Here is the simple technique...*

- Sit or lie down quietly (if lying down, be sure you don't go to sleep!). Close your eyes and deeply relax all your muscles, beginning at your feet and ending at your face.
- Breathe through your nose and become aware of your breathing. As you breathe out, say a word. ("One" was what Benson suggested, but any word will do.) Breathe in, breathe out (repeat

> **W**ant a simple method to achieve Personal Peace? Keep a photograph of loved ones in your wallet or at your workplace.
>
> In one study, it was found that sheep who are temporarily isolated from their flock endure an increase in stress as measured by heart rate, changes in movements and vocalization and hormone levels. But when the sheep were shown photos of other sheep, all symptoms of stress were reversed. Abstract face shapes and goat photos had no effect.
>
> This positive response can be extrapolated to humans, as it involves our highly complex ability to recognize and respond to familiar faces. Though we don't understand precisely how this mechanism works, we do know that the link between face recognition and physiological response is real.

"One"), breathe in, breathe out (repeat "One"), and so on. Breathe naturally and easily.

- Continue for 10 to 20 minutes. You can open your eyes to check the time, but don't use an alarm. When finished, sit or lie quietly for a few minutes.
- Be passive. Ignore distracting thoughts.

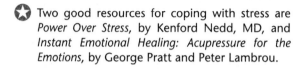

Two good resources for coping with stress are *Power Over Stress*, by Kenford Nedd, MD, and *Instant Emotional Healing: Acupressure for the Emotions*, by George Pratt and Peter Lambrou.

You should do the relaxation response once or twice daily. Don't do it within two hours of eating, as digestion seems to interfere with the effectiveness of the response. At first, you may find it difficult to achieve the relaxation response. You'll be distracted and your head might fill with unrelated thoughts. Try to gently ignore those distractions and focus on your breathing.

You might find it a challenge at first. Perhaps it will seem like a waste of time, but persevere and you'll begin to reap the rewards. People who regularly practice the relaxation response find they have:

- A better awareness of the tension levels in their bodies and thus a better ability to relax in any situation.
- Improved concentration.
- Reduced resting levels of the fight-or-flight portion of the autonomic nervous system.

The Relaxation Response

	FIGHT OR FLIGHT	RELAXATION RESPONSE
Metabolism	up	down
Heart rate	up	down
Blood pressure	up	down
Breathing rate	up	down
Muscle tension	up	down

Meditation

Similar in many ways to the relaxation response, meditation is a state in which the body is relaxed and the mind is calm and focused. Mindfulness, or meditation, is the method the Buddha taught as part of the means to end suffering.

Meditation is the practice of paying attention to the breath and to sensations in the present moment rather than getting lost in random thoughts, whether memories of the past, commentary on the present or anticipation of the future. Meditation has been demonstrated to ease chronic pain, depression, anxiety and stress, improve heart health, boost mood and immunity, and generally improve symptoms associated with many chronic ailments. Meditation is not difficult to learn, and those who meditate regularly are able to achieve a relaxed, meditative state very quickly. The greatest rewards of meditation come with practice and persistence.

Almost all techniques of stress reduction have similar components: Repetition of a sound or word, phrase or prayer...image or physical activity and a passive disregard of everyday thoughts as they occur. For me, silently repeating my mantra, "Trust in God," has a 100 percent track record in pushing any negative thought or emotion out of my mind.

Meditation has measurable effects on health. One study showed a significant lowering of blood pressure and heart rate in black adults, as well as a reduction in atherosclerosis of the carotid artery, which supplies blood to the brain.

Another study showed that African-American teenagers who meditated for 15 minutes twice a day for four months were able to lower their blood pressure a few points. This is significant, because African-Americans suffer disproportionately from hypertension, and if blood pressure can be reduced in teens, they are more likely to enjoy a reduced risk for hypertension as they age.

Scientific evidence shows that people who are meditating experience an increase of activity in the part of the brain that controls metabolism and heart rate. Studies on Buddhist monks show that meditation produces long-lasting changes in the brain activity in areas involving attention, working memory, learning and conscious perception.

A recent study recruited 62 "stressed-out" volunteers and found that those who underwent "mindfulness training" had experienced an average 54 percent reduction in psychological distress by the end of the three-month study. The control subjects had no such reduction. The trainees also reported a 46 percent drop in medical symptoms over the period of the study, compared with a slight increase in the control group.

Meditation involves focusing the mind on an object or word, consciously relaxing the body and repeating a word or phrase. It's ideal to practice meditating twice a day—in the morning and evening. As Gandhi stated, "Meditation is the key to the morning and the latch of the evening." Set aside 10 to 15 minutes to meditate. Find a quiet place and sit comfortably relaxed with eyes open or closed. Choose a phrase to repeat. Feel your body relax and if your mind wanders, return it to your chosen phrase. Remain in this state for 10 to 20 minutes.

Persistent high levels of stress hormones impair memory in people of all ages by affecting brain areas involved in cognitive processing. These stress hormones—glucocorticoids—are normally released in times of stress, and studies show that both short- and long-term exposure to these hormones can have a negative effect on the memory and cognitive processing in both children and adults.

Older adults who experience constantly high levels of stress hormones may also experience as much as a 14 percent shrinkage of the hippocampus—the brain area involved in emotion and memory.

Spirituality and Religious Practice: The Power of Prayer

There is increasing evidence that religious practice such as prayer enhances health. Since antiquity, people of every geographic area, culture, ideology and religious belief system have used prayer as a means to positively affect their daily life and well-being. William James described prayer as "every kind of inward communication or conversation with the power recognized as divine."

Scientific studies suggest that if you want to live longer, frequent attendance at religious services may yield positive health benefits. Even among individuals who attend religious services once a month or more, mortality rates appear to be lower than among people who attend rarely or not at all. These benefits accrue for both Judeo-Christian and non-Judeo-Christian religions, and at least one study demonstrates a positive outcome for people who primarily and regularly practice their prayer in a nonchurch/religious-facility setting.

We know that religiosity or spirituality is associated with lower blood pressure and less risk of developing hypertension. Blood pressure studies show a generally consistent pattern connecting greater religious involvement to lower blood pressure or a lower incidence of hypertension. There is also evidence that religious activity is associated with better blood lipid profiles, with lower ("bad") LDLs and higher ("good") HDLs among those who regularly participate in religious services. Finally, there's evidence that those who worship regularly also enjoy better immune function.

Multiple studies on religion and health indicate "a trend toward better health and less morbidity across the board in the presence of higher levels of religiosity."

If you do regularly practice a religion, you can be encouraged by the positive evidence that this habit enhances your health.

People who are interested in developing their spiritual side may experience fewer hospitalizations and require less long-term care than their peers who are less spiritual.

An interesting study found a connection between spirituality and health care needs. While it's unclear what the exact connection between spirituality and health is, evidence suggests that those who are inclined to develop their spiritual life may reap the rewards of better health.

Personal Peace in an Instant

Stress can appear at any time. While a regular habit of stress-relieving meditation or relaxation response is restorative, it's also very helpful to take full advantage of other simple stress-reducing techniques throughout the day. Many of you probably use one or more of these techniques automatically and unconsciously, but sometimes when you employ a stress-reduction technique consciously and deliberately, it can be more effective.

Here are some simple techniques to bring more peace into your life

• Breathe deeply. Deep, diaphragmatic breathing can be an excellent stress reducer. Research has shown that slowing down and deepening our breaths shifts us from the stress response to the relaxation response. Optimal breathing can not only help reduce stress levels, it can also improve performance.

I often stop and take a few deep breaths to reduce stress in any situation. *Here's how:* Sit or stand comfortably and place your hands on your stomach. (Once you've practiced, you won't need to do this.) Inhale slowly and deeply, letting your abdomen expand like a balloon. Exhale, letting your abdomen fall as you release all the air. Press the air out as you contract your abdomen, pulling it in. Repeat a few times. Relax!

• Listen to music. Music can be an excellent stress reducer. Music has been shown to increase emotional arousal and induce positive emotions. It activates reward centers in the brain and inhibits negative emotions. Anthony Storr states, "Music exalts life, and gives meaning...Music is a source of reconciliation, exhilaration and hope which never fails...An irreplaceable and unreserved transcendental blessing."

Many surgeons, me included, listen to music while operating. A study of 50 male surgeons showed that listening to music can reduce the elevations in blood pressure and heart rate that often accompany performing tasks under pressure.

And music, like photos, can remind us of pleasant events in our past. Have readily available relaxing, soothing tapes and/or CDs in your car, workplace and home. If you're in the habit of listening to talk radio while you drive, now and again switch to a classical or soothing jazz station and feel your body relax as you listen. Put on music that you enjoy while completing chores or while walking the dog. Be an "active" listener and allow the music to alter your mood and relax you.

• Seek fun and friendship. It seems that positive events have a much stronger impact on the immune function than upsetting events have a negative one. Simple activities like a walk in the park, a quiet dinner with friends or a cuddle with the family dog or cat can have immediate results, such as strengthening the immune system and temporarily reducing blood pressure.

Fill your life with pleasurable social events and brief moments of relaxing pleasures. Social contact is a mitigating factor against a host of diseases including hypertension and heart disease. Many studies substantiate that people who enjoy high levels of social relationships tend to live longer than those who do not. In one study, living alone led to a near doubling of the risk for recurrent heart attack or death in patients who had already experienced a heart attack. Make a point of developing and enjoying a strong social support network.

• Embrace nature. Nature is man's refuge from the stresses and complications of daily life. Retreat to nature whenever you can for restorative moments. Whether it's a walk in a park, time spent in the garden, a hike in the mountains or even just a moment spent watching a pigeon on a city street corner, nature brings us back to ourselves and can serve as a sort of meditation.

Mother Earth plays an essential role in our health and well-being, including...

• The health-promoting natural pharmacy in whole foods.

• The gentle caress of the wind and rain on our skin (massage therapy).

• The fragrant smell of flowers and our own pheromones (aroma therapy).

• The magnificent visual images of natural beauty that can be found by everyone each and every day.

• The many pleasing and calming sounds of the natural world (music therapy).

> *Surely there is something in the unruffled calm of nature that overawes our little anxieties and doubts: the sight of the deep-blue sky, and the clustering stars above, seem to impart a quiet to the mind.*
>
> —Jonathan Edwards

• Reduce anger. Anger robs us of health. Too many of us experience anger regularly in our lives and we will ultimately suffer the penalty. In one study of more than 1,000 medical students, it was revealed that those with the highest levels of anger (determined by expressed or concealed anger, gripe sessions and irritability) were at significant risk for developing premature heart attacks versus those with lower levels of anger.

A high level of anger not only serves as a potential trigger for a heart attack, but in this study it was a trigger for causing a premature heart attack. These students with excessively angry responses to stress appeared to initiate biochemical changes marking them for an early heart attack.

> *Consider how much more you often suffer from your anger and grief than from those very things for which you are angry and grieved.*
>
> —Marcus Aurelius Antoninus

Another study of 540 middle-aged Finnish men found that an increase in a measure of their anger expression was associated with an increase in their risk for hypertension. Neal Krause of the University of Michigan School of Public Health found that people who forgive easily tend to enjoy greater psychological well-being and have less depression than those who hold grudges.

A Hawaiian kupuna (elder) expressed it beautifully: "You have to forgive three times. You must forgive yourself, for you will never be perfect. You have to forgive your enemies, for the fire of your anger will only consume you and your family. And perhaps most difficult of all, if you want to find pleasure in your living, you have to forgive your friends, for because they are friends they are close enough to you to hurt you by accident. Forgiving is the meaning of and making of friendship." ❦

OPTIMISM KEEPS YOU HEALTHY

A study of 334 healthy men and women was conducted to see how their "emotional style" related to their vulnerability to colds. All subjects were given nasal drops containing cold viruses, but the subjects with a "highly positive" emotional style developed fewer cold symptoms. People with negative styles didn't get sick significantly more than those with only slightly positive emotions, but those who did reported more discomfort than objective measures would have predicted. Positive thinking pays off.

Bibliography

CHAPTER 1
SuperFoods Rx: The Basics

How Your Diet Is Killing You

Adlercreutz, H. Western diet and Western diseases: some hormonal and biochemical mechanisms and associations. *Scand J Clin Lab Invest* 1990;201(suppl):3-23.

Albanes, D., et al. Antioxidants and cancer: evidence from human observational studies and intervention trials. In: *Antioxidant Status, Diet, Nutrition and Health*. Papas, A.M., ed. CRC Press;1999:497-544.

Albertson, A.M., et al. Consumption of grain and wholegrain foods by an American population during the years of 1990-1992. *J Am Diet Assoc* 1995;95:703-4.

Ascherio, A., et al. Intake of potassium, magnesium, calcium, and fiber and risk of stroke among US men. *Circulation* 1998;98(12):1198-204.

Bantle, J.P., et al. Effects of dietary fructose on plasma lipids in healthy subjects. *Am J Clin Nutr* 2000;72: 1128-34.

Bazzano, L.A., et al. Fruit and vegetable intake and risk of cardiovascular disease in US adults: the first National Health and Nutrition Examination Survey Epidemiologic Follow-up Study. *Am J Clin Nutr* 2002;76(1):93-9.

Brand, J., et al. Food processing and the glycemic index. *Am J Clin Nutr* 1985;42:1192-6.

Centers for Disease Control and Prevention. Chronic diseases and their risk factors: the nation's leading causes of death. Atlanta: Centers for Disease Control and Prevention, 1999.

Coulston, A.M. The role of dietary fats in plant-based diets. *Am J Clin Nutr* 1999;70(suppl):512S-5S.

Davis, C.D. Diet and carcinogenesis. In: *Vegetables, Fruits, and Herbs in Health Promotion*. Watson, R.R., ed. CRC Press;2001:273-92.

DeBoer, S.W., et al. Dietary intake of fruits, vegetables, and fat in Olmsted County, Minn. *Mayo Clinical Proceedings* 2003;78:161-6.

Dock, W. The reluctance of physicians to admit that chronic disease may be due to faulty diet. Reprinted from 1953. *Am J Clin Nutr* 2003;77(6):1345-7.

Fontaine, K.R., et al. Years of life lost due to obesity. *JAMA* 2003;289(2):187-93.

Food and Nutrition Board, Institute of Medicine. Dietary Intake Data from the Third National Health and Nutrition Examination Survey (NHANESIII), 1988-1994. In: *Dietary Reference Intakes*, appendix C. Washington, D.C.: National Academy Press; 2001:594-643.

Fraser, G.E., et al. Effect of risk factor values on lifetime risk of and age at first coronary event. The Adventist Health Study. *Am J Epidemiol* 1995;142:746-58.

Fraser, G.E., et al. Risk factors for all-cause and coronary heart disease mortality in the oldest-old. The Adventist Health Study. *Arch Intern Med* 1997;157: 2249-58.

Fraser, G.E. Associations between diet and cancer, ischemic heart disease, and all-cause mortality in non-Hispanic white California Seventh-Day Adventists. *Am J Clin Nutr* 1999;70(suppl):532S-8S.

Friedenreich, C.M. Physical activity and cancer: lessons learned from nutritional epidemiology. *Nutr Rev* 2001;59(11):349-57.

Fung, T.T., et al. Association between dietary patterns and plasma biomarkers of obesity and cardiovascular disease risk. *Am J Clin Nutr* 2001;73:61-7.

Harnack, L.J., et al. Temporal trends in energy intake in the United States: an ecologic perspective. *Am J Clin Nutr* 2000;71:1478-84.

Kanazawa, M., et al. Effects of a high-sucrose diet on body weight, plasma triglycerides, and stress tolerance. *Nutr Rev* 2003;61(5, Part II):S27-S33.

Kimura, S. Glycemic carbohydrate and health: background and synopsis of the symposium. *Nutr Rev* 2003;61(5, Part II):S1-S4.

O'Dea, K. Clinical implications of the "thrifty genotype" hypothesis: where do we stand now? *Nutr Metab Cardiovasc Dis* 1997;7:281-4.

Ramakrishnan, U. Prevalence of micronutrient malnutrition worldwide. *Nutr Rev* 2002;60(5, Part II):S46-S52.

Rolls, B.J., et al. Portion size of food affects energy intake in normal-weight and overweight men and women. *Am J Clin Nutr* 2002;76(6):1207-13.

Rutledge, J.C. Links between food and vascular disease. *Am J Clin Nutr* 2002;75(1):4.

Micronutrients: The Keys to Super Health

Cao, G., et al. Antioxidant capacity of tea and common vegetables. *J Agric Food Chem* 1996;4:3426-31.

Hennekens, C.H. Antioxidant vitamins and cardiovascular disease. In: *Antioxidant Status, Diet, Nutrition and Health.* Papas, A.M., ed. CRC Press;1999:463-78.

Jacob, R.A., et al. Oxidative damage and defense. *Am J Clin Nutr* 1996;63(suppl):985S-90S.

O'Neill, K.L., et al. Fruits and vegetables and the prevention of oxidative DNA damage. In: *Vegetables, Fruits, and Herbs in Health Promotion.* Watson, R.R., ed. CRC Press;2001:135-46.

Phytochemicals—A New Paradigm. Bidlack, W.R., Omaye, S.T., Meskin, M.S., Jahner, D., eds. Lancaster, PA: Technomic Publishing Co. Inc., 1998.

Phytochemicals as Bioactive Agents. Bidlack, W.R., Omaye, S.T., Meskin, M.S., Jahner, D., eds. Boca Raton, FL: CRC Press LLC, 2000.

Rimm, E.B., et al. Vegetable, fruit, and cereal fiber intake and risk of coronary heart disease among men. *JAMA* 1996;275:447-51.

Shahidi, F., et al. *Phenolics in Food and Nutraceuticals.* Boca Raton, FL: CRC Press LLC, 2004.

Simopoulos, A.P. The Mediterranean diets: what is so special about the diet of Greece? The scientific evidence. *J Nutr* 2001;131:3065S-73S.

Trichopoulou, A., et al. Mediterranean Diet: are antioxidants central to its benefits? In: *Antioxidant Status, Diet, Nutrition and Health.* Papas, A.M., ed. CRC Press;1999:107-18.

Waladkhani, A.R., et al. Effect of dietary phytochemicals on cancer development. In: *Vegetables, Fruits, and Herbs in Health Promotion.* Watson, R.R., ed. CRC Press;2001:3-18.

Wattenberg, L.W. An overview of chemoprevention: current status and future prospects. *Proc Soc Exp Biol Med* 1997;216:133-41.

Wise, J.A. Health benefits of fruits and vegetables: the protective role of phytonutrients. In: *Vegetables, Fruits, and Herbs in Health Promotion.* Watson, R.R., ed. CRC Press;2001:147-76.

The Four Principles of SuperFoods Rx

Anatomy of an Illness as Perceived by the Patient—Reflections on Healing and Regeneration. Cousins, N, ed. New York: Norton, 1979.

Anderson, J.W. Diet first, then medication for hypercholesterolemia. *JAMA* 2003;290(4):531-8.

Appel, L.J. The role of diet in the prevention and treatment of hypertension. *Curr Atheroscler Rep* 2000;2:521-28.

Cao, G., et al. Increases in human plasma antioxidant capacity after consumption of controlled diets high in fruit and vegetables. *Am J Clin Nutr* 1998;68:1081-7.

Carson, R. *Silent Spring.* Boston, MA: Houghton Mifflin, 1994.

Cordian, L. The nutritional characteristics of a contemporary diet based upon Paleolithic food groups. *JANA* 2002;5(3):15-24.

de Lorgeril, M., et al. Mediterranean dietary pattern in a randomized trial. Prolonged survival and possible reduced cancer rate. *Arch Intern Med* 1998;158:1181-7.

de Lorgeril, M., et al. Modified Cretan Mediterranean diet in the prevention of coronary heart disease and cancer. In: *Mediterranean Diets.* Simopoulos, A.P., Visioli, F., eds. Karger Basel, Switzerland 2000;87:1-23.

Eastell, R., et al. Strategies for skeletal health in the elderly. *Proc Nutr Soc* 2002;61(2):173-80.

Fairfield, K.M., et al. Vitamins for chronic disease prevention in adults: scientific review. *JAMA* 2002;287(23):3116-26.

Fan, W.Y., et al. Reduced oxidative DNA damage by vegetable juice intake: a controlled trial. *J Physiol Anthropol Appl Human Sci* 2000;19:287-9.

Fleet, J.C. DASH without the dash (of salt) can lower blood pressure. *Nutr Rev* 2001;59(9):291-7.

Gronbaek, M., et al. Type of alcohol consumed and mortality from all causes, coronary heart disease, and cancer. *Ann Intern Med* 2000;133:411-9.

Gussow, J.D. *This Organic Life: Confessions of a Suburban Homesteader.* White River Junction, VT: Chelsea Green Publishing Company, 2001.

Jenkins, D.J.A., et al. Effects of a dietary portfolio of cholesterol-lowering foods vs lovastatin on serum lipids and c-reactive protein. *JAMA* 2003;290(4):502-10.

Kant, A.K., et al. Dietary diversity and subsequent mortality in the First National Health and Nutrition Survey Epidemiologic Follow-up Study. *Am J Clin Nutr* 1993;57:434-40.

Marlett, J.A., et al. Position of the American Dietetic Association: health implications of dietary fiber. *J Am Diet Assoc* 2002;102(7):993-1000.

Milton, K. Nutritional characteristics of wild primate foods: do the natural diets of our closest living relatives have lessons for us? *Nutr* 1999;15:488-98.

Mozaffarian, D., et al. Cereal, fruit, and vegetable fiber intake and the risk of cardiovascular disease in elderly individuals. *JAMA* 2003;289(13):1659-66.

Nick, G.L. Detoxification properties of low-dose phytochemical complexes found within select vegetables. *JANA* 2002;5(4):34-44.

Pool-Zobel, B.L., et al. Consumption of vegetables reduces genetic damage in humans: first results of a human intervention trial with carotenoids-rich foods. *Carcinogenesis* 1997;18:1847-50.

Pratt, et al. Nutrition and Skin Cancer Risk Prevention. In: *Functional Foods and Neutraceuticals in Cancer Prevention*, Ronald R. Watson, editor, Iowa State Press, 2003:105-20.

Simopoulos, A.P. Essential fatty acids in health and chronic disease. *Am J Clin Nutr* 1999;70(suppl):560S-9S.

Storper, B. Moving toward healthful sustainable diets. *Nutr Today* 2003;38(2):57-9.

Sun, J., et al. Antioxidant and antiproliferative activities of common fruits. *J Agric Food Chem* 2002;50(25):7449-54.

Suter, P.M. Alcohol and mortality: if you drink, do not forget fruits and vegetables. *Nutr Rev* 59(9):293-7.

Thompson, H.J., et al. Effect of increased vegetable and fruit consumption on markers of oxidative cellular damage. *Carcinogenesis* 1999;20:2261-6.

USDA Nutrient Database for Standard Reference. *http://www.nal.usda.gov/fnic/cgi-bin/nut_search.pl*

White, I.R. The level of alcohol consumption at which all-cause mortality is least. *J Clin Epidemiol* 1999;52:967-75.

Willcox, B.J. *The Okinawa Program.* Willcox, B.J., Willcox, D.C., Suzuki, M., eds. New York: Three Rivers Press, 2001.

Willett, W.C., et al. Mediterranean diet pyramid: a cultural model for healthy eating. *Am J Clin Nutr* 1995;61(suppl):1402S-6S.

Willett, W.C., et al. Relation of meat, fat, and fiber intake to the risk of colon cancer in a prospective study among women. *N Engl J Med* 1990;323:1664-72.

Willett, W.C. *Eat, Drink and Be Healthy—The Harvard Medical School Guide to Healthy Eating.* New York: Simon & Schuster Source, 2001.

Willett, W.C. Micronutrients and cancer risk. *Am J Clin Nutr* 1994;59:162S-5S.

SuperFoods Rx in Your Kitchen

American Institute for Cancer Research. As restaurant portions grow, vast majority of Americans still belong to "clean plate club," new survey finds. January 15, 2001. American Institute for Cancer Research home page: *www.aicr.org.* Internet: *http://www.aicr.org/r011501.htm* (accessed 8 November 2001).

American Institute for Cancer Research. New survey shows Americans ignore importance of portion size in managing weight. March 24, 2000. American Institute for Cancer Research home page: *www.aicr.org.* Internet: *http://www.aicr.org/r032400.htm* (accessed 8 November 2001).

Duyff, R.L. *American Dietetic Association Complete Food and Nutrition Guide*, 2nd edition. Hoboken, NJ: John Wiley & Sons, Inc., 2002.

Freedman, D.S., et al. Trends and correlates of class 3 obesity in the United States from 1990 through 2000. *JAMA* 2002;288(14):1758-61.

Hu, F.B., et al. Optimal diets for prevention of coronary heart disease. *JAMA* 2002;299(20):2569-78.

Kant, A.K., et al. A prospective study of diet quality and mortality in women. *JAMA* 2000;283:2109-15.

Krebs-Smith, S.M., et al. The effects of variety in food choices on dietary quality. *J Am Diet Assoc* 1987; 87(7):896-903.

Newby, P.K., et al. Dietary patterns and changes in body mass index and waist circumference in adults. *Am J Clin Nutr* 2003;77(6):1417-25.

Ogden, C.L., et al. Prevalence and trends in overweight among US children and adolescents, 1999-2000. *JAMA* 2002;288(14):1728-32.

CHAPTER 2
The Terrific Twenty-three—The SuperFoods

Apples

Arts, I., et al. Dietary catechins in relation to coronary heart disease among postmenopausal women. *Epidemiology* 2001;12:668-75.

Bazzano, L.A., et al. Dietary fiber intake and reduced risk of coronary heart disease in US men and women: The National Health and Nutrition.

Boyer, J., and R.H. Liu. Apple phytochemicals and their health benefits. *J Nutr* 2004, May 12;3(1):5.

Chinnici, F., et al. Improved HPLC determination of phenolic compounds in cv. Golden Delicious apples using a monolithic column. *J Agric Food Chem* 2004, Jan 14;52(1):3-7.

Conceicao de Oliveir, M., et al. Weight loss associated with a daily intake of three apples or three pears among overweight women. *Nutrition* 2003;19:253-56.

Examination Survey I Epidemiologic Follow-up Study. *Arch Intern Med* 2003, Sep 8;163(16):1897-1904.

Fernandez, M.L. Soluble fiber and nondigestible carbohydrate effects on plasma lipids and cardiovascular risk. *Curr Opin Lipidol* 2001, Feb;12(1):35-40.

Feskanich, D., et al. Prospective study of fruit and vegetable consumption and risk of lung cancer among men and women. *J Natl Cancer Inst* 2000;92:1812-23.

Huxley, R.R., and H.A.W. Neil. The relation between dietary flavonol intake and coronary heart disease mortality: A meta-analysis of prospective cohort studies. *Eur J Clin Nutr* 2003;57:904-908.

Knekt, P., et al. Flavonoid intake and risk of chronic diseases. *Am J Clin Nutr* 2002;76:560-68.

Sable-Amplis, R., et al. Further studies on the cholesterol-lowering effect of apple in humans: Biochemical mechanisms involved. *Nutr Res* 1983;3:325-28.

Sesso, H., et al. Flavonoid intake and risk of cardiovascular disease in women. *Am J Clin Nutr* 2003;77:1400-1408.

Shaheen, S., et al. Dietary antioxidants and asthma in adult-population based case-control study. *Am J Respir Crit Care Med* 2001;16:1823-28.

Wolfe, K., et al. Antioxidant activity of apple peels. *J Agric Food Chem* 2003;5:609-14.

Avocado

Hargrove, R.L., et al. Low fat and high monounsaturated fat diets decrease human low density lipoprotein oxidative susceptibility in vitro. *J Nutr* 2001;131: 1758-63.

Lopez, L., et al. Monounsaturated fatty acid (avocado) rich diet for mild hypercholesterolemia. *Arch Med Res* 1996, Winter;27(4):519-23.

Ruiz-Gutierrez, V. et al. Plasma lipids, erythrocyte membrane lipids and blood pressure of hypersensitive women after digestion of dietary oleic acid from two different sources. *J Hypertens* 1996;14:1483-90.

Unlu, N.Z., et al. Carotenoid absorption from salad and salsa by humans is enhanced by the addition of avocado or avocado oil. *J Nutr* 2005, Mar;135(3):431-36.

Beans

Adlercreutz, H.A., et al. Effect of dietary components, including lignins and phytoestrogens on enterohepatic circulation and live metabolism of estrogens and on sex hormone binding globulin. *J Steroid Biochem* 1987;27:1135-44.

The American Cancer Society, Dietary Guidelines Advisory Committee. Guidelines on diet, nutrition and cancer prevention: reducing the risk of cancer with healthy food choices and physical activity. 1996.

Anderson, J.W., et al. Cardiovascular and renal benefits of dry bean and soybean intake. *Am J Clin Nutr* 1999;70(3 suppl):464S-74S.

Anderson, J.W., et al. Hypocholesterolemic effects of oat and bean products. *Am J Clin Nutr* 1988;48:749-53.

Barampama, Z., et al. Oligosaccharides, antinutritional factors, and protein digestibility of dry beans as affected by processing. *J Food Sci* 1994;59:833-8.

Bazzano, L.A., et al. Legume consumption and risk of coronary heart disease in US men and women: The National Health and Nutrition Examination Survey (NHANES) I Epidemiologic Follow-up Study. *Arch Int Med* 2001;161(21):2573-8.

Bazzano, L.A., et al. Dietary fiber intake and reduced risk of coronary heart disease in U.S. men and women: NHANES I Epidemiologic Follow-up Study. *Arch Intern Med* 2003, Sep 8;163(16):1897-1904.

Brown, L., et al. Cholesterol-lowering effects of dietary fiber; a meta-analysis. *Am J Clin Nutr* 1999;69:30-42.

Choung, M.G., et al. Anthocyanin profile of Korean cultivated kidney bean (Phaseolus vulgaris L.). *J Agric Food Chem* 2003, Nov 19;51(24):7040-43.

Correa, P. Epidemiologic correlations between diet and cancer frequency. *Cancer Res* 1981;41:3685-9.

Costacou, T., et al. Nutrition and the prevention of type 2 diabetes. *Ann Rev Nutr* 2003;23:147-70.

Darmadi-Blackberry, I., et al. Legumes: The most important dietary predictor of survival in older people of different ethnicities. *Asia Pacific Journal of Clinical Nutrition* 2004, June 13(2):217-20.

Deshpande, S.S. Food legumes in human nutrition: a personal perspective. *CRC Crit Rev Food Sci Nutr* 1992;32:333-63.

Geil, P.B., et al. Nutrition and health implications of dry beans: a review. *J Am Coll Nutr* 1994;13:549-58.

Graf, E., et al. Suppression of colonic cancer by dietary phytic acid. *Nutr Cancer* 1993;19:11-9.

Hodge, A.M., et al. Glycemic index and dietary fiber and the risk of type 2 diabetes. *Diabetes Care* 2004, Feb;27:538-46.

Hodge, A.M., et al. Glycemic index and dietary fiber and the risk of type 2 diabetes. *Diabetes Care* 2004, Nov;27(11):2701-706.

Hu, F., et al. Diet, Lifestyle and the Risk of Type 2 Diabetes Mellitus in Women. *N Eng J Med* 2001;790-97.

Institute of Medicine, Food and Nutrition Board. Dietary Reference Intakes: Calcium, Phosphorus, Magnesium, Vitamin D and Fluoride. Washington, DC: National Academy Press, 1999.

Jenkins, D.J.A., et al. Exceptionally low blood glucose response to dried beans: comparison with other carbohydrate foods. *Br Med J* 1980;281:578-80.

Kelemen, L.E., et al. Associations of dietary protein with disease and mortality in a prospective study of postmenopausal women. *Am J Epidemiol* 2005, Feb 1;161(3):239-49.

Kushi, L.H., et al. Cereals, legumes, and chronic disease risk reduction: evidence from epidemiologic studies. *Am J Clin Nutr* 1999;70(suppl):451S-8S.

Mazur, W., et al. Isoflavonoids and lignans in legumes: nutritional and health aspects in humans. *J Nutr Biochem* 1998;9:193-200.

McIntosh, M. A diet containing food rich in soluble and insoluble fiber improves glycemic control and reduces hyperlipidemia among patients with type 2 diabetes mellitus. *Nutr Rev* 2001;59(2):52-5.

Menotti, A., et al. Food intake patterns and 25-year mortality from coronary heart disease: cross-cultural correlations in the Seven Countries Study. The Seven Countries Study Research Group. *Eur J Epidemiol* 1999;15(6):507-15.

Miller, J.W. Does lowering plasma homocysteine reduce vascular disease risk? *Nutr Rev* 2001;59(7):242-4.

Morrow, B. The rebirth of legumes. *Food Technol* 1991; 45(4):96-101.

Pereira, M.A., et al. Dietary fiber and risk of coronary heart disease: A pooled analysis of cohort studies. *Arch Intern Med* 2004, Feb 23;164(4):370-76.

Schafer, G., et al. Comparison of the effects of dried peas with those of potatoes in mixed meals on postprandial glucose and insulin concentrations in patients with type 2 diabetes. *Am J Clin Nutr* 2003;78(1):99-103.

Shutler, S.M., et al. The effect of daily baked bean (Phaseolus vulgaris) consumption on the plasma lipid levels of young, normo-cholesterolemic men. *Br J Nutr* 1989;61:257-63.

Slattery, M.L., et al. Plant foods and colon cancer: an assessment of specific foods and their related nutrients (United States). *Cancer Causes Control* 1997;8:575-90.

van Horn, L. Fiber, lipids, and coronary heart disease: a statement for healthcare professionals from the Nutrition Committee, American Heart Association. *Circulation* 1997;95:2701-4.

Vinson, J.A., et al. Phenol antioxidant quantity and quality in foods: vegetables. *J Agric Food Chem* 1998; 46(9):3630-34.

Blueberries

Amakura, Y., et al. Influence of jam processing on the radical scavenging activity and phenolic content in berries. *J Agric Food Chem* 2000;48(12):6292-7.

Bravo, L. Polyphenols: chemistry, dietary sources, metabolism, and nutritional significance. *Nutr Rev* 1998;56(11):317-33.

Cao, G., et al. Anthocyanins are detected in human plasma after oral administration of an elderberry extract. *Clin Chem* 1999;45:574-6.

Cao, G., et al. Serum antioxidant capacity is increased by consumption of strawberries, spinach, red wine or vitamin C in elderly women. *J Nutr* 1998;128(12):2383-90.

Commenges, D., et al. Intake of flavonoids and risk of dementia. *Eur J Epidemiol* 2000;16:357-63.

Couillard, C. Canadian Cardiovascular Society Annual Congress Meeting, Calgary, Alberta, Oct 23-27, 2004.

Das, D.K., et al. Cardioprotection of red wine: role of polyphenolic antioxidants. *Drugs Exp Clin Res* 1999;25(2-3):115-20.

Erlund, I., et al. Consumption of black currants, lingonberries and bilberries increases serum quercetin concentrations. *Eur J Clin Nutr* 2003;57(I):37-42.

Ferrandiz, M.L., et al. Anti-inflammatory activity and inhibition of arachidonic acid metabolism by flavonoids. *Agents Actions* 1991;32:283-8.

Fuhrman, B., et al. Consumption of red wine with meals reduces the susceptibility of human plasma and low-density lipoprotein to lipid peroxidation. *Am J Clin Nutr* 1995;61:549-54.

Gheldof, N., et al. Buckwheat honey increases serum antioxidant capacity in humans. *J Agric Food Chem* 2003;51(5):1500-5.

Gil, M.I., et al. Antioxidant activity of pomegranate juice and its relationship with phenolic composition and processing. *J Agric Food Chem* 2000;48(10):4581-9.

Girard, B., et al. Functional grape and citrus products. In: *Functional Foods Biochemical & Processing Aspects.* Mazza, G., ed. Lancaster, PA: Technomic Publishing Company, Inc., 1998:139-92.

Hertog, M.G.L., et al. Antioxidant flavonols and coronary heart disease risk. *Lancet* 1997;349:699.

Hertog, M.G.L., et al. Antioxidant flavonols and ischemic heart disease in a Welsh population of men: the Caerphilly study. *Am J Clin Nutr* 1997;65:1489-94.

Hertog, M.G.L., et al. Dietary antioxidant flavonoids and risk of coronary heart disease: the Zutphen elderly study. *Lancet* 1993;342:1007-11.

Hertog, M.G.L., et al. Dietary flavonoids and cancer risk in the Zutphen Elderly Study. *Nutr Cancer* 1994;22:175-84.

Joseph, J.A., et al. Long-term dietary strawberry, spinach, or vitamin E supplementation retards the onset of age-related neuronal signal-transduction and cognitive behavioral deficits. *J Neurosci* 1998;18(19):8047-55.

Joseph, J.A., et al. Oxidative stress protection and vulnerability in aging: putative nutritional implications for intervention. *Mech Ageing Dev* 2000;31;116(2-3): 141-53.

Joseph, J.A., et al. Reversals of age-related declines in neuronal signal transduction, cognitive, and motor behavioral deficits with blueberry, spinach, or strawberry dietary supplementation. *J Neurosci* 1999;19(18):8114-21.

Kay, C.D., et al. The effect of wild blueberry (Vaccinium angustifolium) consumption on postprandial serum antioxidant status in human subjects. Br J *Nutr* 2002; 88(4):389-98.

Keevil, J.G., et al. Grape juice, but not orange juice or grapefruit juice, inhibits human platelet aggregation. *J Nutr* 2000;130(1):53-6.

Knekt, P., et al. Dietary flavonoids and the risk of lung cancer and other malignant neoplasms. *Am J Epidemiol* 1997;146:223-30.

Kopp, P. Resveratrol, a phytoestrogen found in red wine: a possible explanation for the conundrum of the French paradox? *Eur J Endocrinol* 1999;138(6):619-20.

Lansky, E., et al. Pharmacological and therapeutical properties of pomegranate. In: *Proceedings 1st International Symposium on Pomegranate;* Megarejo, P.Martinez, J.J. Martinez J., eds., CIHEAM, Orihuela, Spain, 1998;Pr-07.

Lewis, N.M., et al. Blueberries in the American Diet. *Nutrition Today* 2005;40:92-96.

Maas, J.L., et al. Ellagic acid, an anticarcinogen in fruits, especially in strawberries: a review. *Hortic Sci* 1991;26:10-14.

Mazza, G., et al. Absorption of anthocyanins from blueberries and serum antioxidant status in human subjects. *J Agric Food Chem* 2002;50(26):7731-7.

Mittleman, M. Harvard Medical School. American Heart Association Conference on Cardiovascular Disease and Epidemiology, 1996. *Fam Pract News* 1996;26:8.

O'Byrne, D.J., et al. Comparison of the antioxidant effects of Concord grape juice flavonoids and a-tocopherol on markers of oxidative stress in healthy adults. *Am J Clin Nutr* 2002;76(6):1367-74.

Oregon Berries Web Page: *http://www.oregon-berries.com.*

Paper, D.H. Natural products as angiogenesis inhibitors. *Planta Med* 1998;64:686-95.

Pilaczynska-Szczesniak, L., et al. The Influence of Chokeberry Juice Supplementation on the Reduction of Oxidative Stress Resulting from an Incremental Rowing Ergometer Exercise. *International Journal of Sport Nutrition and Exercise Metabolism* 2005;14: 48-58.

Rimando, A. Pterostilbene as a new natural product agonist for the peroxisome proliferators-activated receptor alpha isoform. Paper presented at the 228th American Chemical Society National Meeting, Philadelphia, PA, August 23, 2004.

Rimando, A., et al. Resveratrol, pterostilbene, and piceatannol in vaccinium berries. *J Agric Food Chem* 2004, Jul 28;52(15):4713-19.

Saija, A., et al. Flavonoids as antioxidant agents: importance of their interaction with biomembranes. *Free Radic Biol Med* 1995;19(4):481-6.

Sanchez-Moreno, C., et al. Anthocyanin and proanthocyanidin content in selected white and red wines. Oxygen radical absorbance capacity comparison with nontraditional wines obtained from highbush blueberry. *J Agric Food Chem* 2003, Aug 13; 51(17):4889-96.

Stacewicz-Sapuntzakis, M., et al. Chemical composition and potential health effects of prunes: a functional food? *Crit Rev Food Sci Nutr* 2001;41(4):251-86.

Sun, J., et al. Antioxidant and Antiproliferative Activities of Common Fruits. *J Agric Food Chem* 2002; 50(25):7449-54.

Suvarna, R., et al. Possible Interaction between warfarin and cranberry juice. *BMJ* 2003, Dec 20; 327(7429):1454.

USDA Database for the Flavonoid Content of Selected Foods. Accessed March 2003. *www.nalusda.gov/fnic/foodcomp.*

Vinson, J.A. Total polyphenol content of selected juices and jams. Personal communication, 2003.

Vinson, J.A., et al. Phenol antioxidant quantity and quality in foods: fruits. *J Agric Food Chem* 2001; 49(11):5315-21.

Broccoli

Cohen, J.H., et al. Fruit and vegetable intakes and prostate cancer risk. *J Natl Cancer Inst* 2000;92(1):61-8.

Conaway, C.C., et al. Disposition of glucosinolates and sulforaphane in humans after ingestion of steamed and fresh broccoli. *Nutr Cancer* 2000;38(2):168-78.

Ernster, L., et al. Biochemical, physiological and medical aspects of ubiquinone function. *Biochem Biophys Acta* 1995;1271:195-204.

Fahey, J.W., et al. Antioxidant functions of sulforaphane: a potent inducer of phase 2 detoxication enzymes. *Food Chem Toxicol* 1999;37:973-9.

Franco, V., et al. Role of dietary vitamin K intake in chronic oral anticoagulation: Prospective evidence from observational and randomized protocols. *Am J Med* 2004, May 15;116(10):651-56.

Haristoy, X., et al. Efficacy of sulforaphane in eradicating Helicobacter pylori in human gastric xenografts implanted in nude mice. *Antimicrob Agents Chemother* 2003, Dec;47(12):3982-84.

Huxley, R.R., and H.A.W. Neil. The relation between dietary flavonol intake and coronary heart disease mortality: A meta-analysis of prospective cohort studies. *Eur J Clin Nutr* 2003;57:904-908.

Jackson, S.J.T., and K.W. Singletary. Sulforaphane inhibits human MCF-7 mammary cancer cell mitotic progression and tubulin polymerization. *Am J Clin Nutr* 2004, Sep;134(9):2229-36.

Jeffery, E.H., et al. Cruciferous Vegetables and Cancer Prevention. In: *Handbook of Nutraceuticals and Functional Foods.* Wildman, R.E.C., ed. Boca Raton, FL: 2001;169-92. CRCS Press LLC.

Michnovicz, J.J., et al. Altered estrogen metabolism and excretion in humans following consumption of I3C. *Nutrition and Cancer* 1991;16:59-66.

Murray, S., et al. Effect of cruciferous vegetable consumption on heterocyclic aromatic amine metabolism in man. *Carcinogenesis* 2001;22(9):1413-20.

Nagle, C.M., et al. Dietary influences on survival after ovarian cancer. *Int J Cancer* 2003, Aug 20;106(2):264-69.

Nestle, M. Broccoli sprouts in cancer prevention. *Nutr Rev* 1998;56(4 Pt 1):127-30.

Osborne, M.P. Chemoprevention of breast cancer. *Surg Clin North Am* 1999;79(5):1207-21.

Pelucchi, C., et al. Fibre intake and prostate cancer risk. *Int J Cancer* 2004, Mar 20;109(2):278-80.

Telang, N.T., et al. Inhibition of proliferation and modulation of estradiol metabolism: novel mechanisms for breast cancer prevention by the phytochemical indole-3-carbinol. *Proc Soc Exp Biol Med* 1997;216: 246-52.

Vallejo, F., et al. Phenolic compound contents in edible parts of broccoli inflorescences after domestic cooking. *J Sci Food and Agric* 2003, Oct;83(14):1511-16.

Van Poppel, G., et al. Brassica vegetables and cancer prevention. Epidemiology and mechanisms. *Adv Exp Med Biol* 1999;472:159-68.

Verhagen, J., et al. Reduction of oxidative DNA-damage in humans by Brussels sprouts. *Carcinogenesis* 1995; 16(4):969-70.

Verhoeven, D.E., et al. A review of mechanisms underlying anticarcinogenicity by brassica vegetables. *Chem Biol Interact* 1997;103(2):79-129.

Verhoeven, D.T.H., et al. Epidemiological studies on brassica vegetables and cancer risk. *Cancer Epidemiol Bio Prev* 1996;5(9):733-48.

Wattenberg, L.W. Inhibition of carcinogenesis by minor anutrient constituents of the diet. *Proc Nutr Soc* 1990;49:173-83.

Zhang, S., et al. Dietary carotenoids and vitamins A, C, E and risk of breast cancer. *J Natl Cancer Inst* 1999; 91:547.

Dark Chocolate

Chevaux, K., et al. Proximate, Mineral and Procyanidin Content of Certain Foods and Beverages Consumed by the Kuna Amerinds of Panama. *J Food Cmpstn & Anal* 2001;14:553-63.

Gertner, J. Eat Chocolate, Live Longer? *The New York Times Sunday Magazine* October 10, 2004;33-37.

Hannum, S.H., et al. Chocolate: A Heart Healthy Food? Show Me the Science. *Nutrition Today* 2002;37:103-109.

Kris-Etherton, P.M., et al. Effects of a milk chocolate bar per day substituted for a high-carbohydrate snack in young men on an NCEP/AHA Step I Diet. *Am J Clin Nutr* 1994;60:1037S-42S.

Kris-Etherton, P.M., et al. The role of fatty acid saturation on plasma lipids, lipoproteins, and apolipoproteins: 1. Effects of whole food diets high in cocoa butter, olive oil, soybean oil, dairy butter, and milk chocolate on the plasma lipids of young men. *Metabolism* 1993;42:121-29.

Lee, C., et al. Cocoa Has More Phenolic Phytochemicals and a Higher Antioxidant Capacity Than Teas and Red Wine. *J Agric Food Chem* 2003;51(25):7292-95.

Mursu, J., et al. Dark Chocolate Consumption Increases HDL Cholesterol Concentration and Chocolate Fatty Acids May Inhibit Lipid Peroxidation in Healthy Humans. *Free Radical Biology & Medicine* 2004;37: 1351-59.

Rein, D., et al. Cocoa inhibits platelet activation and function. *Am J Clin Nutr* 2000;72:30-35.

Schramm, D.D., et al. Chocolate procyanidins decrease the leukotriene-prostacyclin ratio in humans and human aortic endothelial cells. *Am J Clin Nutr* 2001;73:36-40.

Serafini, M., et al. Plasma antioxidants from chocolate. *Nature* 2003;424:1012.

Garlic

Couillard, C. Canadian Cardiovascular Society Annual Congress Meeting, Calgary, Alberta, Oct 23-27, 2004.

Lee, Y.L., et al. Antibacterial Activity of vegetables and juices. *Nutrition* 2003, Nov-Dec;19(11-12):994-96.

Tsao, S.M., et al. Garlic extract and two diallyl sulphides inhibit methicillin-resistant Staphylococcus aureus infection in BALB/cA mice. *J Antimicrob Chemother* 2003, Dec;52(6):974-80.

Honey

Gheldof, N., et al. Buckwheat honey increases serum antioxidant capacity in humans. *J Agric Food Chem* 2003, Feb 26;51(5):1500-505.

Gross, H., et al. Effect of honey consumption on plasma antioxidant status in human subjects. This paper was presented at the 227th American Chemical Society Meeting, Anaheim, CA, March 28, 2004.

Margen, Sheldon, and the editors of the UC Berkeley *Wellness Letter. Wellness Foods A to Z*. New York: Rebus, 2002.

Subrahmanyan, M. A prospective randomized clinical and histological study of superficial burn wound healing with honey and silver sulfadiazine. *Burns* 1998;24:157-61.

White, J.W. Composition of honey. In: *Honey, A Comprehensive Survey,* ed. E. Crane. New York: Crane, Russak & Co., 1975, pp. 157-206.

Kiwi

Duttaroy, A., and A. Jørgensen. Effects of kiwi fruit consumption on platelet aggregation and plasma lipids in healthy human volunteers. *Platelets* 2004, Aug;15(5):287-92.

Dwyer, J.H., et al. Oxygenated carotenoid lutein and progression of early atherosclerosis. The Los Angeles Atherosclerosis Study. *Circulation* 2001;103:2922-27.

LaChance, P.A. Fruits in Preventative Health and Disease Treatment: Nutritional Ranking and Patient Recommendations. Presented at the 38th annual meeting of the American College of Nutrition, Sept 27, 1997, New York.

Margen, Sheldon, and the editors of the UC Berkeley *Wellness Letter. Wellness Foods A to Z*. New York: Rebus, 2002.

Rush, E.C., et al. Kiwifruit promotes laxation in the elderly. 2001 (unpublished).

Oats

Albertson, A., et al. Consumption of grain and whole-grain foods by an American population during the years 1990-1992. *J Am Diet Assoc* 1995;95:703-4.

Bazzano, L.A., et al. Dietary fiber intake and reduced risk of coronary heart disease in U.S. men and women: The National Health and Nutrition Examination Survey I Epidemiologic Follow-up Study. *Arch Intern Med* 2003, Sep 8;163(16):1897-1904.

Boushey, C.J., et al. A quantitative assessment of plasma homocysteine as a risk factor for vascular disease. Probable benefit of increasing folic acid intakes. *JAMA* 1995;274:1049-57.

Cleveland, L.E., et al. Dietary intake of whole grains. *J Am Coll Nutr* 2000;19:331S-8S.

Costacou, T., et al. Nutrition and the prevention of type 2 diabetes. *Ann Rev Nutr* 2003;23:147-70.

Cunnane, S.C. Metabolism and function of α-linolenic acid in humans. In: *Flaxseed in Human Nutrition.* Cunnane, S.C., and Thompson, L.U., eds.Champaign, IL: AOCS Press, 1995:99-127.

Cunnane, S.C., et al. Nutritional attributes of traditional flaxseed in healthy young adults. *Am J Clin Nutr* 1995;61(1):62-8.

de Lorgeril, M., et al. Mediterranean alpha-linolenic acid-rich diet in secondary prevention of coronary heart disease. *Lancet* 1994;343(8911):1454-9.

The Diabetes Prevention Program Research Group. Reduction of the Incidence of Type 2 Diabetes with Lifestyle Intervention or Metformin. *N Eng J Med* 2002;346:393-403.

Fung, T.T., et al. Whole-grain intake and the risk of type 2 diabetes: a prospective study in men. *Am J Clin Nutr* 2002;76(3):535-40.

Harnack, L., et al. Dietary intake and food sources of whole grains among US children and adolescents: Data from the 1994-1996 continuing survey of food intakes by individuals. *Journal of the American Dietetic Association* 2003;103:1015-19. *Harvard Men's Health Watch,* May 2004.

Hodge, A.M., et al. Glycemic index and dietary fiber and the risk of type 2 diabetes. *Diabetes Care* 2004, Feb;27:53846.

Hodge, A.M., et al. Glycemic index and dietary fiber and the risk of type 2 diabetes. *Diabetes Care* 2004, Nov;27(11):2701-706.

Hu, F., et al. Diet, Lifestyle and the Risk of Type 2 Diabetes Mellitus in Women. *N Eng J Med* 2001;790-97.

Jacobs, D.R., et al. Is whole-grain intake associated with reduced total and cause-specific death rates in older women? The Iowa Women's Health Study. *Am J Public Health* 1999;89:322-9.

Jacobs, D.R., et al. Whole-grain intake and cancer: an expanded review and meta-analysis. *Nutr Cancer* 1998;30(2):85-96.

Jacobs, D.R., et al. Whole-grain intake may reduce the risk of ischemic heart disease death in postmenopausal women: the Iowa Women's Health Study. *Am J Clin Nutr* 1998:68(2):248-57.

Jensen, M., et al. Intakes of whole grains, bran, and germ and the risk of coronary heart disease in men. *Am J Clin Nutr* 2004, Dec;80:1492-99.

Johnston, L., et al. Cholesterol-lowering benefits of a whole grain oat ready-to-eat cereal. *Nutr Clin Care* 1998;1:6-12.

Katz, D.L., et al. Acute effects of oats and vitamin E on endothelial responses to ingested fat. *Am J Prev Med* 2001;20(2):1124-9.

Kilkkinen, A., et al. Research Communication: intake of lignins is associated with serum enterolactone concentration in Finnish men and women. *J Nutr* 2003;133(6):1830-3.

Lampi, A.M., et al. Tocopherols and tocotrienols from oil and cereal grains. In: *Functional Foods: Biochemical and Processing Aspects,* vol. 2. Shi, J., Mazza, G., Le Maguer. M., eds. Boca Raton, FL: CRC Press, LLC, 2002: 1-38.

Levine, A.S., et al. Dietary fiber: does it affect food intake and body weight? In: *Appetite and Body Weight Regulation: Sugar, fat and macronutrient substitutes.* Fernstrom, J.D., Miller, G.D., eds. Boca Raton, FL: CRC Press, Inc., 1994:191-200.

Liu, S., et al. Is intake of breakfast cereals related to total and cause-specific mortality in men? *Am J Clin Nutr* 2003;77(3):594-9.

Liu, S., et al. Relation between a diet with a high glycemic load and plasma concentrations of high-sensitivity C-reactive protein in middle-aged women. *Am J Clin Nutr* 2002;75(3):492-8.

Liu, S., et al. Relation between changes in intakes of dietary fiber and grain products and changes in weight and development of obesity among middle-aged women. *Am J Clin Nutr* 2003, Nov;78(5):920-27.

Liu, S., et al. Whole-grain consumption and risk of coronary heart disease: results from the Nurses' Health Study. *Am J Clin Nutr* 1999;70(3):412-9.

Liu, S., et al. Whole-grain consumption and risk of ischemic stroke in women; a prospective study. *JAMA* 2000;284:1534-40.

McKeown, N.M., et al. Whole-grain intake and risk of ischemic stroke in women. *Nutr Rev* 2001;59(5):149-152.

Meyer, K.A., et al. Carbohydrates, dietary fiber, and incident type 2 diabetes in older women. *Am J Clin Nutr* 2000, Apr;71(4):921-30.

Miller, H.E., et al. Antioxidant content of whole grain breakfast cereals, fruits and vegetables. *J Am Coll Nutr* 2000;19(suppl):312S-9S.

Montonen, J., et al. Whole-grain and fiber intake and the incidence of type 2 diabetes. *Am J Clin Nutr* 2003;77(3):622-9.

Oomah, B.D., et al. Flaxseed products for disease prevention. In: *Functional Foods Biochemical & Processing Aspects.* Mazza, G, ed. Lancaster, PA: Technomic Publishing Company, Inc., 1998:91-138.

Pedersen, B., et al. Nutritive value of cereal products with emphasis on the effect of milling. *World Rev Nutr Diet* 1989;60:1-91.

Pereira, M.A., et al. Dietary fiber and risk of coronary heart disease: A pooled analysis of cohort studies. *Arch Intern Med* 2004, Feb 23;164(4):370-76.

Salmeron, L., et al. Dietary Fiber, Glycemic Load and Risk of Non-Insulin Dependent Diabetes in Men. *Diabetes Care* 1997;20:545-50.

Saltzman, E., et al. An oat-containing hypocaloric diet reduces systolic blood pressure and improves lipid profile beyond effects of weight loss in men and women. *J Nutr* 2001;131:1465-70.

Slattery, M., et al. Plant Foods, Fiber and Rectal Cancer. *Am J Clin Nutr* 2004, Feb;79(2):274-81.

Slavin, J. Whole Grains and Human Health. *Nutrition Research Reviews* 2004;17.

Slavin, J., et al. Grain processing and nutrition. *Crit Rev Food Sci Nutr* 2000;40:309-26.

Slavin, J., et al. Plausible mechanisms for the protectiveness of whole grains. *Am J Clin Nutr* 1999;70(3 suppl):459S-63S.

Slavin, J., et al. Whole grain consumption and chronic disease: protective mechanisms. *Nutr Cancer* 1997;27:14-21.

Thompson, L.U. Antioxidants and hormone-mediated health benefits of whole grains. *Crit Rev Food Sci Nutr* 1994;34(586):473-97.

Tousoulis, D., et al. L-arginine in cardiovascular disease: dream or reality? *Vasc Med* 2002;7(3):203-11.

Trusswell, A.S. Cereal grains and coronary heart disease. *Eur J Clin Nutr* 2002;56(1):1-14.

Tsai, C.J., et al. Dietary protein and the risk of cholecystectomy in a cohort of US women:The Nurses' Health Study. *Am J Epidemiol* 2004, Jul 1;160(1):11.

Van Dam, R.M., et al. Dietary patterns and risk for type 2 diabetes mellitus in US men. *Ann Int Med* 2002;136:201-9.

Extra Virgin Olive Oil

Couillard, C. Canadian Cardiovascular Society Annual Congress Meeting, Calgary, Alberta, Oct 23-27, 2004.

Ferrara, L.A., et al. Olive oil and reduced need for antihypertensive medications. *Arch Intern Med* 2000;160:837-42.

Hargrove, R.L., et al. Low fat and high monounsaturated fat diets decrease human low density lipoprotein oxidative susceptibility in vitro. *J Nutr* 2001;131:1 758-63.

Marrugat, J., et al. Effects of differing phenolic content in dietary olive oils on lipids and LDL oxidation: A randomized controlled trial. *Eur J Clin Nutr* 2004, Jun;43(3):140-47.

Masella, R., et al. Extra Virgin Olive Oil Biophenols Inhibit Cell-Mediated Oxidation of LDL by Increasing the mRNA Transcription of Glutathione-Related Enzymes.*J Nutr* 2004, Apr;134(4):785-91.

Menendez, J.A., et al. Oleic acid, the main monounsaturated fatty acid of olive oil, suppresses Her-2/neu (erbB-2) expression and synergistically enhances the growth inhibitory effects of trastuzumab (HerceptinTM) in breast. *Ann Oncol* 2005, Jan 10.

Mittleman, M. Harvard Medical School. American Heart Association Conference on Cardiovascular Disease and Epidemiology, 1996. *Fam Pract News* 1996;26:8.

Morello, J.R., et al. Changes in commercial virgin olive oil (cv Arbequina) during storage, with special emphasis on the phenolic fraction. *J Agric Food Chem* 2004, May;85(3):357-64.

Psaltopoulou, T., et al. Olive oil, the Mediterranean diet, and arterial blood pressure: The Greek European Prospective Investigation into Cancer and Nutrition (EPIC) study. *Am J Clin Nutr* 2004, Oct;80(4):1012-18.

Ruiz-Gutierrez, V., et al. Plasma lipids, erythrocyte membrane lipids and blood pressure of hypertensive women after ingestion of dietary oleic acid from two different sources. *J Hypertens* 1996;14:1483-90.

Stoneham, M., et al. Olive oil, diet, and colorectal cancer: An ecological study and hypothesis. *J Epidemiol Community Health* 2000;54:756-60.

Trichopoulou, A., et al. Cancer and Mediterranean dietary traditions. *Cancer Epidemiol Biomarkers Prev* 2000;9:869-73.

Weinbrenner, T., et al. Olive Oils High in Phenolic Compounds Modulate Oxidative/Antioxidative Status in Men. *J Nutr* 2004;134:2314-21.

Onions

Awash, P.B., et al. The effects of bulb extracts of onions and garlic on soil bacteria. *Acta but Ind* 1984;12:45-49.

Dorant, E., et al. A prospective cohort study on the relationship between onion and leek consumption, garlic supplement use and the risk of colorectal carcinoma in the Netherlands. *Carcinogenesis* 1996, Mar;17(3):477-84.

Fukushima, S., et al. Cancer prevention by organosulfur compounds from garlic and onion. *J Cell Biochem Suppl* 1997;27:100-105.

Gad, C.M., et al. Protective effect of allium vegetables against both esophageal and stomach cancer: A simultaneous case-referent study of a high epidemic area in Jianjsu province, China. *Jpn J Cancer Res* 1999;90:614.

Hu, J., et al. Diet and brain cancer in adults: A case control study in northeast China. *Int J Cancer* 1999;81:20.

Sesso, H., et al. Flavonoid intake and risk of cardiovascular disease in women. *Am J Clin Nutr* 2003;77: 1400-1408.

Shaheen, S., et al. Dietary antioxidants and asthma in adult-population based case-control study. *Am J Respir Crit Care Med* 2001;16:1823-28.

Song, K., and J.A. Milner. The influence of heating on the anticancer properties of onions. *J Nutr* 2001, Mar;131(3s):1054S-1057S.

Wagner, H., et al. Antiasthmatic effects of onions: Inhibition of 5-lipoxygenase and cyclooxygenase in vitro by thiosulfinates and "Cepaenes." *Prostaglandins Leukot Essent Fatty Acids* 1990, Jan;39(1):59-62.

Yang, J., et al. Varietal Differences in Phenolic Content and Antioxidant and Antiproliferative Activities of Onions. *J Agric Food Chem* 2004;52(22):6787-93.

Oranges

Amparo, C., et al. Limonene from citrus. In: *Functional Foods: Biochemical and Processing Aspects,* vol. 2. Shi, J., Mazza, G., Le Maguer, M., eds. CRC Press LLC 2002:169-88.

Baghurst, K. The Health Benefits of Citrus Fruits. Report to Horticulture Australia Ltd.:CSIRO Health Sciences and Nutrition; June 2003.

Block, G., et al. Ascorbic acid status and subsequent diastolic and systolic blood pressure. *Hypertension* 2001;37:261-67.

Costacou, T., et al. Nutrition and the prevention of type 2 diabetes. *Ann Rev Nutr* 2003;23:147-70.

Crowell, P.L. Prevention and therapy of cancer by dietary monoterpenes. *J Nutr* 1999;129(3):775S-8S.

The Diabetes Prevention Program Research Group. Reduction of the Incidence of Type 2 Diabetes with Lifestyle Intervention or Metformin. *N Eng J Med* 2002;346:393-403.

Gey, K.F., et al. Increased risk of cardiovascular disease at suboptimal plasma concentrations of essential antioxidants: an epidemiological update with special attention to carotene and vitamin C. *Am J Clin Nutr* 1993;57(suppl):787S-97S.

Gil-Izquierdo, A., et al. Effect of processing techniques at industrial scale on orange juice antioxidant and beneficial health compounds. *J Agric Food Chem* 2002;50(18):5107-14.

Girard, B., et al. Functional grape and citrus products. In: *Functional Foods Biochemical & Processing Aspects.* Mazza, G., ed., Lancaster, PA: Technomic Publishing Company, Inc. 1998:139-92.

Gorton, H.C., and K. Jarvis. The effectiveness of vitamin C in preventing and relieving the symptoms of virus-induced respiratory infections. *Manipulative and Physiological Therapeutics* 1999;22(8):530-33.

Hakim, I.A., et al. Citrus peel use is associated with reduced risk of squamous cell carcinoma of the skin. *Nutr Cancer* 2000;37(2):161-8.

Hallberg, L., et al. Effect of ascorbic acid on iron absorption from different types of meals. Studies with ascorbic acid rich roods and synthetic ascorbic acid given in different amounts in different meals. *Hum Nutr Appl Nutr* 1986;40:97-113.

Halliwell, B. Vitamin C and genomic stability. *Mutat Res* 2001;475(1-2):29-35.

Jacques, P.F., et al. Long-term vitamin C supplement use and prevalence of early-age-related lens opacities. *Am J Clin Nutr* 1997;66:911-6.

Johnston, C.S. Vitamin C. In: *Present Knowledge in Nutrition,* 8th edition. B.A. Bowman and R.M. Russell, eds. Washington, DC: ILSI Press, 2001;175-83.

Johnston, C.S., et al. People with marginal vitamin C status are at high risk of developing vitamin C deficiency. *J Am Diet Assoc* 1999;99(7):854-6.

Johnston, C.S., et al. Stability of ascorbic acid in commercially available orange juices. *J Am Diet Assoc* 2002;102:525-9.

Joshipura, K., et al. Fruit and vegetable intake in relation to risk of ischemic stroke. *JAMA* 1999;282:1233-39.

Jung, U.J., et al. The Hypoglycemic Effects of Hesperidin and Naringin Are Partly Mediated by Hepatic Glucose-Regulating Enzymes in C57BL/KsJ-db/db Mice. *J Nutr* 2004;134:2499-2503.

Kurowska, E.M., and J.A. Manthey. Hypolipidemic effects and absorption of citrus polymethozylated flavones in hamsters with diet-induced hypercholesterolemia. *J Agric Food Chem* 2004, May 19;52(10):2879-86.

Leonard, S.S., et al. Antioxidant properties of fruit and vegetable juices: more to the story than ascorbic acid. *Ann Clin Lab Sci* 2002;332(2):193-200. Levine, M., et al. Criteria and recommendations for vitamin C intake. *JAMA* 1999;281(15):1415-23.

Liu, L., et al. Vitamin C preserves endothelial function in patients with coronary heart disease after a high-fat meal. *Clin Cardiology* 2002;25:219-24.

Loria, C.M., et al. Vitamin C status and mortality in US adults. *Am J Clin Nutr* 2000;72(1):139-45.

Martini, L., et al. Relative bioavailability of calcium-rich dietary sources in the elderly. *Am J Clin Nutr* 2002;76(6):1345-50.

Nagy, S. Vitamin C contents of citrus fruit and their products: a review. *J Agric-Food Chem* 1980;28(1):8-18.

Pattison, D.J., et al. Vitamin C and the risk of developing inflammatory polyarthritis: Prospective nested case-control study. *Annals of Rheumatic Diseases* 2004, Jul;63(7):843-47.

Proteggente, A.R., et al. The antioxidant activity of regularly consumed fruit and vegetables reflects their phenolic and vitamin C composition. *Free Radic Res* 2002;36(2):217-33.

Sanchez-Moreno, C., et al. Effect of orange juice intake on vitamin concentrations and biomarkers of antioxidant status in humans. *Am J Clin Nutr* 2003;78:454-60.

Tangpricha, V., et al. Fortification of orange juice with vitamin D: a novel approach for enhancing vitamin

D nutritional health. *Am J Clin Nutr* 2003;77(6): 1478-83.

Vinson, J.A., et al. In vitro and in vivo lipoprotein antioxidant effect of a citrus extract and ascorbic acid on normal and hypercholesterolemic human subjects. *J Med Food* 2001;4(4):187-92.

Vinson, J.A., et al. Phenol antioxidant quantity and quality in foods: Fruits. *J Agric Food Chem* 2001;49: 5315-21.

Wang, Q., et al. Pectin from fruits. In: *Functional Foods: Biochemical and Processing Aspects,* vol. 2. Shi, J., Mazza, G., Le Maguer M., eds., CRC Press LLC 2002:263-310.

Yuan, J.M., et al. Dietary cryptoxanthin and reduced risk of lung cancer: The Singapore Chinese Health Study. *Cancer Epidemiol Biomarkers Prev* 2003, Sep;12(9):890-98.

Pomegranates

Aviram, M. et al. Pomegranate juice consumption inhibits erum angiotension converting enzyme activity and reduces systolic blood pressure. *Atherosclerosis* 2001;158:195-98.

Aviram, M., et al. Pomegranate juice flavonoids inhibit LDL oxidation and cardiovascular diseases: Studies in atherosclerotic mice and in humans. *Proc Int Conf Mech Action Nutraceuticals (ICMAN)* 2002;28:49-62.

Gil, M.I., et al. Antioxidant activity of pomegranate juice and its relationship with phenolic composition and processing. *J Agric Food Chem* 2000;48:4581-89.

Pumpkin

Albanes, D., et al. Alpha-tocopherol and beta carotene supplements and lung cancer incidence in the Alpha-Tocopherol, Beta-Carotene Cancer Prevention Study: Effects of base-line characteristics and study compliance. *J Nutr Cancer Inst* 1996;88:1560-70.

The Alpha-Tocopherol, Beta Carotene Cancer Prevention Study Group. The effect of vitamin E and beta carotene on the incidence of lung cancer and other cancers in male smokers. *N Engl J Med* 1994;330:1029-35.

Ascherio, A., et al. Relation of consumption of vitamin E, vitamin C, and carotenoids to risk for stroke among men in the United States. *Ann Intern Med* 1999;130(12):963-70.

Bowen, P.E., et al. Variability of serum carotenoids in response to controlled diets containing six servings of fruits and vegetables per day. *Ann NY Acad Sci* 1993;691:241-3.

Connor, S., et al. Diets low in folic acid and carotenoids are associated with the coronary disease epidemic in Central and Eastern Europe. *J Am Diet Assoc* 2004;104:1793-99.

Cooper, D.A., et al. Dietary carotenoids and certain cancers, heart disease, and age-related macular degeneration: a review of recent research. *Nutr Rev* 1999;57:201-14.

D'Odorico, A., et al. High plasma levels of alpha- and beta-carotene are associated with a lower risk of atherosclerosis: results from the Bruneck study. *Atherosclerosis* 2000;153(1):231-9.

Erdman, J.W., Jr. Variable bioavailability of carotenoids from vegetables. *Am J Clin Nutr* 1999;70:179-80.

Etminan, M., et al. Intake of vitamin E, vitamin C, and carotenoids and the risk of Parkinson's disease: A meta-analysis. *Lancet Neurology* 2005, Jun;4(6):362-65.

Feskanich, D., et al. Prospective study of fruit and vegetable consumption and risk of lung cancer among men and women. *J Natl Cancer Inst* 2000;92:1812-23.

Kohlmeier, L., et al. Epidemiologic evidence of a role of carotenoids in cardiovascular disease prevention. *Am J Clin Nutr* 1995;62(suppl):1370S-6S.

Krinsky, N.I. The antioxidant and biological properties of the carotenoids. *Ann NY Acad Sci* 1998;854:443-7.

Mayne, S.T. b-Carotene, carotenoids and disease prevention in humans. *FASEB J* 1996;10:690-701.

McVean, M., et al. Oxidants and antioxidants in Ultraviolet-induced nonmelanoma skin cancer. In: *Antioxidant Status, Diet, Nutrition and Health.* Papas, A.M., ed. CRC Press 1999;401-30.

Michand, D.S., et al. Intake of specific carotenoids and risk of lung cancer in 2 prospective US cohorts. *Am J Clin Nutri* 2000;72:990-97.

Omenn, G.S., et al. Effects of a combination of beta carotene and vitamin A on lung cancer and cardiovascular disease. *N Engl J Med* 1996;334:1150-5.

Palozza, P., et al. Beta-carotene downregulates the steady-state and heregulin-alpha-induced cox-2 pathways in colon cancer cells. *J Nutr* 2005;135:129-36.

Rock, C.L., et al. Responsiveness of serum carotenoids to a high-vegetable diet intervention designed to prevent breast cancer recurrence. *Cancer Epidemiol Biomarkers Prev* 1997;6:617-23.

Rock, C.L. Carotenoid update. *J Am Diet Assoc* 2003;103(4):423-5.

Schabath, M.D., et al. Dietary carotenoids and genetic instability modify bladder cancer risk. *J Nutr* 2004;134:3362-69.

Stahl, W., et al. Carotenoids and carotenoids plus vitamin E protect against ultraviolet light-induced erythema in humans. *Am J Clin Nutr* 2000;71(3):795-8.

van Poppel, G., et al. Epidemiologic evidence for beta-carotene and cancer prevention. *Am J Clin Nutr* 1995;62(suppl):1393S-1402S.

White, W.S., et al. Ultraviolet light-induced reductions in plasma carotenoids levels. *Am J Clin Nutr* 1988; 47:879-83.

Yeum, K.J., et al. Carotenoid bioavailability and bioconversion. In: *Annual Review of Nutrition*, vol. 22, 2002. McCormick, D.B., Bier, D.M., Cousins, R.J., eds. 2002;483-504.

Yuan, J.M., et al. Dietary cryptoxanthin and reduced risk of lung cancer: The Singapore Chinese Health Study. *Cancer Epidemiol Biomarkers Prev* 2003, Sep;12(9): 890-98.

Zhang, S., et al. Dietary carotenoids and vitamins A, C, E and risk of breast cancer. *J Natl Cancer Inst* 1999;91:547.

Zhao, G., et al. Dietary and Linolenic Acid Reduces Inflammatory and Lipid Cardiovascular Risk Factors in Hypercholesteaclemic Men and Women. *J Nutr* 2004;134:2991-97.

Wild Salmon

Albert, C.M., et al. Fish consumption and risk of sudden cardiac death. *JAMA* 1998;279:23-8.

Bazzano, L.A., et al. Dietary intake of folate and risk of stroke in US men and women;NHANES I Epidemiologic Follow-up Study. *Stroke* 2002, May;33(5):1183-89.

Bhatnagar, D., et al. Omega-3 fatty acids: their role in the prevention and treatment of atherosclerosis related risk factors and complications. *Int J Clin Pract* 2003;57(4):305-14.

Calvo, M.S., et al. Prevalence of vitamin D insufficiency in Canada and the United States: importance to health status and efficacy of current food fortification and dietary supplement use. *Nutr Rev* 2003;61(3):107-13.

Canada Food Inspection Fact Sheet. Food safety facts on mercury and fish consumption. Available at: *http://www.inspection.gc.ca/english/corpaffr/foodfacts/mercurye/shtml*. Accessed June 26, 2002.

Conquer, J., et al. Human health effects of docosahexaenoic acid. In: *Functional Foods: Biochemical and Processing Aspects*, vol. 2. Shi, J., Mazza, G., Le Maguer, M., eds. CRC Press LLC 2002:311-30.

Couillard, C. Canadian Cardiovascular Society Annual Congress Meeting, Calgary, Alberta, Oct 23-27, 2004.

Cunningham-Rundles, S. Is the fatty acid composition of immune cells the key to normal variations in human immune response? *Am J Clin Nutr* 2003;77(5):1096-7.

Dewailly, E., et al. Cardiovascular disease risk factors and n-3 fatty acid status in the adult population of James Bay Cree. *Am J Clin Nutr* 2002;76(1):85-92.

Dewailly, E., et al. n-3 Fatty acids and cardiovascular disease risk factors among the Inuit of Nunavik. *Am J Clin Nutr* 2001;74(4):464-73.

Doleckk, T.A., et al. Dietary polyunsaturated fatty acids and mortality in the multiple risk factor intervention trial (MRFIT). *World Rev Nutr Diet* 1991;66:205-16.

Foulke, J.E. Mercury in fish: cause for concern? FDA Consumer, Sept. 1994. Accessed on FDA Web site at *http://www.fda.gov/fdac/reprints/mercury.html*.

Freedman, D.M., et al. Sunlight and mortality from breast, ovarian, colon, prostate, and non-melanoma skin cancer: a composite death certificate based case-control study. *Occ Environ Med* 2002;59:257-62.

Freeman, M.P. Omega-3 fatty acids in psychiatry: a review. *Ann Clin Psychiat* 2000;2(3):159-65.

Harris, W.S. n-3 Long-chain polyunsaturated fatty acids reduce risk of coronary heart disease death: extending the evidence to the elderly. *Am J Clin Nutr* 2003;77(2):279-80.

He, K., et al. Fish consumption and incidence of stroke: A meta-analysis of cohort studies. *Stroke* 2004, Jul;35(7):1538-42.

Holick, M.F. Vitamin D: the underappreciated D-lightful hormone that is important for skeletal and cellular health. *Curr Opin Endocrinol Diabetes* 2002;9:87-98.

Iribarren, D., et al. Dietary intake of n-3, n-6 fatty acids and fish: Relationship with hostility in young adults—the CARDIA study. *Eur J ClinNutr* 2004, Jan;58(1):24-31.

Jones, P.J.H., et al. Effect of n-3 polyunsaturated fatty acids on risk reduction of sudden death. *Nutr Rev* 2002;60(12):407-9.

Kalijn, S., et al. Dietary intake of fatty acids and fish in relation to cognitive performance at middle age. *Neurology* 2004, Jan 27;62(2):275-80.

Kew, S., et al. Relation between the fatty acid composition of peripheral blood mononuclear cells and measures of immune cell function in healthy, free-living subjects aged 25-72 y. *Am J Clin Nutr* 2003;77(5):1278-86.

Kris-Etherton, P.M., et al. Fish consumption, fish oil, omega-3 fatty acids and cardiovascular disease. *Circulation* 2002;106:2747-57.

Lemaitre, R.N., et al. n-3 Polyunsaturated fatty acids, fatal ischemic heart disease, and nonfatal myocardial infarction in older adults: the Cardiovascular Health Study. *Am J Clin Nutr* 2003;77(2):319-25.

Lewis, N.M., et al. Enriched eggs as a source of n-3 polyunsaturated fatty acids for humans. *Poult Sci* 2000;79(7):971-4.

Luchsinger, J.A., et al. Dietary Factors and Alzheimer's Disease. *The Lancet Neurology* 2004;3:579-87.

Mattson, M.P. Emerging neuroprotective strategies for Alzheimer's disease: Dietary restriction, telomerase activation, and stem cell therapy. *Exp Gerontology* 2000;35:489-502.

Mittleman, M. Harvard Medical School. American Heart Association Conference on Cardiovascular Disease and Epidemiology, 1996. *Fam Pract News* 1996;26:8.

Morris, M.C., et al. Consumption of fish and n-3 fatty acids and risk of incident Alzheimer disease. *Arch Neurol* 2003,Jul;60(7):940-46.

Morris, M.C., et al. Dietary Fats and the Risk of Incident Alzheimer Disease. *Arch Neurology* 2003;60:194-200.

Morris, M.C., et al. Does fish oil lower blood pressure? A meta-analysis of controlled trials. *Circulation* 1993;88:523-33.

Mozaffarian, D., et al. Fish intake and risk of incident atrial fibrillation. *Circulation* 2004, Jul 27;110(4):368-73.

Rose, D.P., et al. Omega-3 fatty acids as cancer chemopreventive agents. *Pharmacol Ther* 1999;83(3):217-44.

Stoll, A.L. *The Omega 3 Connection.* New York: Simon & Schuster, 2001, 24.

Terry, P.D., et al. Intakes of fish and marine fatty acids and the risks of cancers of the breast and prostate and of other hormone-related cancers: a review of the epidemiologic evidence. *Am J Clin Nutr* 2003;77(3):532-43.

Tidow-Kebritchi, S., et al. Effects of diets containing fish oil and vitamin E on rheumatoid arthritis. *Nutr Rev* 2001;59(10):335-7.

Vanschoonbeek, K., et al. Fish oil consumption and reduction of arterial disease. *J Nutr* 2003;133(3):657-60.

Whitemore-Burns, B., et al. Effect of N-3 Fatty Acid Enriched Eggs vs Walnuts on Blood Lipids in Free-Living Lacto-Ovo Vegetarians. *Experimental Biology* 2005, Mar 31-April 5;San Diego, CA, Abstract 591.17.

Woodman, R.J., et al. Effects of purified eicosapentaenoic and docosahexaenoic acids on glycemic control, blood pressure, and serum lipids in type 2 diabetic patients with treated hypertension. *Am J Clin Nutr* 2002;76(5):1007-15.

Ziboh, V.A. The significance of polyunsaturated fatty acids in cutaneous biology. *Lipids* 1996;31(suppl): S249-S53.

Soy

Adlercreutz, H.H., et al. Plasma concentrations of phytoestrogens in Japanese men. *Lancet* 1993;342:1209-10.

Allred, C.D., et al. Soy processing influences growth of estrogen-dependent breast cancer tumors in mice. *Carcinogenesis* 2004, June.

Anderson, J.W., et al. Soy foods and health promotion. In: *Vegetables, Fruits, and Herbs in Health Promotion.* Watson, R.R., ed. CRC Press; 2001:117-34.

Anderson, J.W. Meta-analysis of the effects of soy protein intake on serum lipids. *N Engl J Med* 1995;333(5): 276-82.

Bhathena, S.J., et al. Beneficial role of dietary phytoestrogens in obesity and diabetes. *Am J Clin Nutr* 2002;76(6):1191-1201.

Chang, S.K.C. Isoflavones form soybeans and soy foods. In: *Functional Foods: Biochemical and Processing Aspects,* vol. 2. Shi, J., Mazza, G., Le Maguer, M., eds. CRC Press LLC 2002:39-70.

Desroches, S., et al. Soy protein favorably affects LDL size independently of isoflavones in hypercholesterolemic men and women. *J Nutr* 2004, Mar;134(3):574-79.

Dwyer, J.T., et al. Tofu and soy drinks contain phytoestrogens. *J Am Diet Assoc* 1994;94(7):739-43.

Erdman, J.W., Jr. AHA science advisory: soy protein and cardiovascular disease: a statement for healthcare professionals from the Nutrition Committee of the AHA. *Circulation* 2000;102(20):2555-9.

Guzman-Maldonado, S.H., et al. Functional Products of Plants Indigenous to Latin America: Amaranth, Quinoa, Common Beans, and Botanicals. In *Functional Foods,* ed.G.Mazza. Lancaster, PA: Technomic Publishing Co. Inc., 1998, pp.293-328.

Haub, M.D., et al. Effect of protein source on resistive-training-induced changes in body composition and muscle size in older men. *Am J Clin Nutr* 2002;76(3):511-7.

Jenkins, D.J.A., et al. Effects of high- and low-isoflavone soyfoods on blood lipids, oxidized LDL, homocysteine, and blood pressure in hyperlipidemic men and women. *Am J Clin Nutr* 2002;76(1):365-72.

Kreijkamp-Kaspers, S., et al. Phyto-oestrogens and cognitive function. In: *Performance Functional Foods.* Watson, D.H., ed. CRC Press, Woodhead Publishing Limited, 2003:61-77.

Margen, Sheldon, and the editors of the UC Berkeley *Wellness Letter. Wellness Foods A to Z.* New York: Rebus, 2002.

Matvienko, O.A, et al. A single daily dose of soybean phytosterols in ground beef decreases serum total cholesterol and LDL cholesterol in young, mildly hyper-cholesterolemic men. *Am J Clin Nutr* 2002;76(1):57-64.

Messina, M. Legumes and soybeans: overview of their nutritional profiles and health effects. *Am J Clin Nutr* 1999;70(3 suppl):439S-50S.

Messina, M., et al. Provisional recommended soy protein and isoflavones intakes for healthy adults. *Nutr Today* 2003;38(3):100-9.

Messina, M.J. Emerging evidence on the role of soy in reducing prostate cancer risk. *Nutr Rev* 2003;61(4): 117-31.

Messina, M.J., et al. Soy intake and cancer risk: a review of the in vitro and in vivo data. *Nutrition and Cancer* 1994;21(2)113-31.

Munro, I.C., et al. Soy isoflavones: a safety review. *Nutr Rev* 2003;61(1):1-33.

Nagata, C., et al. Soy product intake is inversely associated with serum homocysteine level in premenopausal Japanese women. *J Nutr* 2003;133(3):797-800.

Ni, W., et al. Anti-atherogenic effect of soya and rice-protein isolate, compared with casein, in apolipoprotein E-deficient mice. *Br J Nutr* Jul;90(1):13-20.

Ogura, C.H., et al. Prevalence of senile dementia in Okinawa. *Intl J Epidem* 1995;24:373-80.

Sagara, M., et al. Effects of dietary intake of soy protein and isoflavones on cardiovascular disease risk factors in high risk, middle-aged men in Scotland. *J Am Coll Nutr* 2004, Feb;23(1):85-91.

Sass, L. *The New Soy Cookbook.* San Francisco, CA: Chronicle Books, 1998.

Setchell, K.D.R., et al. Bioavailability, disposition, and dose-response effects of soy isoflavones when consumed by healthy women at physiologically typical dietary intake. *J Nutr* 2003;133(4):1027-35.

Shurtleff, W., et al. *The Book of Tofu.* Berkeley, CA: Ten Speed Press, 1998, 21.

Steinberg, F.M., et al. Soy protein with isoflavones has favorable effects on endothelial function that are independent of lipid and antioxidant effects in healthy postmenopausal women. *Am J Clin Nutr* 2003;78(1):123-30.

Teixeira, S.R., et al. Isolated Soy Protein Consumption Reduces Urinary Albumin Excretion and Improves the Serum Lipid Profile in Men with Type 2 Diabetes Mellitus and Nephropathy. *J Nutr* 2004;134:1874-80.

Wood, C.E., et al. Breast and uterine effects of soy isoflavones and conjugated equine estrogens in postmenopausal female monkeys. *J Clin Endocrinol Metab* 2004, Jul;89(7):3462-68.

Zhao, G., et al. Dietary and Linolenic Acid Reduces Inflammatory and Lipid Cardiovascular Risk Factors in Hypercholesteaclemic Men and Women. *J Nutr* 2004;134:2991-97.

Zhao, Y., et al. Calcium Bioavailability from Fortified Soymilk and Bovine Milk. Abstract 972.1, *Experimental Biology,* March 31-April 5, 2005, San Diego, CA.

Zhou, J.R., et al. Soy phytochemicals and tea bioactive components synergistically inhibit androgen-sensitive human prostate tumors in mice. *J Nutr* 2003;133:516-21.

Spinach

Beatty, S., et al. Macular pigment and age-related macular degeneration. *Br J Ophthalmol* 1999;83:857-77.

Booth, S.L., et al. Dietary intake and adequacy of vitamin K. *J Nutr* 1998;128(5):785-8.

Braam, L.A.J.L.M.. et al. Vitamin K1 supplementation retards bone loss in postmenopausal women between 50 and 60 years of age. *Calcif Tissue Int* 2003;73:21-26.

Brown, L., et al. A prospective study of carotenoids intake and risk of cataract extraction in US men. *Am J Clin Nutr* 1999;70(4):517-24.

Brown, M.J., et al. Carotenoid bioavailability is higher from salads ingested with full-fat than with fat-reduced salad dressings as measured with electrochemical detection. *Am J Clin Nutr* 2004, Aug 1;80(2):396-403.

Burke, J.D., et al. Diet and Serum Carotenoid Concentrations Affect Macula Pigment Optical Density in Adults 45 Years and Older. *J Nutr* 2005;135:1208-14.

Carson, L., et al. Carotenoids and eye health. *Nutrition and the MD* 2004;30:1-4.

Castenmiller, J.J.M., et al. The food matrix of spinach is a limiting factor in determining the bioavailability of b-carotene and to a lesser extent of lutein in humans. *J Nutr* 1999;129:349-55.

Chasan-Taber, L., et al. A prospective study of carotenoids and vitamin A intakes and risk of cataract extraction in US women. *Am J Clin Nutr* 1999;70(4):431-2.

Colditz, G.A., et al. Increased green and yellow vegetable intake and lowered cancer deaths in an elderly population. *Am J Clin Nutr* 1985;41:32-6.

Ernster, L., et al. Biochemical, physiological and medical aspects of ubiquinone function. *Biochem Biophys Acta* 1995;1271:195-204.

Greenway, H.T., et al. Fruit and vegetable micronutrients in diseases of the eye. In: *Vegetables, Fruits, and Herbs in Health Promotion.* Watson, R.R., ed. CRC Press;2001:85-98.

Hammond, B.R., et al. Macular pigment density is reduced in obese subjects. *Invest Ophthalmol Vis Sci* 2002;43:47-50.

Handelman, G.J., et al. Lutein and zeaxanthin concentrations in plasma after dietary supplementation with egg yolk. *Am J Clin Nutr* 1999;70(2):247-51.

Hu, F.B., et al. A prospective study of egg consumption and risk of cardiovascular disease in men and women. *JAMA* 1999;281(15):1387-94.

John, J.H., et al. Effects of fruit and vegetable consumption on plasma antioxidant concentrations and blood pressure: a randomized controlled trial. *Lancet* 2002;359(9322):1969-74.

Klein, R., et al. The association of cardiovascular disease with the long-term incidence of age-related maculopathy: the Beaver Dam Eye Study. *Ophthalmol* 2003;110(4):636-43.

Landvik, S.V., et al. Alpha-Lipoic acid in health and disease. In: *Antioxidant Status, Diet, Nutrition and Health*. Papas, A.M., ed. CRC Press, 1999:591-600.

Pratt, S. Dietary prevention of age-related macular degeneration. *J Am Optom Assoc* 1999;70(1):39-47.

Richer, S. Lutein—an opportunity for improved eye health. *JANA* 2001;4(2):6-7.

Seddon, J.M., et al. Dietary carotenoids, vitamins A, C, and E, and advanced age-related macular degeneration. Eye Disease Case-Control Study Group. *JAMA* 1994;272(18):1413-20.

Shao, A. The role of lutein in human health. *JANA* 2001;4(2):8-24.

Simopoulos, A.P., et al. Common purslane: a source of omega-3 fatty acids and antioxidants. *J Am Coll Nutr* 1992;11(4):374-82.

Slattery, M.L., et al. Carotenoids and colon cancer. *Am J Clin Nutr* 2000;71(2):575-82.

Steenge, G.R., et al. Betaine supplementation lowers plasma homocysteine in healthy men and women. *J Nutr* 2003;133(5):1291-5.

Zeisel, S.H., et al. Concentrations of choline-containing compounds and betaine in common foods. *J Nutr* 2003;133(5):1302-7.

Tea

Ahmad, N., et al. Antioxidants in chemoprevention of skin cancer. *Curr Probl Dermatol* 2001;29:128-39.

Ahmad, N., et al. Green tea polyphenols and cancer: biologic mechanisms and practical implications. *Nutr Rev* 1999;57(3):78-83.

Arab, L. Tea and prevention of prostate, colon and rectal cancer. Third international scientific symposium on tea and human health: role of flavonoids in the diet. Washington, DC: United States Department of Agriculture, September 23, 2002.

Bell, S.J., et al. A functional food product for the management of weight. *Crit Rev Food Sci Nutr* 2002;42(2):163-78.

Benzie, I., et al. Consumption of green tea causes rapid increase in plasma antioxidant power in humans. *Nutr Cancer* 1999;34:83-87.

Cao, Y., et al. Antiangiogenic mechanisms of diet-derived polyphenols. *J Nutr Biochem* 2002;13(7):380-90.

Chung, F. Tea in cancer prevention: studies in animals and humans. Third international scientific symposium on tea and human health: role of flavonoids in the diet. Washington, DC: U.S. Department of Agriculture, September 23, 2002.

Duffy, S.J., et al. Short- and long-term black tea consumption reverses endothelial dysfunction in patients with coronary artery disease. *Circulation* 2001;104:151-6.

Fujiki, H. Two stages of cancer prevention with green tea. *J Cancer Res Clin Oncol* 1999, Nov;125:589-97.

Geleijnse, J.M., et al. Inverse association of tea and flavonoid intakes with incident myocardial infarction: the Rotterdam Study. *Am J Clin Nutr* 2002;75(5):880-6.

Geleijnse, J.M., et al. Tea flavonoids may protect against atherosclerosis: the Rotterdam Study. *Arch Intern Med* 1999;159(18):2170-4.

Gupta, S.K., et al. Green tea protects against selemite-induced oxidative stress in experimental cataractogenesis. *Exp Eye Res* 2001;73:393-401.

Hakim, I. Tea and cancer: epidemiology and clinical studies. Third international scientific symposium on tea and human health: role of flavonoids in the diet. Washington, DC: United States Department of Agriculture, September 23, 2002.

Hegarty, V.M., et al. Tea drinking and bone mineral density in older women. *Am J Clin Nutr* 2000;71:1003-7.

Lambert, J.D., et al. Piperine enhances the bioavailability of the tea polyphenol(-)-epigallocatechin-3-gallate in mice. *J Nutr* 2004, Aug;134(8):1948-52.

Margen, Sheldon, and the editors of the UC Berkeley *Wellness Letter. Wellness Foods A to Z*. New York: Rebus, 2002.

McKay, D., et al. The role of tea in human health: an update. *J Am Coll Nutr* 2002;21(1):1-13.

Mei, Y., et al. Reversal of cancer multidrug resistance by green tea polyphenols. *J Pharm Pharmacol* 2004, Oct;56(10):1307-14.

Mukamal, K., et al. Tea consumption and mortality after acute myocardial infarction. *Circulation* 2002;105:2476-81.

Nagao, T., et al. Ingestion of a tea rich in catechins leads to a reduction in body fat and malondialdehyde-modified LDL in men. *Am J Clin Nutr* 2005, Jan;81(1):122-129.

Nakayama, M., et al. Inhibition of influenza virus infection by tea. *Lett Appl Microbiol* 1990;11:38-40.

Olthof, M.R., et al. Chlorogenic acid, quercetin-3-rutinoside and black tea phenols are extensively metabolized in humans. *J Nutr* 2003;133(6):1806-14.

Serafini, M., et al. In vivo antioxidant effect of green and black tea in man. *Eur J Clin Nutr* 1996;50:28-32.

Stephanou, A., Role of STAT-1 and STAT-3 in ischaemia/reperfusion injury. *J Cell Mol Med* 2004, Oct-Dec;8(4):519-25.

Tsuneki, H., et al. Effect of green tea on blood glucose levels and serum proteomic patterns in diabetic (db/db) mice and on glucose metabolism in healthy humans. *BMC Pharmacol* 2004, Aug 26;4(1):18.

van het Hof, K.H., et al. Bioavailability of catechins from tea: the effect of milk. *Eur J Clin Nutr* 1998;52:356-9.

Yang, C.S., et al. Effects of tea consumption on nutrition and health. *J Nutr* 2000;130(10):2409-12.

Yang, Y.C., et al. The protective effect of habitual tea consumption on hypertension. *Arch Inter Med* 2004, July;164:1534-40.

Zhu, Q.Y., et al. Regeneration of a-tocopherol in human low-density lipoprotein by green tea catechin. *J Agric Food Chem* 1999;47:2020-5.

Tomatoes

Beecher, G.R. Nutrient content of tomatoes and tomato products. *Proc Soc Exp Biol Med* 1998;218:98-100.

Boileau, T.W., et al. Prostate carcinogenesis in N-methyl-N-nitrosourea (NMU)-testosterone-treated rats fed tomato powder, lycopene, or energy-restricted diets. *J Natl Cancer Inst* 2003, Nov 5;95(21):1578-86.

Edwards, A.J., et al. Consumption of watermelon juice increases plasma concentrations of lycopene and beta-carotene in humans. *J Nutr* 2003;133(4):1043-50.

Etminan, M., et al. The role of tomato products and lycopene in the prevention of prostate cancer: A meta-analysis of observational studies. *Cancer Epidemiol Biomarkers Prev* 2004, Mar;13(3):340-45.

Ford, E.S., et al. Serum vitamins, carotenoids, and angina pectoris: findings from the National Health and Nutrition Examination Survey III. *Annals of Epidemiol* 2000;10(2):106-16.

Fuhrman, B., et al. Lycopene synergistically inhibits LDL oxidation in combination with vitamin E, glabridin, rosmarinic acid, carnosic acid, or garlic. *Antioxid Redox Signal* 2000;2:491-506.

Gartner, C., et al. Lycopene is more bioavailable from tomato paste than from fresh tomatoes. *Am J Clin Nutr* 1997;66:116-22.

Giovannucci, E. Tomatoes, tomato-based products, lycopene, and cancer: review of the epidemiologic literature. *J Natl Cancer Inst* 1999;91(4):317-31.

Hadley, C.W., et al. The consumption of processed tomato products enhances plasma lycopene concentrations in association with a reduced lipoprotein sensitivity to oxidative damage. *J Nutr* 2003;133(3):727-32.

Ishida, B.K., and M.H. Chapman. A comparison of carotenoid content and total antioxidant activity in catsup from several commercial sources in the United States. *J Agric Food Chem* 2004, Dec 29;52(26):8017-8020.

Khachik, F., et al. Lutein, lycopene, and their oxidative metabolites in chemoprevention of cancer. *J Cell Biochem* 1996;22(suppl):236-46.

Lazarus, S.A., et al. Tomato juice and platelet aggregation in type 2 diabetes. *JAMA* 2004, Aug 18;292(7):805-806.

Lazarus, S.A., and M.L. Garg. Inhibition of platelet aggregation from people with type 2 diabetes mellitus following consumption of tomato juice. *Asia Pacific Journal of Clinical Nutrition* 2004;13 (Supple):S65.

Nkondjock, A., et al. Dietary Intake of Lycopene Is Associated with Reduced Pancreatic Cancer Risk. *J Nutr* 2005, Mar;135(3):592-97.

Ribaya-Mercado, J.D., et al. Skin lycopene is destroyed preferentially over beta-carotene during ultraviolet irradiation in humans. *J Nutr* 1995;125(7):1854-9.

Riso, P., et al. Tomatoes and health promotion. In: *Vegetables, Fruits, and Herbs in Health Promotion.* Watson, R.R., ed. CRC Press;2001:45-70.

Rissanen, T.H., et al. Low serum lycopene concentration is associated with an excess incidence of acute coronary events and stroke: the Kuopio Ischaemic Heart Disease Risk Factor Study. *Br J Nutr* 2001;85(6):749-54.

Sesso, H.D., et al. Dietary lycopene, tomato-based food products and cardiovascular disease in women. *J Nutr Jul*;133(7):2336-41.

Snowdon, D.A., et al. Antioxidants and reduced functional capacity in the elderly: findings from the Nun Study. *J Gerontol Med Sci* 1996;51A(1):M10-6.

Stahl, W., et al. Carotenoid mixtures protect multilamellar liposomes against oxidative damage: synergistic effects of lycopene and lutein. *FEBS Lett* 1998;427:305-8.

Stahl, W., et al. Dietary tomato paste protects against ultraviolet light-induced erythema in humans. *J Nutr* 2001;131(5):1449-51.

Stewart, A.J., et al. Occurrence of flavonols in tomatoes and tomato-based products. *J Agric Food Chem* 2000;48:2663-9.

Upritchard, J.E., et al. Effect of supplementation with tomato juice, vitamin E, and vitamin C on LDL oxidation and products of inflammatory activity in type 2 diabetes. *Diabetes Care* 2000;23(6):733-8.

Zhang, S., et al. Measurement of retinoids and carotenoids in breast adipose tissue and a comparison of concentrations in breast cancer cases and control subjects. *Am J Clin Nutr* 1997;66:626-32.

Turkey (Skinless Breast)

Anderson, J.J.B., et al. High protein meals, insular hormones and urinary calcium excretion in human subjects. In: *Osteoporosis.* Christiansen, C., Johansen, J.S., Riis, B.D., eds. Viborg, Denmark: Nørhaven A/S, 1987;240-5.

Bell, J., et al. Elderly women need dietary protein to maintain bone mass. *Nutr Rev* 2002;60(10, part I):337-41.

Bingam, S.A. High meat diets and cancer risk. *Proc Nutr Soc* 1999;58(2):243-8.

Clark, L.C., et al. Effects of selenium supplementation for cancer prevention in patients with carcinoma of the skin: a randomized controlled trial. Nutritional Prevention of Cancer Study Group. *JAMA* 1996; 276:1957-63.

Cordain, L., et al. Plant-animal subsistence ratios and macronutrient energy estimations in worldwide hunter-gatherer diets. *Am J Clin Nutr* 2000;71:682-92.

Eaton, S.B., et al. An evolutionary perspective enhances understanding of human nutritional requirements. *J Nutr* 1996;126:1732-40.

Eaton, S.B., et al. Paleolithic nutrition: a consideration of its nature and current implications. *N Engl J Med* 1985;312:283-9.

Eaton, S.B., et al. Paleolithic nutrition revisited: a twelve-year retrospective on its nature and implications. *Eur J Clin Nutr* 1997;51:207-16.

Eisenstein, J., et al. High-protein weight-loss diets: are they safe and do they work? A review of the experimental and epidemiologic data. *Nutr Rev* 2002;60(7):189-200.

Fung, T., et al. Major dietary patterns and the risk of colorectal cancer in women. *Arch Int Med* 2003;163(3):309-14.

Hamer, D.H., et al. From the farm to the kitchen table: the negative impact of antimicrobial use in animals on humans. *Nutr Rev* 2002;60(8):261-4.

Morris, M.C., et al. Dietary fats and the risk of incident Alzheimer disease. *Arch Neurol* 2003;60(2):194-200.

Norat, T., et al. Meat consumption and colorectal cancer: a review of epidemiologic evidence. *Nutr Rev* 2001;59(2):37-47.

Norrish, A.E., et al. Heterocyclicamine content of cooked meat and risk of prostate cancer. *J Natl Cancer Inst* 1999;91(23):2038-44.

O'Dea, K. Traditional diet and food preferences of Australian aboriginal hunter-gatherers. *Philos Trans R Soc Lond B Biol Sci* 1991;334:233-41.

Pawlosky, R.J., et al. Effects of beef- and fish-based diets on the kinetics of n-3 fatty acid metabolism in human subjects. *Am J Clin Nutr* 2003;77(3)565-72.

Peregrin, T. Limiting the use of antibiotics in livestock: helping your patients understand the science behind the issue. *J Am Diet Assoc* 2002;102(6):768.

Promislow, J., et al. Protein consumption and bone mineral density in the elderly: the Rancho Bernardo study. *Am J Epidemiol* 2002;155:636-44.

Thorogood, M., et al. Risk of death from cancer and ischemic heart disease in meat and non-meat eaters. *BMJ* 1994;308:1667-70.

Walnuts

Ahsan, S.K. Magnesium in health and disease. *J Pak Med Assoc* 1998;48:246-50.

Albert, C.M., et al. Nut consumption and decreased risk of sudden cardiac death in the Physicians' Health Study. *Arch Intern Med* 2002;162(12):1382-7.

Albert, C.M., et al. Nut consumption and the risk of sudden and total cardiac death in the Physicians' Health Study. *Circulation* 1999;98(suppl I):I-582.

Ascherio, A., et al. Intake of potassium, magnesium, calcium and fiber and risk of stroke among US men. *Circulation* 1998;98:1198-1204.

Awad, A.B., et al. Phytosterols as anticancer dietary components: evidence and mechanism of action. *J Nutr* 2000;130:2127-30.

Devaraj, S., et al. g-Tocopherol, the new vitamin E? *Am J Clin Nutr* 2003;77(3):530-1.

Dixon, L.B., et al. Choose a diet that is low in saturated fat and cholesterol and moderate in total fat: subtle changes to a familiar message. *J Nutr* 2001;131(2S-1):510S-26S.

Feldman, E.B. The scientific evidence for a beneficial health relationship between walnuts and coronary heart disease. *J Nutr* 2002;132(5):1062S-1101S.

Fukuda, T., et al. Antioxidative polyphenols from walnuts (Juglans regia L.). *Phytochemistry* 2003, Aug;63(7):795-801.

Garg, M.L., et al. Macadamia nut consumption lowers plasma total and LDL cholesterol levels in hypercholesterolemic men. *J Nutr* 2003;133:1060-3.

Hu, F.B., et al. Dietary fat intake and the risk of coronary heart disease in women. *N Engl J Med* 1997;337:1491-9.

Jiang, R., et al. Nut and peanut butter consumption and risk of type 2 diabetes in women. *JAMA* 2002, Nov 27;288(20):2554-60.

Kris-Etherton, P.M., et al. High-monounsaturated fatty acid diets lower both plasma cholesterol and tricylglycerol concentrations. *Am J Clin Nutr* 1999;70:1009-15.

Kris-Etherton, P.M., et al. Nuts and their bioactive constituents: effects on serum lipids and other factors that affect disease risk. *Am J Clin Nutr* 1999;70(suppl):504S-11S.

Kris-Etherton, P.M., et al. Recent discoveries in inclusive food-based approaches and dietary patterns for reduction in risk for cardiovascular disease. *Curr Opin Lipidol* 2002;13(4):397-407.

Laurin, D., et al. Vitamin E and C supplements and risk of dementia. *JAMA* 2002, Nov 13;288(18):2266-68.

Liu, M., et al. Mixed tocopherols inhibit platelet aggregation in humans: potential mechanisms. *Am J Clin Nutr* 2003;77(3):700-50.

Lovejoy, J.C., et al. Effect of diets enriched in almonds on insulin action and serum lipids in adults with normal glucose tolerance or type 2 diabetes. *Am J Clin Nutr* 2002;76(5):1000-6.

Morgan, J.M., et al. Effects of walnut consumption as part of a low-fat, low cholesterol diet on serum cardiovascular risk factors. *Int J Vitam Nutr Res* 2002, Oct;72(5):341-47.

Morgan, W.A., et al. Pecans lower low-density lipoprotein cholesterol in people with normal lipid levels. *J Am Diet Assoc* 2000;100:312-8.

Morris, M.C., et al. Dietary intake of antioxidant nutrients and the risk of incident Alzheimer disease in a biracial community study. *JAMA* 2002;287(24): 3223-9.

Ostlund, R.E., et al. Effects of trace components of dietary fat on cholesterol metabolism: phytosterols, oxysterols, and squalene. *Nutr Rev* 2002;60(11):349-59.

Reiter, R.J., et al. Melatonin in Walnuts: Influence on Levels of Melatonin and Total Antioxidant Capacity of Blood. Nutrition: *Intl J Applied and Basic Nutr Sciences* 2005;21:920-24.

Ros, E., et al. A walnut diet improves endothelial function in hypercholesterolemic subjects: A randomized crossover trial. *Circulation* 2004, Apr 6;109(13):1609-1614.

Sabaté, J. Nut consumption, vegetarian diets, ischemic heart disease risk, and all-cause mortality: evidence from epidemiologic studies. *Am J Clin Nutr* 1999;70(suppl):500S-3S.

Spiller, G.A., et al. Nuts and plasma lipids: an almond-based diet lowers LDL-C while preserving HDL-C. *J Am Coll Nutr* 1998;17:285-90.

Stevens, L.J., et al. Essential Fatty Acid Metabolism in Boys with Attention-Deficit Hyperactivity Disorder. *Am J Clin Nutr* 1995, Oct;62(4):761-68.

Stewart, J.R., et al. Resveratrol: a candidate nutritional substance for prostate cancer prevention. *J Nutr* 2003;133(7S):2440S-3S.

Tapsell, L.C., et al. Including Walnuts in a Low-Fat/Modified-Fat Diet Improves HDL Cholesterol-to-Total Cholesterol Ratios in Patients with Type 2 Diabetes. *Diabetes Care* 2004, Dec;27(12):2777-83.

Venho, B., et al. Arginine intake, blood pressure, and the incidence of acute coronary events in men: the Kuopio Ischaemic Heart Disease Risk Factor Study. *Am J Clin Nutr* 2002;76(1):359-64.

Watkins, T.R., et al. Tocotrienols: biological and health effects. In: *Antioxidant Status, Diet, Nutrition and Health*. Papas, A.M., ed. CRC Press, 1999:479-96.

Zhao, G., et al. Dietary and Linolenic Acid Reduces Inflammatory and Lipid Cardiovascular Risk Factors in Hypercholesteaclemic Men and Women. *J Nutr* 2004;134:2991-97.

Low-fat or Nonfat Yogurt

Adolfsson, O., et al. Yogurt and Gut Function. *Am J Clin Nutr* 2004;80:245-56.

Bornet, F.R.J, et al. Immune-stimulating and gut-health-promoting properties of short-chain fructo-oligosaccharides. *Nutr Rev* 2002;60(10, part I):326-34.

Chan, J.M., et al. Dairy products, calcium, and prostate cancer risk in the Physicians' Health Study. *Am J Clin Nutr* 2001;74(4):549-54.

Duggan, C., et al. Protective nutrients and functional foods for the gastrointestinal tract. *Am J Clin Nutr* 2002;75(5):789-808.

Fortes, C., et al. Diet and overall survival in a cohort of very elderly people. *Epidemiol* 2000;11(4):440-5.

Gill, H.S., et al. Enhancement of immunity in the elderly by dietary supplementation with the probiotic Bifidobacterium lactis HN019. *Am J Clin Nutr* 2001;74(6):833-9.

Gluck, U., et al. Ingested probiotics reduce nasal colonization with pathogenic bacteria (Staphylococcus aureus, Streptococcus pneumoniae, and beta-hemolytic streptococci). *Am J Clin Nutr* 2003;77(2):517-20.

Heaney, R.P., et al. Effect of yogurt on a urinary marker of bone resorption in postmenopausal women. *J Am Diet Assoc* 2002;102:1672-4.

Hilton, E., et al. Ingestion of yogurt containing Lactobacillus acidophilus as prophylaxis for candidal vaginitis. *Ann Intern Med* 1992;116(5):353-7.

Hojo, K., et al., of Tsurumi University, Yokohama, Japan. Paper presented at the International Association for Dental Research, Baltimore, March 10, 2005.

Hooper, L.V., et al. How host-microbial interactions shape the nutrient environment of the mammalian intestine. In: *Annual Review of Nutrition*, vol. 22, 2002.

McCormick, D.B., Bier, D., Cousins, R.J., eds., Palo Alto, CA: Annual Reviews;283-308.

Isolauri, E. Probiotics in human disease. *Am J Clin Nutr* 2001;73(6, suppl):1142S-6S.

Jelen, P., et al. Functional milk and dairy products. In: *Functional Foods Biochemical & Processing Aspects.* Mazza, G., ed., Lancaster, PA: Technomic Publishing Company, Inc., 1998:357-80.

Kaur, N., et al. Applications of inulin and oligofructose in health and nutrition. *J Biosci* 2002;27(7):703-14.

Kent, K.D., et al. Effect of whey protein isolate on intracellular glutathione and oxidant-induced cell death in human prostate epithelial cells. *Toxicol In Vitro* 2003;17(1):27-33.

Liska, D., et al. Gut restoration and chronic disease. *JANA* 2002;5(4):20-33.

Madden, J.A., et al. A review of the role of the gut microflora in irritable bowel syndrome and the effects of probiotics. *Brit J Nutr* 2002;88(suppl 1):S67-S72.

Mann, G.V., et al. Studies of a surfactant and cholesteremia in the Maasai. *J Nutr* 1974;27:464-9.

Mitral, B.K., et al. Anticarcinogenic, hypo-cholesterolemic, and antagonistic activities of lactobacillus acidophilus. *Crit Rev Microbiol* 1995;21(3):175-214.

Perdigon, G., et al. Antitumour activity of yogurt: study of possible immune mechanisms. *J Dairy Res* 1998;65(1):129-38.

Rachid, M.M., et al. Effect of yogurt on the inhibition of an intestinal carcinoma by increasing cellular apoptosis. *Int J Immunopathol Pharmacol* 2002;15(3):209-16.

Saavedra, J.M. Clinical applications of probiotic agents. *Am J Clin Nutr* 2001;73(6,suppl):1147S-51S.

Salminen, S., et al. Demonstration of safety of probiotic—a review. *Int J Food Microbiol* 1998;44:93-106.

Sanders, M.E. Probiotics: considerations for human health. *Nutr Rev* 2003;61(3):91-9.

Seppo, L., et al. A fermented milk high in bioactive peptides has a blood pressure-lowering effect in hypertensive subjects. *Am J Clin Nutr* 2003;77(2):326-30.

Teitelbaum, J.E, et al. Nutritional impact of pre- and probiotics as protective gastrointestinal organisms. In: *Annual Review of Nutrition,* vol. 22, 2002. McCormick, D.B., Bier, D., Cousins, R.J., eds., Palo Alto, CA: Annual Reviews, 107-38.

Vanit Veer, P., et al. Consumption of fermented milk products and breast cancer: A case-control study in the Netherlands. *Cancer Res* 1989;49:4020-23.

Wong, C.W., et al. Immunomodulatory effects of dietary whey proteins in mice. *J Dairy Res* 1995;62(2):359-68.

Zemel, M.B., et al. Dairy (yogurt) augments fat loss and reduces central adiposity during energy restriction in obese subjects. *FASEB* 2003;17 (5):A1088.

CHAPTER 3
Nutritional Information You Need To Know

Are You Getting Enough Vitamin D?

Holick, M.F. McCollum Award Lecture, 1994: Vitamin D: New horizons for the 21st century. *Am J Clin Nutr* 1994;60:619-30.

Institute of Medicine, Food and Nutrition Board. *Dietary Reference Intakes: Calcium, Phosphorus, Magnesium, Vitamin D and Fluoride.* Washington, DC: National Academy Press, 1999.

van den Berg, H. Bioavailability of vitamin D. *Eur J Clin Nutr* 1997;51 Suppl 1:S76-S79.

Webb, A.R., et al. Influence of season and latitude on the cutaneous synthesis of vitamin D3: Exposure to winter sunlight in Boston and Edmonton will not promote vitamin D3 synthesis in human skin. *J Clin Endocrinol Metab* 1988;67:373-78.

Potassium Power

Colditz, G.A., et al. Diet and risk of clinical diabetes in women. *Am J Clin Nutr* 1992;55:1018-23.

Fiber

Ajani, U.A., et al. Dietary Fiber and C-Reactive Protein: Findings from National Health and Nutrition Examination Survey Data. *J Nutr* 2004;134:1181-85.

Chandalia, M., et al. Beneficial Effects of High Dietary Fiber Intake in Patients with Type 2 Diabetes Mellitus. *N Eng J Med* 2000;342:1392-98.

Guzman-Maldonado, S.H., et al. Functional Products of Plants Indigenous to Latin America: Amaranth, Quinoa, Common Beans, and Botanicals. In *Functional Foods*, ed. G. Mazza. Lancaster, PA: Technomic Publishing Co. Inc., 1998, pp.293-328.

Jensen, M.K., et al. Intakes of whole grains, bran, and germ and the risk of coronary heart disease in men. *Am J Clin Nutr* 2004;80:1492-99.

Ludwig, D.S., et al. Dietary fiber, weight gain and cardiovascular disease risk factors in young adults. *JAMA* 1999;282 (16):1539-46.

Rock, C.L., et al. J Clin Oncol 2004;22:2379 (from Nutrition and the M.D. 2004, Oct;30:6-7).

Wolk, A., et al. Long-term Intake of Dietary Fiber and Decreased Risk of Coronary Heart Disease Among Women. *JAMA* 1999;281:1998-2004.

SuperSpices

Anderson, R.A., et al. Isolation and Characterization of Polyphenol Type-A Polymers from Cinnamon with Insulin-like Biological Activity. *J Agric Food Chem* 2004;52:65-70.

Calucci, L., et al. Effects of gamma-irradiation on the free radical and antioxidant contents in nine aromatic herbs and spices. *J Agric Food Chem* 2003, Feb 12;51(4):927-34.

Khan, A., et al. Cinnamon improves glucose and lipids of people with type 2 diabetes. *Diabetes Care* 2003;26:3215-218.

Otsuka, H., et al. Studies on anti-inflammatory agents. VI. Anti-inflammatory constituents of Cinnamomum sieboldii Meissn [author's transl]. *Yakugaku Zasshi* 1982, Jan;102(2):162-72.

Ouattara, B., et al. Antibacterial activity of selected fatty acids and essential oils against six meat spoilage organisms. *Int J Food Microbiol* 1997, Jul 22;37(2-3):155-62.

Quale, J.M., et al. In vitro activity of Cinnamomum zeylanicum against azole resistant and sensitive Candida species and a pilot study of cinnamon for oral candidiasis. *Am J Chin Med* 1996;24(2):103-109.

Valero, M., and M.C. Salmeron. Antibacterial activity of 11 essential oils against Bacillus cereus in tyndallized carrot broth. *Int J Food Microbiol* Aug 15;85(1-2):73-81.

Wu, X., et al. Lipophilic and hydrophilic antioxidant capacities of common foods in the United States. *J Agric Food Chem* 2004, Jun 16;52(12):4026-37.

Zoladz, P., et al. Cinnamon perks performance. Paper presented at the annual meeting of the Association for Chemoreception Sciences, Sarasota, FL, April 21-25, 2004.

CHAPTER 5
Healthy Menus the Gourmet Way

Eisenberg, M., et al. Correlations between family meals and psychosocial well-being among adolescents. *Arch Pediatrics and Adolescent Medicine* 2004;158:792-96.

Gillman, M.W., et al. Family Dinner and Diet Quality Among Older Children and Adolescents. *Arch Fam Med* 2000;9:235-40.

CHAPTER 7
Lose Weight by Eating Well

The American Institute for Cancer Research. Understanding the Obesity-Cancer Connection. Awareness and Action: *AICR Surveys on Portion Size, Nutrition and Cancer Risk*, p. 7. Available at *http://www.aicr.org/press/awarenessandaction_03conf.pdf.* Accessed March 4, 2004.

Cifuentes, M., et al. Weight loss and calcium intake influence calcium absorption in overweight postmenopausal women. *Am J Clin Nutr* 2004, Jul;80(1):123-30.

Clark, A., et al. *Int J Cardiol* 2001, Aug;80(1):87-88.

Hannum, S.M., et al. Use of portion-controlled entrees enhances weight loss in women. *Obes Res* 2004, Mar;12(3):538-46.

Logue, E.F., et al. Longitudinal relationship between elapsed time in the action stages of change and weight loss. *Obes Res* 2004, Sep;12(9):1499-1508.

Orlet, Fisher J., et al. Children's bite size and intake of an entrée are greater with large portions than with age-appropriate or self-selected portions. *Am J Clin Nutr* 2003, May;77(5):1164-70.

Pereira, M.A., et al. Dairy consumption, obesity, and the insulin resistance syndrome in young adults: The CARDIA Study. *JAMA* 2002;287:2081-89.

Rolls, B.J., et al. Portion size of food affects energy intake in normal-weight and overweight men and women. *Am J Clin Nutr* 2002, Dec;76(6):1207-13.

Sloan, E. A. What, when, and where Americans eat. *Food Technol* 2003;38:91-94

Wansink, B., and J. Kim. Bad Popcorn in Big Buckets: Portion Size Can Influence Intake as Much as Taste. *J Nutr Edu and Behavior* 2005.

Young, L.R., and M. Nestle. Expanding Portion Sizes in the US Marketplace:Implications for Nutrition Counseling. *J Am Diet Assoc* 2003;103:231-4.

CHAPTER 8
Exercise Your Way to Health

Abraham, C., and P. Sheeran, Deciding to exercise: The role of anticipated regret. *British Journal of Health Psychology,* May 2004;9(2):269-78.

Anderson, L.B., et al. All-Cause Mortality Associated with Physical Activity During Leisure Time, Work, Sports, and Cycling to Work. *Arch Intern* Med 2000;160:1621-28.

Berlin, J.A., et al. A meta-analysis of physical activity in the prevention of coronary heart disease. *Am J Epidemiol* 1990;132:612-28.

Cartee, G.D. Aging skeletal muscle response to exercise. *Exerc Sport Sci Rev* 1994;22:91-120.

Clyman, B. Exercise in the Treatment of Osteoarthritis. *Current Rheumatology Reports* 2001;3:520-23.

Colcombe, S., and A.F. Kramer. Fitness Effects on the Cognitive Function of Older Adults: A Meta-Analytic Study. *Psychological Science* (March 2003);14, no. 2, 125-29.

The Diabetes Prevention Program Research Group. Reduction of the Incidence of Type 2 Diabetes with Lifestyle Intervention or Metformin. *N Eng J Med* 2002;346:393-403.

Dunn, A.L., et al. Comparison of lifestyle and structured interventions to increase physical activity and cardiorespiratory fitness: A randomized trial. *JAMA* 1999;281 (4):327-34.

Estabrooks, P.A., et al. Physical activity promotion through primary care. *JAMA* 289, no. 22, 2913-16.

Exercise and Women. *National Health Interview Survey,* 2000.

Frontera, W.R., et al. Strength conditioning in older men: skeletal muscle hypertrophy and improved function. *J Appl Physiol* 1988;64:1038-44.

Frontera, W.R., et al. Strength training and determinants of VO2 max in older men. *J Appl Physiol* 1990;68:329-33.

Get your daughters off the sofa and into the gym. *The Wall Street Journal,* Dec 23, 2003, D1.

Gregg, Edward W., et al., for the Study of Osteoporotic Fractures Research Group. Relationship of Changes in Physical Activity and Mortality Among Older Women. *JAMA* 2003;289:2379-86.

Gulati, M., et al. Exercise Capacity and the Risk of Death in Women. The St. James Women Take Heart Project. *Circulation,* American Heart Association. Abstract available online at *http://circ.ahajournals.org/cgi/content/abstract/01.CIR.0000091080.57509.E9v1.*

Guraloik, J., et al. Maintaining mobility to late life. *Am J Epidemiol* 1993;137:845-57.

Hakim, A.A. Effects on walking on mortality among non-smoking retired men. *N Eng J Med* 1998, Jan 8;338:94-99.

Hawkins, S., et al. Rate and mechanism of maximal oxygen consumption decline with aging: Implications for exercise training. *Sports Medicine* 2003;33:877-888.

Hu, F., et al. Diet, Lifestyle and the Risk of Type 2 Diabetes Mellitus in Women. *N Eng J Med* 2001;790-97.

Ivarsson, T., et al. Physical exercise and vasomotor symptoms in postmenopausal women. *Maturitas* 1998, June 3;29(2):139-46. (Original material from *Harvard Health Letter.*)

The Joys and Benefits of Getting into Shape. *Harvard Health Letter,* July 2002.

Kamel, H.K., et al. Sarcopenia and aging. *Nutrition Reviews* 2003;61:157-67.

Keller, M.C., et al. (in press). A warm heart and a clear head: The contingent effects of weather on human mood and cognition. *Psychological Science.*

Kemmler, W., et al. Benefits of 2 Years of Intense Exercise on Bone Density, Physical Fitness, and Blood Lipids in Early Postmenopausal Osteopenic Women: Results of the Erlangen Fitness Osteoporosis Prevention Study (EFOPS).

Khfgaard, H., et al. Function, morphology and protein expression of aging, skeletal muscle: a cross-sectional study of elderly men with different training backgrounds. *Acta Physiol Scand* 1990;140:41-54.

Lam, T.H., et al. Leisure Time Physical Activity and Mortality in Hong Kong: Case-control Study of All Adult Deaths in 1998. *Ann Epidemiol* 2004;14:391-98.

Lemura, L.M., et al. The effects of physical training on functional capacity in adults. Ages 46 to 90: A meta-analysis. *Journal of Sports Medicine and Physical Fitness* 2000;40:1-10.

Manson, J.E., et al. A prospective study of walking as compared with vigorous exercise in the prevention of coronary heart disease in women. *N Eng J Med* 1999, Aug. 26;341:650-8.

McGuire, D.K., et al. A 30-year Follow-up of the Dallas Bed Rest and Training Study I. Effect of Age on the Cardiovascular Response to Exercise II. Effect of Age on Cardiovascular Adaptation to Exercise Training. *Circulation* 2001;104:1358-66.

McGuire, D.K., et al. A 30-year Follow-up of the Dallas Bed Rest and Training Study I. Effect of Age on the Cardiovascular Response to Exercise I. *Circulation* 2001;104:1350-57.

Milgram, N.W., et al. Learning ability in aged beagle dogs is preserved by behavioral enrichment and dietary fortification: A two-year longitudinal study. *Neurobiol Aging* 2005;26:77-90.

Mora, S., et al. Ability of Exercise Testing to Predict Cardiovascular and All-Cause Death in Asymptomatic Women. *JAMA* 290:1600-1607.

Rockhill, B., et al. Physical Activity and Mortality: A Prospective Study Among Women. *Am J Public Health* 91(4), April 2001, 578-83.

Saris, W.H.M., et al. How much physical activity is enough to prevent unhealthy weight gain? Outcome of the IASO 1st Stock Conference and consensus statement. *Obesity Reviews* 2003;*4:101-14.*

Simonsick, E.M., et al. Risk due to inactivity in physically capable older adults. *Am J Public Health* 1993; 83:1443-50.

Slattery, M., et al. Physical Activity and Colon Cancer: A Public Health Perspective. *Ann Epidemiol* 1997; 7:137-45.

Smith, D.T., et al. Effects of ageing and regular aerobic exercise on endothelial fibrinolytic capacity in humans. *J Physiol* 2003, Jan 1;546(pt.1):289-98.

Smith, K., et al. Two Years of Resistance Training in Older Men and Women: The Effects of Three Years of Detraining on the Retention of Dynamic Strength. *Can J Appl Phys* 2003;28, no. 3, 462-74.

Stone, W.J., et al. Long-term exercisers: What can we learn from them? *ACSM's Health & Fitness Journal,* March/April 2004, 11-14.

Thornton, E.W., et al. Health benefits of tai chi exercise: improved balance and blood pressure in middle-aged women. *Health Promotion International,* 2004;19, no. 1, 33-38.

U.S. Department of Health and Human Services. *Physical Activity and Health: A Report of the Surgeon General.* Atlanta, GA: U.S. Department of Health and Human Services, Centers for Disease Control and Prevention, National Center for Chronic Disease Prevention and Health Promotion, 1996.

Young, D.R., et al. The effects of aerobic exercise and tai chi on blood pressure in older people: Results of a randomized trial. *J Am Geriatrics Soc* 1999;47:277-84.

CHAPTER 9
Better Sleep: Improve Your Life

Campbell, S., et al. Effects of a Nap on Nighttime Sleep and Waking Function in Older Subjects. *J Am Ger Soc* 2005, Jan;(53):48.

Carskadon, M.A. Sleep deprivation: Health consequences and societal impact. *Med Clin N Am* 2004;88:767-76.

Crouch, E.R., et al. Retinal Vascular Changes in Obstructive Sleep Apnea Syndrome. *ARVA* 2005;poster 3278-B831.

Culebras, A. Cerebrovascular disease and sleep. *Curr Neurol Neurosci Rep* 2004;4:164-69.

Engle-Friedman, M., et al. The effect of sleep loss on next day effort. *J Sleep Res* 2003;12:113-24.

Ferrara, M., et al. How much sleep do we need? *Sleep Medicine Reviews* 2001;5 (2):155-79.

Gupta, N.K., et al. Is obesity associated with poor sleep quality in adolescents? *Am J Hum Biol* 2002;14:762-68.

Lamberg, L. Promoting Adequate Sleep Finds a Place on the Public Health Agenda. *JAMA* 2004;2415-17.

Ledger, D. Public Health and Insomnia: Economic Impact. *Sleep* 2000;23:S69-S76.

North American Association for the Study of Obesity, Nov 14-18, 2004, Las Vegas.

Patel, S.R., et al. A Prospective Study of Sleep Duration and Mortality Risk in Women. *Sleep* 2004;27(3):440-44.

Peppard, P.F., et al. Longitudinal study of moderate weight change and sleep-disordered breathing. *JAMA* 2000;284:3015-21.

Sadeh, A., et al. The Effects of Sleep Restriction and Extension on School-Age Children: What a Difference an Hour Makes. *Child Development* 2003;74:444-55.

Spiegel, K., et al. Leptin levels are dependent on sleep duration: Relationships with sympathovagal balance, carbohydrate regulation, cortisol, and thyrotropin. *J Clin Endrocrinol Metab* 2004, Nov;89(11):5762-71.

Taira, K., et al. Sleep health and lifestyle of elderly people in Ogimi, a village of longevity. *Psychiatry Clin Neurosci* 2002;56:243-44.

Van Dongen, H.P., et al. The cumulative cost of additional wakefulness: Dose-response effects on neurobehavioral functions and sleep physiology from chronic sleep restriction and total sleep deprivation. *Sleep* 2003;26:247-49.

Webb, W.B., et al. Are we chronically sleep deprived? *Bull Psychon Soc* 1975;6:47-48.

CHAPTER 10
The Keys to Avoiding Disease

Allen, J.B., et al. The effects of glucose on nonmemory cognitive functioning in the elderly. *Neuropsychologia* 1966;34(5):459-65.

Apovian, C.M. Sugar-Sweetened Soft Drinks, Obesity, and Type 2 Diabetes. *JAMA* 2004;292(8):978-79.

Braam, L.A.J.L.M., et al. Vitamin K1 supplementation retards bone loss in postmenopausal women between 50 and 60 years of age. *Calcif Tissue Int* 2003;73:21-26.

Castillo-Richmond, A., et al. Effects of stress reduction on carotid atherosclerosis in hypertensive African-Americans. *Stroke* 2000;31:568-73.

Cornuz, J., et al. Smoking, Smoking Cessation, and Risk of Hip Fracture in Women. *Am J Med* 1999;106:311-14.

Costacou, T., et al. Nutrition and the prevention of type 2 diabetes. *Ann Rev Nutr* 2003;23:147-70.

The Diabetes Prevention Program Research Group. Reduction of the Incidence of Type 2 Diabetes with Lifestyle Intervention or Metformin. *N Eng J Med* 2002;346:393-403.

Earnest, C.R., et al. Effects of preexercise carbohydrate feedings on glucose and insulin responses during and following resistance exercise. *Strength and Conditioning Research* 2000;14:361.

Furberg, A.S., et al. Serum high-density lipoprotein cholesterol, metabolic profile, and breast cancer risk. *National Cancer Inst* 2004, Aug;96(15):1152-60.

Ginkgo biloba for Alzheimer's disease: "promising evidence." *www.cochrane.org.* October 21, 2002.

Gold, P.E. Role of glucose in regulating the brain and cognition. *Am J Clin Nutr* 1995;61(4 suppl):987S-995S.

Hebert, Le, et al. Annual Incidence of Alzheimer Disease in the US projected to the Year 2000 through 2050. *Alzheimer Dis Assoc Dissord* 2001;15:169-73.

Hodge, A.M., et al. Glycemic index and dietary fiber and the risk of type 2 diabetes. *Diabetes Care* 2004, Feb;27:538-46.

Hodge, A.M., et al. Glycemic index and dietary fiber and the risk of type 2 diabetes. *Diabetes Care* 2004, Nov;27(11):2701-706.

Holick, M.F. McCollum Award Lecture, 1994: Vitamin D: New horizons for the 21st century. *Am J Clin Nutr* 1994;60:619-30.

Hu, F., et al. Diet, Lifestyle and the Risk of Type 2 Diabetes Mellitus in Women. *N Eng J Med* 2001;790-97.

Jiang, R., et al. Nut and Peanut Butter Consumption and Risk of Type 2 Diabetes in Women. *JAMA* 2002;288:2554-60.

Khan, A., et al. Cinnamon improves glucose and lipids of people with type 2 diabetes. *Diabetes Care* 2003;26:3215-218.

Lazarus, S.A., et al. Tomato juice and platelet aggregation in type 2 diabetes. *JAMA* 2004, Aug 18;292(7):805-806.

Lazarus, S.A., and M.L. Garg. Inhibition of platelet aggregation from people with type 2 diabetes mellitus following consumption of tomato juice. *Asia Pacific Journal of Clinical Nutrition* 2004;13 (Suppl):S65.

Liebeerman, L.S. Dietary, Evolutionary, and Modernizing Influences on the Prevalence of Type 2 Diabetes. *Annu Rev Nutr* 2003;23:345-77.

Liebman, B. Breaking Up: Strong Bones Need More Than Calcium. *Nutrition Action* 2005, April;32(3):2.

Luchsinger, J.A., et al. Dietary Factors and Alzheimer's Disease. *The Lancet Neurology* 2004;3:579-87.

Mattson, M.P. Emerging neuroprotective strategies for Alzheimer's disease: Dietary restriction, telomerase activation, and stem cell therapy. *Exp Gerontology* 2000;35:489-502.

Meyer, K.A., et al. Carbohydrates, dietary fiber, and incident type 2 diabetes in older women. *Am J Clin Nutr* 2000, Apr;71(4):921-30.

Mokdad, A.H., et al. The Coming Epidemic of Obesity and Diabetes in the United States. *JAMA* 2001;286:1195-1200.

Morris, M.C., et al. Consumption of fish and n-3 fatty acids and risk of incident Alzheimer disease. *Arch Neurol* 2003, Jul;60(7):940-46.

Morris, M.C., et al. Dietary Fats and the Risk of Incident Alzheimer Disease. *Arch Neurology* 2003;60:194-200.

Morris, M.C., et al. Dietary niacin and the risk of incident Alzheimer's disease and of cognitive decline. *J Neurol Neurosurg Psychiatry* 2004;75:1093-99.

Mukamal, K.J., et al. Prospective study of alcohol consumption and risk of dementia in older adults. *JAMA* 2003;289:1405-13.

National Osteoporosis Foundation. *America's Bone Health: The State of Osteoporosis and Low Bone Mass in Our Nation.* Washington, DC: National Osteoporosis Foundation, 2002.

Ockene, I.S., et al. Seasonal variation in serum cholesterol levels. *Arch Intern Med* 2004;164:868-70

Okello, Ed J., et al. In vitro anti-beta-secretase and dual anti-cholinesterase activities of Camellia sinensis L. (tea) relevant to treatment of dementia. *Phytotherapy Research* 2004;18:624-27.

Olshansky, S.J., et al. A Potential Decline in Life Expectancy in the United States in the 21st Century. *N Eng J Med* 2005, March 17;352(11):1138-45.

Salmeron, L., et al. Dietary Fiber, Glycemic Load and Risk of Non-Insulin Dependent Diabetes in Men. *Diabetes Care* 1997;20:545-50.

Seshadri, S., et al. Plasma homocysteine as a risk factor for dementia and Alzheimer's disease. *N Eng J Med* 2002, Feb 14;346:476-82.

Stranges, S., et al. Relationship of Alcohol Drinking Pattern to Risk of Hypertension: A Population-Based Study. *Hypertension* 2004;44:813-19.

Tillotson, J.E., Pandemic Obesity. *Nutrition Today* 2004, Jan/Feb;39(1):6-9.

Van Dam, R.M., et al. Dietary patterns and risk for type 2 diabetes mellitus in US men. *Ann Int Med* 2002;136:201-9.

CHAPTER 11
How to Achieve Whole Mind/ Whole Body Health

Barnes, V. Impact of transcendental meditation on ambulatory blood pressure in African-American adolescents. *Am J Hypert* 2004, April;17:366-69.

Bonadonna, R. Meditation's Impact on Chronic Illness. *Holist Nurs Pract* 2003;17(6):309-19.

Castillo-Richmond, A., et al. Effects of stress reduction on carotid atherosclerosis in hypertensive African-Americans. *Stroke* 2000;31:568-73.

Comstock, G.W., et al. Church Attendance and Health. *J Chro Dis* 1972;25:665-72.

da Costa, A.P., and K.M. Kendrick. Face pictures reduce behavioural, autonomic, endocrine and neural indices of stress and fear in sheep. *Proc Royal Soc London B* 2004, Oct 7;271:2077-84.

Everson, S.A., et al. Anger expression and incident hypertension. *Psychosom Med* 1998;60:730-35.

Everson, S.A., et al. Hopelessness and 4-year Progression of Carotid Atherosclerosis: The Kuopio Ischemic Heart Disease Risk Factory Study. *Arterioscler Thromb Vasc Biol* 1997;17:1490-95.

Frasure-Smith, N., et al. Gender, depression, and one-year prognosis after myocardial infarction. *Psychosom Med* 1999;61:26-37.

Gardner, J.W., et al. Cancer in Utah Mormon Women by Church Activity Level. *Am J Epidemiol* 1982;116: 258-65.

Graham, T.W., et al. Frequency of Church Attendance and Blood Pressure Elevation. *J Behav Med* 1978;1:37-43.

House, J.S., et al. The Association of Social Relationships and Activities with Mortality: Prospective Evidence from the Tecumseh Community Health Study. Am J *Epidemiol* 1982;116:123-40.

Koenig, H.G., et al. Religion, spirituality, and acute care hospitalization and long-term care use by older patients. *Arch Intern Med* 2004, Jul 26;164(14):1579-85.

Krantz, D.S., et al. Effects of Mental Stress in Patients with Coronary Artery Disease. *JAMA* 2000;283:1800-1802.

Lupien, S.J., et al. Stress hormones and human memory function across the lifespan. *Psychoneuroendocrinology* 2005, Apr;30(3):225-42.

Lutz, A., et al. Long-term mediators self-induce high-amplitude gamma synchrony during mental practice. *Proc Natl Acad Sci USA* 2004, Nov 16;101(46):16369-16373.

McEwen, B.S. Protective and damaging effects of stress mediators. *New Eng J Med* 1998, Jan 15;338:171-79.

Music and Blood-Pressure Reduction. *Harvard Heart Letter* 1995;5 (adapted from JAMA, Sep 21, 1994).

Oleckno, W.A., et al. Relationship of Religiosity to Wellness and Other Health-Related Behaviors and Outcomes. *Psychological Reports* 1991;68:819-26.

Pearsall, P. *The Pleasure Prescription.* Salt Lake City, UT: Publishers Press, 1996.

Polk, D.E., et al. State and trait affect as predictors of salivary cortisol in healthy adults. *Psychoneuroendocrinology* 2005, Apr;30(3):261-72.

Ruo, B., et al. Depressive symptoms and health-related quality of life: The Heart and Soul Study. *JAMA* 2003;290:215-21.

Schneider, R.H., et al. A randomized controlled trial of stress reduction for hypertension in older African-Americans. *Hypertension* 1996;26:820-27.

Selye, H. *The Stress of Life*. NY: McGraw-Hill, 1956;2nd ed., paperback, 1978.

Strike, P.C., and A. Steptoe. Psychosocial factors in the development of coronary artery disease. *Prog Cardiovasc Dis* 2004, Jan-Feb;46(4):337-47.

Toews, J. Soul Care: The Importance of Spirituality in Life and Practice. Exploring Health and Healing. Calgary Health Region, Kananaskis, Canada, June 2005. UC Berkeley *Wellness Letter*, Feb 2005, p. 8.

Votruba, S.B., et al. Prior exercise increases subsequent utilization of dietary fat. *Med Sci Sport Exerc* 2002;34:1757-65.

Votruba, S.B., et al. Prior exercise increases dietary oleate, but not palmitate oxidation. *Obes Res* 2003;11(12):1509-18.

Williams, J.E., et al. Anger proneness predicts coronary heart disease risk: Prospective analysis from the atherosclerosis risk in communities (ARIC study). *Circulation* 2000;101:2034-39.

Williams, K.A., et al. Evaluation of a Wellness-Based Mindfulness Stress Reduction Intervention: A Controlled Trial. *Am J Health Promot* 2001, Jul-Aug;15(6):422-432.

Recipe Index

Index